Introduction to Turkish Business Law

Şebnem Kılıç (ed.)

Introduction to Turkish Business Law

PETER LANG

Bibliographic Information published by the Deutsche Nationalbibliothek
The Deutsche Nationalbibliothek lists this publication in the Deutsche Nationalbibliografie; detailed bibliographic data is available online at http://dnb.d-nb.de.

Library of Congress Cataloging-in-Publication Data
A CIP catalog record for this book has been applied for at the Library of Congress.

ISBN 978-3-631-84889-0 (Print)
E-ISBN 978-3-631-87420-2 (E-PDF)
E-ISBN 978-3-631-87421-9 (EPUB)
10.3726/b19466

Peter Lang – Berlin · Bern · Bruxelles · Istanbul · New York · Oxford · Warszawa · Wien

This publication has been peer reviewed.

www.peterlang.com

Editor's Disclaimer

The views and opinions expressed do not reflect those of the publisher and editor. The responsibility lies on the authors of the chapters. Neither the editor nor the publisher can be held responsible for any errors, omissions, claims, or any consequences arising from the use of information contained herein.

Editor's Note and Acknowledgments

This book is intended to assist readers who are in search of general knowledge about Turkish Business Law. To this end, it draws a broad outline in many parts. Yet, I hope that the grasp of knowledge we provided would constitute a suitable basis for the reader to launch further readings.

Drawing a convenient outline for legal disciplines that are inherently deep-seated requires a challenge in most cases. Fortunately, I had the opportunity to collaborate with some of the most eminent academics in their field, and they contributed to the book. I would like to express my gratefulness to the authors of all chapters. Undoubtedly, without labor and support from my colleagues, this book would not exist. I also would like to express my deepest appreciation to Dr. *Tuğba Semerci Vuraloğlu* and *Halil Mert Özel* for their revisions and voluntary contributions, which have enriched my own chapter.

Publishing is a long process that involves intensive labor as well. I gratefully acknowledge the support of Bahçeşehir University and, especially, the Faculty of Law for rendering the publication of this book possible. I also would like to thank for generous assistance of *Esra Bahşi* from Peter Lang Publishing during all process.

Şebnem Kılıç,
İstanbul, November 2021

Contents

List of Contributors

Assistant Prof. Dr. Evrim AKGÜN
Maritime and Insurance Law, Bahçeşehir University Law Faculty, Istanbul, Turkey.
E-mail: evrim.akgun@law.bau.edu.tr. ORCID ID: 0000-0002-4085-6503.

Associate Prof. Dr. Zafer KAHRAMAN
Civil Law, Bahçeşehir University Law Faculty, Istanbul, Turkey.
E-mail: zafer.kahraman@law.bau.edu.tr. ORCID: 0000-0002-9303-1062.

Assistant Prof. Dr. Şebnem KILIÇ
Labor and Social Security Law, Bahçeşehir University Law Faculty, Istanbul, Turkey.
E-mail: sebnem.kilic@law.bau.edu.tr. ORCID: 0000-0003-3186-8518.

Assistant Prof. Dr. Elif KÜZECİ
Public Law, Bahçeşehir University Law Faculty, Istanbul, Turkey.
E-mail: elif.kuzeci@law.bau.edu.tr. ORCID: 0000-0002-3723-8421.

Prof. Dr. Aslı MAKARACI
Civil Law, Bahçeşehir University Law Faculty, Istanbul, Turkey.
E-mail: asli.makaraci@law.bau.edu.tr. ORCID: 0000-0002-8854-914X.

Associate Prof. Dr. Seda ÖKTEM ÇEVİK
Civil Law, Bahçeşehir University Law Faculty, Istanbul, Turkey.
E-mail: seda.oktem@law.bau.edu.tr. ORCID: 0000-0002-9253-475X.

Assistant Prof. Dr. Tuğba SEMERCİ VURALOĞLU
Commercial Law, Bahçeşehir University Law Faculty, Istanbul, Turkey.
E-mail: tugba.semercivuraloglu@law.bau.edu.tr. ORCID: 0000-0002-0575-0746.

Assistant Prof. Dr. Ayşe ŞAHİN
Commercial Law, Bahçeşehir University Law Faculty, Istanbul, Turkey.
E-mail: ayse.sahin@law.bau.edu.tr. ORCID: 0000-0003-1544-4846.

Associate Prof. Dr. Didem YILMAZ
Constitutional Law, Bahçeşehir University Law Faculty, Istanbul, Turkey.
E-mail: didem.yilmaz@law.bau.edu.tr. ORCID ID: 0000-0001-5354-4114.

Abbreviations

ACP	Act on Consumer Protection
AHREIT	Act on Human Rights and Equality Institution of Turkey
AoA	Articles of association
AOHS	Act on Occupational Health and Safety
APC	Act on the Protection of Competition
Art.	Article
BoD	Board of directors
CC	Turkish Civil Code
CBA	Collective bargaining agreement
CCG	Communiqué on the Corporate Governance
CEO	Chief executive officer
Cf.	Confer
CIP	Code of Industrial Property
CISG	United Nations Conventions on Contracts for the International Sale of Goods
CJEU	Court of Justice of the European Union
CMB	Capital Markets Board
CMC	Capital Markets Code
Contra.	Contrary
CSD	Central Securities Depository
EBC	Execution and Bankruptcy Code
ECHR	European Convention on Human Rights
ECtHR	European Court of Human Rights
Ed.	Edited
e.g.	for example *(exempli gratia)*
EU	European Union
et al.	and others *(et alia)*
ff.	and following *(folios)*
fn.	footnote
GA	General assembly
GDPR	General Data Protection Regulation of EU
GNAT	Grand National Assembly of Turkey
GTC	General terms and conditions
IAA	Insurance Activities Act
ibid.	from the same place (*ibidem*)

ICTs	Information Communication Technologies
i.e.	that is *(id est)*
ILO	International Labour Organization
Iss.	Issue
LA	Labor Act
MÜHF-HAD	Marmara University Faculty of Law – Journal of Legal Studies
no.	number
OECD	Organisation for Economic Co-operation and Development
OJ	Official Journal (of Turkey)
OJ L	Official Journal of the European Communities – Legislation series
para.	paragraph
SMEs	small-sized enterprises
sub-para.	sub-paragraph
Swiss UCA	The Federal Act Against Unfair Competition
TCA	Turkish Competition Authority
TCC	Turkish Commercial Code
TCO	Turkish Code of Obligations
TFEU	Treaty on the Functioning of the EU
The DP Act	Turkish Personal Data Protection Act
The DP Board	The Data Protection Board of Turkey
TPC	Turkish Penal Code
trans.	Translated
UCP	EU Unfair Commercial Practices Directive
UNCITRAL	The United Nations Commission on International Trade Law
USA	United States of America
Vol.	Volume
WTAs	Working time arrangements

Introduction

This book is intended to be of interest to those concern with the legal essentials of Turkish Business Law, including to legal practitioners who engage in business practices internationally as well as to the students who need to acquire general legal knowledge. Therefore, the contributors are encouraged to address this broad audience. We hope that the outcome will appeal to readers from all walks of business life.

In the academic sphere, the book provides a comprehensive conception and normative information on Turkish private law, including Law of Persons and Law of Obligations, Commercial Law, Employment Law, and addresses understudied areas of Business Law such as Data Protection Law, Insurance Law, Competition Law, and the effects of Constitutional Law on Turkish private law.

It also involves legal amendments and juridical developments, notably in the fields of Employment Law, Data Protection Law, and Competition Law in addition to being explanatory in character. Since Business Law is often considered as a subset of private law, this book takes a unique approach by covering new amendments to the Turkish Constitution, which allow individuals to apply to the Constitutional Court and will have an impact on business practices.

Also, the structure aims to provide a simple, coherent framework to the reader. Each chapter commences with an introductory remark by depicting the content and frames the main bibliography in the very beginning. The reader who demands more in-depth knowledge can benefit from the list of further reading at the end of chapters.

Overall, the book is prepared to provide a clear and comprehensive view of the key aspects of Turkish Business Law. Therefore, it involves the relevant chapters to cover the business practices as a whole and aims to help the reader to acquire a general understanding of the subject matters.

The authors of all the chapters, who are my colleagues, are the ones who have an excellent command of the subjects in their respective fields and even pioneering the concepts that they work for Turkish law. We hope that for many years to come, this compilation will serve as a standard reference book for a broad audience.

Assoc. Prof. Dr. Didem YILMAZ*

Chapter I Constitutional Law

Aybay, Rona. *An Introduction to Law.* İstanbul: Der Yayınları, 2020; Gözler, Kemal. *Türk Anayasa Hukuku.* Bursa: Ekin, 2020; Özbudun, Ergun. *Türk Anayasa Hukuku.* Ankara: Yetkin, 2020; Özbudun, Ergun. "Constitutional Law." In *Introduction to Turkish Law*, 21–48. Edited by Ansay, Tuğrul, Wallace Jr., Don and Önay, Işık. 7th ed. Ankara: Seçkin, 2020; Tanör, Bülent and Yüzbaşıoğlu, Necmi. *1982 Anayasası'na Göre Türk Anayasa Hukuku.* İstanbul: Beta, 2020; Teziç, Erdoğan. *Anayasa Hukuku.* İstanbul: Beta, 2020.

Introductory Remarks

As the other parts of social life, the relationships between employers and employees fall under the rules enshrined by the Constitution. The state has the regulatory and oversight power on business activities. It protects, on one hand, the workers' rights and freedoms and, on the other hand, it takes actions to promote the private business activities, thus economic development of the state. The fruitful economic development either of the state or that of the private sector depends on the constitutional structure of the given state.

Modern states, emerged in 16th century, became constitution-based political structures with the effort of constitutionalism movements. This constitutional structure was formed in order to protect individual liberties from any arbitrary interference by the state. The constitutions, by creating the institutionalized state authority, became also the ultimate source of the political power exercised by the state's organs. Hence, the political power that dominates all the social life must be used in conformity with the constitution of each state.

In this chapter, it will be presented a general overview on the political structure and the principal characteristics and protection mechanisms of the fundamental rights and freedoms in Turkish constitutional system. The aim is to highlight the constitutional limits of the political power exercised by states organs and to give basic information on the protection of rights and freedoms especially related to business life.

* Corresponding author.

§ Part I The Essentials of the Political Structure According to the Constitution of 1982

The political structure and fundamental liberties were prescribed in the Constitution, which was enacted in 1982 aftermath of the military intervention occurred on 12 September 1980. This is the current and the third Constitution of the Republic and was amended nineteen times.[1]

The article 2 of the Constitution stipulates the fundamental principles of the Republic: The Republic, respectful to human rights, is a secular, democratic and social state based on the rule of law. The republican form of government (art. 1), its constitutional qualities (art. 2), and the provisions on the flag, official language and anthem, on capital city, and the unity of the state are unamendable (art. 4).

The Constitution begins with a Preamble, which indicates the basic views and principles that the Constitution is based on. As an integral part of the Constitution, the Preamble is binding upon legislative, executive and judicial organs, and administrative authorities and other institutions and individuals (art. 156).

I. Constitutional Bodies of the Republic and Their Functions

A. The Legislature and Legislative Power

The Grand National Assembly of Turkey (GNAT) is vested the legislative authority which can be delegated to neither any other institution nor any branch of government (arts. 6 and 7). It has the supreme power to enact, amend or repeal the laws (art. 87), to supervise and control the executive power (arts. 98, 105, and 106), also it is the only authority empowered to amend the Constitution (art. 175).

The constitutional structure of the Republic was founded upon the legislature. Therefore, the supremacy of the GNAT is still a constitutional principal dated back to the foundation of the Republic. The first Constitution (1924) of the Republic had stipulated that the GNAT was the one and the only representative

---

1 For detailed explanation of the constitutional history of Turkey and previous amendments also see, Ergun Özbudun, "Constitutional Law," in *Introduction to Turkish Law*, edited by Tuğrul Ansay, Don Wallace Jr. and Işık Önay, 7th ed. (Ankara: Seçkin: 2020), 29–33. The constitutional amendment in 2008 was found incompatible with the Constitution, and therefore, annulled by the Constitutional Court with its decision dated 5.6.2008, no. 16/116 (OJ, 22.10.2008, no. 27032).

of the national sovereignty. This principle establishing a unity or a concentration amongst the legislative, the executive and even the judiciary power[2] was modified by the Constitution of 1961,[3] which made the GNAT one of the organs entitled to use sovereign power along with others. Thereof, by distributing the sovereignty across the constitutional organs, this Constitution established true separation of powers in Turkish constitutional system for the first time in the history.

1. *The Structure and the Composition of the GNAT*

Unlike the previous Constitution (1961), the current Constitution (1982) has created a unicameral legislature. The number of deputies is determined in the Constitution (art. 75). Accordingly, the GNAT is composed of 600 deputies elected by popular vote. Elections for the GNAT and presidential elections are held every five years and on the same day. Every Turkish citizen, who fulfills the other legal conditions and is over the age of 18, enjoys the right to elect and be elected (art. 67).

An early election can be initiated either by the GNAT itself or by the President. The former may decide to renew the election on condition of three-fifth majority; the latter may call to election at any time without any condition. In both circumstances, the general and presidential elections are held on the same day. The Constitution provides that if the decision of renewal is initiated by the GNAT when the President enjoys the second term, then the President may be run for a third term (art. 116).

2. *Legislative Function*

The legislative power is vested in the GNAT, which means that following the Constitution, the legislative power is the primary source of general national legal norms. The legislative authority does not have any exclusive legislative domain. All social, economic and political issues can be enacted by the legislature provided that they are in conformity with the Constitution. The latest constitutional

---

2 During the foundation and following period, the "independence courts" that were intended to try the crimes for high treason were composed by the members of the GNAT.

3 For the English version of the Constitution see, Sadık Balkan, Ahmet E. Uysal and Kemal Karpat, trans., *The Constitution of Turkish Republic* (Ankara: 1961), and for online access https://www.anayasa.gen.tr/1961constitution-text.pdf, accessed 17.9.2021.

amendment of 2017 brought a slight modification on that issue which will be explained below.[4]

Beside its law-making function, the GNAT has the power to oversight the executive by several means such as written question, general debate, parliamentary investigation and parliamentary inquiry.[5] Only the parliamentary inquiry may cause criminal liability of the executive, i.e., the President, the deputy presidents and the ministers. The other means serve the GNAT to obtain information as to the general policy from the deputy president and ministers.

3. *Legislative Process*

All deputies are empowered to introduce bill. The President of the GNAT sends the bill to relevant legislative commission, where it is debated for maximum of 45 days and then forwarded to the President of the GNAT attached with a report. The agenda of the GNAT is set by the President of the GNAT.

The quorum for a meeting of the GNAT shall be at least one-third of the total number of members (art. 96). Unless otherwise stipulated in the Constitution, the GNAT makes decisions by absolute majority of those who are present in the general assembly. However, the quorum for decision making cannot, under any circumstances, be less than one plus a quarter of the total number of members.

The President of the Republic either promulgates the laws adopted by the GNAT within 15 days or returns the laws to the GNAT for reconsideration. If the GNAT adopts the law without any amendment and by absolute majority, the President of the Republic shall promulgate the law. However, if any amendments are made on the law by the GNAT, this time, the President of the Republic may return the amended law to the GNAT for reconsideration again.

4. *Legislative Control over the Executive*

Before the last constitutional amendment, the Council of Ministers was bearing political and criminal responsibility, and the President of the Republic was responsible only for criminal matters regarding their duties. This kind of

4 Under this chapter, see infra: *The Regulatory Power of the Executive.*

5 In the English version of the Constitution, the means for criminal liability of the President, deputy presidents and ministers is translated as "parliamentary investigation". But in the doctrine of constitutional law, the phrase "parliamentary inquiry" better describes that means. Here, it is preferred to use the phrase which is appropriately aligned with the doctrine rather than using a contestable translation. See also, https://global.tbmm.gov.tr/docs/constitution_en_2019.pdf, accessed 17.9.2021.

responsibilities was a corollary of the parliamentary system of government. After the establishment of a different kind of presidential system in 2017, the only means that the GNAT holds is the parliamentary inquiry of the President, the deputy presidents and the ministers as prescribed in the articles 105 and 106.[6]

Along with the parliamentary inquiry, members of the GNAT may use several means of parliamentary oversight. According to the article 98, written question is a way of oversight asked by the deputies to the deputies of the President of the Republic or to the ministers in a written form, which is to be answered no later than 15 days. Also, political party groups or at least twenty of the deputies may request opening a general debate on a matter concerning the community and the activities of the state or they may give a motion of parliamentary investigation. The parliamentary investigation is an examination conducted to gather information on a specific matter by a commission formed on this purpose. The main difference of those oversight means from the parliamentary inquiry is that none of them may target directly the President.

B. The Executive and Its Regulatory Powers

The executive power and function is exercised and carried out by the President of the Republic. The executive is not only bound by law but also by the Constitution. According to the article 8 of the Constitution, the executive power must be exercised in conformity with the Constitution and laws.

The President of the Republic assumes the authority of being the head of the state and represents the Republic of Turkey and the unity of the Turkish nation. The President ensures the implementation of the Constitution and functioning of the organs of the state orderly and harmoniously.

The monarchical system of the Ottoman Empire was faded during the war of independence and it was officially terminated in 1922. This transformation on the political governance, which was founded upon the supremacy of the nation represented by the Assembly, was apparent even in the first constituent assembly gathered in 1920. The supremacy of the nation represented by the Assembly has been embedded in the constitutional political structure since then. But the executive, by the virtue of the majority rule in the GNAT, became indirectly the primary political organ regardless of the principle of the legislative supremacy written in those constitutions explicitly.[7] The first military intervention of 27 May 1960 was due to this political shift between the legislative and the

6 Under this chapter, see infra: *Criminal Liability of the Executive.*

7 For similar comments see, Özbudun, "Constitutional Law," 24.

executive. The Constitution of 1961, by intending to frame the executive with the legislative, had established a very fragile relationship between the GNAT and the executive. This Constitution remained in force for 19 years and it was altered by the current Constitution after the second military intervention. The National Security Council, who executed the intervention was in favor of the idea of the strengthening the state, that is the executive, eventually the President of the Republic. It can be asserted that the constitutional amendments on the popular vote for the presidency in 2007 and on the modification of the political system in 2017 stay in the line with this political choice.

The current Constitution adopted following the military intervention of 1980 empowered the political position of the President within the constitutional structure. Political impartiality and non-accountability, the main principles of the former Constitution (1961) of the Republic were weakened by the current Constitution. The President of the Republic was empowered to order and to decide unilaterally on the matters specified in the Constitution without any judicial review. In 2007, after a political crisis triggered during the presidential election, the majority group at the GNAT adopted a constitutional amendment on the popular election of the President of the Republic. Approved at the constitutional referendum held on 21 October 2007 by a 68.95 % majority, this amendment reinforced the political position of the President with numerous unilateral powers exempt from judicial review. This modification led a controversial situation between the Prime Minister and the President who was general president of the political majority. The failed attempt of military intervention occurred in the summer 2016 beget a new amendment that finalized the creation of a powerful executive with the President at the head. Elected by popular vote, the President is no longer required to leave the political membership of their party and is entitled to a very crucial power to intervene to the legislative power.

1. *Formation of Executive*

Since the constitutional amendment of 2007, the President of the Republic is directly elected by popular vote amongst Turkish citizens over 40 years of age who are eligible to be a deputy and have completed higher education. The President of the Republic's term of office is 5 years for two terms at most. The first presidential election was held in 2014.

The latest amendment of 2017, which changed the political system, also amended the procedures for the candidacy. The President of the Republic may be nominated by political party groups, political parties which received at least 5 % of valid votes on their own or collectively in the latest parliamentary elections, or through the petitions of at least one hundred thousand voters. In presidential elections, the candidate who receives the absolute majority of the valid electoral votes is considered the President elect. If absolute majority cannot be obtained in the first ballot, the second ballot shall be held on the second Sunday following the former one. Two candidates who received the greatest number of electoral votes in the first ballot shall run for the second ballot, and the candidate who receives majority of valid electoral votes shall be the President of the Republic. If one of the candidates, who is eligible the right to run for the second ballot, becomes unable to participate in the election for any reason, the second ballot shall be conducted by substituting the vacant candidacy in conformity with the ranking in the first ballot. If only one candidate remains for the second ballot, this ballot shall be conducted as a referendum. The candidate, who receives the majority of the valid electoral votes, shall be elected President of the Republic. If this candidate fails to receive the majority of the valid electoral votes in the election, the presidential election shall be renewed.

The President may appoint one or more deputies and minister among those who are eligible to be a deputy, without any approval of the Assembly but they are obliged to take oath before the GNAT. If a member of the GNAT is appointed as a deputy president or minister, their membership of the GNAT becomes terminated, and their seats remain vacant. The deputies of the President and the ministers are accountable to the President of the Republic, who has authority to remove them from the office.

2. *Criminal Liability of the Executive*

The absolute majority of the member of the GNAT may give a motion of an investigation of the President, the deputy presidents, and the ministers on allegations of perpetration of a crime regarding their duties. This motion has to be approved by three-fifth majority of the GNAT (art. 105–106). It is noteworthy that the procedures of parliamentary inquiry of both, the President and the others appointed by the President, are identical.

The procedure begins with a motion of parliamentary inquiry backed by absolute majority. Once the motion is tabled, a preliminary debate must be organized and then the motion must be accepted by three-fifth majority of the total members of the GNAT by upholding the secrecy of the ballot. After that, a committee of inquiry composed of fifteen members chosen by the candidates of political parties proportionate to their political forces, conducts an investigation within a period of 2 months, which can be renewed only for one time. The final report of the committee of inquiry shall be discussed and for the referral of this report to the Supreme Criminal Tribunal, the decision must be taken by two-thirds of the total number of its members by secret ballot.

The subject of the criminal liability is expressly referred to the *"allegations of perpetration of a crime regarding their duties"* for the deputy presidents and the ministers. Nonetheless, the article related to the criminal liability of the President regulates the investigation of the President *"on allegations of a crime"*. During the discussions on constitutional amendments, those who were in favor commented that this peculiar disposition covers all the criminal liability and results to an extended criminal responsibility of the President which goes beyond the allegations regarding the duties of the President. In our opinion, this interpretation cannot be valid according to the literal wording of the article 148 of the Constitution. This article, which determines the duties of the Constitutional Court, clearly states that the Court, in its capacity as the Supreme Criminal Tribunal, has the duty to *try the offences relating to their functions of those concerned, inclusively that of the President of the Republic.*

By the virtue of the literal wording and the teleological interpretation of the dispositions on criminal liability, it can easily be urged that the procedure of parliamentary inquiry is dedicated only for allegations of perpetration of a crime regarding the duties of the President and deputies of the President. For an ordinary allegation of a crime not related to presidential duties, the general rules of criminal law shall be applied.

3. *Regulatory Power of the President*

The law-making power of the executive was an exception before 2017. According to the article 8, as a rule, the executive, in ordinary times, had disposed a derivative power of regulation. The implementation of a regulatory source was once depended on the very existence of a legislative act. Only in the state of emergency, the executive could have enacted emergency legislation without any authorization act.

With the latest constitutional amendment, the provisions on the state of emergency remained the same but the regulatory power during ordinary time became a primary power for the delimited matters with the insertion of a new kind of norm, called "presidential decree".

Presidential decrees issued by the President of the Republic may only be related on the matters regarding executive power and on matters which are not explicitly granted to legislative authority by the Constitution. Except the state of emergency, the rights and freedoms cannot be restricted by presidential decrees. The President has the power to enact a decree only for the rights and freedoms which are covered in the third section of the Constitution. This implies that only social and economic rights can be regulated by presidential decrees. Furthermore, the GNAT has the power to invalidate a decree by enacting a law on the same matter and when there is a discrepancy between provisions of the presidential decrees and the laws, the provisions of the laws prevail.

Those are general rules provided in the article 104/17 of the Constitution. Nevertheless, there are also several specific constitutional provisions which directly refer to a legal regulation by presidential decrees. On one hand, there is an ongoing debate in the doctrine on whether those clauses correspond to the exclusive power of the executive, or the supremacy of the legislative is still valid also for those specific provisions.[8] On the other hand, the Constitutional Court, with a very weak jurisprudence, implicitly accepted that those provisions create an exclusive regulatory power of the executive.[9]

Beside the presidential decrees, the President may issue presidential decisions and by-laws. Those acts are pure administrative in quality, and their validity depends on their conformity to the relevant legislative act.

Presidential decisions and by-laws come into effect on the date of publication in the Official Journal, and according to the Presidential Decree no. 10 on Official Journal,[10] it lies with the President's discretion to decide to which presidential decision or by-law is to be published.

4. *Budgetary Power of the President*

The revolutionary effect of the Magna Carta was the restriction of the rulers' power to collect taxes by their own discretion. Since this constitutional document, the power to levy taxes passed in the hand of the legislatures. This principal

---

8 For the discussions in the doctrine see also, Oktay Uygun and Egemen Esen (ed.), "Cumhurbaşkanının İşlemlerinin Hukuki Niteliği, Normlar Hiyerarşisindeki Yeri ve Denetimi," *Kamu Hukukçuları Platformu VIII. Toplantısı, 18–19 Ekim 2019, Tam Metin Bildiri Kitabı* (İstanbul: On İki Levha, 2019); Özen Ülgen Adadağ, "Kanun-Cumhurbaşkanı Kararnamesi İlişkisinin Yargısal Denetimine Yönelik Sorunlar," *Anayasa Yargısı Dergisi*, Vol. 36, Iss. 1 (2019): 261–277.

9 For some of sample cases on this issue, see the decisions of the Constitutional Court, dated 22.01.2020, no. 2018/125–2020/4, §6; dated 23.01.2020, no. 2019/31–2020/5, §6; dated 23.01.2020, no. 2019/78–2020/6, §6; dated 11.06.2020, no. 2018/119–2020/25, §6; dated 11.06.2020, no. 2018/155–2020/27, §6; dated 12.06.2020, no. 2019/105–2020/30, §6; dated 25.06.2020, no. 2018/126–2020/32, §6; dated 15.10.2020, no. 2018/124–2020/56, §6; dated 30/12/2020, no. 2019/71–2020/82, §6.

10 OJ, 15.7.2018, no. 30479.

is embedded within the modern constitutionalism no matter which type of political governmental system is chosen. With the wording of the Constitutional Court, "*(t)he authorization of the legislature given to the executive authority to collect public revenues on behalf of the people and to spend those revenues on behalf of the people within the limits set by law and under the control of the legislature is called the budgetary right. In other words, the power of the purse is the right to determine the type and amount of public expenditures, and approve and oversight the consequences of these expenditures, which are afforded by taxes or similar revenues. This right exercised by the representatives elected by the people in democratic countries belongs to the legislatures. The budget is the government's primary responsibility mechanism toward the Assembly.*".[11]

On the other hand, there is an undeniable fact that the executives, by support of the political majority, indirectly in a presidential system or directly in a parliamentary system begin to influence the budgetary power of the legislature. Nevertheless, the democratic legislatures never relinquish their budgetary power. The Turkish Constitution might be conferred as an example to the exception on this matter despite the presence of financial review exercised by the Court of Accounts.

The budget bill is submitted by the President of the Republic to the GNAT at least 75 days before the commencement of the fiscal year. After a consideration within 55 days at the Committee on Budget, the budget bill is to be debated and adopted by the Plenary Assembly before the commencement of the fiscal year.

In the circumstances when the budget act cannot be put into force within due period, the provisional budget law must be enacted, and if the provisional budget law cannot either be enacted, the budget of the previous year must be applied increasingly as per the revaluation rate until the budget act is adopted.

Those constitutional provisions grant to the President to determine the budget without any parliamentary oversight, especially when the President is backed by the majority at the GNAT, or when the President is backed by the coalition which holds the majority.

C. The Judiciary and Judicial Review

Judicial power is exercised by independent and impartial courts on behalf of the Turkish nation. The independence and impartiality of courts and judges are

---

11 See the decision of the Constitutional Court, dated 12.11.2020, no. 2018/162–2020/66, §26 (own translation).

enshrined either by material constitutional provisions and by a special constitutional institution called the Council of Judges and Prosecutors.

The articles between 138 and 141 prescribe the fundamental rules for the independence and impartiality of judiciary. It is constitutionally forbidden to give orders or instructions, to send circulars, to make recommendations and suggestions to courts or judges regarding the exercise of judicial power. In addition, the legislative, executive, and administrative organs are strictly obliged to comply with the court decisions.

The general rules on the guarantee of tenure of judges and public prosecutors rely on two provisions, which prevents any arbitrary intervention to judges and public prosecutors performing their duties (art. 139 and 140). Even though, the Constitution of 1982 modified those guarantees slight in appearance but important in essence, it has pursued the idea enshrined in the Constitution of 1961 to reinforce the constitutional principles on judiciary by an institutional guarantee. However, the current Constitution has assembled judges and public prosecutors under the protection of the same institution, even though those professions are different in nature.

The Council of Judges and Prosecutors is composed of thirteen members. The Minister of Justice and the Undersecretary of the Ministry of Justice are ex-officio members. Four members are (three members among first category civil judges and public prosecutors not having lost the qualifications to be entitled in the first category and one member among first category administrative judges and public prosecutors not having lost the qualifications to be entitled in the first category) appointed by the President. Seven members (three members among the members of the Court of Cassation, one member among the members of the Council of State and three members among academic staff working in the field of law at higher education institutions and lawyers, whose qualifications specified in law) are elected by the GNAT. Two-third majority of total number of the members is required for the first ballot; in case the election cannot be concluded, three-fifth majority of total number of the members is required for the second ballot. In case the members cannot be elected either in the second ballot, the election of the members shall be concluded by lot between the two candidates who received the highest number of votes.

The Council of Judges and Prosecutors, whose president is the Minister of Justice, is the highest authority to conduct the proceedings regarding the admission to the profession of judges and public prosecutors of civil and administrative courts, appointment, transferring to other posts, delegation of temporary powers, promotion, and the entitlement to the first category, and also to make decisions concerning those, whose continuation in the profession is found unsuitable, the imposition of disciplinary penalties and discharges. Since 2010, only the decisions of dismissal from profession may be reviewed by courts.

The form of the organization, established since the enactment of the Constitution, and the composition, as amended in 2017, of the Council is unfortunately opened to the direct influence of the Executive, which blurs the independence of the judiciary.

1. *High Courts*

a. *Overview*

The judiciary system in Turkey is composed of different divisions. According to the division of jurisdiction, the Constitution establishes several High Courts (art. 154, 155, and 158). The High Courts, such as Court of Cassation and Council of State are the last instance courts to review decisions and judgments given by civil and criminal courts and by administrative and tax courts respectively besides their other duties.

As being one of the High Courts, the Court of Jurisdictional Disputes (or Court of Conflicts) is empowered to deliver final judgments to settle the disputes between civil and administrative courts concerning their jurisdiction and judgments.

Established following the Constitution of 1961, the military courts and their appellate courts have been gradually abrogated by constitutional amendments. In 2004, the Courts of State Security as first instance court, and in 2017, High Military Court of Cassation and High Military Administrative Court were abolished. Consequently, there is no longer a division of jurisdiction between civilian judiciary and military judiciary.

b. *The organization of judiciary*

The Turkish judiciary system comprises of a joined construct of first instance courts, regional-level appellate courts and national-level high courts. Accordingly, there are different judicial divisions under this construct. Civil and criminal litigations are settled by criminal and civil courts at the first instance. These courts are also specialized according to the nature of the litigation. For example, regarding the civil procedure, employment courts and commercial courts are also established and specialized by their relevant codes.

By the Act on Civil Procedure no. 6100,[12] which has been put into effect as of October 2011, the litigation phases of civil courts have been significantly

12 OJ, 4.2.2011, no. 27836.

amended. By 2016, another vital change was the implementation of the appellate review as a legal remedy. Appellate courts (Regional Courts of Appeal), which have been introduced before,[13] began to process on 20 July 2016. This legal remedy has a divergent nature from the Court of Cassation. As a rule, the Court of Cassation conducts its review based on written documents without a hearing (art. 369/1 and 2 of Act on Civil Procedure), and it is not bound by the grounds stated in the application. However, in the stage of appeal, as a rule, a hearing is held and the court is bound by the grounds, except for the matters to be examined ex officio (art. 355 and 356 of Act on Civil Procedure).

Accordingly, the decisions of those court of first instance can be brought before the Regional Courts of Appeal. Those appellate courts have the power to review the lower courts' decisions by appraising their conformity with the law and legal procedures.[14] While some decisions are considered as finalized at the stage of appeal, some can be brought to the Court of Cassation for review.

According to this construct, the decisions of the appellate courts regarding civil procedure can be upheld by the Court of Cassation, upheld with correction of decision, or can be rescinded and remanded back to the appellate courts (or to the first instance court in certain cases) for review. If the appellate court persists in its judgment, it, then, holds the decision to resist. In this case, the decision will be reviewed by the Court of Cassation. The decision can be reviewed by the Civil Chamber initially or by the General Assembly of Civil Chambers of the Court of Cassation. If the General Assembly (of Civil Chambers) upholds the Chamber's decision, the case is remanded back to lower courts for review on the same grounds as the initial reversal. Lower courts are no longer able to hold the decision to resist against the decisions of the General Assembly of Civil Chambers of the Court of Cassation (art. 373/7 of Act on Civil Procedure).[15]

In the field of the administrative and tax law, a similar organization scheme can be found. Specific for those disputes, the decisions of administrative and tax courts may be brought to the Regional Administrative Courts of Appeal other

---

13 According to the Act no. 5235 (OJ, 7.10.2004, no. 25606).

14 The Regional Courts of Appeal regarding the civil procedure conducts the appellate review separately as Civil Chamber of, and Criminal Chamber of Regional Courts of Appeal. For further information on appellate courts regarding civil procedure see, Deniz Meraklı Yayla, *Medeni Usul Hukukunda İstinaf Kanun Yolunda Yeniden Tahkikat Yapılması* (Ankara: Yetkin, 2014).

15 For further information regarding civil procedure see, Hakan Pekcanıtez, Muhammet Özekes and Oğuz Atalay, *Medeni Usul Ders Kitabı*, 9th ed. (İstanbul: On İki Levha, 2021), 511 ff.

than those that are already finalized at the first instance courts.[16] Furthermore, for the decisions that are not finalized at the stage of appeal, it is possible to bring them to the Council of State for review.[17]

The general rules of appellate procedure are set up by the Act on Civil Procedure no. 6100, the Act on Criminal Procedure no. 5271, the Act on the Procedure of Administrative Justice no. 2577, and the Tax Procedures Act no. 213.

Furthermore, the individual application according to the article 148/para. 3 of the Constitution may be brought before the Constitutional Court after the exhaustion of this judicial order.

2. Constitutional Court

In order to constrain the legislative authority, thus assuring the supremacy of the Constitution, the Constitutional Court was first established by the Constitution of 1961. Its structure was, and still is, organized in conformity with the European model of centralized judicial review model and maintained by the current Constitution of 1982.

a. Composition

Remarkably amended two times (in 2010 and 2017), the Constitutional Court is composed of fifteen judges. Three members (two members from among three candidates to be nominated by and from among the president and members of the Court of Accounts and one member from among three candidates nominated by the heads of the bar associations from among self-employed lawyers) are elected by the GNAT with the two-thirds majority of the total number of the members for the first ballot, and absolute majority of total number of the members is required for the second ballot. If an absolute majority cannot be obtained in the second ballot, a third ballot is held between the two candidates who have received the majority of the votes in the second ballot; the member who receives the majority of the votes in the third ballot is elected.

Twelve members are appointed by the President. Three of them are appointed among from the presidents and members of the Court of Cassation and two from the Council of State. Three members are nominated by the Council of

---

16 The Regional Administrative Courts of Appeal regarding the administrative procedure conducts the appellate review separately as Administrative Law Chamber of, and Tax Law Chamber of Regional Administrative Courts of Appeal.

17 For further information regarding administrative procedure see also, Ali D. Ulusoy, *İdari Yargılama Kanunu* (Ankara: Yetkin, 2020).

Higher Education from among members of academic staff who are not members of the Council, in the fields of law, economics, and political sciences. The last four members are appointed from among high level executives, self-employed lawyers, first category judges, and public prosecutors, or rapporteurs of the Constitutional Court having served as rapporteur for at least 5 years.

The Constitution prescribes the qualifications for appointment: The members of the academic staff are required to possess the titles of professor or associate professor; lawyers are required to have practiced as a lawyer for at least 20 years; high level executives are required to have completed higher education and to have worked for at least 20 years in public service, and first category judges and public prosecutors with at least 20 years of work experience including their period of candidacy, provided that they all shall be over the age of 45. The members serve for 12 years without the possibility of re-election. The retirement age from the service is 65.

b. Functions

The article 148 of the Constitution of 1982 regulates the primary functions of the Constitutional Court. First, the Constitutional Court exercises the control of conformity of laws, presidential decrees and standing order of the GNAT. The constitutional amendments can only be reviewed for the procedural conformity with the Constitution. As it is mentioned earlier, presidential decrees during the state of emergency are excluded of judicial review. An action of annulment can be initiated by the President of the Republic, the two political party groups having the largest number of members in the GNAT, or at least one-fifth of the total number of members of the GNAT within 10 days for procedural and 60 days for substantial inconformity with the Constitution following the promulgation of the law in the Official Journal (art. 148, 150, and 151). The control of constitutionality may also be initiated by other courts according to the article 152. If, during a trial by court, the court finds ex officio that the law or the presidential decree to be applied for appraising the concrete case is unconstitutional or become convinced of the seriousness of the claim of unconstitutionality submitted by one of the parties to the trial, it refers the law or the presidential decree to the Constitutional Court and postpone the proceedings until the Constitutional Court decides on the issue.

The other functions of the Constitutional Court are to try high public servants for their allegation of crime regarding their duties (art. 148/7); to decide on the request to dissolution of political parties (art. 69) and exercise financial control over the political parties; to review the conformity of the GNAT decision on lifting the immunity of a deputy or on loss of membership of a deputy (art. 85); and decide on individual application (art. 148/3).

The decisions of the Constitutional Court enter in force as of the day of their publication in the Official Journal, and are binding all governmental organs, administration and individuals (art. 153).

II. Hierarchy of Legal Written Norms

A. Constitutional Norms: Constitution, Constitutional Amendments, and Decisions of the Constitutional Court

The Constitution is the principal source of the legal system. The article 11 of the Constitution announces the supremacy of the Constitution and the binding effect of the constitutional provisions. This article is reinforced by the constitutional review of the Constitutional Court whose decisions are binding on the legislative, executive, and judicial organs, on the administrative authorities, and on persons and corporate bodies as binding as the provisions of the Constitution.

The constitutional amendments occupy the same hierarchy as the Constitution, except for constitutional amendments that are unconstitutional.[18]

B. Legislative (Statutory) Norms: Laws, International Agreements (Ordinary) Presidential Decrees, Precedents of High Courts

The second level of the normative hierarchy is occupied by the acts of the legislative authority. Laws (i.e., acts, codes) which are not contrary to the Constitution must be applicable by the executive and judiciary.

The international law is also an important legal source in Turkish system. According to article 90 of the Constitution, "*International agreements duly put into effect have the force of law* and no one can *appeal to the Constitutional Court… on the grounds that they are unconstitutional*". In 2004 by constitutional amendment, it is added a new final clause at this article and clearly differs the impacts of ordinary international agreements and those concerning fundamental rights and freedoms. The latter takes precedence when the provisions of national laws are not in conformity with those international agreements concerning fundamental rights and freedoms. After this amendment all the constitutional

18 The Constitutional Courts that have the authority to review the conformity of legislative acts to the Constitution have built up a jurisprudence which permits them to exercise a material review of constitutional amendments. For these almost entrenched decisions see, Yaniv Roznai, *Unconstitutional Constitutional Amendments, the Limits of Amendments Powers* (Oxford: Oxford University Press, 2017).

organs, not only the judiciary, are bound by the provisions of the international agreements, and shall apply them to the relevant issue when the national laws offer less guarantee.

As previously mentioned, the latest constitutional amendment created a new kind of legal norm called "presidential decree" which must be analyzed in the second row of the hierarchy. A presidential decree gives to the President the power to "legislate". This is not to be considered concurrent legislative power, it is delimitated by content and also by specific conflict resolution rules provided in the article 104/17 of the Constitution, which stipulates that the legislative authority prevails over presidential decrees.

First of all, a presidential decree may be issued only in the matters relevant to the executive authority. This means that the President cannot issue a presidential decree either on judicial matters or on matters that Constitution clearly refers to legislative authority. There are seven constitutional provisions that the Constitution expressly refers to the power to "legislate" by a presidential decree. Those seven provisions are to be found in the articles 104/12, 104/17, 106/11, 108, 118, 123/3 and 119. The last one, which lacks judicial review, necessities a deeper explanation.

The article 119, amended in 2017, poses the causes and rules of declaring a state of emergency. Without foreseeing any differences of degree between them, the states of emergency are listed consecutively in the article such as war, the emergence of a situation necessitating war, mobilization, an uprising, strong rebellious actions against the motherland and the Republic, widespread acts of violence of internal or external origin threatening the indivisibility of the country and the nation, emergence of widespread acts of violence aimed at the destruction of the constitutional order or of fundamental rights and freedoms, serious deterioration of public order caused by acts of violence, occurrence of natural disasters, outbreak of dangerous epidemic diseases or emergence of a serious economic crisis. If one of this causes occurs, the President has the power to declare unilaterally a state of emergency in one region or nationwide for a period not exceeding 6 months. This decision immediately shall be published in the Official Journal and submitted for approval to the GNAT on the same day. After the approval, the legislative authority regresses and the executive authority replaces it in order to reinstate the public order by issuing emergency acts called presidential decrees. Those decrees are, on a considerable scale, different from those of ordinary times because of three reasons:

First, during the state of emergency, the President may intervene in all rights and freedoms in order to restrain or suspend their exercise. The second reason is that the presidential decrees issued during the state of emergency cannot be brought to the Constitutional Court regarding constitutionality according to the article 148 of the Constitution. Before 2016, the Constitutional Court, by teleological interpretation, had created a jurisprudence for the control of the conformity of those emergency acts.[19] However, in 2016, the Court overturned its judgments by a quite strict literal interpretation stating that the only control available is the political one which must be exercised by the GNAT and that it is expressly forbidden to appeal against the emergency regulation to the Constitutional Court due to the wording of "the constituent power".[20] The third reason of difference is related to that issue. In ordinary times, the presidential decrees are not to submitted to the GNAT for an act of parliament. But the new constitutional amendment of 2017 which followed this jurisprudence of the Constitutional Court determined a period of 3 months for the decision of the GNAT. If the GNAT does not decide within this time, the presidential decrees issued during the state of emergency will be annulled automatically.

This very controversial nature of the presidential decree issued during the state of emergency which creates a denial of justice (*déni de justice*) that is why this kind of decree is not and cannot be stated in the hierarchy of legal written norms.

The High Courts, while interpreting a legal provision *enjoy the privilege of laying down rules as effective as the rules of a statute.*[21] The binding effect of those decisions for the lower courts makes them another source of law in the legislative hierarchy.

The judicial review of all legal written norms enumerated here are exercised by the Constitutional Court.

C. Administrative Regulations (Executive Sources): Presidential Decisions, By-Laws and Other Regulatory Sources

There are three different kinds of presidential decision with administrative nature which must be examined in a different row of the hierarchy.

---

19 For the decisions of the Constitutional Court before 2016 see, dated 10.1.1991, no. 1990/25–1991/1; dated 3.7.1991, no. 1991/6–1991/20; dated 26.5.1992, no. 1992/30–1992/36; dated 22.5.2003, no. 2003/28–2003/42.

20 For the decisions of the Constitutional Court see also, dated 12.10.2016, no. 2016/166–2016/159; dated 12.10.2016, no. 2016/167–2016/160; dated 02.11.2016, no. 2016/171–2016/164; dated 02.11.2016, no. 2016/172–2016/165.

For further information on the state of emergency in Turkey see, the Opinion of the Venice Commission, dated 12.12.2016, CDL-AD (2016)037.

21 Adnan Güriz, "Sources of Turkish Law," in *Introduction to Turkish Law*, edited by Tuğrul Ansay, Don Wallace Jr. and Işık Önay, 7th ed. (Ankara: Seçkin, 2020), 16.

On taxation and commercial matters, the Constitution permits the legislature to empower the President to regulate or make modification unilaterally within the limits prescribed in the provisions of the law. According to this authorization, the President may decide to amend the percentages of exemption, exceptions and reductions in taxes, fees, duties and other such financial obligations (art. 73/4) or to introduce additional financial impositions on imports, exports and other foreign trade transactions, except taxes and similar impositions, or to lift them (art. 167/3) by a presidential decision. This kind of decision is the only administrative decision which are based on a much broader regulatory authority awarded to the President than the other type of presidential decisions.

The other administrative presidential decisions are similar to the by-laws issued by the President of the Republic, the ministries and other public corporate bodies relating to their jurisdiction and are issued only to implement the laws and presidential decrees. They are valid as long as they are not contrary to the laws and decrees.

The last types of the presidential decisions are those issued by the President for the nomination to or revocation from office of all public servants of central government or staff of subsidiary institutions.

All legal written norms enumerated here are reviewed by administrative courts at the first instance following the procedural hierarchy among administrative courts. Only the presidential decisions can be sued directly before the Council of State for their conformity with the law and the Constitution.

§ Part II Fundamental Rights and Freedoms

In this part, it will be primarily presented the general outline on fundamental rights and freedoms according to the Constitution and then will be focused on social and economic rights and the protection of those by individual application procedure.

I. General Provisions

A. Nature

The Turkish Constitution contains a very broad list of fundamental rights and freedoms. The liberal principles with a fundament of natural law are expressively stated in the Constitution as "*Everyone possesses inherent fundamental rights and freedoms, which are inviolable and inalienable.*" (art. 12/1). In the second paragraph of the article 12, it is also emphasized that the rights and freedoms impose duties and responsibilities on all individuals toward society, their families, and other individuals. This article indicates the "expectation of bearing the constituent will" from *democracy-loving Turkish sons' and daughters' for the sake of the(ir) motherland and nation.*[22]

Similar to the former Constitution, fundamental rights and freedoms are categorized according to the duties and responsibilities of the state. Individual rights, as known as negative rights, are recognized to all, no matter what the political, economic and social status of individuals is (art. 17–40).[23] This section is followed by social and economic rights which necessitate positive action of the state for their enforceability (art. 41–65).[24] Final category is

22 The wordings *in italic* are for highlighting the quotations mentioned in the last sentence of the Preamble of the Constitution.

23 Art. 17 – Personal inviolability, corporeal and spiritual existence of the individual; Art. 18 – Prohibition of forced labour; Art. 19 – Personal liberty and security; Art. 20 – Privacy and protection of private life; Art. 21 – Inviolability of the domicile; Art. 22 – Freedom of communication; Art. 23 – Freedom of residence and movement; Art. 24 – Freedom of religion and conscience; Art. 25 – Freedom of thought and opinion; Art. 26 – Freedom of expression and dissemination of thought; Art. 27 – Freedom of science and the arts; Art. 28 – Provisions relating to the press and publication; Art. 29 – Right to publish periodicals and non-periodicals; Art. 30 – Protection of printing facilities; Art. 31 – Right to use media other than the press owned by public corporations; Art. 32 – Right of rectification and reply; Art. 33 – Freedom of association; Art. 34 – Right to hold meetings and demonstration marches; Art. 35 – Right to property; Art. 36 – Freedom to claim rights; Art. 37 – Principle of natural judge; Art. 38 – Principles relating to offences and penalties; Art. 39 – Right to prove an allegation; Art. 40 – Protection of fundamental rights and freedoms.

24 Art. 41 – Protection of the family, and children's rights; Art. 42 – Right and duty of education; Art. 43 – Utilization of the coasts; Art. 44 – Land ownership; Art. 45 – Protection of agriculture, animal husbandry, and persons engaged in these activities; Art. 46 – Expropriation; Art. 47 – Nationalization and privatization; Art. 48 – Freedom of work and contract; Art. 49 – Right and duty to work; Art. 50 – Working conditions and right to rest and leisure; Art. 51 – Right to organize unions; Art. 52 – Activities of unions 52; Art. 53 – Rights of collective bargaining agreement and collective agreement; Art. 54 – Right to strike and lockout 54; Art. 55 – Provision of fair wage; Art. 56 – Health services and protection of the environment; Art. 57 – Right to housing; Art. 58 – Protection of the youth; Art. 59 – Development of sports and arbitration; Art. 60 – Right to social security; Art. 61 – Persons requiring special protection in the field of social security; Art. 62 – Turkish citizens working abroad 62; Art. 63 – Protection of historical, cultural and natural assets; Art. 64 – Protection of arts and artists; Art. 65 – The extent of social and economic duties of the state.

dedicated to the political rights that only the citizens may enjoy (art. 66–74).[25]

Those rights are protected by judicial review, and since 2010, the individual application also provides a subsidiary protection. In the original text of the Constitution, the balance between freedoms and the state authority was in favor of the latter. Even though the liberal principles were recognized, the state was also given a broad power to intervene. But the constitutional amendments of 1995, 2001 and 2004 brought so such modifications that, currently, it can be undoubtedly asserted that the European system of human rights is incorporated in the Constitution. Nevertheless, the weakness in the independence of the judiciary remains as a major challenge that needs to be amended.

B. *Equality Before the Law and Prohibition of Discrimination*

One of the core principles of a democratic republican government is the principle of equality. As prescribed in the article 10, the principle of equality before the law "(…) *does not mean that everyone should be bound by the same provisions in all respects. The purpose pursued by this principle is to ensure that those who are in the similar conditions must be subject to the same procedure by laws.*" according to the Constitutional Court.[26] This is a constitutional duty that "*State organs and administrative authorities to act in compliance with the principle of equality before the law in all their proceedings*".

By the constitutional amendment of 2010, positive action for the realization of gender equality was also constitutionalized in the Turkish Constitution. According to the article 10, it is the state's duty to ensure the equality between men and women, and also to take all necessary measures that enable the equality exists in practice. Nevertheless, despite this constitutional provision, the inequality between men and women has not been overcame yet, and the inequality in social life[27] still requires intensified governmental actions.

---

25 Art. 66 – Turkish citizenship; Art. 67 – Right to vote, to be elected and to engage in political activity; Art. 68 – Forming parties, membership and withdrawal from membership in a party; Art. 69 – Principles to be observed by political parties; Art. 70 – Entry into public service; Art. 71 – Declaration of assets; Art. 72 – National service; Art. 73 – Duty to pay taxes; Art. 74 – Right of petition, right to information and appeal to the Ombudsperson.

26 For the decision of the Constitutional Court, dated 13.04.1976, no. 1976/3–1976/23.

27 For a general analysis on social inequality in a market-oriented economic policy without a mature welfare state at Turkey see, Ayşe Buğra, "Social Policy and Different

The protection of equality covers the prohibition of discrimination on language, race, color, sex, political opinion, philosophical belief, religion and sect, or any such grounds protected most strongly by the individual application procedure. The Constitutional Court held with regard to the individual application on the complaint about the difference in treatment after the termination of employment contract that there had been a breach of the principle of equality (the principle as to the prohibition of discrimination) guaranteed in the article 10 of the Constitution.[28] In addition, the Court recently upheld the unconstitutionality claims of some specialist doctors, who work under the Act no. 2547 and are not paid for their duty watch while other staff members are paid under the Public Servants Act no. 657. The Constitutional Court ruled that this difference between doctors was lack of any objective and reasonable justification and there has been a discriminatory interference with the right to property for the doctors who are not paid.[29]

C. State Obligations to Protect Rights and Freedoms

Regarding the realization of the fundamental rights, when the Constitution of 1961 and 1982 were compared, it could be easily deduced that the state has undertaken relatively very weak duty. The imperative wording of the former Constitution has been softened by the latter with using the phrase of "*trying to ensure the prosperity of the individuals*".

This article, never amended, became a source of important protection clause with the decisions of the Constitutional Court relating to individual application. The Court gradually began to refer to this article in order to bring the positive obligation doctrine of the European Court of Human Rights into Turkish protection mechanism. According to this view, the state does not only under the duty to not to interfere arbitrarily to fundamental rights, but also it should respect them and assure their fulfillment with the hand of proper legislation.

Dimensions of Inequality in Turkey: A Historical Overview," *Journal of Balkan and Near Eastern Studies*, Vol. 20, Iss. 4 (2018): 318–331.

28 For the individual application decision of Constitutional Court, Remezan Orak and others, dated 03.02.2016, application no. 2013/2229.

29 For the relevant individual application decisions of Constitutional Court, Tevfik İlker Akçam, dated 03.07.2019, application no. 2018/9074; Ali Akay, dated 15.12.2020, application no. 2017/33784; Yelda Dere, dated 24.03.2021, application no. 2018/10841; Asuman Biçer Yeşilay, dated 13.04.2021, application no. 2018/19742.

D. Restriction Clauses

The state authority had very broad means to intervene in the rights and freedoms especially with the hand of the article 13 of the Constitution. The original provisions had stipulated nine general clauses for restriction with a very large sense. With the constitutional amendment of 2001, this article became a protection clause for the rights and freedoms. The amended article permits only a restriction by law whose purpose must be in conformity with the relevant article. The restriction must be proportional, and the essence of the rights and freedoms must not be infringed. This article is a general clause for restriction. However, two other constitutional provisions must be mentioned on that issue. The first one is related to the delimitation of the social and economic duties of the state; and the second is related to the restriction clause for the rights and freedoms of the aliens/non-citizens.

The social and economic rights and freedoms, due to their nature, generally requires a positive action from the state. The Constitution of 1982 provided a specific article which permits to the state to derogate from its duties in this field. Accordingly, "*the capacity of its financial resources*" set the limit for social and economic rights and freedoms (art. 65).

Also, according to the article 16, the fundamental rights and freedoms of aliens/non-citizens, may be restricted by law compatible with international law.

Those are general principles applicable during ordinary time. Besides, in the article 119, the Constitution establishes a system on the state of emergency. Regarding this differentiated government regime, the article 15 prescribes the general rules on the suspension of fundamental rights during the emergency state. In the first paragraph, the government is empowered to suspend the fundamental rights only if it is necessary for the exigencies of the situation provided that the measures shall be compatible with the international law. Thus, the emergency state does not give any unlimited power to the government. Also, by the second paragraph, a list of core human rights is enshrined which can be exemplified as the individual's right to life, the integrity of his/her corporeal and spiritual existence (except where death occurs through acts in conformity with law of war), the prohibition of compelling anyone to reveal their religion, conscience, thought or opinion, or accusing anyone on account of them, non-retroactivity of offenses and penalties, and the presumption of innocence.

Nevertheless, even though this article strictly delimits the governmental power, the judicial accountability of the government is unprovided due to the lack of judicial review.

E. *Prohibition of Abuse*

As a principle of militant democracy, the prohibition of abuse found its constitutional basis in Turkish law with the constitutional amendment of 1971 within the Constitution of 1961. Known by the locution "*There is no freedom for the enemies of freedom*", the prohibition of abuse became another means for the government to interfere and restrict the fundamental rights. This prohibition, almost word for word, has also been prescribed in the Constitution of 1982.

In 2001, this article wasn't annulled but amended to render the state under the duty not to exercise its power in a way to destroy the fundamental rights and freedoms and not to stage an activity with the aim of restricting them more extensively than the Constitution allows. The Constitutional Court, by a very recent decision, underlined the arbitrariness that can arise by this article and concluded in the relevant case that there has been a violation inflicted by the application of this article for a deputy.[30]

II. Social and Economic Rights and Freedoms

A. *General Overview*

The constitutional principle which is directly related to the economic and social rights and freedoms is declared in the second article of the Constitution as "social state". This principle was, for the first time, constitutionally recognized by the former Constitution. According to the Constitution of 1961, the main duty of the state was to remove all the obstacles to the liberty of the individuals. As it was mentioned both in the Preamble and in the article 10 of the Constitution, this "liberalization" must be realized in every domain including economic and social sphere. This principle is adopted by the current Constitution but in a very different economic setting. The Constitution of 1961 had foreseen the state as an actor to intervene in economic relation in order to fulfill its duties of liberalization. Just before the military intervention in 1980, the state took some decisions which would bring fundamental modifications in economics. Frequently mentioned as "Decisions of 24th of January",[31] those decisions were considered as

---

30 For the relevant individual application decision of the Constitutional Court, Ömer Faruk Gergerlioğlu, dated 1.7.2021, application no. 2019/10634 (OJ, 8.7.2021, no. 31535).

31 For a detailed explanation see, Sadık Rıdvan Karluk and Sevilay Küçüksakarya, "Opening up the Economy of Turkey to the Outside World: The Stabilization Decisions of January 24th 1980, Economic Situation in Pre and Post January 24th Period," in *Chinese Business Review*, Vol. 15, Iss. 6 (2016): 265–281.

the signals for the implementation of the neo-liberal economic plan in Turkey. The current Constitution drafted in this economic setting carries within the articles related to social and economic rights the echoes of such an economic plan, which contradicts to the former Constitution.

The list of economic and social rights and freedoms is very exhaustive and very detailed in content. In this part, not only the right and freedoms related to employment law are enumerated, but also the protection of family, children, youth, elderly or disabled people, protection of health and environment are also put on the duty of the state with separate provisions.

It must be remembered that all those rights and freedoms are also under the protection of international agreements. Turkey has ratified the Convention for the Protection of Human Rights and Fundamental Freedoms and the revised European Social Charter, in addition to ILO Conventions, including the Convention on Freedom of Association and the Protection of the Right to Organise (no. 87, 1948), the Convention concerning the Application of the Principles of the Right to Organise and to Bargain Collectively (no. 98, 1949), and the Convention concerning the Protection of the Right to Organise and Procedures for Determining Conditions of Employment in Public Service (no. 151, 1978). According to the final sentence of the article 90 of the Constitution, those international agreements duly put into effect in Turkish law are directly applicable norms when there is an incompatibility in the national legal provision.[32]

B. *Right and Freedoms Directly Related to Business Law*

Amongst the rights and freedoms directly related to business law, the freedom of work and contract and the free establishment of private enterprises along with

---

On the history of Turkish economy see also, Korkut Boratav, *Türkiye İktisat Tarihi: 1908–2009* (Ankara: İmge Kitabevi, 2011).

32 Also see infra: *Chapter IV – Employment Law*. The Constitutional Court, by its decisions given with the procedure of individual application clearly underlined that the last sentence of the article 90 of the Constitution is an implicit abrogation rule and eliminates the ability to apply the provision of law that conflict with the provision(s) of an international agreement related to fundamental rights and freedoms (Sevim Akat Ekşi, dated 19.12.2013, application no. 2013/2187; Gülsim Genç, dated 6.3.2014, application no. 2013/4439; Neşe Aslanbay Akbıyık, dated 16.04.2015, application no. 2014/5836). This means that all the courts shall apply the international agreement provision when the national law offers less guarantee. But it is worth noting that while this jurisprudence clarifies the direct application of the article 90, it remains silent on the issues arising from the lack of national legislation.

the prohibition of drudgery come to the fore. The Constitution foresees that the state must take measures against the infringements of those rights. For the first, the state must take the necessary measures to raise the standard of living, to protect workers and the unemployed in order to improve the general conditions of labor, to promote labor, to create suitable economic conditions for prevention of unemployment, and to secure labor peace. For the latter, it is the duty of the state to take measures ensuring that private enterprises operate in accordance with national economic requirements and social objectives and in security and stability.

It must be noted that, despite the fact that numerous individual applications to the Constitutional Court have been filed about the prohibition of drudgery over time, no violation decision has yet been issued on this issue.[33]

According to the Constitution, workers have to work suited to their age, sex and capacity. As for the type of works, the minors, women, and physically and mentally disabled persons enjoy special protection with regard to the working conditions. The state has the authority to ensure that workers earn a fair wage commensurate with the work they perform and that they enjoy other social benefits.

In terms of collective employment law, trade-unionism[34] and the right to strike[35] and lockout are also regulated in a very detailed form, and the state must refrain from interfering them. The right to form unions and higher organizations may be enjoyed by the employees[36] and the employers as well. Accordingly, the right to form a union can only be restricted by law on the grounds of national security, public order, prevention of commission of crime, public health, public

---

33 For the sample decisions of the Constitutional Court, Yasemin Balcı, dated 25.7.2017, application no. 2014/8881; Sedat Durmuş, dated 17.4.2019, application no. 2015/14954.

34 For a critical analysis of the constitutional provisions and the implementation in the relevant Acts see also, Banu Uçkan, "From the perspective of EU integration: trade union rights in Turkey," *SEER Journal for Labour and Social Affairs in Eastern Europe*, Vol. 10, Iss. 4 (2007): 108.

35 Tankut Centel, "The right to strike: Turkey," in *The Right to Strike. A Comparative View*, edited by Bernd Waas (The Netherlands: Kluwer Law International, 2014), 537–550. Also, on the compatibility of the prohibition of strike with ILO provisions see, Alptekin Güney and Kemale Arslanova, "Türk Hukukunda Grev Yasakları ve ILO Normları," *Çalışma ve Toplum Dergisi*, Vol. 40, Iss. 1 (2014): 257–272.

36 The right to form unions of public servants has ever been very controversial issue from the enactment of the Constitution. With two constitutional amendments (1995 and 2001), their right to form unions is gradually constitutionalized with explicit dispositions within the articles 51 and 53.

morals, and protecting the rights and freedoms of others. The employees and employers have the right to conclude collective bargaining agreements in order to regulate reciprocally their economic and social position and working conditions while the right to strike is foreseen only when a disagreement arises during the collective bargaining process. Besides, the public servants and other public workers in public institutions have the right to collective agreements. The Public Servants Arbitration Board has been established in accordance with the constitutional amendments of 2010 in order to solve the disagreement arose during the process of collective agreement for public servants and other public workers. The Board's decision is final and has the force of "collective agreement" even though no collective (industrial) action was available. Therefore, the legislature refrained from using the term "collective bargaining agreement" and opted the locution of "collective agreement" by excluding the term "bargaining".

On the other hand, the restrictions are not limited to the public servants. A peculiar provision of the Constitution gives to the legislature the authority to regulate the circumstances and the workplaces, in which strike, and lockout may be prohibited or postponed (art. 54/4 of the Constitution).[37] And, in cases where a strike or a lockout is prohibited or postponed, the Supreme Arbitration Board, established in 2010, settles the collective disputes at the end of the period of postponement. The decision of the Board is final and has the force of a collective bargaining agreement, either in cases of prohibition or that of postponement.

In 2010, the article 54/7 of the Constitution, which prohibits any political strike, was abolished. However, the relevant legal provision (the article 58/3 of the Act on Labour Unions and Collective Bargaining Agreement no. 6356) which implicitly prohibits the political strikes is controversially still in force.

In violation allegations brought before the Constitutional Court through individual applications, the Court's decisions regarding the limitation of trade union activities can be classified under several categories. Penalties imposed on workers for participating in union activities are frequently viewed as a violation of their union rights.[38] Similarly, decisions were taken that were found to violate union rights, since the public authority could not provide sufficient justification

37 Ufuk Aydın, "From the Taft-Hartley Act to Turkish Industrial Relations – Postponement of Legal Strikes: A Legal Borrowing Case," *Comparative Labour Law and Policy Journal*, Vol. 25, Iss. 3 (2004): 365–390.

38 For the relevant individual application decisions of the Constitutional Court, Tayfun Cengiz, dated 18.9.2014, application no. 2013/8463; Ebru Arslan, dated 30.12.2014, application no. 2013/8464; Ertan Rüstem, dated 6.1.2015, application no. 2013/8517; Selda Demir Taze, dated 10.6.2015, application no. 2014/7668; Mehmet Çağdaş Serttaş,

for the strike postponement decisions.[39] Violation decisions on terminations due to unionization[40] or those on interventions that aggravate the status of a union representative as a result of their union activities are also of importance.[41]

Another constitutional provision that is of importance in the sphere is the right to social security, which aims to provide everyone with an institutionalized social insurance corresponding to Bismarck model.[42] The social security organization and related legal provisions have changed all over the years and are still being rebuilt.

Social security rights enshrined in the Constitution are also protected through individual applications to the Constitutional Court. The sample decisions that should be mentioned in this context are those related to property rights violations related to social security rights.[43] In addition, in cases where the Social Security Institution requests the reimbursement of unjustly made payments, in cases where the balance of personal interest and public interest is not considered, a decision of violation may be rendered in cases where a burden is heavily placed on the applicant for the sake of public interest.[44]

---

dated 6.1.2015, application no. 2013/8516; Veysel Kaplan, dated 26.9.2019, application no. 2015/13524.

Cf. The individual application decision of the Constitutional Court, Ahmet Parmaksız, dated 22.5.2019, application no. 2017/29263.

39 For the relevant individual application decisions of the Constitutional Court, Kristal İş Sendikası, dated 2.7.2015, application no. 2014/12166; Birleşik Metal İşçileri Sendikası, dated 9.5.2018, application no. 2015/14862.

40 For the relevant individual application decision of the Constitutional Court, Remezan Orak and others, dated 3.2.2016, application no. 2013/2229.

41 For the relevant individual application decision of the Constitutional Court, Abdülkadir Aksu, dated 20.3.2019, application no. 2015/19791.

42 On the social security system in Turkey, Ayşe Bugra and Aysen Candaş, "Change and Continuity under an Eclectic Social Security Regime: The Case of Turkey," *Middle Eastern Studies* Vol. 47, Iss. 3 (2011): 515–528.

43 For the relevant individual application decisions of the Constitutional Court, Şenal Haylaz, dated 25.2.2015, application no. 2013/3457; Besime Çetin, dated 8.11.2017, application no. 2014/17809; Mehmet Hocaoğlu, dated 15.10.2015, application no. 2013/3207; Mustafa Peker, dated 7.11.2019, application no. 2016/7192; Nurten Esen, dated 10.6.2015, application no. 2013/7970.

44 For the relevant individual application decisions of the Constitutional Court, Tevfik Baltacı, dated 9.3.2016, application no. 2013/8074; Ümit Çakır, dated 28.11.2018, application no. 2015/18918. Cf. Kemal Özcan, dated 12.2.2020, application no. 2017/18560.

III. Protection of Fundamental Rights by Individual Application before the Constitutional Court

The procedure of individual application as a secondary remedy for the protection of human rights was incorporated in the Constitution by the amendment of 2010. According to the new provision added in the article 148, "*Everyone may apply to the Constitutional Court on the grounds that one of the fundamental rights and freedoms within the scope of the European Convention on Human Rights which are guaranteed by the Constitution has been violated by public authorities*."

Along with the Constitution, the rules on the individual application procedure are to be found in the Code on Establishment and Rules of Procedures of the Constitutional Court (no. 6216)[45] between the articles of 45 to 51 and within the internal regulations of the Constitutional Court[46] between the articles of 59 to 84.

This kind of protection mechanism closely resembles, in principle, with those exercised in Germany (constitutional complaint/*Bundersverfassungsbeschwerde*) or in Spain (individual appeal for protection/*recurso de amparo*). The main difference with those remedies relies on the variety of the rights and freedoms which can be brought before the Constitutional Court. If an individual claim that public authorities infringed their rights, in order to make an individual application in Turkish law, those alleged rights or freedoms must be recognized both by the Constitution and by the European Convention of Human Rights. By this provision, it has widely acknowledged that only the rights and freedoms involved in the intersection set of these legal norms constitute the material subject of the Turkish individual application. Even though this provision could have easily been interpreted in a way to encompass almost all rights in the Constitution, the Constitutional Court preferred the interpretation promoting the delimited meaning, and rejected the claims related to the rights outside of the intersection.[47]

---

45 For the Code on Establishment and Rules of Procedures of the Constitutional Court see also, https://anayasa.gov.tr/en/legislation/law-on-constitutional-court/, accessed 17.8.2021.

46 For the internal regulations of the Constitutional Court see also, official website of Constitutional Court https://anayasa.gov.tr/en/legislation/internal-regulations-of-the-court/, accessed 17.8.2021.

47 For the decision of the Constitutional Court on freedom of movement see, Sebahat Tuncel, dated 20.2.2014, application no. 2012/1051, §53; Sare Tekalan, dated 14.10.2020, application no. 2018/34758, §37. On the right to vote during the local election see, Mansur Yavaş and Cumhuriyet Halk Partisi, dated 23.7.2014, application no. 2014/5425, §37; Zeyyat Ceylan, dated 20.10.2020, application no. 2019/14426, §28. On

According to the individual application mechanisms in comparative law, the claims of violation target the action, decision or the omission of the public authorities. In the relevant constitutional provisions translated in English, the terms which are used refers to the "public authorities". Nevertheless, the Turkish version explicitly refers to the "public power" which covers the acts, decisions, omission of the public authorities by including the legislative, executive, the judiciary power of the state. However, according to the article 45/3 of the Code on Establishment and Rules of Procedures of the Constitutional Court, only the judicial decisions may be brought before the Court with the individual application. So, the legislative act and decisions, the presidential decrees and decisions and the other administrative acts and decisions are exempted from this remedy. By the decision given after the appeal for annulment, the Constitutional Court rejected the allegations that those exempted norms are very abstract to cause any current individual violation and didn't find any incompatibility.[48]

As the article 46/1 states, the claim of infringement may be lodged by whose current and personal rights is directly affected. These provisions set the condition for the admissibility *rationae personae.* The aliens may only form an individual application for the rights which are not dedicated only to the citizens. Among legal entities/persons, only private legal entities/persons have the right to individual application for their rights. They cannot apply to the Constitutional Court for the violation of the rights and freedoms for their members. The legal entities of public law are unconditionally exempted for making any individual application. According to the Constitutional Court, this kind of legal entities may not be victim of any infringement of "the public power". However, this approach is incompatible with the comparative law and with the jurisprudence of the European Court of Human Rights.

The article 47 of the Code on Establishment and Rules of Procedures of the Constitutional Court stipulates the rules on the application process and due time for applications. Individual applications may be filed directly or through courts or representations abroad of Turkish Republic within 30 days after the exhaustion of legal remedies. Individual application isn't free from fee.[49]

---

referandum see also, Nurullah Efe and Halkın Kurtuluş Partisi, dated 7.6.2017, application no. 2017/20127, §16.

48 For the decision of the Constitutional Court, dated 1.3.2012, no. 2011/59–2021/34 (OJ, 2.4.2012, no. 28606).

49 In 2020, the fee is 446,90 Turkish Liras (approx. 45 Euros). This amount can be considered as high as to become an obstacle for individual application, even though the individual who proves that she/he is in an economic vulnerability may request for legal assistance.

If an individual application fulfills the conditions of admissibility checked by a commission composed by two members with a decision rendered unanimously, the individual application file is referred to the section composed by five members. The section decides on the merits of the individual application which is terminated by a decision of violation or not. If the section concludes that there has been a violation, it decides to the referral of the case to the relevant judicial authority (the court of first instance) and/or accompanied with a compensation. The section is also empowered to decide to what has to be done in order to rectify the violation (art. 50 of the Code no. 6216).

The decision of the violation concerns primarily the judicial authority (the court of first instance) whose decision has violated the right of the claimant. But according to the article 153 of the Constitution, these decisions are also binding for all other state organs. This means that if the violation is caused by incompatible interpretation of the statute with the Constitution, all other judicial and administrative organs must comply with the decision of the Constitutional Court, and the legislature is under the duty to amend a legal provision in the circumstances of a conflict with the international protection.

In terms of issues falling within the scope of business law, the Constitutional Court gives many decisions addressing the violation of the right to a fair trial in disputes arising from employee-employer relations or the working lives of public servants, apart from the ones previously mentioned.[50] The majority of these are due to the fact that the proceedings over 5 years exceed the reasonable time.[51] In the same vein, by the applications of commercial companies, the decisions are

---

50 For the relevant individual application decisions of the Constitutional Court, Vesim Parlak, dated 20.3.2014, application no. 2012/1034. For the decisions that rely on lack of justification see, Hüseyin Özdemir, dated 25.3.2015, application no. 2013/7455; Bayram Özkaptanoğlu, dated 8.4.2015, application no. 2013/1015.

51 For the relevant individual application decisions of the Constitutional Court, Hayrettin Ekim, dated 20.3.2014, application no. 2013/3442; Celal Aydemir, dated 3.4.2014, application no. 2013/5881; Zeynel Temel Kangal, dated 28.5.2014, application no. 2013/5049; Erdal Küçükali, dated 10.3.2015, application no. 2013/3617; Emine Özden, dated 21.5.2015, application no. 2013/5549. For a sample case where the trial exceeding 3 years is considered as excessive see, Osman Geçer, dated 17.7.2014, application no. 2013/1326. On the other hand, for an individual application decision that considers 3 years reasonable, also cf. Feridun Karaköylü, dated 15.10.2014, application no. 2013/4454.

mostly related to the violation of the right to a fair trial due to exceeding the reasonable time in course of trial.[52]

On the other hand, the decisions addressing the violation of the right to a fair trial are not solely based on the excessive length of the proceedings. There are also decisions on violation of the right to a fair trial given due to the obstruction of the right to access to a court,[53] and due to third party intervention in the case and the breach of equality of arms principle.[54] The decisions on violations of the right to a fair trial due to unpredictable interpretation and application of law are also given by the Constitutional Court.[55] There are also current decisions addressing the violations of the right to a fair trial arising from the cases related to employment security.[56]

In terms of the right to property, the Constitutional Court decides that there has been a violation due to the lack of predictable legal tax clause[57] or due to the application of the recidivism provision to the administrative fines.[58]

---

52 For the relevant individual application decisions of the Constitutional Court, Marmara Mühendislik Müt. San. Tic. Ltd. Şti., dated 15.6.2021, application no. 2018/30350; Nurtek İnşaat Petrol Nakliye Tekstil Gıda Emlak Müşavirliği Sağlık Hizmetleri Turizm Sanayi Ticaret Ltd. Şti., dated 27.1.2021, application no. 2019/18327.

53 For the relevant individual application decisions of the Constitutional Court, Nkt Teknoloji Dağıtım Ticaret Ltd. Şti., dated 24.2.2021, application no. 2018/26844; Aktif Elektik Müh. İnş. San. Ve Tic. Ltd. Şti., dated 26.6.2014, application no. 2012/855; Mustafa Berberoğlu, dated 26.2.2020, application no. 2015/3324; Levent Tütüncü, dated 8.9.2020, application no. 2015/7108; Ahmet Özdoğan, dated 9.1.2019, application no. 2017/26326; Ömer Faruk Eski, dated 21.3.2019, application no. 2016/1253.

54 For the relevant individual application decisions of the Constitutional Court, Zekiye Şanlı, dated 26.6.2014, application no. 2012/931; Murat Yasan, dated 8.1.2020, application no. 2015/6802.

55 For the relevant individual application decisions of the Constitutional Court, Murat Daş, dated 26.6.2014, application no. 2013/3063; Şahin Erol, dated 7.7.2015, application no. 2013/2539.

56 For the relevant individual application decisions of the Constitutional Court, Emin Arda Büyük, dated 2.7.2020, application no. 2017/28079; Berrin Baran Eker, dated 2.7.2020, application no. 2018/23568.

57 For the relevant individual application decision of the Constitutional Court, Türkiye İş Bankası A.Ş. (12), dated 6.10.2021, application no. 2019/1270.

58 For the relevant individual application decision of the Constitutional Court, Barut Turizm Müşavirlik Gıda Ticaret Ltd. Şti., dated 30.6.2021, application no. 2018/12722.

Prof. Dr. Aslı MAKARACI
and Assoc. Prof. Dr. Seda ÖKTEM ÇEVİK*

Chapter II Law of Persons

Ansay, Tuğrul Ş., Wallace, Don, Jr. and Önay, Işık, ed. 2020. Introduction to Turkish Law. Ankara: Seçkin; Bucher, Eugen. "Position of the Civil Law in Turkey in the Western Civilisation." Annales de la Faculté de Droit d'Istanbul, XXXII/49 (2000): 7–23; Dural, Mustafa and Öğüz Tufan. Türk Özel Hukuku: Cilt II, Kişiler Hukuku. İstanbul: Filiz, 2019; Oğuzman, Kemal, Seliçi, Özer and Oktay Özdemir, Saibe. Kişiler Hukuku. İstanbul: Filiz, 2016; Sağlam, İpek. Turkish Family Law. İstanbul: Oniki Levha, 2019.

Introductory Remarks

Civil Law, as one of the main branches of private law, has been fundamentally regulated by the Turkish Civil Code (CC), which is first legislated at 1926 and amended at 2002. The former Turkish Civil Code[1] (no. 743), which had come into force on 17th of February 1926, was adopted with slight amendments from the Swiss Civil Code, and the current Turkish Civil Code[2] (no. 4721) came into force on the first of January 2002. The roots of the Turkish Civil Code depend on the Swiss Civil Code due to the historical developments and the legislature choice. Thereby, it can be seen that the Turkish and Swiss Civil Codes are, apart from the minor changes, identical, and that Turkish and Swiss private law, in a considerable sense, are akin in structure.[3] However, after the last amendments in the Swiss Civil Code, significant differences have emerged between Turkish and Swiss civil law, especially in the field of personal law and family law.

Law of persons is a branch of civil law that generally deals with beginning and end of personality, the legal capacity of persons, registration of personal status and the protection of personality. General provisions regulated in the introductory part of the Turkish Civil Code are applicable to all civil law matters. As a result of this, the general principles governed in the law of persons have a significant role on the other branches of private law. As an example, the provisions on

* Corresponding authors.

1 Turkish Civil Code, no. 743 (*Türk Kanunu Medenisi*), OJ, 04.04.1926, no. 339.

2 Turkish Civil Code, no. 4721 (*Türk Medeni Kanunu*), OJ, 08.12.2001, no. 24607.

3 Eugen Bucher, "Position of the Civil Law in Turkey in the Western Civilisation," *Annales de la Faculté de Droit d'Istanbul*, XXXII/49 (2000): 7 ff.

the legal capacity of persons to enter transactions are applicable to all types of transactions such as business transactions and ordinary transactions.

In the first part of this chapter, general remarks on the Turkish Civil Code will be examined. In the second part, natural persons and legal persons will be analyzed. The topics of the beginning of personality, end of personality, registration of personal status, capatity to act, capacity to be subject of rights, and the protection of personality against others and also against themselves are to be explained under Turkish civil law. Lastly, the legal persons are briefly underlined in order to provide a solid ground for further explanations in the other chapters.

§ Part I General Remarks on the Turkish Civil Code

I. Overview

The current Turkish Civil Code is divided in an introductory part of seven articles followed by four books, which regulate, respectively, the law of persons, the family law, the law of inheritance and the law of property. In addition to this, due to the Article 646 of the Turkish Code of Obligations, the Turkish Code of Obligations completes the Turkish Civil Code as it forms the fifth book of the Civil Code. It should be noted that to express the significance of the Turkish Civil Code, the Turkish Commercial Code is also an integral part of the Turkish Civil Code as it is stated in the Article 1 of the Turkish Commercial Code.

As a whole, the Turkish Civil Code contains totally four parts with an introductory book:

- Preamble (as general principles of civil law)
- Law of Persons
- Family Law
- Law of Inheritance
- Law of Property

II. General Principles

General principles regulated in the introductory part of the Turkish Civil Code are applicable to all civil law matters.

The first Article of the Turkish Civil Code states that the law applies in all relevant matters referred to by the wording and its substance. In the absence of an enforceable provision, the judge shall decide in accordance with customary law, if no such rule exists, decide in accordance with the rule that they would make as if they were legislator. While ruling, the judge shall find assistance from the established doctrine and judicial decisions.

The Article 2 of the Turkish Civil Code governs acting in good faith. Due to this Article, every person must act in good faith when exercising their rights and performing their obligations. The apparent abuse of a right is not protected by the legal order.

The Article 3 of the Turkish Civil Code regulates good faith with a wording that "In cases where the law attaches a legal consequence to good faith, the presence of good faith is rule. However, a person who does not pay due diligence expected from them required by the situation cannot invoke the presence of good faith".

Judicial discretion is stated in the Article 4 of the Turkish Civil Code. According to this article, where the law confers discretionary power on judges, or orders to appriase the requirements of the situation, or good (just) causes, the judge shall decide in accordance with the principles of justice and equity.

The Article 5 of the Turkish Civil Code is stated that the general provisions of this Code and the Code of Obligations apply to all civil law matters to the extent appropriate.

The Article 6 of the Turkish Civil Code regulates burden of proof. According to this rule, unless the law provides otherwise, everyone is obliged to prove the existence of the facts on which they rely on for invoking their rights.

Proof by offical document is governed under the Article 7 of the Turkish Civil Code. Due to this article, official registers and official deeds constitute full evidence for the accuracy of the facts evidenced by them. Unless the law provides otherwise, the proof that their content is not accurate is not required to be in any particular form.

§ Part II Essentials of Law of Persons

Since the main subject of law is social relationships among people, law deals with every legal relationship, in which individuals participate, and regulates these relationships in terms of human benefit. In this sense, law takes persons as a subject from the beginning to the end of their life and existence. Additionally, even after the end of life, problems related to the properties of deceased people are also legally addressed within the scope of inheritance law. This suggests that persons are protected by law from birth to death.

For this reason, firstly the question of who are legally defined as persons will be answered. The concept of personality consists of human beings (real persons-natural persons) and legal persons (legal entities).

Legal persons are artificial personalities, to whom some rights and obligations have been granted by law. A body, which is composed of several human beings or of property, and is recognized by law, is called a legal person. In other words, a group of real persons, who come together individually, or bring their capital or skill for a common social, political and commercial purpose, or a property assigned for those kind of purposes, and acquire personality are called legal persons. This might be exemplified as associations, foundations, corporations, etc.

All persons (including real persons and legal persons) are subject to the rights and obligations. On the other hand, the extent of these rights and obligations differ from person to person.[4] In addition to this, the extent of these also differ depending on the statute of being a real person or a legal person. In other words, legal persons have all the rights and duties other than those, which presuppose intrinsically human attributes, such as gender, age, or kinship.

In this part, firstly natural persons, and then legal persons are to be analyzed.

I. Natural Persons

A. *Beginning and End of Personality*

1. *Beginning of Personality*

Personality is a status of being a person. The beginning of personality of real persons is started at the moment of birth (CC Art. 28/I). In biological meaning, birth is defined as the complete and alive separation of a child from its mother's body. "Complete separation" means leaving the mother's body beyond any doubt. The notion of "to be alive" requires solely a single breath to be taken and be given out. In other words, a child, who has breathed once and couldn't even take another breath, will be defined as born alive.[5] In this sense, the capability of surviving, or to be healthy, or to have mental capacity are not required in order to be a person, and these are not considered as essential elements of personality. The famous saying "a child born from a human is a person" explains that no other requisity

4 Tuğrul Ansay and Işık Önay, "Law of Persons," in *Introduction to Turkish Law*, eds. Tuğrul Ş. Ansay, Don Wallace Jr. and Işık Önay, 7th ed. (Ankara: Seçkin, 2020), 92.

5 Kemal, Oğuzman, Özer, Seliçi and Saibe Oktay Özdemir, *Kişiler Hukuku* (İstanbul: Filiz, 2016), 10 ff.; Mustafa, Dural and Tufan Öğüz, *Türk Özel Hukuku: Cilt II, Kişiler Hukuku* (İstanbul: Filiz, 2019), 17 ff.

is necessarily determined (except leaving mother's body alive and completely) to be considered as having a personality.[6]

It should be noted that as a general principle every person has a right to be the subject of rights. Indeed, due to the Article 28/II of the Turkish Civil Code, a child has legal capacity to be a subject of rights provided that it survives birth. On the other hand, even an unborn child may also be the subject of some of the rights. As subjected to the condition on to be born alive, an unborn child may acquire the rights, which benefits it. For example, if an unborn child exists amongst the heirs, the estate will be distributed after its birth. Similarly, an unborn child may be appointed as a successor.

2. *End of Personality*

a. *Death*

The personality of human being ends at the moment of death. The natural way of extinction of personality is death. Legal definition of death mainly corresponds to the "brain death" in the medical terminology. It is medically defined as the end of life by the way of cessations of functions of the central nervous system. On the other hand, another definition given to death covers the notion of "hearth death". In doctrine, both of these definitions have been encompassed. That is to say, "death is the loss of functions of all the organs of a person".[7]

The meaning of the personality of human being ends with death is that a dead person cannot be the subject of rights. In other words, the personality rights end after dead. For instance, upon a person's death, their estate passes to the successors. By means of a last will that was made when the deceased was alive, they may dispose of their property, and such a will becomes effective at their death. Also, marriage will be dissolved after the death of one of the spouses without requiring a court declaration or a court decision. As a result of this, the matrimonial property is to be divided after death.

As a rule, the death should be determined officially with a document issued by the public authorities. Since the proof of the birth or death of a person is established by the records kept by the civil register, public authority makes a recording according to the identification of the body of deceased. On the other hand, in some circumstances, the person is presumed as a dead person despite of their

---

6 Oğuzman, Seliçi and Oktay Özdemir, *Kişiler Hukuku,* 12; Dural and Öğüz, *Kişiler Hukuku,* 17 ff.

7 Oğuzman, Seliçi and Oktay Özdemir, *Kişiler Hukuku*, 20 ff.; Dural and Öğüz, *Kişiler Hukuku,* 21 ff.

body cannot be identified. For these cases, the Turkish Civil Code regulates both the presumption of death, and the presumption that depends on the declaration of dead in absentia (disappearance). If it is impossible to prove who among a group of people died before or after another, they are all assumed to have died at the same time (CC Art. 29/II). In this circumstances, none of these persons can acquire succession from each other.[8]

b. Presumption of death

Pursuant to the Article 31 of the Turkish Civil Code, the death of a person is deemed proven, even the corpse has not been found, on condition that this person has disappeared in the circumstances, in which their death may be regarded certain. This is called as presumption of death. If no news is received during the set period prescribed by law, the missing person is declared as a presumed dead, and the rights derived from death may be enforced as if the death were proven. If the missing person was married, the marriage dissolves automatically as does in the case of death.[9]

c. Declaration of presumption of dead in absentia (Disappearance)

In some circumstances, presumption of dead in absentia may occur according to the Turkish Civil Code (CC Art. 32–35). If it is highly probable that a person is dead, because of the fact that they disappeared under extremely life-threatening circumstances, or that they has been missing for a long period without any sign of life, the court may declare this person is presumed dead upon the application of those whose rights are dependent on the death. In this case, declaration of presumption of dead in absentia requires a court decision.[10]

The application may be made at least 1 year elapsed after the life-threatening event has occured, or 5 years elapsed after the last sign of life. The court must, by suitable public means, call on any person, who may provide information about the missing person to come forward within a specified period. The period for call shall be at least 6 months from the first public notice (CC Art. 33).

During this process, if the missing person comes forward within the set period or if news on the missing person is received, or if the date of their death

8 Ansay and Önay, "Law of Persons," 94.

9 Oğuzman, Seliçi and Oktay Özdemir, *Kişiler Hukuku,* 28 ff.; Dural and Öğüz, *Kişiler Hukuku,* 26 ff.

10 Oğuzman, Seliçi and Oktay Özdemir, *Kişiler Hukuku,* 30 ff.; Dural and Öğüz, *Kişiler Hukuku,* 30 ff.

is directly proved, the application fails (CC Art. 34). If none of them is occurred during the set period, the missing person is declared as presumed dead, and the rights derived from their death may be enforced as if the death were proven. The declaration of presumed death in absentia has retroactive effect as of the time of the life-threatening event, or that of the last sign of life. (CC Art. 35).

In case of declaration of presumption of death in absentia, if the missing person was married, the declaration does not dissolve the marriage automatically, the annulment of the marriage should be demanded from the court by the spouse (CC Art. 131). The spouse of the missing person, who intends to remarry, must apply to the court to receive a decision regarding the annulment of their marriage to the missing one.

B. Registry of Personal Status

Every fact about the personality (such as birth, death, marriage, divorce, religion, nationality, etc.) are registered in the special registries, which are kept by the public authorities. Birth, death, marriage, and divorce registries are maintained by the Personal Status Officer. Birth, marriage, or death certificates issued by the registrars are also used for proof. As a rule, birth, death, marriage, and other facts related to personal status are proved by these registrations. Unless the contrary is proven, their accuracy is to be presumed. The state assumes liability for erroneous (wrong) registrations. The register authorities must, *ex officio*, rectify mistakes resulting from an obvious oversight or error. Except for the obvious errors, registries may be changed only by a court decision.

C. Persons of Subject of Rights: Capacity

According to Turkish law system, the capacity may be defined in two meanings:

- The capacity to be the subject of rights
- The capacity to act

1. The Capacity to Be the Subject of Rights (Legal Capacity)

The capacity to be the subject of rights is defined as "legal capacity" in Turkish Law (CC Art. 8). This ability simply means to be entitled having the rights and assuming obligations for all persons (real or legal persons) within the boundaries of the legal order. All persons must be equal in terms of being subject of rights and obligations. The only necessity for real persons to enjoy rights is to be born completely alive. All persons, even an unborn child, on conditional to be born alive, are subject of all the rights. In other words, all human beings have the right to enjoy rights, and to assume obligations within legal limits. All real persons, even an unborn child, as noted above, have legal capacity (CC Art. 28/II).[11]

In this context, the provisions of the Turkish Constitution are also of importance. The Turkish Constitution, under the section regulating fundamental rights and freedoms, expressly states that every individual possesses inherent fundamental rights and freedoms, which are inviolable and inalienable (Constitution Art. 12). Every one has the right to life, and the right to the protection of integrity (of their physical and spiritual being) (Constitution Art. 17/I). Also, every one has the right to personal liberty and security (Constitution Art. 19/I).[12]

The equality of all persons as subjects of rights is further enshrined by the Constitution under the Article of 10. Accordingly, "All individuals are equal without any discrimination before the law irrespective of language, race, color, sex, political opinion, philosophical belief, religion or religious sect, or any such grounds. No privilage shall be granted to any individual, family, group, or class".

However, there are some resctrictions on the ability to be the subject of specific rights. As seen in the Article 124 of the Turkish Civil Code, in order to be able to marry, the prospective spouses must have reached 17 years of age.[13] Another example shall be given for foreigners. Foreigners are subject to rights different from that of for Turkish citizens in many cases. A foreigner, for instance, may not own real property within the country as freely as a Turkish national. Some areas of work are also closed to foreigners. Due to the globalization, these restrictions are losing their ground, especially in cases of foreign investment.[14]

Legal persons are also fully subject of legal rights and obligations. The Article 48 of the Turkish Civil Code states this rule in the following way: "Legal persons have the capacity of having rights and incurring obligations except those rights and obligations which presuppose intrinsically human attributes, such as gender, age, or kinship".

Hereby, it must be noted that ability to be subject of rights is a different concept from the capacity to act. For example, a 2-year-old child, or an 80-year-old person may inherit property, have money deposited in their name in a bank, be

---

11 Oğuzman, Seliçi and Oktay Özdemir, *Kişiler Hukuku,* 42 ff.; Dural and Öğüz, *Kişiler Hukuku,* 39.

12 Also see supra: *Chapter I – Constitutional Law.*

13 The extraordinary marriage age is regulated under the Art. 124 of the Turkish Civil Code. For detailed information also see, İpek Sağlam, *Turkish Family Law* (İstanbul: Oniki Levha, 2019), 60.

14 Oğuzman, Seliçi and Oktay Özdemir, *Kişiler Hukuku,* 44 ff.; Dural and Öğüz, *Kişiler Hukuku,* 41 ff.

an obligee or obligor, own a house, or bring a law suit before courts. However, because of a lack of capacity, as will be discussed below, in most of these cases somebody else will act in the name of the child (and possibly the 80-year-old man).[15]

2. *The Capacity to Act*

The capaciy to act means, on the one hand, the capacity to enter into binding transactions, and on the other hand, the capacity to be liable for wrongdoings or torts. Capacity to enter into legal transactions indicates the ability to enter into legally valid transactions (CC Art. 9). The legal validity of a transaction, for example that of a contract, depends on the capacity of the person's, who are parties to this transaction. To have capacity to be liable for torts means that a person may be legally liable if they damages the body, personality, or property of another person. The capacity of suing actions is also regarded including in the scope of the capacity to act.[16]

The capacity to act involves three following conditions:

- Majority (Full age)
- Capacity of judgment
- Not to be interdicted (not to be under guardianship)

a. *Conditions*

aa. *Majority*

There are three types of full age due to Turkish civil law.

(i) *Legal majority:* Legally, the age of majority is 18. One, who has completed 18 years old age, is regarded to have reached the majority (CC Art. 11).

(ii) *Majority by the court decision:* A mature child, who has completed the age of 15, after taking the consent of their parents, and with their own will, and under certain circumstances may be emancipated by the court (CC Art. 12). For example, if a child has to earn their own living, or has to take care of their ill parents, these circumstances are to be regarded as justified legal grounds for majority by the court decision.

---

15 Ansay and Önay, "Law of Persons," 94.

16 Ansay and Önay, "Law of Persons," 95; Oğuzman, Seliçi and Oktay Özdemir, *Kişiler Hukuku*, 53 ff.; Dural and Öğüz, *Kişiler Hukuku*, 52 ff.

(iii) *Majority through marriage:* Marriage renders the minor as major (CC Art. 11/II). A male and a female those are at the age of 17 years old, or those are at the age of 16 years solely under extraordinary conditions provided the permission of the court are entitled to marry; in this case, they acquire majority by means of law (CC Art. 124).

bb. The capacity of judgment

The capacity of judgment is the ability to make fair judgment (power of discernment). In other words, the capacity of judgment means the ability to choose and decide what is right or wrong.

This is also defined in the Article 13 of the Turkish Civil Code, "Persons, who are not able to act reasonably because of minority, mental sickness, mental weakness, drunkenness, or causes similar to these, do not have the ability to make fair judgements".

However, to act in a fair manner or reasonably is a vague concept. It changes from person to person and from time to time. On the other hand, as the Code indicates, there are certain obstacles that impede the ability to make fair judgments. These are as follows:

(i) *Minority (a status before majority*): Infants are completely incapable of making fair judgments. At what age a child starts to act reasonably is a question on incidents, and therefore, must be determined in each concrete case by the judge. Sometimes a 14-year-old child might be more mature than a 16-year-old. Moreover, a child may be able to make fair judgments with respect to certain transactions, on which they has had experience. To illustrate, a child, who works in their fathers' shop, is probably able to make fair judgments on selling goods there on one hand, but on the other hand, the same child will not be able to appreciate the nature of a guaranty contract.

(ii) *Mental illness:* Certain mental sicknesses, such as epilepsy and hysteria, may at times impede the ability to make fair judgments. In these cases, the court may need to determine the facts within the framework of concrete cases.

(iii) *Mental weakness:* Mental weakness, such as imbecility, drunkenness and other similar grounds, may deprive a mature of having legal capacity.

(iv) *Other causes similar to these:* Examples such as sickness with fever and sleepwalking may be given for the other circumstances mentioned in the Article 13 of the Turkish Civil Code.

cc. Not to be interdicted

This is a negative condition. Under certain conditions, a person may be interdicted, which means to be put under guardianship.

Legal grounds for interdiction are cited as minority (if the parental authority has been terminated by means of court, or by natural ways), mental illness or weaknesses, dipsomania or drug addiction, imprisonment over one year, wasteful expenditure (extravagance), or bad treatment of property and private life. Also, the Code stipulates the conditions for voluntary interdiction (CC Art. 404–408).

b. Types of capacity to act

aa. Full capacity

Those of age at full age (majority), having capacity of judgment, and who is not interdicted, depending on afore-mentioned grounds, are defined as full capacitated persons. Fully capacitated persons are entitled to enter all transactions by themselves and liable of all their lawful, or unlawfull actions. Such persons will be bound by the contracts that they have concluded, and they will be liable of torts if they give damage to somebody else, or their property.

bb. Full incapacity

A person, who does not have the ability to make fair judgments, is defined as fully incapacitated person. Their transactions are void, or they cannot incur an obligation, and cannot be put under liability because of their torts. Generally, they have neither transactional nor tortial responsibility. On the other hand, as an exception of this principle, they are accepted to be liable if the principle of equity requires the compensation of damages caused by an incapacitated person. The court may also rule on that a person, lacking the capacity to consent, shall compensate entirely or partially for damages they has caused, depending on the basis of equity (TCO Art. 65). A person, who has temporarily lost their capacity to consent, is liable for any damage having caused during that state unless they can prove that this state originated by no fault of their own (TCO Art. 59).

Incapacitated persons must act through a legal representative, such as a parent or a guardian. However, there some prohibited transactions, which incapacited persons cannot conclude even through their legal representatives. Under these circumstances, their legal representatives cannot act on behalf of incapacited persons. These are specified in the Article 449 of the Turkish Civil Code as follows: Donation, foundation and suretyship. The legal representatives also cannot act on the personal rights closely and directly attached to the incapacitated persons. Only if the incapacited person has any benefit upon the exercise of these personal rights, the legal representative can act.[17]

cc. Limited incapacity
Minors, who have the capacity to make judgments, and interdicted people, who are mature, are of limited incapacity. They are liable in damages arisen through their torts (CC Art. 16/II).

Their contractual capacity may be examined in three groups of transactions: Transactions of own power, transactions with the approval of their representatives, and prohibited transactions.

(i) *Transactions of own power:* Persons of limited capacity have capacity to act some sort of transactions by themselves, without any need of taking assent of their legal representatives. These transactions are those, which do not impose an obligation but only provide benefit to the contractual party. For example, accepting a present or inheriting an estate may be constituted by their own will (CC Art. 16). More precisely, they may only accept benefits that are free of charge, or carry out minor and daily transactions. On the other hand, the transactions regarding strictly personal rights must be assessed differentlly. Personal rights directly and closely associated with personality are defined as strictly personel rights. These are another group of the transactions that should be self-made (for example, a breach of promise of marriage). Under these circumstances, limited incapacitated persons exercise their strictly personal rights independently[18].

(ii) *Transactions with the approval of their representatives:* Limited incapacitated persons may only incur liability with the consent of their legal representative (CC Art. 16/I). Approval may be given before the act or after the act. Approval after the act (after a prior transaction) is referred to as ratification. The approval given before the transaction is referred to as permission. The consent of the legal representative may be given expressly or implicitly. The counterparty is relieved of any obligation if approval is not given within a reasonable period that assigned by the counterparty or that ascertained by a court. As long as approval is given,

---

17 Ansay and Önay, "Law of Persons," 98–99; Oğuzman, Seliçi and Oktay Özdemir, *Kişiler Hukuku,* 80 ff.; Dural and Öğüz, *Kişiler Hukuku,* 69 ff.

18 Ansay and Önay, "Law of Persons," 98; Oğuzman, Seliçi and Oktay Özdemir, *Kişiler Hukuku,* 100 ff.; Dural and Öğüz, *Kişiler Hukuku,* 91 ff.

no one, even the counterparty, can declare the transaction is void.[19] If the limited incapacitated person has induced the counterparty to erroneously assume that they has the capacity to act, the limited incapacitated person is liable for the loss or damage incurred.

(iii) *Prohibited transactions:* Some transactions are prohibited either for the persons of limited incapacity nor of their representatives. These are significant donations, foundation, and suretyship (CC Art. 449). Except of these transactions, persons with limited incapacity may act all of the other contracts through their legal representatives.

3. *Protection of Personality*

The concept of personality requires rights, obligations, capacity, bodily integrity, dignity, health, freedom, name, reputation, and right to be privacy. According to the Turkish Constitution, personality rights are explicitly enshrined.[20]

Personality rights are also recognized by international conventions such as European Convention of Human Rights,[21] United Nations Convention on the Rights of the Child[22] and United Nations Convention on the Elimination of All Forms of Discrimination against Women.[23]

Protection of personality consists of two meanings: Protection of personality against excessive restriction and protection of personality against infringements.

a. *Protection of personality against excessive restriction*

The Article 23 of the Turkish Civil Code regulates that "No person may, entirely or partially, relinquish their legal capacity or their capacity to act. No person may restrain their freedom, or limit their use of it to an extent which contradicts with the law or public morals". In this circumstance, the personality of people is also protected against themselves. This principle involves three aspects: These are legal capacity, capacity to act, and freedoms.

Firstly, the restrictions on the legal capacity can be defined as no person is entitled to sign an agreement, which restricts their legal capacity such as promise

---

19 Ansay and Önay, "Law of Persons," 98; Oğuzman, Seliçi and Oktay Özdemir, *Kişiler Hukuku,* 93 ff.; Dural and Öğüz, *Kişiler Hukuku,* 86 ff.

20 Ansay and Önay, "Law of Persons," 102; Oğuzman, Seliçi and Oktay Özdemir, *Kişiler Hukuku,* 164 ff.; Dural and Öğüz, *Kişiler Hukuku,* 104 ff.

21 OJ, 19.03.1954, no. 8662.

22 OJ, 27.01.1995, no. 22184.

23 OJ, 18.09.2002, no. 24880.

not to marry, or not to make a testamentary for their lifetime.[24] As another example, no person may promise not to bring a law suit to the courts, or never to dispose of their property. No person may promise not to change their domicile in their lifetime, or not to change their political ideas or religious beliefs.[25] No person has the right to end their life such as an euthanasia (also see, the By-Law on Patients Rights, Art. 15).

Secondly, the restrictions on the capacity to act can be defined as no person is entitled to limit their capacity to act. For instance, an employee may not promise not to engage in a similar profession without time limitation.[26] Lastly, no person is entitled to limit their freedoms unlawfully. To illustrate, in an individual employment contract, if an employee promises to work more than 10 years, this contract is to be regarded void. Those contracts whose terms are impossible, unlawful, or immoral are also regarded as void under the Article of 27 of the Turkish Code of Obligations.

b. Protection of personality against infringements

aa. In general

Any person whose personality rights have been infringed upon unlawfully may petition the court for protection from all those who are responsible for the infringement. An infringement on rights is against the law, unless it is justified by the consent of the person, whose rights are infringed, or by an overriding private or public interest, or by the competence granted by law (CC Art. 24).

There are two conditions for the protection of personality against infringements.

(i) *The first condition* is that there should be an attack against personality rights unlawfully. A person, whose bodily integrity is violated under any attack or any offenses or a person, whose personality or property are being damaged or threatened, may be given as an examples of unlawfull attacks against personality. Accusations, libels, slanders, false information, or improper criticism, as well as revealing secrets such as private letters, or listening in on others' telephone calls, or unlawfully publishing images of a person, are all

24 Oğuzman, Seliçi and Oktay Özdemir, *Kişiler Hukuku,* 198; Dural and Öğüz, *Kişiler Hukuku,* 149.

25 Ansay and Önay, "Law of Persons," 104.

26 Also see infra: *Chapter IV – Employment Law.*

deemed actions damage person's honor and dignity, that is, are considered actions against personality.[27]

(ii) *The second condition* is there may not be any grounds for justification. The grounds for justification are the consent of the person, whose rights are infringed, the presence of an overriding private interest, or the presence of overriding public interest, or a granted competence by law (CC Art. 24). The consent of patient for the medical treatments may be given as an example for the grounds of consent of the affected person. And, the emergent treatment applied by the doctor for the patient that lost conscious may be given as an example for an overriding private interest. The publication of news about well-known persons such as politicians, musicians, and scientists will not considered acts against personality because of the presence of an overriding public interest, which is considered as a justification ground.[28] If the publication of news is correct, up to date, and if there is a balance between its substance and form, then it is not considered as an infringement upon personality.

bb. Actions

A person, whose personal rights have been illegally attacked may petition the court for the protection from the infringements (CC Art. 25). The applicant may request the judge:

- to render the danger of infringement prevented,
- to order the cessation of an ongoing infringement,
- to make a declaratory decision that an ending infringement was unlawful, on condition that its effects continue even if the infringement has ended.

The applicant may also request the rectification, or the decision be notified to third parties or be published. The applicant's right to request material and immaterial compensation, and to claim the restitution of profits obtained due to unlawful attack in accordance with the provisions of agency without authority is retained.

(i) *Declaratory action:* It is an action for requesting the court to decide if the violation is contrary to laws or not.

27 Ansay and Önay, "Law of Persons," 102; Oğuzman, Seliçi and Oktay Özdemir, *Kişiler Hukuku,* 206 ff.; Dural and Öğüz, *Kişiler Hukuku,* 152 ff.

28 Ansay and Önay, "Law of Persons," 103.

(ii) *Act of prohibiton:* It is an action for requesting the court to prevent the violation of personal rights or to cease it if the harmful action has already begun.
(iii) *Compensation:* Material or immaterial damage may be demanded to be compensated in case of violation of personal rights. *Material compensation:* It is requested for material damage. Material damage is the substantial damage of loss, which can be compansated with money. It includes medical treatment expenses, the loss of profit, the loss of awaited profit, etc. *Immaterial compensation:* It is requested for immaterial damage. Immaterial damages are psychological damages about mental anguish, grief, and suffering.
(iv) *The restitution of the profits*: It has been earned through the actions contrary to personal rights, profits may also be restituted. For example, an author, who has written the life story of a politician by emboiding with libels, and thereby, has violated the privacy of the given politician, must hand over the profit they has gained from the publication of this book.

In addition to this, the protection of a person's right to their name is specially regulated in the Article 26 of the Turkish Civil Code. This article states that "The individual whose name is in dispute might sue to have their right determined". A person aggrieved by the infringement of their rights to the name, may request the prevention of this violation.

If the use of a name is disputed, the person may apply for a court declaration confirming their rights to the name. If a person is adversely affected because another person is using their name, they may seek an order from the court that prohibits such use, and if the user is at fault, they may bring a claim for damages, and where justified by the nature of the infringement, for compensation.

II. Legal Persons

According to Turkish civil law, the legal persons are cited as associations and foundations. Associations of persons organized as a corporate body having a structure in itself, and independent property communities dedicated to a specific purpose acquire legal personality pursuant to special provisions related to them. Associations of persons and property communities, which pursue an immoral or unlawful purpose, shall not acquire legal personality (CC Art. 47). Legal persons have all the rights and obligations other than those, which presuppose intrinsically human attributes, such as gender, age, or kinship (CC Art. 48). Legal persons gain the capacity to act once their governing bodies have been appointed as required by law and their articles of association.

Pursuant to the article 56 of the Turkish Civil Code, an association is defined as a society formed by unity of at least seven real persons or legal persons for realization of a common purpose other than sharing of profit and by constantly combining their knowledge and studies for this purpose. Every person has the right to form an association without prior permission. The founders of association should possess the capacity to act (CC Art. 57). Associations with a political, religious, scientific, cultural, charitable, social or other non-profit purpose acquire legal personality as soon as indication of the title, object, income sources, membership conditions, organs and organization as well as the list of provisional board of directors stated in the articles of the associations. Members may be admitted to the association at any time. Every real person and legal persons that possess the capacity to act has the right to apply for membership in an association (CC Art. 64).

A foundation is established by the endowment of assets for a specific purpose (CC Art. 101). A foundation can be established through an official deed or through a testamentary disposition. The foundation is regarded as a legal person, when it is being registered in the records kept by the court of the given location (CC Art. 102).

Apart from these legal persons, according to Turkish civil law, there are also different types of legal persons (legal entities) such as commercial companies, which are regulated in the Turkish Commercial Code.[29] Trade unions, political parties, and bar associations are also stated as legal persons due to their special laws.[30]

---

29 See infra: *Chapter V – Commercial Law.*

30 Tuğrul Ansay and Işık Önay, "Legal Persons, Societies and Business Associations," in *Introduction to Turkish Law*, eds. Tuğrul Ş. Ansay, Don Wallace Jr. and Işık Önay, 7th ed. (Ankara: Seçkin, 2020), 107.

Prof. Dr. Aslı MAKARACI
and Assoc. Prof. Dr. Seda ÖKTEM ÇEVİK*

Chapter III Law of Obligations

Ansay, Tuğrul and Önay, Işık. "Law of Obligations." In *Introduction to Turkish Law*, 177–203. Edited by Ansay, Tuğrul, Wallace, Don Jr. and Önay, Işık. 7th ed. Ankara: Seçkin, 2020; Antalya, Gökhan. *Borçlar Hukuku Genel Hükümler Cilt V/1, 1.* Ankara: Seçkin 2019; Antalya, Gökhan. *Borçlar Hukuku Genel Hükümler Cilt V/1, 3.* Ankara: Seçkin 2019; Bucher, Eugen. "Position of the Civil Law in Turkey in the Western Civilisation." *Annales de la Faculté de Droit d'Istanbul*, XXXII/49 (2000): 7–23; Bucher, Eugen. "Law of Contracts." In *Introduction to Swiss Law*, 103–137. Edited by Dessemontet, F. and Ansay, Tuğrul. The Hague: Kluwer/Schulthess, 2004; Erdem, Mehmet. *La Clause Pénale.* Neuchâtel: Étude comparative de droit suisse et de droit turc, 2010; Erdem, Mehmet. *Özel Hukukta Zamanaşımı.* İstanbul: On İki Levha, 2010; Eren, Fikret. *Borçlar Hukuku Genel Hükümler.* Ankara: Yetkin, 2019; Esener, Turhan. *Turkish Business Law I, Contracts and Torts (Law of Obligations).* İstanbul: Boğaziçi University Press, 2000; Helvacı, İlhan. *Turkish Contract Law.* Springer, 2017; Kocayusufpaşaoğlu, Necip. *Borçlar Hukuku Genel Bölüm Birinci Cilt.* İstanbul: Filiz, 2014; Nomer, Haluk Nami. *Borçlar Hukuku Genel Hükümler.* İstanbul: Beta, 2017; Oğuzman, Kemal and Öz, Turgut. *Borçlar Hukuku Genel Hükümler, Volume I.* İstanbul: Vedat Yayıncılık, 2015; Oğuzman, Kemal and Öz, Turgut. *Borçlar Hukuku Genel Hükümler, Volume II.* İstanbul: Vedat Yayıncılık, 2016; Tandoğan, Haluk. *Borçlar Hukuku Özel Borç İlişkileri Cilt I/1.* Ankara: Banka ve Ticaret Hukuku Araştırma Enstitüsü, 1984; Tekinay, Selahattin Sulhi, Akman, Sermet, Burcuoğlu, Haluk and Altop, Atilla. *Borçlar Hukuku Genel Hükümler.* İstanbul: Filiz, 1993; Tercier, Pierre, Pichonnaz, Pascal and Develioğlu, H. Murat. *Borçlar Hukuku Genel Hükümler.* İstanbul: On İki Levha, 2021.

* Corresponding authors.

Introductory Remarks

In the vein of what has been stated in the previous chapter on law of persons, it is widely acknowledged that Turkish civil law roots depend on Swiss civil law due to the historical developments and the legislature choice. More precisely, the historical background of the Turkish Code of Obligations depends on the basis of the Swiss Code of Obligations since both the Turkish Civil Code and the Turkish Code of Obligations were adapted from the Swiss versions. As a result of this, the former Turkish Code of Obligations no. 818[1] had come into force on 22 April 1926 as an adaptation of the Swiss Code of Obligations.

The current Turkish Code of Obligations no. 6098[2] came into force on 1 June 2012. The amendments in the current Turkish Code of Obligations (TCO) are mostly in accordance with the provisions of the Swiss Code of Obligations and the decisions of the Swiss Supreme Court within the framework of the implementation of the relevant provisions. It is obvious that Turkish and Swiss Code of Obligations are, except minor changes, are identical; therefore, this allows the view that Turkish and Swiss private law are closely akin.[3]

When it is assessed within the context of national law, pursuant to the Article 646, the Turkish Code of Obligations is a component part of the Turkish Civil Code (CC). Thus, the general provisions of the Code of Obligations may be applied to all legal relations governed by the Civil Code if there are no special rule governs. Additionally, due to the Article 5 of the Civil Code the general provisions of the Code of Obligations concerning the formation, performance and termination of the contracts also apply to other civil law matters.[4]

The Turkish Code of Obligations which consists of 644 articles has two parts: General provisions and special provisions. The part of general provisions commences with the creation of obligations regarding the obligations arising by contracts (TCO Art. 1–48), torts (TCO Art. 49–76) and unjust enrichment (TCO Art. 77–82). Secondly, the effects of obligation relationship, which

---

1 OJ, 08.05.1926, no. 366.

2 OJ, 04.02.2011, no. 27836.

3 Eugen Bucher, "Position of the Civil Law in Turkey in the Western Civilisation," *Annales de la Faculté de Droit d'Istanbul*, Vol. XXXII, Iss. 49 (2000): 7 ff.
Therefore, under this chapter, in cases where the articles of Turkish and Swiss Code of Obligations overlap, the official English translation of the Swiss Code of Obligations will be quoted. See, www.fedlex.admin.ch, accessed 18.9.2021.

4 Turhan Esener, *Turkish Business Law I, Contracts and Torts* (İstanbul: Boğaziçi University Press, 2000), 1.

are performance of obligations and consequences of non-performance of obligations, are regulated. The other parts contain obligations involving third parties, extinction of obligations (e.g., novation, set-off, prescription, etc.) and special relationships relating to obligations (e.g., joint and several obligationship, conditional obligations, earnest money, forfeit money, contractual penalties, assignment of claims and assumption of debts, etc.). In the special provisions, types of contractual relationships such as sale, special types of sale, exchange contract, gifts, the lease, the loan, the individual employment contract and the special types of it, contract for work, agency contract, contract of surety, etc. are regulated. In addition to this, Turkey is a part of United Nations Conventions on Contracts for the International Sale of Goods (CISG). As a result of this, if there is a dispute, which is arising from an international sale, the provisions of CISG will be applied.

Under this chapter, a brief overview of Law of Obligations in Turkey will be explained in two parts. In the first part, the general provisions of obligation law will be briefly introduced. In the second part the special provisions of obligation law will be analyzed by the method of classifying contracts according to their subject.

In the first part of this chapter, the general provisions of the Turkish Code of Obligations will be briefly evaluated under the topics of; concept of contracts, formation of contracts, interpretation of contracts, validity of the contracts, representation, performance of the contract, default of the obligee, non-performance of the contract, extinction of obligations, joint and several obligationship, assignment of claims and assumption of debts.

In the second part, the focus will be on contracts providing the transfer of ownership, the contracts providing the transfer of using of goods, service contracts and security contracts. Lastly, the Consumer Protection Law will be briefly analyzed as well.

§ Part I The General Provisions of Obligation Law

I. Overview

In the Turkish Code of Obligations, the sources of obligations are cited as contracts, torts and unjust enrichment. A person, who unlawfully causes damage to another either willfully or negligently, is obliged to provide compensation. This obligation is derived from tort. Obligations arising from tort is regulated in TCO between Art. 49–76. Another source of obligation is unjust enrichment, which is regulated in TCO between Art. 77–82. A person, who has enriched their selves without just cause at the expense of another, is obliged to make restitution according to the principle of prohibition of unjust enrichment. On the other hand, the main focus of this part will be the contract as a source of obligation rather than tort and unjust enrichment. Under this chapter, the sources of obligation arising from contracts, the performance of obligation, the extinction of obligations and special relationships relating to obligations will be evaluated.

It should be noted that obligation has several meanings. If there is a contract between parties, this relationship is accepted as obligation relationship. Obligation relationship is binding for the contracting parties. Within the frame of an obligation relationship, there can be multiple obligations separately.[5] Therefore, it also refers to the singular obligations. For example, in a lease contract, the lessor (or landlord) is required to make the object available for its designated use and to maintain it in that condition. In return, the lessee (or tenant) is obliged to pay rent. In this respect, due to the Code of Obligations, the obligation (debt) means a single duty of the obligor (debtor) to fulfill each of promise.

II. Contract: As a Source of Obligation

Contract law is based on the principle of freedom of contract. The principle of freedom of contract contains several aspects. These aspects are cited as[6]:

- Freedom to conclude or not to conclude a contract,
- Freedom to choose the party,
- Freedom of choice of form of contract,
- Freedom to establish the provisions of contract,
- Freedom of extinction of contracts.

---

5 Kemal Oğuzman and Turgut Öz, *Borçlar Hukuku Genel Hükümler, Volume I* (İstanbul: Vedat Yayıncılık, 2015).

6 Necip Kocayusufpaşaoğlu, *Borçlar Hukuku Genel Bölüm Birinci Cilt* (İstanbul: Filiz, 2014), 525–613; Selahattin Sulhi Tekinay, Sermet Akman, Haluk Burcuoğlu and Atilla Altop, *Borçlar Hukuku Genel Hükümler* (İstanbul: Filiz, 1993), 362–364, 369–407; Fikret Eren, *Borçlar Hukuku Genel Hükümler* (Ankara: Yetkin, 2019), 335–365; Oğuzman and Öz, *V. I*, 23 ff.; İlhan Helvacı, *Turkish Contract Law* (Springer, 2017), 35; Eugen Bucher, "Law of Contracts," in *Introduction to Swiss Law*, eds. F. Dessemontet and Tuğrul Ansay (The Hague: Kluwer/Schulthess, 2004), 105; Tuğrul Ansay and Işık Önay, "Law of Obligations," in *Introduction to Turkish Law*, eds. Tuğrul Ansay, Don Wallace, Jr. and Işık Önay, 7th ed. (Ankara: Seçkin, 2020), 180; Haluk Tandoğan, *Borçlar Hukuku Özel Borç İlişkileri Cilt I/1* (Ankara: Banka ve Ticaret Hukuku Araştırma Enstitüsü, 1984), 8 ff.; Gökhan Antalya, *Borçlar Hukuku Genel Hükümler Cilt V/1, 1* (Ankara: Seçkin 2019), 125 ff. and 429 ff.

To maintain the freedom of contract, the provisions of the Turkish Code of Obligations are non-mandatory in principle. However, in some contracts such as consumer contracts and individual employment contracts, the parties are not in the equal positions. Consequently, the weaker party is protected with the mandatory provisions.

The Turkish Code of Obligations frames some types of contracts such as sale contract, lease contract, agency contract, etc. But in Turkish law, as a result of the principle of freedom of contract, the parties may determine their preferred contract types. Franchise agreements and arbitration contracts can be given as an example.

A. *Concept of Contracts*

A contract is a legally binding agreement that is usually concluded between two parties.[7] According to the Article 1 of the Turkish Code of Obligations, the conclusion of a contract requires mutual expression of intent by the parties. The Turkish Code of Obligations refers contract as a bilateral legal transaction. The examples may be given such as sale contract, lease contract, and contract of work, etc. However, it should be noted that contracts rarely may be concluded between more than two parties such as partnership contracts.[8]

Contracts are agreements that create, modify or terminate an obligation. Special types of contracts, which are regulated under the Turkish Code of Obligations, mostly create an obligation. These are called as "contracts creating an obligation".[9]

A bilateral contract (or a *synallagmatic* contract) is a contract in which both parties oblige reciprocal duties. In these contracts, the rights and obligations of the parties are like two sides of a coin.[10] A sale contract is a typical example for the synallagmatic contracts. In sale contracts, the seller promises to transfer the ownership where the buyer promises to pay the sale price. These are mutual promises.[11] If only one party of the contracts undertakes an obligation, these

7 Oğuzman and Öz, *V. I*, 42; Helvacı, *Turkish Contract Law*, 3.
8 Oğuzman and Öz, *V. I*, 42; Tekinay, Akman, Burcuoğlu and Altop, *Genel Hükümler*, 54; Eren, *Borçlar Genel*, 210 ff.; Helvacı, *Turkish Contract Law*, 3.
9 Oğuzman and Öz, *V. I*, 45 ff.; Eren, *Borçlar Genel*, 217 ff.; Esener, *Turkish Business Law I*, 17.
10 Esener, *Turkish Business Law I*, 18.
11 Oğuzman and Öz, *V. I*, 45; Eren, *Borçlar Genel*, 222 ff.; Esener, *Turkish Business Law I*, 18; Ansay and Önay, "Law of Obligations," 179.

contracts are called as unilateral or one-sided contracts. Donation is a unilateral contract in which only the donor undertakes an obligation.[12]

B. *Formation of Contract*

As a general principle in contract law, the contracts are formed by an offer and its acceptance. Expressions of the intent that formulate the contract compose "offer" and "acceptance". In a timeline, the expression declared first is called as offer whereas the second is acceptance.[13]

The main requirement of a valid contractual relationship is the consent of the parties that must be mutual and consistent (TCO Art. 1/I). The expression of the intent may be explicit or implicit (TCO Art. 1/II).

Other elements may be mentioned such as the requirement of the capacity of the persons concluding the contract and the mutual expression of intentions to enter into the contract and be bound by the contract. It implies that a contract only exists as of the moment they mutually expressed the intention to enter into it and be contractually bound, not when they simply agreed on the terms of the contract.[14]

1. *Offer*

An offer is deemed to be a declaration of the intention to be bound under a contract with the content as specified, subject to the acceptance by the addressee. It has to include all the necessary elements of the intended contract, so that the addressee of the offer may only say "yes" or "agreed".[15]

It must be made with the intention of concluding a contract. Lastly, the offer must be addressed to a prospecting contracting party. It may also be addressed to determined or undetermined persons (e.g., to the general public).[16]

A person, who offers to enter into a contract with another person and sets a time limit for acceptance, is bound by this offer until the time limit expires. The

12 Oğuzman and Öz, *V. I*, 45; Eren, *Borçlar Genel*, 222; Esener, *Turkish Business Law I*, 18; Ansay and Önay, "Law of Obligations," 179.

13 Eren, *Borçlar Genel*, 276 ff.; Helvacı, *Turkish Contract Law*, 4.

14 Bucher, "Law of Contracts," 110.

15 Eren, *Borçlar Genel*, 276 ff.; Bucher, "Law of Contracts," 110; Helvacı, *Turkish Contract Law*, 4.

16 Oğuzman and Öz, *V. I*, 51; Eren, *Borçlar Genel*, 277 ff.; Helvacı, *Turkish Contract Law*, 4; Ansay and Önay, "Law of Obligations," 181; Antalya, *Cilt V/1, 1*, 303 ff.; Haluk Nami Nomer, *Borçlar Hukuku Genel Hükümler* (İstanbul: Beta, 2017), 48 ff.

offeror is no longer bound if no acceptance has reached them on expiry of the time limit (TCO Art. 3). Where an offer is made in the offeree's presence and no time limit for acceptance is set, it is no longer binding on the offeror unless the offeree accepts it immediately (TCO Art. 4/I).

Where an offer is made in the offeree's absence and no time limit for acceptance is set, it remains binding on the offeror until such time as they may reasonably expect a response sent duly and promptly has reached them. The offeror may assume that their offer has been promptly received. Where an acceptance sent duly and promptly is late in reaching the offeror and the offeror does not wish to be bound by their offer, they must immediately inform the offeree (TCO Art. 5).

The sending of unsolicited goods does not constitute an offer. The recipient is not obliged to return or keep such goods (TCO Art. 7).

The offeror is not bound by their offer if they have made express declaration to that effect or such a reservation arises from the circumstances or from the particular nature of the transaction. The sending of tariffs, price lists and alike does not constitute an offer unless circumstances indicate otherwise (TCO Art. 8).

An offer is deemed not to have been made if its withdrawal reaches the offeree before or at the same time as the offer itself or, if the withdrawal is communicated to the offeree before they become aware of the offer even if it arrives subsequently (TCO Art. 10).

2. Acceptance

The acceptance must be entirely consistent with the offer; a modification of conditions of the original offer is not an acceptance but is deemed to constitute a counter-offer.[17]

Where the particular nature of the transaction or the circumstances make the expression of the acceptance unlikely to be reasonably expected, the contract is deemed to have been concluded if the offer is not rejected within a reasonable time (TCO Art. 6).

A person, who publicly promises remuneration or a reward in exchange for the performance of an act, must pay in accordance with the promise. If the offeror withdraws their promise before performance has been made, they must reimburse any person, who have confidence in the promise, for their expenditures that are incurred in good faith up to the maximum amount promised unless it is

17 Oğuzman and Öz, *V. I*, 65; Eren, *Borçlar Genel*, 288; Helvacı, *Turkish Contract Law*, 7; Bucher, "Law of Contracts," 110; Antalya, *Cilt V/1, 1*, 331 ff.

proved that such person could not have provided the performance in question (TCO Art. 9).

Due to the TCO Art. 10/II, the principles about the withdrawal of the offer will be applied to the withdrawal of the acceptance.

3. *Standard Terms*

Standard terms are stated under the Turkish Code of Obligations between Art. 20–25. Previously these terms were not regulated in the Turkish Code of Obligations. Standard terms are the terms which are prepared from one of the party previously and unilaterally to use in several numbers of similar contracts. The party, whom prepares the contract, imposes these terms to the counterparty without negotiating or/and discussing (TCO Art. 20/I). The imposed party has only right to say "yes" or "no". Standard terms are used in many contracts in practice.[18]

Under the Turkish Code of Obligations, standard terms are to be assessed according to the three-stage test:

- Control of validity (Enforcement control): The standard terms which are contrary to the benefits of imposed party can be the part of the contract if the preparing party informs the counterparty clearly about the existence and the contents of these terms during concluding the contract and if the imposed party accepts these terms. Otherwise, the standard terms are deemed to be non-written[19] (TCO Art. 21/I).

  Standard terms that are unusual to the purpose of the contract and the nature of the transaction are considered as non-written (TCO Art. 21/II). These terms also may be defined as 'surprising' clauses. For example, the clause concerning that a surety accepts being mortgagee under the standard terms of surety contract is deemed to be non-written.

---

18 Oğuzman and Öz, *V. I,* 160 ff.; Eren, *Borçlar Genel,* 227 ff.; Helvacı, *Turkish Contract Law,* 29; Ansay and Önay, "Law of Obligations," 187. See for detailed information Oğuzman and Öz, *V. I,* 160 ff.; Eren, *Borçlar Genel,* 277 ff.; Helvacı, *Turkish Contract Law,* 29 ff.; Antalya, *Cilt V/1, 1,* 471 ff.; Nomer, *Borçlar Genel,* 78 ff.; Pierre Tercier, Pascal Pichonnaz and H. Murat Develioğlu, *Borçlar Hukuku Genel Hükümler* (İstanbul: On İki Levha 2021), 297 ff.

19 It should be noted that the term "non-written" is not typical for the Turkish Code of Obligations. This term refers to "non-existent". That is to say, invalid standard terms are deemed to be non-existent. See also, Helvacı, *Turkish Contract Law,* 30; Oğuzman and Öz, *V. I,* 163 ff. Also cf. Antalya, *Cilt V/1, 1,* 505.

If the contract consists of invalid standard terms, the valid provisions of the contract exist except the non-written standard terms. The preparing party cannot claim that if the invalid terms did not exist, the contract wouldn't have been concluded (TCO Art. 22).

TCO Art. 24 states that the provisions which give the authority to the preparing party to make amendments to the provisions of a contract regarding general terms or to make new arrangement in such type of a contract unilaterally shall be deemed to be non-written.

- Control of interpretation: If a standard term is not clear and understandable or is ambiguous, it is interpreted to the disadvantage of the preparing party (TCO Art. 23).
- Control of content: The provisions which are detriment to the imposed party according to the principle of good faith cannot be entitled to the contract as a standard term (TCO Art. 25). The provisions which violate moral principles due to the lack of balance between the interests of the parties are held invalid. As a typical example, it can be given the terms which give the preparing party the authority to terminate the contract or to amend the contract unilaterally.

4. *Form of Contracts*

Pursuant to the TCO Art. 12/I, the validity of a contract is not subject to compliance with any particular form unless a particular form is prescribed by. In the absence of any provision to the contrary on the significance and effect of formal requirements prescribed by law, the contract is valid only if such requirements are satisfied (TCO Art. 12/II). This principle is called as freedom of form of contract which is underlined under TCO Art. 12/I. It is also referred to as the principle of no requirement as to form.

Consequently, a contract may be written or orally. For example, a sale contract of movable property may be made written or orally same as contract of lease for movable of immovable property. But there are some form requirements which arises from law or from the consent of the contracting parties. The law requires that certain contracts be done in a specific form for the validity.[20] In this

20 Oğuzman and Öz, *V. I*, 140 ff.; Eren, *Borçlar Genel*, 301 ff.; Helvacı, *Turkish Contract Law*, 20; Ansay and Önay, "Law of Obligations," 188; Antalya, *Cilt V/1, 1*, 527 ff.; Tercier, Pischonnaz and Develioğlu, *Genel Hükümler*, 233.

The reasons for this requirement are as follows: (1) to invite the parties to consider the contract and (2) to provide certainty regarding the terms of the contract. Moreover, in certain cases, the legislature sets stricter form requirements (the official

circumstances, the requirement also applies to any amendment to the contract with the exception of supplementary collateral clauses that do not conflict with the original document. Where the parties agree to make a contract subject to formal requirements not prescribed by law, it is presumed that the parties do not wish to assume obligations until such time as those requirements are satisfied (TCO Art. 17).[21]

In some cases, the written form is required to provide ease of proof. Due to the Code of Civil Procedure Art. 200; if the value of contract exceeds 4,880 Turkish Liras[22] at the time of its conclusion, the claimant must prove the existence of the contract by specific evidence, which is not subject to the judge's discretion, such as a deed.[23]

There are different types of the written form: Simple written form, qualified written form and official form.

- Simple written form: A contract required by law to be in writing must be signed by all persons on whom it imposes obligations. Unless the contrary is stipulated by law, a signed letter or the original copy of a telegram that has been signed by the obliged party is deemed to be in writing. Moreover, recoverable texts that are sent by fax or similar means or by secure electronic signature are considered to be in writing, provided that they are confirmed (TCO Art. 14).[24]
  Signatures must be appended by hand by the contracting parties. As it is mentioned above, the secure electronic signature is considered to be in writing.[25]

---

form) in order to provide a secure foundation for official registries. See, Helvacı, *Turkish Contract Law,* 20. For detailed information also see, Oğuzman and Öz, *V. I,* 139 ff.; Eren, *Borçlar Genel,* 299 ff.; Antalya, *Cilt V/1, 1,* 528.

21 If the parties agree on a written form without providing any specifications as a condition for the validity of the contract, the provisions governing the legal written form apply to the contractual form requirement (TCO Art. 17/II). See also, Oğuzman and Öz, *V. I,* 158; Helvacı, *Turkish Contract Law,* 20.

22 The given limit is valid for 2022. It should be noted that this amount may be revised by law in the following years.

23 Oğuzman and Öz, *V. I,* 138; Eren, *Borçlar Genel,* 306; Helvacı, *Turkish Contract Law,* 19; Ansay and Önay, "Law of Obligations," 189. See also, the Code of Civil Procedure Art. 200.

24 Oğuzman and Öz, *V. I,* 144; Eren, *Borçlar Genel,* 308 ff.; Helvacı, *Turkish Contract Law,* 22.

25 See, Digital Signature Act no. 5070 of 15.1.2004 (OJ, 23.01.2004, no. 25355).

A signature reproduced by mechanical means is legally recognized as sufficient only where such reproduction is customarily permitted, and in particular in the case of signatures on large numbers of issued securities (TCO Art. 15). Blind persons may sign the contract by themselves or request the testimony of a witness while signing it (TCO Art. 15/III).
The examples of contracts which must be concluded in simple written form for validity by law are given as the promise of gift donation (TCO Art. 288/I), assignment of claims (TCO Art. 184), etc.

- Qualified written form: Some certain contracts are required a special written form for validity by law. This written form is called as qualified written form. Suretyship contracts are one of the significant examples of the contracts required qualified written form. Due to TCO Art. 583, a contract of surety must be in writing and that the date and maximum amount of the surety's liability must be indicated in the surety's own handwriting. If the contract of surety is joint and several, this fact must also be included on the surety bond in the surety's handwriting.[26] Another example can be given as the provision in the Article 538 of CC purporting to handwritten testamentary. This article states that a handwritten must be entirely in the testator's handwriting (including the year, the month and the day it was made) and must be signed by the testator.
- Official form: Due to the Turkish Code of Obligations, some contracts require official form for validity. The example of these contracts may be given as sale contracts for immovable property (TCO Art. 237/I). Accordingly, sale contracts for immovable property must be concluded by a land register officer. Contracts purporting to transfer the ownership of immovable property must be made before a land registry officer and authenticated by the officer[27] (Land Registry Act Art. 26).[28]

Due to the Turkish Code of Obligations Art. 15/I, a secure electronic signature will have the same legal force and effect as a handwritten signature. However, Digital Signature Act Art. 5/II governs that security contracts (e.g., a surety, guarantee, pledge, etc.) and transactions that are subject to an official form (e.g., the sale of immovable property, mortgages, etc.) or a specific procedure (e.g., marriage) cannot be signed by an electronic signature.

26 Oğuzman and Öz, *V. I*, 141; Eren, *Borçlar Genel*, 319; Helvacı, *Turkish Contract Law*, 21; Ansay and Önay, "Law of Obligations," 189.

27 Oğuzman and Öz, *V. I*, 149 ff.; Eren, *Borçlar Genel*, 319; Helvacı, *Turkish Contract Law*, 21.

28 Land Registry Act no. 2644 of 22 December 1934 (OJ, 29.12.1934, no. 2892).

C. *Interpretation of Contracts*

When assessing the form and terms of a contract, the true and common intention of the parties must be ascertained without dwelling on any inexact expressions or designations they may have used either in error or by way of disguising the true nature of the agreement (TCO Art. 19/I). In some cases, it is not possible to determine the parties' common intention. In this case, the judge shall interpret the declarations of the intent.

"The principle of mutual trust and confidence" governs the interpretation of a party's declaration of intent, which means that the declaration must be interpreted not in the sense of what the declaring party may have intended nor in accordance with the literal meaning of the wording, but in the sense that the addressee could in good faith attribute to it. Herewith, the principle of mutual trust and confidence aims to protect the best interest of the parties.[29]

D. *Validity of the Contracts*

1. *Generally*

In the concluding the contract, if there is a lack of mutual consent of the parties, then the contract is not considered as a valid contract. This type of invalidity is called as in-existence.

There are some conditions required for the valid contract. If a contract established contrary to these validity conditions, then the contract is considered as a null (void) contract. A void contract does not yield any legal consequences, starting from the beginning of the conclusion of the contract. It should be clarified that the terms of a contract may be freely determined within the limits of the law. Clauses that deviate from those prescribed by law are admissible only where the law does not prescribe any wording in sense of mandatory provision or where any deviation from the legally prescribed terms would not contravene public policy, morality, or personal rights (TCO Art. 26).

A contract is void if its terms are impossible, unlawful or immoral. However, where the defect pertains only to the certain terms of a contract, those terms alone are void unless there is a cause to assume that the contract would not have been concluded without them (TCO Art. 27).

29 Ansay and Önay, "Law of Obligations," 183; Bucher, "Law of Contracts," 112–113; Helvacı, *Turkish Contract Law,* 53 ff. For detailed information see Eren, *Borçlar Genel,* 152 ff.; Kocayusufpaşaoğlu, *Genel Bölüm,* 331 ff.; Oğuzman and Öz, *V. I,* 69 ff.

In addition to this, also the lack capacity of the parties, simulation of contract and violation of form requirement are another reasons for invalidity.[30]

Lastly, a voidable (annullable) contract is a contract affected by a defective declaration of one of the parties such as mistake, fraud, duress and unfair advantage.

2. *Mistake, Fraud and Duress*

"Dissensus" is the absence of contractual consent with the consequence that no contract at all came into existence even if the parties believed to have concluded it. Dissensus arises when two parties agree upon the same term but understand it differently, so much so that both interpretations are equally admissible in the light of particular circumstances. If one of the interpretations prevails against the other, the contract exists but the counterparty may claim relieve resulting from "mistake, fraud or duress".[31]

a. Mistake

According to the Turkish Code of Obligations Art. 30, a party laboring under a fundamental error when entering into a contract is not bound by this contract.

There are two types of mistakes in the frame of the Turkish Code of Obligations. These are mistake in expression and mistake in motive.

aa. Mistake in expression

An error is particularly fundamental in the following cases:

- Where the party acting in error intended to conclude a contract different from that to which is consented (for example, when a person who wants to sign a lease contract concludes a sale contract),
- Where the party acting in error has concluded a contract relating to a subject matter other than the intended matters, or concluded it with a person other than the intended person where the contract relates to a specific person (for example, when a person who wants to buy mobile phone from Internet declares their intent to buy a laptop, or a person wants to conclude an employment agreement with X sends the proposal to Y and the latter accepts it),
- Where the party acting in error has promised to make a significantly greater performance or has accepted a promise of a significantly lesser consideration than it is actually intended (for example, when a parent wants to conclude a

---

30 Amongst, for the requirements as to form of contracts, under this chapter see supra: *4. Form of Contracts.*

31 Bucher, "Law of Contracts," 113.

private lesson agreement for their child with teacher X who has a good command of English, but they sends the proposal to teacher Y who does not speak English),
- Where the error related to specific facts which the party acting in error considered to be a necessary basis for the contract in good faith (for example, when the buyer wants to buy 1,000 pairs of socks from the seller, but they makes the proposal to buy for 100 pairs).

However, where the error relates solely to the motive for concluding the contract, it is not fundamental. Calculation errors do not render a contract any less binding but must be corrected (TCO Art. 31).

bb. Mistake in motive

If there is a discrepancy between a party's knowledge and the actual circumstances relevant to the contract when entering into a contract, such a discrepancy is deemed to be a mistake in motive. A mistake in motive, as a rule, is not considered as a fundamental error (material mistake) since whoever is wrong must suffer the consequences.[32] However, in certain cases, a mistake in motive is deemed to be fundamental. These conditions are as follows[33]:

- A party must be mistaken about one or more facts that form the basis of the contract;
- The mistake must be related to a substantial component of the contract for the mistaken party. If this is the case, the mistaken party had known of the mistake, the contract would not have been concluded at all or would not have been concluded under the same conditions;
- It must be the case that the mistaken party's true motive is known or could be known by the counterparty; and
- According to the principle of good faith in business relations, the claim that the mistake affects the validity of the contract must be justifiable (TCO Art. 32).

The commonly used example of mistake in motive is given such as that: A person buys a painting considering that it was painted by Van Gogh, but in real, it is not painted by Van Gogh.

---

32 Oğuzman and Öz, *V. I*, 92 ff.; Eren, *Borçlar Genel*, 426–427; Helvacı, *Turkish Contract Law*, 69; Antalya, *Cilt V/1, 1*, 374 ff.; Tercier, Picshonnaz and Develioğlu, *Genel Hükümler*, 271 ff.

33 Oğuzman and Öz, *V. I*, 93 ff.; Eren, *Borçlar Genel*, 426–427; Helvacı, *Turkish Contract Law*, 69–70; Antalya, *Cilt V/1, 1*, 386 ff.; Tercier, Picshonnaz and Develioğlu, *Genel Hükümler*, 276 ff.

Where the party acting under fundamental error (mistake in expression or mistake in motive) does not declare within 1 year to the counterparty that it is intended to either not honor the contract, or not seek restitution for the performance made, the contract is deemed to have been ratified. The 1-year period runs as of the date on which the party acting under fundamental error has been aware of the error (TCO Art. 39).

A person may not invoke an error in a manner contrary to good faith. In particular, the party acting in error remains bound by the intended contract provided the counterparty accepts this contract (TCO Art. 34).

A party acting in error and invoking that this error to evade the validity of the contract is liable for any damage arising from the nullity of the contract where the error is attributable to this party's own negligence, unless the counterparty knew or should have known of the error. In the interests of equity, the court may award further damages to the person suffering damage (TCO Art. 35).

b. Fraud

A party induced to enter into a contract due to the fraud of the counterparty is not bound by it even if the error is not fundamental. A party, who is the victim of fraud by a third party, nonetheless remains bound by the contract unless the counterparty knew or should have known of the fraud at the time the contract was concluded (TCO Art. 36). For instance, that is a case of fraud if a seller trades a reproduction painting of Van Gogh in a famous art gallery, as if it was an original painting.

If the party exposed to fraud does not declare within 1 year to the counterparty that it is intended to either not honor the contract, or not seek restitution for the performance made, the contract is deemed to have been ratified. The 1-year period runs from the time that the fraud was discovered. The ratification of a contract that is made voidable due to fraud does not automatically exclude the right to claim damages (TCO Art. 39).

c. Duress

A party entered into a contract under duress from the counterparty or a third party is not bound by this contract. Where the duress originates from a third party and the counterparty neither knew nor need to have known of it, a party under duress who wishes to be released from the contract must pay compensation to the counterparty where equity so requires (TCO Art. 37).

A party is regarded under duress if it is comprehensible to believe that there is imminent and substantial risk to the party's own life, limb, reputation, or property or to those of a person close to themselves. The fear of another person pursuing a legitimate claim is considered duress only where the straitened circumstances of the party under duress have been exploited by the claimant in order to extort excessive benefits (TCO Art. 38). For instance, X wants to buy Y's house, but Y does not want to sell it. When X threatens Y that if Y does not take the offer, they would kill Y, abduct Y's child, or burn down their house, it is an example of duress.[34]

Where the party acting under duress does not declare within 1 year to the counterparty that it is intended to either not honor the contract, or not seek restitution for the performance made, the contract is deemed to have been ratified. The 1-year period runs from the time that the duress ended. As with fraud, the ratification of a contract that is made voidable due to duress or fraud does not automatically exclude the right to claim damages (TCO Art. 39).

3. *Unfair Advantage*

Where there is a clear discrepancy between performance and consideration under a contract concluded as a result of one party's exploitation of the other's straitened circumstances, inexperience or thoughtlessness, the person suffering damage may declare within 1 year not to honor the contract and to demand restitution of any performance already made. The 1-year period commences on the time he finds out his inexperience, thoughtlessness. In any case, these rights cannot use after the 5 years as of the beginning of the contract (TCO Art. 28). For example, this is the case when a couple sells their high-value house for considerably less than its true value due to financial difficulties.[35]

E. Representation (Agency)

In general, the parties enter into contracts by the act of themselves. However, in some circumstances, the parties could not conclude the contract by themselves, they need to be represented by a representative (agency).[36]

If a representative acts in the name of and on behalf of a principal, the contract is formed between the principal and the third party. For instance, when a customer enters into a credit contract with a bank clerk who is the representative of the Bank, the contract binds the Bank.

---

34 Helvacı, *Turkish Contract Law,* 74.

35 Helvacı, *Turkish Contract Law,* 78.

36 Oğuzman and Öz, *V. I,* 210 ff.; Eren, *Borçlar Genel,* 477; Esener, *Turkish Business Law I,* 79; Antalya, *Cilt V/1, 1,* 580 ff.; Tercier, Pichonnaz and Develioğlu, *Genel Hükümler,* 137.

The provisions on representation are regulated under the Articles 40 to 48 of the Turkish Code of Obligations.

1. Effect of the Representation

According to TCO Art. 40/I, the rights and obligations arising from a contract made by a representative in the name of another person accrue directly to the person represented, and not to the representative. In this relationship there exists three persons. These are: The representative, the represented person (principal) and the third party. In this situation, the contract is concluded between the represented person and the third party. In other words, the rights and obligations occur between the principal and the third party. The representative is not one of the contracting parties. Because of this, the representative does not have any rights or obligations arising from the contract.

In general, the representative might declare acting as a representative. Where the representative did not inform the third parties as such when making the contract, the rights and obligations arising from there accrue directly to the principal only if the third party needed to have inferred the representation relationship from the circumstances or did not care with whom they made the contract. Where such authorization is conferred by means of the transaction itself, its scope is determined by this transaction (TCO Art. 40/II).

Where a principal grants such authorization to a representative, and informs the third party thereof, the scope of the authorization conferred on the representative is determined according to the wording of the communication made to the third party (TCO Art. 41/II).

If a person enters into a contract without having authorization to act on behalf of a principal, the rights and obligations do not accrue to the latter unless the principal ratified the contract. In case of unauthorized representation, the third party has the right to request the principal to ratify this contract within a reasonable time. If in this reasonable time the ratification is not provided, then the third party would not be bound by the contract. However, if the principal ratifies this contract, the third party will be bound by the contract from the time of conclusion.[37]

If the principal refuses expressly or implicitly to ratify, the action may be brought for compensation against the person, who pretended as the representative (against the unauthorized representative). This compensation includes all the damages caused by the invalidity of the contract. If the unauthorized

37 Oğuzman and Öz, *V. I*, 241; Eren, *Borçlar Genel*, 507; Helvacı, *Turkish Contract Law*, 85.

representative proves that the third party knew, or need to have known the lack of authorization, then the representative will not be liable for the compensation. If the unauthorized representative is at fault, the court may order them to pay further damages on grounds of equity (TCO Art. 47).

The principal may restrict or revoke the authorization given to the representative at any time without prejudice to any rights acquired by those involved under existing legal relationships, such as an individual contract of employment, a partnership agreement or an agency agreement. The principal is avoided to waive this right in advance. There is an important point regarding the restriction or revocation of the authorization of the representative: If the principal has expressly or de facto announced the authorization that conferred, the principal may not invoke its total or partial revocation against a third party acting in good faith unless the principal has likewise announced such revocation.

2. *The Expiration of the Representation*

The death, incapacity, bankruptcy and other circumstances may affect the authorization of the representative. The authorization conferred by means of a legal transaction expires in the case of loss of capacity to act, bankruptcy, death, or declaration of the presumed death of the principal or that of the representative. However, if the principal and the representative agree or the nature of the transaction is inferred so, then the authorization of the representative does not expire (TCO Art. 43).

When the authorization of the representative is expired, they must return the instrument indicating their authorization or they must deposit it with the court. If the principal or their legal successors have omitted to insist on the return of such instrument, they are liable to the bona fide third parties for any damage arising from that omission (TCO Art. 44). Until such time as a representative becomes aware that their authorization has expired, their actions continue to give rise to the rights and obligations on the part of the principal or the latter's legal successors as if the representative's authorization still existed. This does not apply in cases, in which the third party is aware that the representative's authorization has expired (TCO Art. 45).

F. *Performance of the Contract*

The fulfillment of an obligation can be defined as performance.[38] The obligor (debtor) must perform what they are obliged to perform.

38 Eren, *Borçlar Genel,* 1021; Ansay and Önay, "Law of Obligations," 194; Gökhan Antalya, *Borçlar Hukuku Genel Hükümler Cilt V/1, 3* (Ankara: Seçkin 2019), 42; Nomer, *Borçlar Genel,* 293; Tercier, Pichonnaz and Develioğlu, *Genel Hükümler,* 328.

An obligor may be obliged to give (for example, transfer of ownership of a car or real estate, etc.), to do (for example, construction of a building, writing a book, etc.), or not to do (for example, not to disclose any confidential information) something.[39]

If the obligor fulfills their obligation, the obligation extinguishes. If a claim ceases to exist by virtue of being satisfied, or in some other manner, all accessory rights such as mortgage, pledge, surety and interests likewise extinguish. Interest that has accrued may be claimed only if that right is conferred on the obligee by the contract, or it is evident from the circumstances. The specific provisions governing interest on immovable property, securities and composition agreements are reserved.[40]

There are some significant principles regarding performance of obligation in TCO:

- The obligor (debtor) is not obliged to discharge their obligation in person unless so required by the obligee (TCO Art. 83).
- An obligee (creditor) may refuse partial payment of the debt where the total debt is determined and due. If the obligee accepts partial performance, the obligor cannot abstain from performing the part of the debt acknowledged by them (TCO Art. 84).
- The place of performance is determined by the intention of the parties as stated expressly, or it might be evident from the circumstances.

The place of performance: Except where otherwise stipulated, the following principles on the place of performance apply:

- Pecuniary debts must be paid at the place where the obligee is resident at the time of performance.
- Where a specific object is owed, it must be delivered at the place where it was located when the contract was concluded.
- All other obligations must be discharged at the place where the obligor was resident at the time they arose (TCO Art. 89).

39 Helvacı, *Turkish Contract Law,* 93; Tercier, Pichonnaz and Develioğlu, *Genel Hükümler,* 328.

40 Oğuzman and Öz, *V. I,* 250 ff.; Eren, *Borçlar Genel,* 1022; Helvacı, *Turkish Contract Law,* 93.

The time of performance: If the time of performance is not stated in the contract or evident from the nature of the legal transaction, the obligation may be discharged or called in immediately (TCO Art. 90).

In addition, the Article 97 of TCO is a significant provision regulating the order of performance in bilateral contracts. A party to a bilateral contract may not demand performance until they has discharged or offered to discharge their own obligation, unless the terms or nature of the contract allow them to do so at a later time.

Payment currency: Pecuniary (material) debts must be discharged in national currency, in which the debt was incurred. In Turkey, the national currency is the Turkish Lira. A debt expressed in a currency other than the national currency may be discharged according to the national currency at the rate of exchange that applied on the day it falls due, unless literal performance in foreign currency is required by inclusion in the contract of the expression 'actual currency' or words to that effect. However, if the obligor does not perform their obligation on the due date, the obligee may demand of the obligor to perform the debt literally in foreign currency, or in the national currency according to the rate of exchange on the due date or on the date of actual performance (TCO Art. 99).[41] Accordingly, the obligee has right to opt one of these options.

G. Default of the Obligee

The obligee is in default if they refuses to accept performance properly offered to them without good cause, or if they abstain to carry out necessary preparations that they are obliged for the obligor to fulfill their own debt (TCO 106).

The default of the obligee gives some rights to the obligor.[42] According to TCO Art. 107, if the obligee is in default, the obligor has the option of depositing the object at the expense and risk of the obligee, thereby discharging their obligation. The court decides which place should serve as depositary; however, merchandise may be deposited in a warehouse without need for a court decision.

If the characteristics of the object or the nature of the transaction preclude a deposit, or if the object is perishable or gives rise to substantial maintenance costs or storage costs, provided to give the obligee a formal reminder, the obligor

41 Oğuzman and Öz, *V. I*, 289 ff.; Eren, *Borçlar Genel*, 1093 ff.; Antalya, *Cilt V/1, 3*, 161 ff.; Tercier, Pichonnaz and Develioğlu, *Genel Hükümler*, 383 ff.; Nomer, *Borçlar Genel*, 307 ff.; Helvacı, *Turkish Contract Law*, 104.

42 Oğuzman and Öz, *V. I*, 258 ff.; Eren, *Borçlar Genel*, 1142 ff.

may dispose of the object by open sale and may deposit the sale prices with the court's permission. If the object is traded on a quoted stock exchange or has market price or its value is low in proportion to the costs involved, the sale need not be open, and the court may authorize it without prior reminder (TCO Art. 108).

The obligor is entitled to take back the object deposited providing the obligee has not declared to accept the deposited object or providing the deposit has not resulted in the removal of a pledge. As soon as the object is taken back, the claim and all accessory rights become effective again (TCO Art. 109).

If the obligation does not relate to delivering objects, and the obligee is in default, the obligor may withdraw from the contract in accordance with the provisions governing default of the obligor (TCO Art. 110).

H. Non-Performance of the Contract

1. Generally

The aim of the party entering into the contractual relationship is to obtain "correct performance" that is fulfilled completely and properly as promised by the counterparty. The breach of the contract is referred as contractual liability.[43] For example, in a lease contract, the lessee (tenant) who does not perform their promise (to pay the rental fee) is liable to the lessor because of the breach of the contract.

The liability of the parties to a contract is, according to the wording of the Code, a liability under the condition of fault of the party not performing correctly (TCO Art. 112). This principle is complemented and qualified by a presumption of fault: The burden of proof is on the non-performing party causing damage, who may show that their non-performance, or delayed or defective performance, was caused by elements independent of their responsibility.[44]

As a rule, a party of the contract, who is not performing their dept correctly, must be liable for the damages by compensating the failure of performance or its imperfections. The damage resulting from the non-performance of obligation is mentioned as "positive damage". Positive damage includes both actual damage (*damnum emergens*) and the deprivation of the opportunity to obtain a benefit or to avoid a loss (*lucrum cessans*).[45]

---

43 Eren, *Borçlar Genel,* 1153; Esener, *Turkish Business Law I,* 9.

44 Oğuzman and Öz, *V. I,* 408; Eren, *Borçlar Genel,* 1162; Bucher, "Law of Contracts," 116; Antalya, *Cilt V/1, 3,* 216 ff.; Nomer, *Borçlar Genel,* 337.

45 Oğuzman and Öz, *V. I,* 383; Eren, *Borçlar Genel,* 1184 ff.; Helvacı, *Turkish Contract Law,* 154; Bucher, "Law of Contracts," 116.

The obligor is generally liable for any fault attributable to them. The scope of such liability is determined by the particular nature of the transaction and in particular is judged more leniently where the obligor does not stand to gain from the transaction. In addition to this, the provisions governing liability in tort apply *mutatis mutandis* to a breach of contract (TCO Art. 114).

As a general principle, the obligor is liable for the damages arising from their non-performance of obligation. However, the parties may agree that the obligor will not be liable for such damage. An agreement for the non-liability of the obligor may be decided by the parties as a clause in the contract. Such clauses are referred to as "exemption clauses". In addition to this, the parties may also make a separate agreement that excludes the obligor's liability. Such agreements are referred to as "non-liability agreements" or "agreements excluding the obligor's liability" (release of liability). The Turkish Code of Obligations accepts the validity of such agreements. However, the Code sets certain restrictions on the contractual exclusion of liability. According to TCO Art. 115, the parties may agree that the obligor is not liable to pay the damages in cases where the obligor is at slight negligence.[46] Any agreement made in advance that purports to exclude liability in case of intent or gross negligence is null and void.

Any prior exclusion of liability for slight negligence may be deemed void provided the exemption occurs from the employment contract signed between the obligor and the obligee (TCO Art. 115/II). In addition to this, due to TCO Art. 115/III, such prior agreement indicating that the obligor shall not be liable for slight negligence shall be strictly null and void in case of a service, profession or art requiring specialization that carried out exclusively with the permission granted by competent authorities or law.

The obligor is also liable for the conducts of the associates, who are delegated by obligor to exercise a contractual obligation. This liability may be limited or excluded by prior agreement (TCO Art. 116/I). However, if a service or profession or art requiring specialization, which can only be carried out with the permission of competent authorities or law, then any agreement concluded in advance that purports to exclude the obligor's liability for the conducts of associates is null and void (TCO Art. 116/III).[47]

---

46 Oğuzman and Öz, *V. I*, 406 ff.; Eren, *Borçlar Genel*, 1217 ff.; Antalya, *Cilt V/1, 3*, 411 ff.; Nomer, *Borçlar Genel*, 343 ff.; Helvacı, *Turkish Contract Law*, 152, 158.

47 Oğuzman and Öz, *V. I*, 423 ff.; Eren, *Borçlar Genel*, 1200 ff.; Antalya, *Cilt V/1, 3*, 421 ff.; Nomer, *Borçlar Genel*, 345 ff.; Helvacı, *Turkish Contract Law*, 162.

2. *Default of the Obligor*

a. *General rule*

As a rule, a delay in performance of the obligation does not automatically create the obligor's default by itself. According to TCO Art. 117/I, in order for an obligor to fall into default, the obligation must be due, the obligor must fail to perform the obligation and the obligee must give notice for performance.[48] If an obligation is due but not fulfilled by the obligor, the default of the obligor occurs as soon as they receives a formal reminder from the obligee.

In several circumstances, there is no need for the formal reminder. If there is a deadline for the performance of obligation that has been set by agreement or determined as a result of a duly exercised right of determination reserved by one party, or in case of a tortfeasor, or in case of a person acting in bad faith, who is unjustly enriched; the obligor is automatically in default on expiry of the deadline (TCO Art. 117/II).

An obligor in default is liable in damages for late performance and even for accidental damages (TCO Art. 118–119). They may discharge themselves from such liability by proving that their default occurred through no fault of their own or that the object of performance would have suffered the accidental damage to the detriment of the obligee even if the performance would have been fulfilled correctly. As a general consequence of the default, the obligor must perform the obligation nearby their liability for the compensation.

An obligor in default on payment of a pecuniary debt must pay default interest. If the value of the damage suffered by the obligee exceeds the default interest, the obligor is also liable for this additional damage unless they can prove that they is not at fault (TCO Art. 120–122). The parties might agree on the rate of interest in the contract. Otherwise, the rates that are cited in the Act on Statutory Interest and Default Interest (no. 3095) will be applied.

b. *Consequences of default of obligor for bilateral contract*

If the obligor under a bilateral contract is in default, the obligee is entitled to set an appropriate time limit for subsequent performance or to ask the court to set such time limit.

If performance has not been rendered by the end of that time limit, the obligee may compel the obligor to render the performance in addition to suing for damages in connection with the delay, or provided they makes an immediate

48 Oğuzman and Öz, *V. I*, 457 ff.; Eren, *Borçlar Genel*, 1224 ff.; Antalya, *Cilt V/1, 3*, 479 ff.; Nomer, *Borçlar Genel*, 365 ff.; Helvacı, *Turkish Contract Law*, 167.

declaration to this effect, they may instead forego subsequent performance, and either claim damages for non-performance or withdraw from the contract at all.

If the obligee claims damages for the non-performance instead of the performance, these damages are referred as "positive damages". Positive damages are damages which are resulting from the non-performance of the obligation. Positive damage includes both actual damage (*damnum emergens*) and the deprivation of the opportunity to obtain a benefit or to avoid a loss (*lucrum cessans*).

The obligee can also withdraw from the contract. An obligee withdrawing from a contract may refuse the promised consideration and demand the return of any performance already made. In addition, they may claim damages for the lapse of the contract, unless the obligor can prove that they were not at fault. These damages are referred as "negative damages". Negative damages are damages that would not have been suffered by the obligee if the contract would not have been concluded (TCO Art. 123–125).[49]

However, in some circumstances, setting a time limit is not required:

- Where it is evident from the conduct of the obligor that a time limit would serve no purpose,
- Where performance has become pointless to the obligee as a result of the obligor's default,
- Where the contract makes it clear that the parties intended that the performance takes place at or before a precise point in a timeline.

3. *Contractual Penalty*

When the parties enter into a legal transaction, the obligee would like to protect themselves from non-performance or defective performance of the obligor. That is why the parties determine contractual penalty mostly in their contracts in practice. The obligee is relieved to prove the quantum of the damage due to the penalty clauses.[50]

In practice, the parties generally agree on a fixed amount of money as a penalty. But also, any act offering a benefit to the counterparty such as an obligation

---

49 Oğuzman and Öz, *V. I*, 498 ff.; Eren, *Borçlar Genel*, 1259; Antalya, *Cilt V/1, 3*, 553 ff.; Nomer, *Borçlar Genel*, 394 ff.; Ansay and Önay, "Law of Obligations," 200.

50 Oğuzman and Öz, *V. I*, 529 ff.; Eren, *Borçlar Genel*, 1323; Helvacı, *Turkish Contract Law*, 259; Tercier, Pichonnaz and Develioğlu, *Genel Hükümler*, 475 ff.; Nomer, *Borçlar Genel*, 471; Mehmet Erdem, *La Clause Pénale* (Neuchâtel: Étude comparative de droit suisse et de droit turc, 2010).

to give or to do may be determined by the parties as a penalty.[51] For instance, in a contract for work, the parties agree on that the contractor will finish the work in a definite time, and if the contractor fails to do so, then the business owner may demand a penalty of 20,000 Turkish Liras from the contractor.

A penalty clause is an accessory right that is attached to the promised obligation. As a result of this, if the promised obligation is void, the penalty clause will, then, be void.[52]

If the parties promise a penalty for non-performance or defective performance of a contract, unless they agreed otherwise, the obligee may either compel the obligor for performance or claim the penalty. If the penalty is agreed for the failure of promised performance to be rendered complying with the stipulated time or place of performance, the obligee may claim the penalty in addition to performance provided they has not expressly waived such right or accepted the performance without reservation. This is not applicable if the obligor can prove that they has the right to withdraw from the contract by paying the penalty (TCO Art. 179).

The obligee may claim the penalty even if they has not suffered any damage. If the damage suffered exceeds the amount of the penalty, the obligee may claim further compensation only if they can prove that the obligor was at fault (TCO Art. 180).

The parties are free to determine the amount of the contractual penalty. The penalty may not be claimed where its purpose is to reinforce an unlawful or immoral promise or, unless otherwise agreed, where performance has been prevented by circumstances beyond the obligor's control. At its discretion, the court shall reduce penalties that it deems excessive (exorbitant) according to TCO Art. 182.

I. Extinction of Obligations

If an obligor fulfills their obligation, the obligation extinguishes. In other words, an obligation become extinct by the performance. In addition to this, there are several reasons for extinction of obligations. If a claim ceases to exist by virtue of being satisfied or in some other manner, all accessory rights such as mortgage, pledge, surety and charges likewise extinguish. Interest that has accrued may be claimed only if that right is conferred on the obligee by the contract, or it is

51 Helvacı, *Turkish Contract Law*, 262.

52 Oğuzman and Öz, *V. II*, 535 ff.; Eren, *Borçlar Genel*, 1325; Helvacı, *Turkish Contract Law*, 261.

evident from the circumstances. The specific provisions governing interest on immovable property, securities and composition agreements are reserved (TCO Art. 131).[53]

1. *Extinction by Agreement*

If the obligor and obligee agree on the extinction of the obligation arising from their contractual relationship through an extinction agreement, the obligation will be extinguished. According to an extinction agreement, an obligation may be extinguished wholly or partly. No particular form is required for the extinction of an obligation by agreement even where the obligation itself could not be assumed without satisfying certain formal requirements stipulated by law or determined by the parties (TCO Art. 132).

2. *Novation*

Novation is one of the causes of extinction of the obligation so that the contracting parties extinguish the obligation by creating a new obligation relationship. Novation is governed under the Articles of 133 to 134 of TCO. To illustrate, when there was a sale agreement between the parties in which the buyer must pay 10,000 Turkish Liras, the parties making a new agreement which converts the cause of the buyer's obligation into a loan agreement is an example for novation.[54]

If a new obligation relationship is contracted by the contracting parties, there is no presumption that the former one novated; rather, novation must be explicitly intended. In particular, in the absence of agreement to the contrary, novation does not result from the signature of a bill of exchange in respect of an existing debt, or from the issue of a new borrower's note or a contract of surety.

The posting of individual entries in a current account does not result in novation alone. However, there is a presumption of novation if the balance on the account has been drawn and acknowledged by the counterparty. If a special security exists for one of the account entries, unless otherwise agreed, such security is retained even if the balance on the account is drawn and acknowledged.

53 Oğuzman and Öz, *V. I*, 533 ff.; Eren, *Borçlar Genel*, 1460 ff.; Nomer, *Borçlar Genel*, 413; Helvacı, *Turkish Contract Law*, 93.

54 Helvacı, *Turkish Contract Law*, 200.

3. *Merger*

If the capacities of the obligor and the obligee may merge in the same person, the obligation is deemed extinguished by the merger. To put it another way, an obligation is deemed extinguished by merger where the capacities of obligor and obligee are united in the same entity. In the event of de-merger, the obligation is revived. The specific provisions governing charges on immovable property and securities are reserved (TCO Art. 135).

4. *Impossibility (Performance Becomes Impossible)*

Impossibility has two aspects: One of them is initial impossibility, which occurs at the time of the conclusion of the contracts. In this situation, if there is an objective impossibility, the contract is, then, null. To illustrate, if there is a sale contract which is concerning a certain object such as a jewelry and if the stated object has been entirely corrupt before the formation of the contract, then the contract is void.[55] If there is a subjective impossibility, the contract is valid, and the obligor may be liable for their non-performance.

The other aspect of the impossibility is subsequent impossibility. Subsequent impossibility arises after the conclusion of the contract. In this case, due to TCO Art. 112, the obligee can claim for damages if the obligor is liable for the impossibility. An obligation is deemed extinguished where its performance is made impossible by circumstances not attributable to the obligor. To illustrate, in a sale contract for the exchange of a certain object, the obligation extinguishes if, after the conclusion of the contract, this certain object is devastated due to an event for which the obligor is not liable, such as an earthquake.[56]

In a bilateral contract, the obligor, who is released from the debt due to the impossibility, must restitute the consideration that already received from the counterparty in accordance with the provisions of unjust enrichment and loses the right to demand for the claims that have not yet been performed. However, this does not apply to cases in which, by law or contractual agreement, the risk passes to the obligee prior to performance (TCO Art. 136).

5. *Hardship (and Disappearance of the Contractual Basis)*

One of the basic principles in contract law is sanctity of the contracts (*pacta sund servanda*) which is also accepted in Turkish law system. According to this principle, the parties of the contract are bound to the terms of the contract under any

55 Helvacı, *Turkish Contract Law*, 204.
56 Helvacı, *Turkish Contract Law*, 205.

conditions in accordance with the principle of good faith and predictability of the law.[57] However, in some circumstances due to the changing conditions, it is not equitable to expect the obligor's performance. Especially, if the circumstances which take place during the formation of the contract change significantly due to the unforeseen events, the obligor cannot be expected to perform their obligation. In this situation, the contractual basis disappears because of contingencies (*Wegfall der Geschäftsgrundlage*).[58] When contingencies frustrated the purpose of the contract and undermine its basis, insisting on the performance of the obligor may be contrary to the principle of good faith, equity and justice.[59]

TCO Art. 138 regulates the adaptation of contracts in case of hardship. In this case, the disadvantaged party may apply to the court and demand the adaptation of the contract according to the changing conditions. If the judge cannot adapt the contract to the new conditions, the disadvantaged party may withdraw from the contract, and the contract become extinct retrospectively (*ex tunc*). However, if there is a continuing contract between the parties, then the disadvantaged party, as a rule, may terminate the contract instead of withdrawing from it, and the contract become extinct prospectively (*ex nunc*).[60]

Because of the Coronavirus (COVID-19) pandemic, many contractual relationships have been affected. In the doctrine, the Coronavirus pandemic is considered as an example of hardship and frustration of purposes.

6. *Set-Off*

If the contracting parties owe each other sums of money or are obligated to perform identical obligations, and on condition that both claims have fallen due, each of the contracting parties may set off their debt against their claim. The obligor may assert the right of set-off even if the corresponding claim is contested. A claim that has been prescribed may be set-off provided that it was not prescribed when it became eligible for set-off.

A set-off takes place only if the debtor notifies the creditor of his intention to exercise his right of set-off. Once this has occurred, to the extent that they cancel

57 Oğuzman and Öz, *V. I*, 559 ff.; Eren, *Borçlar Genel*, 540 ff.; Murat Develioğlu, *the Adaptation of Contracts*, http://www.erdem-erdem.av.tr/publications/law-post/, accessed 18.9.2021.

58 For detailed information see also, Başak Baysal, *Sözleşmenin Uyarlanması, BK m. 138 Aşırı İfa Güçlüğü* (İstanbul: On İki Levha, 2020).

59 Develioğlu, ibid.

60 Oğuzman and Öz, *V. I*, 564; Eren, *Borçlar Genel*, 547; Helvacı, *Turkish Contract Law*, 208.

each other out, the claim and countervailing claim are deemed to have been satisfied as of the time they first became susceptible to set-off.

7. Prescription

The general principle is that claims are subject to prescription. When an obligation is prescribed, the obligation is valid, but it is now regarded as a natural (imperfect) obligation. That implies that the obligor may either perform the prescribed obligation or assert a defense that the claim is prescribed.[61] If the obligor raises this defense, the judge must dismiss the case unless this defense is not against to the principles of good faith (CC Art. 2/II). All claims prescribe after 10 years unless otherwise provided by law (TCO Art. 146).

In certain cases, the prescription period is determined as 5 years by the legislator. Pursuant to the sub-paragraphs of TCO Art. 147, the following claims become prescribed after 5 years[62]:

1. periodic payments such as rent, capital interest and wages. However, if the rental fee is to be paid non-periodically or if the capital interest is to be added to the capital, these claims become prescribed after 10 years. Furthermore, default interest is not covered by this article.
2. accommodation fees at such places as hotels, motels, bed and breakfasts and resorts and food and beverage costs at restaurants and other such places;
3. claims arising from small-scale retail sales and work performed by artisans on a small scale;
4. in a partnership, claims arising out of the partnership contract, which are between partners or between each partner and the partnership; claims arising between the directors, agents or auditors of the partnership and the partnership itself or the partners;
5. claims arising from agency contracts, commission and agent contracts or brokerage contracts except those relating to commercial brokerage fees; and
6. claims arising from the contracts for work, except those relating to non- or improper performance by the contractor at gross fault (*culpa lata*).[63]

---

61 Eren, *Borçlar Genel*, 1433 ff.; Helvacı, *Turkish Contract Law*, 217. For detailed information see also, Mehmet Erdem, *Özel Hukukta Zamanaşımı* (İstanbul: On İki Levha, 2010).

62 Helvacı, *Turkish Contract Law*, 218.

63 Helvacı, *Turkish Contract Law*, 218.

The prescription period commences to start when the obligation is due (TCO Art. 149/I). The 2-year term regarding tort and unjust enrichment obligations commences only when the claim and the identity of the obligor is known to the obligee (referred to as basic period). However, an "ultimate period" is also stipulated that those claims become prescribed 10 years after the event causing damage or enrichment, regardless of whether the obligee is aware of the incident (see, the Articles 72 and 82 of TCO).[64]

In some circumstances, the prescription period does not commence and, if it does, is suspended. Some of these circumstances are as follows: the claims of children against their parents, until the children reach the age of majority, the claims of spouses against each other during the marriage, the claims of the household employees against the employer during the employment relationship, for as long as the obligor owns the claim's usufruct, for as long as the claim cannot be brought before a court due to the objective reasons. At the end of the day on which the causes of prevention or suspension cease, the prescription period commences, or resumes if commenced before (TCO Art. 153).

Furthermore, the prescription period is interrupted in several circumstances. If the obligor acknowledges the claim, in particular, if they makes interest payments or partial payments, gives an item in pledge or provides surety; if the obligee has recourse to the court or arbitral tribunal by submission of a statement of claim or defense, or for proceeding enforcement of a debt or submitting a petition for bankruptcy (TCO Art. 154). If the prescription period is interrupted, a new period commences from the beginning. In this situation the new period has the same duration as the preceding one.[65]

J. Joint and Several Obligationship

Obligors become jointly and severally liable for a debt by stating that each of them intends to be individually liable for performance of the entire obligation. However, only in cases specified by law, obligors are joint and severally liable without such a statement of intent required (TCO Art 162).

In case of joint and several obligationship, an obligee may at their discretion request a partial performance of the obligation from each jointly and severally liable obligor (co-obligors) or else a full performance from any one of them. All the obligors are liable for the obligation until the entire obligation has been fully performed.

---

64 Oğuzman and Öz, *V. II*, 72 ff., 496 ff.; Bucher, "Law of Contracts," 132.

65 Oğuzman and Öz, *V. I*, 593 ff.; Eren, *Borçlar Genel*, 1445 ff.

Unless the jointly and severally liable obligors agree in their relationship otherwise, each of them undertakes an equal share of the payment promised to the obligee. A jointly and severally liable obligor, who pays more than their share, may request all other co-obligors for the excessed part. Amounts that cannot be recovered from one of joint and severally liable obligors must be undertaken by other co-obligors in equal shares (TCO Art. 167).

A jointly and severally liable obligor with right of recourse against other co-obligors is subrogated to the rights of the obligee to the extent that of the latter has been satisfied. The obligee is liable if they promotes the legal position of one of jointly and severally liable obligors to the detriment of the others (TCO Art. 168).

K. Assignment of Claims and Assumption of Debts

A claim arising from a contract or from other sources of obligations, such as a tort or unjust enrichment, may be transferred to third parties. A claim may be transferred by an agreement, by a court order or as a requisite of law.[66] According to TCO Art. 183, an obligee may assign a claim to which they is entitled to a third party without the obligor's consent unless the assignment is forbidden by law or contract or is prevented by the nature of the legal transaction. The obligor may not assert against any third party an objection to the assignment on the grounds that it was excluded by agreement, if the third party acquires the claims in reliance on a written acknowledgment of debt, in which there is no mention of any prohibition of assignment.

The assignment agreement must be made in written form. It is a requirement for validity. In other words, an assignment is valid only if concluded in writing. However, no particular form is required for a promise to enter into an assignment agreement (TCO Art. 184).

As a result of an assignment agreement, the claim is transferred to the assignee. Furthermore, the obligor must perform their obligation to the assignee. If the obligor performs their obligation to the assignor, as a rule, their obligation is deemed not fulfilled. However, before the assignment agreement has been brought to their attention by the assignor or the assignee, if the obligor makes payment in good faith to the former obligee, or, in the case of multiple assignments, to a subsequent assignee that acquires the claim, the obligor is, then, deemed fulfilled their obligation (TCO Art. 186).

---

66 Oğuzman and Öz, *V. II*, 556; Eren, *Borçlar Genel*, 1370 ff.; Nomer, *Borçlar Genel*, 488; Helvacı, *Turkish Contract Law*, 269.

The assignment of a claim includes all preferential and accessory rights except those that are inseparable from the person of the assignor (TCO Art. 189/I). More precisely, by the assignment of claims, all accessory rights such as mortgage, pledge, surety and likewise are also transferred.[67] Pursuant to TCO Art. 189/II that is not mandatory, accrued interest is also transferred with the assignment of the claim.

The obligor may raise any objections, which they was able to raise to the assignor's claims when they first learned of the assignment, also to the assignee's claims. The obligor may set the claims undue, when they learned of the transfer, off against their debt, provided that the debt falls due before or at the same time of the due date of assigned claims (TCO Art. 188).

If assignment is made for valuable consideration, it implies that the assignor warrants the existence of the claim at the time of assignment and the solvency of the obligor. If there is no valuable consideration for the assignment or there is a claim assigned to someone else in accordance with law, the assignor or the former obligee is not even responsible for the existence of the claim and the solvency of the obligor (TCO Art. 191).

Assumption of a debt is an agreement that changes the obliged party (obligor) within the individual obligation relationship and that must be concluded between the obligee and the third party, who intends to assume the debt. Due to TCO Art. 195, the person who promises to undertake a debt by the assignment agreement with the obligor, is under liability to be released from the debt either by performing in person or undertaking the debt with consent of obligee. The obligor may not compel performance of the obligation by the party assuming the debt until the obligor has discharged their obligations under the agreement on assumption of debts. If the former obligor is not released from their debt, they may request that the new obligor provides security.

There is no specific form requirement for the validity of the agreement of assumption of a debt, which is concluded between the obligor and the third party.[68]

As a legal consequence of assumption of a debt, the new obligor is obliged to perform the debt whereas the former obligor is no longer obliged to perform. Another consequence of the assumption of a debt is that the accessory rights are

---

67 Oğuzman and Öz, *V. II*, 575 ff. According to CC Art. 891, the assignment of a claim secured by a mortgage contract is valid without entry in the land register.

68 If the promising party is obliged to discharge the obligor without consideration, this agreement must be in writing. Since such an agreement creates a promise of a donation (TCO Art. 288/I).

not affected by the change of obligor unless they are inseparable from the identity of the former obligor. However, the responsibilities of the third party who provides pledges and that of the surety in favor of the obligee resume only if they give their written consent to the assumption of debt (TCO Art. 198).

§ Part II The Special Provisions of Obligation Law

I. Overview

The Turkish Constitution guarantees the freedom of contract that is one of the basic principles of the Turkish Code of Obligations (Art. 48 of Constitution). Due to this principle, various types of contracts can be concluded. The parties may agree on a type of contract which is covered in the Turkish Code of Obligations. Accordingly, the Turkish Code of Obligations governs special kinds of contracts such as sale contract (Art. 207–281), exchange contract (Art. 282–284), gift contract (Art. 285–298), lease contract (Art. 299–378), loan contract (Art. 379–392), employment contract (Art. 393–447), agency contract (Art. 502–514), contract for work (Art. 470–486), surety contract (Art. 581–603), etc. In addition to this, the contracting parties may determine type and content of their contract by their own choice within the limits of the law. This right of choice is also based on the principle of freedom of contract.

As a result of freedom of contract, the parties may create "sui generis contracts", "mixed contracts" or "combining contracts". These contracts are named as unnamed contracts that are not regulated under any codes but created by the parties as a consequence of freedom of contract. Sui generis contracts consist of combination of elements that are not included in the types of contracts regulated in the law. Mixed contracts are those, in which the elements of a contract that regulated in the law and the unspecified elements blended together in a way not foreseen by the law. "Combining contracts", on the other hand, are those in which fates of multiple contract types have interconnected.[69]

The contracts which are regulated under codes may be provided not only in the Turkish Code of Obligations but also, they may be provided in other special codes. As an example, financial leasing contracts and factoring contracts are governed by a special code no. 6361 enacted on 21 November 2012. Another

69 Tandoğan, *V. I / 1*, 11; Saibe Oktay, "İsimsiz Sözleşmelerin Geçerliliği, Yorumlanması ve Tamamlanması," *İstanbul Üniversitesi Hukuk Fakültesi Mecmuası*, Vol. 55, Iss. 1–2 (1996): 263 ff.; Erden Kuntalp, *Karışık Muhtevalı Akit* (Ankara: Banka ve Ticaret Hukuku Araştırma Enstitüsü, 2013), 1 ff.

significant example is consumer contracts which are governed in the Act on Consumer Protection (ACP) that applies to contracts related to the supply of goods and services where one party is the consumer and the other is seller/supplier. Consumer contracts can be exemplified as sale contracts, installments sales, subscription contracts, package tour contracts, pre-paid house contracts, loan contracts, distance contracts, etc. The main task of ACP is to protect consumers by the regulations introduced and to strengthen the contractual rights of consumers against sellers/suppliers. However, certain contract types are regulated in the Turkish Code of Obligations and in the special codes both. The employment contract may be given as an example that is explained below.[70]

Within the regulations of the Turkish Code of Obligations, the contracts are divided into groups considering their content. In this consideration, the contracts which are regulated in the Turkish Code of Obligations can be basically classified as contracts providing the transfer of ownership, the contracts providing transfer of usage and benefit, service contracts and security contracts.[71] In this chapter, the contracts which are regulated in the Turkish Code of Obligations will be explained by the method of classifying their content since it will be difficult to analyze all these types of contracts detailed. The focus of this explanation will be especially on the differences of the contracts from each other. Lastly in this part, the Consumer Protection Law will be briefly explained as well.

II. Contracts Providing Transfer of Ownership

These types of contracts are contracts which aim to create an obligation of the transfer of the ownership of the property. Sale contracts, exchange contracts, and gift (donation) may be given as an example of those contracts that provide transfer of ownership. These kinds of contracts create an obligation of the transfer of ownership.

Contract for sale is a contract whereby the seller undertakes to deliver the item sold and transfer ownership to the buyer in return for the sale price, which the buyer undertakes to pay to the seller. In this contract, exchange for receiving property, the buyer agrees to pay a sale price which is an amount of money. This exchange is the distinctive feature of a sale contract from an exchange contract and from any sui generis contract. If the buyer agrees to fulfill a performance other than paying a sale price, these will be, then, deemed an exchange contract

70 See infra: *Chapter IV – Employment Law.*

71 Tandoğan, *V. I/1*, 2 ff.; Aydın Zevkliler and Emre Gökyayla, *Borçlar Hukuku Özel Borç İlişkileri* (İstanbul: Vedat, 2020), 27 ff.

or a sui generis contract. The rules governing sale contracts also apply to the contracts of exchange in the sense that each party to the exchange is considered as seller in respect of the object promised by them, and as buyer in respect of the object promised to them. If one party is obliged to transfer of ownership, and the counterparty is obliged to render a service, then there will be a sui generis contract. For example, if the parties agree on the transfer of the ownership of a mobile phone for 5,000 Turkish Liras, this contract is considered as a sale contract. On the other hand, if the parties agree on the transfer of the ownership of a mobile phone in the exchange of the ownership of a necklace, this contract is considered as an exchange contract. A sui generis contract then exists if the parties agree on the transfer of the ownership of the mobile phone in exchange of the performance such as a singing at a concert.

A sale contract has special types which will be classified as to the subject of the contract such as sales for personal property and sales for real property, and as to the type of paying sale price such as installment sale, pre-paid sale and cash payment sale. Sale by sample, sale on test and inspection, and auction sales can be given as another special types of sale contracts.

It should be noted that, since 1 August 2011, the United Nations Convention on Contracts for the International Sale of Goods (CISG) became a part of Turkish national law. As a result of this, if there is a dispute that is arising from an international sale, the provisions of CISG will be applied. The aim of the CISG is to provide a consistent and equitable framework for contracts for the international sale of goods. In practice, the CISG, in a considerable scale, contributes to providing certainty in commercial transactions and reducing transaction costs.[72] The CISG provides standardized legislation for the international sale of goods and applies to every contract that are concluded for the sale of goods between the parties with a business premises inside contracting states. In addition to this, CISG applies to contract of sale of goods between parties whose business premises are in different states when the rules of private international law led to the application of the law of a contracting state. Under Turkish Law, if there is a contract that is covered by CISG's scope of application, the provisions of CISG will be regulated.[73]

72 See also, https://uncitral.un.org/, accessed 7.8.2021.

73 For detailed information on the application and provisions of CISG see also, Yeşim M. Atamer, *Uluslararası Satım Sözleşmelerine İlişkin Birleşmiş Milletler Antlaşması (CISG) Uyarınca Satıcının Yükümlülükleri ve Sözleşmeye Aykırılığın Sonuçları* (İstanbul: Beta, 2005).

In this consideration, it should be noted that option contracts also establish a sale relationship with a unilateral declaration of will. By the purchase, repurchase, and pre-purchase agreements, the right to purchase the goods with a unilateral declaration of intent is given to the one of the parties.

The gift (donation) contract, which is another contract aimed at the transfer of the ownership, is regulated under TCO Art. 285. According to the article 285 of TCO, a gift is any *inter vivos* disposition, in which a person uses their assets to enrich another without receiving an equivalent consideration. As a general principle, the promise of a gift is valid only if done in writing. The gift contract is divided into sub-categories. For example, it is deemed as a gift hand to hand when the conclusion of the contract and transferring the ownership take place at the same time. Additionally, if the value of an asset is 100,000 Turkish Liras but it is transferred as 50,000 Turkish Liras for the aim of donation, this transaction is considered as a mixed donation.

III. Contracts Providing Transfer of the Right of Usage and Benefit

In these contracts, the transfer of the right of usage and benefit is agreed by the parties with the exchange of payment or without any payment. As it can be understood from the definition, these contracts will be classified as into two: The contracts provided the transfer of the right of usage and benefit in return of rental fee and those that provide the transfer of the right of usage and benefit without fee. A loan for use is contract whereby the lender agrees to leave the use of chattels without any fee. The purpose of the contract of loan for use is the temporary use of the object loaned by the borrower. The loan for use is defined in the TCO Art. 379. According to this article, a loan for use is a contract whereby the lender promises to make an object available for the borrower's use free of charge, and the borrower promises to return it to the lender after they have used and profited from it. The borrower may make use of the loaned object only for the purpose stipulated in the contract if there is any, or for its normal purpose or the purpose entailed by its nature. The borrower bears the ordinary costs of maintenance and, in the case of loaned animals, in particular the costs of feeding them. If the loan for use is for indefinite term, it comes to an end as soon as the borrower has made use of the object as promised or when the period, during which such use could have been made, has expired. Further, the lender is entitled to reclaim the object before the due date for return, if the borrower uses the object against the purpose of the contract, damages the object, or permits a third party to use it, or in case of unforeseen circumstances occur which renders the lender in urgent need of the object.

Apart from a loan for use (*commodatum*), according to the Article 386 of TCO, a loan for consumption (*mutuum*) is defined as a contract whereby the lender promises to transfer the ownership of a sum of money or of other consumable goods to the borrower in return of that, the borrower promises to return objects of equal quantity and quality to the lender. In other words, it entails simply the return of the equivalent and not the identical object. By a loan for consumption, if it is not stipulated that a certain day in order the loan will be due or any notification period or not determined that the loan is to be due immediately when requested back, the borrower is not obliged to return the loan until 6 weeks have passed since the first request.

Leases are contracts in which a lessor (landlord) grants a lessee (tenant) the use of an object in in return for rent. Lease contract is regulated between the Articles 299 to 378 in TCO. Due to the provisions of TCO, lease contract is divided in three sub-categories: general provisions of lease contract, the provisions of leases of residential and roofed commercial premises and the provisions of usufructuary lease. The common feature of these provisions is that most of them are mandatory provisions. The aim of this approach is to protect the tenant and to strengthen the contractual rights of the lessee. As a consequence of this, even if the contract is expired, the contract is extended for an indefinite period of time. As to the fixed term contracts for the leases of residential and roofed commercial premises, due to Art. 347 of TCO, the contract is extended automatically unless the lessee terminates the contract. In this point of view, to protect the lessee who is in the weaker position against the lessor, the causes of termination of leases of residential and roofed commercial premises are stipulated limited.

On the change of ownership, to protect the lessee one of the most significant provision is stipulated in the Article 310 of TCO. Due to this provision, after conclusion of the contract, if the lessor alienates the object for any reason, the lease passes to the acquirer together with ownership of the object.

In addition to this, in the leases of residential and roofed commercial premises, the adjustment on the rental fees is subject to certain rules aiming to protect the lessee. Pursuant to TCO Art. 344, the agreement of the parties regarding the rental fee to be applied in the renewed lease periods are valid provided that the increase rate of the consumer price index computed according to 12-month averages in the previous lease year. According to TCO Art. 344/II, if the parties of the lease contract do not determine the increase rate on this matter, the rental fee will be determined by the judge on an equitable basis, considering the condition of the leased property, provided that the increase rate does not exceed the increase rate of the consumer price index computed according to 12-month averages in the previous lease year. Also, the Article 344/III regulates that, regardless of whether an agreement has been made by the parties on this matter, the judge will determine the rental fee to be applied in lease agreements for more than 5 years or renewed after 5 years, on an equitable basis, considering the increase rate of the consumer price index computed according to 12-month averages, the condition of the leased property, and the comparable rental fees. For lease contracts concluded in foreign currency, the rental fees can be amended at earliest 5 years have passed. On the other hand, rental fees can be amended, or the contract can be terminated prematurely on condition that the conditions arise cited in TCO Art. 138 in reference to a disappearance of the contractual basis (TCO Art. 344/IV).

IV. Service Contracts

The contracts aiming at the accomplishment of service that are regulated in the Turkish Code of Obligations are divided into sub-categories: "contract for work", "the agency contract" and "general contract of service (employment contract)", "the brokerage contract" and "commission contract".

It should be noted that the general contract of service (i.e., employment contract) that will be evaluated in detail in the following chapter[74] is regulated between the Articles 393 to 447 of the Turkish Code of Obligations. Solely to protect the employee, who is the weaker party of the contract, a special code is regulated containing mostly absolutely or relatively mandatory provisions to assure this protection (referred to as Labor Act). Employment contract is concluded between employer and employee which is defined in TCO Art. 393. Due to this article, by means of an employment contract, the employee undertakes to work dependently in the service of the employer for a definite or indefinite period and the employer undertakes to pay the employee a wage based on the amount of time they works (time wage) or the tasks they performs (piece work).

Contract for work may be given as another types of service contracts and is defined in TCO Art. 470. According to this article, a contract for work is a contract whereby the contractor undertakes to carry out work and the business owner undertakes to pay them for that work. In a contract for work, the activity aimed for achieving the promised result is carried out by an independent contractor. Therefore, the correct performance of the debt is regardless of the effort involved in the activity performed. The activity might be related to a work that has a tangible existence or been embodied in a material property or it might

74 See infra: *Chapter IV – Employment Law.*

be related to an intangible work. As an example, sewing a dress is regarded as a work, likewise a performance in a scene is regarded as such.[75]

According to the employment contract, the employee is obliged to work in the service of employer under the authority of the employer performing in a dependent manner and to follow the instructions given by the employer during the contract. The employee undertakes to provide with a certain service, work or activity to the employer rather than with a result produced by the performance. In the employment contract, the employer is entitled to issue general directives and specific instructions regarding the performance of the work and the conduct of the employees in their business or household. On the other hand, in the contract for work, there is no such a dependent relationship between the contractor and the business owner. As a rule, the contractor performs independently while carrying out the work. However, in some circumstances, it is intrinsically possible that the business owner may direct the contractor. Nevertheless, this cannot be construed that the contractor is under the order, supervision or control of the business owner while carrying out the work.[76]

A contract regarding the manufacture of a furniture in return for a payment may be given as an example for the contract for work. The business owner must pay for the work on completion or delivery. If the work is delivered in stages and payment is made in installments, the amount due for each stage of the work is payable upon the delivery of relevant stage. If the price was determined only as an approximate amount or not determined in advance at all, it does not prevent the conclusion of the contract, and the amount is determined according to the value of the work carried out and the expenses incurred by the contractor. If the parties decide that no price will be paid, then there exists no longer a contract for work. In this circumstance, this contract may be deemed as either a sui generis contract,[77] or a mixed contract.[78] For example, the construction contract in return for land share is considered as a mixed contract. In this contract, the construction is indebted in return for the commitment to transfer the land share

75 Fikret Eren, *Borçlar Hukuku Özel Hükümler*, 5th ed. (Ankara: Yetkin, 2017), 689 ff.

76 Eren, *Borçlar Özel*, 599; Öz Seçer, *Eser Sözleşmesinin İş Sahibi Tarafından Tam Tazminatla Feshi*, 1st ed. (Ankara: Yetkin, 2016), 30; Zevkliler and Gökyayla, *Borçlar Özel*, 507. See also, the decision of Turkish Court of Cassation, General Assembly of Civil Chambers, dated 06.04.2010, no. 3–727/75.

77 Alper Gümüş, *Borçlar Hukuku Özel Hükümler, Volume II* (İstanbul: Vedat, 2014), 6; Haluk Tandoğan, *Borçlar Hukuku – Özel Borç İlişkileri, Volume II* (Ankara: Banka ve Ticaret Hukuku Enstitüsü, 1989), 24.

78 Zevkliler and Gökyayla, *Borçlar Özel*, 496.

under the joint ownership. It should be reiterated that in the contract for work, there is a promise of conclusion, and the contractor is responsible for the failure to obtain the result.[79]

The agency (proxy) contract is governed between the Articles 502 to 512 of the Turkish Code of Obligations. According to TCO Art. 502, an agency contract is a contract whereby the agent undertakes to conduct certain business or provide certain services in accordance with the terms of the contract. Remuneration is not a requisite, but payable where it is agreed or customary. Service contracts that are not covered by any other specific type are subject to the provisions of agency contract.

As it is understood from the definition, in agency contract there is not a promise that the work will continue for a definite or indefinite period as in the individual employment contract. In addition to this, as in the contract for work, there is no promise regarding the obtaining of a specific result. The agent is not responsible if they cannot achieve the result despite their diligent and faithful performance.[80] However, the agent is liable to the principal for the diligent and faithful performance of the service entrusted to them. The loyalty, which is essential for the individual employment contract, is not of that much importance for the agency contract.[81] When viewed in this aspect, it should be noted that the situations of the agent and the contractor are similar in terms of independence in service, profession or art requiring specialization. It should be reiterated that the agent, who undertakes to conduct certain work or provide certain services on behalf of the principal within the agency contract, may obtain a result due to their performance, even though is not obliged to provide such a result. Nevertheless, the point is not to achieve the result desired by the principal, but to perform the work or service in accordance with the duty of care.[82]

As a typical example of an agency contract, the attorney contract and the medical treatment contract between the doctor and the patient can be mentioned. In both contracts, the agent is not liable if they has not achieved the result even if they has fulfilled their performance diligently and faithfully. However, in both cases, both the doctor and the attorney will be held responsible for even the slightest negligence, since their service can be regarded as a profession or art

79 Zevkliler and Gökyayla, *Borçlar Özel,* 510 ff.
80 Zevkliler and Gökyayla, *Borçlar Özel,* 637.
81 Eren, *Borçlar Özel,* 600.
82 Zevkliler and Gökyayla, *Borçlar Özel,* 637.

requiring specialization that carried out exclusively with the permission granted by competent authorities or law.

V. Security Contracts

Another distinction regarding contracts is the security contracts. Contracts for the purpose of collateral are named as personal securities. In this type of contracts, a third party guarantees that a result will be obtained. A contract that provides personal security is referred as the contract of surety, which is defined in TCO Art. 581. According to this article, under such a contract, the surety undertakes as against the obligee of the principal obligor to vouch for performance of the obligation.

Contract of surety is concluded between the surety and the obligee. If the principal obligor does not fulfill their obligation, the surety is obliged to indemnify the loss. Therefore, contract of surety is commonly used in business transactions in order to protect obligors from damages against the failure of the obligor to fulfill obligations. Within this contract, the obligation of the principal obligor and the obligation of the surety are independent from each other.[83] The obligation of the surety has an ancillary nature. That is to say, the obligation arises from contract of surety is an accessory undertaking and it is, therefore, not binding where the principal obligation is not valid.

According to TCO Art. 582, for a contract of surety, the existence of a valid primary obligation prerequisites. A future or conditional obligation may be guaranteed by means of a contract of surety only provided that the primary obligation takes effect. A person, who stands surety for performance of an obligation resulting from a contract, by which is not binding on the principal obligor due to the error or incapacity to make a contract, is liable for such obligation subject to the concrete conditions of event and the principles that govern surety, if they was aware of the defect that vitiating the contract at the time they gave their commitment. The same applies to any person, who stands surety for performance of an obligation, which is time-barred by prescription period for the principal obligor. Unless the law provides otherwise, the surety may not waive in advance the rights conferred on them due to this title.

---

83 Gülçin Elçin Grassinger, *Kefilin Alacaklıya Karşı Sahip Olduğu Savunma İmkanları* (İstanbul: Alfa, 1996), 13 ff.; Burak Özen, *6098 Sayılı Türk Borçlar Kanunu Çerçevesinde Kefalet Sözleşmesi* (İstanbul: Vedat, 2012), 51 ff.; Gümüş, *V. II*, 531; Serkan Ayan, *Kefalet Sözleşmesinde Kefilin Sorumluluğu* (Ankara: Adalet, 2013), 13 ff.; Zevkliler and Gökyayla, *Borçlar Özel*, 703 ff.

Due to TCO Art. 598, the surety is released as soon as the principal obligation is extinguished for whatever reason. Therefore, the obligee must prove the existence of a valid principal obligation.

The contract of surety is divided into different kinds which are basically regarded as simple surety, joint and several surety and co-surety.

Simple surety is regulated in TCO Art. 585. According to said article, the obligee may resort to a simple surety only after they has resorted to the principal obligor. However, in certain cases, it is possible to resort directly to who undertakes the simple surety. There are as follows:

In the case the obligor declared bankrupt or came to a composition agreement or obtained a definitive certificate of loss as a result of the proceedings against, or in the case the obligor is granted time for composition agreement, or in the case that the legal proceedings brought against the obligor in Turkey become impossible or significantly impeded.

If the claim, before or during the suretyship, is secured by a pledge, a simple surety may request that the claim be satisfied from the pledges first, provided that the obligor has not been declared bankrupt or granted time for composition agreement. Only for the exceptions in the law, it may be resorted to the surety directly, instead of the principal obligor. However, it is possible to agree in the contract that also in those cases, the obligee must first resort to the principal obligor.

Joint and several surety is regulated in TCO Art. 586. Pursuant to this article, if the surety has accepted to undertake an obligation by appending the phrase of "joint and several" literally or any equivalent phrase in meaning, the obligee may resort to the surety without having resort to the principal obligor or before converting the immovable pledge into money. However, for this to be applied, the obligor must be delayed in performance or clearly insolvent or the reminder must remain ineffective.

Unless it is agreed in the contract, joint and several liability may only arise by law. However, according to the principle cited within the Turkish Commercial Code (TCC) referred to as a "presumption of solidarity", the parties to a contract regarding an obligation of a commercial nature are presumed to be jointly liable to the obligee (TCC Art. 7).

Co-surety is also regulated in TCO Art. 587. Where two or more persons stand surety for a single divisible principal obligation, each of them is liable as a simple surety for their own share and as collateral surety for the shares of the others.

A contract of guarantee is another form of creating personal security. It is difficult to draw a distinction between contract of guarantee and contract of surety.

The main difference between two contracts is that the contract of guarantee is an independent contract creating a principal obligation whereas the obligation arises from the contract of surety is an accessory undertaking and it is, therefore, not binding if the principal obligation is not valid. In case of the contract of guarantee, even if the principal obligation is not valid, the guarantor is liable for damages resulting by the third party's non-performance of the obligation.[84]

The contract of guarantee has two sub-categories: Pure guarantees and collateral guarantees. A pure guarantee is commonly used to guarantee against the losses of an investor or to assure a fixed profit ratio in the course of their operations.[85] For example, the promise that if certain stocks are purchased, the stock will increase by 25 %, if otherwise, the guarantor will pay the difference is deemed as a pure guarantee.[86] Collateral guarantee is a contract that requires the existence of a primary obligation and by which the guarantor undertakes, in case the primary obligor fails to perform their obligation, to pay damages arising from such failure.[87]

VI. Consumer Protection Law

As mentioned above, the Turkish Code of Obligations is based on the principal of freedom of contract. As a consequence of this, within the contractual relationship, as a rule, the contracting parties are in an equal position with each other. However, in some contractual relationships, the contracting parties are not in reality in an equal position. One of the most notable examples is individual employment contracts in which the employer has a stronger position than the employee. Similarly, in the consumer contracts, the consumer has a weaker position than the buyer/supplier. To strike a balance between the parties and to assure the protection of weaker party in the frame of consumer contracts, consumer protection law has emerged from the 20th century. To this end, the former Act on the Consumer Protection (no. 4077)[88] was adopted in Turkey. However,

---

84 Tandoğan, *V. II*, 812 ff.; Özen, *Kefalet Sözleşmesi*, 24; Gümüş, *V. II*, 658; Eren, *Borçlar Özel*, 766 ff.; Zevkliler and Gökyayla, *Borçlar Özel*, 707; Lale Sirmen, "Secured Transactions," in *Turkish Business Law*, eds. Tuğrul Ansay and Eric C. Schneider (Ankara: Seçkin 2014), 67.

85 Sirmen, "Secured Transactions," 67.

86 Tandoğan, *V. II*, 807; Özen, *Kefalet Sözleşmesi*, 26 ff.; Zevkliler and Gökyayla, *Borçlar Özel*, 705 ff.

87 Özen, *Kefalet Sözleşmesi*, 23; Gümüş, *V. II*, 655; Zevkliler and Gökyayla, *Borçlar Özel*, 706; Sirmen, "Secured Transactions," 67.

88 OJ, 23.02.1995, no. 22221.

due to changing circumstances the protection provided by this act remained inefficient and detailed provisions were needed for effective protection of consumers. As a result of this, the current Act on Consumer Protection (no. 6502)[89] is adopted. Pursuant to the Article 1 of the Act on Consumer Protection (ACP), the purpose of this law is maintaining health and safety of the consumer in accordance with the public interest and protecting their economic interests, redressing their losses, assuring them protection against environmental hazards, enlightening the consumers and taking measures that arise awareness, encouraging the solidarity of consumers with self-help incentives and promoting voluntary organizations with the aim of creating public policies.

With the current ACP, the scope of implementation has expanded. Consumer transaction is defined as any contract, including any contract of work, transportation contract, brokerage contract, insurance contract, contract of agency or attorney contract, banking contract or any other similar contract, or legal transaction that is instituted on any goods or service market between any natural person or legal entity, public legal entities, who acts for commercial or professional purposes or any natural person or legal entity, who acts on behalf or on the account of any such natural person or legal entity, and consumer.

Consumer contracts, such as installment sales, distance contracts, subscription contracts, package tour contracts, sales through campaigns and other prepaid sales and consumer credit contracts are regulated by special provisions of the ACP. In addition to these contracts, the pre-paid house selling contracts are deemed as consumer transaction to ensure the protection of consumer specifically against the problems arising from the construction sector in Turkey. Some of consumer contracts which are governed by the ACP, such as installment sales, package tour contracts, distance contracts, consumer credit contracts and housing finance contracts must be concluded in written form and contain specific terms required by law. In addition, in the vast majority of the consumer contracts, the consumer has a withdrawal right. Pursuant to ACP Art. 83/I, any cases which are not regulated in this Law, shall be governed by general provisions.[90]

---

89 OJ, 07.11.2013, no. 28835.

90 For detailed information on Consumer Protection Law see also, M. Alper Gümüş, *6502 Sayılı Tüketicinin Korunması Hakkında Kanun Şerhi (Madde 1–46), Volume I* (İstanbul: Vedat, 2014); Murat Aydoğdu, "6502 Sayılı Tüketicinin Korunması Hakkında Kanun'un Getirdiği Yeniliklere Genel Bakış, Sözleşmeye Aykırılık, Ayıplı İfa Kavramlarına Getirdiği Farklı Yaklaşım ve Bu Konuda Önerilerimiz," *Dokuz Eylül Üniversitesi Hukuk Fakültesi Dergisi*, Vol. 15, Iss. 2 (2013): 1–62; Murat Aydoğdu,

One of the most significant consequences of a contract which is qualified as a consumer contract is related to the resolution of disputes. ACP Art. 73/A introduced a compulsory mediation for the resolution of consumer disputes. Besides this resolution method, ACP Art. 68 governs that at least one committee must be formed in each city and borough and stipulates a special application procedure based on monetary limits. The monetary limits of the applications to be made to the consumer arbitration committees for 2021 has been adopted. Accordingly, it is compulsory to apply to the borough arbitration committees for consumer conflicts in respect of any dispute, the amount of which is less than 7,550 Turkish Liras, and to the city arbitration committees for consumer problems in respect of any dispute, the amount of which is less than 11,330 Turkish Liras, and to the city arbitration committees for consumer conflicts in respect of any dispute, the amount of which is between 7,550 to 11,330 Turkish Liras in the cities with metropolitan status. Any application to the arbitration committees for consumer conflicts in respect of any dispute, the amount of which exceeds the foregoing amounts, shall be inadmissible.[91]

Consumer courts has jurisdiction for proceedings involving disputes arising from consumer transactions and consumer-oriented practices (ACP Art. 73/I). Due to ACP Art. 70/III, either party may appeal against the decision of an arbitration committee for consumer conflicts before the consumer court seated at the location, where such arbitration committee is seated, within a period of 15 days as of the date of notification of the decision. It must be noted that any such contest shall not prevent the contested decision of the arbitration committee from being enforced. However, if it is claimed, the judge may cease the enforcement of the decision of the arbitration committee by the way of the imposition of an interim injunction.

Further Readings

Atamer, Yeşim M. *Uluslararası Satım Sözleşmelerine İlişkin Birleşmiş Milletler Antlaşması (CISG) Uyarınca Satıcının Yükümlülükleri ve Sözleşmeye Aykırılığın Sonuçları*. İstanbul: Beta Yayınevi, 2005.

Tüketici Hukuku Dersleri (Ankara: Adalet, 2015); Yeşim M. Atamer, *Kredi ve Diğer Finansman Sözleşmelerinde Tüketicinin Korunması* (İstanbul: On İki Levha, 2016); Lale Sirmen, "Consumer Protection Law," in *Turkish Business Law*, ed. Tuğrul Ansay and Eric C. Schneider (Ankara: Seçkin 2014), 29 ff.

91 These amounts can be amended every year with the communiqués published in the Official Journal.

Atamer, Yeşim M. *Kredi ve Diğer Finansman Sözleşmelerinde Tüketicinin Korunması*. İstanbul: On İki Levha, 2016.

Ayan, Serkan: *Kefalet Sözleşmesinde Kefilin Sorumluluğu*. Ankara: Adalet Yayınevi, 2013.

Aydoğdu, Murat. "6502 Sayılı Tüketicinin Korunması Hakkında Kanun'un Getirdiği Yeniliklere Genel Bakış, Sözleşmeye Aykırılık, Ayıplı İfa Kavramlarına Getirdiği Farklı Yaklaşım ve Bu Konuda Önerilerimiz." *Dokuz Eylül Üniversitesi Hukuk Fakültesi Dergisi, Vol. 15, Iss. 2* (2013): 1–62.

Aydoğdu, Murat. *Tüketici Hukuku Dersleri*. Ankara: Adalet, 2015.

Baysal, Başak. *Sözleşmenin Uyarlanması, BK m. 138 Aşırı İfa Güçlüğü*. İstanbul: On İki Levha, 2020.

Develioğlu, Murat. "The Adaptation of Contracts." http://www.erdem-erdem.av.tr/publications/ (Accessed 18.9.2021).

Elçin Grassinger, Gülçin. *Kefilin Alacaklıya Karşı Sahip Olduğu Savunma İmkanları*. İstanbul: Alfa Basın Yayın Dağıtım, 1996.

Eren, Fikret. *Borçlar Hukuku Özel Hükümler*. 5th ed. Ankara: Yetkin, 2017.

Gümüş, M. Alper. *Borçlar Hukuku Özel Hükümler, Volume II*. İstanbul: Vedat Kitapçılık, 2014a.

Gümüş, M. Alper. *6502 Sayılı Tüketicinin Korunması Hakkında Kanun Şerhi (Madde 1–46), Volume I*. İstanbul: Vedat Kitapçılık, 2014b.

Kuntalp, Erden. *Karışık Muhtevalı Akit*. Ankara: Banka ve Ticaret Hukuku Araştırma Enstitüsü, 2013.

Oktay, Saibe. "İsimsiz Sözleşmelerin Geçerliliği, Yorumlanması ve Tamamlanması." *İstanbul Üniversitesi Hukuk Fakültesi Mecmuası, Vol. 55, Iss. 1–2* (1996): 263–296.

Özen, Burak. *6098 Sayılı Türk Borçlar Kanunu Çerçevesinde Kefalet Sözleşmesi*. İstanbul: Vedat Kitapçılık, 2012.

Seçer, Öz. *Eser Sözleşmesinin İş Sahibi Tarafından Tam Tazminatla Feshi*. Ankara: Yetkin Yayınları, 2016.

Sirmen, Lale. "Consumer Protection Law." In *Turkish Business Law*, 29–45. Edited by Ansay, Tuğrul and Schneider, Eric C. Ankara: Seçkin, 2014a.

Sirmen, Lale. "Secured Transactions." In *Turkish Business Law,* 59–75. Edited by Ansay, Tuğrul and Schneider, Eric C. Ankara: Seçkin, 2014b.

Tandoğan, Haluk. *Borçlar Hukuku – Özel Borç İlişkileri, Volume II*. Ankara: Banka ve Ticaret Hukuku Enstitüsü, 1989.

Zevkliler, Aydın and Gökyayla, Emre. *Borçlar Hukuku Özel Borç İlişkileri*. İstanbul: Vedat Kitapçılık, 2020.

Asst. Prof. Dr. Şebnem KILIÇ*

Chapter IV Employment Law

Aybay, Rona. *An Introduction to Law*. İstanbul: Der Yayınları, 2020; Centel, Tankut. *Introduction to Turkish Labour Law*. Springer, 2017; Çelik, Nuri, Caniklioğlu, Nurşen and Canbolat, Talat. *İş Hukuku Dersleri*. İstanbul: Beta, 2020; Dereli, Toker. *Labour Law in Turkey*. Alphen aan den Rijn: Kluwer Law International, 2015; Ekmekçi, Ömer and Korkusuz, Refik. *Turkish Individual Labour Law*. İstanbul: On İki Levha, 2020; Esener, Turhan. *Turkish Business Law I, Contracts and Torts (Law of Obligations)*. İstanbul: Boğaziçi University Press, 2000; Esener, Turhan and Yarsuvat, Ömür. *Turkish Business Law II*. İstanbul: Boğaziçi University Press, 2000; Süral, Nurhan and Kılıçoğlu, Mustafa. "Labor Law." In *Introduction to Turkish Business Law*, 161–184. Edited by Ansay, Tuğrul and Schneider, Eric C. The Netherlands: Kluwer Law International, 2014; Süzek, Sarper. *İş Hukuku*. İstanbul: Beta, 2020.

Introductory Remarks

Everyone, who is engaged in a business activity by working, is not the subject of the discipline of employment law per se. There is a legal difference between the employee, who works as a chief operator in the workplace, and the business owner, who comes to his own workplace every day. Both are running a working activity; however, their legal status is different. This small-scale example is expandable; yet, a similar fundamental difference is striking in each case: Dependent work.[1]

In this respect, employment law examines a specific contractual relationship. Some works independently in business life. These are called "independent contractors" or "freelancers", although there are some differences in themselves. Accordingly, independent employees are not the subject matter of this discipline.

* Corresponding author.

1 The term of "dependency" in this context is also widely known and used as "subordination".

In terms of employment law, which covers an important and enormous part of business activities, the legal relations between the employee that works dependently, and the employer are the main subject of examination. Another aspect of employment law covers the collective industrial relations between organized interest groups of employees and employers, which is out of the scope of this chapter.

In this chapter, a brief overview of the regulations on individual employment relationship in Turkey will be provided. To this end, first, historical background and general remarks on employment law will be outlined. Following that, the features and the types of individual employment contract will be explained. Then, within the framework of this contract, the concepts of employee and employer and the rights and obligations of given parties arising from the employment contract will be examined. One of the most important issues in terms of employment law is the protection of employees against the termination of contract as a vulnerable party of the contract. Therefore, the legal regulations regarding termination will be featured broadly. Finally, current debates of employment law will be highlighted.

§ Part I Essentials of Employment Law

I. Historical Background of Employment Law

According to the traditional narrative, employment law (or labor law, which often used interchangeably) was born parallel with the emergence of the Industrial Revolution. In today's expression, "the first" Industrial Revolution symbolizes the transition to new production processes with steam power mostly in Europe and the United States. Following this, the second Industrial Revolution commences by mass production with the aid of electric power, and it lasts from the mid-19th century until the early 20th century, and it took place in a broader geographical scope respectively.

The understanding of law of the first period had considered industrial relations within the framework of contract law as many other contractual relationships and covers it by the Law of Obligations. As the fundamental codification regulating the contractual relations, the Code of Obligations was based on the principle of freedom of contract.

It is not possible to conceive the freedom of contract without the adoption of autonomy of will. Originally, the theory of autonomy of will was the ideological base of the freedom of contract perception of the 19th century following the French Revolution. This point of view grants general authorization by legal order to individuals to regulate their private relations with others freely and with having been intervened as scarce as possible.[2] As a rule, a free individual may limit their freedom at their own will by the virtue of a contract. This is the base of freedom of contract in private law.

This perception intrinsically avoids any intervention to the contracts by the state. On the other hand, social outcomes following the Industrial Revolution required industrial relations to be handled differently. This period in history was remarkable by the low wages, working with long hours, and without paid vacations. At first, these difficult and unsafe working conditions had been considered as the choice of the employees, who conclude employment contracts under these terms "freely". Over time, it was yet seen that the fiction of "legal equality" of the contracting parties couldn't be provided effectively in reality. Because of the hierarchy between the parties based on the dependency that was established by the employment contract, one of the parties (the employee) was in a vulnerable position, and because of the financial circumstance at the beginning they was suffering from the lack of bargaining power. Therefore, the idea to protect the weaker party of this contract with legal instruments was developed. These instruments were realized basically in two ways: by the legalization of the unions that were once considered as an illegal intervention to the free will of individuals, and by state intervention. Afterwards, labor movement (trade unionism) has expanded, and many of industrialized states put into effect various protective regulations regarding the working conditions gradually. Most importantly though, first in Germany, the "social state" was introduced, and the protection shield for the vulnerable population in society was formed. A similar process occurred in many industrialized countries gradually, and this approach is mainly preserved until the 1980s. Although globalization and increasing competition in the market and new approaches regarding flexible employment conditions have emerged today, the core of employment law is still based on the principle of the protection of the employee.[3]

---

2 Rona Aybay, *An Introduction to Law* (İstanbul: Der Yayınları, 2020), 105–106; Turhan Esener, *Turkish Business Law I, Contracts and Torts* (İstanbul: Boğaziçi University Press, 2000), 73–75.

3 Nuri Çelik, Nurşen Caniklioğlu, and Talat Canbolat, *İş Hukuku Dersleri* (İstanbul: Beta, 2020), 4 ff., 23 ff.; Sarper Süzek, *İş Hukuku* (İstanbul: Beta, 2020), 9. See also, Öner Eyrenci, Savaş Taşkent, Devrim Ulucan and Esra Baskan, *İş Hukuku* (İstanbul: Beta, 2020); Ercan Güven and Ufuk Aydın, *Bireysel İş Hukuku* (Eskişehir: Nisan, 2020); Hamdi Mollamahmutoğlu, Muhittin Astarlı and Ulaş Baysal, *İş Hukuku Ders Kitabı* (Ankara: Lykeion, 2021).

In brief, employment law is the first branch of law, which protects the weaker party of the contractual relationship as a discipline. After that, this approach is also embraced by other branches of law such as regulations on consumer law and law of residential leases. The aim of employment law is to create an effective balance between parties by removing the imbalance imposed by the employer. For this reason, unlike the law of obligations, imperative regulations prevail in employment law in order to compensate for the weaker position of employees. Thereby it has detached from the branch of the law of obligations that mainly based on freedom of contract and has gained recognition as a distinct law discipline.[4]

II. The Position of Employment Law as to the Division of Law

According to the main division of law, which is based on the major legal tradition that each law system belongs to, Turkey is one of the civil law countries.[5] Civil law systems generally traced back to Romano-Germanic law tradition, and fundamental legal concepts that rooted in those traditions have been developed, to a greater or lesser degree, similar in basis yet varied over many years. In essence, a civil law system may be defined as a system of codified law.[6]

In the civil law countries, the commonly accepted classification leans on the traditional division between "public law" and "private law". This division is arranged according to the subject-matter and the nature of the rules applied by law.[7] Besides, the distinction between public and private law is made according to whether one of the parties having the authorization of the state. In principle, public law embraces those rules, which regulate the relations between private individuals and the public authority, as well as the state structure. In contrast to the branches of public law, branches of private law regulate the relationship between private persons none of whom having a superior position. As much as state intervention increases, the branch of law becomes increasingly related to public law domain. Due to overriding intervention of the state, the characteristics of both public law and private law have intertwined in the field of employment law.

4 Çelik, Caniklioğlu, and Canbolat, *İş Hukuku Dersleri*, 5–6; Süzek, *İş Hukuku*, 10, 37 ff.

5 Mehmet Nur Tanışık, *Turkish Labor Law* (Ankara: Office of Defense Cooperation Press, 1995), 4.

6 Aybay, *An Introduction to Law,* 55 ff.

7 Aybay, *An Introduction to Law*, 65–66.

According to the prevalent opinion in Turkey, employment law, even that it has significant characteristics of private law, falls within the intersection of the public and private law domains.[8] Precisely, employment law is defined as a "mixed branch" that the characteristics of both private and public law converge, even though Turkish legal system has a distinctive approach between public and private law domains as a civil law system.

III. The Development of Turkish Employment Law

The development of employment law has also been relatively late similar to the experience of late industrialization in Turkey.[9]

The advent of industrialization mainly by the public authority rendered the public sector particularly important in terms of Turkish industrial relations. However, work relationship in the public sector is, as a rule, the subject of administrative law (as a branch of public law).[10] In fact, the status of dependent work covers the status of public (civil) servants as well as that of employees. Nonetheless, public servants carry out this dependent work under the public authority, not under a private entrepreneur. The public authorities appoint them with a unilateral declaration of will, they do not recruit with the mutual will of the contracting parties. Moreover, it is hardly needful to remark that public servants have barely bargaining power. All considered, this type of work, as a rule, is not based on a contractual relationship within the domain of private law. By comparison, the employment contract is a private law contract, despite of the

---

8 Aybay, *An Introduction to Law*, 124 ff.; Çelik, Caniklioğlu, and Canbolat, *İş Hukuku Dersleri*, 3; Süzek, *İş Hukuku*, 45.

9 For further information on historical development of employment law see also, Toker Dereli, *Labour Law in Turkey* (Alphen aan den Rijn: Kluwer Law International, 2015) 45 ff.; the Melda Sur, "General Framework and Historical Development of Labor Law in Turkey," *Comparative Labor Law and Policy Journal*, Vol. 30, Iss. 2 (2009): 183–197.

10 In Turkish law, there are also those, who work in the public sector under some form of administrative contracts and are not engaged in the administration of the State. However, this type of work, if not less in quantity, is out of the scope of individual employment law. On the other hand, as the third category, there are also those, who work with service contracts as public service workers and are within the scope of individual employment law. Hence, it is not distinctive whether the counterparty is a public or private sector employer. Nevertheless, as a rule, what is stated under this chapter applies to those working in the private sector, even those, who are within the scope of the Labor Act no. 4857.

fact that the employees have low bargaining power in contract negotiations, or that the state interferes, on a considerable scale, with their freedom of contract. This suggests that the work relationship of public servants and that of employees are to be evaluated separately.

In conclusion, the work of public servants is based on a "status relationship" between them and the state, and their legal status is out the scope of the Labor Act (while it is mainly determined by the Public Servants Act no. 657 and with numerous statutory decrees). Whereas the legal status of employees historically has followed a different line under employment law.

A. *Milestones in the History of Turkish Employment Law*

1. *Reform Period*

The origins of employment law might be traced back to the close past. Before the *Tanzimat* (literally means "Reform"), which was the reform period of the Ottoman Empire, manufacturing of goods mainly depended on the production of craft guilds. The work relationship was traditionally dominated by customary law and the rules and standards of those guilds.[11] By the *Tanzimat*, non-agricultural production had grown gradually. Thereafter, the rudimentary regulations on work in mines were introduced into law first in the history.[12]

2. *Constitutional Monarchy Period*

The Constitutional Monarchy Period commences in 1876 with the promulgation of the Ottoman Constitution. Following this, a quasi-employment contract was regulated in 1877 under the section of lease contracts in *Mecelle*, which might be defined as the Ottoman Civil Code.[13] Nevertheless, it is not conceivable to construe this contract equated with the employment contract in today's context. The content of this was consisted of personal and moral commitment intensely, unlike a contemporary employment contract.

On the other hand, after a brief period, the constitutional monarchy was interrupted. Yet in 1908, it was reinstated and restored by new amendments known as the 2nd Constitutional Monarchy.[14] During those periods, industrial actions accelerated due to the construction of railroads and investments in banks and

11 Çelik, Caniklioğlu, and Canbolat, *İş Hukuku Dersleri*, 7; Süzek, *İş Hukuku*, 11.

12 Çelik, Caniklioğlu, and Canbolat, *İş Hukuku Dersleri*, 7; Sur, "General Framework and Historical Development of Labor Law in Turkey," 189; Süzek, *İş Hukuku*, 11–12.

13 Tankut Centel, *Introduction to Turkish Labour Law* (Springer, 2017), 3.

14 Tanışık, *Turkish Labor Law*, 3.

mines. Plenty of strikes were declared all around the country.[15] Upon this, any strike was forbidden and the development of the collective employment relations in Turkey had interrupted.

3. *Republican Period*

After the transition from the Ottoman Empire to the Republic of Turkey, the employment relationship was in a rapid change in terms of legal regulations. Just before the promulgation of the Republic, whereas the "Independence War" was still ongoing, the Turkish Parliament adopted the Act on the Rights of Miners in the Coal Basin of Ereğli Province to remediate the working conditions in mines in 1921.

Furthermore, various legal regulations regarding the employment relationship, in amount and in content, have been passed by Parliament. Notably, the regulations on week holiday came into force in 1924 and as an important threshold, the Code of Obligations was enacted in 1926 as the reception of the Swiss Code of Obligations (*Obligationenrecht*). Nevertheless, this reference Code had a liberal approach, rather than containing the protective provisions for the employees.

As the national industry was promoted, the need for the protection of the employees had gradually become evident. Then, the drafts for the first Labor Act were prepared. An equally significant event of this period was that Turkey became a member of the International Labour Organization (ILO) in 1932. Following that, the first Labor Act no. 3008 that had been prepared with the help and advice of experts from ILO was adopted in 1936.[16] On the other hand, this new code regulated individual employment relationships rather than collective industrial relations. Throughout this period, strikes and lockouts were remained prohibited.

Most significantly, this Labor Act that repealed later made a distinction between the employees working in physically and those working in intellectually. This approach contracted the scope of the Act by excluding the employees working in intellectual manner. Therefore, the first Labor Act provided a limited protection to the employees for the early Republican period.

---

15 Centel, *Turkish Labour Law*, 3; Sur, "General Framework and Historical Development of Labor Law in Turkey," 190.

16 Centel, *Turkish Labour Law*, 4. Yet, it came into effect in 1937.

4. *Constitution of 1961*

The Constitution of 1961 is a new phase for employment law of Turkey. First in the history, the principle of welfare (social) state and the basic principles regarding the employment relationship were enshrined in the Constitution. The Constitution of 1961 introduced numerous social and economic rights, such as the right to work, the right to rest, right to organize and collective bargaining with the right to strike of the employees, and the social security right.

Another important legal development of this period is the adoption of twin acts, Act on Trade Unions (no. 274) and the Act on Collective Bargaining Agreement, Strike and Lockout (no. 275) in 1963. It should be noted that with the enforcement of the Constitution of 1961, Turkey adopted a fundamentally new economic, social and legal order, not solely in terms of employment law but entirely.[17]

On one hand, the Constitution of 1982, the successor to the Constitution of 1961, reiterated the social state principle and the list of previously enshrined economic and social rights, on the other hand, it also adopted various restrictions for collective bargaining and industrial actions.

5. *The Current Situation*

By the 1980s, the factory-based employment structure (the bulk of employees that work in the factories with indefinite term contracts and commonly are covered by collective bargaining agreements) changed over time following the globalization of markets. With the automation of manufacturing and the widespread use of digital technologies, a new production phase called industry 3.0 has been started. In the view of that change, intellectual effort of employees becomes prominent because of the implication of information technologies for employment. The employee profile gradually changed and working under the contracts for definite periods or for flexible wages become widespread. Therefore, the "flexibility" gained importance, and the demands regard to the amendment of legal regulations have increased. A new approach to regulate employment relationships has emerged. On the other hand, those flexible standards that demanded are likely to cause employees to work precariously.

As the corollary of that change, the fundamentals of employment law have shaken and were opened to discussion. These conflicting interests create a challenge for the contemporary employment law. One of the current solutions

17 Centel, *Turkish Labour Law*, 5; Dereli, *Labour Law in Turkey*, 48 ff.; Süzek, *İş Hukuku*, 13. See also, Çelik, Caniklioğlu, and Canbolat, *İş Hukuku Dersleri*, 13.

of employment law to this can be defined as an integrated strategy called "flexicurity". The term "flexicurity" refers to combining those flexible working standards with the protective ones, with the aim of attaining the required balance between flexibility and security. In Turkey, this approach has received much attention in the past decades.[18]

Because of the pressuring economic and social challenges, it was a social need to have comprehensive regulations on employment relations with a new perspective. For these purposes, in 2003, a new Labor Act no. 4857[19] was adopted taking flexibility into account, whereas a certain degree of employment security is also provided.

Besides that, the current Constitution has been changed various times. Following the constitutional amendments dated in 2017, the structure of the state and the sources of employment law have changed fundamentally.[20] By the last amendments in the Constitution, "presidential decree" is a newly introduced legal source amongst the other traditional regulations. The president of the Republic may, in ordinary times, issue those decrees insofar they shall not regulate the fundamental rights other than social and economic rights that are enshrined in the Constitution. This type of decree has the power of law and has been regarded as a new and important legal source of Turkish legal system. On the other hand, the Council of Ministers that was the only authority being able to issue "the regulations", was abrogated. Therefore, "the regulations" are no longer present among the codified (executive) sources. Yet, hitherto existing regulations are still in force while there is no constitutional authority to issue new ones.

B. General Remarks on Turkish Employment Law

1. The Major Laws for Employment

According to Turkish employment law, a general codification regulating all kinds of employment relationship has not been preferred. It has rather a fragmented structure. In view of that, from the regulations of the Turkish Code of Obligations (*lex generalis*) to that of special codes (*lex specialis*) there are numerous legislative sources that effect the employment contract. It will be seen, therefore, the

18 See also, Toker Dereli, "Flexicurity and Turkey's New Labor Act: Problems and Prospects," in *Labor and Employment Relations in a Globalized World*, eds. Toker Dereli and others (Springer, 2014): 135–158.

19 OJ, 10.06.2003, no. 25154.

20 See supra: *Chapter I – Constitutional Law*. See also, Aybay, *An Introduction to Law*, 50 ff.

followings are not presented to provide an exhaustive list. There might be various legislative sources other than those with respect to the concrete case.

a. The Turkish Code of Obligations

Within the regulations of the Turkish Code of Obligations, general terms and special terms are divided, and under special terms, the contracts are divided into groups considering their content. The contracts aiming at the accomplishment of service[21] are also divided into several sub-categories, such as "contract for work", "the agency contract" and "(individual) employment contract".

Amongst them, the agency contract has the general application domain. The regulations on agency contract may be applied to the concrete case provided that a contract cannot be classified under other types of contracts that aiming at the accomplishment of service regulated by the Turkish Code of Obligations. Another type is the contract for work that can also be defined as "contract *for* service", distinguishing from the "contract *of* service" (employment contract). In case of contract for work, the business owner requests the (independent) contractor to produce and deliver a work in return for a price that she is obliged to pay as an owner. To put it more simply, the independent contractor is imposed an obligation to reach a specific result by the outcome of their independent performance.

On the other hand, the employment contract has a distinctive feature and key component apart from the other contracts that fall in the same group. Under the employment contract, employee accomplishes a service under the authority of the employer. Therefore, dependency, which also knowns as subordination, is the distinctive feature of the employment contracts.[22] Another key component to remember, employment relationship spreads over time and it requires 'continuity' of services as based on ongoing relationship. That is, it is not essential to reaching a specific result for obtaining a wage, but the process of performing a service itself is decisive.

Under the section of the Turkish Code of Obligations, the general regulations on the employment relationship have been introduced and specifically the term of "(general) contract of service" has been preferred. However, it is accepted no

21 Esener, *Business Law I*, 23. Also, see supra: *Chapter III – Law of Obligations*.

22 Çelik, Caniklioğlu, and Canbolat, *İş Hukuku Dersleri*, 88, 178; Süzek, *İş Hukuku*, 229; Nurhan Süral and Mustafa Kılıçoğlu, "Labor Law," in *Introduction to Turkish Business Law*, eds. Ansay, Tuğrul and Schneider, Eric C., 2nd ed. (The Netherlands: Kluwer Law International, 2014), 163.

difference between the legal content of the term of "employment contract" and the term of "contract of service" in the doctrine, and those are used interchangeably.[23] Under this chapter, the term of employment contract will be used to refer to a work relationship based on a dependent work between the employee (who serves) and the employer (who pays a wage in return).

b. *The Act on Employment Courts*

Courts specific to the underlying codes are a common practice for the civil law systems. There is, therefore, usually separate civil court system that assesses the concrete cases whether those are consistent with the legislation, and that interprets the specific codes. Under Turkish employment law, there is another subdivision under the civil courts.

According to the Act on Employment Courts (no. 7036), courts specific to the employment relationships are introduced and those courts hear and determine the concrete cases relating to employment disputes. More importantly, with the new amendments, the mediation procedure between contracting parties prior to court hearings become mandatory for most employment disputes.

c. *The Occupational Health and Safety Act*

The Occupational Health and Safety Act (no. 6331)[24] was enacted in 2012. Hereby first in the history, the rules and standards on occupational health and safety have been aggregated under one single codification for all workers without regard to the type of working relationship. The consequence is that all workers including the employees, public servants, and quasi-employees (apprentices and trainees) are exposed to the same legal standards only in terms of occupational health and safety measures.

d. *The Act on Trade Unions and Collective Bargaining Agreements*

The current legislation regarding the regulations on the collective employment law has been enacted in 2012, titled The Act on Trade Unions and Collective Bargaining Agreements (no. 6356).[25] The aim of this Act can be defined as three-staged. First, it is to regulate the principles and the procedures on the establishment, management, audit, and other activities of unions that are organized by the interest groups of employees and employers (as social counterparts).

23 Çelik, Caniklioğlu, and Canbolat, *İş Hukuku Dersleri*, 187; Süzek, *İş Hukuku*, 233.
24 OJ, 30.06.2012, no. 28339.
25 OJ, 07.11.2012, no. 28460.

Another is to regulate the collective bargaining process and the standards on collective labor agreements that the social counterparts determine their economic, social, and working conditions mutually. Lastly, it is to regulate the settlement of collective disputes through peaceful means or strikes and lockouts.

In conclusion, it is widely accepted that the employment relationship is characterized by an imbalance of power between employer and individual employee. On the other hand, collective bargaining and collective disputes can be defined as countervailing instruments to evade the low bargaining power of individual employees. Therefore, the fundamentals and standards of collective employment law differ from that of individual employment law.

e. The Labor Act

Currently, the special regulations that are in effect for the employment relationships in industrial and service sectors are contained mainly in the Labor Act no. 4857. The Labor Act preempts *lex generalis* in respect to the employment relations that are covered by its scope.[26]

On the other hand, there exist other special regulations that referred to as the Maritime Labor Act and the Press Labor Act. The regulations of these acts are also applicable for the employees, who work within their scope. However, throughout this chapter, the provisions of the Labor Act no. 4857 are to be featured exclusively, and it will be referred to as the "Labor Act" hereinafter (LA).

In conclusion, the above-mentioned acts are not isolated sets of rules, rather they are interrelated in practice. Within the framework of this chapter, those regulations will be mentioned, if pertinent. Yet, it should be reiterated that this chapter will, in a broad sense, focus on the individual employment relationships that are covered by the Labor Act no. 4857, which has the widest application scope in the industry, and in the service and the manufacturing sector.[27]

2. Basic Principles of Employment Law

a. The principle of protection of the employees

With the detachment of the employment law from the law of obligations over time and the occurrence as an independent and separate discipline, its principles

---

26 Süzek, *İş Hukuku*, 40. See also, Çelik, Caniklioğlu, and Canbolat, *İş Hukuku Dersleri*, 160 ff.

27 Under this chapter, see infra: *Part II – The Scope of the Labor Act.*

and standards have also developed. In this process, the employment law has been characterized by the provisions protecting the weaker party of the contract.[28] The rationale of the independence of the employment law can be traced back to the presumption that the employee should be protected.

Therefore, it is possible to say that the primary purpose and the basic principle of employment law is the protection of the employee. That requires to strike a balance in favor of the employee against the unfettered exercise of prevailing bargaining power of the employer.

On the other hand, this purpose should not be understood as simply protecting the employee economically. This principle also addresses the protection of the employee's personality, dignity, health, and integrity, that is, the protection of all fundamental rights and freedoms of the employee within the framework of the employment relationship.[29] By the virtue of the state interventions direct towards this purpose, the minimum standards regard to employment relationship are determined and that provides for the employees a protection shield.

b. The principle of restricted freedom of contract

The freedom of contract, which is the basic principle of the law of obligations, has multiple aspects. At first, it refers to the freedom to determine whether to enter a contractual relationship. Secondly, parties are afforded discretion on the type and the subject matter of the contract. In this sense, freedom of contract means determining the content of the contract by the choice of the contracting parties.[30]

Third, it includes the freedom to determine whether to extinguish a contractual relationship. Undoubtedly, none of those have been granted to the parties without any restriction. For instance, the contracts as to commit an illegal act (or crime) or to impose on one of the parties promising to change domicile, not to marry or not to have a child, and slavery or usurious contracts are considered illegal and void. In general, the justification of these restrictions is founded on public order or good morals.[31] On the other hand, it does not change the

---

28 Kübra Doğan Yenisey, *İş Hukukunun Emredici Yapısı* (İstanbul: Beta, 2014), 4, 11 ff.; Ömer Ekmekçi and Refik Korkusuz, *Turkish Individual Labour Law* (İstanbul: On İki Levha, 2020), 3 ff.; Esener, *Business Law I*, 76.

29 Süzek, *İş Hukuku*, 17. See also, Çelik, Caniklioğlu, and Canbolat, *İş Hukuku Dersleri*, 28.

30 Esener, *Business Law I*, 73 ff. Also, see supra: *Chapter III – Law of Obligations*.

31 Esener, *Business Law I*, 76. See supra: *Chapter III – Law of Obligations – Validity of Contracts*.

basic principle: "Freedom of contract is the general rule and restraint is the exception".

When it comes to employment law, it is seen that the scope of freedom of contract is immensely curtailed. In some cases, the employer is enforced to enter a new employment relationship with their former employee. Likewise, the freedom to determine the content of the employment contract is highly restricted. An employment contract aims to regulate the working conditions. However, in most of the cases, minimum working standards are already set by "mandatory provisions" and the clauses of the contract are subject to those binding rules laid down by applicable laws.

In addition, protection of the employee against termination is one of the domains of employment law that intensively regulated. Therefore, the employer's freedom of contract is also severely constrained in terms of termination of the employment contract. All considered, this suggests that the restricted freedom of contract is the general rule in the field of employment law.

In essence, the laws for employment provide a narrow framework for the contracting parties. Thus, it is important to distinguish working standards laid down by applicable law from the actual working conditions established through private employment contracts. This narrow legal framework in question is generally provided by the virtue of relatively mandatory provisions and less frequently by absolutely mandatory provisions. The relatively mandatory provision means that deviations from them can be made to protect the employee, thereby the applicable rule can be changed by contract only if the deviation is in favor of the employee. Whereas absolutely mandatory provision is a rule that the parties can by no means deviate from, even if the agreed working conditions are in favor of the employee.

As can be understood, the relative mandatory provisions serve more to the purpose of protecting the employee. The restrictive effect of those is only for the employer so that they are known as relatively mandatory. When the employee can convince the employer to undertake an obligation above the minimum standard set by applicable rule, as a rule, the bargaining power of this employee should be preserved, and the negotiated obligation should not be deemed invalid. On the other hand, the purpose of applicable rule is not always to protect the employee. Sometimes the justification that led the legislator to prefer to draw a narrow framework for the contracting parties is to maintain the public order, not solely to protect the employee. In such cases where it is the aim that the standards in applicable rule never be exceeded, the subject matter is to be regulated by absolute mandatory provisions. Besides, although they are less in quantity, there are also complementary provisions in the employment law that let the parties to deviate from the standards set in the applicable the law by their choice without any restriction.[32]

Accordingly, it is important to determine which of these categories the relevant rule falls into. This determination is mostly an interpretation issue shaped by doctrinal views and decisions of judicial authorities. Pursuant to the precedent ruling of the Court of Cassation, "There is no doubt that the provisions regarding the employment law are, as a rule, considered as relatively mandatory rules. In this sense, the rights provided by applicable provisions constitute a base for the employees, it can be exceeded by more favorable conditions, but cannot be lowered below that. In other words, the restrictive effect of public order in such cases is only for the employer".[33] Therefore, in case of doubt, it is appropriate to interpret a rule regarding employment relationship as relatively mandatory. In conclusion, it has been seen that the restricted freedom of contract is inherent to employment law and will be in the predictable future.

c. *Principle of adaptation*

As mentioned above, in employment law, the prevalence of regulations protecting the weaker party of the contract and the significant effect of the restricted freedom of contract distinguished it from the law of obligations. Depending on this progress, the basic principles of the employment law gained certain characteristics. On the other hand, since it is a contractual relationship based on private law, it is not possible for employment law to be completely detached from the domain of the law of obligations and civil law. It can easily be seen that employment law is in close relation with the law of obligations and civil law.[34]

Therefore, the boundaries of this close relation must be drawn. As stated, the rules of civil law and the law of obligations are of a general nature compared to applicable rules of employment law. In the case, where there is a legislative gap regarding employment law, yet if there is a general term on this issue amongst the provisions of the Civil Code or the Code of Obligations, this term is to be applied to the concrete case.

The legislative gap might arise from an explicit gap (as an unregulated space through legislative omission) or in some cases, from an implicit gap. In the case

32 See also, Centel, *Turkish Labour Law*, 14–15.

33 The decision of Turkish Court of Cassation, 9th Civil Chamber, dated 10.4.1970, no. 101/3487 (own translation, quoted in Süzek, *İş Hukuku*, 35). See also, Çelik, Caniklioğlu, and Canbolat, *İş Hukuku Dersleri*, 25.

34 Çelik, Caniklioğlu, and Canbolat, *İş Hukuku Dersleri*, 18 ff.; Süzek, *İş Hukuku*, 39 ff.

of implicit gap, there might exist a specific regulation in the general terms yet applying this general term to the employment relationship might have some drawbacks. Due to the critical difference between underlying principles of the law of obligations and that of employment law, this creates a challenge. On the one hand, the freedom of contract is promoted, on the other hand, the protection of employee is prominent. Therefore, the direct application of the existing general term might cause results contrary to the purposes and principles of employment law. In this case, the general term must be applied only to the extent that it is appropriate. If it is not, it must be adapted to the requirements of employment law by interpretation. In other words, the direct application of general term depends on the condition that it complies with the purpose and characteristics of employment law. Otherwise, the adaptation is a must.[35]

d. The complementary principle of interpretation: Interpretation in favor of the employee

In employment law, in case the legislation contains ambiguity and vagueness, the approach of interpretation in favor of the employee should be applied in principle, according to the vast majority of leading legal scholars.[36] Also, with respect to the precedent ruling of the Court of Cassation, "Considering the historical reasons that forced the legislator to enact special provisions for the employment relationship and adopt the principle of protection of the employee against the employer, and in addition to that, considering that the wording of the legal provisions should be discerned in the light of the purpose, it is concluded that, in case of uncertainty as a result of interpretation of the provisions, the adoption of the meaning in favor of the employee is one of the basic principles of employment law".[37]

However, that does not suggest that general principles of law and the primary principles of interpretation might be ignored. Primary principles are also to be followed in course of interpretation of regulations regarding employment law. Most significantly, it is possible to frame those as "purposive (*teleological*)

35 Süzek, *İş Hukuku*, 41 ff.

36 Centel, *Turkish Labour Law*, 16; Çelik, Caniklioğlu, and Canbolat, *İş Hukuku Dersleri*, 27–28; Cf. Süzek, *İş Hukuku*, 23.

37 The decision of Turkish Court of Cassation, General Assembly of Civil Chambers, dated 25.1.1978, no. 3435/23 (own translation, quoted in Süzek, *İş Hukuku*, 23). Also see, the decision of Turkish Court of Cassation, 9th Civil Chamber, dated 8.5.2006, no. 5938/12950, *Çalışma ve Toplum Dergisi*, 10/3 (2006): https://www.calismatoplum.org/, accessed 18.7.2021.

approach", "interpretation in accordance with the Constitution" and "prohibition on interpretation contrary to law (*interpret contra legem*)".

The purposive approach in the course of interpretation is mainly adopted in Turkish legal system as is in the decisions of Court of Justice of European Union (CJEU).[38] Referring to this approach, the aim is to resolve the legal uncertainty by reference to the purpose of the rule (*ratio legis*), general scheme, and prescribed measure within as well as the legal context to which it refers.[39] In other words, even though, the first phase in order to determine the meaning of a legal rule is to discern the wording of it, the plain meaning is not solely decisive (as opposed to literal approach). Besides that, according to this approach, during the process of interpretation, parliamentary preparations and discussions regarding to the drafts are also considered as are they by historical approach. Yet, those are not the main indicators of purposive interpretation. The aim of purposive approach is not only to reveal the purpose of the legislator that once having prescribed the rule, but also to objectively reveal the preference of the rule among the conflicting interests by considering the conditions of the period when it will be interpreted.[40] The core of the purposive interpretation can be described as revealing the "spirit of the rule".

Most provisions in employment law are protective for employees in nature. Therefore, it is, as a rule, expectable that the conclusion reached by purposive approach may coincide with the conclusion reached by the principle of protection of the employee. Nevertheless, it is not always the case. If an explicit meaning of a rule cannot be reached by taken purposive approach and general rules of interpretation into account, only then the principle of interpretation in favor of the employee should be applied. However, prior to this phase, purposive and primary rules of interpretation may lead to the opposite conclusion to protection of employee. If the meaning becomes certain by general rules of interpretation, the principle to protect employee cannot be primary approach to be relied upon, but rather it is a complementary tool.[41] This is also compatible with the approach of CJEU. Even though CJEU adopted the purposive approach, this does not lead

---

38 This is also compatible with the approach adopted by most EU member states. See, Niall O'Connor, "Interpreting Employment Legislation Through a Fundamental Rights Lens: What's the Purpose?," *European Labour Law Journal*, 8/3 (2017): 197.

39 O'Connor, 196–197. See also, Aybay, *An Introduction to Law*, 47 ff.

40 Süzek, *İş Hukuku*, 25–26.

41 Süzek, *İş Hukuku*, 23.

the CJEU to undermine the explicit wording of any rule in order to protect the employee.[42]

It should also be noted that in addition to purposive approach, an interpretation contrary to law is prohibited. It suggests that a meaning that contradicts the precise and explicit wording of the rule is avoided during the process of interpretation. Last, but not least, while interpreting a rule, a meaning compatible with the Constitution should be preferred. According to Hirsch as a leading scholar, "justices should look at the legislative sources through tinted spectacles overlaid by the Constitution" and take constitutional approach in consideration.[43]

Apart from the essence of statutory interpretation, principles of contractual interpretation are also of importance for the employment relationship. There are some interpretive tools specific to employment contract compatible with the characteristic of employment law.

In course of an employment dispute before court, if it raises a question of how to interpret a contract, as a rule, the wills of the contracting parties shall be examined in the light of the principle of mutual trust and confidence. According to this, it is assumed that the one party shall express their will as a reasonable and honest person and that the counterparty also shall understand this declaration as a reasonable and honest receiver.[44] It enables the parties to reach the closest result what they intended to accomplish with the contract.

However, even in the light of theory of trust, the wording of a rule in the contract might not be sufficient to determine the wills of parties. In such cases, the meaning of the rule is to be construed compatible with the aim to protect the employee. This is also a requirement of the principle of interpretation against the party that supplied the term (*contra proferentem*), which in most cases the party that drafted the contract is the employer.[45] Considering all, these suggest that the principle of interpretation in favor of the employee is also an interpretive tool to resolve contractual uncertainty.

---

42 See, the CJEU's decision of Bowden and Others for this approach, dated 4.10.2001, C-133/00 Bowden and Others (European Court Reports 2001 I-07031). See also, O'Connor, 199, 205.

43 Ernest E. Hirsch, "Anayasanın Özel Hukuk Kurallarına Etkileri," *Birinci Türk Hukuk Kongresi'ne Sunulan Tebliğler* (Ankara: Türkiye Barolar Birliği Yayınları, 1972), 3 ff. and 13.

44 On the other hand, it should be noted that the interpretive tools for the collective bargaining agreements are a special issue that should be taken separate approach.

45 Süzek, *İş Hukuku*, 33.

This is also applicable in cases there is an ambiguity regarding the incidents such as the failure to determine how the facts occurred or to detect concrete events in the disputes. In other words, if the incident underlying the dispute cannot be determined, the doubts on incidents should also be commented in favor of the employee.

On the other hand, it should be recalled that, according to court practices, the primary principles and general rules of law should be considered during the process of interpretation. Even if the meaning of a rule is still not explicit, then the conclusion in favor of the employee is to be reached.

As another significant aspect of contractual interpretation, the courts are not bound to follow the traces determined by the parties and are eligible to rule on the appropriateness and legality of the form and substance of an employment contract. To put it more simply, courts are not bound to take the legal assessments of the contracting parties into consideration.

In the final analysis, employment law has interpretive tools in specific to legislation and contracts regarding employment relationship. Nevertheless, interpretive tools are beset by the concrete case. There is no need for interpretation when there is sufficient clarity on the meaning of the rule, term, or true facts in the concrete case. In those cases, there is notoriously no need to apply interpretive tools specific to employment law.

IV. The Legal Sources of Employment Law

The term 'sources of law' is generally understood to mean (official and unofficial) legal institutions that set out applicable rules. Every country has its own government structure and a selection for own list of legal sources.[46] The first chapter already begins by examining those sources in the light of the Constitution of the Republic.[47] Therefore, in this chapter, the explanations regarding the legal sources specific to employment law will be merely featured.

A. *Official Sources*

Official sources are divided into three kinds headed by the Constitution: Statutory (legislative) sources, regulatory (executive) sources, and judicial sources.

46 Aybay, *An Introduction to Law*, 49 ff. See also, Centel, *Turkish Labour Law*, 15 ff.

47 Related to what is presented within this subheading also see supra: *Chapter I – Constitutional Law*.

Relevantly, another division amongst official sources, that is international sources and national sources, is also commonly used.

1. Constitution

As being one of civil law countries, legislation is the most important national source of law. According to the hierarchy of codified rules, the Constitution is the most prominent (supreme) national source. It is followed by codes, acts, and statutory decrees, and presidential decrees. The determination of the hierarchy of rules and list of legal sources has undoubtedly importance in terms of employment law. The following list is a summary of sources of employment law in an order from the most to the least binding.

Primarily, constitutional rules determine governmental structure and organs of the state. Above and beyond, the Constitution enshrines the fundamental rights and freedoms of all persons before law.[48] Hereby, the provisions of Constitution lay down a general framework for employment relationship.

Furthermore, in the Constitution, Turkish Republic is described as a democratic, secular and social state that governed by rule of law and lay on the principles set forth in the Preamble (within the article 2). By the nature of the social (welfare) state, the state shall remove the economic and social barriers before the fundamental rights and freedoms of the persons to the extent which those obstacles are contrasted with the founding principles of the state (in accordance with the article 5).

In view of individual employment law, freedom to conduct a business (free enterprise) and freedom of contract, right to work, and rights regarding the working conditions along with right to rest and leisure are also enshrined in the articles 48 through 50 of the Constitution respectively under the section of social and economic rights and duties.

2. Statutory Sources

a. National sources

Statutory (legislative) sources following the Constitution are also known as primary sources and they are followed by executive sources. Those sources overall cover codes, laws, acts, or statutes and contain abstract and general rules to meet the needs and requirements of society.[49] The provisions of codes and specifically that of labor acts have always been the major means of establishing working

48 See supra: *Chapter I – Constitutional Law.*

49 Aybay, *An Introduction to Law*, 50 ff. See also, Centel, *Turkish Labour Law*, 9 ff.

standards. Those are mentioned under the subheading for the major laws for employment above.[50] It should be reiterated that there exist various acts and statutes that regulate the employment relationship to some extent except those mentioned.

It is also noteworthy that statutory decrees and international agreements have also force of law as has presidential decrees in accordance with the new amendments of the Constitution.

b. International sources

Official sources are, also, studied within separate and yet interrelated categories: National and international sources. As regards to employment law, some specific conventions have a high value.

The importance of international conventions is that when it is put into effect duly, it has the force of law. For instance, ILO conventions that are ratified by Turkey have force of law. All international conventions that duly ratified are deemed to be at equal rank with national laws (with statutory sources) regardless of the content and domain they regulated.[51]

On the other hand, in case of a conflict between the provisions of national laws and that of international conventions concerning fundamental rights and freedoms, the provisions of such international conventions shall be taken as the basis of the judgment provided that they have been duly ratified by Turkey. In other words, according to Constitution, in the case of a conflicting provision on the same matter between national laws and international agreements concerning fundamental rights and freedoms, the provisions of international agreements shall be applied.

However, this prerogative has sparked a debate on the nature of provisions within the international conventions. The provisions of conventions, to the large extent, can only be invoked before the national judicial organs once the relevant provisions are adopted in a national act or statute. Therefore, the debates in the doctrine continue due to the distinction made between the provisions of international conventions whether they are directly applicable (self-executing) or indirectly applicable (non-self-executing).[52] It is worth mentioning that it is an ongoing controversial issue in the field of employment law.[53]

---

50 Under this part, see supra: *The Major Laws for Employment.*

51 See also, Rona Aybay, "Uluslararası Antlaşmaların Türk Hukukundaki Yeri," *Türkiye Barolar Birliği Dergisi*, 70 (2007): 198.

52 Centel, *Turkish Labour Law*, 17–18; Dereli, *Labour Law in Turkey*, 67; Süzek, *İş Hukuku*, 93 ff. See also, Aybay, "Uluslararası Antlaşmalar," 202, 207.

53 Also see supra: *Chapter I – Constitutional Law.*

In this sense, ILO conventions are of particular importance for employment relationship. ILO, as an independent agency of United Nation, is charged with drawing up universal working standards mainly in the form of Conventions and Recommendations. Being a member state of ILO since 1932, Turkey ratified 59 ILO conventions so far, and 55 of them are in force.

Besides the conventions and recommendations of ILO, research papers and brief notes that supplied by ILO Commissions are important advisory texts for the member states. For instance, ILO Future of Work Centenary Initiative has been developed by the establishment of the Global Commission on the Future of Work in August 2017. Next, "Work for a Brighter Future Report" that promotes human-centered approach in order to overcome current challenges of labor market was published in 2019 by this Commission.[54]

Along with ILO, Turkey has signed and ratified numerous "bilateral labor agreements (BLAs)" since 1961 as a country that supplies labor to foreign countries. Out of the bilateral labor agreements to which Turkey is a party, thirteen (two with Germany) are in force and there are also twenty-nine social security agreements. Furthermore, due to Turkey's EU accession negotiations, EU acquis also has a relative impact on national law by the process of approximation of national legislation to the EU *acquis communautaire*.[55] In most cases of employment law, EU acquis has been used as the justifications of national provisions in some degree.

3. *Regulatory (Executive) Sources*

a. *By-laws*

Referring to the back, regulations and the Council of Ministers that once had competence to issue regulations both are abrogated. Parliament, as a rule, issues legislative sources, and grants the public authorities the discretion in a lesser extent to issue "by-laws" and "other regulatory sources" executively. Even though, hitherto existing regulations are still in force, the existing regulations had never been outnumbered in the employment law.

Due to the last constitutional amendments, by-laws are the main executive sources. These rules are issued for the purpose of ensuring the application of

54 See, ILO Report of Global Commission on the future of work: Work for a brighter future (Geneva: ILO, 2019). See also, https://www.ilo.org/global/topics/future-of-work/ , accessed 18.7.2021.

55 Centel, *Turkish Labour Law*, 19–20; Süzek, *İş Hukuku*, 98; Süral and Kılıçoğlu, "Labor Law," 162.

codes and acts by ministries and public authorities related to their domains of operation in accordance with legislative sources.[56]

There are various by-laws that regulate working conditions such as "By-law on annual paid leave", "By-law on working periods pursuant to the Labor Act", "By-law on Overtime Work and Work for Extra Hours pursuant to the Labor Act", and "By-law on the Minimum Wage".

Tab. 1. Official regulations vs. Workplace regulations
It should be emphasized that the term of regulation might be used in different context. The existing (official) regulations and by-laws are very different from the regulations or instructions issued by the employer as a private actor. The instructions issued by the employer at the workplace are one of the unofficial sources of law, rather than an official one. Those are, in most cases, called under various names such as "Internal Regulations", "Workplace Regulations", etc.

b. Other regulatory sources

Presidential decisions are also of importance for employment law, since the decisions on the appointments of officers or postponement of strikes might be put into effect by the presidential decisions.

There, also, exists a cluster of communiques and circulars adopted by the Ministry of Family, Labour, and Social Services amongst other regulatory sources of the employment law. An important part of them is on social security law and occupational health and safety issues. Those might be exemplified as communiques on premium incentives for employers, communiques on healthcare practices or communiques on classification of workplace hazards.

4. Judicial Sources

When a dispute is brought to court, justices determine which set of rules is applicable in the concrete case and reach a decision by discerning in facts. In other words, the justices are responsible for ensuring that the law is followed in each case. Whereas the jury system is never adopted and the division of labor between judges and jurors is not embraced by Turkey, a kind of labor of division

56 See also, Centel, *Turkish Labour Law*, 12. Some of scholars use the term of "by-laws" in place of regulations in the doctrine, and the term of "regulations" in place of by-laws. However, the contents of terms are crucial. See, Dereli, *Labour Law in Turkey*, 64 ff.

between courts is adopted traditionally. Therefore, employment disputes are settled by specific first instance courts.[57] According to the former judicial structure, the decisions of the lower court (one of the first instance courts) were being upheld or reversed by the Court of Cassation upon request. Recently, in order to reduce backlog in courts, the legislator converted the structure of courts into three-tier system as first instance courts (local courts), second instance courts (regional courts of appeal), and the high instance (the Court of Cassation) actually as of 2016. The start of proceedings in the appellate courts following those amendments have particular importance for the cases regarding disputes on employment security since it is presently avoided in such cases to recourse to the Court of Cassation. In conclusion, at the second tier, appellate court's decision on employment security becomes final.

Due to civil law tradition, the decisions issued by judge, as a rule, do not have a binding effect on subsequent cases. Nevertheless, judicial sources (decisions of the courts) might lead the exercise of law complementarily. According to private disputes, main judicial sources are decisions of the Constitutional Court, the Court of Cassation, and regional courts of appeal.

On the other hand, there exists exception for the binding effect of court decisions. The first, the decisions of the Constitutional Court have a binding effect on everyone, including every person and every institution regardless of whether they are public or private law entity (art. 11 of the Constitution). Due to the new amendments to Turkish Constitution, which provides individuals to apply to the Constitutional Court, the decisions of individual application issued by the Constitutional Court will have an ever-increasing impact on employment relationship.[58]

Another equally important aspect is that unifying decisions (unification decisions or awards) of the Court of Cassation (*in Turkish "İçtihadı Birleştirme Kararı"*) have, exceptionally, power of law. When there is a conflict between different chambers of high court, the Committee for Unification of Precedents may gather and may render a 'unification of decisions of different chambers of the High Court with the intent of eliminating conflicting opinions on jurisprudence. Hereby, the Committee may formulate universally acceptable principle on the specific subject. There are several unifying decisions (unification decisions or awards) of the Court of Cassation that have specific importance for the employment relationship.

57 Under this part, see supra: *The Act on Employment Courts.*
58 For further information also see supra: *Chapter I – Constitutional Law.*

Nevertheless, as a rule, decisions supplied by judicial bodies to settle employment disputes are of complementary sources of the employment law. International court decisions are also considered as judicial sources in accordance with the article 90/last paragraph of the Constitution and illuminate the content of international agreements that have the force of law.

Tab. 2. Customary law

There are also unwritten rules among the legal sources. The main unwritten source is customary law. There exist legal requirements in order an ordinary social conduct to be considered as "a customary rule". There should be a general belief in the society that it is obligatory to comply with the given conduct and there should be a continuous conduct practice since ancient times.[a] If the legislator refers to those customary rules in an applicable rule, they become "customary law" and justices may apply them before the courts they presided. Accordingly, in rare cases of employment law, the law refers to customary rules. For instance, the time intervals for daily breaks can be determined according to local customs by the virtue of contracts (art. 68 of LA).

[a]Aybay, An Introduction to Law, 51 ff.

B. Unofficial Sources

Unofficial sources contain the rules set forth by private parties to regulate the employment relationship. Those also have a hierarchy among themselves such as have the codified rules.

According to the hierarchy of the unofficial sources, collective bargaining agreement is the most prominent source. It is followed by individual employment contracts, internal regulations, entrenched workplace practices, and at the lowest tier, the right to manage of the employer.

1. Collective Bargaining Agreements

A collective bargaining agreement (CBA) is a contract that is signed between the trade unions of employees and employers' associations or single employers (that not a member of any association). Such contract generally consists of the provisions concerning wages and working conditions and stands at the top of the hierarchy of unofficial sources. The reason for this is its distinctive position between private law contracts.

As is common knowledge, a contractual relationship forms a basis only for the contracting parties and creates "relative" rights. This means that each party has a right to claim against merely the counterparty. As a result, the creditor can demand only from his debtor to fulfill his promise, not from the third parties that are excluded from the contractual relationship. Accordingly, a relative right can only be violated by the debtor, it cannot be violated by the third parties. In the view of employment contract, it also establishes relative rights. This suggests that the employees will be able to direct their claims merely to their employer in the contractual relationship. In response to that, the employers will direct their demands merely to the employees.

Conversely, the provisions of the CBA have a direct effect both on the members of the signatory parties and on the signatory parties themselves.[59] In principle, the provisions laid down by a collective bargaining agreement are to be applied directly and mandatorily[60] between the parties to individual employment contracts, who are not the signatory of the CBA but mutually bound by the individual employment contract. Those deemed to be bound by the collective bargaining agreement are not merely the signatories, but the members of parties to a collective agreement (in some cases, individual employers who are direct parties to a CBA).

The general terms regulating the CBA and the discussions on interpretive tools for those agreements fall outside the scope of this chapter.[61] On the other hand, its distinctive position is of importance for the legal sources of employment law. The parties of the CBA, like the legislator, set rules that regulate an

59 In some cases, a CBA may also contain the provisions that impose obligations to directly its signatories and regulates the relationship between the contracting parties except the normative part that has direct effect on the individual employment contracts. This part is known as the contractual part of the CBA.

60 As a rule, collective bargaining agreement takes precedence over the individual employment contract. On the other hand, in the light of the principle of favorability, the individual employment contract precedes over the collective bargaining agreement insofar it contains more favorable provisions for the employee. The question of whether an individual contract contains more favorable provision is to be solved in the light of the concrete case by requiring using interpretive tools.

61 See also, Centel, *Turkish Labour Law*, 12–13, 213 ff.; Dereli, *Labour Law in Turkey*, 242 ff. For further information see, Ekmekçi, Ömer, Korkusuz, M. Refik and Uğur, Ömer, *Turkish Collective Labour Law* (İstanbul: On İki Levha, 2020); Fevzi Şahlanan. *Toplu İş Hukuku* (İstanbul: On İki Levha, 2020); A. Can Tuncay and F. Burcu Savaş Kutsal. *Toplu İş Hukuku* (İstanbul: Beta, 2019).

abstract employment relationship and provisions of the CBA have a direct effect on individual employment contracts in the similar way that of the codes have. This is known as "normative function" or "normative legal efficacy" of collective bargaining agreements. Therefore, an important exception to the relative impact of contracts is collective bargaining agreements. Such normative effect of collective agreements substantively resembles the effect of the codes and normative part of a CBA has force of law in material sense. As the corollary of that, the CBA is a sort of contract with the form of a contract but with the substance of code in material sense and has a prominent position amongst the unofficial sources of employment law.

2. Individual Employment Contracts

Even though the individual employment contract is placed at the second tier in the hierarchy of unofficial sources, it is inconceivable that other sources come into effect without the existence of an employment contract. In other words, the employment relationship established by the employment contract has a constituent effect. Due to this importance, the components of (individual) employment contract will be featured below in detail.[62]

3. Workplace Regulations (Internal Regulations)

In the most cases of practice, the rules on the operations of workplace and workflow are supplied unilaterally by the employers and presented to their employees without any bargaining opportunity. Those rules that contain general and uniform regulations are called as "workplace regulations" or "internal regulations". Although these regulations have same legal effect in nature, they may have different names for each workplace or they can be specific to certain subject matters (e.g., Dress Code, Disciplinary Regulations, Personnel Regulations, etc.).

In some countries, the workplace regulation has been specially arranged in order to eliminate the drawbacks that this will cause, and its legal framework has been determined strictly by the legislator. However, in Turkish law, the framework has not been constrained. On one hand, the employers do not oblige to regulate a workplace regulation, it is optional for the employers. On the other hand, the subject matters to be regulated are neither limited. In other words, the working conditions that can be regulated by workplace regulations are not

62 Under this chapter, see infra: *Part II – Form and Substance, and Types of Employment Contract.*

restricted by law. According to the article 22 of the Labor Act, the law is explicitly clear on this point, the workplace regulation has been counted as one of the legal sources that drawing up working conditions. Unless its terms do contradict with the mandatory regulations sided at higher in the hierarchy, they may contain rules on details of working conditions, regulations regarding the employer's right to management and work organization.[63]

With the confirmation of the employee, those regulations supplied by the employer in advance convert into an annex to the employment contract. Undoubtedly, in this case, the employer should enable the employee to have "reasonable means of knowledge" regarding the content. In case that those terms enter into force with the employee's confirmation, they are also subject to review by courts. Those regulations that were drafted before and to regulate many relationships not by considering the situation of the concrete employee are similar to the "standard terms" of the contract that regulated within the Turkish Code of Obligations (article 20 to 25 of TCO).[64] In this respect, these provisions, which are general terms in nature, may be applied in terms of workplace regulations supplied unilaterally by the employer.[65]

On the other hand, the consistency of the terms of the workplace regulation which "reserves the right to change the working conditions for the employer" with mandatory provisions of law is controversial. The overwhelming opinion in the doctrine on this matter is that reservations to enable one of the parties (of the employers in most cases) to change the working conditions unilaterally are deemed as "not written", as are regulated in the standard terms and conditions (art. 24 of TCO). The major opinion is that those provisions of TCO shall have efficiency in terms of employment law due to the lack of specific provisions in the Labor Act.[66] However, there are also contrary opinions in the doctrine. The decisions of the Court of Cassation on this subject have also uneven history. Therefore, the discussions on this subject are ongoing.

---

63 Centel, *Turkish Labour Law*, 13–14; Çelik, Caniklioğlu, and Canbolat, *İş Hukuku Dersleri*, 269; Süzek, *İş Hukuku*, 63.

64 For further information see also, Orhan Ersun Civan, *Genel İş Koşulları* (İstanbul: Beta, 2015).

65 Çelik, Caniklioğlu, and Canbolat, *İş Hukuku Dersleri*, 270–271; Süzek, *İş Hukuku*, 63 ff. Also see supra: *Chapter III – Law of Obligations – Standard Terms.*

66 Çelik, Caniklioğlu, and Canbolat, *İş Hukuku Dersleri*, 270; Süzek, *İş Hukuku*, 69.

The workplace regulations, in some cases, may change the current working conditions. The employer is already able to make changes to the contract in the scope of the right to manage. Apart from this, when the changes are substantial,[67] the employer can only make those changes by following the relevant rules. Accordingly, for substantial changes regarding the working conditions to be enforceable, following steps must be taken: First, the written proposal must be notified to the employees individually, and then written confirmation of the employee is required within 6 working days (art. 22 of the LA). In case that the current working conditions are amended substantially by the workplace regulations, this procedure must be applied. It should be remembered that these workplace regulations are completely different from those issued by the public authorities.[68]

4. *Entrenched Workplace Practices*

"Entrenched workplace practices" emerge from the repetition of some actual practices that the employer puts these into effect on their own initiative. Those actual practices in the workplace may gain permanence over time. The important part is that entrenched workplace practices are such working conditions that are unilaterally applied by the employer. A practice that derives its legal source from the law or the employment contract does not qualify as an entrenched workplace practice. For instance, if the employer provides transportation for commuting which is indebted under the contract, here it is not possible to deem this condition in terms of workplace practice.

On the other hand, if this does not arise from a contractual or legal obligation, a workplace practice may be in question. If the employer puts into effect a practice not based on a provision foreseen by the law or not based on a common will arising from the mutual agreements of the parties, then confidence may have been built among the employees on that this practice will continue. In accordance with the rule of good faith and in the light of relationship

67 Changes that cannot be expected from the employee or that the employee cannot be forced to tolerate the new conditions are deemed as substantial changes: Süzek, *İş Hukuku*, 679 ff., 688. Under this chapter, also see supra: *Part III – Legal Regulations on the Change in Working Conditions.*

68 Under this part, also see supra: Table 1: Offical regulations vs. Workplace regulations.

of trust between employee and employer, if confidence of the employees might be deemed as reasonable, the said practices are considered an annex to the employment contract and become binding as if that they arise from common will of the parties.

It is a legal source adopted by doctrine and constant jurisprudence of courts. Therefore, its conditions were mainly ascertained through court decisions. According to Court of Cassation, such a practice should be of a general nature. For this, the practice specific to limited departments can be regarded as general, insofar there is no individual application. In addition, the application must be carried out under the same conditions and must have gained a certain continuity.[69]

Confidence must have been built in employees that those practices will continue in the future and in the same way. The test on whether this confidence is reasonable is to be determined according to the concrete case in accordance with the rule of good faith. On the other hand, the Court of Cassation approves the practices to be entrenched for to have continued for 3 years in a row or to be repeated three times.[70] Nevertheless, it is not possible for a practice to be deemed as entrenched in case the employer makes a reservation in advance to change the practice. In this case, employees will not have a reasonable expectation that should be protected due to the rule of good faith. Moreover, the rights and benefits granted as a result of error do not convert into workplace practices.[71]

In sum, if the employers do not reserve explicitly their right to repeal or change those practices in advance, it is necessary to get the consent of employee for the change or repeal of an entrenched workplace practice.

69 Centel, *Turkish Labour Law*, 14; Çelik, Caniklioğlu, and Canbolat, *İş Hukuku Dersleri*, 272 ff.; Süzek, *İş Hukuku*, 76 ff.

70 Çelik, Caniklioğlu, and Canbolat, *İş Hukuku Dersleri*, 273; Süzek, *İş Hukuku*, 77–78. See also, the decision of Turkish Court of Cassation, 9th Civil Chamber, dated 16.11.2015, no. 21153/32270.

71 Çelik, Caniklioğlu, and Canbolat, *İş Hukuku Dersleri*, 275; Süzek, *İş Hukuku*, 79.

Tab. 3. Entrenched workplace practices vs. Customary law

It is conceivable that entrenched workplace practices to be compared to the customary law. On the other hand, there are several differences between them. For the formation of customary law, much longer period is required. Contrary to that, being applied three times consistently in the same way is sufficient for the formation of an entrenched workplace practice. Besides, for the formation of customary law, the belief that the compliance of those is obligatory is required. Whereas it is not necessary for the formation of entrenched workplace practices that employer has a belief that these workplace practices are binding.

To put it more simply, a workplace practice might become a binding rule regardless of the intention of the employer. Even if the employer doesn't expect the legal consequence, this practice might convert into an annex of the contract. The key point is the level of trust between the employer and employees and the confidence of the employees in the continuity of those rights and benefits in the future and in the same way.

5. *Right to Manage of the Employer*

Every problem that may arise in the employment relationship may not be resolved with the legal resources listed above. Due to the continuity of services, the regulations on employment relationship must be able to respond to changing needs during the process. In other words, it is not possible to anticipate and arrange every concrete event in advance. In practice, these needs can be met through the rules embodied by the employer's right to manage. However, it is undoubted that this kind of discretionary power that granted to only one party of the contract should be exercised in accordance with the above-mentioned regulations and the rule of good faith.

In principle, the right to manage of the employer serves to concretize the job and job-related principles determined abstractly in the contract. It also includes the rules put into effect by the employer to establish a workplace order. It is prevalently accepted that the legal source of right to manage is the employment contract itself.[72] On the other hand, the article 399 of TCO also refers to the right to manage of the employers.

72 Çelik, Caniklioğlu, and Canbolat, *İş Hukuku Dersleri*, 276 ff.; Süzek, *İş Hukuku*, 79 ff.

According to the historic comment of Storey, the right to manage of the employer can be defined as the residue of discretionary powers left to employer when the mandatory rules of law and collective agreements have been subtracted.[73] It holds true also for Turkish employment law.[74] This suggests that the right to manage of the employer (discretionary power) in question is at the bottom tier of the unofficial legal sources of employment law. Therefore, the employer should not violate the mandatory rules of above-mentioned sources while exercising the right to manage.

§ Part II Basic Concepts, Coverage and Employment Contract

I. The Concept of the Employee

A. The Definition of the Employee

According to the article 2 of the Labor Act, the concept of employee is defined as "any person working under an employment contract in any job for wages". In order to be considered as an employee, performing any task/work or any job should be done for a wage. In other words, one who performs unpaid work cannot be identified as an employee.[75]

Also, the employee should be a real person, who is personally liable for the performance and carries out the work under dependence on the employer.[76] There are several different aspects of such a dependent relationship. These are mainly defined as legal dependence, personal dependence, and economic dependence, interacting with one other.[77] Dependency distinguishes the employee from the others who perform a work/task. Since dependence is the distinctive

---

73 John Storey, *The Challenge to Management Control* (K. Page: London, 1980), 41. See also, Centel, *Turkish Labour Law*, 14–15; Melda Sur, "The Fundaments and Limits of Managerial Prerogative in Turkish Labor Law," *Comparative Labor Law and Policy Journal*, 30/2 (2009): 313–333.

74 For further information see, Aydın Başbuğ, *İşverenin Yönetim Hakkı ve Çalışma Şartlarında Değişiklik* (Ankara: Alter, 2008).

75 For the prohibition on forced labor, see supra: *Chapter I – Constitutional Law.*

76 Çelik, Caniklioğlu, and Canbolat, *İş Hukuku Dersleri*, 89, 304; Dereli, *Labour Law in Turkey*, 77 ff., 101 ff.; Ekmekçi and Korkusuz, *Turkish Individual Labour Law*, 20. See also, Centel, *Turkish Labour Law*, 31, 33.

77 Süzek, *İş Hukuku*, 133 ff., 224.

feature, the employee is to be subordinated by the employer within the employment relationship.[78]

It indicates that the employment relationship creates an intense bond between the contracting parties and the dependency in the employment contract is closely related to the personality of the employee. The employee is also surrounded by physical conditions, with participating in an organization pre-set by the employer. Therefore, the authority of giving orders and instructions that used by the employer, on a considerable scale, affects the personality of the employee.

This construct inevitably establishes a hierarchy between the contracting parties. Corollary of that, in an employment relationship, the highest level of command and instruction authority rests with the employer. Thus, it is of importance to decide who the decision-making authority in this relationship is. However, the presence of a dependent work/subordination can be debatable in some cases. The distinction between (dependent) employees and independent contractors have been traditionally made by checking the facts and eliciting the owner of discretionary power over the work process.

B. *Fact-Checking*

Whether a person is an independent worker, or an employee is determined by several factors. Those facts that indicate a dependent work has been developed by judicial precedents in time.[79] To start with, it should be noted that the courts are not bound by the determinations of the contracting parties, which may at times attempt to conceal the underlying reality. Depending on the verdict from the fact-checking, the court appraises the case.

The main purpose is to elicit whether the person is working under the subordination of the counterparty or not. There are several issues that need to be enlightened, they are not, however, confined to the following:

- Who supplies the materials? As a rule, it is the employer's responsibility to provide the employee with necessary tools and equipment.
- Has the party the right to refuse the duty/project/customer assigned by the counterparty?

As a rule, the employee has no right to reject any work or project and to refuse any customer. If they have the right to reject a project by accepting the risk

78 Centel, *Turkish Labour Law*, 29 ff.; Çelik, Caniklioğlu, and Canbolat, *İş Hukuku Dersleri*, 89; Dereli, *Labour Law in Turkey*, 101; Süzek, *İş Hukuku*, 229; Süral and Kılıçoğlu, "Labor Law," 163.

79 Süzek, *İş Hukuku*, 229 ff.

of less income, the partnership can prevail over when the other elements are also considered.

- Who has the right to decide on the allocations of working and rest periods according to set schedules? The employer is the one who has the highest level of authority to organize their business and to manage execution of works performed by the employees.
- Where is the promised task performed? Generally, the independent contractor does the work at their place whereas the employee works within the sphere of a business organization of someone else.
- How is the work performed? As a rule, the employee performs an ongoing work rather than set projects that have certain end points.
- Who covers the costs of work and is liable for the business risk? The business risk is incumbent on the employer; therefore, the financial risk cannot be allocated to the employees.

Undoubtedly, none of them are decisive on their own. Instead, one or more criteria can offset the absence of the others. In each concrete case, a decision is reached by evaluating all and similar issues cumulatively.[80] Thereby, the court shall elicit the true substance of the contract and ascertain the legal consequences deriving from this reality.

C. Current Debates

Globalization has made a significant impact on the nature and profile of labor force. In addition, new economic models have been emerging today. As the industrial revolution did previously, web 2.0 and industry 4.0 also evolve today's employment relationships. This transformation has generated new business areas, such as "gig work" (gig economy) and "crowdsourcing" (platform economy).[81] Traditional foundations of employment law are affected adversely by new economic models, in which temporary positions are common and organizations contract for short-term engagements.

---

80 Süzek, *İş Hukuku*, 226–227.

81 Both are briefly described as a system created by the Internet users jointly and by sharing. However, there is a difference. The crowdwork describes tasks performed remotely via online platforms, whereas the gig work refers to the tasks organised via applications but completed in physical sphere. See, Valerio De Stefano, "Introduction: Crowdsourcing, the Gig-Economy and the Law," *Comparative Labor Law and Policy Journal*, 37/3 (2016): 461–470.

The important question is whether it is possible to define these groups as workers. Lack of continuity is the most important problem. In addition, the responsibilities such as supply of equipment and establishment of business organization are left to the workers. Since especially crowdworks are offline, the management of occupational safety and health is also difficult to provide. Another important issue is the collective aspect of employment law. These models have potential to render collective rights ineffective, since it is not possible for these workers to act with solidarity.[82]

The most typical example of gig workers is the Uber case. Disputes between the Uber platform and Uber drivers have been brought before the courts in many countries. Numerous cases have been filed in the United States, France, and the United Kingdom. Having considered various tests of worker/employee status, the courts either assessed that the drivers were entitled to the minimum wage and holiday pay since they are "workers"[83] or they were entitled to all as "employees". The decisions were issued by considered and weighed up all circumstances in the concrete case.

However, in each country, the legislators are expected to dissolve this issue. Apparently, the debate will continue, since it is probably too early to suggest permanent legal remedies against the current problems of employment law.[84] On the other hand, dependency (subordination) is still an integral part of this contract. Although how the dependency is defined varies according to which criterion

---

82 ILO Report for G20, Digital platforms and the world of work in G20 countries: Status and Policy Action (Italia: G20, 2021) 18, 20, 22. See also, Michael Doherty and Valentina Franca, "Solving the 'Gig-saw'? Collective Rights and Platform Work," *Industrial Law Journal*, 49/3 (2020): 352–376.

83 Uber BV v Aslam and others (2021) United Kingdom Supreme Court 5. However, in the United Kingdom, status of "worker" affords the drivers some -but not all- of the employment rights that are granted to the employees, while in Turkish employment law, there is no middle status defined as neither employee nor independent contractor.
See also decisions in the USA and France that reclassify Uber drivers as "employees": Court of Appeal of California, People v. Uber Technologies, Inc. (22.10.2020) A160701, A160706; Paris Court of Appeals, January 10, 2019, 6–2, n°18/08357.

84 See, ILO Working Paper 27, Platform work and the employment relationship (Geneva: ILO, 2021). See also, Kübra Doğan Yenisey, "Endüstri 4.0, Üretimin Değişen Yapısı ve İş Hukuku," *Toprak İşveren Dergisi*, Iss. 120 (2019): 1–7; Dilek Dulay Yangın, "Endüstri 4.0, Dijitalleşme ve İş Hukukunun Geleceği-Dijital Platformların Ortaya Çıkardığı Hukuki İlişkiler Çerçevesinde Değerlendirilmesi," *İstanbul Hukuk Mecmuası*, 78/3 (2020): 1209–1237.

is applied, undoubtedly it is not possible to conceive an employment contract without a dependent relationship.

II. The Concept of the Employer

A. *Definition of the Employer*

According to the article 2 of the Labor Act, the employer is defined as "(…) a real or corporate person or a non-corporate institution or organization, who employs the employees". Accordingly, the employer can be either a real person/real entity or a legal person/legal entity. Whereas the employee should be a real person, the employer might even be an organization that lacks legal personality.[85]

It is worth noting that in this relationship, the employer is the decision-maker and the highest authority to command and control according to the chain of command in the business.[86]

B. *The Representative of the Employer*

The concept and the responsibility of the representative of the employer are regulated in the Labor Act. These are persons, acting on behalf of the employer and taking charge in the management of the work, workplace, or enterprise. The authority of the representative of the employer is confined to the authority given by the employer to this person.[87]

In this context, the employer is directly responsible for the transactions and legal actions done by the representative of the employer. For instance, the general manager who manages the whole enterprise, the managers who manage the whole workplace, the personnel managers, and the chiefs, all of them are the employers' representatives, who have different levels of representation authority and management control. They exercise a derivative authority, and act on behalf of their employer in limited to their authorization. Not necessarily senior levels, but employees at any level can be assigned as the representative of the employer based on the authorization of the employer. The way the position is named in the business is not decisive.

---

85 Centel, *Turkish Labour Law*, 35; Çelik, Caniklioğlu, and Canbolat, *İş Hukuku Dersleri*, 100 ff.; Dereli, *Labour Law in Turkey*, 82; Süzek, *İş Hukuku*, 143.

86 Süzek, *İş Hukuku*, 143. For further information see also, Murat Engin, *Türk İş ve Sosyal Güvenlik Hukukunda İşveren* (İstanbul: BASİSEN, 1993).

87 Centel, *Turkish Labour Law*, 46; Çelik, Caniklioğlu, and Canbolat, *İş Hukuku Dersleri*, 102; Dereli, *Labour Law in Turkey*, 84.

But on the other side of the coin, the representatives of the employer work under an employment contract in most cases and are legally employees. As a legal consequence of this relationship, a representative of the employer has no responsibility, arising from the private law regarding the transactions they has done on behalf of the employer.[88] However, representatives may be exposed to the criminal sanctions due to their actions. The rationale is the principle of individual criminal responsibility.[89]

C. *The Definition of the Sub-Contractor*

Sub-contracting is one of the most important aspects of fragmentation of employment structures. Fissuring of business activities that were once managed internally draws an increasing attention all around the world.[90]

In the frame of Turkish employment law, the Labor Act defines a specific form of sub-contractor nexus (art. 2 of LA).[91] The legal regulations are intended

---

88 Ekmekçi and Korkusuz, *Turkish Individual Labour Law*, 23; Süzek, *İş Hukuku*, 155; Süral and Kılıçoğlu, "Labor Law," 163.

On the other hand, special regulations also govern the responsibilities of some employer representatives such as CEOs or CFOs, who work under employment contracts in substance. For example, according to TCC 553, when the founders, members of the board of directors, directors, and liquidators violate their obligations arising from the law and the articles of association, they are liable for the damages they cause to both the company, the shareholders and the company's creditors.

Also, according to APC, the employer representatives playing an important role in the violation of competition law will be subjected to the penalties along with the undertaking itself. See infra, *Chapter VI – Competition Law – Sanctions against Prohibited Anti-Competitive Behaviors.*

89 Süzek, *İş Hukuku*, 155. See also, Centel, *Turkish Labour Law*, 48; Dereli, *Labour Law in Turkey*, 84.

90 See, ILO Report, Non-standard employment around the world: Understanding challenges, shaping prospects (Geneva: ILO, 2016). See also, David Weil, *The Fissured Workplace* (Cambridge: Harvard University Press, 2014); Charles Wynn-Evans, "A Solution to Fissuring? Revisiting the Concept of the Joint Employer," *Industrial Law Journal*, 50/1 (2020): 70–103.

91 Therefore, the special term "sub-employment relationship" instead of sub-contractor relationship is also used. See, Ekmekçi and Korkusuz, *Turkish Individual Labour Law*, 29.

See also, Çelik, Caniklioğlu, and Canbolat, *İş Hukuku Dersleri*, 104 ff.; Süzek, *İş Hukuku*, 157 ff. For further information see, İbrahim Aydınlı, *Türk İş Hukukunda Alt İşveren İlişkisi ve Muvazaa Sorunu* (Ankara: Seçkin, 2021).

to provide employment protection against the fissuring of the workplace and the fragmented employment relationship. However, in order to apply these regulations in a concrete case, there are some prerequisites.

The first condition is the existence of the main employer. It means that they should have employer status by employing their own employees in their own workplace. Similarly, the sub-contractor, namely the sub-employer, should have employer status by employing their employees. The sub-contractor relationship may be established in the works related to the production of goods or services, carried out by the main employer. In other words, the sub-contractor should run a business that is linked to the main employer's business.

Tab. 4. Sample case 1
If the employer, who products goods for the market, needs an additional building in the premises of the workplace and contracts with a contractor for this construction, it cannot be conceived the sub-contractor relationship is present. Since the construction work is not linked to the business of the main employer.

Another condition regards the type of the work outsourced by the main employer. According to the regulations of the Labor Act, the establishment of the sub-contractor relationship for the primary works and auxiliary works is arranged differently from each other. There is a constraint when this relationship is established for the principal work or a part of the principal work of the main employer. Only those primary works that require expertise due to the business and technological reasons can be outsourced. However, a sub-contractor relationship can be established for all sorts of auxiliary works linked to the main employer's production of goods or services without such limitation. In most cases, those are auxiliary works depending on the production of goods or services carried out in the workplace, such as cleaning, catering, personnel transportation, security services, technical maintenance, etc.

Also, the work should be done in the workplace of the main employer. The sub-contractor, who provides the main employer with a service, should lead their employees to perform their work at the workplace of the main employer. In other words, if the employees of sub-contractor continue to work in the workplace of their contractual employers, then it cannot be conceived as a sub-contractor relationship which raises the legal consequences specified in the Labor Act. As the last condition, the employees of the sub-contractor should be dedicated to the work of the main employer.

When these conditions are available, the joint liability has been seen as a mean to enhance liability by involving putative employer (main employer) rather than solely a contractual employer (sub-contractor), as both have overlapping workplaces. Consequently, should these conditions meet, the employers are regarded as jointly liable against the claims of the employees of the sub-contractor rising from the relevant nexus.[92]

III. The Concept of Workplace

A. *Definition of Workplace*

The workplace is defined as a unit that incorporates various assets under the article 2 of the Labor Act. Accordingly, the employer unites all sorts of assets under the same organization to produce goods or services, which is the sole purpose of workplace. In this sense, the workplace is legally seen as a business organization under the same management, that is, an organizational unit.[93]

These can be tangible and intangible assets that are brought together to produce goods or services. The human (labor) factor is also considered amongst them. In this respect, premises affiliated to the workplace are considered within the concept of workplace. Those premises affiliated to the workplace form integrity with the main workplace and there is an organic bond between them. More precisely, there should be a connection between the two spaces in terms of the nature and execution of the work. If a space does not form such integrity with the main workplace, then it might be considered as an independent and separate workplace, not as part of "workplace premises".

Further, the facilities for rest, breastfeeding or sleep, parking lots, garages, loading-unloading docks, and ramps are add-ons of the workplace. Also, all

---

92 Centel, *Turkish Labour Law*, 40 ff.; Çelik, Caniklioğlu, and Canbolat, *İş Hukuku Dersleri*, 123; Dereli, *Labour Law in Turkey*, 87–88; Ekmekçi and Korkusuz, *Turkish Individual Labour Law*, 29; Süzek, *İş Hukuku*, 165.

On the other hand, the collusion between contractor and business owner in case of sub-contractor relationship is regulated differently. For further information see, Centel, *Turkish Labour Law*, 42 ff.; Çelik, Caniklioğlu, and Canbolat, *İş Hukuku Dersleri*, 140 ff.; Ekmekçi and Korkusuz, *Turkish Individual Labour Law*, 31 ff.; Süzek, *İş Hukuku*, 169.

93 Çelik, Caniklioğlu, and Canbolat, *İş Hukuku Dersleri*, 145; Ekmekçi and Korkusuz, *Turkish Individual Labour Law*, 25; Süzek, *İş Hukuku*, 189; Süral and Kılıçoğlu, "Labor Law," 163.

The term "establishment" is also used for the workplace in a broad meaning. See, Centel, *Turkish Labour Law*, 51; Dereli, *Labour Law in Turkey*, 92 ff.

kinds of equipment used in the activities carried out or the services performed are evaluated within the scope of workplace premises. For example, vehicles such as automobiles, buses, and trucks, graders, cranes, forklifts, grabs, bulldozers on highways, etc.

Under Turkish employment law, the construct of a workplace differs from that of an enterprise. The distinctive feature of a workplace unit is its purpose. It intends to produce goods or services, while the latter intends to make a profit. In other words, a workplace has a technical purpose rather than an economic one. Undoubtedly, a good or service with economic value can be produced in the workplace. However, this production is done to attain a technical purpose; in other words, the purpose of profit is not in the foreground unlike enterprises.[94]

B. *Transfer of Workplace*

The employer may transfer their workplace to another person, which might engender uncertainty and risk for the claims of the employees. According to the protective provisions of the Labor Act, the transfer of workplace by a legal transaction has been attached to various legal consequences in order to mitigate its detrimental effects to the employees.

In case of transfer by a legal transaction,[95] the transferor and the transferee are jointly liable for the claims of the employees that were incurred before the transfer and are payable at the time of transfer (art. 6/3 of LA). The liability of the transferor is limited to 2 years as of the date of transfer, whereas there is no such

94 Çelik, Caniklioğlu, and Canbolat, *İş Hukuku Dersleri*, 157; Kübra Doğan Yenisey, *İş Hukukunda İşyeri ve İşletme* (İstanbul: Legal, 2007), 32 ff.; Süzek, *İş Hukuku*, 192. See also, Centel, *Turkish Labour Law*, 52 ff.; Dereli, *Labour Law in Turkey*, 97 ff.

On the other hand, when the enterprise consists of a single workplace, technical and economic purpose might be intertwined. See, Doğan Yenisey, *İşyeri ve İşletme*, 35.

95 Therefore, these provisions exclude transfer by inheritance. The transfer of workplace entailed by liquidation due to the bankruptcy of the employer is also excluded from the application of this provision (art. 6/6 of LA).

See also, Gülsevil Alpagut, *İşyerinin Devri ve İş Sözleşmesini Fesih Hakkı* (İstanbul: Beta, 2010), 66 ff.; Ercüment Özkaraca, *İşyeri Devrinin İş Sözleşmelerine Etkisi ve İşverenlerin Hukuki Sorumluluğu* (İstanbul: Beta, 2008), 42 ff.; Süzek, *İş Hukuku*, 194.

limitation for the liability of the transferee except preclusion periods for the relevant claims.[96] Neither the transferor nor the transferee can misuse the transfer to justify the termination of employment contracts. The employee cannot terminate the contract by alleging detrimental effects of transfer alone. On the other hand, the cases of termination based on just cause or any cases, which necessitate terminating the contract due to the economic and technological reasons or due to any change in the business organization other than the transfer are reserved.[97]

However, the legal consequences of transfer of workplace entailed by merger, division or conversion of the companies have been stipulated divergently by Turkish Commercial Code (see, art. 158, 178 and 190).[98]

IV. Form and Substance, and Types of Employment Contract

A. *Substance of Employment Contract*

The Labor Act defines the content of an individual employment contract (art. 8 of LA). In this context, the employment contract should comprise three ingredients: Performance of a work, service or task (a job), payment of a certain wage and the presence of dependency (subordination).[99] In general, dependent work is the work done at the place and time determined by the employer, with the technical support to be provided by the employer and under the authority and supervision of the employer.[100]

---

96 However, even for the transferor employer, a two-year is not applicable in terms of claims based on severance pay. See also, Çelik, Caniklioğlu, and Canbolat, *İş Hukuku Dersleri*, 151, 722; Süzek, *İş Hukuku*, 199, 779.

97 Centel, *Turkish Labour Law*, 55; Çelik, Caniklioğlu, and Canbolat, *İş Hukuku Dersleri*, 153; Dereli, *Labour Law in Turkey*, 94; Süzek, *İş Hukuku*, 200.

98 Centel, *Turkish Labour Law*, 56; Çelik, Caniklioğlu, and Canbolat, *İş Hukuku Dersleri*, 153; Dereli, *Labour Law in Turkey*, 95; Ekmekçi and Korkusuz, *Turkish Individual Labour Law*, 27 ff.; Süzek, *İş Hukuku*, 204 ff.

For further information see, Mustafa Alp, "Yeni Türk Ticaret Kanunu'na Göre Bölünme, Tür Değiştirme ve Tür Değiştirmenin İş İlişkilerine Etkisi," *Çalışma ve Toplum Dergisi*, 32/1 (2012): 51–74.

99 Centel, *Turkish Labour Law*, 67; Çelik, Caniklioğlu, and Canbolat, *İş Hukuku Dersleri*, 176 ff.; Dereli, *Labour Law in Turkey*, 101; Süzek, *İş Hukuku*, 223 ff.

100 Under this chapter, also see supra: *Part I – Basic Principals of Employment Law*.

Tab. 5. Principal obligations
Under each contractual relationship, the parties might undertake various obligations. Some of those obligations flow from the contract is called "principal obligations". This suggests that such obligations characterize the contractual relationship by composing the distinctive feature of each contract. Considering the individual employment contract, payment of wage is the principal obligation for the employer, in return for that, performing a job/task is the principal obligation for the employee. Those promises that characterize the employment relationship, and "dependent relationship" (subordination) between the contracting parties are the distinctive features of an individual employment contract. Therefore, an employment relationship without those characteristics is unconceivable.

In this vein, the subject matter of employment relationship might cover a wide range of activities. The type of work performed by the employee, or the qualifications of the contracting parties are of no importance. Even an artistic work might be undertaken by the employee in the frame of employment contract provided that the given employee has been working independently.[101] Likewise, the employer may be a public legal entity, a ministry or a municipality, or an association, a foundation or a company, even an organization that lacks legal personality. These factors have no bearing on the determination of "employment relationship".

Furthermore, the employment contract constitutes a continuing obligation relationship.[102] In the employment contract, the employees are entitled to get paid even without obtaining a result provided that they are ready to work, and the contracting parties intend to constitute a continuing legal bond that rolls over. Therefore, it is classified amongst continuing contracts as a leading example.[103]

101 Centel, *Turkish Labour Law*, 67; Süzek, *İş Hukuku*, 223.

102 Centel, *Turkish Labour Law*, 70; Çelik, Caniklioğlu, and Canbolat, *İş Hukuku Dersleri*, 187; Süzek, *İş Hukuku*, 233.

103 Süzek, *İş Hukuku*, 311. See also, Maija Halonen-Akatwijuka and Oliver Hart, "Continuing Contracts," *The Journal of Law, Economics, and Organization*, 36/2 (2020): 284 ff.

B. Form of Contract

There is a common misunderstanding with regards to the form of contracts. Contrary to popular belief, an oral agreement or even an implicit one is generally no less binding than a written one. In other words, a contract does not require formality except for the certain cases.[104]

In this context, the employment contract is not bound to any requirement as to form unless otherwise prescribed by law. For instance, "on-call contracts", "team contracts" and "definite term contracts for more than one year" are the examples that law prescribed otherwise. These specific contracts should be concluded in writing.

On the other hand, if the employment contracts to be concluded in writing are concluded without complying with this form, legal consequence of this is controversial. According to one view, the form is a condition providing ease of proof, while according to opposing view, it is a condition of validity.[105]

In cases where no written contract is required, the employer shall provide the employee a written statement consisting of general and special working conditions, daily or weekly working time, the duration of the contract, basic wage and wage supplements, if any, and the rules on termination process at latest in 2 months (art. 8/3 of LA).

C. Types of Employment Contract

1. Definite Term and Indefinite Term Contracts

The contracting parties might agree upon the date, on which the employment contract is going to be ended from the very beginning. Those contracts are called as "definite term contracts", synonymously as "fixed-term contracts". In contrast, the employment contracts without any specific expiry date are defined as indefinite term contracts, synonymously as open-ended contracts.[106]

The employees who work under a definite term contract cannot benefit from the provisions of employment security and can claim severance pay only if the contract is ended before the expiry date (premature termination) when the other

---

104 See supra: *Chapter III – Law of Obligations – Form of Contracts.*

105 See, Centel, *Turkish Labour Law*, 89; Süzek, *İş Hukuku*, 310. Alternatively, conversion is accepted as the repercussion of noncompliance with the form requirement, according to another viewpoint. For instance, a definite term contract for more than one year that concluded orally is converted to an indefinite term contract. See also, Çelik, Caniklioğlu, and Canbolat, *İş Hukuku Dersleri*, 191 ff.; Süzek, *İş Hukuku*, 313.

106 For further information on form of this contract, also see supra: *Form of Contract.*

conditions are also available. In brief, the employees work under definite term contracts are, as a rule, in a disadvantageous position. On the other side of the coin, those types of contracts can be regarded more attractive to the employers than indefinite term contracts.[107]

Therefore, the cases in which, the Labor Act allows the conclusion of a definite term contract, are limited (art. 11 of LA). This implies that the conclusion of contracts for indefinite term is rule, and that of for definite term is exception.[108] Accordingly, under the provision of the Labor Act, the parties may conclude a definite term contract based on one of the objective reasons listed in the Act. A definite term employment contract without these reasons is legally considered an indefinite term contract from the very beginning irrespective of the previous arrangement made by the contracting parties.[109]

The stated objective reasons might be either the presence of a fixed-term job, a need for the completion of a specific job or the emergence of a specific incident (art. 11/1 of LA). In addition, there is another limitation as to the successive definite term contracts (also known as chain contracts). A definite term contract cannot be concluded more than once, unless there is a "substantial reason", which requires the conclusion of successive definite term contract repeatedly (art. 11/2 of LA).

As a sum, the Labor Act requires the presence of one of the objective reasons for the conclusion of definite term contract at the time of conclusion and requires a substantial reason for the extension of those contracts.[110] If there is no substantial reason at the time of extension, the contract is to be deemed for an indefinite term from the very beginning (art. 11/2 of LA).

It can be questioned whether there is a difference between objective reasons and substantial ones. According to overwhelming majority in the doctrine, the substantial reasons correspond the content of the objective reasons specified in

---

107 Centel, *Turkish Labour Law*, 71; Çelik, Caniklioğlu, and Canbolat, *İş Hukuku Dersleri*, 189; Ekmekçi and Korkusuz, *Turkish Individual Labour Law*, 42–43.

108 Çelik, Caniklioğlu, and Canbolat, *İş Hukuku Dersleri*, 190; Süzek, *İş Hukuku*, 239. For further information see, Yeliz Bozkurt Gümrükçüoğlu, *Türk İş Hukuku'nda Belirli Süreli İş Sözleşmesi* (İstanbul: Vedat, 2012).

109 See also, Dereli, *Labour Law in Turkey*, 186.

110 Centel, *Turkish Labour Law*, 73; Çelik, Caniklioğlu, and Canbolat, *İş Hukuku Dersleri*, 195; Ekmekçi and Korkusuz, *Turkish Individual Labour Law*, 44; Süzek, *İş Hukuku*, 239; Süral and Kılıçoğlu, "Labor Law," 166. Cf. Dereli, *Labour Law in Turkey*, 105.

the article 11 of the Labor Act.[111] In other words, those reasons should be present either in the time of the conclusion or that of extension.[112]

It is worth noting that another limitation regards the differential treatment between the employees who work for indefinite term and definite term (art. 12/1 of LA). An employee working under a contract for definite term should not be subjected to differential treatment in relation to the comparable employee working under a contract for indefinite term, unless there is a reason justifying the different treatment.[113] The Labor Act also intends to prevent wage disparity between the employees who work for indefinite term and definite term. Therefore, it mandates that the wages and other monetary benefits that are divisible based on time period shall be paid to the given employee according to the length of service by being calculated proportionately to the wage of comparable the employees who work for an indefinite term (art. 12/2 of LA).

2. Part-Time and Full-Time Contracts

Part-time work is one of the traditional forms of non-standard employment. The article 13/para. 1 of the Labor Act denotes that the employment contract shall be considered a part-time contract if the normal weekly working time of the employee has been arranged considerably shorter than a comparable full-timer. Therefore, it is a must to identify the phrase of "considerably shorter". According to the article 6 of By-Law on Working Times Regarding the Labor Act, the phrase of "considerably shorter" implies an upper limit by defining part-time work as work up to two-thirds of normal working hours of full-timer.

Another important point is the limitation on the differential treatment between the employees who work for part-time and full-time. The employer should treat those employees equally unless there is a justifying reason for the differential treatment (art. 13/2 of LA).

In this regard, the wage rates should be set same for part-timers and full-timers. The wages and other monetary benefits that are divisible to be accorded

111 Çelik, Caniklioğlu, and Canbolat, *İş Hukuku Dersleri*, 200, fn. 121; Süzek, *İş Hukuku*, 249, fn. 90; Süral and Kılıçoğlu, "Labor Law," 166.

112 Nevertheless, under the provisions of TCO, definite term contracts are divergently prescribed (art. TCO). For further information see, Süzek, *İş Hukuku*, 239, fn. 55.

113 The comparable employee is the one who works in same position, in same workplace and has same qualifications under the indefinite term contracts (art. 12/3 of LA). In this context, the reasons that justify different treatment may be educational status, seniority, and degree of skills or similar reasons. See also, Centel, *Turkish Labour Law*, 75; Dereli, *Labour Law in Turkey*, 106.

to part-timers must be paid in accordance with the length of their working time proportionate to those accorded to a comparable full-timer (art. 13/2 of LA). Therefore, part-timers should receive "pro-rata" not only the wage benefits, but also non-wage benefits (child allowances, meal allowances, etc.) comparable to those of full-timers. In addition, part-timers are also able to enjoy the collective rights such as freedom of association, the right to collective bargaining and the right to strike, in the same manner as full-timers.[114]

The forms of part-time work vary over a wide range in practice. In some cases, working time arrangements may involve either very short hours or no foreseeable fixed hours, such as "on-call contracts" prescribed by the article 14 of LA. Furthermore, remote work has also been evaluated within this context by the legislator and regulated under the same article in 2016 (art. 14/para. 4–7 of LA). In the aftermath of the COVID-19 outbreak, the various forms of remote work have become widespread.[115]

3. *Employment Contracts with Trial Clause*

A clause prescribing trial (probation) period is not an inextricable part of the employment contracts. It is entirely up to the wills of contracting parties to agree on trial period in the employment contracts.[116] In order to establish this type of contract, the parties should agree on a specific arrangement prescribing trial period in the employment contract.[117]

On the one side, the purpose of trial period is to enable employers to evaluate the employee's aptitudes, personality, discipline at work, efficiency, and whether the fact that employee is suitable for the business. On the other side, it intends to enable employees to evaluate whether the working conditions and work are suitable for them. During this period, both the employer and the employee are enabled to terminate the employment contract without giving any reason and without having to comply with the notice period (art. 15/2 of LA).

Those contracts that involve trial clause may not be conceived of as two separate contracts, as such one for the duration of the trial period and another

---

114 Çelik, Caniklioğlu, and Canbolat, *İş Hukuku Dersleri*, 211. See also, Dereli, *Labour Law in Turkey*, 107; Süzek, *İş Hukuku*, 262; Süral and Kılıçoğlu, "Labor Law," 165.

115 Çelik, Caniklioğlu, and Canbolat, *İş Hukuku Dersleri*, 228. See also, Ekmekçi and Korkusuz, *Turkish Individual Labour Law*, 49 ff.

116 Çelik, Caniklioğlu, and Canbolat, *İş Hukuku Dersleri*, 239; Süzek, *İş Hukuku*, 254.

117 Centel, *Turkish Labour Law*, 79; Çelik, Caniklioğlu, and Canbolat, *İş Hukuku Dersleri*, 239; Süzek, *İş Hukuku*, 254; Süral and Kılıçoğlu, "Labor Law," 164.

one at the end of this period. Instead, solely one contract is of concern.[118] The beginning of the contractual relationship is the date on which the employee starts working, not the day on which the trial period expires. In other words, the expiry of the trial period is not to be conceived as a new beginning. After the end of trial period, the contractual relationship pursues where it left off. The impact of the expiry of trial period is the reversion to the standard termination procedure.

In case of an arrangement on trial period by individual employment contracts, the duration must not exceed 2 months as a rule (art. 15/1 of LA).[119] These contracts enable both parties to terminate the contract without observing notice period during trial period. On the other hand, other obligations and rights of the contracting parties remain intact during this period.[120]

Tab. 6. Overlying of different contract types

It should be noted that those contract types might be intertwined and not exclude one other. In practice, these are not isolated sets of provisions. This implies that one type of contract may also have the characteristics of another one. Accordingly, a part-time employment contract might be concluded for an indefinite term or definite term, as well as with a trial clause, and vice versa. For instance, if the employee works 5 hours a day, and only 3 days a week, it is regarded as part-time work. If no expiry date is determined, and then it is also considered as an "indefinite term contract" as well as a part-time employment contract. However, if the same contract is concluded for 2 years, it is, then, classified as both a "definite term contract" and a "part-time contract".

V. The Scope of the Labor Act (no. 4857)

While employment law covers employment relationships in general, all different labor acts apply to different employment relationships. The Labor Act no. 4857 has the widest scope of application in industry, in service and in the manufacturing

118 See also, Dereli, *Labour Law in Turkey*, 109.

119 For further information on specific sectors and arrangement made by collective bargaining agreements see also, Centel, *Turkish Labour Law*, 79; Çelik, Caniklioğlu, and Canbolat, *İş Hukuku Dersleri*, 239; Süzek, *İş Hukuku*, 255.

120 Çelik, Caniklioğlu, and Canbolat, *İş Hukuku Dersleri*, 240; Dereli, *Labour Law in Turkey*, 110; Ekmekçi and Korkusuz, *Turkish Individual Labour Law*, 51.

sector. Therefore, under this chapter, in a broad sense, the focus will lie on the individual employment relationships that are covered by the Labor Act.

According to the article 4 of the Labor Act titled "exceptions", the provisions of the Act (no. 4857) shall not apply to the following activities and employment relationships:

- Sea and air transport activities,
- In the workplaces and the enterprises for agricultural and forestry activities employing a minimum of 50 employees (50 inclusive),
- Any agricultural construction work that falls within the scope of family economy,
- In handicraft work activities that are performed in homes by the efforts of members of a family and their relatives up to the third degree (3rd degree inclusive) without the participation of anyone from the outside,
- Domestic (household) services,
- Apprentices,
- Sportsmen,
- Those undergoing rehabilitation programs,
- In the workplaces employing three or fewer employees by complying with the definition of the article 3, sub-para. a of the Act on Tradesmen and Artisans Societies no. 5362.

On the other hand, some activities that are cited in the rest of the article are excluded from the exceptions, such as loading and unloading operations to and from ships at ports and docks, and all ground operations related to air transport.[121]

VI. The Obligations of the Contracting Parties

A. The Obligations of the Employee

The obligations arising from the employment contract for the employee are classified into three categories as the obligation to perform a job/work or a task (principal obligation), the obligation to obey and to be loyal (or duty of loyalty).

---

121 For further information see, Centel, *Turkish Labour Law*, 58; Çelik, Caniklioğlu, and Canbolat, *İş Hukuku Dersleri*, 160 ff.; Dereli, *Labour Law in Turkey*, 97 ff.; Ekmekçi and Korkusuz, *Turkish Individual Labour Law*, 35–38; Süzek, *İş Hukuku*, 210 ff.

1. Obligation to Perform a Job/Work or a Task (Principal Obligation)

The obligation to perform a work is the principal obligation of the employee. As a rule, the employee's performance obligation must be fulfilled duly and in person by the employee. This is inherent in the principal obligation of the employee, and this principal obligation imposes the obligation on the employee to perform all kinds of work undertaken by the employment contract. What the employee will do or how they will perform the work in frame of an employment relationship is determined by legal regulations and collective bargaining agreements along with the individual employment contracts. On the other hand, a strictly specific job definition is unlikely provided with the written regulations in practice. Therefore, the content of the obligation is determined by evaluating all kinds of work falling within the scope of the profession or task, or the works that can be requested from the employee under the rule of good faith.[122] In other words, the content of performance varies in every concrete case.

In some cases, the contracting parties may amend the content of this obligation by choice. Yet, the changes in substantial issues regarding the working conditions (including the changes to the definition of the job/work) are subjected to the consent of the employee.[123]

The employee must fulfill this obligation with due diligence by using reasonable skill and care in the work. On the other hand, this is not a separate obligation rather a complementary in nature; it is tied to the obligation to perform a job. In other words, since the obligation to perform the work also covers "the obligation to perform the work with care and diligence", an imperfect performance in the sense of care and diligence is to be construed as a direct violation of the principal obligation (obligation to perform the work).[124]

2. Obligation to Obey

The obligation to obey requires the employee to comply with the employer's instructions, which are in conformity with legal regulations. This obligation is regulated within the article 399 of the TCO more broadly than the Labor Act. According to the article 399 of the TCO, the employer is able to give general and

---

122 Çelik, Canikliоğlu, and Canbolat, *İş Hukuku Dersleri*, 307; Süzek, *İş Hukuku*, 341. See also, Centel, *Turkish Labour Law*, 103; Ekmekçi and Korkusuz, *Turkish Individual Labour Law*, 58.

123 Under this chapter, see infra: *Part III – Legal Regulations on the Change in Working Conditions.*

124 Süzek, *İş Hukuku*, 341. See also, Dereli, *Labour Law in Turkey*, 122.

specific instructions regarding the performance of the work and the behaviors and attitudes of the employees at the workplace. The employees are obliged to comply with them to the extent that the rule of good faith requires.[125]

Instructions clarifying the content of the obligation to perform the work are considered within the principal obligation.[126] If the employee disobeys those instructions, it is construed as the violation of obligation to perform the work. The scope of those instructions varies from a broad outline to a fully developed performance specification.

On the other hand, obeying instructions and orders regarding the behaviors and attitudes of the employees at the workplace is considered as a separate obligation. In general, those are in relation to the business organization such as door controls and other organizational norms applied in the premises of workplace. Disobedience to those instructions is no longer considered within the violation of principal obligation, but it constitutes a violation in specific to the obligation to obey.[127]

3. *Duty of Loyalty (Obligation to Be Loyal)*

Duty of loyalty is defined as the act of working by the employee in accordance with the honesty and loyalty. According to the article 396 of the TCO, the employee must act honestly and faithfully in the protection of the employer's rightful interests. More precisely, the Court of Cassation describes this obligation as "*not harming the counterparty's personality, properties and other legally protected assets upon performing contractual obligations, (...) avoiding all kinds of behaviors that may endanger the purpose pursued by the contract, particularly those that may weaken the mutual trust between parties*".[128]

Accordingly, the content of duty of loyalty can be manifest itself as to do something (such as the obligation to act in accordance with the benefit of the employer) or refrain from doing something (such as the obligation to avoid behaviors that may harm the employer) in terms of employee actions. To

---

125 Centel, *Turkish Labour Law*, 109; Çelik, Caniklioğlu, and Canbolat, *İş Hukuku Dersleri*, 313 ff.; Dereli, *Labour Law in Turkey*, 123; Ekmekçi and Korkusuz, *Turkish Individual Labour Law*, 59.

126 Ekmekçi and Korkusuz, *Turkish Individual Labour Law*, 59.

127 Dereli, *Labour Law in Turkey*, 124; Ekmekçi and Korkusuz, *Turkish Individual Labour Law*, 59; Süzek, *İş Hukuku*, 346.

128 See, Turkish Court of Cassation, 9th Civil Chamber decision, dated 01.02.2010, no. 13571/1815 (own translation, quoted in *Çalışma ve Toplum Dergisi*, 26/3 (2010): https://www.calismatoplum.org/, accessed 18.7.2021).

illustrate, the employee is obliged to keep the business information confidential (mostly trade secrets) and not to compete against the employer during the employment contract due to the duty of loyalty.[129]

The scope of the duty of loyalty (and that of duty of confidentiality) is to be determined by the employee's position in the workplace. Within the duration of contract relationship, either the competition with the employer or the release of confidential information is treated as a violation of the duty of loyalty. As a rule, once the contractual relationship has ended, the freedom of enterprise revives for the employee. They may be employed in the rival companies or may set up a competing establishment against the former employer following the end of the employment contract.

Should the employer require the employee be obliged to maintain confidential business information even after the termination of the employment relationship, the employer may propose for a confidentiality (or non-disclosure) agreement. Otherwise, since the underlying duty of loyalty has already vanished, the duty of confidentiality, as a rule, expires when the employment relationship ends. On the other hand, under the article 396/4 of the TCO, in cases where the legitimate interest of the employer justifies that, duty of confidentiality may endure beyond the end of the contract. This case exceptionally does not necessitate any specific confidentiality agreement. Nevertheless, the scope of legitimate interest of the employer is a controversial issue in doctrine.[130]

It must be stated that a confidentiality agreement is not a contract that inherently prevents the employee from competing with the former employer. It only prevents the employee from revealing the confidential information of the former employer.[131] The non-compete obligation is also treated as an aspect of the duty of loyalty during the period in which the employment contract is in progress so that it expires when the employment relationship ends. On the other hand, it becomes an independent obligation after the end of the employment contract only if there is a non-compete agreement.[132]

---

129 Centel, *Turkish Labour Law*, 107; Çelik, Caniklioğlu, and Canbolat, *İş Hukuku Dersleri*, 317–318; Ekmekçi and Korkusuz, *Turkish Individual Labour Law*, 60; Süzek, *İş Hukuku*, 347. See also, Arzu Ertürk Arslan, *Türk İş Hukukunda İşçinin Sadakat Borcu* (İstanbul: On İki Levha, 2010).

130 Süzek, *İş Hukuku*, 348, fn. 30.

131 For further information see also, Turkish Court of Cassation, 9th Civil Chamber decision, dated. 11.10.2016, no. 15516/17659, *Çalışma ve Toplum Dergisi*, 54/3 (2017).

132 Centel, *Turkish Labour Law*, 108; Çelik, Caniklioğlu, and Canbolat, *İş Hukuku Dersleri*, 323; Ekmekçi and Korkusuz, *Turkish Individual Labour Law*, 61.

Non-compete clauses within the employment contract (or separate agreement as to the non-competition) are subject to the articles 444 to 447 of the TCO. Following are required for such an agreement to be valid: The employee, who concludes a non-compete agreement, must have the legal capacity to act and the agreement must be in writing. These prerequisites allow the employee to have a thorough understanding of the prohibition's reach.

However, even if these prerequisites are met, such an agreement cannot be concluded with every employee or in every circumstance. There are several conditions for the parties to conclude an agreement on a non-compete: First, the employer must have a legitimate interest worth legal protection. In this sense, the employee should be able to reach the information regarding the economic and technological capacity or the customers of the employer, and any information that provides the employer with competitive advantage. Also, a risk that the employee may cause a considerable loss in case of their competition against the former employer should be present. In other words, this information must bear the potential to cause considerable damages for the former employer if the employee reveals it or it is exploited by the rivals.[133]

As a second condition, prohibition on competition should be limited to such an extent that it does not endanger the economic future of the employee, since those prohibitions likely constrain the prospective employment options of the employees and weaken their economic freedom. To this end, the provisions of the TCO regulate certain limits that must be adhered to for concluding those contracts in terms of the period of the prohibition, the prohibited geographical area and work scope (art. 445/1).[134]

If the scope of the non-compete agreement exceeds those limits in any manner, provisions of the Code of Obligation provide the court with discretion to appraise the contract's validity or to intervene to the given contract by constricting the exceeding scope of non-compete obligation.[135] More precisely, either the court might invalidate the contract or reduce the scope of prohibited area or work as well as shorten the period of non-compete obligation.

On the other hand, the legal consequence of a valid non-compete agreement is that the employee, who violates the contract, is undertaken to compensate

---

133 Çelik, Caniklioğlu, and Canbolat, *İş Hukuku Dersleri*, 328–329; Süzek, *İş Hukuku*, 350.

134 For further information see also, Centel, *Turkish Labour Law*, 108; Çelik, Caniklioğlu, and Canbolat, *İş Hukuku Dersleri*, 330 ff.; Dereli, *Labour Law in Turkey*, 125 ff.; Ekmekçi and Korkusuz, *Turkish Individual Labour Law*, 61 ff.; Süzek, *İş Hukuku*, 352.

135 Süzek, *İş Hukuku*, 354. For further information see, Polat Soyer, *Rekabet Yasağı Sözleşmesi* (Ankara: Adalet, 1994).

all the losses of employer due to the violation.[136] In addition, the contracting parties may agree on a penalty clause within the agreement. If a contractual penalty is included in the agreement, the employee shall pay the specified amount without requiring the employer to prove the presence or the quantum of the damage. However, if any damages in excess of the penalty amount are proven, the employee is obligated to compensate these further damages only if they are at fault in this case.[137]

B. *The Obligations of the Employer*

The obligations arising from the employment contract for the employer are mainly classified into three categories as the obligation to pay wage (principal obligation), the obligation to protect the employee and the obligation of equal treatment.

1. *The Obligation to Pay Wage (Principal Obligation)*

a. *General overview*

The obligation to pay wage is the principal obligation of the employer in return for the performance of the employee and the compulsory element of the employment contract. To put it another way, it is impossible to conceive an employment contract that doesn't include any wage payment.[138]

The basic wage is an amount of money to be paid in return for the work of the employee and in cash.[139] The importance of the basic wage lies in fact that it should be paid in cash, namely, as money. The rationale for this is that cash allows the employee to circulate and convert money without any delay. However, payment instruments such as promissory note, bill of exchange or cheques do not provide this opportunity and are, thereby, prohibited as an instrument for wage payments (art. 32/4 of the LA).[140]

---

136 Süzek, *İş Hukuku*, 355.

137 Çelik, Caniklioğlu, and Canbolat, *İş Hukuku Dersleri*, 325 ff.; Süzek, *İş Hukuku*, 356. Also, see supra: *Chapter III – Law of Obligations – Contractual Penalty.*

138 Süzek, *İş Hukuku*, 361. See also, Centel, *Turkish Labour Law*, 111; Çelik, Caniklioğlu, and Canbolat, *İş Hukuku Dersleri*, 335; Ekmekçi and Korkusuz, *Turkish Individual Labour Law*, 63.

139 Centel, *Turkish Labour Law*, 111; Süzek, *İş Hukuku*, 362.

140 Also, payment in foreign currency or payment fixed to foreign currency is no longer possible with some exceptions (According to the Presidential Decision [dated 2018, no. 85] that amends the Cabinet Decision on the Protection of the Value of Turkish Currency no. 32, and to the subsequent amendment communiqués). As a rule, the

Premiums, bonuses, commission fees, and pay shares are examples of "wage supplements" that might be provided by the employer in addition to the basic wage. Total wage covers basic wage and those wage supplements, if any. In other words, these payments constitute the total wage altogether. On the other hand, those provided economic benefits should be continuous in order to be considered as the part of total wage. Unlike basic wage, the wage supplements might be paid both in cash and in kind. That is to say, they might be paid by provision of goods such as food or clothing aid in practice.[141]

Besides, for some periods, during which the employee has not worked, the employees are able to claim social wages. Accordingly, the social wage is described as a wage, which is paid regardless of whether the employee has worked actually but in consideration of social needs. These can be exemplified as the wages paid on week holidays, national holiday and public holidays.[142]

Tab. 7. Net wage vs. Gross wage

In terms of legal deductions from wages, there is a separate classification. The leftover wage after any legal deductions is referred to "net pay" or "net wage". Yet, the entire amount before these legal deductions is referred to as the "gross wage".

Wage systems or forms of wage payment There are various payment systems such as per piece pay rate, lump sum, percentage pay and time-based pay, etc.[143] The commonly used form of wage payment is time-based pay. In this case, payment is made based on a certain time frame, during which the work performed, such as day, week or month. Therefore, the amount of work produced during that period is not important for this payment system.

On the other hand, time-based pay applies to both salaried employees and hourly employees, which are distinct from one other. For white collar employees,

amount of the wage can only be paid in national currency for the employees residing in Turkey. The main exceptions are foreign employees residing in Turkey and the employees residing in Turkey on condition that the performance is to be fulfilled abroad.

141 Süzek, *İş Hukuku*, 376.

142 Süzek, *İş Hukuku*, 362. Under this chapter, see also: *Rest Periods*.

143 Centel, *Turkish Labour Law*, 111 ff.; Çelik, Caniklioğlu, and Canbolat, *İş Hukuku Dersleri*, 339 ff.; Dereli, *Labour Law in Turkey*, 156; Ekmekçi and Korkusuz, *Turkish Individual Labour Law*, 64 ff.; Süzek, *İş Hukuku*, 363 ff.

set salary is more common, in which the salaried employees get paid a fixed amount of money regardless of how many hours they work in a week/month unlike hourly employees. In case of absenteeism of the salaried employees due to sickness, leave or any similar reasons, their set salary shall not be deducted.[144] Adversely, the wages of hourly employees shall be deducted in those cases. However, both receive their pay at predetermined time intervals, such as week or month, according to time-based pay.

Amount of wage If the amount is specified in the contract, this amount is considered as contractual wage on condition that it is not less than the legal minimum wage. The legal minimum wage is determined by the "Minimum Wage Determination Commission". This amount is to be considered as national minimum wage.[145] If there is no determination in the contract, the employer is obliged to pay the wage of a comparable employee, which cannot be determined less than minimum wage (art. 401 of TCO).

There are also some protective rules for the wage amounts. For instance, the transfer, assignment and seizure of the wage (except seizure to pay off the alimony arrearage) can only be up to one-fourth of the monthly wage (art. 35 of LA; see also, art. 410 of TCO).

Place of payment The employers, who employees 5 employees in Turkey overall, are obliged to pay the net wages remained after legal deductions to the bank account of the employees (art 32/2–3 of LA; see also, art. 6–8, 10 of By-Law on the Payment of Wages, Premiums, Bonuses and all kinds of Remunerations via Banks). Payment via bank accounts is optional for the rest of employers. In case of payment in-kind, the wage supplements as goods or services can be provided in the workplace. In other words, it is appropriate to remunerate payable wage supplements to the bank accounts (for the bonus, the premium, etc.) or to deliver them to the employees within the workplace (for providing goods).[146]

Time of payment It is a binding rule that the wage is paid at the latest once a month (art. 32/5 of LA). The employee must perform the work first, only after then they may claim for their wages.[147] As an example, the employee, who works

144 Ekmekçi and Korkusuz, *Turkish Individual Labour Law*, 65; Süzek, *İş Hukuku*, 363.

145 Ekmekçi and Korkusuz, *Turkish Individual Labour Law*, 68. Currently, the amount is determined 3,577 Turkish Liras as gross wage for 2021. Yet, it will be regularly revised in the following periods by the Minimum Wage Determination Commission.

146 Süzek, *İş Hukuku*, 377.

147 See, Centel, *Turkish Labour Law*, 118.

in November, receives the wage of this performance within December. In field of Employment Law, the only exception is provided for the journalists by legal regulations. The journalists are paid at the beginning of each work period (art. 14/1 of the Press Labor Act). On the other hand, by contractual arrangements, the parties may agree upon that the wage of employee is to be paid at the beginning of each work period before the relevant performance is fulfilled.

Proof of payment The obligation to pay wage is incumbent on the employer. Since the employer is obliged to pay the wages, it is, then, the employer who has to prove the payment in case of any dispute.[148] During court proceedings, the common practice is to enquire about the median wages of comparable employees by referring to professional organizations and trade unions.

b. Legal consequences of non-payment

Some employees who meet certain conditions are entitled to get a maximum of 3 months' wage from the Wage Guarantee Fund if their employers have financial difficulties. Apart from this, there are two options for the employees who are exposed to non-payment of the wages: to terminate the employment contract immediately or to refrain from fulfilling the obligation to work. In both cases, they may claim special interest rate for non-payment.

If the wage is not paid in due time, the employee is able to terminate the contract immediately without following the notice periods (art. 27/II, sub-para. e).[149] Besides, if 20 days have passed since the due date for payments, the employees can refrain from working, when the wages of employees are unpaid without any compelling reason (art. 34 of LA). In this case, non-performance of the employees cannot be considered as a strike, even though a group of employees in the workplace refrains from working together. Termination of the contract of these employees by the employer is also prohibited. To reiterate, for the latter option, the non-payment of the employer should not be based on a compelling reason and should last at least 20 days as of the due date for payment.

Nevertheless, according to early decisions of Court of Cassation, the employees cannot claim wage payment for the days that they refrain from working.[150]

---

148 Centel, *Turkish Labour Law*, 118; Dereli, *Labour Law in Turkey*, 155; Süzek, *İş Hukuku*, 379.

149 Under this chapter, also see infra: *Part IV – The Cases for Termination with Just Cause for the Employee.*

150 Cf. Centel, *Turkish Labour Law*, 119; Çelik, Caniklioğlu, and Canbolat, *İş Hukuku Dersleri*, 359; Süzek, *İş Hukuku*, 385. For other late but significant decisions see also, Çelik, Caniklioğlu, and Canbolat, *İş Hukuku Dersleri*, 359, fn. 796.

Tab. 8. Reminder about waiting periods
It should be underlined that the waiting period of 20 days is only for the option of refraining from working. More precisely, the employee is not obliged to wait for 20 days if they opt for immediate termination in case of the non-payment of wages.

Either case, a special interest rate may be claimed by the employee as the wage interest. "The highest interest rate charged to bank deposits" shall be applied for the wages not paid on due date (art. 34/1 of LA). This interest rate applies to all kinds of wage payments including premiums, bonuses, and other fees that qualify as such.

On the other hand, prescription period for the claims regarding unpaid wages is 5 years from the due date (art. 32 of LA). It means that any obligation regarding principal payments or interests of unpaid wages would be turned into imperfect obligation after 5 years from the due date, even though the employment contract is still in force.

2. The Obligation to Protect the Employee

As it is commonly embraced, labor is not a commodity to be traded in markets for the lowest price; employees are human beings with rights, needs, and aspirations.[151] This perception requires the protection of employee's personal rights, health, and physical integrity above all. In this sense, the obligation to protect the employee covers this requirement.[152]

The obligation to protect the employee during the contractual relationship is first perceived as the protection of employees' health and physical integrity by considering occupational safety and health in the workplace. The employer should provide the employee with protective tools and materials along with necessary information on the work process. Within this framework, the employer is obliged to inspect the work process and to build a proper business organization for health and physical integrity of the employees.[153]

---

151 See, ILO Report of Global Commission on the future of work: Work for a brighter future (Geneva: ILO, 2019), 38.

152 For further information see also, Erdem Özdemir, *İş Sağlığı ve Güvenliği Hukuku Dersleri* (İstanbul: Vedat, 2020).

153 Centel, *Turkish Labour Law*, 123; Dereli, *Labour Law in Turkey*, 127; Süzek, *İş Hukuku*, 409 ff.

Nonetheless, it is only the one facet of this obligation. In addition, the scope covers the protection of the employee from physical and sexual harassment, along with psychological harassment known as mobbing.[154] The employer should also protect the personal data of the employees and not disclose them in violation of the law.[155] As is obvious, the scope of this obligation is, by definition, extensive.[156] However, it can be defined as the establishment of an occupational safety and health (OSH) management system by the employer[157] and basically divided into three parts:

a. The obligation to take occupational safety and health measures

There is a special regulation on OSH management in Turkish law, known as the Act on Occupational Health and Safety no. 6331 (AOHS). According to AOHS, with some exceptions, the occupational health and safety boards should be established in specific workplaces (art. 22 of AOHS). On the other hand, all employers, as a rule, are imposed to employ specific professionals to ensure OHS management (art. 6/1, sub-para. a of AOHS).[158] The employer appoints followings amongst its employees: Occupational safety specialists, workplace physicians, and only for specified most dangerous works, health staff other than those.

According to the Act no. 6331, the employer is obliged to prevent occupational risks by taking all kinds of measures including training and providing information, organizing the work process properly, etc. The state of the current science and technological developments determines the degree of the employer's obligation to take measures (art. 4/1 of AOHS; art. 417/2 of TCO).

---

154 Centel, *Turkish Labour Law*, 125 ff.; Çelik, Caniklioğlu, and Canbolat, *İş Hukuku Dersleri*, 368 ff.; Ekmekçi and Korkusuz, *Turkish Individual Labour Law*, 75 ff.; Süzek, *İş Hukuku*, 399–400.

155 Çelik, Caniklioğlu, and Canbolat, *İş Hukuku Dersleri*, 382; Süzek, *İş Hukuku*, 402 ff.

156 Dereli, *Labour Law in Turkey*, 127 ff.; Ekmekçi and Korkusuz, *Turkish Individual Labour Law*, 76, 170 ff.

157 According to ILO, the system should contain the main elements of policy, organizing, planning and implementation, evaluation and action for improvement, which requires continual improvement. See also, Guidelines on occupational safety and health management systems, ILO-OSH 2001 (Geneva: ILO, 2009).

On the other hand, it must be reminded that these guidelines are not legally binding and are not intended to replace national regulations. Also see, Levent Akın, "İş Sağlığı ve Güvenliğinde İşyerinin Örgütlenmesi," *AÜHFD*, 54/1 (2004): 1–60.

158 However, for some public institutions and small and medium-sized enterprises, the enforcement of the relevant provision has been postponed to 31.12.2023 (art. 38/1, sub-para. a-1 of AOHS).

The employer should also assess the risks within the workplace. This also has importance, because the primary purpose of occupational safety and health measures is to eliminate or minimize risks in the workplace (art. 3/1, sub-para. ö of AOHS).

Employers cannot evade the obligation to protect the employee by pleading the economic reasons. In the case of an occupational accident caused by failure to take occupational health and safety measures, the employer is to be held liable. The employer cannot assert their poor financial status or financial insufficiency to avoid legal responsibility.[159]

b. The obligation to inspect

The employer is also obliged to audit whether the occupational safety and health measures taken in the workplace are followed by the employees and supervise the implementation of the relevant measures.[160] The investigation of the origin and underlying causes of work-related diseases and accidents, documentation of them and risk assessments within the workplace are also of importance.

Furthermore, it is not an abstract obligation. When assigning a job to an employee, the employer should examine the employee's appropriateness to this position in every case. According to the circumstances of each employee, the employer is also obliged to take special measures. This includes constantly observing employee health surveillance, considering the health and safety risks to which the employees are exposed in the workplace. Moreover, for all employees working in dangerous and most dangerous jobs, the employer is obliged to receive a health report periodically (art. 15/2 of AOHS).

c. The obligation to provide training

To provide training is conceived as an important part of the occupational safety and health measures. Trainings need to be associated with specific risks in the workplace. The employer should provide the employees with comprehensible instructions and adequate information. Thereby, the employer enables to maintain an organization in compliance with the rules of occupational safety and health.

In return for this, it is also necessary for the employees to obey the rules regarding occupational safety and health and to follow the relevant instructions.

---

159 Süzek, *İş Hukuku*, 409 ff. See also, Centel, *Turkish Labour Law*, 124.

160 Çelik, Caniklioğlu, and Canbolat, *İş Hukuku Dersleri*, 396 ff.; Dereli, *Labour Law in Turkey*, 128.

If employees the employee endangers safety of the workplace by disobeying the rules, their employment contracts can be terminated by the employer immediately based on just cause (art. 25/II, sub-para. 1 of LA).

Tab. 9. The regulations of AOHS
While the employees are obliged to obey the rules, they also have some rights. Pursuant to AOHS, the employees, who face serious and imminent danger, may apply to the Occupational Health and Safety Board. If there is no Board within the workplace, the employees may apply to the employer directly. In this case, the employers should immediately decide on an effective action against the occupational risks on their own (art. 13/1 of AOHS). If the Board or the employer confirms the presence of a serious and imminent danger in accordance with the employee's request, or if the danger is unavoidable, the employee may also refrain from working until the necessary actions are taken. In this case, for the days off due to the occupational hazards and risks, this period is payable (13/3–4 of AOHS). This is different from the rule that is to be applied in case of refraining from work due to the unpaid wages. On the other hand, until the danger is eliminated, the work may be suspended in part or in the whole by administrative authorities, depending on the degree of risk (art. 25/1 of AOHS). However, the article 13 of LA is not applicable in the case of suspension of work. Yet, even in case of suspension, the employees are also entitled to get paid for this period even though they had not worked (art. 25/6 of AOHS). As another option, the employees may also immediately terminate their employment contracts by just cause, if the necessary measures are not taken despite their request.

3. *The Obligation of Equal Treatment*

In essence, the article 10 of the Constitution regulates equality.[161] Furthermore, recently Human Rights and Equality Institution of Turkey has established in 2016. The Act having established the Institution (AHREIT) has inherently addressed this issue. The purpose of this Act; inter alia, is to protect and promote human rights, and to provide assurance for the right to equal treatment (art. 1 of AHREIT). Moreover, the article 3 of AHREIT regulates the principle of equality and the prohibition of discrimination.

161 See supra: *Chapter I – Constitutional Law.*

In specific to employment relationships, the article 5 of the Labor Act both prohibits discrimination and establishes a basis for equal treatment in a broad meaning.[162] Accordingly, unless there are justifying reasons, as a rule, the employer should not make any distinction between the comparable employees.

Under the article 5 of the Labor Act, absolute prohibitions regarding the following reasons are issued: Language, race, gender, political thought, philosophical belief, religion and sect and similar reasons. Besides that, under the article 5/3 of the Labor Act, a distinction based on pregnancy or gender cannot be justified either unless biological or work-related reasons so require.

Additionally, the employer should not discriminate against the employee comparing to type of the contract. For example, different treatment between employees with definite term contracts and indefinite term, or different treatment between employees with part-time contracts and full-time contracts are prohibited unless the presence of justifying reasons (art. 5/2 of LA). However, if there is a reason justifying the differential treatment, then the treatment does not constitute a discriminatory action.

In case of violation of the prohibition on discrimination in course of application for an employment contract, the legal consequence is different. In this case, there is no concluded contract yet. Therefore, any failure to conduct negotiations in accordance with the rule of good faith may only result in *culpa in contrahendo* responsibility.

On the other hand, for the discriminative actions during contractual relationship or at the termination process, the Labor Act stipulates special regulations. The compensation to be paid shall amount to the wage of the employee for up to 4 months (art. 5/6 of LA), except for the termination of contract by the employer based on unionization. In addition to this amount, the employees, who have suffered from discrimination, can also claim the rights they have been deprived of. For instance, if a female employee had not been promoted due to her gender, she may also claim the shortfall amount of the wages that she would have received if she had been promoted.

As a rule, the employee is obliged to prove that the employer acts in contradiction with the prohibition on discrimination. Yet, if the employee reveals any

---

162 Dereli, *Labour Law in Turkey*, 135; Ekmekçi and Korkusuz, *Turkish Individual Labour Law*, 73–75. However, it is widely accepted in doctrine that the article 5 of LA excludes the obligation of equal treatment in narrow meaning. See also, Çelik, Caniklioğlu, and Canbolat, *İş Hukuku Dersleri*, 435 ff.; Süzek, *İş Hukuku*, 452 ff.; Gaye Burcu Yıldız, *İşverenin Eşit İşlem Yapma Borcu* (Ankara: Yetkin, 2008).

proof that strongly demonstrates the possibility of a violation, the employer is under an obligation to prove otherwise (art. 5/7 of LA). In other words, in case that a discriminatory action is strongly demonstrated, the burden of proof is shifted to the employer. Finally, the employee may also terminate the contract immediately due to the discriminatory actions exposed during the employment relationship.[163]

However, the obligation of equal treatment in narrow meaning differs from the scope of the prohibition of discrimination. The employer's obligation of equal treatment in narrow meaning can be defined as an obligation to act equally to the comparable employees amongst a community.[164] Therefore, it is conceived that the prohibition of discrimination is related to fundamental rights, whereas the obligation of equal treatment in narrow meaning is rather related to the right of management of the employer.[165]

§ Part III Working Conditions

I. The Legal Regulations on Working Time

There are various regulations on the working conditions within the Labor Act since the protective nature of employment law manifests itself largely while the employees perform their jobs.

A. Normal Working Time

According to the Labor Act, working time is maximum 11 hours daily and 45 hours weekly. As an exception, the normal working time for miners working underground is maximum 7.5 hours daily and 37.5 hours weekly (art. 63/para. 1 and para. 2 of LA).

The term of normal working time mainly refers to the actual working time of the employee. However, in accordance with the provisions of the Labor Act, the employee is regarded to have worked even though they did not actually in those cases stated in the article 66 of LA. The time elapsed in these cases is

163 Ekmekçi and Korkusuz, *Turkish Individual Labour Law*, 74. Cf. Dereli, *Labour Law in Turkey*, 136–137.

164 See also, Centel, *Turkish Labour Law*, 128 ff.

165 For further information see, Çelik, Caniklioğlu, and Canbolat, *İş Hukuku Dersleri*, 435 ff.; Süzek, *İş Hukuku*, 458 ff. See also, Kübra Doğan Yenisey, "Harmonisation of Turkish law with EU's regulations in respect of equal treatment," *Managerial Law*, 47/6 (2005): 235–256.

included in the account of working time. That can be exemplified as the period elapsed on the road, during which the employee is assigned by the employer to work somewhere other than the workplace, and the period elapsed, during which the employee is ready for the work to be done without having worked. Also, the period required for the employee to arrive or depart the halls or main working spaces in underground or underwater works, and the periods required for female employees, who are breastfeeding, to express milk for their children are accounted as working time.

It is also counted as working time the time elapses during the mass transportation of employees in the works that require employees to be gathered and brought to the workplaces settled at a distance from the main premises, such as construction, protection, maintenance, and modification of railways, highways and bridges, etc. On the other hand, it is hardly needful to remark that the time elapsed while commuting cannot be counted as working time. That is, this provision does not cover the time elapses during the transportation between the residence of the employee and the workplace.[166]

A maximum of 45 hours is, as a rule, the maximum time that an employee can normally work in a week. According to the Labor Act, the weekly working time shall be divided equally by the working days of the week. Nevertheless, otherwise may be agreed by the contracting parties (art. 63/1 of LA). This suggests that an equal distribution of working hours through the working days is not a mandatory rule. It is applicable only if not agreed otherwise.[167]

B. Shift Work and "Balancing (Equalization) of the Working Hours" (WTAs)

There are several flexibility models for arranging working hours that are adopted by ILO as "balanced working time arrangements". On the other hand, overtime work is not in itself a type of arrangement of working hours (WTA).[168] Types of WTAs might differ according to the national regulations. A few of them are explicitly regulated in Turkish employment law.

166 Centel, *Turkish Labour Law*, 141; Çelik, Caniklioğlu, and Canbolat, *İş Hukuku Dersleri*, 744; Ekmekçi and Korkusuz, *Turkish Individual Labour Law*, 87; Süzek, *İş Hukuku*, 803.

167 Centel, *Turkish Labour Law*, 138; Çelik, Caniklioğlu, and Canbolat, *İş Hukuku Dersleri*, 737; Dereli, *Labour Law in Turkey*, 139; Süzek, *İş Hukuku*, 799; Süral and Kılıçoğlu, "Labor Law," 167.

168 See, Guide to developing balanced working time arrangements (Geneva: ILO, 2019), 3 ff.

Shift work is one of those arranged in the Labor Act (art 76/2 of LA; see also, By-Law on Special Procedures and Principles Regarding Shift Works[169]). The most common shift systems are the two-shift or three-shift fixed systems (at least three shifts in a 24-hour period). When the workplace operates non-stop during the whole week, shifts are, then, considered as "continuous operations".[170]

Another configuration is the model of "hours averaging schemes" that is referred to as "balancing (equalization) of working hours" in Turkey. The model of hours averaging scheme allows for changes in daily and weekly working hours over longer periods than 1 week. These arrangements enable variations in normal working hours within certain legal limits, such as maximum daily hours and length of the reference period.[171]

According to the Labor Act, on the condition that the contracting parties have agreed, the weekly work scheme (the distribution of working hours through weekly periods) can be arranged differently (art. 63/2). Some weeks of the scheme can be determined as intensified working period and some of them as diluted, over total period within which the hours are averaged. This is called "balancing (equalization) of the working hours" in the Labor Act (art. 63/2). The consent for the implementation of equalization is required either by the individual employment contract or by the collective bargaining agreement.[172]

To prevent the cycle of excessive overtime, the reference period is introduced. As a rule, the reference period in Turkey, which means over the period within which the hours are averaged, is 2 months. Within a time period of 2 months, the average weekly working time of the employee must not exceed normal weekly working time (in general, 45 hours per week). As an exception, this (equalization) period may be increased up to 4 months only by collective bargaining agreements.[173] In those cases, where the equalization period is applied, the

---

169 OJ, 07.04.2004, no. 25426.

170 See, Guide to developing balanced working time arrangements (Geneva: ILO, 2019), 13.

171 See, Guide to developing balanced working time arrangements (Geneva: ILO, 2019), 23.

172 Whether the implicit consent to be sufficient is controversial in the doctrine. For further discussions see, Çelik, Caniklioğlu, and Canbolat, *İş Hukukụ Dersleri*, 738–740, fn. 2563–2567; Dereli, *Labour Law in Turkey,* 140; Süzek, *İş Hukuku*, 800, fn. 11–13.

173 In the tourism sector, the reference period is exceptionally four months, and it can be extended to six months by collective bargaining agreements. See, the current amendment in the last sentence of the art. 63/2 of LA.

employee is not considered as undertaken an overtime work since the average of working hours is still fewer than 45 hours weekly (art. 41/1 of LA).

On the other hand, due to the periodic adjustment, if the average period exceeds normal working hours, overtime pay is to be paid based on working hours during the reference period.[174] In addition, to evade the excessive work of the employees, daily working time must not exceed 11 hours even in case of equalization period (art. 63/2 of LA). If the employee works more than 11 hours daily, that is also considered as overtime work.

Tab. 10. Sample case 2

For instance, an employee, who works 5 days a week, might work 10 hours per day for 3 weeks and then 6 hours per day for the next 3 weeks within the reference period of 6 weeks. In this case, the average working hour for the entire 6 weeks would be 8 hours per day, and overtime pay is not required even for the intensified working period.

ILO also promotes the adoption of "advance notice period". It refers to a minimum period required for notifying employees of changes in their working schedules due to the shift to hours averaging scheme. Herewith, it enables the employees to maintain work-life balance and to arrange their personal lives. A minimum advance notice period of 24 to 48 hours is highly suggested by ILO.[175]

However, in Turkish law, there is no such requirement to observe the notice period before implementing the hours averaging scheme. Likewise, there is no restriction on the equalization periods to follow each other at the end of each reference period.

Other configurations such as "staggered hours" and "flexi-time" arrangements have not been regulated in the Labor Act either. Nevertheless, there is no legal impediment to establish different starting and finishing times for different employee groups in the same workplace or to establish periods of "core hours" for the employees.

---

174 Centel, *Turkish Labour Law*, 138; Çelik, Caniklioğlu, and Canbolat, *İş Hukuku Dersleri*, 739; Dereli, *Labour Law in Turkey*, 141; Süzek, *İş Hukuku*, 803.

175 See, Guide to developing balanced working time arrangements (Geneva: ILO, 2019), 24.

C. Overwork Time and Work at Extra Hours

Overtime refers to all hours worked by the employee in excess of regular working hours. The regulations on overtime commonly set two thresholds: First, the maximum standard working time (often called "normal working hours") indicating a threshold, above which working time is considered as overtime; second, the maximum total working time including overtime.[176] The national threshold used for determination of overtime varies depending on the relevant acts. A similar threshold has been set according to the Labor Act: Working hours must not exceed 11 hours per day including overtime work and 45 hours per week. An annual limit has also been drawn, which is 270 hours excluding normal working hours (art. 41/8 of LA). However, maximum weekly working hours (including overtime) have not been arranged in the Labor Act.

In accordance with provisions of the Labor Act, overtime work is mainly defined as a working period exceeding 45 hours per week. In addition, the current Labor Act introduced a new concept that is called as "work at extra hours". By mutual agreement, the weekly working time may be arranged fewer than 45 hours per week. If the employee works longer than the weekly working time that is arranged in the contract, even if it is not exceeded to 45 hours, then "work at extra hours" is in question (art. 41/3 of LA).

It must be reiterated that contractual working time can deviate from the statutory working time provided that it is in favor of the employees. At a national level, overtime is regulated by a combination of individual employment contracts and collective bargaining agreements.

1. The Classification of Overtime Work

The classification of overtime work can be divided into three categories as "ordinary overtime work", "compulsory overtime work" and "overtime work at the state of emergency". According to the provisions of the Labor Act, the reasons for ordinary overtime work are defined as the general benefits of the country or the reasons such as the need arising from the nature of the work or the need for a rise in production (art. 41/1 of LA).

An overtime work may also be undertaken for compulsory reasons such like either in the case of a breakdown and those, when an actual or potential risk exists, or in the case of urgent work to be performed for the safety of machinery,

176 ILO Information Sheet no. WT-2, dated May 2004.

tools or equipment, or for compelling reasons (art. 42/1 of LA). These cases are defined as compulsory overtime work.[177]

"Overtime work at the state of emergency" is another category prescribed in the Labor Act. If it is deemed necessary to work in such workplaces that meet the requirements of the defense of the country during any mobilization period, the President may expand the daily working duration to the maximum working capacity of the employees according to the type of operations and the degree of need (art. 43/1 of LA).

It is safe to say that ordinary overtime work is routine. Most of the cases depend on the needs arising from the nature of the work or for an increase in the production. Corollary of this, compulsory overtime work and overtime work at the state of emergency are exceptional cases in practice.

2. *The Legal Requirements and the Limits*

The employer, as a rule, cannot unilaterally decide to run overtime work. The approval of the employee is a requisite. In accordance with the Labor Act, the written approval of the employee must be obtained in order to run ordinary overtime work (and work at extra hours) (art. 41/7 of LA). The approval of the employee for overtime work (and work at extra hours) might also be obtained through an employment contract or collective bargaining agreement in advance. However, the consent of the employee is not required to undertake overtime work for the other categories. That is, for compulsory overtime work and overtime work at the state of emergency, the approval of the employee is not sought (art. 42/2 and 43/2 of LA).

For the overtime works requiring approval, the employees who gave their consent at the beginning might, then, give up approving and withdraw their consent by giving written notice to the employer 30 days in advance (art. 9/2 of By-Law Regarding Overtime Work and Work at Extra Hours).

The Labor Act provides for an upper limit for overtime work considering the health and personality of the employees. Accordingly, the sum of the overtime shall not exceed 270 hours in a year. Also, the daily working time cannot exceed 11 hours as a rule (art. 41/8, 63/2 of LA). Furthermore, the workplace physician or the physician of the Social Insurance Institution may prevent some employees

---

177 The distinction between compelling reasons (*force majeure*) and compulsory reasons has ever been controversial in the doctrine, it has particularly sparked new debates in the aftermath of the epidemic. See also, Çelik, Caniklioğlu, and Canbolat, *İş Hukuku Dersleri*, 752, fn. 2617; Süzek, *İş Hukuku*, 810, fn. 30.

from working overtime or at extra hours by prescribing a medical report, even if the employee has already given the approval (art. 8/1, sub-para. (b) of By-Law Regarding Overtime Work and Work at Extra Hours).

There are also additional protective regulations to prevent some of the vulnerable labor groups from working in excessive hours (for the protection of youth and for the protection of miners working underground see, art. 41/9 and 71 of LA; for the protection of night shift employees see also, art. 41/6 of LA).[178]

3. *The Legal Consequences of Overtime Work*

It's important to distinguish between the legal consequences of ordinary overtime work and that of other categories. As a general legal consequence of overtime work, the wage for each hour of overtime is to be paid by a 50 % increase in the amount of normal working wage per hour.[179] For work at extra hours, the wage for each hour of extra work is to be paid by a 25 % increase in the amount of normal working wage per hour (art. 41/2 and 41/3 of LA).

Addition to that, overtime work is not necessarily awarded with monetary payments. The Labor Act allows the employee to exercise leisure time instead of being paid the increased wage in the case of ordinary overtime work. They may also exercise 1 hour and 30 minutes of leisure time (by a 50 % increase for each hour) instead of being paid an increased wage when they undertake overtime work (art. 41/4 of LA).[180] They may also exercise 1 hour and 15 minutes of leisure time if they work at extra hours (by a 25 % increase for each extra hour). The leisure time is granted exclusively upon the request of the employee. To put it another way, the employee has a sole discretion. It suggests that the employer

---

178 ILO has also determined five significant aspects of decent work within the frame of working time, or "decent working time". These five aspects focus on: promoting health and safety; advancing the productivity and sustainability of the enterprises; being "family-friendly" and improving work-life balance; promoting gender equality; and offering workers a degree of choice and influence over their hours of work (See, Guide to developing balanced working time arrangements (Geneva: ILO, 2019), 3 ff.)

179 According to the ILO Hours of Work (Industry) Convention, 1919 (no. 1), the rate of pay for overtime work should not be less than one-and-one-quarter times of the regular rate. Yet, Turkey has not ratified this Convention.

180 In Turkey, the rate of the overtime pay is arranged divergently for the miners working underground. It stipulates that except for compulsory state and the state of emergency, the employees working in underground mine services cannot be undertaken to work overtime; yet, in the event of exceptional cases, they are entitled to overtime pay at least by a 100 % increase for each hour (art. 41/para. 9–10 of LA).

cannot force the employee to exercise leisure time to evade having to pay the increased wage.[181]

While the approval of the employee for overtime work can be obtained in advance by the employer at the beginning of the contract, the declaration of the will stating the choice of the employee to exercise leisure time must be obtained in writing when the necessity for overtime work arises.[182] It is not possible to determine the choice of the employee by a clause within the collective bargaining agreement or employment contract in advance.

For the cases of compulsory overtime work and overtime work at the state of emergency, an increased wage is still to be paid for the employees, yet the employee cannot exercise leisure time instead of receiving an increased wage in return for compulsory overtime work or overtime work at the state of emergency.

II. The Legal Regulations on Rest Periods

Rest periods are periods of time given to the employees for purposes such as meeting their fundamental needs and restoring their physical strength.[183] These periods can be classified as daily, weekly and annual. The right to rest is also enshrined by the Constitution (art. 50) together with the provisions of the Labor Act. The rest periods of the employees, who are subject to the Labor Act, are briefly explained below.

A. Rest Periods

1. Daily Break (Work Break)

Pursuant to the Labor Act, the employees shall be granted a rest break at an average time of daily working time. The length of daily breaks is regulated as follows (art. 68 of LA):

- Fifteen minutes for works lasting 4 hours or less,
- Half an hour for works lasting more than 4 hours and up to seven and a half hours (seven and a half hours inclusive),
- One hour for works lasting more than seven and a half hours,

---

181 Centel, *Turkish Labour Law*, 144; Çelik, Caniklioğlu, and Canbolat, *İş Hukuku Dersleri*, 781 ff.; Dereli, *Labour Law in Turkey*, 151; Süzek, *İş Hukuku*, 830.

182 Süzek, *İş Hukuku*, 830. See also, Çelik, Caniklioğlu, and Canbolat, *İş Hukuku Dersleri*, 782.

183 Çelik, Caniklioğlu, and Canbolat, *İş Hukuku Dersleri*, 786; Ekmekçi and Korkusuz, *Turkish Individual Labour Law*, 94; Süzek, *İş Hukuku*, 834.

These daily breaks are minimum and, as a rule, must be given to employees continuously. However, these periods may be used intermittently by the virtue of contracts or by considering the environmental and seasonal conditions, regional customs and quality of the work (art. 68/2–3 of LA).

The period elapses during daily break is not counted as paid time (the last sentence of art. 68 of LA). However, during the work break, if the employee remains in control of the employer or is maintained ready for any work that might be ordered by the employer, this so-called break shall, then, be counted within the working hours.[184]

2. *Week Holiday*

Week holiday is regulated by a special and separate law issued as the Act on the Week Holiday no. 394. Its scope is also specifically arranged.

For all types of factories, workshops, stalls, shops, stores, offices, commercial enterprises, industrial and commercial establishments in cities with a population of ten thousand or more, it is required to provide 1-day holiday per week. Accordingly, the employees are entitled to a rest period for at least 24 hours without interruption in every 7-day period.

Within the articles of the Act no. 394, Sunday is specifically indicated as week holiday. In general, this rest period is exercised on weekends. Therefore, it is commonly referred to as weekend holiday (paid weekend).[185] Nevertheless, within the scope of service and entertainment industry, employees typically enjoy their week holidays on the weekdays rather than the weekends.

Pursuant to the related provisions, the employees shall be granted at least 24 hours of uninterrupted rest in a 7-day period on condition that they have worked on the working days before the holiday. This period is counted as paid time, the amount paid is referred to as a social wage.[186]

3. *National Holiday and Public Holidays*

There is a special act regulates national holidays and public holidays known as Act on National Holiday and Public Holidays no. 2429.

---

184 Centel, *Turkish Labour Law*, 147; Çelik, Caniklioğlu, and Canbolat, *İş Hukuku Dersleri*, 788; Dereli, *Labour Law in Turkey*, 153; Süzek, *İş Hukuku*, 836.

185 Ekmekçi and Korkusuz, *Turkish Individual Labour Law*, 95. See also, Çelik, Caniklioğlu, and Canbolat, *İş Hukuku Dersleri*, 789 ff.; Süzek, *İş Hukuku*, 838.

186 Centel, *Turkish Labour Law*, 150; Çelik, Caniklioğlu, and Canbolat, *İş Hukuku Dersleri*, 793; Süzek, *İş Hukuku*, 840. See also, Dereli, *Labour Law in Turkey*, 170.

The 29th of October, when the Republic was declared in 1923, is the National Holiday. The official ceremony is held on behalf of the State only for the Republic Day. The national holiday starts on the 28th of October at 13.00 and continues to the 29th of October.

In addition, apart from religious holidays (Eid), 23rd of April, 19th of May, 30th of August, New Year's Day, 1st of May, and 15th of July are counted as public holidays. On the other hand, although contractual arrangements are not forbidden, the legal regulations do not require the employees to be given a bank holiday.

These periods are counted as paid time, the amount paid is referred to as a social wage.[187] On the other hand, the provisions of the special acts of the organizations that are required to work continuously due to their nature are reserved. Private businesses can be exempted from these regulations, yet they are required to close on National Holiday in principle.

B. Annual Paid Leave

The annual paid leave period, in particular, should be highlighted. Also, it is specifically enshrined by the Constitution for the purpose of providing the employees with leisure and recreation time so that they continue to work with the same zeal and efficiency after the rest (art. 50 of the Constitution). It also serves the aim to protect the health and safety of the employees. To such an extent that the employees cannot relinquish this right even on their own initiative (art 53/2 of LA).

1. Length and Entitlement

The employees, who have worked for at least 1 year, including the entire contract duration from the day they begin to work, are granted annual paid leave according to the Labor Act (art. 53/1). The length of the service will be calculated by combining the periods, in which the employee worked in one or several workplaces of the same employer (art. 54/1 of LA).

Annual paid leave period is to be awarded to the employees according to the length of their services as follows (art. 53/4 of LA):

- For those with a service period up to 5 years, the length of annual paid leave cannot be less than 14 days,

187 Centel, *Turkish Labour Law*, 152; Çelik, Caniklioğlu, and Canbolat, *İş Hukuku Dersleri*, 798 ff.; Süzek, *İş Hukuku*, 845. See also, Dereli, *Labour Law in Turkey*, 171–172.

- For those with a service period of at least 5 years, but less than 15 years, the length of annual paid leave cannot be less than 20 days,
- For those with a service period of 15 years and more, the length of annual paid leave cannot be less than 26 days.

However, the length of annual paid leave for those, who are aged 18 and under, as well as those, aged 50 and older, cannot be less than 20 days without regard to their length of service (art. 53/5 of LA). The length of annual paid leave can also be increased with individual employment contracts and collective bargaining agreements (art. 53/6 of LA).

As a rule, the employer should provide the annual paid leave that the employee requested without interruption. Nevertheless, the period of annual paid leave may be divided into a maximum of three parts, provided that one part must not be less than 10 days under the agreement of the parties (art. 56/1–3 of LA). The employer is obliged to keep the records, which demonstrate the schedules of annual paid leaves of the employees working in the workplace (art. 56/6 of LA).

2. *The Conversion of Unused Annual Paid Leaves into Money*

It is hardly needful to remark that even though the employees do not work actually during paid leave, they are entitled to acquire their regular wages. It is why this leave is referred to as paid leave. More precisely, the employer is obliged to pay the wage of this period in cash and in advance (art. 57/1 of LA).

The employees may occasionally offer the employer to work even during paid leave in exchange for getting paid twice as much. The right to paid annual leave is indispensable and inalienable. Therefore, this offer is unacceptable to the employer, and the employee cannot demand to be paid twice times of the regular rate and cannot waive from enjoying this right even by choice.

According to the Labor Act, getting paid a wage instead of taking annual leave is permitted in one situation if it is impossible to exercise this right. In other words, if an employment contract is terminated without annual paid leave being exhausted, the employer is required to pay the appropriate wage only for the unused annual leave after the termination. The wage that corresponds to the period of unused annual leaves does not become demandable and payable until the contract is terminated.[188]

The said wage is calculated based on the wage on the last day of the contract (art. 59/1 of LA). In addition, the prescription period for the wages of unused

---

188 Centel, *Turkish Labour Law*, 157; Çelik, Caniklioğlu, and Canbolat, *İş Hukuku Dersleri*, 816 ff.; Dereli, *Labour Law in Turkey*, 177, 180; Süzek, *İş Hukuku*, 860.

paid leaves commences from the expiry date of the employment contract and it is 5 years (art. 32/8 of LA).

Tab. 11. Commencement of prescription period
The prescription period is similarly 5 years for unpaid wages, but it commences as of the date that the obligation to pay wage become due. For the wage of unused paid leave, on the other hand, the prescription period commences from the expiry date of the employment contract, deviating from the rule for unpaid wages.

III. Legal Regulations on the Change in Working Conditions

If the changes made in the working conditions are within the scope of the employer's right to manage, they are not of substantial nature. The changes that disrupt the balance between the parties to the detriment of one party, in other words, that worsen the working conditions in an extent that the employee cannot be expected to endure, are considered substantial.[189] As a rule, the changes in the workplace, wage or in the description of job are substantial in nature.[190]

Substantial changes to be made in working conditions based on the employment contract or in conditions attached to the contract arising from internal regulations or entrenched workplace practices can only be implemented after the employee receives a written proposal from the employer and approves them in accordance with the manner required by the law.

More precisely if there is a substantial change, the employee must approve these changes in written form and within 6 working days after receiving the written proposal. The changes that are not in conformity with this procedure and not approved by the employees shall not bind the employees (art. 22/1 of LA). It means that employee's silence cannot be construed as an implicit approval. In case of rejection (or that of silence of the employee) the contract remains the same as before.[191] In other words, the proposal of substantial change cannot affect the contract on its own. Also, a general announcement to the employees for substantial changes will not be sufficient.[192] The employer must inform each

189 Çelik, Caniklioğlu, and Canbolat, *İş Hukuku Dersleri*, 611 ff.; Süzek, *İş Hukuku*, 673.

190 Çelik, Caniklioğlu, and Canbolat, *İş Hukuku Dersleri*, 613.

191 Çelik, Caniklioğlu, and Canbolat, *İş Hukuku Dersleri*, 615; Dereli, *Labour Law in Turkey*, 211; Süzek, *İş Hukuku*, 680.

192 Çelik, Caniklioğlu, and Canbolat, *İş Hukuku Dersleri*, 616; Dereli, *Labour Law in Turkey*, 211; Süzek, *İş Hukuku*, 680.

individual employee in person with the written proposal for substantial changes. This is a general rule that applies to all employees covered by the Labor Act, regardless of whether they have employment security.

Substantial changes in working conditions may be made only upon the consent of the employee. Under the provisions of the Labor Act, the employee is entitled to terminate the employment contract with just cause, if the employer insists on not implementing unchanged working conditions in force without regards to get the approval of the employee.

On the other hand, if the employee does not accept the proposal for change within this period, the employer may terminate the contract by observing the notice period. Yet, in this respect, there is a difference between the employees with employment security and employees without that. The employer can terminate the contract of an employee, who has employment security, provided that it was declared in written form indicating that the proposed change was based on a valid reason or there was another valid reason for termination.[193]

It must be remembered that the changes that are not substantial can be amended without this procedure observed.[194] By mutual agreement, the contracting parties may always change working conditions. Yet, the changes in working conditions cannot be retroactive (art. 22/2 of LA).

§ Part IV Termination of the Employment Contract

Even though it is the most common way, termination is not the only way for the extinction of an employment contract; extinction of contract other than termination is also of importance. Accordingly, the cases that cease the contractual relationship are to be examined under two groups:

- Extinction other than termination: Death of employee, another agreement as to the dissolution of the contract (extinction by agreement), the expiration of definite term, etc.
- Extinction by termination of the contract.

193 Dereli, *Labour Law in Turkey*, 211; Süral and Kılıçoğlu, "Labor Law," 172. Cf. Süzek, *İş Hukuku*, 686.

194 Çelik, Caniklioğlu, and Canbolat, *İş Hukuku Dersleri*, 612; Süzek, *İş Hukuku*, 673.

I. Extinction Other than Termination

A. *Extinction by Agreement* (İkale)

As in the other private law contracts, the employment contract may also be extinct by an agreement between the previous contracting parties. The parties hereby conclude another contract with the aim of eliminating the before-founded contractual relationship between them. Such an agreement cannot be legally considered as a way of termination since it is bilateral.

In other words, termination is a process that enables the contractual relationship dissolved by a unilateral declaration of one of the parties. It is not subject to the approval of the counterparty. However, an agreement as to the extinction of the employment contract requires bilateral compromise.[195] That is a different legal way from the termination process. In practice, extinction by agreement rather than termination may have some drawbacks for the employees. Some principles have been adopted by the Court of Cassation and have become entrenched over time, since this type of agreement is not constrained by the Labor Act.[196]

On the other hand, it is also possible to end one or more of the obligations arising from the employment contract by an agreement of the contracting parties. This is distinct from extinction of the entire contract by mutual assent. This type of agreement (on release from obligations) is not regulated in the Labor Act, but in Turkish Code of Obligations that entered into force in July of 2012 (art. 420). Before 2012, several principles were adopted by precedent rulings of Court of Cassation also on this issue.[197] However, after 2012, the article 420 of TCO lays down explicit and strictly defined requirements for a valid agreement on the extinction of an obligation arising from an employment contract.[198]

---

195 Çelik, Caniklioğlu, and Canbolat, *İş Hukuku Dersleri*, 460 ff.; Dereli, *Labour Law in Turkey*, 184; Ekmekçi and Korkusuz, *Turkish Individual Labour Law*, 103; Süzek, *İş Hukuku*, 517 ff.

196 Çelik, Caniklioğlu, and Canbolat, *İş Hukuku Dersleri*, 462; Ekmekçi and Korkusuz, *Turkish Individual Labour Law*, 104; Süzek, *İş Hukuku*, 519. See also, Turkish Court of Cassation, 9th Civil Chamber decision, dated 14.09.2015, no. 17239/25415, *Çalışma ve Toplum Dergisi*, 51/4 (2016); 22th Civil Chamber decision, dated. 03.02.2014, no. 402/1341, *Çalışma ve Toplum Dergisi*, 41/2 (2014). For further information see also, Muhittin Astarlı, *İş Hukukunda İkale* (Ankara, Turhan, 2016).

197 Çelik, Caniklioğlu, and Canbolat, *İş Hukuku Dersleri*, 685; Süzek, *İş Hukuku*, 793.

198 Çelik, Caniklioğlu, and Canbolat, *İş Hukuku Dersleri*, 686 ff.; Süzek, *İş Hukuku*, 794 ff.; Süral and Kılıçoğlu, "Labor Law," 173. For further information see also, Şahin Çil, *İş Hukukunda İbraname* (Ankara: Yetkin, 2013).

It is hereby important to note that it is possible for the parties to cease a contractual relationship entirely or a specific obligation arising from this root with the mutual assent provided that they observe the constraints adopted by precedent rulings, or legal requirements stated in the article 420 of TCO.

B. *Expiration of Specific Period (for Definite Term Contracts)*

A definite term contract shall automatically be extinct by the expiry of the period indicated by the parties when the contract was concluded. As a rule, no further legal action is required for the extinction of those contracts that have been concluded for a specific period. Therefore, the expiration of such a contract cannot be legally regarded as a way of termination.[199]

C. *The Death of the Employee*

Although, as a rule, the death of the employer does not result in the extinction of the employment contract, the death of the employee necessarily leads to this consequence (art. 440 of TCO).[200] Since the personality of the employee is of particular importance, the employee cannot delegate their obligation to perform a job to another person (or to legal successors). As a result, if the employee dies, the employment contract becomes extinct.

On the other hand, if the employer dies, the contract, as a rule, continues with the decedent's legal successors (art. 441/1 of TCO). However, personal care service obligations cease upon the death of the employer as a notable exception to this rule.[201] In other words, if the employment contract is based on the employer's personality and it is important to whom the employee is caring, then as an exception, the employment contract is regarded extinct when the employer is dead in such a case (art. 441/2 of TCO).

---

199 Centel, *Turkish Labour Law*, 170 ff.; Çelik, Caniklioğlu, and Canbolat, *İş Hukuku Dersleri*, 471; Dereli, *Labour Law in Turkey*, 185–186; Süzek, *İş Hukuku*, 519.

200 Centel, *Turkish Labour Law*, 170; Çelik, Caniklioğlu, and Canbolat, *İş Hukuku Dersleri*, 468; Dereli, *Labour Law in Turkey*, 185; Ekmekçi and Korkusuz, *Turkish Individual Labour Law*, 105; Süzek, *İş Hukuku*, 521.

201 Centel, *Turkish Labour Law*, 170; Çelik, Caniklioğlu, and Canbolat, *İş Hukuku Dersleri*, 471; Dereli, *Labour Law in Turkey*, 185; Ekmekçi and Korkusuz, *Turkish Individual Labour Law*, 105.

II. Extinction by Termination of the Contract

According to the general principles, the contracting parties have the right to terminate the contract without the counterparty's approval or consent. Termination is a right that allows each of parties to end a contract with a unilateral declaration of will.[202] However, the party terminating the contract must serve to the counterparty a termination notice. As a result, termination declaration allows the employment contract to be ended either after a certain period (termination notice) or immediately (summary dismissal).

Thereby, types of termination can be divided into two groups: "Immediate termination with just cause (summary dismissal)" and "termination at will". The circumstances of termination with just cause are those, in which the declaration of termination produces instant results as soon as it reaches the counterparty. Termination at will, on the other hand, means that after a certain waiting period has lapsed, the contract will be regarded terminated.

A. Termination with Just Cause

It is noteworthy that the right to terminate the contract with just cause is possible both for definite (fixed) term contracts and indefinite-term contracts. The right to terminate the contract with just cause is also granted to both the employee and the employer without regard to the type of the employment contract.

Those circumstances that the parties cannot be expected to continue the contractual relationship in accordance with the principle of good faith are defined as reasons for termination with just cause.[203] These reasons for termination with just cause are stipulated separately for the employee and the employer in line with the twin provisions of the Labor Act (art. 24 and 25). Then each of the articles regulates just causes by classifying them into three circumstances such as cases of health concerns, cases of immoral, dishonorable or malicious conduct, and cases of compelling reasons (*force majeure*).

---

202 Centel, *Turkish Labour Law*, 171; Çelik, Caniklioğlu, and Canbolat, *İş Hukuku Dersleri*, 477; Süzek, *İş Hukuku*, 522 ff.; Süral and Kılıçoğlu, "Labor Law," 168.

203 Süzek, *İş Hukuku*, 691 ff. See also, Centel, *Turkish Labour Law*, 185; Çelik, Caniklioğlu, and Canbolat, *İş Hukuku Dersleri*, 626; Dereli, *Labour Law in Turkey*, 212 ff.

1. *The Cases for Termination with Just Cause for the Employee (art. 24 of LA)*

In such cases, the employee may terminate the employment contract before the expiry of the period if it is a definite (fixed) term contract, or without observing any notification period if it is an indefinite term contract.

a. *Cases of health concerns*

In the following situations, the employee has the right to terminate the contract immediately due to health concerns:

If the employee's health or life is jeopardized as a result of the nature of the job agreed upon in the contract, or if the employer, their representatives, or another employee who is regularly near the employee contracts an infectious disease or a disease incompatible with the designated work, the employee is no longer required to give notice period in such cases.

b. *Cases of immoral, dishonorable, or malicious conduct, and alike*

The second group is the cases that do not comply with the principle of good faith and morals and resemble these reasons. Accordingly, the employee may terminate the contract immediately in the following cases:

- If the employer misleads the employee by stating the conditions of work incorrectly or by giving the employee false information concerning any essential point of the contract when the contract concluded, only if this deception is related to the essential (substantial) terms of the contract (art. 24/II, sub-para. a), the employee may terminate the contract immediately.
  However, the misinformation or staying speechless regarding less significant matters (such as secondary terms) that will not lead to the deception cannot result in the termination of the contract with just cause.
- If the employer is guilty of any speech or action committing an offense against the honor or reputation of the employee or a member of the employee's family, or if the employer harasses the employee sexually (art. 24/II, sub-para. b).
- If the employer harasses or intimidates the employee or a member of the employee's family, or encourages, incites, or compels the employee or a member of the employee's family to act against the law, or if the employer commits a crime that requires imprisonment against the employee and a member of the employee's family, or if the employer makes unfounded, grave accusations against the employee that jeopardize the employee's honor and dignity (art. 24/II, sub-para. c).

- When the employee is exposed to sexual harassment within the workplace by another employee or third parties, and despite reporting it to the employer, if the employer fails to take the necessary measures (art. 24/II, sub-para. d).
- If the employer fails to calculate or pay the employee's wage in accordance with the law or the terms of the contract (art. 24/II, sub-para. e).
- In cases where it is determined to be paid the wage per piece or per the amount of work, and the employer gives the employee less work/piece than they are able to do, if the wage discrepancy is not compensated on a time basis by the employer, and if the working conditions are not applied (art. 24/II, sub-para. f).

As is obvious, each of those cases that enable the employee to terminate the contract immediately mainly focus on acts of gross misconduct. When the employer commits such conduct, it destroys the trust between the contracting parties.[204]

c. Cases of compelling reasons (force majeure)

Compelling reasons arise out of circumstances that are other than the defect of the counterparty; however, they force the party to terminate the contract. These cases are not explicitly enumerated in the Labor Act.

If there are any compelling reasons that will require the work to be ceased for more than 1 week at the place of employment, the employee may terminate the contract immediately. Floods, earthquakes, etc. may be defined as compelling reasons.[205]

It's worth mentioning that the right to terminate does not exist during the first week after the cessation of work. For the first week, a suspension period is required, and the contract can be terminated neither immediately nor by following notice periods by the employee. The employee can terminate the employment contract immediately only if the cessation of work lasts longer than a week.[206]

---

204 Çelik, Caniklioğlu, and Canbolat, *İş Hukuku Dersleri*, 628; Süzek, *İş Hukuku*, 691. See also, Centel, *Turkish Labour Law*, 185.

205 Centel, *Turkish Labour Law*, 189; Çelik, Caniklioğlu, and Canbolat, *İş Hukuku Dersleri*, 636; Dereli, *Labour Law in Turkey*, 214; Ekmekçi and Korkusuz, *Turkish Individual Labour Law*, 115; Süzek, *İş Hukuku*, 714.

206 Dereli, *Labour Law in Turkey*, 169; Ekmekçi and Korkusuz, *Turkish Individual Labour Law*, 115; Süzek, *İş Hukuku*, 508. On the other hand, if another just cause occurs during the suspension period, then the employee may terminate the contract based on this emerging situation. See also, Süzek, *İş Hukuku*, 513.

2. *The Cases for Termination with Just Cause for the Employer (art. 25 of LA)*

The employer's right to terminate the contract with just cause is regulated slightly different in the Labor Act. As is in the preceding article, the employer may terminate the employment contract immediately before the end of the fixed term if it is a definite term contract or without observing the notification period if it is an indefinite term contract in the following cases.

Similar to the reasons for the employee, the reasons for the employer are also gathered in three main groups:

a. *Cases of health concerns*

- If it is determined by the Health Committee that the employee's disease is incurable and it is inconvenient for the employee to continue work in the workplace, the employer may terminate the contract immediately (art. 25/I, sub-para. b).
- It is also possible for the employee to be contracted a disease due to their own intent or loose living or dipsomania. If the employee, who has contracted the disease due to such reasons, does not continue to work for 3 consecutive working days or more than 5 working days in a month, the employer may terminate the employment contract immediately (art. 25/I, sub-para. a).

However, in some cases the employee may be unable to continue working owing to a disease or an accident even though the concrete example does not fall within one of the above-mentioned circumstances. In such circumstances, the employer must provide the employee with a period of time before initiating the immediate termination process. Accordingly, this (suspension) period is to be calculated by adding 6 weeks to the notice period of the given employee, which will be determined by their seniority. Even after this period has expired, if the employee still cannot recover and return to work, then the employer may terminate the employment contract immediately.[207]

- That is to say, in cases of absenteeism due to a disease or accident which are not attributable to the cases stated in the article 25/I, sub-para. a, the employer

---

It must be noted that during this period for one week, the employee is paid half wages according to the article 40 of the Labor Act.

207 Çelik, Caniklioğlu, and Canbolat, *İş Hukuku Dersleri*, 638; Süzek, *İş Hukuku*, 693. See also, Ekmekçi and Korkusuz, *Turkish Individual Labour Law*, 115 ff.

is entitled to terminate the contract with just cause, only if recovery from the illness or injury continues for more than 6 weeks beyond the notice periods.

In addition, for female employees, the diseases caused by pregnancy or by confinement (during postpartum) are specially regulated. In this case, the duration of maternity leave granted to the female employee shall be added to abovementioned suspension period. In other words, only after these periods (the whole period granted to her for notice period + the maternity leave period + 6 weeks), if she is still unable to return to the work, then the employer may terminate the contract immediately.[208]

b. Cases of immoral, dishonorable, or malicious conduct, and alike

Similar to the causes of termination for the employee, the second group is the cases that do not comply with the principle of good faith and morals and resemble these reasons. The employer may terminate the contract immediately if the following cases are present:

- If the employee misleads the employer by making incorrect statements or by misinforming the employer that they pretend to have requisite qualifications or conditions for one of the essential terms of the contract, even though they have not them when the contract concluded (art. 25/II, sub-para. a), the employer may then terminate the contract immediately.
  It should be noted that it is only the case if the misleading the employer (by the employee) is related to the essential (substantial) terms of the contract and only if the employee remains silent while the rule of good faith requires them to speak.[209] Misleading or misinformation regarding the issues other than essential points does not grant the employer the right to terminate the contract immediately, and neither does it provide the employee such a right.
- If the employee is guilty of any speech or action committing an offense against the honor or reputation of the employer or a member of the employer's family, or if the employee makes unfounded, grave accusations against the employer that jeopardize the employer's honor and dignity (art. 25/II, sub-para. b).

---

208 See also, Ekmekçi and Korkusuz, *Turkish Individual Labour Law*, 116; Süzek, *İş Hukuku*, 693. Cf. Centel, *Turkish Labour Law*, 190.

209 Centel, *Turkish Labour Law*, 190; Çelik, Caniklioğlu, and Canbolat, *İş Hukuku Dersleri*, 640; Süzek, *İş Hukuku*, 694.

- If the employee sexually harasses another employee of the employer (art. 25/II, sub-para. c).
- If the employee harasses the employer, a member of the employer's family, or a fellow employee in the workplace (that is to say, such behavior towards other employees may also lead to the termination with just cause by the employer), or if the employee arrives the workplace drunk or taken narcotics or uses these substances within the workplace (art. 25/II, sub-para. d).
- If the employee commits a dishonest act against the employer, such as a breach of trust, theft or disclosure of the employer's trade secrets (art. 25/II, sub-para. e).
- If the employee commits a crime within the premises of the workplace, which is punishable with 7 days or more imprisonment without probation (art. 25/II, sub-para. f).
- If the employee is absent from work for two consecutive working days or three days within 1 month, or the next working day after rest periods twice in a month, without any justification or permission from the employer (art. 25/II, sub-para. g).
- If the employee insists on not performing the duties assigned to do, despite being reminded and cautioned (art. 25/II, sub-para. h).
- Either deliberately or through negligence, if the employee endangers safety of the workplace or damages machinery, equipment or other tools or materials in their care, and only if the damage cannot be compensated by their 30-day wage (art. 25/II, sub-para. ı).

In such cases, the employer cannot be expected to continue the contract.[210] Insomuch that it is not aimed to protect the contractual relationship even throughout the notice period. The employer may terminate the contract immediately without observing the notice periods but observing the time limit stated in the article 26 of the Labor Act.

c. Cases of compelling reasons (force majeure)

The occurrence of a circumstance that prevents the employee from working in the workplace for more than 1 week is a compelling reason for the employer to terminate the contract immediately.[211] Also, in case that the employee is detained

210 For further information see also, Centel, *Turkish Labour Law*, 192–193; Çelik, Caniklioğlu, and Canbolat, *İş Hukuku Dersleri*, 640 ff.; Süzek, *İş Hukuku*, 694 ff.

211 It must be noted that the employee is paid half wages for one week also in this case (art. 40 of LA). See also, Centel, *Turkish Labour Law*, 195.

or arrested, if absenteeism exceeds the suspension period, the employer may terminate the contract immediately. In this case, the suspension period will be so long as the employee's notice period, which will be determined by their seniority.[212]

As a result, if the employee commits a crime on the premises of the workplace, which is punishable with 7 days or more imprisonment without probation, the employer may terminate the contract immediately for the reasons based on the cases against rule of good faith (namely, on the cases of immoral, dishonorable or malicious conduct). If, on the other hand, the employee has been taken into custody or arrested (regardless of whether within the workplace premises), and their absence from work exceeds the notice periods, the employer may terminate the contract immediately for compelling reasons.

3. *The Procedure for Termination with Just Causes*

According to the article 26 of the Labor Act, the right to terminate the contract with just cause based on immoral, dishonorable or malicious conduct or other similar behaviors (art. 24/II and 25/II) should be exercised within the time limit.[213] For these cases, the right to terminate must be exercised within 6 working days both for the employee and the employer.

The time limit to exercise this right for each party expires after 6 working days as of the date, on which the party has learned of that the counterparty has conducted in this manner (basic period), and it expires in any case 1 year after the conduct has occurred (ultimate period). However, if the employee gains material benefits owing to their immoral, dishonorable or malicious conduct, a 1-year (ultimate) period shall not be applied.

On the other hand, any time limit has not been stipulated by the Labor Act for the cases of termination based on other paragraphs (for the paragraphs of I and III).[214] This cannot be construed that there are no restrictions for the cases other than the conducts that violate the principle of good faith and morals; the parties should also exercise the right to terminate the contract with just cause within a reasonable period in any other case.

---

212 However, the employee is not entitled the right to claim half wages for suspension period in case of absenteeism due to arrest or detention. See, Süzek, *İş Hukuku*, 707.

213 Centel, *Turkish Labour Law*, 196; Çelik, Caniklioğlu, and Canbolat, *İş Hukuku Dersleri*, 672; Dereli, *Labour Law in Turkey*, 221; Ekmekçi and Korkusuz, *Turkish Individual Labour Law*, 118; Süzek, *İş Hukuku*, 715.

214 Çelik, Caniklioğlu, and Canbolat, *İş Hukuku Dersleri*, 672; Süzek, *İş Hukuku*, 716. Contrary, Centel, *Turkish Labour Law*, 196.

Tab. 12. Appraise of the presence of a just cause
The employers may claim that they have terminated the contract with just cause and proceed to terminate the contract immediately. As is obvious, the evaluation of the employer on the presence of a just cause is not binding for the courts. The court, therefore, is to appraise whether, in fact, a just cause is present in the concrete case or not.

The difference between the just cause and the valid reason is based on their effects on the contractual relationship. Just causes are severe enough that they exceed the gravity of valid reasons. If the employment relationship has become unsustainable and the basis for trust in the contractual relationship has completely collapsed, the right to terminate the employment contract with just cause shall be granted to both parties. Under these circumstances, the parties cannot be expected to continue the contractual relationship even for the period of notice.[215]

B. Unjust Termination

The party terminated the employment contract with just cause is obliged to prove their claim, as a rule. In other words, the burden of proof lies with the party terminating the contract. The party, who is under the burden of proof, might withstand all kinds of evidence.

On the other hand, an unjust termination will occur if the employee or the employer terminates the employment contract immediately without the presence of above-mentioned circumstances, or even though one of these circumstances presents, if the contract is terminated after the time limit has expired.[216]

Since the termination process differs for the employees who are covered by employment security system, an unjust termination is a case for employment relationships that are excluded from employment security. An unjust termination may be a case also in a definite term employment contract: For instance, an unjust termination might occur if the employee or the employer terminates a definite term contract before the expiry date claiming that one of the aforementioned circumstances existed, even though it did not.

215 For further information see also, Süzek, *İş Hukuku*, 555 ff.; 584 ff.

216 Çelik, Caniklioğlu, and Canbolat, *İş Hukuku Dersleri*, 674; Süzek, *İş Hukuku*, 725. See also, Centel, *Turkish Labour Law*, 198 ff.

Under the 1st paragraph of the article 438 of TCO, if the employer terminates the contract without a just cause, the employee is entitled to compensation equal to the wage for the notification period in the employment contracts with an indefinite term. In the employment contracts with a definite term, the employee is entitled to compensation equal to the wage for the remaining period. Furthermore, the 3rd paragraph of the article states that the judge may appraise a compensation of up to 6 months' wages depending on the unique characteristic of concrete case. The article 439 of TCO, on the other hand, regulates the unjust termination of the employee.

It should be noted that the articles regulating compensation for unjust termination have relatively a broad application for the definite term contracts in practice.[217]

C. Termination at Will

Termination at will is a right that enables both parties to terminate the employment contract unilaterally provided that to notify the counterparty and to observe the designated period. As a rule, only indefinite term contracts are subjected to the termination by the way of observing notice period.[218] In other words, as a rule, for the occurrence of the right to terminate the contract at will both for the employer and the employee, the existence of an indefinite term contract is necessary and sufficient.[219]

1. The Notice (Notification) Period

The party, who wills to terminate a contract, does not need to wait for the occurrence of a just cause, yet it is obliged to wait for a specific period known as the notice (notification) period. In case of an employment contract with indefinite term, the declaration as to the termination must be notified to the counterparty before a certain period (the art. 17 of LA). According to the article, employment contracts are deemed terminated after the following periods:

---

217 Cf. Çelik, Caniklioğlu, and Canbolat, *İş Hukuku Dersleri*, 674, fn. 2264; Süzek, *İş Hukuku*, 726 ff.

218 Centel, *Turkish Labour Law*, 172; Çelik, Caniklioğlu, and Canbolat, *İş Hukuku Dersleri*, 484; Dereli, *Labour Law in Turkey*, 188; Ekmekçi and Korkusuz, *Turkish Individual Labour Law*, 106 ff.; Süzek, *İş Hukuku*, 524; Süral and Kılıçoğlu, "Labor Law," 169.

219 It should be remembered that this right is limited in case of employment security for the employers. Under this part, also see infra: *Termination of the Contract in Case of Employment Security.*

- two weeks following the notification for the employees who have worked for less than 6 months.
- four weeks following the notification for the employees who have worked between 6 months to one and a half years,
- six weeks following the notification for the employees who have worked between one and a half years to 3 years,
- eight weeks following the notification for the employees who have worked for more than 3 years.

The terminations made in compliance with these periods are defined as "lawful termination" in practice.[220] On the other hand, in case of an unlawful termination, that is, terminations made without complying with the notice period, the party who fails to observe the notice period shall compensate for their failure. In practice, compensation payable for the unlawful termination notices is referred to as "notice pay" (notice compensation). Even though in the cases of the absence of specific loss, such as when the employee immediately finds a new job or when a new employee immediately replaces the resigned employee, the affected party may claim the notice pay from the counterparty, who failed to adhere to the notice period.[221]

Accordingly, the employee has right to claim a compensation equal to their wages that would have accrued up to the end of the notice period in case the employer fails to terminate the contract by observing the notice period. Likewise, in case the employee fails to terminate the contract by observing due period, the employer has the right to claim a compensation from the employee equal to the employee's wage that would have accrued up to the end of the notice period if the employee had worked. In other words, the notice pay is a compensation paid to the party, who has been exposed to unlawful termination, by the counterparty, who does not comply with the required procedure.[222]

In practice, when the employer terminates the employment contract, they pay notice pay in advance and in cash, which relieves them of having to observe the notice period. It is stipulated by law and requires a payment in full by the employer (art. 17/para. 5 of LA). It should be highlighted that the right to terminate the

---

220 Süzek, *İş Hukuku*, 539.

221 Centel, *Turkish Labour Law*, 176; Çelik, Caniklioğlu, and Canbolat, *İş Hukuku Dersleri*, 495; Dereli, *Labour Law in Turkey*, 193; Süzek, *İş Hukuku*, 540.

222 Centel, *Turkish Labour Law*, 175 ff.; Çelik, Caniklioğlu, and Canbolat, *İş Hukuku Dersleri*, 485; Dereli, *Labour Law in Turkey*, 193 ff.; Süzek, *İş Hukuku*, 539; Süral and Kılıçoğlu, "Labor Law," 169.

employment contract by upfront payment of notice pay rather than waiting until the end of the notice period is granted to the employers alone.[223]

Tab. 13. The effect of notice period on the contractual relationship
During the notice period, the employment contract continues as an obligation relationship as it was before. During this period, both the employer and the employee are required to perform all obligations resulting from the employment contract.[b] In course of notice period, if a just cause for immediate termination arises for one of the parties; this party may terminate the contract immediately, before the end of notice period. The beginning of the notice period does not preclude the right to terminate the contract with just cause. [b] See also, Süzek, *İş Hukuku*, 532; Dereli, *Labour Law in Turkey*, 190 ff.

Regardless of which party notifies the counterparty of the termination, permission for seeking a new job must be granted to the employee without deduction from their wages accrued up during notice period.[224] The duration of this permit cannot be less than 2 hours a day and cannot combine with another paid holiday (art. 27/para. 1 of LA). If the employer fails to give the employee this permit, they shall pay the employee's wage with 100 % increase in addition to the wage the employee would have earned even without working (art. 27/para. 3 of LA).[225]

2. *Malevolence Compensation (In the Case of Abusive Termination)*

In principle, the employer is not obliged to assert to the employee any reason for their decision on termination at will when the employees are not covered by the employment security system. On the other hand, there may have been employer decisions derived from malevolence within the termination process. In this case, the gravity of the misconduct by the employer is of importance. If the decision of

223 Centel, *Turkish Labour Law*, 175; Çelik, Caniklioğlu, and Canbolat, *İş Hukuku Dersleri*, 492 ff.; Dereli, *Labour Law in Turkey*, 192; Ekmekçi and Korkusuz, *Turkish Individual Labour Law*, 107; Süzek, *İş Hukuku*, 536; Süral and Kılıçoğlu, "Labor Law," 169.

224 Çelik, Caniklioğlu, and Canbolat, *İş Hukuku Dersleri*, 490 ff.; Ekmekçi and Korkusuz, *Turkish Individual Labour Law*, 107, 126; Süzek, *İş Hukuku*, 533. Cf. Centel, *Turkish Labour Law*, 174.

225 For the discussion on the difference between the wording of 2nd and 3rd paragraphs of the article 27 see, Çelik, Caniklioğlu, and Canbolat, *İş Hukuku Dersleri*, 492; Süzek, *İş Hukuku*, 535.

the employer amounts to malevolent conduct, the employees, who are excluded from employment security, are entitled to malevolence compensation.[226]

Accordingly, if the employer terminates the employment contract in a violation of the principle of good faith, it causes the abuse of right to terminate the contract and the employer is, then, obliged to pay three times the amount of notice pay (art. 17/para. 6 of LA). In practice, the former is referred to as "abusive termination" and the latter as "malevolence compensation". In addition to the malevolence compensation, if the employer, who has terminated the contract in malevolent conduct, did not comply with the notice period at the same time, the employer must also compensate the notice pay, which is a sanction for non-compliance with the notice period alone.[227]

It is notable that the same is not true for the employees who abuse their right to terminate the contract. That is to say, the employer cannot claim such compensation on the grounds that the employee abused the right to terminate the contract.[228]

On the other hand, the burden of proof regarding the presence of malevolence in the termination process is incumbent on the employee. Since the presence of goodwill is rule and malevolence is exception.[229]

III. Termination of the Contract in Case of Employment Security

Employment security is a system that aims to protect the confidence of employees on they will remain in employment life and to provide them with a shield of protection against the risk of income variations as a result of job loss.[230] ILO has also offered its members various instruments for employment protection legislation, and specifically adopted a convention known as "C158 Termination of Employment Convention", which has been also ratified by Turkey.[231]

---

226 Çelik, Caniklioğlu, and Canbolat, *İş Hukuku Dersleri*, 500; Dereli, *Labour Law in Turkey*, 195; Süzek, *İş Hukuku*, 543. See also, Süral and Kılıçoğlu, "Labor Law," 169–170.

227 Çelik, Caniklioğlu, and Canbolat, *İş Hukuku Dersleri*, 501; Ekmekçi and Korkusuz, *Turkish Individual Labour Law*, 129; Süzek, *İş Hukuku*, 544.

228 However, the employers may claim for compensation based on rule of good faith and general principles of TCO. See also, Centel, *Turkish Labour Law*, 176 ff.; Süzek, *İş Hukuku*, 549.

229 Süzek, *İş Hukuku*, 551. See also, Çelik, Caniklioğlu, and Canbolat, *İş Hukuku Dersleri*, 501; Dereli, *Labour Law in Turkey*, 195.

230 See also, Dereli, *Labour Law in Turkey*, 198 ff.; Ekmekçi and Korkusuz, *Turkish Individual Labour Law*, 108 ff.

231 OJ, 18.06.1994, no. 21964.

Accordingly, the employment security system was introduced into Turkish law in 2002, and the relevant provisions are gradually revised on a large scale since the current Labor Act was enacted (in 2003).[232] What counts here is that the procedure for the termination of the employment contract of employees covered by employment security has been regulated in an extensively different way.

For those, who are out of the scope of employment security, the only limitation on the employer's right to terminate the contract is the prohibition on the abuse of this right (the prohibition on malevolence in termination). In case of absence of employment security, as a rule, it is sufficient for the employer to inform the employee of the termination of the contract and to pursue the employment relationship for a certain period.[233]

On the other hand, the procedure for dismissal of the employees, who are covered by employment security, is subjected to the certain rules. Thus, by this system, the employer's freedom to terminate a contract is more restricted compared to the dismissal of employees excluded from employment security. In order for the occurrence of the right to terminate, a valid reason must arise in case of employment security. Additionally, it must be noted that the legal constraints on the termination of employment contract in this scope are only applicable for the termination at the initiative of the employer.

By the provisions of employment security, the birth of the employer's right to terminate the contract has been linked with the existence of valid reasons. The Labor Act introduces certain rules regarding the termination procedure and imposes the burden of proof on the employer, who claims the existence of a valid reason. The Act also stipulates a special process for reinstatement in case of invalid termination.

A. *The Requirements for Employment Security*

1. *Exclusion of Certain Categories of the Employees or the Enterprises*

The provisions of employment security do not contain rules that are applicable to every employee and every enterprise without any exception. Although the aim is to cover as many employees as possible, the employment security system

232 Çelik, Caniklioğlu, and Canbolat, *İş Hukuku Dersleri*, 509 ff.; Süzek, *İş Hukuku*, 555. For further information see, Fevzi Demir, *En Son Yargıtay Kararları Işığında İş Hukuku ve Uygulaması* (İzmir: Albi, 2018).

233 Centel, *Turkish Labour Law*, 177; Çelik, Caniklioğlu, and Canbolat, *İş Hukuku Dersleri*, 507; Süzek, *İş Hukuku*, 552 ff.; Süral and Kılıçoğlu, "Labor Law," 169.

only exists under certain conditions (see, art. 18 of LA). In order to benefit from employment security, the following requirements are to be met:

to be an employee covered by the Labor Act or the Press Labor Act As mentioned in the previous parts, there are several acts in effect regarding employment relationships, and each of them has specific coverage. The provisions on employment security are regulated within the Labor Act. Therefore, employment security is applicable for the cases within its coverage if the other requirements are also available. Additionally, by means of a special provision in the Press Labor Act (art. 6), it is also applicable for the cases within the coverage of the Press Labor Act.

to be employed in the workplaces employing at least 30 employees According to this requirement, the feature of the enterprise is also important. Small-sized enterprises (such as some of SMEs) that employ less than 30 employees are excluded.[234] Of the calculation, all employees working in the workplaces of the employer that are in the same branch of activity are taken into consideration. For instance, those employees that are on sick leave or maternity leave are included in the total number of the employees. However, persons such as apprentices, trainees, and the employees of the sub-contractor are not considered since they are not the employees of the given employer or any other employer.

to be an employee, who has at least six months of seniority For the determination of the seniority of at least 6 months, the entire period during which the employment contract continues shall be taken into account. If the employee works intermittently with the same employer or if they have worked in different workplaces of the same employer, the periods spent are counted together.[235] This condition is not required for those working underground (art. 18/1 of LA).

to be an employee, who works under an indefinite term employment contract The employees, who work under a definite term contract, cannot benefit from employment security. In other words, employment security is granted to the employees working under indefinite term contract solely.

---

234 For the criticism of this requirement see also, Centel, *Turkish Labour Law*, 177; Çelik, Caniklioğlu, and Canbolat, *İş Hukuku Dersleri*, 513–514; Süzek, *İş Hukuku*, 559. Cf. Dereli, *Labour Law in Turkey*, 199; Süral and Kılıçoğlu, "Labor Law," 169.

235 However, the decisions of different chambers of Court of Cassation on the calculation of seniority are inconsistent. See also, Çelik, Caniklioğlu, and Canbolat, *İş Hukuku Dersleri*, 522; Süzek, *İş Hukuku*, 565.

to not be such an employers' representative that is excluded In order to benefit from employment security, the employee should not be one of the certain types of the employer's representative. In accordance with the Labor Act, the provisions of employment security shall not be applied to either the employers' representatives and their assistants who direct and manage the whole enterprise; or the employers' representatives, who direct and manage the whole of the workplace (not the enterprise) provided that having the authority to hire and dismiss the employees.

Accordingly, those, who manage the whole workplace but do not have the authority to hire and dismiss the employees, are not excluded from employment security such as the branch managers of banks.[236] As another example, the personnel managers or managers of human resources, who are authorized to hire or dismiss the employees, are covered by employment security since they do not have the authority to manage the whole of the workplace. In summary, not every employer representative, but specific employer representatives with certain qualifications are excluded from employment security. Others shall benefit from employment security if they meet the other requirements.[237]

In addition, the authority to hire and dismiss employees must be a real authority, not a symbolic alone. That is to say, if the represented employer decides who will be hired and be dismissed at the final stage, it means the approval of the employer is required for the recruitment, and the authority of the representative is a dependent competence. As a result, these representatives who do not have such independent authority (autonomy) are not excluded.[238]

2. *Justification for Termination and Invalid Reasons*

Employees with these qualifications are considered within the coverage of employment security. Under this circumstance, the employer must follow a

236 Even though, the branch managers of the banks might be authorized as commercial representative in practice, it is probable for them to be unauthorized to hire and dismiss the employees through their employment contracts or workplace (internal) regulations. For further information on commercial representatives see infra: *Chapter V – Commercial Law – Part I.*

237 Çelik, Caniklioğlu, and Canbolat, *İş Hukuku Dersleri*, 524; Dereli, *Labour Law in Turkey*, 200; Ekmekçi and Korkusuz, *Turkish Individual Labour Law*, 109; Süzek, *İş Hukuku*, 569.

238 Çelik, Caniklioğlu, and Canbolat, *İş Hukuku Dersleri*, 525.

special procedure when terminating indefinite term contracts of the employees, who fall within the scope of employment security.

In this case, the employer must assert justification for termination, which implies that they must assert the presence of any valid reason in order to terminate the contract. This is different from the justifications based on just causes. The difference between a valid reason and a just cause is not explicitly regulated by the Labor Act. By inference, the valid reason is deemed a justification that is not sufficient to provide a reason for the immediate termination of the employment contract on one hand, but not so simple that the employee's warning is sufficient on the other hand.[239] In case of a valid reason, it affects the employer's confidence and the contractual relationship negatively.

Accordingly, valid reasons for termination are qualitatively less severe than just causes. However, those reasons that are required for valid termination must also involve a certain degree of severity. In other words, even though valid reasons are not as grave as the just causes, they severely and adversely affect the normal process of the work, workflow, and the workplace.[240]

Tab. 14. Reminder about the justification for termination
If the employee is not covered by employment security, the employer is not required to assert any justification for the termination. It is sufficient to observe the notice periods for a lawful termination unless the employer conducts in a manner that contradicts the rule of good faith. If an employee benefits from employment security, observing the notice periods is not sufficient. The justification for termination must be based on a valid reason, and the required procedure must be followed. It must be noted that in the presence of a just cause, the right to terminate the contract immediately arises even for the contracts covered by employment security.

239 Centel, *Turkish Labour Law*, 179; Çelik, Caniklioğlu, and Canbolat, *İş Hukuku Dersleri*, 527 ff.; Dereli, *Labour Law in Turkey*, 202; Süzek, *İş Hukuku*, 585.

240 For instance, without the employer's permission or a legitimate reason, if the employee is absent from work for two consecutive days, this conduct constitutes a just cause. Accordingly, frequent sick leaves that constantly affects the workflow negatively, even if the non-performance of employee never reaches a severity of just cause, it constitutes a valid reason. On the other hand, not all misconduct of the employee can be considered as a valid reason for termination. Likewise, seldomly arriving late to the workplace does not even provide a valid reason for termination since it does not reach a certain level of culpable act. See also, Süzek, *İş Hukuku*, 585.

According to the Labor Act, the valid reasons must be arisen either from the conduct or the performance of the employee or from the operational requirements of the enterprise, the workplace, or the work itself.[241] In addition, situations that do not constitute a valid reason for termination are also regulated separately.

a. The valid reasons connected with the conduct and performance of the employees

The reasons arising from the performance of the employee These can be exemplified as being less productive than the average employee performing similar works; or having performance that is lower than predicted from the qualifications suggested by the employee, or the gradually reduced concentration of the employee, etc. This sort of valid reasons might also include similar justifications such as tardiness, being reluctant to learning, frequent illness of the employee, or the inadequate compliance of the employee, etc.
The reasons arising from the conduct of the employee These reasons have diversified over time by court decisions. They involve the cases such as frequent absenteeism, asking for money from colleagues, causing discomfort in the workplace, inciting co-workers against the employer, performing the assigned job improperly despite being cautioned, making long phone calls that halt the workflow, having serious conflicts with supervisors or with colleagues, etc.

Any socially negative behavior of the employee or any attitude of them that contradicts rules of social conduct and morals cannot be considered a valid reason unless it has a detrimental impact on the relevant employment relationship. Therefore, it is not sufficient for these examples to have occurred alone, but they should also adversely affect the work environment or production in the workplace.[242]

b. The reasons connected with the operational requirements of the enterprise, the workplace or the work

This sort of valid reasons is divided into two groups as external and internal reasons. On the one hand, the examples of external reasons are the reduced material and sales opportunities, the decrease in demands and orders, energy shortage, economic crisis in the country, etc. On the other hand, the internal

241 For further information see also, Centel, *Turkish Labour Law*, 179–180; Çelik, Caniklioğlu, and Canbolat, *İş Hukuku Dersleri*, 533 ff., 541 ff.; Dereli, *Labour Law in Turkey*, 202; Süzek, *İş Hukuku*, 573 ff., 583 ff.

242 Çelik, Caniklioğlu, and Canbolat, *İş Hukuku Dersleri*, 566; Süzek, *İş Hukuku*, 593.

reasons might consist of introducing new working methods into the workplace, reducing the size of workforce, implementing the new technologies, etc.

c. *Invalid reasons for termination*

The Labor Act also regulates which situations cannot be construed as a valid reason (art. 18/para. 3 of LA). In particular, the following shall not constitute a valid reason for the termination:

- To participate in trade union activities outside the working hours or with the approval of the employer during working hours (sub-para. a)
- To act as trade union representative in the workplace (sub-para. b)
- To apply to the administrative or judicial authorities against the employer or to participate in an initiated process in order to follow the rights arising from the legislation or the contract (sub-para. c)
- Race, color, gender, marital status, family obligations, pregnancy, birth, religion, political opinion, and similar reasons (sub-para. d)
- Failure to continue working during the periods prohibited by the Labor Act for female employees (during the maternity leaves) (sub-para. e)
- Temporary absenteeism of the employees during the relevant suspension period, which is regulated as just cause due to illness or accident (sub-para. f).[243]

Tab. 15. The occurrence of the employer's right to terminate the contract
In case of lack of employment security, no reason is required for the occurrence of the employer's right to terminate the contract. The employer has such a right; it is sufficient not to abuse it to make a lawful termination. On the other hand, in case of employment security, the occurrence of the employer's right to the terminate the contract depends on the presence of one of the valid reasons.

3. *Notice of Termination*

The distinctive feature of employment security system is that the notice of termination procedure is regulated differently except for the length of notice period. As a rule, after the counterparty receives the notice of termination, the

243 For further information see, Centel, *Turkish Labour Law*, 180; Çelik, Caniklioğlu, and Canbolat, *İş Hukuku Dersleri*, 564; Dereli, *Labour Law in Turkey*, 203; Süzek, *İş Hukuku*, 594. Under this part, also see supra: *Termination with Just Cause*.

contractual relationship continues for a certain time (i.e., for notice period) until the designated period expires. The only exception is the termination with just cause, which is also defined as immediate (summary) termination.[244]

Tab. 16. The Press Labor Act

According to the Press Labor Act, which has a special coverage for the employment relationships of journalists, the periods for notice are regulated differently. Pursuant to the Press Labor Act, the termination of the employment contract of a journalist with a minimum of five consecutive years of service shall become effective 3 months after receiving the notice of termination. The notice period shall be 1 month for journalists whose length of service is less than 5 years. It should be reminded that these special notice periods are to be considered for journalists covered by employment security.

Whereas the notice of termination is not subjected to any form to be valid in general, the termination procedure of employment security is regulated differently. In case of employment security, the employer is obliged to notify the employee in writing of termination and indicate a valid reason in a clear and precise manner within this statement (art. 19/1 of LA). Besides, in case of the assertion that contract was terminated due to the employee's performance or conducts, the employer is, then, obliged to provide affected employees with an opportunity to defend themselves before notice of termination (art. 19/2 of LA). However, this is not required for the cases of immoral, dishonorable or malicious conducts of the employees, since the employer's right to terminate the contract under the grounds set forth in the article 25/II is reserved.

It must be noted that this procedure applies only to the employees covered by employment security. For others, termination can be done, albeit verbally. In other words, unless the employment security provisions are applicable, there is no requirement to provide a cause for termination. This means that, as a rule, in the event of termination at will, both parties to the employment contract are obliged solely to follow the notice period. However, in the case of employment security, the employer must assert a valid reason for termination precisely and in writing and must adhere to required procedure at all.

244 Under this part, also see supra: *Termination with Just Cause*.

4. *The Requirement on Taking Measures to Avert Termination (Ultima ratio Principle)*

In case of employment security, the employer is obliged to take adequate measures to avert termination. In practice, it is also defined as "the principle of last resort" or "ultimate remedy principle".[245] It is a requirement arising from the aim of the employment security system, not from the wording of the provisions, and a principle established by preamble of the article, and promoted by court decisions and the doctrine.[246] According to this principle, if the need for termination can be dissolved by other measures, the termination process should not be initiated at the earliest opportunity, since termination must represent the last possible resort.

ILO Recommendation no. 166 also encompasses guidance as to the measures which could be adopted to avert termination. In this regard, the offered measures include, inter alia, freezing recruitment, restricting overtime and reducing normal working hours, spreading the redundancy over a certain period of time to allow natural elimination, retraining, and redeployment, offering early retirement to volunteers, etc.

Despite the presence of valid reasons, if the direct implementation of termination without such measures is applied first, according to court decisions, such termination is deemed invalid based on ultima ratio principle.[247] Accordingly, before having applied to the termination, the employer should remove the overtime or should reduce the working hours if necessary. In some cases, providing the employees with plausibly affordable training is also advised.[248]

5. *Burden of Proof*

Another legal consequence introduced by the employment security system concerns the burden of proof. Under the provisions of the Labor Act, the employer has the obligation to prove the presence of a valid reason. In addition,

---

245 Dereli, *Labour Law in Turkey*, 202; Ekmekçi and Korkusuz, *Turkish Individual Labour Law*, 110.

246 Çelik, Caniklioğlu, and Canbolat, *İş Hukuku Dersleri*, 559; Süzek, *İş Hukuku*, 602; Süral and Kılıçoğlu, "Labor Law," 170.

For further information see, Ali Güzel, Karar İncelemesi, İşletmesel Kararların Keyfilik Denetimine Tabi Olması ve Geçerli Nedenle Fesihte Son Çare (Ultima Ratio) İlkesinin Gözetilmesi, *Çalışma ve Toplum Dergisi*, 1/4 (2005): 159–182.

247 Çelik, Caniklioğlu, and Canbolat, *İş Hukuku Dersleri*, 558, fn. 1701; Süzek, *İş Hukuku*, 604 ff.

248 Süzek, *İş Hukuku*, 606.

if the employee asserts that the termination was based on another reason, and the alleged reason was on appearance, the employee is, then, obliged to prove this assertion. However, at the first stage, the burden of proof is incumbent on the employer (art. 20/2 of LA).[249]

B. *Proceeding against Invalid Termination*

Even though the termination of the employment contract is based on a valid reason, if the employer has failed to comply with the required procedure, the employee covered by employment security is eligible to claim invalid termination. Likewise, although the notice period and required procedure are observed, if there is no valid reason at the time of termination notice, termination is, then, regarded as an invalid one.

If the employee asserts the presence of an invalid termination, they should contest to the employer's termination. Nonetheless, new provisions within the Act on Employment Courts (no. 7036) have been put into force in 2017 and they amended the relevant articles of the Labor Act. Hence, the mediation procedure is mandatory for employment disputes from now on. Therefore, the employee must first consult the mediator within 1 month from the date of receiving of termination notice (art. 20/1 of LA).

The Labor Act also stipulates that if the parties agree, the dispute may be brought to the private arbitrator within the very same time by the mutual assent of the contracting parties, which must be given after the termination. This consent is not valid when such an arbitrator agreement has been concluded between the parties while the contract is being negotiated between the parties or while it is in force.[250] Once the parties have agreed to settle the dispute before the arbitrator, the opportunity to apply to the court is no longer applicable.[251]

On the other hand, if the employee prefers a judicial remedy, they first apply to the mediator on due time. During the negotiations before the mediator, if the reconciliation is reached, then the dispute dissolves. If the mediation procedure could not solve the dispute, only after that, the employee may apply to the court within 2 weeks (art. 20/1 of LA).

---

249 See also, Centel, *Turkish Labour Law*, 182; Çelik, Caniklioğlu, and Canbolat, *İş Hukuku Dersleri*, 582 ff.; Dereli, *Labour Law in Turkey*, 207; Süzek, *İş Hukuku*, 619; Süral and Kılıçoğlu, "Labor Law," 170.

250 Çelik, Caniklioğlu, and Canbolat, *İş Hukuku Dersleri*, 581; Süzek, *İş Hukuku*, 616.

251 Süzek, *İş Hukuku*, 616.

It is also notable that if the contract of employee covered by employment security is terminated by the employer allegedly on a just cause, the employee is eligible to initiate the proceedings also against this termination, as in the case of termination by the employer providing no valid reason.

Tab. 17. The main aim of the employment security system
It must be remembered that the employees covered by employment security cannot claim malevolence compensation for abusive termination, and vice versa, the employees, who are excluded from employment security, cannot claim reinstatement (and employment security compensation). Furthermore, as a rule, an employee covered by employment security cannot directly claim specific compensations without first claiming the reinstatement. Since the main aim of the system is to provide reinstatement rather than a compensation for lack of reinstatement.

C. Legal Consequences of Invalid Termination

At the end of mediation process, if the parties reach no reconciliation, then the employee may apply to labor courts within 2 weeks as of the date on which the final report of mediator has been recorded.

According to employment security provisions, the employee can file a lawsuit with a request exclusively for reinstatement in case of allegedly invalid termination. In other words, the employee is not eligible to demand for attaining relevant compensations directly. Thereafter, the court grants a declaratory decision[252] on validity of termination and resolves the legal uncertainty.

When the claim of the employee is upheld by the court, the employee should apply to the employer for reinstatement within 10 working days from the notification of the finalized court decision.[253] If the employee does not apply to in due time, the process turns out to contrary. Due to a delay or failure to apply to the employer, the termination that made before becomes "valid" despite the fact that it was previously determined to be invalid by the court (art. 21/6 of LA). Such an employee can claim notice pay and severance pay if the other conditions are available. However, this employee, who does not apply for reinstatement,

252 Çelik, Caniklioğlu, and Canbolat, *İş Hukuku Dersleri*, 590–591; Süzek, *İş Hukuku*, 617, 623, 626 ff.

253 The relevant court decision becomes final at the second tier if the decision of the first instance court is objected. Under this chapter, also see supra: *Part I – Judicial Sources.*

cannot claim the relevant compensations since the termination is no longer an invalid one.[254]

If the employee applies to the employer for reinstatement to the work and if the employer reinstates the employee, it is deemed that the employment contract continues without any interruption between the parties. The initial termination process dissolves. On the other hand, the period of time between the termination notice and the finalized court decision is considered idle time for the employee. Even though the employer had invited the employee to work, this period had elapsed without the employee working and should be compensated by the employer. However, in accordance with the Labor Act, the employee shall be paid a maximum of 4 months' wage for this idle time, not be paid for the whole period. In other words, irrespective of whether the employee is reinstated, the employee may claim this compensation for the idle time, but equal to 4 months' wage in maximum. The compensation for idle time should be calculated on the amount of total wage.[255]

If the employee applies to the employer for reinstatement in due time, the employer has an option not to reinstate the said employee. To put it more accurately, the employment security does not absolutely force the employer to reinstate the employee. Pursuant to the Labor Act, if the employer does not reinstate the employee to their previous position/job within 1 month after the application, the employer shall be obliged to pay employment security compensation for a minimum amount of 4 months wages to a maximum of 8 months wages of given employee. It must be reiterated that the employment security compensation is not provided in all cases, it is paid on condition that the employee is not invited for reinstatement by the employer after the due application alone.[256]

If the employee, who applied to the employer for reinstatement, was not invited by the employer, the employment contract shall be deemed terminated by the employer on the date of the rejection of the application for reinstatement or on the date, which the limited period (1 month) has expired.[257]

---

254 Çelik, Caniklioğlu, and Canbolat, *İş Hukuku Dersleri*, 589; Dereli, *Labour Law in Turkey*, 209; Ekmekçi and Korkusuz, *Turkish Individual Labour Law*, 111; Süzek, *İş Hukuku*, 635.

255 Çelik, Caniklioğlu, and Canbolat, *İş Hukuku Dersleri*, 601; Dereli, *Labour Law in Turkey*, 210; Süzek, *İş Hukuku*, 646. Under this chapter, also see supra: *Part II – The Obligation to Pay Wage.*

256 Çelik, Caniklioğlu, and Canbolat, *İş Hukuku Dersleri*, 593; Süzek, *İş Hukuku*, 643. See also, Ekmekçi and Korkusuz, *Turkish Individual Labour Law*, 111 ff.

257 Çelik, Caniklioğlu, and Canbolat, *İş Hukuku Dersleri*, 591; Dereli, *Labour Law in Turkey*, 209; Süzek, *İş Hukuku*, 639.

The amount of employment security compensation cannot be increased by mutual agreements of the parties. These regulations cannot be changed through collective bargaining agreements, individual labor agreements or official regulations, even if they are in favor of the employee (see, last paragraph of the article 21 of LA). In addition, this compensation is calculated on the amount of basic wage of the employee.[258]

IV. Severance Pay

Ending of the employment contract has several legal consequences. One of the most important consequences has been severance pay. In fact, the future of severance pay remains uncertain. While the former Labor Act (no. 1475) was repealed in favor of the current Act (no. 4857), the former regulation on severance pay remained in effect. The aim was to repeal this regulation (art. 14 of the former Labor Act) in a short time and to replace them with a severance pay fund. However, this replacement was suspended due to the pressure from the opposition and the social counterparts. The discussion on the repeal of the relevant provision is still ongoing.[259] Apart from the discussions, severance pay is still applicable and defined as a sum of money payable to the employees in case of the extinction of an employment contract. It is of importance for the employees following the termination process of the employment contract.

First, severance pay is not payable or applicable for all employment contracts. For instance, it is applicable for the employment contracts subject to the Labor Act, but not for the contracts subject to the provisions of the Turkish Code of Obligations. The coverage of each labor act must be considered separately. On the other hand, the severance pay is a right granted to the employees alone. Therefore, public servants are not eligible for severance pay.[260]

Besides, in order to be eligible for severance pay, the employment contract needs to be ended in accordance with one of the cases defined in the applicable law (art. 14 of the former Labor Act no. 1475).

---

258 Çelik, Caniklioğlu, and Canbolat, *İş Hukuku Dersleri*, 593; Dereli, *Labour Law in Turkey*, 210; Süzek, *İş Hukuku*, 643. Under this chapter, also see supra: *Part II – The Obligation to Pay Wage.*

259 For further information see, Centel, *Turkish Labour Law*, 199–200; Çelik, Caniklioğlu, and Canbolat, *İş Hukuku Dersleri*, 688; Dereli, *Labour Law in Turkey*, 228; Süzek, *İş Hukuku*, 752 ff. Cf. Süral and Kılıçoğlu, "Labor Law," 172.

260 Centel, *Turkish Labour Law*, 201; Çelik, Caniklioğlu, and Canbolat, *İş Hukuku Dersleri*, 689; Süzek, *İş Hukuku*, 752.

A. *Requirements for Severance Pay*

1. *Seniority of Minimum One-Year*

The employee may be entitled to severance pay only after the seniority of minimum 1 year at the same workplace or several workplaces of the same employer. In other words, the length of the seniority shall be calculated by considering employee's length of service at the same workplace or multiple workplaces of the same employer together. The seniority of the employee is the period that begins with the actual work in the workplace and continues until the end of the employment contract.[261]

2. *Special Cases Defined by Law*

Provided that the first requirement has been met, severance pay is to be paid if one of the specific cases stipulated by law is available (art. 14 of the former Labor Act no. 1475).

a. *The termination with just cause by the employee*

The circumstances that grant to the employee to terminate the employment contract with just cause are listed in the article 24 of the Labor Act. If the employee terminates the employment contract based on a cause listed in all paragraphs of this article, they shall, then, be entitled to the severance pay. On the other hand, if the employee terminates the employment contract at will, severance pay is not demandable. In other words, it is not applicable in case that the employee resigns by observing notice period.[262]

b. *The termination by the employer excluding the cases listed in the art. 25/II of LA*

In case of termination by the employer at will, it is to be paid. That is to say, if the employer terminates the contract by following notice periods, then the employee may demand the severance pay.

---

261 Centel, *Turkish Labour Law*, 203 ff.; Çelik, Caniklioğlu, and Canbolat, *İş Hukuku Dersleri*, 707 ff.; Dereli, *Labour Law in Turkey*, 232; Ekmekçi and Korkusuz, *Turkish Individual Labour Law*, 120; Süzek, *İş Hukuku*, 770 ff.

On the other hand, for different decisions of Court of Cassation on computing of suspension periods see also, Çelik, Caniklioğlu, and Canbolat, *İş Hukuku Dersleri*, 706; Ekmekçi and Korkusuz, *Turkish Individual Labour Law*, 121.

262 Centel, *Turkish Labour Law*, 201; Çelik, Caniklioğlu, and Canbolat, *İş Hukuku Dersleri*, 691; Süzek, *İş Hukuku*, 760.

In addition, if the employer terminates the employment contract with just cause due to the health concerns or compelling reasons, the employee may still claim the severance pay from the employer.[263] On the other hand, in case the employment contract is terminated by the employer due to the circumstances that do not comply with the principle of good faith and similar reasons, then the employee cannot demand the severance pay.

c. The peculiar conditions

In addition, severance pay is also to be paid under special circumstances defined by the former Labor Act (no. 1475). Accordingly,

- If the employee has terminated his employment contract due to 'regular military service', he is to be entitled to the severance pay.
- If the employee has voluntarily terminated the employment contract in order to be granted an old-age pension or a lump sum payment from funds or institutions established according to the social security regulations, they are eligible for severance pay. In cases where retirement is facilitated,[264] severance pay is also granted to those, who terminate the contract while they have been waiting to reach retirement age.
- If a newly married female employee, who has voluntarily terminated the contract, shall be entitled to the severance pay on condition that she has terminated the contract within 1 year from her marriage.

According to the decisions of the Court of Cassation, the employees do not have to observe notice period if they leave their jobs for reasons such as regular military service, marriage, or retirement.[265] In these cases, the employees are eligible to terminate the contract without observing notice periods, and they may demand severance pay.[266]

---

263 Centel, *Turkish Labour Law*, 201; Süzek, *İş Hukuku*, 755.

264 Çelik, Caniklioğlu, and Canbolat, *İş Hukuku Dersleri*, 695 ff.; Dereli, *Labour Law in Turkey*, 230 ff.; Süzek, *İş Hukuku*, 762 ff.

265 For the relevant decisions see, Süzek, *İş Hukuku*, 768. Cf. Çelik, Caniklioğlu, and Canbolat, *İş Hukuku Dersleri*, 702; Süzek, *İş Hukuku*, 769.

266 In practice, the Court of Cassation rules that a married female employee being solicited for a new position after receiving severance pay is not an abuse of right. See, Centel, *Turkish Labour Law*, 202.

The same applies for the retired employees, who enjoy the facilitated retirement. There is no obstacle for them to be recruited in a new job after the termination enabled them to obtain severance pay. See, Süzek, *İş Hukuku*, 763, 765.

- Another circumstance is the death of the employee. Undoubtedly, in this case, those who shall be entitled to obtain severance pay are only legal successors of the deceased employee.

B. *Amount of Severance Pay*

The amount of severance pay is calculated by multiplying the amount of the employee's seniority by the last 30 days' wage amount. In other words, the employees may demand a severance pay equal to 30-day wage for each full year that they spend under the employment contract as of the first working day. On the other hand, there is an upper limit for annual amount of severance pay. The annual amount may not exceed the maximum pension bonus granted to a public servant at the highest rank for 1 year of their service. The constraint on the upper limit is absolutely mandatory rule; in other words, is immutable law.[267]

The wage to be taken as basis The wage to be taken as basis to calculate the severance pay is the total wage. Accordingly, that wage shall include any regular benefits paid to the employee. The important thing is their continuous character. Those benefits that are the one-time bonus or premiums granted to the employees are not considered in the calculation of total wages since they are not continuous.[268]

Seniority period Accurate determination of seniority period is also of importance. The payment shall be made *pro rata*. This means that periods less than 1 year are to be calculated proportionally. For instance, if the employee has a seniority of 2 years and 6 months, they receives 1-month total wage for each full year and half-month total wage for 6 months. However, this compensation is not proportionally paid to employees, whose seniority does not exceed 1 year.[269]

---

267 Çelik, Caniklioğlu, and Canbolat, *İş Hukuku Dersleri*, 729; Dereli, *Labour Law in Turkey*, 240; Ekmekçi and Korkusuz, *Turkish Individual Labour Law*, 122–123; Süzek, *İş Hukuku*, 787. Cf. Centel, *Turkish Labour Law*, 208.

268 Centel, *Turkish Labour Law*, 207; Çelik, Caniklioğlu, and Canbolat, *İş Hukuku Dersleri*, 725 ff.; Dereli, *Labour Law in Turkey*, 238; Süzek, *İş Hukuku*, 785; Süral and Kılıçoğlu, "Labor Law," 172.

269 Çelik, Caniklioğlu, and Canbolat, *İş Hukuku Dersleri*, 705; Ekmekçi and Korkusuz, *Turkish Individual Labour Law*, 122.

C. *Interest Rate for Late Payment*

After the termination, the employee may demand interest rate by claiming that severance pay is not paid on a timely basis or nor paid at all, the court shall then decide an interest rate at the highest rate applicable to the deposit accounts for unpaid severance pay specifically (art. 14/11 of the former Labor Act no. 1475).

D. *Prescription Period*

The prescription period is 5 years for severance pay (additional art. 3 of LA). Last but not least, severance pay is a distinct sort of compensation from other types of employee claims and should not be confused with notice pay, malevolence compensation or employment security compensation, etc. These are not employees' claims that necessarily follow each other. For instance, irrespective of whether the notice period is duly given, the employee may also demand the severance pay, if the requirements for severance pay are available. It holds true also for the type of contract; it is not important for the employee to work under a definite term or indefinite term contract in order to receive severance pay.[270]

V. Concluding Remarks

The recent breakthroughs in technology are not on the agenda of employment law only because of their effects on the gig economy or the sharing economy. There is also concern that the developments in AI technology will result in the loss of millions of jobs. It is estimated that nearly 50 % of the activities (of the tasks rather than specific jobs) that people do currently are automatable. As a result, it is assumed that the challenges such as rising inequality and even outright unemployment will inevitably arise in the foreseeable future amongst certain categories of working people.[271] The relevant transition is projected to produce a major disruption with detrimental impacts on labor market.

On the other hand, the concepts of basic income and decent work stand out among the current issues of employment law. Decent work has recently become a universal goal, not only for providing a fair income, but also for paving a way for a larger social and economic growth and strengthening individuals and

---

270 The important point is whether there is a termination that gives the right to severance pay rather than the type of contract. See also, Çelik, Caniklioğlu, and Canbolat, *İş Hukuku Dersleri*, 704; Süzek, *İş Hukuku*, 754.

271 Martin Ford, *Articles of Intelligence: The truth about AI from the people building it* (Birmingham: Packt Publishing, 2018), 650, 673.

communities.[272] Accordingly, decent work and its pillars have been introduced as the integral elements of the new 2030 Agenda for Sustainable Development.[273] Also, the concept of "social protection floors" is established by ILO and the United Nations agencies. It refers to a set of basic social security guarantees that involve basic income security and access to health care. To this end, the extension of social security measures to provide a basic income to all in need of such protection is promoted.[274]

The concept of universal (unconditional) basic income has also been incorporated to these debates. It refers to providing a certain amount of income to everyone, without determining their needs or questioning their means by means-test. It is argued that to provide an income not only to people in need, but to all will reduce bureaucracy and paperwork, and diminish the administrative cost of social benefits, in which paperwork and means-test are unavoidable. It also aims to prevent the stigmatization of the vulnerable groups on one hand, and on the other hand, to ensure inclusion of those, who are excluded from the society.[275] In this context, the debates on basic income are also carried out in Turkey.[276] However, these are not yet legally adopted solutions.

Further Readings

Akın, Levent. "İş Sağlığı ve Güvenliğinde İşyerinin Örgütlenmesi." *Ankara Üniversitesi Hukuk Fakültesi Dergisi*, Vol. 54, Iss. 1 (2004): 1–60.

Alp, Mustafa. "Yeni Türk Ticaret Kanunu'na Göre Bölünme, Tür Değiştirme ve Tür Değiştirmenin İş İlişkilerine Etkisi." *Çalışma ve Toplum Dergisi*, Vol. 32, Iss. 1 (2012): 51–74.

272 See also, Guidelines on decent work and socially responsible tourism (Geneva: ILO, 2017); Guidelines on decent work in public emergency services (Geneva: ILO, 2018).

273 See for further information on the United Nations Sustainable Development Summit 2015, involving 17 sustainable development goals (SDGs), https://sustainabledevelopment.un.org/post2015/summit, accessed 17.8.2021.

274 See also, the ILO Social Protection Floors Recommendation, 2012 (no. 202). For further information on Turkish social law and social security law see, Tankut Centel, *Turkish Social Law* (Springer, 2021); Dereli, *Labour Law in Turkey,* 38 ff.; Ali Güzel, A. Rıza Okur and Nurşen Caniklioğlu, *Sosyal Güvenlik Hukuku* (İstanbul: Beta, 2020); A. Can Tuncay and Ömer Ekmekçi, *Sosyal Güvenlik Hukuku Dersleri* (İstanbul: Beta, 2019).

275 The Basic Income European Network (BIEN) was founded in 1986, and then became the Basic Income Earth Network in 2006. For further information see also, https://basicincome.org/, accessed 17.8.2021.

276 Şebnem Gökçeoğlu Balcı, *Tutunamayanlar ve Hukuk* (Ankara: Dost, 2007).

Alpagut, Gülsevil. *İşyerinin Devri ve İş Sözleşmesini Fesih Hakkı*. İstanbul: Beta, 2010.

Astarlı, Muhittin. *İş Hukukunda İkale*. Ankara: Turhan, 2016.

Aybay, Rona. "Uluslararası Antlaşmaların Türk Hukukundaki Yeri." *Türkiye Barolar Birliği Dergisi*, Vol. 70 (2007): 187–213.

Aydınlı, İbrahim. *Türk İş Hukukunda Alt İşveren İlişkisi ve Muvazaa Sorunu*. Ankara: Seçkin, 2021.

Başbuğ, Aydın. *İşverenin Yönetim Hakkı ve Çalışma Şartlarında Değişiklik*. Ankara: Alter, 2008.

Bozkurt Gümrükçüoğlu, Yeliz. *Türk İş Hukuku'nda Belirli Süreli İş Sözleşmesi*. İstanbul: Vedat, 2012.

Centel, Tankut. *Turkish Social Law*. Springer, 2021.

Civan, Orhan Ersun. *Genel İş Koşulları*. İstanbul: Beta, 2015.

Çil, Şahin. *İş Hukukunda İbraname*. Ankara: Yetkin, 2013.

De Stefano, Valerio. "Introduction: Crowdsourcing, the Gig-Economy and the Law." *Comparative Labor Law and Policy Journal*, Vol. 37, Iss. 3 (2016): 461–470.

Demir, Fevzi. *En Son Yargıtay Kararları Işığında İş Hukuku ve Uygulaması*. İzmir: Albi, 2018.

Dereli, Toker. "Flexicurity and Turkey's New Labor Act: Problems and Prospects." In *Labor and Employment Relations in a Globalized World*, eds. Toker Dereli and others (Springer, 2014): 135–158.Doğan Yenisey, Kübra. "Harmonisation of Turkish law with EU's regulations in respect of equal treatment." *Managerial Law*, Vol. 47, Iss. 6 (2005): 235–256.

Doğan Yenisey, Kübra. *İş Hukukunda İşyeri ve İşletme*. İstanbul: Legal, 2007.

Doğan Yenisey, Kübra. *İş Hukukunun Emredici Yapısı*. İstanbul: Beta, 2014.

Doğan Yenisey, Kübra. "Endüstri 4.0, Üretimin Değişen Yapısı ve İş Hukuku." *Toprak İşveren Dergisi*, Iss. 120 (2019): 1–7.

Doherty, Michael and Franca, Valentina. "Solving the 'Gig-saw'? Collective Rights and Platform Work." *Industrial Law Journal*, Vol. 49, Iss. 3 (2020): 352–376.

Dulay Yangın, Dilek. "Endüstri 4.0, Dijitalleşme ve İş Hukukunun Geleceği-Dijital Platformların Ortaya Çıkardığı Hukuki İlişkiler Çerçevesinde Değerlendirilmesi." *İstanbul Hukuk Mecmuası*, Vol. 78, Iss. 3 (2020): 1209–1237.

Ekmekçi, Ömer, Korkusuz, M. Refik and Uğur, Ömer. *Turkish Collective Labour Law*. İstanbul: On İki Levha, 2020.

Engin, Murat. *Türk İş ve Sosyal Güvenlik Hukukunda İşveren*. İstanbul: BASİSEN, 1993.

Ernest E. Hirsch. “Anayasanın Özel Hukuk Kurallarına Etkileri.” *Birinci Türk Hukuk Kongresi'ne Sunulan Tebliğler*. Ankara: Türkiye Barolar Birliği Yayınları, 1972.

Ertürk Arslan, Arzu. *Türk İş Hukukunda İşçinin Sadakat Borcu*. İstanbul: On İki Levha, 2010.

Eyrenci, Öner, Taşkent, Savaş, Ulucan, Devrim, and Baskan, Esra. *İş Hukuku*. İstanbul: Beta, 2020.

Ford Martin. *Articles of Intelligence: The truth about AI from the people building it*. Birmingham: Packt Publishing, 2018.

Gökçeoğlu Balcı, Şebnem. *Tutunamayanlar ve Hukuk*. Ankara: Dost, 2007.

Güven, Ercan and Aydın, Ufuk. *Bireysel İş Hukuku*. Eskişehir: Nisan, 2020.

Güzel, Ali. “Karar İncelemesi, İşletmesel Kararların Keyfilik Denetimine Tabi Olması ve Geçerli Nedenle Fesihte Son Çare (Ultima Ratio) İlkesinin Gözetilmesi.” *Çalışma ve Toplum Dergisi*, Vol. 1, Iss. 4 (2005): 159–182.

Güzel, Ali, Okur, A. Rıza and Caniklioğlu, Nurşen. *Sosyal Güvenlik Hukuku*. İstanbul: Beta, 2020.

Halonen-Akatwijuka, Maija and Hart, Oliver. “Continuing Contracts.” *The Journal of Law, Economics, and Organization*, Vol. 36, Iss. 2 (2020): 284–313.

Mollamahmutoğlu, Hamdi, Astarlı, Muhittin and Baysal, Ulaş. *İş Hukuku Ders Kitabı Cilt I*. Ankara: Lykeion, 2021.

O'Connor, Niall. “Interpreting Employment Legislation Through a Fundamental Rights Lens: What's the Purpose?.” *European Labour Law Journal*, Vol. 8, Iss. 3 (2017): 193–216.

Özdemir, Erdem. *İş Sağlığı ve Güvenliği Hukuku Dersleri*. İstanbul: Vedat, 2020.

Özkaraca, Ercüment. *İşyeri Devrinin İş Sözleşmelerine Etkisi ve İşverenlerin Hukuki Sorumluluğu*. İstanbul: Beta, 2008.

Soyer, Polat. *Rekabet Yasağı Sözleşmesi (BK md. 348–352)*. Ankara: Adalet, 1994.

Storey, John. *The Challenge to Management Control*. K. Page: London, 1980.

Sur, Melda. “The Fundaments and Limits of Managerial Prerogative in Turkish Labor Law.” *Comparative Labor Law and Policy Journal*, Vol. 30, Iss. 2 (2009a): 313–333.

Sur, Melda. “General Framework and Historical Development of Labor Law in Turkey.” *Comparative Labor Law and Policy Journal*, Vol. 30, Iss. 2 (2009b): 183–197.Şahlanan, Fevzi. *Toplu İş Hukuku*. İstanbul: On İki Levha, 2020.

Tanışık, Mehmet Nur. *Turkish Labour Law*. Ankara: Office of Defense Cooperation Press, 1985.

Tuncay, A. Can and Ekmekçi, Ömer. *Sosyal Güvenlik Hukuku Dersleri*. İstanbul: Beta, 2019.

Tuncay, A. Can and Savaş Kutsal, F. Burcu. *Toplu İş Hukuku*. İstanbul: Beta, 2019.

Weil, David. *The Fissured Workplace*. Cambridge: Harvard University Press, 2014.

Wynn-Evans, Charles. "A Solution to Fissuring? Revisiting the Concept of the Joint Employer." *Industrial Law Journal*, Vol. 50, Iss. 1 (2020): 70–103.

Yıldız, Gaye Burcu. *İşverenin Eşit İşlem Yapma Borcu*. Ankara: Yetkin, 2008.

Reports & Guidelines

ILO Information Sheet no. WT-2, dated May 2004.

Guidelines on occupational safety and health management systems, ILO-OSH 2001. Geneva: ILO, 2009.

ILO Report. Non-standard employment around the world: Understanding challenges, shaping prospects. Geneva: ILO, 2016.

Guidelines on decent work and socially responsible tourism. Geneva: ILO, 2017.

Guidelines on decent work in public emergency services. Geneva: ILO, 2018.

Guide to developing balanced working time arrangements. Geneva: ILO, 2019.

ILO Report of Global Commission on the future of work: Work for a brighter future. Geneva: ILO, 2019.

ILO Report for G20, Digital platforms and the world of work in G20 countries: Status and Policy Action. Italia: G20, 2021.

ILO Working Paper 27, Platform work and the employment relationship. Geneva: ILO, 2021.

Asst. Prof. Dr. Ayşe ŞAHİN
and Asst. Prof. Dr. Tuğba SEMERCİ VURALOĞLU*

Chapter V Commercial Law

Arkan, Sabih. *Ticari İşletme Hukuku*, 27th ed. Ankara: Banka ve Ticaret Hukuku Enstitüsü, 2021; Bahtiyar, Mehmet. *Ortaklıklar Hukuku*, 15th ed. İstanbul: Beta, 2021; Bahtiyar, Mehmet. *Ticari İşletme Hukuku*, 21th ed. İstanbul: Beta, 2020; Poroy, Reha and Tekinalp, Ünal and Çamoğlu, Ersin. *Ortaklıklar Hukuku Vol. I*, 15th ed. İstanbul: Vedat Kitapçılık, 2021; Poroy, Reha and Tekinalp, Ünal and Çamoğlu, Ersin. *Ortaklıklar Hukuku Vol. II*, 14th ed. İstanbul: Vedat Kitapçılık, 2019; Poroy, Reha and Yasaman, Hamdi. *Ticari İşletme Hukuku*, 18th ed. İstanbul: Vedat Kitapçılık, 2019; Tekinalp, Ünal. *Sermaye Ortaklıklarının Yeni Hukuku*, 5th ed. İstanbul: Vedat Kitapçılık, 2020; Ülgen, Hüseyin, Helvacı, Mehmet, Kendigelen, Abuzer, Kaya, Arslan and Nomer Ertan, Füsun. *Ticari İşletme Hukuku*, 5th ed. İstanbul: Vedat Kitapçılık, 2015.

Introductory Remarks

When a venture is realized with the aim to earn profit, rules to be applied differs from the rules to be applied to non-commercial legal transactions. In Turkish private law, the main principles, and norms to be applied to business transactions and the actors of the business, "the merchants", either as solo entrepreneur in its simplest form or as companies, as more complex business corporations, are regulated in the Turkish Commercial Code (TCC) no. 6102 (in force as of 01.07.2012). Turkish Commercial Code is codified in very close conformity with EU law, and the relevant EU directives, that will be mentioned further in each related part.

Turkish commercial law comprises of three main branches, which can be stated such as the law of commercial enterprise regulated in the first book of the TCC, the company law regulated in the second book of the TCC, and the law of negotiable instruments regulated in the third book of the TCC, which consists of six books in total. In this chapter, the first two books, i.e., "the law of commercial enterprise" and "the company law" will be treated under Part I and Part II.

---

* Corresponding authors.

In the first part, following an overview of the commercial law theories and the historical background of commercial law, the main pillars of the law of commercial enterprise, such as the commercial enterprise and its essential elements, the merchant, the merchant assistants, and the unfair competition rules will be addressed.

In the second part will be explained briefly and to the point norms and principles to be applied to commercial companies. Basic rules that govern the establishment, the management through corporate organs, the rights and obligations of the shareholders, the securities, and the rules on the dissolution of a company will be presented within the framework of a "life circle of a company". Due to broad application of the TCC provisions of joint stock companies, in some extent to cooperatives and limited liability companies as well, will be examined basically joint stock companies as a model-example to give an overview of the Turkish company law.

Certainly, there are other sub-branches that could be gathered under the umbrella of commercial law such as capital market law, intellectual property law, competition law, banking law, energy law, etc. each being subject to a whole different and specific body of legislation; however, they will not be examined in this book but will only be mentioned shortly.

In close connection with company law, the capital market law is codified in the Capital Markets Code (CMC) no. 6362, which was enacted on 30 December 2012, following the entry into force of the TCC. As stated in the preamble of the CMC, the new CMC Draft was based on a Twinning Project in the form of European Union Pre-Accession Assistance. However, later, it has turned into an original text with a non-interventionist manner, based on the principle of "*targeted only at cases where the action is needed*". The CMC mainly comprises regulations regarding publicly held corporations; the issue of capital market instruments, public disclosure, and issuers; capital market institutions and activities; exchanges in Capital Markets Association of Capital Markets of Turkey and other institutions; supervision and measures in capital markets; actions requiring administrative fine and capital market crimes and principles regarding the Capital Markets Board (CMB).

In close connection with the law of commercial enterprise, the intellectual property law is regulated in conformity with European Union law, the relevant EU directives, and regulations. The codification approach reflects the main distinction based on Bern Convention and Paris Convention which regulate copyrights and industrial property rights separately. In this respect, copyright law is codified in the Code of Intellectual and Artistic Work no. 5846 and industrial property rights are codified in a separate Code, the Code of Industrial

Property (CIP) no. 6769. The Industrial Property Code covers and protects a limited number of industrial rights, those rights concerning "trademark", "geographical indication", "design" and "patent". Other industrial rights such as trade secrets, are not specifically codified in the CIP or in the TCC, can be protected according to unfair competition rules of the TCC. A particular legal regime to protect the business name (trade name) of the merchant and the enterprise name are also codified in TCC 39–53.[1]

§ Part I Law of Commercial Enterprise

I. Commercial Law Theories and the Historical Background of Commercial Law

Although commercial and economic activities had occurred in the early stages of human history, at the beginning based on the swap, and latterly based on exchange for money, and augmented during the reign of the Roman Empire, a separate and independent "commercial law" did not exist yet in those ancient times. The first commercial legal concepts such as the simplest partnership models, "*commendas*" or "*compagnias*" and payment models adapted to long-distance trade, the "*bill of exchange*", had been created and used among merchants in the late 12th and 13th centuries, in Europe.[2] Roman law system, which was followed in Europe in the middle age as well, was basic and was not corresponding needs of the commerce evolving significantly in the middle age in central Europe and Anatolia, through silk and spice roads. This need for special rules has drawn merchants to get organized under consortiums the "*loncas*" i.e., "guilds", and follow commercial customs and usages adopted by the guilds, and since then a separate "commercial customary law" i.e., "*ius mercatorium*" has begun developing.[3] Not written and not compiled yet in a Code, "*ius*

---

1 For further explanations concerning business name (trade name) see, Ünal Tekinalp and Mehtap Mertol Digili, *Commercial and Economic Law in Turkey* (Croydon: Kluwer Law International, 2016), 97 ff.

2 Sophus A. Reinert and Robert Fredona, "Merchants and the Origins of Capitalism," in *Forthcoming in Routledge Companion to the Makers of Global Business*, ed. Teresa da Silva Lopes, Christina Lubinski, Heidi Tworek (Boston: Harvard Business School, 2018), 12 ff.

3 The word "*lex mercatoria*" has been first used in the "Fleta Codes", in which commercial customary rules had been gathered in 1293 in the United Kingdom. See, Arzu Oğuz, "Hukuk Tarihi ve Karşılaştırmalı Hukuk Açısından Uluslararası Ticaret Hukuku," *Journal of Ankara University Faculty of Law*, 50, no. 3 (2001): 21.

mercatorium" was rather in the form of commercial practices and customary law which arose basically in the trade fairs, expositions, and markets of the time. Since then, commercial customary law has become one of the legal sources of commercial law (regulated in TCC 2).

Other milestones in the business history are maritime trades and geographical discoveries of the new world at the late 15th and 16th centuries. The significant evolvement of the commerce was due to the Mediterranean Sea trade carried out by the Italian city-states and later the Atlantic Sea commerce following the geographical discoveries. Thus, considerable amount of wealth was collected by European traders. Merchants became part of a well-accepted social class of the time. It took a long time indeed for "traveler merchant type" to transform into "sedentary merchant" who will not need to travel anymore to trade and who will conduct their business in their commercial enterprise through their intermediaries and agents, which is closer to today's real person merchant.

In that epoque customary commercial rules were being applied between merchants, and the application area of these rules was defined with reference to the merchant title of the parties. Thus, commercial law would be defined as the "law of merchant", a set of rules to be applied to a certain class in the society during the early modern period. This legal system, in which the application area of the commercial law was defined based on the concept of the merchant, as the "*sujet*" of the commerce, is called "subjective system" or "subjective theory" of the commercial law.

Trade of products such as gold, silver, silk, and spices, following geographical discoveries and colonization (colonialism) of the new continents and civilizations in the 15th and 16th centuries had accumulated an enormous amount of money in Europe. This accumulation of "capital" and all the new international trade routes and networks resulted in the augmentation and diversification of the commercial activities and the rise of the new sectors such as investment, banking and insurance and caused an economic and commercial expansion in Europe which is described as a "commercial revolution".

On the other hand, technical inventions led to mechanization, which paved the way for the industrial revolution. All these economic and scientific developments alongside the political changes such as the French Revolution in 1789 were the beginning of a completely new age in every area of life, as it was for legal systems as well. The French Revolution and its principles such as "*égalité*", "*liberté*" had big impact, not only on politics and the economy (i.e., arise of Adam Smith's economic liberalism) but also on the basic principles of commercial law as well. Commercial law was no longer defined upon only a certain class and was no longer formulated by the chambers, i.e., "guilds", which were structured as closed associations giving certain powers and privileges only to their members. Thus, commercial law was not reserved anymore to a certain class, but rather was considered as rules to be applied to everyone, who engages in commercial transactions, regardless of their merchant title, in light of freedom of contract, reflecting the "*principe de liberté*" of the French Revolution. This legal system, which defines the application area of the commercial law with reference to commercial acts and transactions, is called the "objective system" or the "objective theory", which focuses on the commercial acts and transactions i.e., "object" of the commerce.

In the late 19th century and 20th century, the modality of commercial activity has changed and evolved dramatically following the industrial revolution.[4] The technology revolution created heavy industry, which allowed mass production in big factories, which were characteristics of the second industrial revolution.

This affected commercial activities enormously; business models such as "commercial enterprise", "limited liability company", and then big corporations and "holding companies" had begun to be founded. This was followed by the rise of the first corporate law and anti-trust law regulations in European countries, in the USA and in the reign of Ottoman Empire as well following the European models. As a result, the objective theory based on the concept of "commercial act", or "commercial transaction" was not sufficient anymore to explain commercial activities. Therefore, as a new approach, commercial law was defined hence forth with reference to the "commercial enterprise", i.e., a business structure under which commercial activities are carried out by the merchant, who gathers both capital and labor under an economic organization. This system based on "commercial enterprise", is called the "modern system" or the "modern theory".

However, as it is the case for Turkish law, today's commercial law codification is based mostly on a synthesis of all the three theories and the TCC stipulates provisions concerning "merchant", "commercial transactions", and "commercial enterprise".[5] The commercial enterprise, refers to the simplest and basic commercial structure in which business activity can be conducted, indicates the "form" and "organization" of the business. The merchant is the businessman, who conducts the business and realizes the business transactions, therefore constitutes the "*sujet*" or the "actor" of the business. And finally, commercial law

---

4 For details and impact of the industrial revolution on the employment law, see supra: *Chapter IV – Employment Law.*

5 Sabih Arkan, *Ticari İşletme Hukuku* (Ankara: Banka ve Ticaret Hukuku Enstitüsü, 2020), 6; Mehmet Bahtiyar, *Ticari İşletme Hukuku,* 21st ed. (İstanbul: Beta, 2020), 10.

attributes legal consequences to commercial transactions, which constitute the "object" of the business.

II. The Main Pillars of the Law of Commercial Enterprise

A. The Commercial Enterprise

1. The Importance of Commercial Enterprise

To illustrate, imagine a big bread factory which operates close to wheat fields in the countryside and engages in many transactions with farmers, suppliers, intermediaries, and customers, which can be defined as the "stakeholders" i.e., all the related interest groups of such business. The factory can be operated either under the legal status of a corporation with legal personality or with the legal status of a partnership, which has no legal personality, or can be managed just by one solo entrepreneur. In this example, the factory would be legally qualified as a "commercial enterprise", and the small pastry shop, the customer that buys regularly bread from the factory would be legally qualified as "tradesman enterprise", i.e., a small commercial enterprise.

The commercial enterprise and the tradesman enterprise have an important role in Turkey's economy. The TCC mainly codifies commercial provisions to be applied to commercial enterprises and covers an important part of the transactions and legal relationships of these enterprises with their stakeholders. However, many of these transactions, especially different type of contracts, e.g., the sale contract, are codified in the Turkish Code of Obligations (TCO).

The commercial enterprise is attributed the qualification to be the core and central concept of the first book of the TCC. This means that many rules and concepts in the first book have been described based on the commercial enterprise. For example, the "merchant" is defined upon the commercial enterprise, as "*an entrepreneur who runs a commercial enterprise completely or partially on its own behalf*" (TCC 12); the "commercial transaction" is also defined with reference to commercial enterprise, as a "*transaction which is related to commercial enterprise*" (TCC 3) and is subjected to TCC provisions that differ from the provisions to be applied to consumers or customers.[6]

---

6 For the meaning of "commercial transaction" according to TCC 3 and 19; and for the question whether commercial companies may be party to consumer transactions see also, Şafak Narbay and Muhammed Akkuş, "Ticari İş Niteliğinin Belirlenmesi ve Ticari İş – Tüketici İşlemi Ayrımı," in *Sabih Arkan'a Armağan*, ed. İsmail Kırca et al. (İstanbul: On İki Levha, 2019), 853–855. For the assessments concerning criteria

The reflection of the "commercial enterprise" theory can be observed in the codification manner as well, since the title of TCC's first book is "commercial enterprise". Nevertheless, interestingly only one article, the Article 11 regulates the commercial enterprise. Whereas twelve articles, the Articles 12 to 23, regulate the merchant and two articles, the Articles 3 and 19, regulate commercial acts and transactions, among the 123 articles of the first book in total.

2. *Definition and Legal Nature*

Since the application area of the TCC depends on the presence of a commercial enterprise, the critical question will be how to define a commercial enterprise and identify in a particular case, especially distinguish a commercial enterprise from the tradesman enterprise. TCC 11 defines the concept of commercial enterprise and stipulates main characteristics and necessary legal elements of a commercial enterprise: "*Commercial enterprise is an enterprise where activities, aiming to generate income exceeding the limit foreseen for the tradesmen enterprise, are carried out continuously and independently*." Based on this definition in the TCC, there can be deduced four main elements of the commercial enterprise:

The first element is the existence of an "economic enterprise", meaning an economic unit under which an organization is made by the merchant, by gathering capital and labor, to make profit. The second element is the scale/the size of the enterprise. Not any economic enterprise, but an enterprise in a certain scale would be defined as a commercial enterprise; thus, a small size enterprise would not constitute a commercial enterprise. This second element is expressed in TCC 11 under the expression the commercial enterprise shall have "the purpose of generating income beyond the limit of tradesmen enterprise". In other words, not any enterprise but an enterprise which aims to generate income beyond tradesmen will be considered as a commercial enterprise.

But which are the criteria to determine whether the size of an economic enterprise is small or not? Would the supermarket in your neighborhood be qualified as a commercial enterprise or a tradesman enterprise? The answer determines the application area of the Commercial Code, and the relative secondary legislation. This is of vital importance since the TCC sets out less protective legal regime for the merchant, with the ground that merchant must behave with due care. But if the answer is "tradesman enterprise" then it will be subject in principle to an entirely different legal regime and different Code, the Act on Tradesmen

in TCC 19/2 see, İsmail Kırca, "Ticari İş ve Ticari Hükme Dair," *Batider,* 34, no. 3 (2018): 6 ff.

and Artisans Societies no. 5362 which sets out different rules, less formalities for smaller enterprises (TCC 15).

The distinguishing criteria are not regulated in TCC 11. The second paragraph of TCC 11 refers to a President's decision, as follows "*The monetary threshold between the commercial enterprise and the tradesman enterprise is determined by the President's decision*". But the President's decision has not been enacted yet, thus the Cabinet Decision (no. 2007/12362, dated 21.07.2007 still in force) will be applied. The Cabinet decision refers to tax law regulations to distinguish, which is indeed a very indirect way of codification. According to the above-mentioned Cabinet Decision, especially the amount of yearly income of the enterprise is taken into consideration, as well as the tax exemption system given to small enterprises.

The third element is the continuity of the business. One-time based businesses, contracts or transactions would not be qualified as commercial enterprise. The fourth element is the independence of the economic enterprise, which means that the enterprise should not be "controlled by" or "dependent on" any other natural person or legal entity, other than the owner of the enterprise. For instance, although a branch office is also an economic structure, it would not be considered as a commercial enterprise since it is under the control of the central office and thus has no legal or administrative independence.

3. *Transfer of the Commercial Enterprise*

a. *Introduction*

Corporations may engage in restructuring transactions such as mergers and acquisitions, division or conversion, which have been regulated in a very comprehensive manner, in the first and common part of the second book and between the Articles 134 and 194 of the TCC. Both merger and acquisitions and the transfer of an enterprise have the consequence of passing of all the assets to the acquiring company. The difference between these two is with regard to the legal status of the entrepreneur. After the transfer, the transferor entrepreneur will have no more connection with the transferred enterprise, no more rights or claims on it. Whereas in case of mergers and acquisitions, shareholders of the transferor company will keep on having connection with the acquiring company, by exchanging their existing shares with the new shares, i.e., shares of the acquiring company (TCC 140). In TCC 194, the commercial enterprise is synthesized with corporate restructuring transactions, i.e., its conversion into a corporation or vice versa is possible. For example, a corporation which intends to continue as a smaller business may transform into a commercial enterprise. Furthermore, a commercial enterprise may merge with a corporation as well, which would also differ from the simple transfer of the commercial enterprise. These transactions have been regulated in the second book of the TCC, in the subsection on corporate restructuring transactions; thus, those transactions concerning the commercial enterprise has been included into restructuring transactions whereas the event of "merging" or "transfer" of commercial enterprises solely, is regulated in an older provision, in TCO 203.

Under this chapter, among all these transactions we will address mainly the transfer of a commercial enterprise which is regulated in TCC 11/3 and will point out the most important traits of the transfer of a commercial enterprise.

b. Main traits of the transfer

What are the requirements for a valid transfer? In case the enterprise comprises various types of assets, such as real estate, vehicles, or movable properties, e.g., machines and devices, how will all these assets be transferred?

A question would be whether the commercial enterprise has a legal personality or not. Once a business structure has a legal personality, it has a separate patrimony other than its members' personal assets, and all its assets form a unit, and the corporation itself might be party to legal transactions. Having legal personality also allows the legal entity to engage in legal transactions and to have separate rights and obligations from its members.

However, the commercial enterprise is not attributed legal personality in Turkish law. Nevertheless, according to TCC 11, all the assets and debts of a commercial enterprise form all together an economic and legal unit, which can be subject of legal transactions such as transfer, pledge, lease agreements, usufruct or can be brought as a capital contribution in a company, and also can be subject to inheritance. Article 11/3 accepts "principle of integrity" and allows the transfer of the assets of a commercial enterprise as just one unit. The possibility to transfer all of them as one unit and with just one transaction, i.e., "*una actu*", allows the merchant to sell all its business easier, by preserving its integrity and value. This is expressed in TCC 11/3 as follows "*The commercial enterprise can be transferred as a whole without the need for separate mandatory transactions for the transfer of assets included and may be subject to other legal transactions.*".

If the transfer of the commercial enterprise were not regulated specifically in TCC 11, the merchant would have to make separate transaction for each of the assets and follow different form requirements for each transaction and economically this would not be as profitable and advantageous as in case of selling all the business as one unit.

TCC 11/3 sets written form requirement and registration in the commercial register for the transfer agreement. Parties shall conclude a written transfer agreement and clearly indicate assets that they want to exclude from the scope of the agreement. Other mandatory contract clauses are the "sale price" and the "payment terms" and the "unconditional statement indicating that commercial enterprise is transferred as a unit in a manner that ensures its continuity".

Although there are discussions concerning the effect of the registration, whether it is declaratory or constitutive, in Turkish law the majority is of the opinion that the transfer takes effect upon the registration (Art. 133/3 of the Regulation of Commercial Register). In other words, all the actives included in the scope of the agreement will be transferred at the date of the registration of the transfer in the official commercial register.

How about the scope of the transfer? Can the parties determine the scope freely or can they exclude some of the assets from the scope of the transfer, for example a valuable antique painting of the grandfather, of the founder of the family business? As long as enough assets that would allow the enterprise to operate after the transfer are included in the contract, parties can determine actives to be transferred as they wish in light of the freedom of contract. Therefore, the answer is surely positive for the antique painting but would not be positive e.g., for the weaving machines which are essential for the manufacture in case of a transfer of a fabric factory.

According to TCC 11/3, unless otherwise agreed by the parties, the transfer agreement is deemed to include fixed assets, business value, tenancy right, business name and other intellectual property rights and assets that are permanently allocated for the business.

How about the debts of the business enterprise? Can the parties exclude totally or partially debts from the scope of the transfer agreement? This is a very controversial subject in Turkish law. According to classical opinion, all the active and passive assets constitute a legal and economic unit and must be transferred altogether. This opinion relies on the "theory of security", which implies that actives constitute a kind of security for the debts; therefore, debts cannot be separated, and actives and passives can only be transferred as an indivisible unit altogether. Thus, such contractual clause excluding debts partially or completely would not be valid. Among the defenders of this approach, one opinion is that in case parties incorporate a clause that the transferee will not be liable for some of the debts, such contract clauses would be binding only for the contracting parties and not for the third parties.[7] On the other hand, there are also opinions that such restrictive clauses would be binding if notified or announced to the creditors.[8] Another opinion contends that debts can be excluded from the scope of the transfer only with the approval of the creditor.[9]

Nevertheless, there are also opinions defending a more liberal approach that favor the will of parties. According to this approach, some or all debts can be totally or partially excluded from the scope of the contract by mentioning explicitly in the contract and notifying or announcing generally to the creditors, thus the excluding clause would be also binding for third parties as well.[10]

c. Legal consequences of a transfer

The main legal consequence of the transfer is that all the actives and passives, i.e., assets and debts of the enterprise are transferred to the transferee. The other important consequence is regarding the liability of parties. The third consequence is that the transferor unless owns other commercial enterprises, loses its legal status of "merchant".

Regarding debts and liability, in the law of obligations, a debtor can transfer a debt to a third party, (i.e., a third party may undertake someone else's debt) only with the approval of the creditor, by reason of the fact that change of the debtor might be risky for the creditor. Thus, this change should be approved (TCO 198).

Regarding debts and liability, a particular system is regulated in case of a transfer of a commercial enterprise. According to TCO 202, the transferee, upon the transfer, should notify or announce creditors with a notice published in the Commercial Register Gazette. The transferee becomes liable for all the debts from the date of notification or announcement. Thus, all debts of the enterprise are transferred by just one transaction (by the "notification or the announcement") and the moment of passing of debts is different than the moment of passing of actives.

However, the transferor remains responsible for the debts, jointly and severally with the transferee for 2 years. This period, for due debts, begins from the

7 Arkan, Ticari İşletme Hukuku, 46–47.

8 Halil Arslanlı, *Kara Ticaret Hukuku Dersleri Umumi Hükümler*, 3rd ed. (İstanbul: Fakülteler Matbaası, 1960), 116.

9 Reha Poroy and Hamdi Yasaman, *Ticari İşletme Hukuku* (İstanbul: Vedat Kitapçılık, 2019), 48–49.

10 Mehmet Fatih Arıcı, *Ticari İşletmenin Aktif ve Pasifi ile Devri* (İstanbul: Vedat Kitapçılık, 2008), 144 ff.; Abuzer Kendigelen et al., *Ticari İşletme Hukuku*, 4th ed. (İstanbul: Vedat Kitapçılık, 2015), 200 ff.

date of notification or announcement; for debts that will be due, starts from the date of maturity. Thus, for a transfer of a commercial enterprise there is no need for the creditors' approval, that requirement is replaced by the "double" liability, i.e., joint and several liability of the transferor for 2-years period and the transferee for the prescription period of debts.

4. *Pledge on Movables in Commercial Transactions*

a. *Pledge through registration*

To maintain its continuity, a commercial enterprise, will need in most of the cases bank loan which can be taken out usually only in return of sufficient securities. The answer to the question of which type of security a merchant might give would be "personal guarantees" or "collateral securities" according to the general principles of property law. Collateral properties could be categorized such as "pledge on movable properties" or "pledge on real estate/mortgage/unmovable properties". Nevertheless, the fact that in most of the cases, the enterprise does not own the building, in which it operates, may prevent the merchant to give a pledge over unmovable property.

On the other hand, except for the separate situations stipulated in the law, a pledge over movable assets requires in principle consignment of the assets to the pledgee, which is actually an ancient and universal principle concerning pledge on chattels, i.e., movables (CC 939/1). In property law, this is called "pledge with consignment requirement" where the pledgor (the debtor) cannot use those assets after pledge. However, if this general requirement were to be applied in commercial affairs, the pledged assets would have to be delivered and consigned to the bank, and the enterprise would not be able to use its pledged assets which are necessary to run the business. On the other hand, from the perspective of the bank (the creditor), the consignment would constitute a burden of safekeeping pledged assets and cause extra expenses.[11] In other words, the consignment requirement does not fit to the nature of commercial and industrial transactions.

This incompatibility of "consignment requirement" in commercial affairs led to adoption of secured transactions legislations worldwide. The UNCITRAL Model Law on Secured Transactions[12] regulated in 2016 takes the lead in this legislative reform, concerning security rights on all types of tangible and intangible

---

11 Arkan, Ticari İşletme Hukuku, 48.

12 See the text of UNCITRAL Model Law on Secured Transactions (2016) at https://uncitral.un.org/sites/uncitral.un.org/, accessed 10.08.2021.

movable property of the business enterprises, which also tackled the legal developments in Turkish law.[13]

In this respect, the general framework in Turkish law concerning pledge on movables with registration is as follows: In the Turkish Civil Code, as an exception to the consignment rule, it is allowed to pledge through registration over movables that are subject to an official register (CC 940/2, 979). Pledge of motor vehicles by registration in the traffic register or pledge of ships (TCC 1014) can be given as examples of this exceptional regime stipulated in CC 940/2.[14]

However, CC 940/2 has a limited coverage; hereby in Turkish law, a special Code concerning "Pledge on Commercial Enterprise"[15] was adopted in 1971. This Code had a very restrictive approach limiting both parties and assets that could be subject to pledge, since pledge without consignment is an exception.

b. The "New Code"

With the ground that the above-mentioned Code was excessively restricting commercial pledge, and with the impact of international approaches, especially the UNCITRAL Model Law on Securities, in Turkey a new Code titled "Code on Pledge over Movables in Commercial Affairs" ("the new Code")[16] has been accepted in 20.10.2016. Thus, a non-possessory pledge based on a centralized electronic registry has been adopted. The new Code aims to facilitate access to finance by expanding the scope of the pledgeable movables, providing publicity, and offering alternative ways of converting the pledge into money.

Alongside the new Code, comprehensive secondary legislations have been issued by the Ministry of Trade, more precisely three regulations, respectively "The Regulation on Registry of Pledged Movable" ("the first Regulation"), "The Regulation on the Establishment of the Right of Pledge in Commercial Transactions and Use of Rights after Default" ("the second Regulation"), and "The Regulation on Valuation of Movable Assets in Commercial Transactions".[17]

The first Regulation concerns rules regarding the new official public Registry established for the pledged movables under the new Code. Accordingly, the new

13 See for assessments concerning Model Law, Spyridon V. Bazinas, "The UNCITRAL Model Law on Secured Transactions," in *International and Comparative Secured Transactions Law Essays in honour of Roderick A Macdonald,* ed. Spyridon V. Bazinas and Orkun Akseli (Oxford: Hart Publishing, 2017), 56 ff.

14 Bahtiyar, Ticari İşletme Hukuku, 44.

15 Code no. 1447 (OJ, 28.07.1971, no. 13909).

16 Code no. 6750 (OJ, 28.10.2016, no. 29871).

17 OJ, 31.12.2016, no. 29935.

public electronic Registry of Pledged Movables has been established under the supervision of the Ministry of Trade and within the Notaries Association of Turkey. Thus, to make a valid pledge, a pledge agreement shall be prepared electronically or in writing. The pledge agreement prepared electronically shall be signed with a secure electronic signature. Afterwards the agreement shall be registered in the Registry of Pledged Movables. The registration has a constitutive effect; the pledge right can be asserted to third parties only upon registration.

Although the new Code comprises 21 articles, the second Regulation contains 44 articles and stipulates many details that are not mentioned in the new Code, concerning the form of the agreement, clauses to be included, the scope and the parties, the registration of the agreement, pledge systems, the advancement system, the fixed degree system, and especially the foreclosure. In addition, there have been several amendments in the Articles 4, 5, 7, 11, 14, 15, 18 of the new Code in 2018[18] and in the Article 5 of the new Code in 2021.[19]

c. The scope of the new commercial pledge

The aim to ease the commercial pledge can be observed in many parts of the new Code, which broadens the scope of the parties and assets and thus favors the loan taker, i.e., the debtor. The pledge contract can be concluded by the credit institutions with the merchant, the tradesman, the farmer, the producer association, self-employed real person, or legal entity or can be concluded between the merchants and/or the tradesmen (Art. 3 of the new Code). Herewith, are included in the scope of the parties, persons other than typical business actors, such as "the farmer", "the producer association" or "self-employed person". Thus, the regulation has expanded in such a way that it covers even the economic activities which are not "commercial" in the meaning of TCC 3.[20]

Even the Code title is "movable assets", both "movable assets" (chattels) and "rights" can be pledged under this Code and are listed in an unlimited manner in the Article 5. Thus, the Code extended enormously the scope of the assets that can be pledged. Assets, which could not be pledged under the former Code, such as existing or expectant receivables, right of tenancy, working assets such as raw materials, earnings and revenues, consumables, stocks and not only existing but expectant assets can be subject to pledge under the new regime. However, receivables are not among the favorite security of the banks since the contract

18 Amending Code no. 7099 (OJ, 10.03.2018, no. 30356).
19 Amending Code no. 7263 (OJ, 03.02.2021, no. 31384).
20 Poroy and Yasaman, *Ticari İşletme Hukuku*, 63.

might concern an assignment prohibiting clause. On the other hand, "working assets" have no stable value and structure and are prone to merge or mingle with other assets.

Contrary to the former Code, the new Code allows pledge of every single movable asset individually and does not require as a must the pledge of the entire enterprise. The enterprise can be subject to pledge under the new Code, but with one condition. If movable assets listed in the first paragraph meet the debt, no pledge can be established on the entire enterprise (Art. 5/2 of the New Code). In case the pledge is made in respect of the enterprise, any assets allocated to the business at the time of establishment of the pledge are considered included in the pledge.[21] Pledge over entire commercial enterprise or tradesman enterprise shall be notified to the trade registry or tradesman registry.

d. Foreclosure possibilities

The new Code, on the other hand, aims to protect the creditor as well, by providing the pledgee (the bank in most of the cases) with four different possibilities of foreclosure of the pledged assets, in the event of non-payment of the debt in due time (Art. 14 of the new Code). The first possibility is to demand the passing of the ownership. If the creditor is placed in the first row, they can demand the transfer of ownership of the pledged asset from the enforcement office pursuant to the Article 24 of the Execution and Bankruptcy Code (EBC) no. 2004. The second option is that the creditor may transfer its receivables to asset management companies operating in accordance with the Banking Code no. 5411. In this case, asset management companies will have the pledge row of the creditor. The third possibility concerns assets that are not subject to the transfer of possession. The creditor can obtain and use the right of leasing and licensing of these assets. The third possibility can be used especially when intangible assets, such as intellectual property rights, are subject to pledge contract. Finally, the fourth option is the most classical and older method, the creditor can request the conversion into cash and can follow up the process according to general provisions of the EBC. Certainly, the Article 14 of the new Code states the foreclosure methods in a general manner. However, the procedure to be followed has been regulated in detail in the above-mentioned second Regulation.

---

21 For the question whether working assets will be included into the scope of the contract in case of a pledge on the entire enterprise see also, Gökhan Antalya and Faruk Acar, *Ticari İşlemlerde Taşınır Rehni* (İstanbul: Aristo, 2017), 71–72.

B. Title of Merchant and Related Consequences

1. The Title of "Merchant"

a. For natural persons

As above-mentioned, the concept of merchant has been described based on the commercial enterprise. As defined in TCC 12/1, a merchant is a person who runs a commercial enterprise completely or partially on its own behalf. Three cumulative conditions arise from this provision in order for a person to be considered "a merchant": existence of a commercial enterprise, running/operating this enterprise and lastly operating it completely or partially on its own behalf.

Some noteworthy remarks regarding these criteria are as follows:

The entry of the enterprise to the commercial register has in principle a declaratory effect. TCC 12/2 introduces an exception to the criterion of operating the commercial enterprise. The person who has notified the public of opening a commercial enterprise by means of circulars, newspapers, radio, TV, and other announcements or has registered their enterprise in the commercial register and announced the situation is deemed a merchant. The person who is deemed a merchant has the legal status of a merchant and can enjoy the rights attached to this title as well as bears the obligations.

TCC 12/3 introduces an exception to the criterion of existence of a business enterprise. The person, who pretends that a business enterprise exists, is also held liable to "bona fide third parties" as if being a merchant. A person who is responsible as a merchant cannot enjoy the rights of being a merchant but bears the obligations of being one.

Lastly, since the last criterion to be considered a merchant is to run the enterprise on its own behalf or as an ordinary partner, if the enterprise is operated on behalf of someone else, the title of merchant will also belong to the represented person. Although the law mentions "operating the enterprise on its own behalf", it need not be on its own account as well. Hence, the silent partner or indirectly represented person cannot be considered a merchant.[22]

b. For legal persons

TCC 16 introduces the following quaternion for legal persons deemed merchant: Commercial companies, associations, foundations, and the organizations

22 Arkan, Ticari İşletme Hukuku, 130; Bahtiyar, Ticari İşletme Hukuku, 107–108.

and institutions established by public legal entities to be managed and commercially operated in accordance with the provisions of private law.

Commercial companies: According to TCC 124/1, collective company, commandite company, joint stock company, limited liability company and cooperatives are commercial companies. Despite the letter of law, it is controversial whether cooperatives are in nature of commercial companies.

Although the other commercial companies mentioned in TCC 124/1 are established for profit purposes, it is argued that cooperatives are not established for profit purposes and therefore cannot be considered as trading companies; the word "institution" used in the Article 1 of Cooperatives Law no. 1163 was also seen as supporting this argument. The major opinion in the doctrine on this matter is that cooperatives are commercial companies since the wording of Article 1 of Cooperatives Law has been changed into "partnership"; cooperatives also pursue an economic purpose, although not in the form of making and distributing profits; also, the reference made in the Article 98 of Cooperatives Law to the joint stock company provisions in the TCC shows that cooperatives are getting closer to joint stock companies. On the other hand, the precedents of the Court of Cassation on this subject have also uneven history. Discussions on the subject are still ongoing.[23]

All commercial companies have legal personality. The legal entity itself has the title of merchant, that is, the legal entity and the title of merchant is acquired simultaneously. In other words, commercial companies gain the title of legal entity and merchant at the same time as soon as they are registered in the commercial register.

Associations: They, like companies, are unities of persons. However, while associations are for social (moral) purposes, companies are for-profit (for material purposes). Although associations follow non-pecuniary purposes (not for-profit organizations), they can operate commercial enterprises. In order for associations to gain the title of merchant in accordance with TCC 16, they should operate commercial enterprise to achieve their purpose and should not be a public benefit association. Associations that meet these two conditions gain the title of merchant.

---

23 See, İsmail Kırca, "Kooperatiflerin Tacir Niteliği Hakkında Yargıtay'ın Tutumu: Kanuna Aykırı Yorum mu Yoksa Örtülü Boşluk Doldurma Gayreti mi?," *Batider*, 33/2 (2017): 5 ff.

Foundations: Contrary to the former TCC, the current TCC 16 regulates the conditions for foundations to acquire the title of merchant. These cumulative conditions are operating a commercial enterprise to achieve their purposes and not spending more than half of their income on public affairs.

Institutions and organizations belonging to public legal entities: According to TCC 16, the institutions and organizations that are established by the state, special provincial administration, municipality and village and other public legal entities to be managed in accordance with the provisions of private law or operated commercially in accordance with their founding laws are also considered merchants.

c. For association of shipowners

According to TCC 1064/1, a union that is formed by more than one person in order to operate a ship owned by them in the form of shared (joint) ownership in maritime trade and to gain benefits on the name and account of all of them pursuant to a contract is called association of shipowners. Association of shipowners has no legal personality. Pursuant to TCC 17, the provisions regarding the merchant are also applied to the association of shipowners.

d. For dominant undertakings

TCC 195 regulates the group of companies by introducing the dominance criteria regarding the relationship of a trading company with another commercial company. It stipulates that the subsidiary companies that are directly or indirectly affiliated with the controlling (parent) company will form a group of companies together with the parent company. However, if the dominant of the group is an "undertaking" whose head office is located in the country or abroad, the provisions regarding the group of companies will be applied and the dominant undertaking will be considered a merchant (TCC 195/5). The scope of the concept of "undertaking" is quite wide so that real persons, legal entities under private or public law, and even entities that do not have legal personality may be considered undertakings and therefore merchants.[24]

---

24 For detailed information on this new merchant group formed within TCC 195 see, Arkan, *Ticari İşletme Hukuku*, 142; Özlem Karaman Coşkun, "6102 sayılı Türk Ticaret Kanunu'nda Teşebbüs Kavramı ve Tacir Sayılmasının Sonuçları," *MÜHF-HAD*, 21, no. 1 (2015): 107 ff.

2. *Loss of the Title of "Merchant"*

Real persons lose their title of merchant upon the deletion of their registration from the commercial register. The merchant who leaves the trade may be subject to the proceedings of bankruptcy for one more year as if their title is still in effect.

Legal persons lose their title of merchant when their business name deleted from the commercial register upon completion of the liquidation procedures. Legal persons, such as associations and foundations, who can acquire the title of merchant provided that certain additional conditions exist, lose their title of merchant if one of these conditions disappears.

Termination of association of shipowners is regulated in TCC 1082 ff. When one of the reasons set forth in this article occurs, the liquidation procedures of the association of shipowners will be carried out and the registration in the commercial register will be deleted.

The title of merchant of the dominant undertaking also expires in the case of loss of one of the conditions for acquiring the dominant undertaking status.

3. *Consequences of Being "Merchant"*

a. *Being subject to insolvency*

Pursuant to the Article 43 of Execution and Bankruptcy Code (EBC), persons subject to bankruptcy are examined through four groups:

- Merchants are subject to bankruptcy due to all kinds of debts, whether ordinary or commercial.
- Persons deemed to be merchants (TCC 12/2) are subject to bankruptcy the same as merchants.
- Persons subject to merchant's provisions may also become insolvent such as responsible persons as merchants (TCC 12/3) and association of shipowners (TCC 17).
- Some persons, although not merchants, are subject to bankruptcy due to the special provisions. The trader who abandons the trade loses their title. However, as this title continues for 1 year, bankruptcy may be requested (EBC 44). Partners of collective and commandite company can be subject to bankruptcy due to the partnership's debts (TCC 238/2, 240, 317). Bank managers and auditors; managers of capital market institutions and their partners holding more than 10 % of the shares are also subject to bankruptcy due to the special provisions prescribed by the law under certain circumstances (Art. 110 of Banking Code no. 5411, CMC 98).

b. Registration to the commercial register

Merchants have to register to the commercial register within 15 days from the date of opening their commercial enterprise (TCC 40/1). Since enterprises are registered, the merchant must also register their other businesses, if any.

c. Registration to the Chambers and Unions

Merchants have to register with the Chambers of Commerce and, if necessary, the Chambers of Industry and Unions in their regions.

d. Obligation to choose and use a business name

Pursuant to TCC 18, 39 ff. and the relevant secondary legislation, the merchants are obliged to choose a business name, register it and use it in their commercial activities.

e. Subject to the presumption of commercial affair

The affairs of merchant are, as a rule, of a commercial in nature. The exception to this rule for real person merchant is as follows as stated in TCC 19/1:

The debts of a merchant are deemed commercial based on the presumption that the debts are related to their commercial enterprise unless the merchant explicitly informs the counterparty that debts are not related to the commercial enterprise, or unless the nature of the transaction requires to be considered ordinary.

f. Being subject to commercial customs

According to TCC 2, commercial customs and traditions are applied to the merchants in an absolute manner. However, the implementation of commercial customs for non-merchants depends on the condition that these people know or need to have known about the existence of customs and traditions.

g. Keeping commercial books

Pursuant to the provisions of TCC 18/1 and 64 ff., the merchants are obliged to keep commercial books. The answers to the questions of which types of merchants will keep which books and which books are subject to which approval and when, are regulated in TCC 64 and within the relevant secondary legislation. However, as required in the provisions of the tax laws, there might be other accounting books that must be kept in addition. Bookkeeping has importance for various reasons such as conclusive force as evidence in favor of or against the merchant under certain conditions (see, Art. 222 of Code of Civil Procedure no. 6100).

h. Acting as a prudent businessperson

Merchants are obliged to act like a prudent businessperson in their commercial activities (TCC 18/2). In terms of the criterion of prudence, the appropriate standard to be applied is objective; whether a reasonable merchant in the same position would have behaved similarly under the same conditions determines the prudence.[25]

For instance, a bus operator, who should take their passengers safely to their destination, is obliged to choose stopover and resting places appropriately, and take measures to prevent any harm to the health and interests of their passengers. Otherwise, they would not be considered to have acted prudently.[26]

TCC 18/2 is a gap-filling provision and includes "burdens" in the form of imposing certain actions on the trader that they have not previously undertaken under the contract or that of encumbering the merchant. In a recent decision, the Court of Cassation even decided that the burden of the bank was heavier than that of other merchants. According to the decision of the Court of Cassation General Assembly of Civil Chambers, the obligation of banks to act prudently in all their transactions as merchants does not differ from any merchant; even the prudence and diligence obligation expected from banks is undoubtedly heavier. It should be admitted that the obligation of banks, which are trust based institutions, to carefully protect the deposits they receive against counterfeiters has increased even more.[27]

Due to this obligation, it is accepted that the merchant cannot claim their loss based on inexperience or thoughtlessness, based on the unfair advantage provision in TCO 28 and can only rely on the reason that their circumstances are straitened.[28]

i. The right to claim fees and interest

According to TCC 20, the merchant may demand commission/fees for their work and services, as well as interest for their advances and expenses, even if

---

25 Nomer Ertan et al., *Ticari İşletme Hukuku*, 285.

26 Arkan, Ticari İşletme Hukuku, 154.

27 Turkish Court of Cassation, General Assembly of Civil Chambers decision, dated 16.6.2020, no. 3092/400: https://www.lexpera.com.tr/, accessed 10.08.2021.

28 Nomer Ertan et al., *Ticari İşletme Hukuku*, 285–286.

by telegram, or, with the registered electronic mail system using a secure electronic signature.[34]

In the former TCC, the phrase "for the validity of notices and warnings" was included. Currently, although it is explained in the Preamble that this condition is no longer a requirement for validity but a condition that provides ease of proof (requirement as to form), the nature of the form is still controversial in the doctrine due to the provision of TCO 12/2. According to TCO 12/2, the form envisaged in the law for contracts will constitute a requirement for validity as a rule, and it is accepted to be applicable in other legal transactions as well.[35]

n. Facility in exercising the right to retain

The Article 950 of Turkish Civil Code regulates the right to retain; that is, in the presence of certain conditions, the creditor is given the right to keep some of the debtor's property until the debt is paid. The exercise of this right depends on the fulfillment of three conditions: The creditor must possess a movable property (chattels) or securities belonging to the debtor with the consent of the debtor; the creditor's receivable must be due; the retained objects must be intrinsically connected with the receivable.

The facility brought for the use of the right to retain by the merchants emerges in terms of the third condition, and the right to retain can be used even if there is no connection between the claim and possession (CC 950/2). In other words, even if the claim and possession arise from different reasons and different contracts, the merchant has the right to retain.

o. Being subject to special provisions in commercial sales and exchange of goods contracts

After it is stated in TCC 23 that commercial sales and exchange of goods contracts between merchants are bound to the relevant provisions of the TCO as a rule, some special provisions are also included about such contracts. In order for these special provisions regulated in TCC 23 to be applicable, there must be a sale and exchange of goods between the merchants concerning their commercial enterprises.

In TCC 23, mainly three special regulations have been introduced regarding the rights of the buyer in the contracts to be partially fulfilled, the seller's right to

---

34 For more information regarding secure electronic signature see, Law Firm Pekin and Pekin, "The Electronic Signature Law in Turkey," *Digital Evidence and Electronic Signature Law Review*, 1 (2004): 33 ff.

35 See Arkan, *Ticari İşletme Hukuku*, 170; Bahtiyar, *Ticari İşletme Hukuku*, 125.

demand the sale of the goods in the event of buyer's default, and the obligations of the buyer in case the sold is defective.[36]

p. Being subject to special provisions in transactions between commercial enterprises for the purpose of supply of goods and services

TCC 1530/para. 2–8 is based on the aim of compliance with the EU Directive 2011/7/EU of the European Parliament and of the Council of 16 February 2011 on combating late payment in commercial transactions,[37] and as it can be understood from its rationale, it brings protection to SMEs producing goods and services against large enterprises (store chains, supermarkets, shopping malls, etc.).[38]

r. Opportunity to make a jurisdiction agreement

According to the Article 17 of the Code of Civil Procedure no. 6100, merchants or public legal entities may agree on the competence of one or more courts for a dispute that has arisen or may arise between them. Unlike commercial companies, since all business of natural person merchants will not be regarded commercial, a natural person merchant should not be able to put an authorization clause in the contract in matters not related to their business.[39]

C. Merchant Assistants

It is simply ineluctable for merchants to carry out their business with assistance due to the large field of activity and business volume. Therefore, merchants benefit from other people who are called assistants of merchants and appointed by them while carrying out the activities related to their business.

Merchant assistants are divided into two main groups as dependent and independent assistants. The first of them work under the order, supervision, and control of the merchant and especially in the merchant's workplace, while the latter mostly has a separate business apart from the merchant's business.

Dependent and independent assistants are also divided into two as those who are authorized to represent the merchant and those who are not. In this chapter,

---

36 For detailed information see Ülgen et al., *Ticari İşletme Hukuku*, 289 ff.; Arkan, *Ticari İşletme Hukuku*, 174 ff.

37 OJ L 48, 23.2.2011, 1–10: https://eur-lex.europa.eu/legal-content/en/ accessed 10.08.2021.

38 For detailed information see, Yeşim Atamer and Gül Okutan-Nilsson, "Para Alacaklısının Geç Ödemelere Karşı Korunmasına İlişkin Yeni TK m. 1530 Düzenlemesi ve Uygulama Alanı," *Batider*, 29/3 (2013): 31 ff.

39 Nomer Ertan et al., *Ticari İşletme Hukuku*, 282; Bahtiyar, *Ticari İşletme Hukuku*, 135.

among dependent assistants only those who are authorized to represent the merchant will be briefly explained, who are commercial representative (TCO 547 ff.), commercial agent (TCO 551) and commercial traveller (TCO 448 ff.).[40]

In the group of independent assistants, agent has an authorization to represent the merchant (TCC 102 ff.). However, the commissioner (TCO 532 ff.) is authorized to represent the merchant indirectly, not directly, whereas the broker is deprived of such authority. Besides, while the agent's relationship with the merchant is continuous, the broker and the commissioner need to be assigned by the merchant on a case basis.

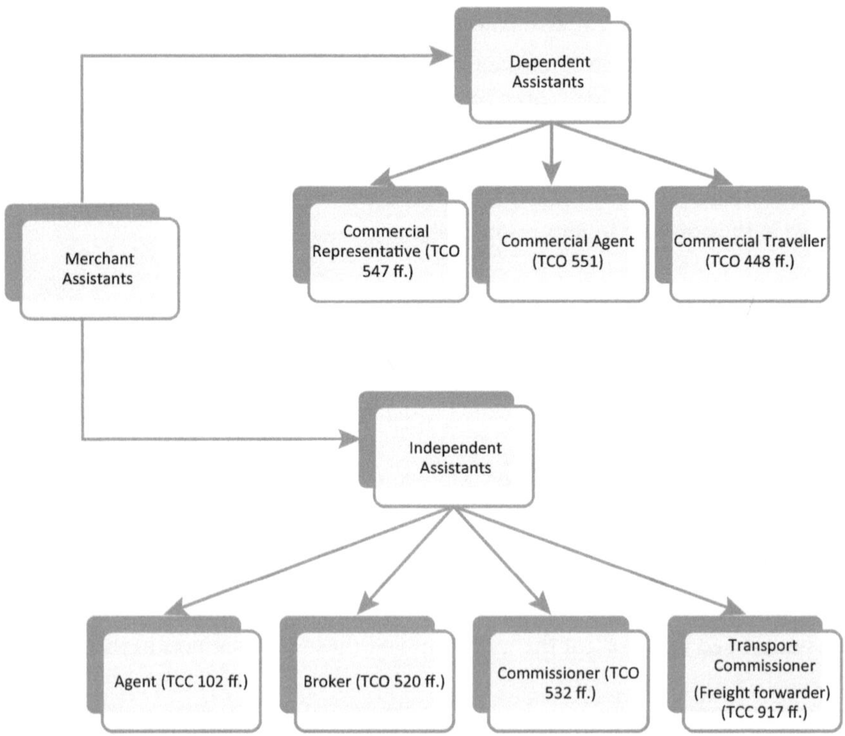

Tab. 1. Merchant Assistants

40 For those who also have employment contracts with the merchant, see supra: *Chapter IV – Employment Law.*

1. *Dependent Assistants*

a. *Commercial representative*

Who is the commercial representative? A commercial representative is a person who has been expressly or tacitly authorized by the owner of the commercial enterprise to conduct the business and to sign per procuration (signing by proxy) under the commercial business name in the transactions related to the business (TCO 547). They have the widest authority among merchant assistants and hence are called as merchant's other self (*alter ego*).

How are they appointed? A commercial representative may only be appointed to conduct the business of a commercial enterprise and may only be appointed by the merchant (owner of the commercial enterprise). The decision to appoint a commercial representative is in principle left to the discretion of the merchant. However, it is obligatory to appoint a fully authorized commercial representative located in Turkey to the head of the branches in Turkey of the enterprises whose headquarters are located abroad (TCC 40/4).

The merchant must give notice of the granting of the commercial representatives for entry in the commercial register. However, they are bound by the actions of the commercial representative even before the registry, since the registration has no constitutive effect but has a declaratory effect.

What are the scope and limits of representation authority? The fact that the scope and limits of the representation authority of the commercial representative are determined by law, independently of the will of the merchant, meets the need for trust in the business life and eliminates third-party concerns about the representative's authority. According to TCO 548, in dealings with bona fide third parties, the commercial representative is deemed authorized to make a commitment by signing bills of exchange in the name of the owner of the enterprise and to carry out on their behalf for all types of transactions that fall within the scope of the commercial operations and business affairs of the merchant. Although they have the widest authority among other merchant assistants as mentioned above, this authority is not unlimited.

Limitations set forth in the law: According to TCO 548/2, the commercial representatives cannot alienate or encumber the immovable assets unless they are given explicit authority, or the field of the enterprise is already immovable trade.

Limitations arising from the will of the merchant: Pursuant to TCO 549, the merchant may impose two types of limitations on the authority of the representative, both of which may also coexist. These limitations, which can be asserted to everyone on the condition that they are entered and published in the commercial register, are restricting the business affairs to a specific branch or granting only the joint power of attorney. Other limitations of authority such as limitation in terms of quantity and subject cannot be entered in the commercial register and those limitations have no legal effect on bona fide third parties.[41]

Limitations arising from auxiliary nature: Although not explicitly stated in the law, it is accepted in doctrine and practice that there are some limitations arising from the nature of representation or assistantship and that some transactions can only be made by the merchants themselves such as transferring the commercial enterprise, requesting the bankruptcy of the merchant, acquiring a partner in the business, pledging the business, appointing another commercial representative.[42]

What are the reasons for termination of representation authority? TCO 554 regulates the expiration of the powers of commercial representatives and commercial agents jointly as follows: Dismissal and resignation; death of the representative and loss of the capacity of judgment; transfer and liquidation of the commercial enterprise, termination of the legal entity of the merchant (TCO 43/2, TCC 251); bankruptcy of the merchant; death or incapacity of the merchant (if commercial companies is in question) if it is determined to be the reason for termination, extinguishes the authority.

Even if the commercial representative's authorization has not been entered in the commercial register, its registry and announcement is mandatory when its authority expires. Otherwise, the good faith of third parties is protected (TCO 550).

b. Commercial agent

Who is the commercial agent? According to TCO 551, a commercial agent is a person authorized by the owner of the commercial enterprise to manage

41 Bahtiyar, Ticari İşletme Hukuku, 222.
42 Bahtiyar, Ticari İşletme Hukuku, 222.

or conduct out some of their businesses without granting them the authority of commercial representative. A hotel manager is an example of a general authorized commercial agent whereas a receptionist or a cashier in a restaurant is a special authorized commercial agent.

How are they appointed? A commercial agent may be appointed explicitly or tacitly by the merchant or commercial representative and may only be appointed to a commercial enterprise. In principle, neither conferral nor withdrawal of the commercial agent's authority is subject to registration and announcement. However, opting for a written form provides ease of proof (for exceptional regulations requiring registration and announcement, see TCC 371/7 and 629/3).

What are the scope and limits of representation authority? The authority of the commercial agent (both general and special) only extends to the activities that fall within the scope of the usual commercial operations of the enterprise, or that are normally connected with the transactions in question. However, a commercial agent cannot take out loans, sign bills of exchange or conduct litigation unless explicitly granted such powers as stated in TCO 551/2. Moreover, the commercial agent is also not authorized to do *a fortiori* the work that the commercial representative cannot carry out such as alienating or encumbering the immovable property. The representation authority of the general commercial agent may be limited as desired by the merchant, provided that it is notified to third parties with letter, notice, circular, etc.

What are the reasons for termination of representation authority? The reasons for termination in terms of commercial agency resemble the above-mentioned reasons for commercial representative (see TCO 554). However, unlike the commercial representative, since the appointment of the commercial agent cannot be registered, the withdrawal of the authorization is not subject to the registration. Hence, giving prompt notice to third parties of the termination of the authority is also required, as well as withdrawal of a certificate of authorization if it has been issued at the time of appointment or afterward. Otherwise, the merchant will be liable for the actions of the unauthorized agent to the bona fide third parties (TCO 42/3, 44).

c. Commercial traveller

Who is the commercial traveller? The commercial traveller is the person who undertakes to act as an intermediary on a continuous basis in the execution of all kinds of transactions outside the business, or in case of a written agreement to perform the works specified in this agreement on behalf of the employer, who is the owner of the commercial enterprise, in exchange for a salary (TCO 448).

As stated in the definition, the relationship between the merchant and the commercial traveller is of a continuous nature, which also distinguishes commercial traveller from the broker. The commercial traveller is appointed to expand the field of activity of the enterprise, to spread it to other places. The merchant who wants to expand their activity may choose to open a branch, or if the business volume in that place is not suitable, may choose to benefit from the services of a -mobile- commercial traveller instead of establishing a fixed office. The commercial traveller, unlike the agent, is an assistant dependent on the merchant. Since it is regulated in the section on service contracts in the TCO, the commercial traveller's contract and related problems also constitute the subject of employment law due to their status of employee.[43]

Conclusion and content of the commercial traveller's contract, obligations and authority of the commercial traveller, special obligations of the employer and the reasons and conditions to terminate this continuous contract are regulated in the Articles 449 to 460 of the TCO.

2. *Independent Assistants*

a. *Agent*

Selling goods and services through an agency provides the merchant with economic advantages and legal conveniences. As a function, the agency frees the merchant from operating in the country or abroad by opening a branch or appointing a dependent assistant in a place other than the place, where the business is headquartered. In this way, the merchant ("the principal" of the agent) will have the opportunity to sell/market their goods and services by making a contract through the agency or directly with the contracts made by the agent.[44] Therefore, one of the main reasons for the preference for the agency is not to impose a burden on the merchant in advance and to pay the agent if a positive result is obtained from the activities of the agency.

---

43 For further information on employee status see supra: *Chapter IV – Employment Law.*

44 Arslan Kaya, *Acentelik Hukuku Şerhi* (İstanbul: Beta, 2016), 5.

Who is the agent? As defined in TCC 102, an agent is a person who, without having a legal position attached to the enterprise, in contrast to a commercial representative, commercial agent, sales officer, or employee of the commercial enterprise, takes the profession of intermediating in contracts that concern a commercial enterprise in a certain place or region on a permanent basis or that of making them on behalf of that merchant.[45]

Since the agent is an independent merchant assistant, they have their own independent business. If this business is a commercial enterprise, which is usually the case, then the agent also has the title of merchant (TCC 12).

The two types of agency, the intermediary agent and the agency authorized to make a contract, can be both natural and legal persons. The difference between these two agencies is important in terms of the form of the contract. Pursuant to TCC 107/1, the agency authorization to make a contract on behalf of the merchant must be given in writing.

The agreement for the abolition of the monopoly right, which is defined as the agency's exclusive right to make transactions or operate within the certain place and region where they will operate, must also be made in writing (TCC 104).

Who are subject to agency provisions? According to TCC 103, persons who are permanently authorized to make contracts on account of a local or foreign merchant, but on their own behalf and who make transactions in Turkey on behalf and account of foreign merchants who do not have a head office or branch in Turkey are subject to the provisions regarding the agency as well.

How about analog innominate contracts? In practice, contracts made under names such as dealer or distributor often appear as one of the contracts that are legally deemed agency or related to the agency in terms of content. In this respect, it is important to distinguish agency from other contracts and to determine the provisions to be applied. The most common innominate contracts are that of relating exclusive distributor and franchisee:

Exclusive distributor Exclusive distributor buys the goods to be sold from the merchant; sells to their customers on their own name and account. Their profit is

45 See and cf. the definition in German law, Georg Vorbrugg and Dirk H. Mahler, "Agency and Distributorship Agreements under German Law," *International Lawyer (ABA)*, 19, no. 2 (1985): 608.

the difference between the purchases and sell price. On the other side, the agency receives a certain fee from the merchant and acts either as an intermediary or on behalf of the merchant. Besides, while the monopoly right is a mandatory element of the exclusive distribution agreement, it can be removed from the agency contract in writing if desired so.

Franchisee In franchising, a merchant grants franchisee a privilege, that is, an authority to market and distribute their goods and services to another merchant within the framework of a contract. Franchiser also trains and supervises the franchisee's personnel. More importantly, franchiser grants the franchisee the right to use the franchiser's business name, brand, identification marks, production procedures and secrets, and technical and commercial know-how. Franchise agreement has been used frequently in Turkey in the recent years. This agreement is not regulated in the law as is in most European countries[46] and contains element of different contracts such as sale, exclusive distribution, simple agency, license and agency. The main differences from the agency contract are that franchisee acts on its own behalf and account; pays a franchise fee to the franchiser that grants the franchisee the right to use the trademark and operating system; benefits from the technical and commercial know-how of the merchant. Besides, the monopoly right is an absolute mandatory element in franchise agreement as in exclusive distribution agreement.

What are the obligations of the agent? The agent should safeguard the principal's interests, inform the principal about the financial situation and changes in the market, follow the given instructions, take preventive measures to avoid damage on goods, send the money belonging to the principal, and non-compete unless otherwise agreed in writing.

What are the obligations of the principal-merchant? The principal-merchant should provide the agent with the necessary documentation to enable the agent to perform their activities successfully; pay the agreed or customary fee on all transactions that the agent facilitated or concluded during the agency relationship and for the transactions made directly by the merchant within the monopoly zone (TCC 113–115); pay extraordinary expenses (TCC 117) and

46 There is no uniform or standardized European franchise law as well. See, Luciana Bassani, Rebecca Bedford, Arthur L. Pressman, Jean-Philippe Turgeon, Dagmar Waldzus, "Applicable Law and Jurisdiction in Franchising, Commercial Agency and Distribution Agreements," *International Journal of Franchising Law,* 13, no. 6 (2015): 5.

pay interest when the agent is entitled in accordance with TCC 20. Besides, the agent has a special lien on movable property and securities in respect of the goods that are in their possession due to the agency until the receivables are paid (TCC 119).

What are the conditions for termination of an agency agreement? Where the agency contract is entered into for an indefinite period, it can be terminated by giving 3 months' notice of termination. Where the agency contract is concluded for a definite period, it expires without notice of termination. However, where a fixed-term agency contract is tacitly extended by both parties on expiry of its duration, it is deemed to be extended for an indefinite period. In cases of death, bankruptcy or loss of capacity to act of the principal or the agent, TCO 513 is applied, and the contract ends unless the nature of the agency business requires, or the contract indicates otherwise. In addition, both the principal and the agent may at any time terminate the contract on the basis of a just cause[47] (TCC 121).

Portfolio compensation[48]: After the agency agreement is terminated, the principal-merchant continues to benefit from the portfolio (clientele) created by the agent. There was no normative regulation in the former TCC no. 6762 regarding the demand for the portfolio as opposed to the case that it is included in the EEC Directive and therefore in the laws of all EU member states. However, judicial decisions filled the gap in the law (*casus omissus*) and it was decided that the agency would be entitled to "portfolio compensation" under certain conditions.

Currently, TCC 122 regulated the portfolio compensation, with inspiration from the German Commercial Code (§ 89b, claim to indemnity) and the Swiss Code of Obligations (418u, compensation for clientele) in a comprehensive manner.[49] Noteworthy points of the provision can be underlined as follows:

---

47 For the explanations and examples of just cause see, Kaya, *Acentelik Hukuku Şerhi*, 207–212.

48 As is stated in the Preamble of TCC 122, although the phrase "compensation" has been used, the claim cannot be understood in the classical sense as compensation for asset damage. However, the doctrine still adopts the approach that the demand is broadly directed towards redressing the damage. For the criticism of the terminology preference in TCC 122, see Kaya, *Acentelik Hukuku Şerhi*, 240.

49 For German law see and cf. Vorbrugg and Mahler, "Agency and Distributorship Agreements under German Law," 616–618.

The three conditions that must be met cumulatively in order to be entitled to the portfolio compensation are that the merchant derives substantial benefits, even after the termination of the contract, from business relationships with the new customers found by the agent; the agency loses its right to the commission for the work done or to be done in a short time with the customers it has brought to the business, depending on the termination of the contract; and such demand is equitable having regard to the characteristics and conditions of the concrete case.

Pursuant to TCC 122/3, the portfolio compensation does not arise when the agent has terminated the contract without the principal's action to justify the termination, or when the principal has terminated the contract for just cause due to the agent's culpable conduct.

Portfolio compensation is regulated as an inalienable right in the law; it cannot be waived in advance and this right must be claimed within 1 year after the termination of the contract (TCC 122/4). This provision regarding the portfolio compensation shall also be applied in the termination of an exclusive distribution agreement and in similar continuous contractual relationships that give exclusive rights as long as it is not contrary to equity (TCC 122/5).

Non-compete agreement: In principle, the agent becomes free after the agency relationship ends, and if they wish, they can continue the agency profession in the area they want, including the area where the terminated relationship was pursued previously. However, this may not always be possible. The parties, often with the principal's request or even pressure, may decide that the non-compete clauses will have effect even after the termination of the contract. The conditions regarding the non-compete agreement, which were not regulated in the former TCC, are regulated in TCC 123.[50]

b. Broker

It may be difficult for the parties who want to enter into a contractual relationship to find each other for the reasons such as operating in separate places or speaking different languages. The activities of intermediaries called brokers are used to eliminate such difficulties, to bring together the people who want to make a contract, to prepare a suitable environment for the conclusion of the

50 For detailed information regarding non-compete agreement see, Arslan Kaya, "Post Contractual Non-Compete Agreements Concerning Agents, Distributors and Franchisees," *Annales de la Faculté de Droit d'Istanbul*, 47, no. 64 (2015): 43 ff.

contract, and even to assist the parties. The legal nature of the people referred to as real estate agents in practice is actually brokerage.[51]

The brokerage agreement does not depend on a form of validity; but the real estate brokerage, which constitutes an exception, depends on the written form (TCO 520/3).

Since broker is an independent merchant assistant, they have their own independent business. If this business is a commercial enterprise, then the broker also has the title of merchant (TCC 12). The broker only alerts the principal to an opportunity to conclude or to facilitate the conclusion of a contract, mediates the parties to form a contract, brings the parties together, often participates in contract negotiations, and even prepares the draft of the contract. The brokerage must be for a fee. Otherwise, the provisions governing simple agency contracts are to be applied (TCO 520/2, 502 ff.).

While the broker's obligation is to mediate the contract and protect the interests of both parties, the broker's right is to request a fee and, if the principal has undertaken to reimburse them under the contract, the expenses.

c. Commissioner

Commission agreement is regulated in TCO 532 ff. (see also, specific regulations regarding certain types of commission agreements, TCC 917 ff.; CMC 37 ff.; Art. 47 ff. of Law no. 5174, etc.)

Who is the commissioner? According to TCO 532, a commissioner is a person who undertakes the purchase and sale of securities or chattels, in return for a commission, on their own behalf but for the account of another. This is not a closed enumeration (that is to say, not *numerus clausus*); the provisions of the commission in TCO apply to other commission as well as securities and chattels (see and cf. TCO 546/3 and TCC 917 ff.).

Since the broker is an indirect representative, as a rule, a second transaction is required in order to transfer to the principal the rights and obligations arising from the transaction with the third party (trader) (TCO 40/3).

However, where the representative did not declare their title when making the contract, the rights and obligations arising therefrom accrue directly to the person represented, only if the other party must have inferred the agency relationship from the circumstances or did not care with whom the contract was made (TCO 40/2). Thus, the rights and obligations pass directly to the principal.

51 Bahtiyar, *Ticari İşletme Hukuku*, 243–244.

Secondly, according to TCO 509/1 (see TCO 532/2), where the agent acting on the principal's behalf acquires claims in their own name against third parties, such claims pass to the principal if the principal has fulfilled all the obligations towards the agent.

Obligations of the commissioner are acting in accordance with the principal's instructions, protecting the principal's interests and keeping the principal informed, and transferring rights and obligations to the principal (TCO 533–536).

The commissioner has the right to request a fee, which is called commission and is usually paid as a percentage of the sale price. A commissioner who assumes liability for the performance by the third party is also entitled to special remuneration, which is called "*del credere* commission" (TCO 537). The commissioner may also request costs and interest according to TCO 538. Pursuant to TCO 541, the commissioner has a special lien in respect of the goods on commission and the sale proceeds until the receivables are paid. Lastly, commissioners may act for their own account under certain circumstances according to TCO 543–545.

d. Transport commissioner (Freight forwarder)

Who is the freight forwarder? A transport commissioner or a freight forwarder, who in return for payment, undertakes to transport goods. They transport goods as a profession and carry or forward goods for the consignor's account but in their own name (see TCC 917 ff.; cf. TCC 918/3). In practice, most of the shipping agencies usually have this title. If the freight forwarder carries passengers, not goods, then the provisions governing simple agency contracts apply.

The freight forwarder must carefully select the carrier to whom the goods will be transported, protect goods and keep them in good condition until delivery, provide the carrier with documents and information about the goods, and notify the trader if there is any damage or defect (TCC 918).

On the other hand, the freight forwarder has the right to demand a fee, and the fee is paid upon delivery of the goods to the carrier (TCC 920–921). If the freight forwarders transport the goods themselves, they are also considered as the carrier. In this case, in addition to the fee they will demand for their own activity, they may also ask for the usual transportation fee (TCC 926). Besides, the freight forwarder has a special lien according to TCC 923 (see also, CC 950–953).

The freight forwarders are responsible for the loss and damage of the goods in their possession, in accordance with the provisions of the carrier's responsibility (TCC 928/1).

All claims are subject to a 1-year prescription period in accordance with TCC 930 (cf. 3-years prescription period according to TCC 930/2, 855/5).

D. *The Unfair Competition Rules*

1. *General Remarks*

Unfair competition rules are codified with a very comprehensive approach, essentially in TCC 54–63, which constitute the normative fundament of the unfair trade practices in Turkish law. In addition, TCO 57 regulates dishonest behaviors between non-merchants, professionals such as doctors or lawyers, as a source of liability.[52] Among the other legislative regulations can be cited the Act on the Prevention of Unfair Competition in the Importation no. 3577, which covers "unfair importation" that is subject to damping or subvention and sets special type of sanctions. Finally, there are few other regulations in the field of consumer law, within the Act on Consumer Protection, and in field of intellectual property law within the Code of Intellectual and Artistic Work.[53]

The main purpose of the unfair competition rules is to ensure "fair and undistorted competition for the benefit of all participants". "Fair competition" (fair trade) means behaviors that are in conformity with both the provisions of the law and general principles of good faith, business ethics, and deontology. "Undistorted" means a competition free from fraud or deception (Preamble of the Art. 54/1). The fundamental principle underlying the unfair competition rules is the rule of "good faith" (TCC 54/2). A quick answer to the question which behaviors would fall under unfair competition, is given in TCC 54/2 as follows: "All the acts and commercial practices that are deceptive or otherwise contrary to good faith, affecting relationships between competitors or between suppliers and customers are considered unfair and against law.".

Pursuant to TCC 54/2, for a behavior, or a commercial practice to be identified as unfair competition,

- It must be contrary to good faith,
- It must affect or is likely to affect the market, the relationships between competitors or suppliers and customers.[54]

---

52 Gül Okutan Nilsson, "Unfair Trade Law," in *Introduction to Turkish Business Law*, ed. Tuğrul Ansay and Eric C. Schneider, (Ankara: Seçkin, 2014), 113.

53 Okutan Nilsson, "Unfair Trade Law," 113.

54 It means that there is no need for a competitive relationship between the parties.

For a behavior to be identified as an unfair competition practice, it is not necessary that the offender has benefited or is faulty, or any damages have occurred.

TCC 54 and 55, concerning the substantial law, take as a reference the Swiss Federal Act Against Unfair Competition (Swiss UCA) of 19 December 1986, which regulates unfair competition behaviors with an expanding approach.[55] Thus, Federal Act codifies the whole unfair competition area in one single Code similarly with German and Austrian legal systems.[56]

Following the Swiss UCA, TCC 54 and 55 set high standards of protection, both by expanding the circle of interests to be protected and increasing the number of unfair behaviors and categories stated in TCC 55. Not only competitors, but suppliers and customers as well, not only merchants but consumers and all the other participants are included into the circle of interest groups to be protected. "All the participants" refer to competitors, suppliers, customers, and consumers and generally the economy and the public interest. Through this expanding circle, unfair competition rules adopt macro-objectives, and customers and business associations and consumer associations are given the right to make claims under unfair competition rules.

Commercial law mostly deals with business transactions based on commercial contracts and the articles of association of the companies which constitute a corporate contractual relationship. However, there can be a whole lot of conflict arising out of unfair and dishonest commercial behaviors among merchants who are not party to the same contract. Not all, but a big part of the unfair competition practices is concerned with tortious acts, thus the unfair competition rules are usually defined as "commercial tort law".

Last but not least, the scope of unfair competition rules is closely linked with competition law which is codified in the Act on the Protection of Competition no. 4054 (APC). These two branches regulate "competition" and protects similar group of interests, and their overall objective are similar. In this context, the APC generally aims to ensure an "unrestricted" competition, i.e., free trade, as well as to attach results to hindered and restricted competition (Preamble of the

55 See the Preamble of TCC 54; On the other hand, it must be noted that the provisions concerning procedural matters of the Swiss UCA are not taken as a reference in the unfair competition rules of the TCC.

56 For a comparison between the Swiss UCA and EU UCP Directive 2005/29/EC see, Peter Jung, "UCP-Directive and Swiss Law against Unfair Competition," *Journal of European Consumer and Market Law* 5, no. 2 (2016) 102–106. See the UCP 2005/29/EC Directive (OJ L 149/22, 11.06.2205) concerning unfair commercial practices at https://eur-lex.europa.eu/eli/dir/2005/29/oj, accessed 10.08.2021.

Art. 54). However, protection methods and sanctions differ one from the other. Unfair competition rules regulate the limits and the general frame of the right to compete in business, thus have rather a restrictive approach. Nevertheless, competition law aims to encourage the competition and forbids the behaviors that are restricting the competition and free trade. From a general perspective can be mentioned that these two branches incline to codify different facets of competition.[57]

2. *The Unfair Business Practices (TCC 55)*

The most common unfair trade practices are regulated in TCC 55, in a very comprehensive way, under six paragraphs, i.e., six main categories that comprise twenty-one sub-paragraphs in total. Neither the main categories nor the sub-paragraphs are limitative. Therefore, although a situation is not mentioned in TCC 55, can still be defined as an act of unfair competition if it bears the above-mentioned essential elements stated in TCC 54/2.[58]

The first category consists of unfair advertising and sale methods contrary to the principle of good faith and other similar unlawful practices (Art. 55/1-a). This is the most comprehensive category with twelve sub-paragraphs. This paragraph concerning examples of unfair advertising and sale methods, can be defined as the main category, that is to say, the main pillar of unfair practices. Most of the examples gathered under paragraph (a) had been codified in the former TCC no. 6762 as well. In the first five sub-paragraphs are regulated generally misleading, false, and deceptive statements and advertisements.

- The first sub-paragraph is "*denigrating others*", includes acts of vilifying, veiling, underestimating, and depreciating "others". Under the first sub-paragraph, there should be a written or verbal statement, this statement should concern others or their goods, business products, prices, activities, or commercial affairs and this statement should be "false", "misleading", or "unnecessarily hurtful".[59] "Denigrating prices" is included into the scope of the first situation. Nowadays statements or advertisements on the online platforms are often being subject to unfair competition claims. In a recent decision of the Turkish Court of Cassation concerning the comparison of tariffs of different electric

57 See *infra: Chapter VI – Competition Law.*

58 See, the Preamble of TCC 55.

59 Poroy and Yasaman, *Ticari İşletme Hukuku,* 395; Nomer Ertan, *Haksız Rekabet Hukuku* (İstanbul: On İki Levha, 2016), 132.

energy providers on a website (www.akillitarife.com), the Court ruled that the comparison of tariffs *per se* does not lead to unfair competition, it should be analyzed tariffs of the plaintiff and assess whether the statements of the defendant on the website are contrary to the truth, thus aiming to mislead the consumers, to drive the customers away from the plaintiff, and whether the rival companies are protected or not, by focusing on whether an objective comparison is made by the defendant in order to inform the consumers.[60]

- "*Deceptive statements or deceptive advertising*" includes making unrealistic, exaggerating or misleading statements about "themselves", or "their" commercial enterprise, business signs, goods, business products, activities, prices, stocks, sales campaigns, and business relationships, or putting the third party ahead of the competition through the same means. The Court of Cassation has considered the case as deceptive in the event of the statement made by the defendant on their website where several famous firms and people were presented as their clients. However, the defendant was a former employee of the plaintiff, and these firms and people were in fact customers of the plaintiff in the concrete event.[61]
- "*Using fake professional titles or diplomas*" includes, although one has not received any diplomas or awards, pretending to have those, trying to evoke the thought that one has an exceptional talent, or using incorrect profession names and symbols.
- "*Creating confusion*" includes following out behaviors that cause confusion with someone else's goods, business products, activities, or affairs. This is realized mostly by using similar/same trademark, or business name of the competitor or imitating their business products or services, thus creating an appearance that confuse the customers. The Court of Cassation has considered the case as an unfair and confusing situation under this sub-paragraph in the event that the former employee put on the market a computer software, which is very similar to the plaintiff's original software.[62] Likewise imitating, e.g., the interface and design of the competitior's website could fall under this sub-paragraph as well.
- "*Comparative advertising*" includes comparing themselves, their goods, business products, activities, prices with others, their goods, business products

---

60 Turkish Court of Cassation decision, dated 09.12.2020, no. 904/5766 (https://www.legalbank.com/, accessed 10.08.2021.)

61 Turkish Court of Cassation decision, dated 15.02.2021, no. 1506/1247 (https://www.lexpera.com.tr/, accessed 10.08.2021.)

62 Turkish Court of Cassation decision mentioned in the previous fn. 61.

or prices, in such a manner that is "untrue", "misleading", "unnecessarily denigrating the competitor" or "unnecessarily exploiting its reputation"; or putting the third party ahead in similar ways. In Turkish practice, mobile phone operator companies widely use comparative advertising. In one of such cases, Turkcell, a mobile operator company, used a map of "only Turkcell attracting destinations" in their advertisements, which involved an implicit comparison. The plaintiff stated that these data were false and misleading. They argued that Turkcell put itself in an advantageous position and its rivals in a disadvantageous position. The first instance court accepted the existence of unfair competition, and the Court of Cassation upheld this decision.[63]

In principle comparative advertising is not forbidden, not illegal *per se*. This sub-paragraph indicates the necessary conditions for a comparative advertising to be assessed as an act of unfair competition. Comparative advertising is unlawful, if the comparison is objectively untrue, misleading, or unnecessarily denigrating the competitor, or exploiting the competitor's reputation. Comparative advertising is regulated in the Article 61/5 of the Act on Consumer Protection no. 6502 and in the Regulation on Commercial Advertising as well.[64] These regulations concerning comparative advertising in Turkish law is fairly in line with the EU Directive 2006/114 EEC concerning misleading and comparative advertising.[65]

- In the following sub-paragraphs 6, 7, 8, 9, are regulated also deceptive tactics and sale methods that are used to influence the decision making of customers and conduct them to buy products, with a misleading, misinforming, pressuring manner. These includes "*hunting with a sample*" (6); "*misleading the customer about the true value of the offering*" (7) which is realized by offering additional promotions and gifts; "*aggressive sales*" ("hard selling") (8) by which customers are forced to purchase by being put into the psychological state of feeling obliged; "*concealing*" (9) is misleading consumer by concealing the properties, quantity, intended use or hazards of goods, work products or activities.
- Lastly, in the sub-paragraphs 10, 11, 12 are regulated the cases of unfair competition that are directly related to the protection of the consumer. The aim is

63 Turkish Court of Cassation decision, dated 04.11.2015, no. 5113/11559 (https://www.lexpera.com.tr/, accessed 10.08.2021).

64 OJ, 15.01.2015, no. 29232.

65 OJ L 376/21, 27.12.2006 (https://eur-lex.europa.eu/legal-content/en/, accessed 10.08.2021).

to protect the consumer against vague, misleading, and deceptive expressions and phrases in consumer loans, installment sales or similar sales conditions, used in the contracts or examples of forms related to these, announcements, or advertisements. Form and contract examples that hide the price of the goods, terms of installment, cost of installments, actual cost, are unfair under these sub-paragraphs.[66]

The second category concerns behaviors of directing others to breach or terminate their contract (55/1-b). Normally only parties of a contract can be liable due to breach or the unlawful termination of the contract. However, third parties may lead one of the parties to breach or terminate the contract unlawfully. In this case, third parties' behavior to direct, or induce parties, customers, consumers, or employees to breach or terminate their contract, so that they can make a contract with the terminated party, would constitute unfair competition under this category.[67]

The third category concerns unauthorized use of other people's business products (55/1-c). This provision is regulated to protect the business products such as, sale catalogs, business accounts or business plans, and similar products that are important for commercial activity but cannot be qualified as intellectual property rights and thus do not benefit from the intellectual property law protection. To reiterate, this paragraph does not intend to protect intellectual property rights. It is a broad application of the labor principle and aims to prevent unjustified exploitation of the labor and experience of others, in other words, the free-riding on others.[68]

The fourth category concerns unlawful disclosure of business secrets; in particular, "using" or "disclosing" to others information and business secrets of the producer that are obtained secretly or without permission or otherwise unlawfully obtained (55/1-d). Although, in many legal systems business secrets benefit from a specialized legal protection as an industrial property right, they

66 The Preamble of TCC 55.

67 This category is a specialized version of TCO 49/2, according to which the one who willfully causes damages to a third party with an immoral act is liable. Although, willfulness and immorality are the requirements for the liability under TCO 49/2, those are not required under TCC 55/1-b. See the Preamble of TCC 55. See also, Okutan Nilsson, "Unfair Trade Law," 114–115; Poroy and Yasaman, *Ticari İşletme Hukuku,* 446–447.

68 Okutan Nilsson, "Unfair Trade Law," 115.

are not described and regulated specifically in Turkish law but can be protected under this paragraph.

The fifth category codifies behaviors that do not comply with the terms of business. According to this paragraph, especially those, who do not comply with rules which are imposed on competitors by law or contract, or with the business rules that are common in a profession or environment, would be considered to have behaved unfairly (55/1-e).

The sixth and final category codifies the use of general terms of contract that are contrary to good faith as a source of liability (55/1-f). The provision mentions specifically under which conditions, general terms of contract would be against good faith. According to TCC 55/1-f, there must be use of pre-formulated general terms in a misleading manner and to the detriment of the other party and the general terms must significantly deviate from the legal regulations or must stipulate distribution of the rights and obligations that are significantly contrary to the nature of the contract. On the other hand, the concept of general terms and conditions is basically regulated and defined in TCO 20/1. Under which conditions general terms and conditions will be considered unwritten or null are set forth in TCO 20 ff.[69] The sanctions attached in the TCO differ from the sanctions regulated in the TCC, in this respect is highly controversial whether the legal regime in the TCO can be applied to merchants as well.[70]

3. *The Sanctions of the Unfair Business Practices*

a. *Types of legal actions and the civil liability claims*

Legal actions: In TCC 56/1 are set out the civil liability claims, and the legal actions that can be brought before the commercial court in the presence of unfair acts, as follows:

- Legal action for establishing the unlawful nature of the act,
- Legal action for the prohibition of unfair competition,

69 For the conditions under which TCO 20 ff. can be applied to merchants in commercial transactions see, Yeşim Atamer, "Genel İşlem Koşulu mu Bireysel Pazarlıkla Kurulan Sözleşme mi? Tüketici ve Tacir İşlemleri Açısından Karşılaştırmalı Olarak Başvurulabilecek Değerlendirme Kriterleri," in *Yeni Türk Borçlar Kanunu ve Yeni Türk Ticaret Kanunu Sempozyumu Makaleler, Tebliğler*, ed. Çiğdem Kırca (İstanbul: Vedat Kitapçılık, 2013), 129 ff.

70 For discussions see, Poroy and Yasaman, *Ticari İşletme Hukuku*, 462; Okutan Nilsson, "Unfair Trade Law," 115.

- Legal action for the elimination of the unlawful situation occurred due to unfair competition, correction of the statements in case unfair competition is made with false or misleading statements, and destruction of the tools and goods that are effective in committing unfair competition only if is inevitable for the prevention of infringement,
- Legal action for compensation for damages and losses, in the presence of fault,
- Legal action for moral compensation, in the presence of the conditions stipulated in TCO 58.

A regulation made to facilitate the proof of claims for damages is that the plaintiff may claim the calculation of the compensation based on the value of the benefit deemed possible to be obtained by the defendant (TCC 56/1).

Publication of the court judgment: At the request of the winning party, the court may also rule the final court decision to be published and announced. The form and the scope of the publication shall be determined by the court. The losing party shall bear the expenses (TCC 59).

Interim injunctions: At the request of the person who has the right to make a claim, the court may decide on interim injunctions such as maintenance of the current situation, restitution of the situation occurred due to unfair competition, prevention of unfair competition and correction of false or misleading statements, and other measures, in accordance with provisions of the Code of Civil Procedure no. 6100 concerning interim injunctions (TCC 61/1).

In addition, upon the request of the person who has right to make a claim, in case its interests are being violated, the goods that require criminal sanctions may be seized during import or export by the custom authorities as an interim measure. Just after in case a lawsuit is not filed in the relevant court or an interim injunction decision is not provided by the court, within 10 days from the notification of the injunction or seizure decision of the customs administrations, the decision of the administration to confiscate shall be cancelled (TCC 61/2, 4).

b. Parties of the legal action

The Plaintiff: Anyone, competitors in the first place, whose customers, credibility, professional reputation, business activities, or other economic interests are harmed or in such danger due to the unfair competition, have right to file claims that are provided in TCC 56. Further, customers, whose economic interests are harmed or who may face such a danger, can also make "all the claims" stated in TTC 56/1 except the request for the destruction of tools and goods (TCC 56/2). Chambers of commerce and industry, chambers of tradesmen, securities exchange, and other professional and economic associations authorized to protect their members' economic interests according to their statutes can file claims stated in sub-paragraphs (a), (b) and (c) of TCC 56/1 (TCC 56/3). Likewise, non-governmental organizations that protect the economic interests of consumers according to their statutes and public institutions can file claims stated in sub-paragraphs (a), (b) and (c) of TCC 56/1 (TCC 56/3).

The Defendant: In principle, unfair competition lawsuits can be filed against the person who has committed the unfair competition act, who is usually the competitor. However, the defendant might be the customers or third parties other than competitors or merchants as well.[71]

Another noteworthy regulation concerns the execution of the court judgment to third parties, who are not party to the lawsuit. The Court decision concerning prohibition and elimination (TCC 56/1-b, 56/1-c) may also be executed against third parties, who have directly or indirectly obtained goods subject to unfair competition, from the defendant for commercial purposes (TCC 56/4).

If the act of unfair competition is committed by employees or workers, while performing their services or business, the claims stated in the sub-paragraphs (a), (b) and (c) of TCC 56/1 can also be brought against their employers (TCC 57).

Liability of press, broadcasting, communication, and information enterprises: In case the unfair competition act has been committed through any kind of press, broadcasting, communication and information enterprises, and through organizations that will become operational as a result of future technical developments, the claims stated in sub-paragraphs (a), (b) and (c) of TCC 56/1 can be filed only against the owner of what is published in the press; what is viewed on the screen, computer or similar media platforms; with the owners of the audio broadcast or what is in any way transmitted and against the owners of the announcement (TCC 58/1). In addition, for press and media related unfair competition acts, are stipulated many other alternative persons who can be filed as defendant, including the owner of the press or media agency. In the following sub-paragraphs of TCC 58/1, the conditions under which they can be filed are regulated.

---

71 For the question whether the consumer can be held liable for unfair competition see, Füsun Nomer Ertan, "Haksız Rekabet," in *Yürürlüğünün 7. Yılında ve Yargıtay Kararları Işığında Türk Ticaret Kanunu Sempozyumu – III (Tebliğler–Tartışmalar) 18 Ekim 2019*, ed. Arslan Kaya (İstanbul: On iki Levha, 2020), 22.

The claims stated in sub-paragraphs (a), (b) and (c) of TCC 56/1 cannot be brought and an injunction cannot be decided against the service provider; especially if it has not initiated the transmission of the unfair competition act, did not select, or change the recipient or the content of the transmission. However, if the negative consequences of the unfair competition act will be extensive or the damage will be significant, the court, by listening to the relevant service provider, may decide on interim injunction concerning termination or prevention of the unfair competition practice (TCC 58/4).

c. Criminal liability

Besides the civil liability, criminal liability as well is provided in the TCC, which is mostly in conformity with the Swiss UCA. Although in the Swiss UCA, a few practices (Article 7 and 8) are excluded from the scope of the criminal liability, in Turkish law all the practices in the sub-paragraphs are regulated as criminal acts as well (TCC 62/1-a).

How the criminal liability will be applied to legal entities? In case an act of unfair competition is committed by the legal entities during the conduct of their business, partners or organ members acting or must act on behalf of the legal entity shall have the criminal liability set forth in TCC 62. In case the unfair competition act is committed in relation to the business activity of the legal entity, it may be also decided on the security measures specific to legal entities (TCC 63).

d. Prescription

The legal actions stated in TCC 56 prescribes after 1 year from the date the party, who has the right to sue, learns the acts and in any case 3 years after the date of their occurrence. However, in case the unfair competition act constitutes an act that requires a criminal sanction under the Turkish Penal Code no. 5237 and that is subject to longer prescription, this longer period is also valid for civil law claims (TCC 60).

§ Part II Essentials of Turkish Company Law

I. General Remarks on Turkish Company Law

Turkish company law is regulated in the second book of TCC, in between the Articles 124–644. The second book consists of one general section and special sections concerning every type of commercial companies. TCC no. 6102, in force as of 01.07.2012, brought drastic changes in Turkish company law, introducing many new provisions and regulations with the idea to expand corporate governance to private companies and set better standards for shareholders and minority protection.[72] Additionally, have been introduced regulations that facilitates and clarifies the functioning of the board of directors and the general assembly. TCC imported certain institutions of the capital market law concerning publicly-held companies, for private companies, such as registered share capital system and advanced dividend distribution. TCC also sets new principles of liability in joint stock companies.

Turkish company law takes as a reference mostly Swiss company law and is inspired by the provisions of the Swiss Code of Obligations concerning commercial companies, especially in the area of joint stock companies. Turkish company law is also very much in line and harmonized with EU company law directives such as the Directive 2017/1132 which codifies a large part of the EU company law, the Directive 2019/2121 which codifies rules on cross-border conversions and divisions and the Directive 2009/102/EC which sets out rules on single-member companies. Consequently, decisions of Swiss Federal Court and European Court of Justice concerning corporate law that fall under the scope of the harmonized area are taken into consideration in Turkish company law as well.[73]

A. Legal Types of Companies in Turkish Law

TCC 124 enumerates with an exhaustive listing commercial companies as follows: "collective company", "commandite company", "joint stock company", "limited liability company" and "cooperative company".[74] Commercial companies are classified under two main categories in TCC 124/2 as "capital companies" that are joint stock companies, limited liability companies and shared commandite companies, and as "personal companies" that are collective companies and simple commandite companies. Legal consequences are attached to this classification; For example, concerning restructuring transactions, such as merger, division or conversion, the question in which transaction which type of companies can engage, depends upon this qualification (TCC 137, 160, 181). Additionally, the kind of capital that can be brought to a company, the

72 Sıtkı Anlam Altay, *Yeni Türk Ticaret Kanunu ve Şirketim, Deloitte Türkiye Raporu* (İstanbul: 2011), 2 ff.

73 For further information see, Arslan Kaya et al., ed. 2020. *Approximation of Turkish Law with European Union Law Private Law.* İstanbul: İstanbul Üniversitesi Yayınevi.

74 For discussions concerning the merchant title of cooperatives see under this chapter, *Part I – The Title of "Merchant" For Legal Persons.*

administration structure, decision-making mechanisms, calculation of the majority and certain quorums (e.g., TCC 151), whether the personal creditor could demand a sequestration on the share of the partners (TCC 133), and the dissolution grounds varies depending on whether the entity is classified as a capital company or a personal company.

Thus, entrepreneurs are offered possibility to choose among different legal models, one that suits the most to their venture and expectations. There is no possibility to establish another type of commercial company with legal personality aside from those. In case entrepreneurs would not prefer any of these models, they may choose "simple partnership" which has no legal personality, and which is regulated in TCO and thus subject to a more liberal legal regime under the law of obligations. Subsequently it is easier to establish and manage a partnership with less formalities. However, the fact that simple partnership has no legal personality, can bring forth certain legal disadvantages such as impossibility to attribute the titles of "contract party", "debtor" or "creditor" to a partnership, thereby partners are personally, jointly and severally liable for the partnership's debts against the creditors.

Among all these types of companies, the provisions concerning joint stock companies have a wide range of application and apply to limited liability companies and shared commandite companies and cooperatives as well, due to the referring articles (TCC 644, TCC 565/2 and Article 98 of the Act on Cooperatives no. 1163). Additionally, joint stock companies and limited liability companies have the biggest share in Turkish business practice in terms of number and the volume of business transactions.[75]

Furthermore, business corporations in certain sectors, such as banks, insurance companies, holdings, public companies, leasing companies, factoring companies, consumer finance and card services companies, independent audit companies and many other, can be established only as joint stock company. Although these companies are subject to their specific legislation, TCC provisions concerning joint stock companies apply as general provisions when there is no regulation in their specific legislation (TCC 330). This gap-filling feature is another fact enhancing the importance of TCC provisions concerning joint stock companies.

---

75 As of September 2021, the number of companies by type is as follows: collective companies 10,810, commandite companies 1,918, cooperatives 84,232, joint stock companies 160,084, limited liability companies 968,761. For data bulletin of Turkish Ministry of Trade for September 2021 see, https://ticaret.gov.tr/, accessed 02.10.2021.

Due to the above-mentioned particularities of the legislative system and the total economic value of joint stock companies, in this chapter, the main features of joint stock companies will be explained. To be able to draw a general picture of commercial companies in Turkish law, joint stock company will be taken as a basic model, which is believed that would provide an insight into the general systematic of the Turkish company law.

B. The Principle of "Limited Liability" and "Lifting the Corporate Veil" as an Exception

One of the basic principles of corporate law is the limited liability of the shareholders both in the joint stock companies and the limited liability companies. This can be seen as a step forward in the evolvement of corporate structure and as an incentive for business development allowing the entrepreneur to differentiate its personal assets from the assets allocated to business, and thereby protect its personal assets from the company's creditors.

However, this fundamental principle is prone to be abused, through behaviors contrary to good faith (CC 2). The legal personality is apt to be used as a tool to hide behind and drain assets of the company, syphoning out cash and funds, and run away from company's creditors. Subsequently since the beginning of 2000s, Turkish commercial courts and the Court of Cassation have elaborated the criteria for lifting the veil to hold liable either shareholders who are behind the veil of the debtor company or sister companies which have close links with the debtor company. A particular judicial approach has been adopted in years to determine those close links between the connected companies. The "identity of shareholders" i.e., common ownership, the "identity of the directors", the "identity or similarity of the business names" and "identity or similarity of their business activities" are considered as close links and expressed with a special terminology, the "organic links" in Turkish judicial precedents.[76] Alongside the criterion of "close links", the Turkish doctrine also accepts three more situations, in which the veil can be lifted, with reference to theory of "lifting the veil" or "piercing the veil". Those additional conditions where the veil can be lifted are "commingling of the assets", "inadequate capital" and "foreign administration".[77]

---

76 These criteria are confirmed with the latest decision of Turkish Court of Cassation, General Assembly of Civil Chambers, dated 01.07.2020, no. 2019/808–2020/504 (https://www.lexpera.com.tr/, accessed 19.9.2021).

77 For detailed explanation of the theory with reference to German law see, Veliye Yanlı, *Anonim Ortaklıklarda Tüzel Kişilik Perdesinin Kaldırılması ve Pay Sahiplerinin Ortaklık Alacaklılarına Karşı Sorumlu Kılınması* (İstanbul: Beta, 2000), 86 ff.

Although, in comparative law, in several common law systems courts have the tendency to abstain from applying the theory of piercing the veil, due to the idea of "*caveat emptor*"[78] (i.e., the counterpart shall be careful and diligent while engaging in transaction with the debtor), this theory has a wide application area within the decisions of commercial courts and the Court of Cassation in Turkey.

C. *Group of Companies*

Turkish company law, taking as a reference the "*German Aktiengesetz*" provisions regarding "*Konzern*"s, is one of the legislative systems that codifies with distinct rules group of companies with a comprehensive approach in the second book of TCC, in Articles 195–209. The aim of TCC provisions is mainly to protect "subsidiaries and their related interest groups", such as their shareholders, and creditors, against the unlawful use of control of the dominant undertaking.[79] The center and focus of TCC provisions on corporate groups is to regulate the liability of the dominant undertaking and of its directors, against shareholders and creditors of the subsidiary company which has a separate legal personality (TCC 202, 206, 209). To determine the scope of these provisions, one fundamental provision is the TCC 195, which sets forth criteria of dominance to establish links and the control relationship between the dominant companies and other companies, which all have separate legal personalities. Pursuant to TCC 195 within the corporate group, the parent and the subsidiary companies are bound to each other, either with the corporate control instruments based on the shareholder title of the parent company, or with the dominance agreement made between the parent and the subsidiary, or by other means. Corporate groups can be structured under pyramid shape or bunch of grapes shape, i.e., may have evolved on a horizontal level or vertical level.[80] Other TCC provisions on corporate groups are directed to facilitate the management of the group through

78 For a comparative analysis of the theory see, Cheng-Han Tan and Jiangyu Wang and Christian Hofmann, "Piercing the Corporate Veil: Historical, Theoretical & Comparative Perspectives," *Berkeley Business Law Journal* 16, no. 1 (2019): 161. For the theory of lifting the veil in British law see also, Paul L. Davies and Sarah Worthington, *Principles of Modern Company Law* (London: Sweet & Maxwell, 2016), 205–206.

79 For details of Turkish law on group of companies see, Gül Okutan Nilsson, "National Report on Turkey," in *Groups of Companies. Ius Comparatum – Global Studies in Comparative Law*, Vol. 43, ed. R. Mariano Manóvil (Cham: Springer, 2020), 400 ff.

80 Ünal Tekinalp, Reha Poroy and Ersin Çamoğlu, *Ortaklıklar Hukuku II*, 14th ed. (İstanbul: Vedat Kitapçılık, 2019), 710 ff., N 2004 ff.

regulations concerning the transmission of information from subsidiaries to the parent company (TCC 199–200), the obligation of notification, the registration and announcement of the acquisition of shares with certain thresholds (TCC 198), the mutual participation of companies (TCC 201), the special audit (TCC 207), and the right of the parent to squeeze-out the minority shareholder from the subsidiary company (TCC 208).

II. The Life Cycle of a Company

A. *How is a Company Managed? "Organs of a Joint Stock Company"*

1. *Division of Labor*

Since legal entities may obtain rights, and undertake obligations only through their organs, joint stock companies are managed and run by their two mandatory organs, i.e., two corporate bodies: "The board of directors" (BoD) and "the general assembly" (GA).

The relationship between the general assembly and the board of directors is based on the principle of segregation of duties i.e., "division of labor", which presents an egalitarian system between the two corporate bodies. Every organ has its own exclusive area of competencies and duties. The Article 698/1 of the Swiss Code of Obligations stipulating that "the general assembly is the supreme corporate body" is not adopted in Turkish law. TCC 374 empowers the board of directors as the generally entitled administrative organ on the overall management of the company except on the issues that are left to the general assembly by explicit stipulations in law or the articles of association (AoA). In this respect, the question, which is also pointed out in the Preamble of TCC 408, whether certain power and duties of the board can be transferred to the general assembly or be subject to approval of the general assembly is controversial in Turkish corporate law.[81]

Although there are few discussions contrary to the former TCC no. 6762, there has not been regulated an auditing or controlling system as an internal "corporate body" of the company. This does not mean there is no auditing at all. Financial control of the company's annual accounts is carried out by the independent audit companies or certified public accountants who need to have special license and be entitled according to their related professional legislation. The

81 For the discussions and especially for the opinion that duties other than TCC 375 may not be transferred to the general assembly see, İsmail Kırca, Feyzan Hayal Şehirali Çelik and Çağlar Manavgat, *Anonim Şirketler Hukuku - Vol. 1 - Temel Kavram ve İlkeler Kuruluş Yönetim Kurulu* (Ankara: Sözkesen Matbaacılık, 2013), 533–538.

independent financial auditing is regulated in TCC 397–401. It is mandatory for large scale companies, both for joint stock companies and limited liability companies that pass over certain thresholds. The criteria concerning the scale of the companies have been determined by the cabinet decree; however, these criteria are being updated (usually decreased) in course of time, to expand the scope of the independent audit.

2. *The Board of Directors*

Joint stock companies are managed and represented by the board of directors (BoD). BoD is in charge of the company's overall management, corporate governance and representation of the company. BoD is authorized to take all the decisions necessary for the realization of the business purpose of the company, except those left under the authority of the general assembly by the law and the articles of association (TCC 374).

a. *Organizational Structure of the Board of Directors*

aa. *Appointment and Dismission*

Appointment and dismission: The board members are appointed and dismissed, in principle, by the general assembly, i.e., the shareholders, with a simple majority calculated based on the capital share (TCC 418). The initial board members at the time of the foundation of the company are appointed in the articles of associations.

Cooptation: Only in one situation, the board members may be appointed by the board itself. For any reason, if the membership on the board becomes vacant, the board of directors shall temporarily appoint a member and submits them for the approval of the subsequent general assembly. The member selected in this way serves until the general assembly meeting, if approved, completes the term of their predecessor (TCC 363). Although there is no regulation in TCC concerning the substitute member, is accepted generally by the doctrine that a substitute member might replace the vacancy and would not be subject to the procedure stated in TCC 363, as long as it is stipulated in the articles of association and accordingly elected in the previous general assembly.[82]

---

82 Kırca, Şehirali Çelik and Manavgat, *Anonim Şirketler Hukuku Vol. 1*, 401; Bahtiyar, Mehmet. *Ortaklıklar Hukuku*, 15th ed. (İstanbul: Beta, 2021), 233.

How does the assignment of the board members end? The board members are appointed for a term of maximum 3 years. Directors' assignment ends after the expiration of 3 years term of office unless they are reappointed for a second or third term (TCC 362). On the other hand, directorship terminates automatically without any action, where a member, is declared bankrupt, or its capacity is restricted by the court, or loses the legal requirements for membership, or loses the qualifications stipulated in the articles of association (TCC 363/2).

Can shareholders dismiss directors? Shareholders can vote for dismissal of directors in the GA with an ordinary quorum (TCC 418). Like any other decision of the GA, a decision concerning dismissal shall be, in principle, indicated explicitly in the meeting agenda. And the GA can take decisions only concerning items mentioned on the agenda. The meeting agenda shall be included in the announcement made to convene the GA and the invitation letters sent to the shareholders at least 2 weeks prior to the GA meeting (TCC 414). This helps shareholders to make necessary preparations before the general assembly, through examining the GA documents, the financial statements, annual directors' report, audit reports and profit distribution proposal of the BoD, either at the company's headquarter or at its branches at least 2 weeks before the GA meeting.

However, dismissal of directors has been facilitated in terms of the agenda requirement. More precisely, directors can be dismissed at any time with the decision of the GA, either in the presence of a relevant item on the meeting agenda or based on just causes. In other words, although "dismissal" is not mentioned explicitly on the meeting agenda, directors can be dismissed, especially in every ordinary general assembly. Because the "approval of financial statements" which is an item that is included per se on the agenda of every ordinary GA meeting, it is considered related with the "dismissal of the board members and election of new ones" (TCC 413/2).

bb. The Composition and the Organizational Structure

Composition: In private joint stock companies, the board of directors may consist of one or more members, there is no upper limit. The "board" composed of just one member constitutes an easier decision-making mechanism without any deadlock risk and is in conformity with one-person company (TCC 338). Each year, the BoD appoints a president among its members and at least one vice-president substituting for the president in its absence. It may be envisaged in the AoA that the president and the vice-president, or one of them shall be elected by the general assembly (TCC 366/1). The BoD may also set up committees and commissions to monitor the progress of the business, to report on the issues to be presented to the BoD, to have their decisions enforced or for internal audit purposes (TCC 366/2).

For publicly-held companies, in the Communiqué on the Corporate Governance (CCG) of the CMB there are envisaged particular requirements concerning the organization of the BoD, such as the prerequisite of minimum number of five members for example (CCG 4.3.1).[83] Additionally, prerequisites concerning executives and non-executive members, independent board members and the conditions a board member shall meet to be qualified independent member and the requirement to establish committees are set forth in a detailed manner within the corporate governance principles (CCG 4.3, 4.5).

Legal entities as the board member: Not only real persons, but also legal entities, for example another joint stock company or a limited liability company, a foundation or an association can be attributed the legal status of "board member", i.e., director in the board of directors. The basic idea here is to attribute the liability arising out the acts and transactions of the person sitting on the chair of director to the legal entity, not to its real person representative. Where a legal entity is elected as a member of the board, together with the legal entity, only a real person can be registered in the commercial register and announced as the representative of the legal entity. On behalf of the legal entity, only this registered representative can attend the meetings and vote (TCC 359/2). Thus, the legal status of "director" belongs to the legal entity and the legal entity can change the person registered at any time (TCC 364/1).

How about public legal entities? Can they have an impact on the administration of joint stock companies? There are two different articles regarding the position of public legal entities in the board of directors. The first one requires a specific regulation in the articles of association and concerns joint stock companies that operates in the public services. Public entities, such as state, special provincial administration, municipality, village and other public authorities, regardless of their shareholder status, may be accorded in the articles of association the right to appoint a representative in the board of directors (TCC 334). The second regulation concerns public legal entities that have shareholder status in a joint stock company. These public legal entities or their real person representatives can be appointed as the board member (TCC 359/5). Thus, public authorities, according to these regulations, through directorship, may have an impact on a joint stock company's administration.

83 Communiqué on Corporate Governance II-17.1 (OJ, 03.01.2014, no. 28871).

How about different groups of shareholders? Can they have an impact on the administration of a joint stock company? In the articles of association may be accorded the right to be represented in the board of directors to "certain category of shares", or to shareholders who constitute a "certain group with certain features and qualifications", or to "minority shareholders" (TCC 360). This serves as a tool of democratic representation of different groups of shareholders in the administration.

b. The Powers and Duties of the Board of Directors

aa. The Overall Management and Direction

The powers and duties can be classified under two main categories: The "daily management duties" and the "non-transferable duties" which concerns the overall direction and supervision of the company, namely the power to determine long-term management, finance, investment and dividend policies and strategies of the company. The non-transferable duties that are part of the overall direction are listed in TCC 375 as follows:

(a) The first sub-paragraph (a) sets out the duty of overall management and giving instructions, which consist of determination of the general business policies and strategies, namely the objectives of the company in terms of investment, finance, dividend policies and the tools to achieve them, the control of the budget (Preamble of 375/1-a).

(b) The sub-paragraph (b) implicates the duty to determine the company's management organization. This duty includes arranging the organizational chart of the management, i.e., different positions at different levels of the management. The organizational chart is a diagram that shows the bottom-up relationships, job descriptions of everyone in the management, the sub-departments, and the relationships between them. This chart allows the board of directors to assess the entire management and evaluate the role of the officials at different positions. It is intended to monitor the use of human resources (Preamble of 375/1-b).

(c) The sub-paragraph (c) imposes on the board the duty to establish the necessary order for financial planning to the extent required for the management of the company. This includes the organization of the accounting department, setting basic principles of keeping books and records, and the establishment of an "internal-audit" system if necessary.

(d) The sub-paragraph (d) charges the board with the duty and power of appointment and dismissal of officers who are responsible for the daily management and operations and who have signing authority. Manager, president, and vice-president are among the most common officer titles; however, additional titles can be used as well.

(e) The sub-paragraph (e) sets out the overall supervision duty and imposes on the board the duty to supervise whether officers in the management act in accordance with laws, the articles of association, internal directives, and written instructions of the board of directors, i.e., the duty to supervise the compliance with law and company directives.

(f) The sub-paragraph (f) states, on one hand, the duty of keeping the share book, the board of directors' resolution book and general assembly meeting and negotiation books, on the other hand, the duty of preparation of the directors' annual report and submission to the general assembly, preparation of the general assembly meetings and execution of the general assembly resolutions.

(g) The sub-paragraph (g) states an obligation to notify the court in the presence of insolvency.

bb. Delegation of the Power and Duties

The above-mentioned duties stated in TCC 375 cannot be delegated to the general assembly or the committees or other departments or any other person. *Argumentum a contrario*, the management duties which are out of the scope of TCC 375 can be delegated totally or partially, either to some of the board members or to third parties outside the board, who would be named as "executive officers". Directors who delegated partially or completely the transferable power and duties would be named as non-executive members (Preamble of 367). In publicly-held companies, majority of the BoD shall consist of non-executive members (CCG 4.3.2).[84]

Although in certain legal systems has been adopted "dualist regime", i.e., two-tier system in which there are two different boards as the management board and the supervisory board[85]; in Turkish company law "monist regime" is adopted, the corporate administration is based on single-board structure (TCC 367/2). On the other hand, with the delegation of management or representation powers pursuant to TCC 367/1 and 370/2, two different functions of the BoD, the

84 Communiqué on Corporate Governance II-17.1 (OJ, 03.01.2014, no. 28871).

85 For the rights and duties of the supervisory board as a corporate body in German corporate law see, Jean J. Du Plessis, Bernhard Grossfeld, Claus Luttermann, Ingo Saenger, Otto Sandrock and Matthias Casper, *German Corporate Governance in International and European Context* (Berlin: Springer, 2017), 133 ff.

"management" and the "supervision" functions can be separated. Accordingly, three different models of administration can be adopted. First, the system of TCC can be preserved, i.e., management powers and duties are not to be transferred, and then would belong exclusively to the board. Second, some of the management duties can be transferred to professional managers, i.e., to "CEOs"; for example, the power to "decide and sign on behalf of the company sale and supply contracts of above one million Turkish Lira value" could be transferred to two professional managers who are not from the board. Third, all the management powers may be transferred to professional executives, and thus can be created an administrative model closer to, but still different than, the "dualist regime" where would exist one management board and one supervisory board.[86]

In order to delegate the duties, the board shall be given power to delegate by the AoA and shall prepare an internal directive which sets out the division of labor, and finally shall take a decision concerning delegation (TCC 367). The internal directive contains provisions on the transfer of the duties and organizes also the "management", including sub-departments such as production, marketing, accounting, and the job descriptions with an organizational chart. Additionally, the internal directive should include powers of decision and assignment and the principles regarding technical, commercial, and legal management of the enterprise.

Liability for the delegated duties: The delegation of the duties and competencies brings along the transfer of the liability as well for the transferred duties to the delegated executives. Still the board conserves the non-transferable duty of supervision concerning delegated duties. TCC sets criteria to clarify the conditions under which the board can be held liable for the delegated duties. According to TCC 553/2, organs or persons transferring a duty or power arising out the law or the articles of association are, in principle, not responsible for the acts and decisions of the delegated managers, unless it is proved that they did not exercise reasonable care in the election of the delegated persons. Especially, they have a duty of care while appointing them. Also, they have a more comprehensive overall duty to supervise the managers as well (TCC 375/1-e).

---

86 For detailed explanations see, Sıtkı Anlam Altay, *Yönetim Yetkilerinin Devrinin Sorumluluğa Etkileri*, (İstanbul: Vedat Kitapçılık, 2011), 50 ff.; Sıtkı Anlam Altay, *Şirketin Merkezine Doğru Yolculuk: CEO, Deloitte Türkiye Raporu* (İstanbul: 2016), 6–7; In the event that a company adopts two-tier board, the relationship between the two boards, whether will be any reporting from the management to the supervisory board, may be regulated in the internal directive (Preamble of TCC 367).

Herewith, the overall supervision duty is prone to being applied in an expanding manner on a grey area. Thereby, the law indicates certain criteria to clarify the boundaries of the supervision duty. According to TCC 553/3, the board members who delegated power, cannot be held liable for violations of the law or the AoA, which are beyond their control. This "non-liability" for violations beyond control cannot be invalidated by bringing forward the duty of care. Thus, should be examined in every case whether members delegating the duties have control over the transactions made by the delegated managers or not.

cc. Representation of the Company

Unless otherwise stipulated in the articles of association, or the BoD is composed of single member, the power of representation belongs jointly to the board of directors, to be used with double signature (TCC 370). Thus, any two of the board members are entitled to sign transactions to represent the company. The board of directors determines how and by who the company will be represented and shall submit the notarized copy of the decision appointing persons authorized to represent the company and indicating the scope and manner of their representation to the commercial register to be registered and announced (TCC 373).

Bona fide third parties' trust in the fact that representatives of a company have the power to represent the company in all matters is protected. Thus, the representation power cannot be restricted in principle. The restrictions concerning "amount" or "subject" cannot be asserted to bona fide third parties, can be considered only as internal instructions. However, pursuant to TCC 371/3, as an exception to the rule, only two types of restrictions can be stipulated validly in the AoA: First, the authority of representation may be restricted with the business activities of the headquarter or the branch offices. Second, the restrictions concerning the joint use of representation power can be set out. These restrictions shall be registered in the commercial register and announced, thus may be asserted to third parties.

Furthermore, another reflection of the protection of third parties trust can be seen in TCC 371/4, according to which the fact that a transaction is contrary to the articles of association or general assembly decision, will not prevent bona fide third parties from applying to the company for the related transaction.

c. Board Meetings

The underlying idea of TCC articles concerning board meetings, is to facilitate meetings and functioning of the decision-making mechanisms and allow the administration to run effectively the company without any unreasonable hesitation, blocking factors or hindrance coming from internal factors. This approach can be observed in the following regulations regarding board meetings and decision-making mechanisms, except for a few regulations.

Convening the BoD: As distinct from the general assembly which usually convenes once in a year, the BoD, as a flexible and constantly functioning body, can gather, hold meetings, and take decisions whenever it is necessary. There is not a specific rule indicating when and how frequently the board shall meet. However, frequency, times, and place of meetings and the procedure of convocation may be regulated in the internal directive or in the AoA.[87] The board is convened by the president, or the vice-president in its absence. The law assigned each board member the right to request in writing the president to call the BoD for a meeting (TCC 392/7).

Quorums: The BoD is gathered with the absolute majority of the members and takes its decisions with a majority of those present at the meeting (TCC 390/1, unless there is a divergence in the AoA aggravating the quorum for decision-making). If the votes are equal and thus the decision cannot be taken, that issue is left to the following meeting. If the equality of the votes continues in the second meeting, the proposal is deemed to be rejected (TCC 390/3).

Circular decision-making: Can decisions be taken without having to gather in a physical meeting place? There are two possibilities to take decision without any necessity to meet. One is the "circular decision-making", according to which, the BoD decisions may be taken by obtaining the written approval of the majority of the total number of members to a proposal made by one of the members on a certain subject, written in the form of a decision. For this, the proposal on a certain subject written in the form of a decision should be presented by one of the board members to all the other members. The requirement that the same suggestion should be made to all board members is a condition of validity. And as negative condition, none of the members should request a meeting to be held (TCC 390/4).

Meeting online: Secondly, there is possibility for directors to participate online, either to a meeting held in a physical place or to a meeting held completely online on the condition that are stipulated in the AoA (TCC 1527/1). In other words, it is possible to organize board meetings either completely online or as hybrid meetings. In the latter, members can participate electronically to a meeting held in a physical place, at the headquarter of the company for example, which

87 Kırca, Şehirali Çelik and Manavgat, *Anonim Şirketler Hukuku Vol. 1*, 482.

can be defined as a physical meeting with an electronical participation. In both meetings, provisions regarding BoD meeting and decision quorums stipulated in the Law or the AoA are applied in the same way (TCC 1527/1). The prerequisites for an online or hybrid BoD meeting on the part of the company, are set forth in the related Communiqué of Ministry of Trade.[88]

Voting in person: Concerning the decision-making mechanisms of the board, a restricting rule regarding voting is that the directors shall vote in person, i.e., cannot give procuration to others and cannot vote to represent each other (TCC 390/2).

Signing the decisions: The validity of the decisions depends on their being written and signed by the members who participated in the meeting (TCC 390/5). Recordings in the minutes of the meeting that a member voted against the decision can help prove that the member in question has no fault or responsibility for that decision.

d. Rights and Obligations of Directors of the Company

Rights: Although powers and duties and the liability of the board of directors are, in principle, of collective nature, the rights and obligations tend to be of individual essence, since they arise out of the contract between the board members and the company. This can be observed especially in case of pecuniary rights such as "remuneration", "honorarium", "premium" or "dividend participation", amount of which shall be determined either in the AoA or by the general assembly (TCC 394). There is no upper limit concerning the "amount" or the "number" of pecuniary rights that may be given to a member. In publicly-held companies is envisaged a disclosure requirement of the financial rights provided for board members and executives via annual report (CCG 4.6).[89] The non-pecuniary rights such as participating to the board meetings and voting, the right to have information (TCC 392), the right to request in writing the president to call the BoD for a meeting (TCC 392/7) are rather powers which help performing management duties.[90]

---

88 Communiqué on Boards Other than the General Assembly of Joint Companies That Will Be Made Electronically in Commercial Companies (OJ, 29.08.2012, no. 28396).

89 Communiqué on Corporate Governance II-17.1 (OJ, 03.01.2014, no. 28871).

90 Ünal Tekinalp, *Sermaye Ortaklıklarının Yeni Hukuku*, 5th ed. (İstanbul: Vedat Kitapçılık, 2020), 283–285 N. 12–113 - 12–115.

Duties: One of the most important duties is a general kind of obligation, the "duty of care" that goes along with all the other duties of the directors and implies that BoD shall perform all their duties with due diligence. The duty of care sets out an "objective standard of care", that is, a standard of care expected from a director holding a similar position in a similar company (TCC 369). The duty of care is shaped by the principle of "business judgment rule" according to which, directors cannot be held liable for business decisions that are taken based on the necessary research and information, with the belief that they act in the best interest of the company. For example, where a pharmaceutical company intends to buy a land for new investments, before taking the necessary decision to buy one of the land options, the BoD shall make all the necessary research concerning lands and compare prices of similar offers and options. The diligent behavior will help the BoD to take the right business decision or at least to be considered as have taken it. Otherwise, the BoD could be deemed not to have acted in accordance with the "business judgment rule" or due care.

Other duties regulated in the law can be enumerated such as the duty of loyalty, i.e., the obligation to safeguard and act for the company's best interests in good faith (TCC 369/1), to comply with the principle of equal treatment (TCC 357), prohibition of participating discussions (TCC 393), prohibition of competition (TCC 396), prohibition of making transactions with the company (TCC 395/1) and prohibition of borrowing cash from the company (TCC 395/2).

e. Sanctions

aa. Liability of the Board of Directors

General remarks and the defendant: Alongside with the nullity of BoD decisions, the main sanction of directors' faulty acts and transactions causing damages to the company, shareholders, or third-party creditors is the civil and criminal liability of the board members (TCC 553, 562/8–11). Under this section will be addressed mainly directors' liability. However, in TCC 553, civil liability of the directors is regulated together with the liability of managers, founders and liquidators who thereby all are subjected to same principles and rules of liability. It is accepted in Turkish law that "de facto" organs, i.e., persons who are not officially appointed but have determinant effect on the direction can be held liable under TCC 553 as well.[91] Liability of the auditors is regulated in the following Article, in TCC 554 with similar principles.

---

91 Tekinalp, *Sermaye Ortaklıklarının Yeni Hukuku*, 435 N. 16–57.

Conditions of the liability: TCC 553 is the main article that regulates the general liability for business administration and management, incorporation, and liquidation of the company. General conditions for corporate liability are the breach of duty arising out the law or the AoA of the company (unlawfulness), fault on the part of the responsible persons, occurrence of damages, and adequate causal link between the faulty conduct and damages.[92] In addition to TCC 553, "specific liability grounds" are regulated separately in TCC 549 to 552, with the idea that certain unlawful acts are of greater importance and riskier for the company. These situations are based on more severe principles against the responsible persons and sets out liability without fault for the persons who committed the act. And for those who only participated in the act, is envisaged liability in the presence of their fault. TCC 549 sets liability for preparation unlawful documents and making unlawful statements concerning certain transactions, such as incorporation of the company, increase and decrease of its share capital, merger, division, conversion and issuance of securities. TCC 550 sets liability for false statements about share capital and knowing the inability of payment of the investors. TCC 551 is concerning illegality of the evaluation of the capital in kind. Also, TCC 552 forbids fundraising unlawfully by making a call to the public by any means to establish a company or increase the capital of the company.

The claimant: In case directors or managers violate by fault their obligations arising out the law and or the AoA of the company, they are liable for damages they have caused both to the company, the shareholders, and the creditors of the company as well. Accordingly, the company, the shareholders and the creditors can sue directors and managers. In principle the current BoD is entitled to file the claim in the name of the company. However, in case the defendant is the current BoD, a trustee shall be appointed to represent the company (CC 427).[93]

Shareholders and creditors may have direct loss claim or indirect loss claim with a derivative action (TCC 553). That is to say, damages incurred directly by the company can be claimed either by the company or the shareholders (TTK 555/1). The compensation issued in a derivative action is to be performed to the company. The idea is to compensate indirectly shareholders' losses by compensating the company's. However, this is the drawback of the shareholder derivative action. Thereby the legislator intended to balance shareholder/plaintiff's

---

92 Marc Bauen and Robert Bernet, Swiss Company Limited by Shares Company Law/Merger Law/Stock Exchange Law/Tax Law (Zürich: Schulthess, 2007), 186.

93 Bahtiyar, *Ortaklıklar Hukuku*, 390.

interests by providing them an advantage concerning expenses of their derivative claim. That is, the court may decide in cases where litigation expenses and attorney's fees cannot be imposed on the defendant, if legal and material reasons justify, for distribution between the shareholder and the company according to equity (TCC 555/2).

On the other hand, creditors can claim company's losses (i.e., their indirect losses) to be performed to the company only in company's bankruptcy. During bankruptcy, the claims of the shareholders and the creditors shall be asserted in the first place only by the bankruptcy administration. If the bankruptcy administration does not assert the claim, then each shareholder or the creditor may substitute the claim (TCC 556). Shareholders and creditors can claim their direct losses to be performed directly to themselves in the event that those losses do not derive from the company's losses (TCC 553).

Joint and several liability: In addition to GA resolutions in the sphere of BoD, the company is being run in principle collectively with the board decisions, hence the liability is also "collective", that is, joint and several liability, i.e., directors are jointly and severally liable for all the damages they caused. However, this aggravated joint and several liability regime in favor of the claimant is balanced with the principle of "differentiated" joint and several liability in favor of the defendants/ responsible persons. Differentiated liability means that each director can be held liable against the claimant only in proportion of their own fault ratio. That is, each of the responsible persons can be held liable for damages only to the extent that the damage is personally attributable to them depending on their own fault and the circumstances (TCC 557/1).

Individual liability: Exceptionally, in few situations, there may be individual liability in such cases where a member acts contrary to prohibition of competition (TCC 396) or to prohibition of making transactions with the company (TCC 395/ 1) or borrowing cash from the company (TCC 395/2). Provisions concerning prohibition of competition and making transactions with the company are not mandatory, directors may be given permission or approval for competing or making such transactions with the company; however, the prohibition of borrowing is mandatory, meaning that not any permission or approval may be given by shareholders, i.e., by the GA.

Discharge from liability: Shareholders may take a decision in the GA to release directors, managers and auditors from the general management liability. The resolution of the GA concerning discharge of directors from liability is subject to a simple quorum, and effective only for the facts covered by the discharge.

The resolution of discharge extinguishes the right to sue of the company and the shareholders who voted for the resolution or who have acquired the shares knowing the discharge. Claims of other shareholders expires 6 months after the resolution of discharge (TCC 558/2). Indirect loss claims are not affected by the discharge.[94] As a reaction to a practice occurred in Turkish law, following Court of Cassation decisions, a particular regulation has been adopted in TCC 558/1 which indicates that the general assembly cannot take a decision to revoke a resolution of discharge taken previously by the GA.[95]

Prescription: Other than discharge from the liability, the prescription time can be asserted by the defendants as a plea within the liability action. The right to seek compensation against those responsible persons, expires in 2 years from the date on which the plaintiff learned of the loss and the responsible, and in any case, 5 years from the day of the defendant's act that caused damages. If the unlawful act constitutes a criminal act subject to a longer prescription time according to the Penal Code, this will be also applicable to the compensation action (TCC 560).

Burden of proof: The liability of the members of the BoD is essentially based on the breach of the contract that is between the company and directors with fault. In case a liability claim is made against the board members, in order to be held liable for the damaging acts or transactions, they must be at fault. Accordingly, the plaintiff shall prove the presence of damages, the breach of a duty, the defendant's fault and the causal link between the act and the damages. In this respect, the question on whom the burden of proof of the fault lies on is highly controversial in Turkish law. Although in the law of obligations, in the event of breach of contract the burden of proof is on the defendant, in corporate law with reference to the wording of TCC 553 is commentated that the burden of proof is on the plaintiff, i.e., the company or the shareholders. Court of Cassation's decisions tend towards to accept this approach that the plaintiff shall prove the fault. However, there are contrary opinions defending that the burden of proof shall be on the defendant, i.e., "the directors", who have better access to the necessary documents and accounting books, among other things, allowing

---

94 Tekinalp, *Sermaye Ortaklıklarının Yeni Hukuku*, 473 N 16–142.

95 Under this chapter for the minority right to oppose to discharge from liability of the establishment and capital increase as a negative minority right (TCC 559), see infra: *Part II – Minority Rights.*

directors to demonstrate that they have been acted with due care and they were not at fault.[96]

Is a decision of general assembly required for the liability suit? Another controversial issue is whether a corresponding decision is required to be taken in the general assembly, in case a lawsuit will be filed by the company against directors. A part of the doctrine defends that since in TCC 553 contrary to former TCC 341, is not required explicitly the decision of the general assembly, then the GA decision is not required under the current TCC no. 6102. However, a big part of the doctrine is of the opinion that a general assembly decision is required.[97]

bb. Invalidity of BoD Decisions

Another sanction of the board transactions contrary to law is the invalidity of the BoD decisions. In accordance with general principles concerning legal transactions (TCO 27) and provisions concerning invalidity of GA decisions (TCC 445 ff.), invalidity of BoD decisions can be classified under three categories, as inexistence, nullity, and annulability.

aaa. Inexistence

Although inexistence of BoD decisions is not regulated in the law, it is accepted that BoD decisions which lack formal constituent conditions, such as decisions contrary to quorum regulations, are deemed to be inexistent.[98]

---

96 For this opinion and the discussions see, İsmail Kayar and Yurdal Özatlan, "Anonim Şirket Yönetim Kurulu Üyelerinin Sorumluluğu Davasında Kusur ve İspat," *Terazi Aylık Hukuk Dergisi Özel Sayı* 14, (2019): 27 ff.

97 For the opinion that a general assembly decision is required due to TCC 379/3-c see, Abuzer Kendigelen, *Yeni Türk Ticaret Kanunu: Değişiklikler, Yenilikler ve İlk Tespitler*, 3rd ed. (İstanbul: On İki Levha, 2016), 308, fn. 164; Altay, *Yönetim Yetkilerinin Devrinin Sorumluluğa Etkileri*, 236; Mehmet Bahtiyar, "Anonim Şirket Adına Yönetim Kurulu Üyelerine Karşı Açılacak Sorumluluk Davasında Genel Kurul Kararının Gerekli Olup Olmadığı Sorunu," in *Prof. Dr. Seza Reisoğlu Armağanı* (Ankara: Bankacılık Enstitü Yayınları, 2016), 393–414. For the opinion that both the board of directors and the general assembly shall be entitled see, Mehmet Helvacı, "Anonim Ortaklık Tarafından Yönetim Kurulu Üyelerine Karşı Açılacak Sorumluluk Davalarında Genel Kurul Kararının Gerekli Olup Olmadığı Sorunu – Düşünceler ve Değerlendirmeler," *Yürürlüğünün 5. Yılında ve Yargıtay Kararları Işığında Türk Ticaret Kanunu Sempozyumu – 20 Ekim 2017* (İstanbul: On iki Levha, 2018), 156 ff.

98 Kırca, Şehirali Çelik and Manavgat, *Anonim Şirketler Hukuku Vol. 1*, 510.

bbb. Nullity

The nullity of board decisions has been regulated in TCC 391 which is a new provision and did not exist in the former TCC no. 6762. Slightly differentiating from its Swiss reference (Swiss Code of Obligations 714), TCC 391 reflects a new approach regarding the sanctions for unlawful board transactions. Not only shareholders but all the related persons who have legal interest may request from the court that a board decision that is contrary to law shall be declared null, same as in the event of inexistence. The grounds for nullity of decisions are regulated in a non-exhaustive manner in TCC 391, as follows especially:

- Decisions that are "contrary to the principle of equal treatment";
- Decisions that "do not comply with the basic structure of the joint stock company or do not comply with the principle of protection of share capital";
- Decisions that "violate the inalienable rights of the shareholders or restrict or complicate their use";
- Decisions that "concern non-transferable powers of other organs or indicate the transfer of these powers"

Other than those indicated in TCC 391, BoD decisions of which the subject is impossible or decisions that are contrary to mandatory provisions, public order, morality, and personal rights will be deemed null and void pursuant to TCO 27.[99]

ccc. Annulability

Contrary to the regulations concerning annulability of the GA decisions (TCC 445 ff.), there is not a general provision that regulates annulability of the BoD decisions. Exceptionally in registered share capital system, both in private companies and publicly-held companies, can be filed an action for annulment of the BoD decisions, concerning capital increase, issuance of privileged shares and restriction of preemptive rights, within 30 days beginning from the announcement of the decision (TCC 460/5, CMC 18/6). In addition, in publicly-held companies can be filed an action for annulment of the BoD decisions concerning advance dividend distribution as well in the presence of the conditions cited in CMC 18/6 (CMC 20/2). Furthermore, in simplified mergers, an action for annulment of the BoD decision concerning merger can be filed within 2 months beginning from the announcement of the decision in the trade registry, and in cases where the announcement is not required, from the date of registration (TCC 192/2). All the mentioned provisions allow annulment for those kinds of decisions that are normally specific to the GA, but that have been included

99 Kırca, Şehirali Çelik and Manavgat, *Anonim Şirketler Hukuku Vol. 1*, 521.

in the authority of the BoD through these exceptional provisions. Finally, the question whether the BoD decisions other than the mentioned regulations can be subjected to annulment is mostly answered negatively in Turkish doctrine. Although the approach of the Court of Cassation is not consistent.[100]

cc. Conflict of interests (prohibition of participating proceedings TCC 393)
There is not a general provision that regulates particularly conflict of interests that directors face in private joint stock companies. However, directors need to comply with the prohibition of participating to negotiations and decisions concerning their personal interests. The scope of the prohibition and the situations that are considered as conflict of interest are regulated in TCC 393 which includes prohibition to participate both in discussions and voting. Pursuant to Art. 393, directors cannot participate in negotiations on matters in which their personal interests, or such interests of their relatives contradict the best interest of the company. The decision should concern "personal", not "corporate" i.e., external interests of the member, or its relatives and should not relate to the interests attached to their director or shareholder status in the company. This prohibition is mandatory, as well as the prohibition of cash borrowing.

The sanction of acting contrary to the prohibition is shown in TCC 393/2. In principle, the liability lies on the director, who is in conflict of interest, in the event of occurrence of damages due to such decision. However, in case the conflict of interest is known objectively, not only the member in question acting in violation of this provision, but also the members who do not object the attendance of the member in question can be held liable as well.

Nevertheless, the question whether the board decision taken in violation of the prohibition would be valid is highly controversial in Turkish law. Especially, during the former TCC, which has no provision concerning the nullity of the board decisions, many opinions defended that the violation of the prohibition results only in the liability of directors, but not in the invalidity of the decision.[101] However, newer opinions following the current TCC no. 6102 defend the nullity of the decision in case that the mandatory quorum could not be obtained without the vote of the member in question. In this case, the decision shall be, then, considered null and void.[102]

---

100 For further explanations see, Kırca, Şehirali Çelik and Manavgat, *Anonim Şirketler Hukuku Vol. 1*, 522 ff.

101 For discussions see, Bahtiyar, *Ortaklıklar Hukuku*, 239.

102 Kırca, Şehirali Çelik and Manavgat, *Anonim Şirketler Hukuku Vol. 1*, 499.

3. *General Assembly*

a. *Duties and powers*

The general assembly (GA) is the other mandatory corporate body of the joint stock company that convenes at least once a year and when necessary, with the participation of the shareholders or their representatives. The GA is the decision-making body of the company and those decisions made by the GA are also valid for the shareholders who are not present at the meeting or who cast negative votes (TCC 423). In principle, the shareholders use their rights regarding company at the GA (TCC 407; cf. TCC 437 and 445 ff.).

Each of the corporate bodies has its own sphere of duties that it cannot, in principle, delegate to the other body and shall not allow other body to encroach upon.[103] TCC 408, which stipulates that the GA shall take decisions in cases expressly determined by law and the articles of association, has also indicated the non-transferable duties and powers of the GA in the second paragraph. According to this provision, without prejudice to the non-transferable duties and powers stipulated in various provisions, the matters that fall under the inalienable authority of the GA are as follows:

- Amendment of the articles of association (AoA);
- Election of the members of the BoD, their terms of office, determination of their salaries and rights such as attendance fee, bonus and premium, decision on their release and discharge;
- Election and dismissal of the auditor, with the exceptions stipulated in the law;
- Taking resolutions regarding the annual accounts, management report, the allocation of the disposable profit, the determination of the dividends and the shares of profits, the use of the reserve fund including capitalizing or adding to the profit to be distributed;
- Dissolution of the company, with the exceptions stipulated in the law;
- The wholesale of a substantial amount of company assets

The GA has also the authority to take a resolution on the merger (TCC 151), division (TCC 173) and conversion (TCC 189), the appointment (TCC 536/1) and dismissal of the liquidator (TCC 537/1) of the joint stock company. Apart from those directly envisaged in the law, duties and powers may be given to the GA by the AoA in matters explicitly stipulated in the law (TCC 340, 408/1).

---

103 Bauen and Bernet, *Swiss Company Limited by Shares Company Law*, 136.

In one-person joint stock companies, the single shareholder has all the powers of the GA. The validity of the resolutions to be taken by the single shareholder in the capacity of the GA depends on the condition that these resolutions are in writing (TCC 408/3).

b. The GA meetings

aa. Meeting Types, Time, Place and Agendas

Meeting Types: The GA meetings may convene on ordinary and extraordinary basis (TCC 409) in terms of the time they are held; and in terms of whether the shareholders who want to attend physically, gather physically (TCC 415 ff.) and electronically (electronic participation, TCC 1527–1528) and in terms of whether the GA convenes upon a call and without any call (TCC 410 and 416).

Meeting Time: Pursuant to TCC 409/1, an ordinary GA convenes within 3 months starting from 31 December (until the end of March), which is the end of each operating period (accounting period due to tax laws). The provision for the 3-month period is not directly sanctioned but is regulatory. Failure to hold or delay the ordinary GA meeting may lead to the liability of the members of the BoD pursuant to TCC 553 ff. If the ordinary meeting is postponed one or more times because the quorum is not met (TCC 418) or the minority requests (TCC 420), the following meetings are also considered as ordinary meetings.

Extraordinary meetings, on the other hand, are meetings held, when necessary, without a specific period (TCC 409/2), depending on the need. It can sometimes be done several times a year or not done at all for years.

As mentioned above, a meeting can be held with electronic participation without sharing the same physical space. However, a purely virtual meeting is not allowed, it is only possible to hold a meeting with partly physical and partly electronic participation (hybrid meetings).[104]

Pursuant to TCC 1527/5, "Participation, expressing opinions and voting in the general assembly of joint stock companies by electronic means give rise to any legal consequences of physical participation and subsequent voting therein". However, since this type of participation and voting requires some technical infrastructure and detailed procedural regulation, the implementation was dependent on the issuance of a regulation. By the entry into force of

104 Bahtiyar, *Ortaklıklar Hukuku*, 154 and fn. 210.

the regulation,[105] the implementation of the system of participating and voting in the general assemblies by electronic means has become mandatory only for listed companies, whereas other companies may voluntarily apply the electronic meeting and voting procedure.

Meeting Place: Unless there is a contrary provision in the AoA, the meetings are held at the place where the company headquarter is located (TCC 409/3). In the AoA, it may be foreseen that the GA meetings shall be held in a place other than the company headquarters, or even abroad.

The Regulation on the Procedures and Principles of the General Assembly Meetings of Joint Stock Companies and Ministry Representatives to Attend These Meetings[106] (The Ministry Representatives Regulation) Article 8 states that unless otherwise provided, the GA meetings shall be held within the boundaries of the local administrative unit where the company's headquarters is located. Also in cases where the address of the meeting is not specifically stipulated in the AoA, the authority to determine meeting place belongs to those who call the meeting. Furthermore, in order for the meeting to be held in a place other than the boundaries of the local administration unit where the company headquarters is located, or abroad, this must be regulated specifically in the AoA.

Meeting Agendas: The agenda is determined by the person who called the GA meeting (TCC 413/1). However, the ordinary meeting should be held every year and the minimum agenda should be decided on the issues listed in TCC 409 and Ministry Representatives Regulation Article 13. At these meetings, the negotiations and resolutions are made regarding the election and dismissal of the BoD, the annual accounts, management report, the allocation of the disposable profit, the determination of the dividends and the shares of profits, discharge of the board members and other matters that are relevant to the activity period and deemed necessary. The extraordinary meeting agenda, on the other hand, is naturally not specified in the law, since the need for the meeting also determines its agenda.

The principle of commitment to the agenda applies in joint stock companies which means subjects that are not on the agenda, whether ordinary or

---

105 For detailed information see the secondary legislation set forth by the Ministry of Trade, "The Regulation on Attendance at the General Assembly Meetings of Joint Stock Companies by Electronic Means" (OJ, 28.08.2012, no. 28395); "The Communiqué on Electronic General Meeting System Applicable at the General Assemblies of Joint Stock Companies" (OJ, 29.08.2012, no. 28396).

106 OJ, 28.11.2012, no. 28481.

extraordinary GA, cannot be negotiated or resolved, without prejudice to the exceptions in the law (TCC 413/2). Pursuant to this principle, the agenda of the meeting, which is determined in advance, shall be shown in the announcement and invitation letters. As a rule, no discussion or decision can be made on matters that are not mentioned on the agenda.

The first exception is regulated in TCC 413/3 that states the dismissal of the members of the BoD and the election of the new ones are considered to be related to the discussion of the annual accounts. With this regulation, the GA has been given the opportunity to dismiss the members of the BoD at each ordinary GA meeting.

According to TCC 364/1, which constitutes another exception to the principle of commitment to the agenda, "even if the members of the BoD are appointed by the articles of association, they can always be dismissed by the decision of the general assembly, if there is a relevant item on the agenda or even if there is no item on the agenda, in case of a justifiable reason".

Finally, in accordance with the relevant provisions of the law, some minority rights and individual rights may be exercised during the GA meeting, although there is no item on the agenda. It is possible to request the negotiation of the annual reports be postponed 1 month (TCC 420), to request a special audit (TCC 438 ff.), to object the release of responsibility arising from establishment, and capital increases (TCC 559) independently of the agenda.[107]

bb. Authorized Persons to Call the GA to the Meeting

The Board of Directors (TCC 410/1): Whether it is an ordinary or extraordinary meeting, the authority to convene the general assembly rests with the BoD. The BoD uses this authority by convening and taking decisions. If the call to the ordinary meeting is not decided despite the due time, or if the call for an extraordinary meeting is not made when there was a need, the responsibility of the BoD arises (TCC 553 ff.). The members of the BoD whose term of office has expired may also call the GA for a meeting.

Shareholder (TCC 410/2): As regulated in TCC 410/2, if the BoD cannot convene or cannot take a decision to convene the general assembly despite meeting, or if the BoD is not present, even the owner of a single share may apply to the court and request permission to convene the general assembly, in this case the court's decision is final. With this regulation, the consequences of absence of corporate body within the meaning of TCC 530 are prevented to some extent.

107 See also, the Ministry Representatives Regulation Article 25.

Minority Shareholders (TCC 411 ff.): According to TCC 411, one or more shareholders together representing at least 10 % of the share capital and 5 % of the share capital of the publicly-held joint stock companies may also convene the GA meeting in writing by stating the compelling reasons and the items of agenda. If it is to be already convened, minority shareholders may demand an item be placed on the agenda. With the AoA, the right of call may be granted to the shareholders with a smaller share. Both demands are made through a notary public. If the BoD accepts the call, the GA is called for a meeting to be held within 45 days at the latest; otherwise, the call is made by the claimants.

In TCC 412, it is regulated that if the demand of the minority regarding the convocation is rejected or not answered within seven working days by the BoD, the commercial court of first instance in the place where the company headquarter is may decide to convene the GA upon the application of the same minority shareholders. If the court finds it appropriate to be summoned, it appoints a trustee and indicates in its decision the duties and powers of the trustee. Unless there is a necessity, the court conducts its decision based on written documents without a hearing; the decision is final.

Liquidators (TCC 410/1): In companies in liquidation, liquidators are also authorized to convene the GA on matters related to their duties.

Bankruptcy Administration (EBC 226): Since the legal representative of the bankrupt company is the bankruptcy administration in liquidation by bankruptcy, it can convene the GA.

Trustee (CC 427): Apart from TCC 412, the appointment of a trustee may come to the fore pursuant to general provisions. In the absence of the managing body of the company, if a trustee has been appointed instead of the BoD pursuant to CC 427/4, the trustee may also convene the GA.

cc. Convocation Form

Meeting upon Invitation: In the GA meetings to be held upon an invitation, the form of the call is determined in TCC 414 and the Ministry Representatives Regulation Article 10. The invitation announcement is made as shown in the AoA, on the websites of the companies that are subject to the obligation to open a website, and also with the announcement to be published in the Commercial Register Gazette. This invitation shall be made at least 2 weeks prior to the date of the meeting, excluding the announcement and meeting days. In addition to the announcement, holders of registered shares and the shareholders who have submitted a share certificate or a document proving being shareholder and who have notified their addresses beforehand shall be notified of the date of the GA meeting and of the agenda and the newspapers, in which the announcement is or will be published through service of a registered mail with return receipt.

In terms of publicly-held corporations, the provisions of CMC 29/1 and 2 shall apply. According to CMC 29/1, publicly-held corporations are obliged to invite their general assemblies to the meeting as indicated in the AoA, with an announcement published in the corporation's website and Public Disclosure Platform and other places determined by the Board. This call shall be made at least 3 weeks prior to the meeting date, excluding the announcement and meeting days. In CMC 29/2, it is stipulated that the first paragraph of TCC 414 (registered mail procedure) shall not be applied to the registered shares traded on the exchange.

Meeting without Invitation (Universal Meeting, TCC 416): In case the owners or representatives of all shares are present and if no objection is raised, a meeting can be held without complying with the invitation procedure. In this method, which is widely used especially in small and family-type private corporations, all provisions other than those related to the call shall be followed (such as the agenda, the presence of a Ministry representative if necessary, meeting, voting, decision-making, preparation of the meeting minutes).

A universal meeting may take decisions as long as the meeting quorum exists. Thus, when a shareholder leaves the meeting, the resolution-making ability of the GA without an invitation ceases from that moment on. In this case, the meeting quorum (representation of all the shares) required for the universal meeting to validly discuss and pass binding resolutions is sought not only at the opening of the meeting but also during the meeting.

dd. Authorization to Attend the GA Meetings, List of Attendees and Voting Rights

Authorization to Attend the GA Meetings: According to TCC 407/2, managing directors and at least one member of the BoD should be present at the GA meeting.

Pursuant to TCC 415/1, the shareholders whose names are included in the "list of attendees" drawn up by the BoD may attend the GA meetings. While this list is being prepared, it is based on the share book records for uncertified shares or registered share certificates and the temporary share certificates regarding the shares that are not monitored in terms of records.

List of Attendees: As stated in TCC 417/3, the list of persons able to attend the GA is signed by the president of the BoD and made available at the location of the GA before the meeting. The list specifically indicates the shareholders' names and surnames or positions, addresses, amounts of shares held, nominal values of shares, their groups, company issue capital and paid-in amount or issued capital and spaces for signatures of those who would attend the meeting directly or by proxy holder. Thereafter, according to TCC 417/4, the list signed by those attending the GA gains the title "List of Attendees". On the other hand, as in stated TCC 417/1, Central Securities Depository (CSD) records will be used for bearer shareholders and the owners of the dematerialized shares. Those who initiate convocation for the GA meeting, will use the shareholders list provided by CSD for bearer shareholders and dematerialized share owners (CMC 13), while maintaining the list of attendees.

It is regulated in TCC 417/5 that the procedures and principles regarding obtaining the shareholders list from CSD, the prohibition of the transfer of the shares limited to the day of the GA meeting, and other related issues are determined by a communiqué of the CMB regarding the shares monitored in dematerialized form pursuant to CMC 13,[108] and by the Ministry of Trade for bearer shares. As it is stated in the Communiqué[109] that has been recently issued by Ministry of Trade in line with the law, shareholders who have bearer shares, are required to register their shares to CSD's "Bearer Shares Registration System" until 31 December 2021 to be able to continue exercising their shareholder rights given by the law. The shareholders will no longer be able to exercise their rights if they fail to register to the system until the given date.

Voting Rights: For uncertified shares, registered share certificates or the temporary share certificates, the shareholders registered in the share book, or the person authorized by them in writing exercise their shareholding rights. The person who proves that he is the owner of the bearer share certificate and is notified to CSD has the authority to use his shareholding rights (TCC 426/1 and 2).

If there is a usufruct on a share, the right to vote is exercised by the usufructuary, unless otherwise agreed. However, usufructuary is liable in damages to the shareholder for any failure to take due account of the latter's interests when exercising them (TCC 432/2).

Real persons must represent their identity cards and representatives of the legal entities must submit power of representation (TCC 415/2). Each shareholder

---

108 See, the Communiqué on the Procedures and Principles of Keeping Records Regarding Dematerialized Capital Market Instruments, II-13.1 (OJ, 07.08.2014, no. 29081).

109 See, the Provisional Art. 1 of the Communiqué of 06.04.2021.

who attends the GA in person or through their representative, physically or electronically, has at least one voting right (TCC 434/2) and voting right takes effect with the payment of the minimum amount (TCC 344, 459/3, 460/3) of the share price (cash capital debt) determined by law or by the AoA (TCC 435). However, restrictions on the number of votes cast by holders of multiple shares may be imposed in the AoA.

Lastly, where one share of stock is owned by several beneficiaries, those beneficiaries may exercise the rights attaching to the share of stock only through a common representative (TCC 432/1).

ee. Representation and Types of Representation in the GA Meetings

Most of the shareholders' rights are exercised in the GA meetings. However, due to reasons such as health issues, density of the workloads, geographical distance and disinterest, shareholders may be unable to attend the GA meetings in person. This might result in power gaps in the GA meetings, or the takeover of the control by particular minority shareholders. To avoid such unintended consequences, the shareholders are given the right to attend meetings and vote by proxy, allowing them to express their wishes and exercise their rights even if they are unable to attend in person. Also, according to TCC 425, the shareholder may represent their shares at the GA meeting by themselves or may have them represented by a third party who need not be a shareholder. Besides, the AoA stipulating that the representative be a shareholder are invalid.

As stated in the Regulation on Attendance at General Assembly Meetings of Joint Stock Companies by Electronic Means, the beneficial owners[110] to attend the GA meeting by electronic means in person or by proxy holder should notify accordingly via Electronic General Meeting System (e-GEM). In case of attendance at the GA meeting by representation, identity data of such proxy holder should be registered in e-GEM. Authorization may be made in the same manner in case of physical attendance. The beneficial owner may vest general powers in their proxy holder as a whole or separately for each agenda item (Art. 7/1 and 2).

A person exercising participation and voting rights as a representative must comply with the instructions of the represented party. However, violation of the instruction does not invalidate the vote. The rights of the represented against the representative are reserved (TCC 427/1).

---

110 The beneficial owner means any real or legal person entitled to attend and vote at the general assembly of a joint stock company as per the provisions of the TCC (the Regulation on Attendance at General Assembly Meetings of Joint Stock Companies by Electronic Means Art. 4/1-f).

A person in possession of a bearer share certificate due to pledge, right to retain, bailment or loan agreement, and similar agreements may exercise the shareholding rights only if specially authorized to do so by the shareholder in writing (TCC 427/2).

As for the types of representatives, the TCC also envisaged new types of representatives regarding representation at the GA meetings: The governing officer as representative, the independent representative, the corporate representative (TCC 428) and the custodian as representative (TCC 429). However, within the scope of the amendments made with the Law no. 7099,[111] TCC 428 was abolished and only TCC 429 regarding the custodian is preserved.

Although the law does not contain classification in terms of representative types, representation in the doctrine divided into two main groups under the headings of individual representation and collective representation. Under the heading of individual representation, ordinary representative and the custodian representative were discussed; while the governing officer as representative, the independent representative, and the corporate representative were also discussed under the heading of collective representation. Since TCC 428 has been abolished, there is no need to explain collective representation anymore. Although the concept of ordinary representative is not encountered in the law, the ordinary representative should also be mentioned in order to differ it from the custodian:

Ordinary Representative: The ordinary representative is the representative within the meaning of the general provisions, and the authority to represent must be given in writing (TCC 426, see and cf. the Ministry Representatives Regulation Art. 18/7 that seeks notarized power of attorney).

Custodian as Representative: The term depositor should be understood as a person who registers their share or leaves the share certificate to a person physically and wants to have them represented in the GA. If the person to whom the share certificate is entrusted is also equipped with the right to represent the shareholder in the GA, it will be considered as the custodian (depositor's representative). As in stated in TCC 429/3, the procedures and principles regarding the custodian are regulated in the Ministry Representatives Regulation Art. 44 ff. The authority to represent must be given in writing pursuant to TCC 426/1 and TCC 427/2 as well.

111 OJ, 10.03.2018, no. 30356, Art. 23.

Pursuant to TCC 429/1, if the custodian is authorized to use the participation and voting rights arising from the shares and share certificates entrusted to them, they must apply to the depositor before each GA meeting for instructions on how to vote. And as stated in TCC 429/2, if the instruction has not been received even though it was requested in time, the custodian exercises voting rights in accordance with the general instructions of the depositor; in the absence of such an instruction, the vote is cast in the favor of the motions proposed by the BoD.

ff. Quorums in the GA Meetings

Since the decisions taken in the GA bind all of the shareholders whether they attend the meeting or not, the legislator envisaged that there should be a certain amount of participation in order to hold the meeting and take decisions. Quorums may vary according to the agenda item, not according to the type of meeting, and if a quorum is not achieved at the first meeting, the applicable law considers lower quorums sufficient at the following meeting in some cases. In addition, while taking a decision, affirmative votes are sought to provide the quorum for the decision; that is, it is generally accepted that abstentions will be counted negatively in tallying (as the rejection of the resolution).

Simple (Ordinary) Quorums: Unless an aggravated quorum is stipulated in the law or in the AoA, the GA convenes with the presence of the owners or representatives of the shares that meet at least one fourth of the capital. This quorum must be maintained throughout the meeting. If this quorum is not achieved in the first meeting, no quorum is required for the second meeting to be held. Decisions are made with the majority of the votes present at the meeting (TCC 418).

In the Preamble of TCC 418, it is stated that this provision is a repetition of the articles 372 and 378 of the former TCC. However, as a novelty in Article 418, it is stipulated that the quorum that meets at least one quarter of the capital must be preserved during the meeting. This implication contradicts the principle that each decision taken within the framework of the agenda is independent of the other. Thus, for example, if the meeting quorum is broken after three of the four items constituting the agenda of the GA are resolved, it has become controversial in the doctrine whether the previously taken decisions will also be considered invalid.[112]

112 For discussions see, Mehmet Bahtiyar, "Anonim Şirket Genel Kurulunda Toplantı Yetersayısının "Toplantı Süresince Korunması" Şartına İlişkin TTK. 418/1 Hükmünün Değerlendirilmesi," in *Prof. Dr. Hamdi Yasaman'a Armağan*, eds. Ercüment Erdem et al. (İstanbul: On İki Levha, 2017), 59 ff.

Aggravated Quorums: The law envisaged aggravated quorums for taking decisions on some issues. Especially in the AoA amendments, different quorums are sought. Although aggravated quorums are regulated in TCC 421, there are also provisions containing aggravated quorums other than this article (such as TCC 151, 173, 189). In addition, privileges in voting right are not applicable for resolutions to be taken for amendments to the AoA, release and the initiation of a liability action (TCC 479/3).

Unless there is an aggravating provision in the law or in the AoA, resolutions amending the AoA are taken with the majority of the votes present at the GA, where at least half of the company's capital is represented. If the meeting quorum stipulated in the first meeting is not achieved, a second meeting can be held within 1 month at the latest. The meeting quorum for the second meeting is that at least one third of the company's capital is represented at the meeting (TCC 421/1).

The AoA amendment resolutions regarding the relocation of the headquarter of the company abroad and the imposing obligations and secondary obligations (incidental duties) to cover the balance sheet losses are taken unanimously by the owners or representatives of the shares constituting the entire capital. The same provision applies to publicly-held corporations with reference to CMC 29/3 (TCC 421/2). If this quorum is not achieved in the first meeting, the same quorum shall be sought in the following meeting (TCC 421/4).

In TCC 421/3, the affirmative votes of the owners or representatives of the shares constituting at least 75 % of the share capital are sought for the amendments to the AoA for the complete change of the scope of the company, the introduction of privileged shares and the restriction on the transferability of registered shares. If this quorum is not reached in the first meeting, the same quorum shall be sought in the following meeting (TCC 421/4).

Quorums in CMC: In CMC, different quorums are regulated for publicly-held corporations. According to CMC 29/3, to the GA meetings of publicly-held corporations, TCC 418 shall be applicable, unless aggravated quorums are foreseen in CMC or in their AoA by clearly indicating a ratio, except decisions regarding the transfer of the headquarter abroad and imposing an obligation or a secondary obligation for covering the balance sheet losses. The provision of CMC 29/6 is reserved and CMC 29/6 states that "As long as aggravated quorums are not foreseen in their AoA by explicitly indicating a ratio, the affirmative votes of the two-thirds of shares with voting rights participating in the GA without any requirement of meeting quorum shall be required in publicly-held corporations for the acceptance by the GA of decisions concerning the restriction of the preemptive rights, the authorization of the BoD to restrict preemptive rights in authorized capital system, reduction of capital and the significant transactions determined according to CMC 23/1. However, as long as aggravated quorums are not foreseen in the AoA, if at least half of the voting rights representing the share capital are present at the meeting, decision shall be taken with the majority of the shares participating in the meeting and holding a voting right.".[113] Lastly, pursuant to CMC 33/4, "Among corporations which are deemed to be publicly-held because of the number of shareholders, those which do not prefer that their shares be traded on the exchange according to CMC 16, may be excluded from the scope of this Law with a GA decision to be taken with affirmative votes of at least two-thirds of the total number shareholders or with three fourths of the total votes.".

Is it possible for quorums to be changed by the AoA? The AoA provisions diminishing the quorums mentioned in the law are invalid. However, in accordance with the clear expression of the law (TCC 418 and 421, CMC 29), quorums can be aggravated by the AoA. Nonetheless, CMC 29 states that a provision in the AoA making solely a reference to TCC or to the related article number without writing its content shall not be considered as a contrary provision that aggravate quorums in publicly-held corporations.

gg. How to Conduct the GA Meetings

The Ministry Representative attends the GA meetings of companies determined in accordance with TCC 333, that is, whose establishment and amendments to the AoA are subject to authorization. Alongside to this provision, the Ministry Representatives Regulation Article 32/1 regulates which GA meetings require the participation of the Ministry Representative:

The Ministry Representative must be present at the GA meetings convened with the agenda of increasing or decreasing the capital, switching to the registered capital system, exiting the registered capital system or increasing the registered capital ceiling, amendment of the AoA regarding changing the field of

113 As an example of the significant transactions mentioned in the provision, publicly-held corporations becoming a party to merger or division transactions, conversion, creating privileges or changing the content or subject of existing privileges are counted. In addition, the Capital Markets Board is authorized to determine transactions of this nature. For detailed information on the significant transactions and criticism of the quorums in CMC 29/6 see, Tuğba Semerci Vuraloğlu, *Sermaye Piyasası Kanunu'na Göre Anonim Ortaklıkta Ayrılma Hakkı,* (İstanbul: On İki Levha, 2018), 259 ff. and 350 ff.

activity, merger, division or conversion. The Ministry Representatives Regulation Article 32/1 also obliges a Ministry Representative to be present at the GA meetings of companies that implement the electronic participation system in the GA, all general assembly meetings to be held abroad, and special assembly meetings for privileged shareholders to be held abroad. According to TCC 422, the meeting minutes are signed by the meeting chairmanship and the Ministry Representative; otherwise they are invalid.[114]

In publicly-held corporations, according to CMC 95, the CMB may send an observer, without any voting rights, to the GA meetings when it deemed necessary.

According to TCC 419/2, the BoD prepares an internal directive containing the rules regarding the working principles and procedures of the GA, the minimum elements of which will be determined by the Ministry of Trade, and puts it into effect after the approval of the GA. Minimum elements to be included in the internal directive are determined as follows according to the Ministry Representatives Regulation Article 41: Entrance to the meeting place and opening of the meeting, establishment of the meeting chairmanship,[115] duties and powers of the meeting chairmanship, actions to be taken before proceeding to the discussion of the agenda and the agenda, the procedure for speaking and voting at the meeting, preparation of the meeting minutes, and actions to be taken at the end of the meeting.

Discussions and resolutions taken at the GA meeting are recorded in the minutes by the meeting chairmanship. The minutes are signed by the chairmanship of the meeting and by the Ministry Representative in the meetings, where the Ministry representative is required, or a Ministry Representative is assigned upon request. In one-person companies, it is obligatory for the shareholder or their representative present at the meeting to sign the meeting minutes. In the Ministry Representatives Regulation Article 26/2, the issues that should be included in the minutes are arranged in detail. The meeting minute is of great

---

114 For discussion of the type of invalidity also see, Erdoğan Moroğlu, *Anonim Ortaklıkta Genel Kurul Kararlarının Hükümsüzlüğü* (İstanbul: On İki Levha, 2020), 126 and fn. 208; Mehmet Bahtiyar, "Anonim Şirketlerde Genel Kurul Toplantı Tutanağı ve Özellikle Kararların Hükümsüzlüğüne Etkileri," in *Prof. Dr. Ersin Çamoğlu'na Saygı Günü, Şirketler Hukukunun Güncel Sorunları Sempozyumu, 30.10.2017, Bildiri Kitabı* (İstanbul: Özyeğin Üniversitesi Hukuk Fakültesi Yayını, 2019), 37 ff.

115 According to the Ministry Representatives Regulation Article 14/2, in one-person companies, it is not obligatory to form a chairmanship and to prepare the list of those who can attend the GA meeting.

importance in that it has the function of proving the resolutions taken and the elections held in the GA.

As stated in TCC 422/2, the BoD is obliged to immediately submit a notarized copy of the minutes to the trade registry directorate and to register and announce the matters subject to registration and announcement in these minutes. Besides, the meeting minutes should also be immediately published on the company's website (if any available).

c. Invalidity of the GA resolutions

The majority rule is necessary, especially in larger corporations, since it is unreasonable to expect all shareholders to gather and agree on items that fall under the GA meeting's remit. However, there is a risk that the majority might use their voting rights for self-serving purposes, leaving the minority or other shareholders to bear the brunt of the burden.[116] The applicable law provides for a detailed set of rules laying down the nullity and voidability grounds and the procedure to be followed in order to challenge the GA resolutions.

The necessary conditions for the existence and validity of the GA resolutions are determined by various provisions of the law, and if a resolution is in contradiction with these provisions in terms of its formation and content, and the AoA regulated within the framework of these, it is legally invalid. Invalidity arises in four ways depending on the nature of the legal rule which was violated: Inexistence, nullity, voidability and pending invalidity.

aa. Inexistence

Violation of the constitutive/formal mandatory provisions stipulated for the emergence of a legal transaction leads to a deficiency in the elements of the transaction and this transaction, thereby, is deemed inexistent. Inexistence might always be asserted and be requested of a determination of inexistence by anyone with an interest and might be taken into account by the judge on its own accord (*ex officio*). The court decision is declaratory.

For instance, if the call is not made by an authorized person or body, or, except for the exception in TCC 416, if a meeting is held and a decision is taken without a call, or if a decision is taken without voting, then, inexistence sanction is applied. In a similar manner, a GA resolution is inexistent when there is not a GA meeting or is a voting has taken outside the meeting, when the Ministry Representative was not present at the meeting despite that they are required to

116 Carsten Gerner-Beuerle and Michael Schillig, *Comparative Company Law* (New York: Oxford University Press, 2019), 428.

attend, when a meeting is held according to TCC 416 although a shareholder or their representative is not present or objects to this universal meeting.[117]

The Court of Cassation and the majority in the doctrine are of the opinion that the decisions taken without complying with the meeting and decision quorums will also be subject to inexistence sanction.[118]

bb. Nullity

Although nullity sanction was not regulated in the former TCC, it was accepted that the provisions regarding nullity of legal transactions (i.e., TCO 27/1 states that a contract is void if its terms are contrary to the mandatory provisions of the law, morality, public order, personal rights or whose subject is impossible.) could also be applied in terms of the GA resolutions with reference to general provisions. As stated above, anyone with interest may request from the court the GA resolution that is contrary to law to be declared null. The grounds for nullity, which are regulated in a non-exhaustive manner, are also listed as follows in current TCC 447:

The resolutions of the GA

- that remove or restrict the right to participate in the general meeting, the minimum voting right, the right to take legal action or other inalienable shareholder rights[119] arising from the law;
- that restrict the shareholders' rights to obtain information, examination and inspection beyond the legally permissible extent, or

117 For detailed information see, Moroğlu, *Anonim Ortaklıkta Genel Kurul Kararlarının Hükümsüzlüğü*, 77 ff.; İsmail Kırca, Feyzan Hayal Şehirali Çelik and Çağlar Manavgat, *Anonim Şirketler Hukuku Vol. 2/2 Genel Kurul Kararlarının Hükümsüzlüğü* (Ankara: Sözkesen Matbaacılık, 2016), 4–11.

118 Ersin Çamoğlu, Reha Poroy and Ünal Tekinalp, *Ortaklıklar Hukuku I*, 15th ed. (İstanbul: Vedat Kitapçılık, 2021), N. 722a; Kırca, Şehirali Çelik and Manavgat, *Anonim Şirketler Hukuku Vol. 2/2 Genel Kurul Kararlarının Hükümsüzlüğü*, 10. On the other hand, Moroğlu is of the opinion that violation of the provisions regarding quorums will lead to an action for annulment, since this only protects the interests of the shareholders. For further information see, Moroğlu, *Anonim Ortaklıkta Genel Kurul Kararlarının Hükümsüzlüğü*, 134–140.

119 The rights that are not possible to be limited or completely removed even with the consent of the shareholder, which are legally recognized and protected not only for the benefits of the shareholder, but also due to the basic structure of the joint stock company, are considered inalienable. Participating to the GA, being represented in the GA, and minimum voting rights can be given as examples. Also see, Tekinalp, *Sermaye Ortaklıklarının Yeni Hukuku*, N. 14–28 to N. 14–32a.

- that disregard the basic structures of the joint stock company or the provisions on capital protection.

It is arguable whether a maximum period of time should be set in order to assert the nullity. In fact, after a long period of time, claiming nullity may be deemed contrary to the principle of good faith enshrined in CC 2 according to the specifics of the concrete case, and the case may be rejected. The fact that, according to CMC Art. 92/1, sub-para. b, the CMB has been authorized to file a lawsuit for the determination of nullity or inexistence within 5 years is open to criticism, especially in terms of determination of inexistence.[120]

cc. Pending Invalidity

Although there is no violation that leads to the sanction of inexistence or nullity, there might be a need for the fulfillment of some additional conditions for a transaction to gain legal validity, and then pending invalidity comes to the fore. If the additional condition is fulfilled, the transaction is completely valid, otherwise, it becomes completely invalid. The transaction has been pending as invalid in the meantime. To illustrate, in cases stipulated in TCC 454, if the general assembly's resolution to amend the AoA has adversely affected holders of the existing preference shares, the implementation of the resolution requires the approval of those privileged shareholders. Invalidity might always be the subject of a determination or objection and is taken into account by the judge on its own accord (*ex officio*).

dd. Action for Annulment

As a rule, majority principle stands in taking decisions in joint stock companies (TCC 418, 421). Decisions taken in the GA are also binding for those who do not attend the meeting and those who attend the meeting and vote against the decision (TCC 423). For this reason, it is common to file an annulment action against the GA resolutions in practice.

What are the substantive law conditions of the case?

- There must be a general assembly resolution in the first place. In this sense, it is accepted that the resolutions of rejection, the resolutions of minority shareholders, and the resolutions of the privileged shareholders board (TCC 454) will also be included among the GA resolutions.
- The GA resolution must be in violation of the law, the AoA, or/and the principle of good faith.

120 Bahtiyar, *Ortaklıklar Hukuku*, 194.

- There must be causal link between the GA resolution and the violation. In other words, the exercise of the right to action for annulment is attributed to the fact that the violations listed in the provision were effective in the decision of the GA. The claim that the violation was effective in the decision must be proven by the plaintiff during the trial.

Who are the parties to the litigation? What are the conditions of litigation and term of litigation?

- **Plaintiff**

Shareholders: The law makes a dual distinction between those who attend the meeting and the cases which each shareholder can be parties to the litigation regardless of whether they attend or not.

According to TCC 446/1, sub-para. a, shareholders who attended the meeting and voted against (negatively) to the resolution must have their dissent recorded in the minutes in order to file an action for annulment. In that case, those who voted in favor of the resolution (yeas), abstained, and those who did not record their dissent despite voting against, cannot file a lawsuit. It is possible, but not mandatory, for dissent to be justified.[121]

As stated in TCC 446/1, sub-para. b, shareholders, regardless of whether they attend the meeting or not, whether they vote against or not, claiming that the call to the meeting is not duly made or the agenda is not announced properly, that those who are not authorized to attend the meeting attended the meeting and voted, that they are unjustly prevented to attend the GA or to vote can file an action for annulment providing that those violations were effective in taking the resolution.

In addition, a shareholder whose voting rights are suspended can also file an action for annulment. Lastly, it is generally accepted in the doctrine that a shareholder who has filed an action for annulment must maintain this title until the final judgment of the case and, if necessary, prove it at every stage of the case. Therefore, unlike in cases of total succession such as death and company

---

121 It is a controversial issue whether opposition can be made at any time during the GA meeting. According to the Court of Cassation, if dissent has been given at a stage before the resolution, the action for annulment should be dismissed. For the criticism of this approach of the Court of Cassation, also see, Veliye Yanlı, "Muhalefetin Tutanağa Geçirtilmesi ve Bu İşlemin Zamanı Sorunu – Genel Kurul Kararlarının İptali Davası Bağlamında," *Batider* 37/2 (2021): 5 ff.

mergers, if the plaintiff has transferred all of their shares, the case should not be heard and should be dismissed.[122]

The board of directors: Since the body responsible for implementing the GA resolutions is the BoD, when the GA takes a resolution that can be annulled, the BoD is also given the right to file an action for annulment (TCC 446/1, sub-para. c). The BoD must first convene and take a decision to file an action for annulment (TCC 390).

Each board member: Each board member has the right to file an action for annulment, on condition that the implementation of the resolution is of such a nature that will lead to personal liability in legal and/or criminal terms (TCC 446/1, sub-para. d). The court must investigate the existence of the aforementioned condition on its own accord (*ex officio*).

The CMB in terms of publicly-held corporations: In the CMC, Capital Markets Board has also been given the right to file a lawsuit for the annulment of the GA resolution in certain circumstances. According to CMC 23/2, CMB may file suit for the annulment of the GA resolutions regarding significant transactions according to the provisions of the TCC. A similar but more comprehensive provision is regulated in CMC 92 as well.

- **Defendant**

The defendant is the company, and the BoD represents it. However, if the BoD has filed a lawsuit, a trustee must be appointed to represent the company. In case of bankruptcy of the company, the bankruptcy administration, in case of liquidation for reasons other than bankruptcy, the liquidator may represent the company in the action for the annulment of the resolutions taken regarding the transactions for the purpose of liquidation. In other matters, the BoD shall still represent the company.[123]

ee. What are the Conditions and Terms of the Litigation?

An action for annulment must be filed within 3 months from the date of the GA resolution (TCC 445).

The competent and authorized court is the commercial court of first instance where the company headquarters is located (TCC 445). Simple jurisdictional procedure applies (TCC 1521).

---

122 See Abuzer Kendigelen, "İptal Davası Açma ve Pay Sahipliği Sıfatının Cüz'î Halefiyet (Payların Devri) Sonucu Değişmesi," in *Prof. Dr. Hayri Domaniç'e 80. Yaş Günü Armağanı Vol. 1*, ed. Abuzer Kendigelen (İstanbul: Beta, 2001), 307 ff.

123 Bahtiyar, *Ortaklıklar Hukuku*, 204–205.

The day of the hearing with regard to the case of nullity or annulment is duly announced by the BoD and disclosed on the company's website. Actions for annulment trials do not begin before the expiry of 3 months. If more than one lawsuit is filed, these lawsuits are brought together (TCC 448/2). At the request of the company, the court may order the plaintiffs to provide security against possible damages. The court determines the quality and amount of the security (TCC 448/3).

Filing an action for annulment or determination of nullity shall not prevent the execution of the resolution, without prejudice to the responsibility of the BoD. However, the court may decide to postpone the execution of the decision after taking the opinion of the members of the board (TCC 449).

If the court accepts the case, the final judgment binds all shareholders, company organs and the members of bodies whether they are parties to the case or not. The BoD must immediately register a copy of the judgment of the court with the trade registry and publish it on the website (TCC 450).

4. Shareholders' Rights and Obligations

a. Obligations of the shareholders

aa. Capital Debt (Single Debt Principle)

Since joint stock company is a capital company, membership of the company is accordingly capital-related rather than being connected to person of the shareholder, i.e., shareholders financial participation matters.[124]

Without prejudice to the exceptions listed in the law, shareholders have only one debt, one legal obligation; and it is the obligation to perform the share price committed for the shares owned and the premium exceeding the nominal value of the share, if any (TCC 480/1, 329/2). Therefore, the "Single Debt Principle" applies to joint stock companies. After the capital debt is fulfilled, the shareholders cannot be put under further financial or personal obligation without their consent.

If the share capital of the registered share has not been fully paid, the title of debtor belongs to the shareholder and if more than one person has acquired a share together, they are jointly liable for the debt (TCC 7/1). The approval of the company is also required for the transfer of the registered shares that have not been fully paid for (TCC 647/3); since this transaction also requires the

---

124 Bauen and Bernet, *Swiss Company Limited by Shares Company Law*, 87.

transfer of debt (TCO 196). In case of company's approval, the responsibility of the former owner of the share for the capital debt ends as a rule (TCC 501, 491).

If the *cash capital* has been committed, at least 25 % percent of the nominal value of the shares is paid before the registration, and the rest is paid within 24 months at the latest after the registration (TCC 344, 459/3 and 460/5). If the share capital was paid partially at incorporation, according to TCC 481, the board of directors can request the outstanding amount from the shareholders through announcement, unless there is a contrary provision in the AoA. In the announcement, the amount of the debt, the date of payment and the place of payment must also be clearly indicated.

If *capital in kind* has been committed, the capital debt becomes due upon the registration of the company. Capital investment of movables, immovables, rights and receivables depending on the form of transfer, commitment and savings stages of the transaction are regulated in the general provisions of commercial companies (TCC 128 ff.)

What are the sanctions for failure to fulfill share capital? As regulated in TCC 128 ff., in case of not observing the obligation to pay in full in good time, the company may request and sue for delayed performance; may levy an execution.

Also, in a joint stock company, non-performance of the cash capital also gives the company the right to demand *default interest* without the need for a warning (TCC 482/1).

In addition, when the shareholder still fails to pay despite a reminder from the board of directors, the shareholder runs the risk of *forfeiture*.[125] Thereby, the board of directors is authorized to replace the defaulting shareholder with deprivation of his rights arising from the participation commitment and partial payments, and to cancel the share certificate if it has been given to it (TCC 482/2).

In the AoA, the defaulting shareholder may be stipulated to pay a *contract penalty* as well (TCC 482/3). The forfeiture sanction is also applied here (TCC 483/1). The contractual penalty here is of the type added to the performance. In other words, the contractual penalty is cumulatively applied alongside of the other sanctions in case of failure to fulfill share capital. Otherwise, the principle of protecting capital (assets) would be damaged.

Compensation may also be requested from the defaulting shareholder (TCC 482/4). In particular, the company may request compensation for the deficits that are not covered by the payments of the new (replaced) shareholder (TCC 483/3–4).

---

125 Bauen and Bernet, *Swiss Company Limited by Shares Company Law*, 92.

bb. Secondary Liabilities (Incidental Duties)

In a joint stock company, in cases where the transfer of shares is bound to the company's consent (TCC 491 ff.), certain recurring liabilities, a performance other than capital debt, at regular intervals (periodically) and the subject of which is not money, can be imposed on the shareholders by the AoA. The duty to perform and its scope are to be set out in the share certificates and temporary share certificates (TCC 480/4). The AoA may stipulate contractual penalties for any case of failure to comply/properly comply with the secondary liabilities (TCC 481/2).

In this context, for example, the shareholders of a company who operates in tomato paste industry may be obliged to deliver a certain amount of tomatoes to the company at each harvest. Such liabilities move the joint stock company away from being capital-based to some extent and bring personalized nature to the fore, similar to cooperatives.[126]

cc. Loyalty Obligation

There is no legal regulation that imposes loyalty obligations on shareholders in joint stock companies. For this reason, the majority in the doctrine is of the opinion that the partners do not have such an obligation and the fact that the company is private will not change this result. The minority view, on the other hand, argues that the shareholders came together to realize a common purpose, and that acts contrary to this purpose should be avoided, and CC 2 confirms this result.

dd. Confidentiality Obligation

Within the scope of the shareholder's right to receive information, the shareholder has the right to request information on certain issues from the BoD and auditors at the GA meetings; disclosure of information can only be refused on the grounds that if the requested information is given, company secrets will be disclosed or a company's interest that needs to be protected will be endangered (TCC 437/2 and 3).

The examination of the commercial books and correspondence of the company that concerns the question of the shareholder is only possible with the express permission of the GA or the decision of the BoD. If permission is obtained, the examination can also be carried out through a specialist. Learned company secrets must also be kept at all times. However, the concept of "company secret" has not been defined and what it covers is open to discussion.

126 Bahtiyar, *Ortaklıklar Hukuku*, 282.

b. Rights of the shareholders

aa. In Terms of Qualifications

aaa. Financial Rights

- **Right to Receive Dividends**

Among the shareholder's financial rights, the right to a dividend is paramount and is the result of the capital invested. Each shareholder has the right to participate in the net profit for the period decided to be distributed to the shareholders in accordance with the provisions of the law and the AoA (TCC 507/1).

Although the regulations regarding the dividend right are included in the TCC, some special regulations have been made in the CMC (CMC 19 and Communiqué on Dividends[127]). Apart from the aforementioned special regulations, the provisions of the TCC will also be applied in publicly-held corporations.

Pursuant to TCC 408/2d and 409/1, the decision authority on whether to distribute profit and its amount is with the GA, but it is obligatory to comply with some conditions stipulated by the law and the AoA regarding distribution and its amount.

Dividends may only be distributed from balance sheet profit and from special reserves created for profit distribution purpose (dividend reserves, TCC 509/2). Whether the company is profitable or not is determined according to the annual balance sheet (TCC 508/2). Also, the profit made must be real; dividends received unfairly and maliciously must be returned to the company (TCC 512 and 513); this issue also leads to the responsibility of the BoD according to TCC 553 ff. The GA resolution is taken by simple meeting and decision quorums (TCC 418) and upon the distribution resolution of the GA, the right to dividend turns into an independent right to claim and it becomes possible to transfer it to others.

There is an important connection between the dividends and the reserves: According to TCC 523/1, the dividend to be distributed to the shareholders cannot be determined unless the statutory reserves and reserves stipulated in the AoA are deducted in accordance both with the law and the AoA. In other words, the profits realized are not distributed in their entirety; reserves stipulated by law or the AoA must remain with the company.

---

127 II-19.1, OJ, 23.01.2014, no. 28891.

It is controversial in the doctrine whether the distribution of profit is compulsory or not.[128] In principle, the GA is not obliged to distribute balance sheet profit to the shareholders. The dividend cannot be paid out until it has been fixed by the GA resolution and the principle of equal treatment must be upheld at all times.

- **Preemptive Rights**

The priority right granted to existing shareholders in order to purchase new shares to be issued as a result of capital increases in proportion to their shares in the company's capital in order to retain their level of shareholding (or issued capital in registered capital system) is called the preemptive rights (the right to purchase new shares, TCC 461/1). If preemptive right was not granted, the shares created by the capital increase could be given directly to others or to specific shareholders; thereby, the ratio and power of the other shareholders in the company capital could be weakened gradually and shareholders would have suffered a dilution of their voting rights and earnings.

According to TCC 461, with the capital increase decision of the GA, the preemptive right may be limited or removed only if there are justified reasons and with the affirmative vote of at least 60 % of the share capital. In particular, the reasons as the public offering, the takeover of the company, parts of the company or shareholdings and the participation of the employees to the company are considered justifiable.

The BoD determines the principles of exercising the preemptive right with a decision and gives the shareholders at least 15 days with this decision. The decision is registered and announced in the Commercial Register Gazette and also published on the company's website, if any (TCC 461/3).

The provisions of the TCC regarding the preemptive right, in principle, are also applicable to publicly-held corporations. As an exception, CMC regulates the authorization of the BoD with the AoA to remove or restrict the preemptive right in capital increases of companies with registered capital (CMC 18/5, cf. TCC 460/4). If there is no such provision in the AoA or if the BoD has not used this authority, the partners will have preemptive right. In case the BoD restricts or removes this right, it is possible to file an action for annulment (CMC 18/6, TCC 460/5).

---

128 See Tekinalp, *Sermaye Ortaklıklarının Yeni Hukuku*, N. 14–35a; Bahtiyar, *Ortaklıklar Hukuku*, 286–287.

The preemptive right arises in capital increases made from external sources and in capital increases made through the creation of new shares. Increases from internal resources and external resources, but without creating new shares (increasing the nominal values of existing shares) do not give rise to preemptive right. This right is not a bonus right, it is completely different in nature from the right to receive gratis shares in increases from internal resources (bonus issue). The right to receive gratis shares cannot be waived (TCC 462/3); whereas the preemptive right can be removed or limited (TCC 461/2). Shareholders who want to exercise their preemptive right shall make a request within the stipulated time and pay the price of the new shares they will receive (TCC 461, CMC 12 and 18). Sanctions for breach of capital debt may be imposed on the shareholder who undertakes to purchase new shares but does not pay the price.

- **Right to Interest Before Commencement of Operations**

As a rule, no interest is paid against the capital in a joint stock company (TCC 509/1). This prohibition is based on the fact that the shareholders are not creditors but persons participating in the company assets, and therefore they can only benefit from the profit, but cannot claim back the capital they have invested. However, pursuant to TCC 510, a certain amount of interest may be paid to the shareholders out of the investment account for the time required to prepare and build up the company prior to commencement of full operations, provided that it complies with Turkish Accounting Standards. The AoA shall also determine how long the interest payments will continue, limited to this period.

In order for the said payment to be made, it must be regulated in the AoA and also specify how long it will take at the latest. The "time" here should not be understood as a definite date, but should be broadly interpreted to include a certain stage to be reached. For example, the preparatory period interest in the AoA can be regulated that it will end with "start of production …" or "end of trial production …".

- **Right to a Share in Liquidation Procedures**

In case of the company's dissolution, each shareholder has the right to benefit from liquidation surplus (a pro rata share of the liquidation proceeds), unless otherwise stipulated in the AoA (TCC 507/1). In all cases of dissolution, except for the cases that do not require liquidation, the company's legal entity does not disappear immediately after the reason for dissolution has occurred, and the liquidation of assets is required for the dissolution of the legal entity (TCC

536 ff.). If there is a liquidation surplus as a result of these transactions, it should be distributed to the shareholders in proportion to the share capital they paid and their privileges, if any, unless otherwise stipulated in the AoA. As a rule, distribution is made in cash, after 3 months have elapsed from the third invitation to the creditors and unless otherwise stated in the AoA or the GA resolution (TCC 543/3).

bbb. Personal Rights

- **Right to Participate in GA Meetings and Related Rights**

As a rule, each shareholder has the right to attend the GA meetings in person or through his/her representative, to speak and express his/her opinion, to vote in taking decisions, and to file an action for annulment if the conditions exist (TCC 407 ff.; 415, 425, 427 ff., 445 ff.).

A shareholder may be excluded from the GA meetings only if there are justifiable reasons and as a last resort (*ultima ratio*). Other than this exception, all partners enjoy the right to participate to the GA meetings. There are also other rights related to participation in the GA: as being invited formally to the GA meetings in accordance with the law and the AoA (TCC 409 ff.), being notified to the agenda in advance (TCC 413), being kept some documents available for inspection before the GA meeting (TCC 437/1).

The most important of the rights related to the right to participate in the GA is *the right to vote*. The shareholder is entitled to vote as soon as the amount provided for by law or by the AoA has been fully paid up (TCC 425). As per TCC 434/1, shareholders exercise their voting rights in proportion to the total nominal value of their shares. Each shareholder has at least one voting right, even if he owns only one share; however, the number of votes to be given to those holding more than one share may be limited by the AoA (TCC 434/2). In addition, with the AoA, privileged shares can be created in voting, and some shares may be granted more voting rights than others (TCC 478–479). The right to vote cannot be waived in advance, nor can this right be revoked by other partners. In other words, the right to vote is an inalienable right.

Shareholders vote at least one (and more if privileged in votes) for each share, as a rule, according to the nominal value of the share they own, and if they have more than one share, according to the total nominal value. But the abovementioned TCC 434/2 not only binds the right to vote to the shareholder in one respect, but also indirectly allows some shares to be left without votes, by regulating the upper limit on the number of votes to be cast by those who have more than one share.

Freezing of the voting rights and *exclusion of the voting rights* have different effects. In cases where the right to vote is frozen (such as TCC 201/1, 389, 497/3), not being able to vote is permanent and related to all agenda items. Exclusion of the voting rights, on the other hand, is not permanent and is related to a specific agenda item (see TCC 436, CMC 17/3 and 29/6) and does not prevent the shareholder from participation in the GA meeting and exercising voting and other shareholding rights concerning other agenda items that do not lead to exclusion.

In TCC 436/1, it is regulated that the shareholders are not entitled to vote "in negotiations concerning a personal business or transaction or a lawsuit in any judicial institution or arbitrator ..." between themselves and their relatives and the company. In other words, exclusion of the voting rights occurs in transactions in cases of facing a conflict of interest.

According to TCC 436/2, board members and those who have been involved in company management are excluded from their voting rights on resolutions on the discharge of the board members. However, this exclusion shall not constitute an obstacle to voting as the representative of another shareholder.

- **Right to Influence the Management and Audit of the Company**

Shareholders do not have the right to manage and audit, as there must be a BoD and an independent auditor. However, the shareholders contribute to the management and control in a broad sense by using their individual rights, minority rights and other tools specified in the law. For example, since managers and auditors are mainly elected by the GA, the shareholders indirectly affect the management and audit by attending the GA and voting in the election; when necessary, they may file a complaint and dismissal request to the GA; make a complaint to the Ministry of Trade; sue for liability; provoke auditors against managers; request a special audit; challenge resolutions of the GA in the court.

- **Right to Information and Inspection Rights**

In order for the shareholder to consciously and effectively use the rights granted to him by law or by the AoA, he should also have knowledge of the company activities in order to avail himself of his rights. For this purpose, a regulation has been included in TCC 437 under the subheading of "Right to information and inspection right" that cannot be abolished or limited by the AoA or the GA resolution (TCC 437/6).

Firstly, the financial statements, consolidated statements, annual business report of the BoD, audit reports and the recommendations of the BoD on profit distribution shall be kept available to the shareholders for their inspection at the headquarters and branches of the company at least 15 days before the ordinary

GA meetings. In addition, the first two documents must remain open for any shareholders' inspection for a period of 1 year following the GA meeting (TCC 437/1).

The shareholder may request information from the BoD about the company's affairs and from the auditors about the audit method and results in the GA; the obligation to provide information in the group of companies also includes subsidiary companies within the framework of TCC 200. The information to be given must be qualified, attentive and truthful in accordance with the principles of good faith and accountability. If a shareholder has been given information outside the GA meeting, the same information should be given to the other shareholders who make a request, within the same scope, even if there is no item on the agenda (TCC 437/2).

When shareholder's interest to right to information clashes with the company's legitimate interest in confidentiality, the company may refuse to provide information in order to protect company's legitimate interest in safeguarding secrecy and avoid impair competitiveness (TCC 437/3).

Examining the company's books and correspondence, which concerns the question of the shareholder, is subject to the explicit permission of the GA or the decision of the BoD. The examination can be done through an expert (TCC 437/4). The shareholder whose request for information or examination is left unanswered, unfairly rejected, postponed or not met within the meaning of this article, may apply to the commercial court of first instance in the place where the company's headquarters is located, within 10 days following the rejection, and in other cases after a reasonable period of time. The court may also include the order and form of giving the information outside the GA. The court's decision on this matter is final (TCC 437/5).

- **Right to Request a Special Audit**

The special audit, like the right to information, is a tool for providing shareholders with access to information about the company's operations so that they can make well-informed decisions about exercising other shareholder rights such as challenging the resolutions of the GA or suing for liability.

The TCC has granted every shareholder at the GA meeting the right to request a special audit to ensure that certain events are clarified, if such an audit is necessary in order to exercise their rights and provided that the right to information and inspection rights has already been exercised before. If the GA approves this request, the company or each shareholder may request the appointment of a special auditor by applying to the commercial court of first instance in the place where the company headquarters is located, within 30 days (TCC 438). If the right of a shareholder to request a special audit used in accordance with TCC 438 is rejected by the GA, one or more shareholders together representing at least 10 % of the share capital and 5 % of the share capital of the publicly-held joint stock companies or whose shares have a nominal value of at least one million Turkish Liras, may apply to the court within 3 months and request the appointment of a special auditor. If the petitioners demonstrate convincingly that the incorporators or corporate bodies have infringed the law and the AoA and thus harmed the company or the shareholders, the special auditor is appointed by the court (TCC 439).

bb. In Terms of Usage

aaa. Majority Rights

Since the majority principle applies in joint stock companies (TCC 418, 421), the shareholders influence and contribute to the formation of the majority and decision-making by participating and voting in the GA. Although the GA is a broadly authorized decision-making body of the company, the powers of the majority are not unlimited.

bbb. Minority Rights

In accordance with the majority principle, the decisions taken by the GA also bind the shareholders who did not attend the meeting or who voted against the meeting despite their participation (TCC 423). However, the legislator, in order to save the minority shareholders from the domination of the majority and strike a balance between majority and minority shareholders granted certain rights or paved the way for entitlement by the AoA (TCC 360) sometimes by showing the ratio (TCC 411–412, 420, 439–440, 531 and 559) and sometimes without showing them (TCC 486/3). Through these rights, the majority can be prevented from making a decision on the relevant issue (negative minority rights) or some actions can be taken on behalf of the company despite the majority (positive minority rights). Thus, a balance is maintained between majority and minority shareholders in the prevention or resolution of conflicts of interest in the company.[129]

- **Negative Minority Rights**
  - Prevention of settlement and release: Pursuant to TCC 559, the responsibilities of the founders, members of the BoD, auditors, arising from the establishment of the company and the capital increase cannot be removed by

129 Bahtiyar, *Ortaklıklar Hukuku*, 297.

settlement and release until 5 years have passed from the registration of the company. Even after this period, settlement and release is possible only with the decision of the GA. However, if the shareholders representing 10 % of the share capital and 5 % of the share capital of the publicly-held joint stock companies oppose, a settlement and release decision cannot be taken.

- Aggravated majority: As mentioned above, the law stipulates aggravated meeting and decision quorums in order to take resolutions on some issues in GA meetings, and that besides these quorums, simple quorums can be aggravated by the AoA (TCC 418, 421). In such cases, the minority has the opportunity to prevent the formation of quorums and thus the taking of certain decisions.

- **Positive Minority Rights**
  - Right to be represented in the BoD: Pursuant to TCC 360, the minority may be granted the right to be represented on the BoD, provided that it is stipulated in the AoA. In this context, it can be foreseen that the members of the BoD will be elected from among the minority or among the candidates proposed by them. The election of the candidate from among the minority or proposed by the minority cannot be refused by the general meeting unless there is a good cause. However, the right to be represented in this way cannot exceed half of the number of board members in publicly-held joint stock companies.
  - Right to convene the GA to a meeting and to include an item on the agenda: As explained above,[130] one or more shareholders together representing at least 10 % of the share capital and 5 % of the share capital of the publicly-held joint stock companies may also convene the GA meeting and if it is to be already convened, minority shareholders may demand an item be placed on the agenda (TCC 411–412).
  - Right to demand postponing the discussions of the financial statements: If one or more shareholders together representing 10 % of the share capital and 5 % of the share capital of the publicly-held joint stock companies requests, the discussion of the financial statements and related matters are postponed to 1 month later, without any need for a GA resolution on this demand, with the decision of the chairman of the meeting (TCC 420).
  - Right to an independent and professional audit: Pursuant to TCC 399/4b, upon the request of the shareholders constituting one tenth of the capital

130 Under this chapter, see supra: *Part II – Authorized Persons to Call the GA to the Meeting.*

and one twentieth of the publicly-held joint stock companies, the court may appoint another auditor by listening to the relevant parties and the elected auditor, especially if there are well-founded personal reasons for the elected auditor, especially if there is a suspicion that he/she is acting biased.

- Right to request a special audit: As explained above[131], if the right of a shareholder to request a special audit used in accordance with TCC 438 is rejected by the GA, shareholders representing at least 10 % of the share capital and 5 % of the share capital of the publicly-held joint stock companies or whose shares have a nominal value of at least one million Turkish Liras, may apply to the court for the appointment of a special auditor (TCC 439).
- Right to request the issuance of share certificates: TCC 486/2, amended by Law No. 7262, made it obligatory to print the bearer shares within 3 months at the latest after they have been paid in full, and to inform CSD regarding the bearer shareholders and the shares they hold before they are distributed.[132] On the other hand, another minority right is regulated in TCC 486/3. If the minority requests, the registered share certificate shall be printed and distributed to all registered shareholders.
- Right to request the dissolution of the company for just cause: As it will be explained below,[133] in case of justifiable reasons, shareholders representing at least 10 % of the share capital and 5 % of the share capital of the publicly-held joint stock companies may file an action before the commercial court for the dissolution of the company (TCC 531).

ccc. Individual, Vested and Inalienable Rights

Shareholders can use many of their rights on their own, especially to participate in the GA, to express an opinion and to bring motions on the planned agenda items, to vote, to take legal action challenging resolutions of the general meeting or legal action for liability. These rights are of individual nature, and some of these rights have been described as vested rights, and some rights have been described as inalienable. In other words, TCC includes the concept of vested rights as in former TCC, and besides it, it also indicates "inalienable rights" (TCC 452/1). The determination of the inalienable right and its limits

131 Under this chapter, see supra: *Part II – Personal Rights.*

132 Under this chapter, see infra: *Part II – Issuing Bearer Share Certificates (The recent amendment).*

133 Under this chapter, see infra: *Part II – Dissolution based on justifiable grounds (TCC 531).*

are of great importance in terms of the exercise of the rights, whether the waiver is valid or not, and the type of invalidity to be applied (TCC 391/c and 447/a).

- **Vested Rights**

The restriction or removal of vested shareholder rights may be possible only with the consent of the affected shareholder. As stated in the doctrine, certain rights can be recognized as vested in the AoA and new vested rights can also be created with the AoA, whereas inalienable rights cannot be created by the AoA.[134] Examples of vested rights are the rights arising from the fact that the company is a Turkish national or that the shareholder cannot bear any debt other than capital debt (TCC 480/1 and 421/2), as well as the rights stipulated in the law and the AoA that can be limited or removed only by the affirmative vote of all shareholders.

- **Inalienable Rights**

Inalienable rights are those rights that are legally recognized, protected, and whose limits are indicated, when necessary, the limitation or removal of which does not depend on the consent of the shareholder, that is, cannot be taken from him even with his consent. These are the rights granted not only to protect the interests of the owners, but also to protect the basic structure of the joint stock company.[135]

Examples of the inalienable rights are being treated equally, participating in the GA, the right to be represented in the GA, minimum votes, the rights to take legal actions or to assert other compulsory rights conferred by law, the right to information and inspection, the right to request the conduct of a special audit, the rights deriving from the basic structure of the joint stock company (such as anonymity, freedom of share transfer, limited liability, being subject to independent auditing, accountability of directors), the rights of the shareholder arising from the principle of protection of capital (e.g., the prohibition of issuing stock below par).

5. *Securities*

a. *Classification of Securities*

General remarks: Private joint stock companies have possibility to issue various types of securities such as, "capital shares" through capital increase, "dividend

134 Tekinalp, *Sermaye Ortaklıklarının Yeni Hukuku*, N. 14–25.
135 Tekinalp, *Sermaye Ortaklıklarının Yeni Hukuku*, N. 14–28.

rights certificates", "bonds", and "other debt instruments". Through securities, joint stock companies collect funds and, thus, finance their business activities. On the counterpart, investors gain "dividend" or "interest", i.e., harvest the production of their investment.

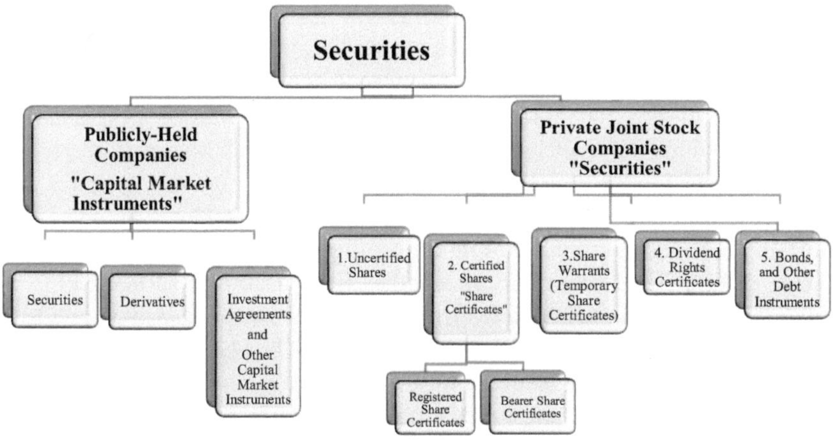

Tab. 2. Classification of the Securities

Classification of the securities: Although in private joint stock companies, main financial investment tools are the "securities", in capital market law, general term is the "capital market instrument", which has a far broader coverage, comprises in addition to securities, the "derivatives" and the "investment agreements" as well. Furthermore, other new capital market instruments can be created and classified as such by the Capital Market Board, which is the official public institution that supervises and regulates financial markets and publicly-held corporations in Turkish law (CMC Art. 3/1, sub-para. ş). Naturally, in the capital market law, there are significantly more type of financial instruments traded in financial markets. Whereas in private joint stock companies, securities can be classified with reference to the rights they accord to their owner, basically as "share of stock" either uncertified, or certified as "share certificates", "temporary share certificates (share warrants)", "dividend rights certificates", "bonds" and "other debt instruments".

Meaning and types of shares of a corporation: A "share" of a corporation represents the smallest part of the registered capital, either certified or uncertified, and grants shareholding rights to its owner.[136] Shares of a company are created and can take effect legally upon the registration of the company's foundation or registration of the capital increase in the commercial register (TCC 486/1). Shares must be at a minimum nominal value of one Turkish cent and this value can be upgraded only a cent and in multiples (TCC 476/1). Shares issued against this rule will be invalid, however the issuers are jointly and severally liable against persons who incurred damages (TCC 476/2). Joint stock companies may issue shares with different nominal values classified under different share groups. The legal status of a shareholder in the company depends on the proportion of the total nominal value of its shares to the share capital. Shares (uncertified) can be classified, according to several criteria such as non-voting shares and shares with voting right or priced shares and gratis shares. However, one of the most important distinction is the one concerning privileged shares and common shares, distinguished according to whether they accord privileged rights or not.[137] The privileges may be concerning shareholders rights such as dividend right, voting right or preemptive right etc. (TCC 478–479, 360, 421/3,6). TCC provide special provisions concerning privileged shares and aim to safeguard privileged shareholders' interests (TCC 454).

b. Issuing Share Certificates

aa. General Remarks

While shares are created *ipso iure* upon registration, joint stock companies may also issue "share certificates" or "temporary share certificates" that would represent shares. Share certificates can be essentially classified under two main categories based on the modality of the transfer: "bearer share certificates" and "registered share certificates" (TCC 484/1).[138] The type of share certificates must be indicated in the AoA (TCC 339/2-d).

One can wonder the aim of issuing share certificates in a company. A share certificate represents the share and does not cause any change on the legal status, rights and obligations of the shareholder, but rather serves as a tool to facilitate legal transactions to be made on the shares, such as transfer or consigning of shares, establishing pledge or usufruct on shares, or other similar transactions.

---

136 Also see, Communiqué on Shares VII-128.1, Article 4/1–p (OJ, 22.06.2013, no. 28685).

137 Bauen and Bernet, *Swiss Company Limited by Shares Company Law*, 53.

138 Although it was very controversial in the past years, recently the opinions both in the court decisions and in the doctrine have been to accept that registered share certificates have the legal qualification of "certificates to order" for a long time.

The share certificate demonstrates rights and the legal status of the shareholder, thereby must indicate certain information; company's title, share capital amount, incorporation date, the capital amount on this date, the arrangement of the issued share certificate, the date of its registration, type and nominal value, how many shares it contains (TCC 487/1). In addition to these, the registered share certificate indicates the name and surname or trade name of the owners, and the place of residence and the amount of the share price paid (TCC 487/2). Accordingly, the certification serves as a tool to enhance the transferability of the shareholder position which is the one essential feature of joint stock companies.[139] The share certificates must be signed by at least two of the persons authorized to sign on behalf of the company (TCC 487/1). Registered share certificates, as indicated by the name, are registered in the company's share book (TCC 487/2).

Notwithstanding in publicly-held corporations, securities and capital market instruments, i.e., publicly traded stocks, are dematerialized, with few exceptions, and no more physical certificates are issued. Capital market instruments are held and subject to legal transactions and trade only through the electronic registry system conducted by the Central Securities Depository (CMC Art. 13).

bb. Issuing Bearer Share Certificates (The recent amendment)

The board of directors shall print share certificates and distribute them to shareholders within 3 months from the date of full payment of bearer share price (TCC 486/2). Accordingly, cannot be issued bearer share certificates for shares that have not been fully paid. Those issued in violation of this rule are void. Bona fide beneficiaries with good faith have right for compensation (TCC 484/2).

Another requirement concerning bearer share certificates has been recently added in TCC 486/2 and 489, within the new drastic amendments made in TCC concerning notification of bearer share certificates by the Act on the Prevention of Financing the Proliferation of Weapons of Mass Destruction no. 7262[140] (Articles 28–34). The aim of the amendments is to assure a more transparent shareholder structure concerning bearer shares which are inherently prone to be anonymous and hide its owner. The information concerning both the bearer shareholders and the shares they hold shall be notified by the private joint stock companies to the Central Securities Depository before the distribution of the share certificates to the shareholders (TCC 486/2).

With this regulation the owners of bearer share certificates will be registered and tracked in private joint stock companies. The overall aim of the amendment

139 Bauen and Bernet, *Swiss Company Limited by Shares Company Law*, 54.
140 OJ, dated 31.12.2020, no. 31352 (in force as of 01.04.2021).

is to prevent the use of bearer share certificates as means of terror financing, proliferation, and money laundering, in conformity with the OECD Financial Action Task Force (FATF) Recommendations.[141]

On the international level is emphasized especially by the OECD Global Forum that "*(…) the anonymity of bearer share owners allows for potential abuses and jurisdictions shall implement some form of transparency mechanism, either by abolishing, immobilizing, or dematerializing bearer shares/warrants*".[142] And also in FATF Recommendations is indicated that "*(…) countries should take measures to prevent the misuse of bearer shares and bearer share warrants, for example by applying one or more of the following mechanisms: (a) prohibiting them; (b) converting them into registered shares or share warrants (for example through dematerialization); (c) immobilizing them by requiring them to be held with a regulated financial institution or professional intermediary; or (d) requiring shareholders with a controlling interest to notify the company, and the company to record their identity*".[143]

Consequently, in this respect, in Turkish company law have been adopted measures for the transparency of the ownership of bearer share certificates. TCC requires that the registration shall be carried by a public authority, through a public and electronic bearer shares registration system, rather than the company itself. Pursuant to TCC 486/2, 489, private joint stock companies shall notify the Central Securities Depository, of their bearer shareholders and their bearer shares, before distributing share certificates to the shareholders. The information concerning bearer shares and bearer shareholders, shall be registered electronically to Central Securities Depository's "Bearer Shares Registration System" by the company representatives. Thus, the Central Securities Depository, in addition to publicly-held companies' dematerialized shares, will monitor and register bearer share certificates of private companies as well.

141 For FATF Recommendations no. 24, 2012 text updated to 2020 see, https://cfatf-gafic.org/, accessed 18.9.2021.

142 Consequently, it is reported that "more than thirty jurisdictions have amended their legal frameworks to eliminate or immobilize bearer shares, only few jurisdictions still allow unregistered bearer shares". See the report of Inter-American Development Bank & OECD, A Beneficial Ownership Implementation Toolkit (2019), 31–32 (https://www.oecd.org/tax/transparency/beneficial-ownership-toolkit.pdf, accessed 18.9.2021).

143 For FATF Recommendations, 94 N. 14 see also, https://cfatf-gafic.org/, accessed 18.09.2021.

Holders of bearer share certificates are required to apply to the company for the registration to Central Securities Depository's "Bearer Shares Registration System" until 31.12.2021. Otherwise, shareholders will no longer be able to exercise their rights, until the necessary application is made. Those who do not apply or notify is punished with an administrative fine according to TCC 562/13. (TCC provisional Art. 14).

cc. Issuing Registered Share Certificates/Temporary Share Certificates
Where the board takes a decision to issue or the minority shareholders request, registered share certificates shall be issued and distributed. This right to request issuing of registered share certificates did not exist in the former TCC, is newly adopted as a minority right in TCC 486/3. Until share certificates are issued, in the meanwhile "temporary share certificates" can be issued in place of the share certificates. Issuing temporary share certificates is practically easier and faster than the issuing of the share certificates. Herewith, companies may issue, for a transitory period, temporary share certificates which grant similar advantages of share certificate. Temporary share certificates are subjected to same legal regime as registered share certificates, in other words, the articles of TCC regarding registered share certificates are to be applied to temporary share certificates by analogy (TCC 486/2).

c. The Modality of the Transfer

Uncertified shares: The modality of the transfer varies upon the type of the shares. Uncertificated shares should be transferred similarly to the regulations on the assignment of claims. In case the shares are fully paid, shares can be transferred with a written agreement, in conformity with the TCO provisions concerning assignment of claims (TCO 183, 184). However, in case the shares are not fully paid, provisions concerning both assignment of claims and assumption of debts (TCO 195) should be applied. To transfer a debt, the approval of the creditor is required. Consequently, the company as the creditor in this context should approve the transfer. Finally, the transfer must be registered in the share book.

Bearer share certificates: Bearer share certificates are not registered in the share book and the owner is not indicated on the certificate. Within the new amendments in force as of 01.04.2021, the modality of the transfer of bearer share certificates has been drastically changed. Before the amendment, the transfer of possession of the certificate was sufficient for a transfer of bearer share certificates.

According to the new regulation, the consignment of the certificate solely does not suffice; a notification to the Central Securities Depository must be made as well. Thus, the transfer of bearer share certificates takes effect against the company and third parties, only upon the notification of the transfer by the transferee to the Central Securities Depository (TCC 489/1). In case the transferee applies to the company, the transfer notification can be made by the company as well (Art. 5/1 of the Communiqué of 06.04.2021).[144]

In case the Central Securities Depository is not notified, the holders of bearer share certificates cannot use their share-related rights arising from the TCC until the notification is made (TCC 489/1). Notification of bearer share certificates to the Central Securities Depository, and the procedures and principles regarding registration, and the fees to be charged in this context are to be determined with the above-mentioned Communiqué regulated by the Ministry of Trade (TCC 489/4).

Registered share certificates and temporary share certificates (warrants): To be transferred, registered share certificates must be endorsed, and consigned to the transferee (TCC 490/2), and the transferee must be registered in the share book. Registered share certificates can be transferred without any limitation unless otherwise stipulated in the law or in the articles of association (TCC 490/1). Temporary share certificates will be transferred the same manner as the registered share certificates since the provisions concerning registered share certificates will be applied by analogy to temporary share certificates (TCC 486/2).

d. Restrictions on the Transferability

aa. Restrictions Arising out the Law

Since joint stock companies are of corporate structure with anonymous ownership, in principle shares of a joint stock company can be transferred freely without any limitation (TCC 490/1).[145] Exceptionally there can be restrictions

---

144 OJ, 06.04.2021, no. 31446.

145 Concerning the transfer of shares to foreign investors there are no restrictions in TCC or in the Act on Foreign Direct Investment no. 4875. However, in case a share transfer made to a foreign investor is a foreign investment under the Code on Foreign Direct Investment (Art. 2/b-2, ii), there is a requirement of notification to public authorities. For details see, Bilgin Tiryakioğlu, "Foreign Investment," in *Introduction to Turkish Business Law*, ed. Tuğrul Ansay and Eric C. Schneider (Ankara: Seçkin, 2014), 239–240.

on the transferability, arising out the law or the AoA. There can be restrictions arising from special legislation, such as Banking Code no. 5411 (Art. 18), or Act on the Protection of Competition no. 4054 (Art. 7/1), in which may be required a special permission to the share transfer of a public authority for certain type of joint stock companies in special sectors. On the other hand, a general restriction arising out the TCC, is concerning joint stock companies' registered shares that are not fully paid. These shares can be transferred only with the approval of the company (TCC 491/1). The company may abstain from giving an approval to such transfer only if the transferee's ability to pay is in doubt and the security requested by the company is not provided. However, the approval of the company is not necessary in case of a passing through "inheritance", "sharing of inheritance", "matrimonial property regime", or by "compulsory execution" (TCC 491/1).

bb. Statutory Restrictions

TCC allows statutory restrictions, but only for registered shares, and regulates restrictions distinctly for shares listed on the stock exchange (TCC 495 to 498) and shares that are not listed (TCC 492, 493, 494). However, concerning publicly-held companies a specific legal regime is set out by the Art. 137/3 of CMC which restricted substantially the application area of TCC 495/1–2.

aaa. In private joint stock companies (TCC 493)

With regard to shares that are not listed (unlisted shares) in private joint stock companies, where there is a need to preserve certain features of the company, e.g., the composition of the shareholders of the company, may be set out restrictions on the transferability of the shares, however the transfer cannot be prohibited. The regime concerning unlisted shares regulated in TCC 492, 493, 494 is quite in line with Articles 685a, 685b, 685c of the Swiss Code of Obligations. Thereby it may be stipulated in the AoA that the transfer of the registered shares is subject to the approval of the company (TCC 492/1) and the company may abstain from giving approval in three situations:

- By asserting an "important reason" (good cause) stipulated in the AoA (TCC 493/1),
- By suggesting to the transferor, to acquire their shares at the real value at the time of application (TCC 493/1).
- Or in case the transferee abstains from declaring explicitly that has received the shares on their own name and account (TCC 493/3).

TCC 493/2 defines the notion of important reason and draws a framework: "Important reasons" can only be grounds regarding the composition of the circle of shareholders which shall justify the refusal of the approval, in terms of business activity or the economic independence of the enterprise. For example, a clause in the AoA of a construction company which mentions that "registered shares can only be transferred to engineers, otherwise the company reserves its right to refuse giving approval to the transfer" would be qualified as a valid clause, since it indicates an important reason according to TCC 493/2. However, in the event of passing of unlisted shares through "inheritance", "sharing of inheritance", "property regime between spouses" or "debt enforcement proceedings", the company may not refuse based on an important reason but may refuse only by offering to acquire the shares at their real value (TCC 493/4).

Consequences of a refusal of a share transfer (TCC 494): Concerning shares that are not listed, in the event of refusal of a share transfer ownership of the shares and all rights attached to the shares remain belonging to the transferor. This is called the "theory of unity" (TCC 494/1). The transferee obtains neither the status of shareholder nor the ownership of the shares, i.e., the transfer would have no legal effect against the company. However, in the event of acquisitions with no regular transfer, this rule changes, and is replaced by "theory of division", which applies in case the shares are acquired due to "inheritance", "division of inheritance", the provisions of the "property regime between spouses" or "debt enforcement proceedings". To put it more accurately, the ownership of the shares and the pecuniary rights arising from those shall pass immediately. However, the right to attend the general assembly and voting rights shall pass to the transferee only upon with the approval of the company. In this respect, the moment of acquiring pecuniary rights and administrative rights is not the same. Pecuniary rights and non-pecuniary administrative rights are differentiated in terms of the acquiring time.

bbb. In publicly-held companies (CMC 137/3, TCC 495)

With regard to listed shares of the publicly-held companies, especially for those acquired from the stock exchange, has been adopted a different legal regime in capital market law, and thus no room is left for any restrictions. Pursuant to the Article 137/3 of CMC it cannot be abstained from registering in the share book the shares of publicly-held corporations purchased on the stock exchange. Whereas concerning the shares of the publicly-held companies that are not traded in the stock exchange, the above mentioned TCC 493 and 494 will be applied (Art. 137/3 of CMC).

Thereby due to the Article 137/3 of CMC, the application area of TCC 495–497 which set the main legal regime of restrictions for listed shares, is limited substantially. To what extent the applicability of those articles is restricted, and which articles, in which situation can be applied, is highly controversial in Turkish law.[146] Concerning listed shares, TCC 495/1 allows only restrictions to limit the number of shares to be acquired on the stock exchange. More specifically, only restrictions concerning an upper limit based on capital and expressed as a percentage, i.e., only a percentage clause, may be stipulated in the AoA (TCC 495/1). However, as stated before, the question whether TCC 495/1 have any applicability in publicly-held corporations is controversial.

6. *Dissolution of Joint Stock Companies*

a. *The Dissolution Phase*

aa. *Meaning of Dissolution, General Dissolution Grounds and Other Provisions*

The meaning of dissolution: The termination of the life circle of a company is codified in the 10th subsection under the title of "dissolution and liquidation" in TCC 529 to 548. This subsection regulates mainly situations causing dissolution and the liquidation procedure. The dissolution is the last phase before the ultimate ending, i.e., before the legal personality is completely extinct and removed from the commercial register. During this phase, business activities of the company cease, only compulsory transactions serving the aim of liquidation can be realized, in principle by the liquidators.

The general dissolution grounds (TCC 529): In which situations do joint stock companies dissolve? In principle, a company may dissolve, in the presence of situations indicated either in the TCC, or in the articles of association, or in case of a general assembly decision subject to a qualified quorum stated in TCC 421/3-4 (TCC 529/1-d). Dissolution grounds of joint stock companies are of corporate nature, such as in case of considerable loss of the equity capital, bankruptcy of the company (TCC 476/2), or legal or factual impossibility to carry out commercial business activities. The grounds for dissolution are generally and mainly, but not limited to, cited in TCC 529, which begins with the expiration of the term indicated in the AoA. A company will dissolve, in principle, upon the expiration of its term *ipso iure*.[147] However, despite the expiry of the term, if the business carries on running, the company will become indefinite without any necessity

146 For discussions see Bahtiyar, *Ortaklıklar Hukuku*, 321; See Yanlı, Veliye and Okutan Nilsson, Gül. "Kaydileştirilmiş Paylar Bakımından Pay Defteri Gerekli Midir?." in *Prof. Dr. Sabih Arkan'a Armağan*, (İstanbul: On İki Levha, 2019), 1327–1349.

147 *Ipso iure* refers to the situations upon which the company ends automatically without any further decision of the court or general assembly.

to change the term clause in the AoA or take a decision in the general assembly (TCC 529/1-a). Secondly is cited the "realization", or the "impossibility" of the subject of the business as an *ipso iure* termination. For example, a joint stock company founded to support a consortium of construction of a big shopping mall project becomes dissolved *ipso iure* upon the completion of the project or upon the objective impossibility of construction due to the discovery of an ancient archeological site located under the construction area (TCC 529/1-b). Another ground cited in TCC 529 is the declaration of company's bankruptcy by the court, upon which the bankruptcy procedure regulated in the Execution and Bankruptcy Code no. 2004 shall be applied and the liquidation procedure shall be conducted by the bankruptcy administration.

Undercapitalization (TCC 376): There are few other provisions which set forth situations upon which the company terminates *ipso iure*. One of those is the undercapitalization set forth in TCC 376/2, according to which if two-thirds of the total of the capital and legal reserves is unrequited due to damage, the company automatically terminates unless the general assembly takes the necessary decisions stipulated in the law. In the event of capital loss indicated in TCC 376/2 the general assembly shall be called immediately and shall decide either to settle with one third of the capital (capital decrease) or to complete the capital (capital increase).[148] Other than the dissolution due to capital loss, the restructuring transactions, mergers, divisions and conversions result in dissolution as well, but in these situations the acquired company or the converting company dissolves without any liquidation procedure.

Dissolution by court decision (TCC 353, TCC 210/3): TCC 353 and TCC 210/3 are other provisions concerning dissolution by the court decision. TCC 353 sets out a dissolution lawsuit that can be filed within the 3-months period beginning from the registration and announcement of the company. This lawsuit can be filed by the board of directors, shareholders, creditors of the company and the Ministry of Trade in the event of violation of the provisions of law during the foundation of the company. The main idea underlying is that the registration of a company has a "healing effect" on the deficiencies and violations of law that occurred during the foundation of a company. Consequently, contrary to

148 The decisions which shall be taken by the GA under TCC 376/2 are enumerated on a broader extent by the Articles 7–11 of the Communiqué of the Ministry of Trade About Procedures and Principles on the Implementation of Article 376 of the TCC (OJ, 15.09.2018, no. 30536). This Communiqué is amended recently by the amending Communiqué published in the OJ, 26.12.2020, no. 31346.

classical approach of law of obligations concerning contracts, cannot be claimed nullity or inexistence of a commercial company based on those deficiencies. However, a lawsuit for dissolution with a proactive effect in TCC 353 can be filed only within 3 months beginning from the foundation of the company.

TCC 210/3 also sets out another lawsuit for dissolution, which can be claimed by the Ministry of Trade in case of violation of public order. In case commercial companies engage in transactions contrary to public order or contrary to subject of business or in preparations in this direction or are determined to engage in collusive business and activities, a lawsuit for dissolution can be filed by the Ministry of Trade, within 1 year after the preparations or activities are learned. This is regarded as one of the regulations that serves for the public supervision on all type of the commercial companies under TCC.

bb. Specific Dissolution Grounds

Lack of organs (TCC 530): A particular lawsuit for dissolution is based on the lack of the organs is regulated in TCC 530. In the event one of the mandatory organs of the company are not available, the BoD cannot be formed or convened, or the general assembly is not or cannot be convened for an extended period of time, shareholders, creditors or the Ministry of Trade may request the dissolution of the company by the commercial court. The meaning and the coverage of "lack of organs" and the "extended period of time" are not explained in TCC 530. To exemplify, deadlock in decision-making process, where the number of affirmative votes and negative votes are equal, and the fact that the GA decisions cannot be taken due to deadlocks can be considered as a lack of organ as well. Besides, where a general assembly has not been convened for 3 or 4 years consecutively, this may be considered as an extended period of time and lead to lack of organ.

The court, upon hearing directors, may decide to give the company a certain time for rectification to bring the company's situation into compliance with law. If the situation is not rectified within due time, the court will order dissolution of the company. The judicial discretion of the court to give time for rectification is the reflection of the principle of "ultima ratio", according to which the dissolution shall be the last resort.

Dissolution based on justifiable grounds (TCC 531): Pursuant to TCC 531, in the presence of justifiable reasons, minority shareholders may request the dissolution of the company by the commercial court. After the current TCC entered into force, since 2012, this lawsuit has been one of the most filed amongst company law lawsuits. Dissolution based on the justifiable grounds, was not regulated in the former TCC for joint stock companies, was regulated only for personalized companies, i.e., the collective company, limited liability company and the general partnership. TCC 531, unlike those regulations, is accorded the quality of a minority right in joint stock companies. Thereby infringement of shareholders' rights has the predominance among the unjustifiable reasons. Especially infringement, severe and constant violation of the right to obtain information and examination, the right to receive dividends and the regular decrease on the dividends distributed, severe violation of the preemptive rights, the fact that the general assembly has been called to the meeting many times in violation of the law and alike can be considered justifiable reasons as cited in the Preamble and in the doctrine in Swiss and Turkish law.[149] Another pillar of justifiable reasons covers situations concerning mostly financial situation of the company, such as the company's constant loss, financial disruption due to poor management, systematic siphoning or draining company's assets, or lasting deadlocks in the general assembly.

As stated before, the concept of "minority shareholder" means not any non-controlling shareholder, but non-controlling shareholder which represents a certain threshold and thus benefits from the specific minority rights. Accordingly, owners of the shares representing at least one tenth of the capital in private joint stock companies and one twentieth of the capital in publicly-held corporations are considered minority shareholders in Turkish company law. One particularity is that, although the threshold is defined both for private and public companies in TCC 531, it is generally accepted that this lawsuit is not appropriate to be filed in publicly-held corporations,[150] since their shareholders, that is, "small investors", may benefit from different rights and options to easily leave the company.[151]

Another particularity of this lawsuit is that the court is given a broader discretionary power than usual, than other dissolution lawsuits. Despite the existence of the reasons that justifying the dissolution, the court, which is of the opinion that it would be more convenient economically and rationally to keep the company alive, may decide to the dismissal of the minority shareholder from the company with the actual value of their shares as of the date closest to the decision instead

---

149 For various examples of justifiable grounds see, Ayşe Şahin, *Anonim Ortaklığın Haklı Sebeple Feshi* (İstanbul: Vedat Kitapçılık, 2013), 157 ff.

150 For this opinion and other controversial legal questions see, Füsun Nomer Ertan, "Haklı Sebeple Fesih Anonim Ortaklığın Haklı Sebeple Feshi Davası – TTK m. 531 Üzerine Düşünceler," *İstanbul Üniversitesi Hukuk Fakültesi Mecmuası* 73, no. 1 (2015): 423.

151 For the appraisal right of shareholders in publicly-held corporations see, Semerci Vuraloğlu, *Sermaye Piyasası Kanunu'na Göre Anonim Ortaklıkta Ayrılma Hakkı*, 173 ff.

of dissolving the company. Undoubtedly, so many legal questions arise when the court decides the plaintiff is dismissed from the company, such as who will buy and pay shares of the dismissed shareholder, whether the other (usually controlling) shareholders can buy the shares or not, how the share price will be evaluated, and up to what percentage the company can buy the dismissed partner's (and its own) shares, and so on.[152] Another controversial question is whether the dismissal claim can be directed by the plaintiff to other shareholders. This claim has been subject to one of the latest decisions of the Court of Cassation, which has approved both the first instance court and the reginal court of appeal decisions, by rejecting the applicability of TCC 531 for dismissal of another shareholder other than the plaintiff.[153]

Besides the court may also decide to another "appropriate" and "acceptable" alternative solution. The notion of alternative solution is not defined in TCC 531. This provision constitutes an exception in terms of discretionary power of the court, which is in principle framed with the request of the plaintiff. However, in Turkish and Swiss doctrine, are generally stated and discussed that the court can decide to the distribution of the profits, the appointment of a minority representative to the board of directors, the decrease of the capital. On the other hand, any change on the articles of association, e.g., incorporating a clause concerning an obligation to distribute profits, or invalidity or change of the decisions of the GA or the BoD taken previously, change of members in the BoD, and division of the company are being discussed and are rather controversial both in the doctrine and Court of Cassation decisions.

b. Liquidation Procedure

General remarks: When entrepreneurs decide to close down their company, they shall request removal of the corporation from the commercial register. However, before this, they need to follow up a liquidation procedure which might take anywhere from 3 to 12 months, or even longer in some cases, depending on the legal and financial situation of the company. During the liquidation, the company still exists and preserves its legal personality but operates only with a limited aim to complete the liquidation.

---

152 For further explanation concerning above-mentioned questions see, Şahin, *Anonim Ortaklığın Haklı Sebeple Feshi,* 416 ff.

153 See, the decision of Turkish Court of Cassation, 11th Civil Chamber, dated 02.12.2019, no. 2019/915–2019/7720 (www.legalbank.com, accessed 17.9.2021).

Liquidators: Liquidation is mainly realized by liquidators who are appointed either by the general assembly or by the articles of association or by the court in case they cannot be appointed by first two ways, or in case the dissolution takes effect upon a court decision. The duties and powers of the organs become limited with transactions which are mandatory for the liquidation, but which cannot be done by the liquidators. This radical change should be announced to third parties by adding the wording of "in liquidation" to the business name of the company.

Procedure: Within the liquidation procedure, liquidators shall complete the ongoing transactions of the company. If necessary, they collect the outstanding portions of the share prices that have not been paid yet, liquidate, and sell the assets, and pay company's debts (if don't exceed the assets) (TCC 542). In the event of wholesale of a substantial part of the company assets, there should be taken a decision by the GA with a qualified quorum (TCC 538/2). It should be followed the procedure to call the creditors. The creditors shall be called upon, with three announcements with an interval of 1 week, to report their claims to the liquidators and shall be informed that the company has come to a dissolution (TCC 541/1). Unless 3 months have passed from the date of the call made to the creditors for the third time, the remaining assets cannot be distributed. To the extent that there is no danger for the creditors depending on the situation, the court may authorize the distribution within 3 months (TCC 543/2). Finally, after debts are paid and the share prices of shareholders are refunded, the remaining funds will be distributed among shareholders in proportion of their share and privileged rights, unless otherwise agreed in the AoA (TCC 543/1). Upon the end of the liquidation, the business name of the company will be removed from the register. Deletion is requested by the liquidation officers from the register office. Upon request, deletion is registered and announced (TCC 545/1).

Additional liquidation: A legal procedure that did not exist in the former TCC is the additional liquidation procedure, regulated in TCC 547. Although the liquidation is completed and the company register has been already removed, related persons may find out that additional liquidation transactions are necessary. Therefore, either of the last liquidators, the BoD, shareholders, or the creditors is given the right to request from the commercial court the re-registration of the company until the liquidation is ultimately completed (TCC 547).

Withdrawal of the liquidation: Shareholders can decide to withdraw from the liquidation under the situations and conditions stated in TCC 548. If the company dissolves due to the expiration of the term or due to a decision of the general assembly, the general assembly may decide to withdraw from liquidation and carry on the business. This decision must be taken with a qualified quorum of at least 60 % of the capital. It also requires that the distribution of company assets among the shareholders should not have started yet. The liquidators shall register the GA decision to withdraw from liquidation (TCC 548/1).

Further Readings

Altay, Sıtkı Anlam. *Yönetim Yetkilerinin Devrinin Sorumluluğa Etkileri.* İstanbul: Vedat Kitapçılık, 2011a.

Altay, Sıtkı Anlam. *Yeni Türk Ticaret Kanunu ve Şirketim, Deloitte Türkiye Raporu.* İstanbul: 2011b.

Altay, Sıtkı Anlam. *Şirketin Merkezine Doğru Yolculuk: CEO, Deloitte Türkiye Raporu.* İstanbul: 2016.

Antalya, Gökhan and Acar, Faruk. *Ticari İşlemlerde Taşınır Rehni.* İstanbul: Aristo, 2017.

Arıcı, Mehmet Fatih. *Ticari İşletmenin Aktif ve Pasifi ile Devri.* İstanbul: Vedat Kitapçılık, 2008.

Arslanlı, Halil. *Kara Ticaret Hukuku Dersleri Umumi Hükümler.* İstanbul: Fakülteler Matbaası, 1960.

Atamer, Yeşim. "Genel İşlem Koşulu mu Bireysel Pazarlıkla Kurulan Sözleşme mi? Tüketici ve Tacir İşlemleri Açısından Karşılaştırmalı Olarak Başvurulabilecek Değerlendirme Kriterleri." In *Yeni Türk Borçlar Kanunu ve Yeni Türk Ticaret Kanunu Sempozyumu Makaleler, Tebliğler*, 103–137. Edited by Çiğdem Kırca. İstanbul: Vedat Kitapçılık, 2013.

Atamer, Yeşim and Okutan-Nilsson, Gül. "Para Alacaklısının Geç Ödemelere Karşı Korunmasına İlişkin Yeni TK m. 1530 Düzenlemesi ve Uygulama Alanı," *Batider* 29, no. 3 (2013): 31–82.

Aydoğan, Fatih and Emirler, Gizem Melike. *Turkish Commercial Code.* İstanbul: On İki Levha, 2021.

Bahtiyar, Mehmet. "Anonim Şirket Adına Yönetim Kurulu Üyelerine Karşı Açılacak Sorumluluk Davasında Genel Kurul Kararının Gerekli Olup Olmadığı Sorunu." In *Prof. Dr. Seza Reisoğlu Armağanı*, 393–414. Edited by Arkan, Sabih and Özkorkut, Korkut. Ankara: Bankacılık Enstitü Yayınları, 2016.

Bahtiyar, Mehmet. "Anonim Şirket Genel Kurulunda Toplantı Yetersayısının "Toplantı Süresince Korunması" Şartına İlişkin TTK. 418/1 Hükmünün Değerlendirilmesi." In *Prof. Dr. Hamdi Yasaman'a Armağan*, 59–102. Edited by Erdem, Ercüment et al. İstanbul: On İki Levha, 2017.

Bahtiyar, Mehmet. "Anonim Şirketlerde Genel Kurul Toplantı Tutanağı ve Özellikle Kararların Hükümsüzlüğüne Etkileri." In *Prof. Dr. Ersin Çamoğlu'na Saygı Günü, Şirketler Hukukunun Güncel Sorunları Sempozyumu*, 30.10.2017, Bildiri Kitabı, 37–66. İstanbul: Özyeğin Üniversitesi Hukuk Fakültesi Yayını, 2019.

Bassani, Luciana, Bedford, Rebecca, Pressman, Arthur L., Turgeon, Jean-Philippe and Waldzus, Dagmar. "Applicable Law and Jurisdiction in Franchising, Commercial Agency and Distribution Agreements," *International Journal of Franchising Law*, 13, no. 6 (2015): 3–34.

Bauen, Marc and Bernet, Robert. *Swiss Company Limited by Shares Company Law/Merger Law/Stock Exchange Law/Tax Law*, Zürich: Schulthess, 2007.

Bazinas, Spyridon V. "The UNCITRAL Model Law on Secured Transactions." In *International and Comparative Secured Transactions Law Essays in honour of Roderick A Macdonald*, 55–76, Edited by Spyridon V. Bazinas and Orkun Akseli. Oxford: Hart Publishing, 2017.

Davies, L. Paul and Worthington, Sarah. *Principles of Modern Company Law*, 10th ed. London: Sweet & Maxwell, 2016.

Gerner-Beuerle, Carsten and Schillig, Michael. *Comparative Company Law*, New York: Oxford University Press, 2019.

Helvacı, Mehmet. "Anonim Ortaklık Tarafından Yönetim Kurulu Üyelerine Karşı Açılacak Sorumluluk Davalarında Genel Kurul Kararının Gerekli Olup Olmadığı Sorunu - Düşünceler ve Değerlendirmeler." In *Yürürlüğünün 5. Yılında ve Yargıtay Kararları Işığında Türk Ticaret Kanunu Sempozyumu - 20 Ekim 2017*, 143–176. Edited by Kendigelen, Abuzer. İstanbul: On iki Levha, 2018.

Jung, Peter. "UCP-Directive and Swiss Law against Unfair Competition." *Journal of European Consumer and Market Law*, 5, no. 2 (2016): 102–106.

Karaman Coşkun, Özlem. "6102 sayılı Türk Ticaret Kanunu'nda Teşebbüs Kavramı ve Tacir Sayılmasının Sonuçları." *MÜHF-HAD*, 21/1 (2015): 107–166.

Kaya, Arslan. "Post Contractual non-Compete Agreements Concerning Agents, Distributors and Franchisees." *Annales de la Faculté de Droit d'Istanbul*, 47, no. 64 (2015): 43–61.

Kaya, Arslan. *Acentelik Hukuku Şerhi*. İstanbul: Beta, 2016.

Kaya, Arslan et al., eds. *Approximation of Turkish Law with European Union Law Private Law*. İstanbul: İstanbul Üniversitesi Yayınevi, 2020.

Kayar, İsmail and Özatlan, Yurdal. "Anonim Şirket Yönetim Kurulu Üyelerinin Sorumluluğu Davasında Kusur ve İspat." *Terazi Aylık Hukuk Dergisi Özel Sayı* 14 (2019): 17–30.

Kendigelen, Abuzer. *Yeni Türk Ticaret Kanunu: Değişiklikler, Yenilikler ve İlk Tespitler,* 3rd ed. İstanbul: On İki Levha, 2016.

Kendigelen, Abuzer. "İptal Davası Açma ve Pay Sahipliği Sıfatının Cüz'î Halefiyet (Payların Devri) Sonucu Değişmesi." In *Prof. Dr. Hayri Domaniç'e 80. Yaş Günü Armağanı Vol. 1*, 307–331. Edited by Kendigelen, Abuzer. İstanbul: Beta, 2001.

Kırca, İsmail. "Kooperatiflerin Tacir Niteliği Hakkında Yargıtay'ın Tutumu: Kanuna Aykırı Yorum mu Yoksa Örtülü Boşluk Doldurma Gayreti mi?." *Batider* 33, no. 2 (2017): 5–25.

Kırca, İsmail. "Ticari İş ve Ticari Hükme Dair." *Batider* 34, no. 3 (2018): 5–17.

Kırca, İsmail, Şehirali Çelik, Feyzan Hayal and Manavgat, Çağlar. *Anonim Şirketler Hukuku - Vol. 1 - Temel Kavram ve İlkeler Kuruluş Yönetim Kurulu.* Ankara: Sözkesen Matbaacılık, 2013.Kırca, İsmail, Şehirali Çelik, Feyzan Hayal and Manavgat, Çağlar. *Anonim Şirketler Hukuku, Vol. 2/2 Genel Kurul Kararlarının Hükümsüzlüğü.* Ankara: Sözkesen Matbaacılık, 2016.

Moroğlu, Erdoğan. *Anonim Ortaklıkta Genel Kurul Kararlarının Hükümsüzlüğü,* İstanbul: On İki Levha, 2020.

Narbay, Şafak and Akkuş, Muhammed. "Ticari İş Niteliğinin Belirlenmesi ve Ticari İş - Tüketici İşlemi Ayrımı." In *Sabih Arkan'a Armağan*, 823–881. Edited by İsmail Kırca et al. İstanbul: On İki Levha, 2019.Nomer Ertan, Füsun. "Haklı Sebeple Fesih Anonim Ortaklığın Haklı Sebeple Feshi Davası - TTK m. 531 Üzerine Düşünceler." *İstanbul Üniversitesi Hukuk Fakültesi Mecmuası*, 73, no. 1 (2015): 421–440.

Nomer Ertan, Füsun. *Haksız Rekabet Hukuku*. İstanbul: On İki Levha, 2016.

Nomer Ertan, Füsun. "Haksız Rekabet." In *Yürürlüğünün 7. Yılında ve Yargıtay Kararları Işığında Türk Ticaret Kanunu Sempozyumu - III (Tebliğler-Tartışmalar) 18 Ekim 2019*, 21–32. Edited by Arslan Kaya. İstanbul: On iki Levha, 2020.

Oğuz, Arzu. "Hukuk Tarihi ve Karşılaştırmalı Hukuk Açısından Uluslararası Ticaret Hukuku." *Journal of Ankara University Faculty of Law*, 50, no. 3 (2001): 11–53.

Okutan Nilsson, Gül. "Unfair Trade Law." In *Introduction to Turkish Business Law*, 111–119. Edited by Ansay, Tuğrul and Schneider, Eric C. Ankara: Seçkin, 2014.

Okutan Nilsson, Gül. "National Report on Turkey." In *Groups of Companies. Ius Comparatum - Global Studies in Comparative Law*, Vol. 43, 399–422. Edited by Manóvil, R. Mariano. Cham: Springer, 2020.

Du Plessis, Jean J., Grossfeld, Bernhard, Luttermann, Claus, Saenger, Ingo, Sandrock, Otto and Casper, Matthias. *German Corporate Governance in International and European Context*. Berlin: Springer, 2017.

Reinert, Sophus A. and Fredona, Robert. "Merchants and the Origins of Capitalism," In *Forthcoming in Routledge Companion to the Makers of Global Business*, 1–36. Edited by Teresa da Silva Lopes et al. Boston: Harvard Business School, 2018.

Semerci Vuraloğlu, Tuğba. *Sermaye Piyasası Kanunu'na Göre Anonim Ortaklıkta Ayrılma Hakkı*. İstanbul: On İki Levha, 2018.

Şahin, Ayşe. *Anonim Ortaklığın Haklı Sebeple Feshi*. İstanbul: Vedat Kitapçılık, 2013.

Tan, Cheng-Han, Wang, Jiangyu and Hofmann, Christian. "Piercing the Corporate Veil: Historical, Theoretical & Comparative Perspectives." *Berkeley Business Law Journal*, 16, no. 1 (2019): 140–204.

Tekinalp, Ünal and Mertol Digili, Mehtap. *Commercial and Economic Law in Turkey*. Croydon: Kluwer Law International, 2016.

Tiryakioğlu, Bilgin. "Foreign Investment." In *Introduction to Turkish Business Law*, 233–244. Edited by Ansay, Tuğrul and Schneider, Eric C. Ankara: Seçkin, 2014.

Vorbrugg, Georg and Mahler, Dirk H. "Agency and Distributorship Agreements under German Law." *International Lawyer (ABA)*, 19, no. 2 (1985): 607–621.

Yanlı, Veliye. *Anonim Ortaklıklarda Tüzel Kişilik Perdesinin Kaldırılması ve Pay Sahiplerinin Ortaklık Alacaklılarına Karşı Sorumlu Kılınması*. İstanbul: Beta, 2000.

Yanlı, Veliye. "Muhalefetin Tutanağa Geçirtilmesi ve Bu İşlemin Zamanı Sorunu – Genel Kurul Kararlarının İptali Davası Bağlamında." *Batider*, 37, no. 2 (June 2021): 5–36.Yanlı, Veliye and Okutan Nilsson, Gül. "Kaydileştirilmiş Paylar Bakımından Pay Defteri Gerekli Midir?." In *Prof. Dr. Sabih Arkan'a Armağan*, 1327–1349. Edited by Prof. Dr. İsmail Kırca et al. İstanbul: On İki Levha, 2019.

Assoc. Prof. Dr. Zafer KAHRAMAN*

Chapter VI Competition Law

Aslan, İ. Yılmaz. Rekabet Hukuku. 5th ed. Bursa: Ekin Kitabevi, 2017; Aşçıoğlu-Öz, Gamze. Avrupa Topluluğu ve Türk Rekabet Hukukunda Hakim Durumun Kötüye Kullanılması. Ankara, 2000; Cengiz, Dilek. Türk Rekabet Hukukunda Uyumlu Eylem ve Bu Eylemin Hukuki Sonuçları. İstanbul: Beta Yayınevi, 2006; Güven, Pelin. Rekabet Hukuku Ders Kitabı. Ankara: Yetkin Yayınları, 2009; İkizler, Metin. Rekabet Hukukunda Uyumlu Eylemler. Ankara: Seçkin Yayınevi, 2005; Jones, Alison, and Sufrin Brenda. EC Competition Law, Text, Cases, and Materials. 2nd edition. New York: Oxford University Press, 2004; Kahraman, Zafer. Rekabet Hukuku Açısından Oligopolistik Bağımlılık. İstanbul: Beta Yayınevi, 2008; Whish, Richard. Competition Law. Edited by LexisNexis. 5th ed. London, 2003.

Introductory Remarks

The free competition remains at the heart of the liberal economy. Therefore, the competition law protecting and promoting a sound economic environment is crucial for all companies and businesses operating in the market.

This chapter will focus on the competition law in Turkey, in seven parts. In the first part, a brief overview and the salient features of the Turkish competition law will be introduced. The legislation and the Competition Authority will be explained as well. In the second part, the undertaking will be defined with its elements, and then, in the third part, the relevant market which sets the framework for the application of the competition law will be described. In the following parts, the prohibitions on cartel and on the abuse of dominant position will be analyzed. Afterwards, the control of concentrations will be handled and in the last part, the sanctions, fines and remedies will be examined.

* Corresponding author.

§ Part I Introduction

I. Overview

Turkey is a liberal economy, which functions under the laws of supply and demand. It is characterized by private ownership, free trade, self-interested economic agents, optimized buying and selling platforms, secure access to finance, competition, and limited government intervention. Given its basic structure and components, it can be defined as an economic system directed by market dynamics.

The liberal economy prescribes an environment where actions performed by individuals to gain benefits and by undertakings to maximize profits are converted into social welfare. In theory, it is argued that free markets, made up of economic agents who act in their own self-interest, deliver the best possible social and economic outcomes when the markets are left to their own devices. The metaphor of "invisible hand", introduced by Adam Smith, has been employed in economics to explain that the mechanisms through which beneficial social and economic outcomes may arise from the accumulated self-interested actions of individuals, none of whom intends to bring about such outcomes.[1]

Hence, the basic principle of the liberal economy is the assumption that economic relations are focused on free competition. In short, the liberal economy depends on the existence of a sound competition environment.[2]

In the economic sense, the competition is characterized by economic rivalry amongst the economic players for attracting the maximum number of customers and making most of the profit.[3] The players in the market, strive to acquire more customers, thereby increase their sales of goods and services, and consequently, their profits.

The concept of competition forms the basis of an efficiently operating liberal market system. It protects the independence of the decisions of market actors as well as their actions in the pursuit of their own interests, while also ensuring social justice and economic efficiency. It is clear that competition between firms is the lifeblood of strong and effective markets, because a sound competitive market structure encourages firms to continually adapt their competitive power in line with the prevailing market conditions. This encourages firms to innovate

---

1 Adam Smith, *The Theory of Moral Sentiments*, 1759; Adam Smith, *An Inquiry into the Nature and Causes of the Wealth of Nations*, 1776.

2 Mustafa Ateş, *Rekabet Hukukuna Giriş*, 2nd ed. (Ankara: Adalet Yayınevi, 2019), 43.

3 Ateş, *Rekabet Hukukuna Giriş*, 38.

by reducing slack, putting downward pressure on costs, and providing incentives for the efficient organization of production. Thus, competition is a central driver for productivity growth in the liberal economy.

The competition among actors involved in commercial activities leads to more efficient production and business management, and also promotes using fewer sources, production at lower costs, technological innovations and developments. As a result of this, it will be possible to buy products with better quality at lower prices, and public welfare will increase. It means that the mere existence of an effective competition creates a consumer-friendly market as a side effect because individuals or firms, in order to maximize their profits, strive to win customers' business by achieving the lowest level of costs and prices, developing new products or services or exploiting particular strengths, skills or other advantages to meet customer needs more effectively than their competitors. This increases quality and decreases prices of the goods and services offered in the market, which helps consumers get a good deal.

On the other hand, if markets are left to their own devices, there is a risk that undertakings within those markets tend to avoid competition in order to maximize their profits. They may start a predatory race in which, instead of competing, they may choose to enter into collaborations with negative effects on social welfare and economic development, or to utilize their economic power through abusive or exclusionary practices. They may set barriers to entry into the markets deterring potential competitors from entering, or abuse costumers, or oblige rivals to exit, to confine them to market niches, or to prevent them from expanding, leading to restriction of competition, which ultimately decline social welfare and cause consumer harm.

In brief, it is highly important to protect the effective competition, which ensures the proper functioning of the liberal economy, and contributes to general welfare with increasing economic efficiency.

In order to secure that end, the competition law is emerged as a body of law which seeks to assure competitive markets. Its main purpose is to remedy some of the situations in which the free-market system breaks down. It is implemented to ensure and protect the proper functioning of the liberal economy.

II. Legislation

The competition law in Turkey has bloomed in the 1990's, in the positive atmosphere created by the Customs Union between the European Union and Turkey and is still going through various improvements.

The law drafted by the legislature to regulate such competition is known as the "Act no. 4054 on the Protection of Competition[4]" ("APC") which finds its legal basis in the article 167 of the Turkish Constitution mandating for the State to form its policies with an eye on the objective of protecting free markets. It states that "*The State shall take measures to ensure and promote the sound, orderly functioning of the money, credit, capital, goods and services market and prevent the formation, in practice or by agreement, of monopolies and cartels in the markets.*" Therefore, the principal reason in drafting the APC is the duty and responsibility placed on the state to take measures to prevent monopolies and cartels.

Another important reason is the Association Agreement (Ankara Agreement) signed between Turkey and European Economic Community on October 12, 1963, which specifies that the principles mentioned in the provisions of the Treaty of Rome concerning competition must be adopted by Turkey.

It should be noted that various regulations are drafted by the State, and communiqués are issued by the Turkish Competition Authority (TCA) regarding the competition law since the adoption of the APC.

III. Salient Features of the Turkish Competition Law

A. *The Purpose*

The competition law aims to protect and promote the liberal market economy by maintaining and preserving an effective competition in the market.[5]

According to the article 1 of the APC, "*the purpose of this Act is to prevent agreements, decisions and practices preventing, distorting or restricting competition in markets for goods and services, and the abuse of dominance by the undertakings dominant in the market, and to ensure the protection of competition by performing the necessary regulations and supervisions to this end.*"

It means that the competition law protects the liberal market against anti-competitive behaviors, which may be conducted by the undertakings operating in the market, in order to avoid the risks of competition. The competition implies that there will be winners and losers. In the absence of the rules of competition law, it is highly possible that competitors tend to prevent competition because nobody wants to be at the downside of the economic contest.

---

4 OJ, 13.12.1994, no. 22140 (Date of Adoption: 7.12.1994).

5 Zekeriyya Arı, "Rekabet Hukukunda Amaç Sorunu," *Süleyman Demirel Üniversitesi İktisadi ve İdari Bilimler Fakültesi Dergisi* 8, no. 3 (2003): 27–48; Ateş, *Rekabet Hukukuna Giriş*, 191; Pelin Güven, *Rekabet Hukuku Ders Kitabı* (Ankara: Yetkin Yayınları, 2009), 27.

It should be noted that each economic player struggle to maximize its profits and acquire more market share, thereby defeat all the rivals and force them to be withdrawn from the market. Since the task is challenging, undertakings, which risk losing their potential profits as a result of competition, may take a different path than competing. They would rather avoid or eliminate the risk of losing through anti-competitive behaviors. They may create cartels, or abuse their dominant position, or adversely affect the competitive environment via concentrations.

The competition law prohibits anti-competitive behaviors in order to maintain and preserve an effective competition in the market. This objective has two perspectives: First, the competition law ensures the equality of the competitive conditions in the market for all economic players by preventing the market actors' restrictive (anti-competitive) behaviors, and second, it maintains the proper functioning of market mechanisms by providing the framework for any competitive activity in a relevant market.

B. *The Scope*

According to the traditional doctrine of territorial jurisdiction, a state may exercise powers over resources and persons within its territory, regardless of the nationality of a person or undertaking. However, the "effects doctrine" gives rise to the extraterritorial application of the competition law when the investigated anti-competitive behavior affects the internal market of the Republic of Turkey.[6] This doctrine implies that the national competition law will extend to foreign market forces, participants and activities, if they cause an "adverse effect" on competition within the domestic market.[7]

In this matter, the article 2 of the APC states that;

> *Agreements, decisions and practices which prevent, distort or restrict competition between any undertakings operating in or affecting markets for goods and services within the boundaries of the Republic of Turkey, and the abuse of dominance by the undertakings dominant in the market, and any kind of legal transactions and behavior having the nature*

---

6 Gülören Tekinalp and Ünal Tekinalp, "Türk Rekabet Hukukunda Etki İlkesi," in *Prof. Dr. Tuğrul Ansay'a Armağan*, ed. Sabih Arkan and Aynur Yongalık (Ankara: Turhan Kitabevi, 2006), 333; Bilgin Tiryakioğlu, *Rekabet Hukukundan Doğan Kanunlar İhtilâfı* (Ankara, 1997), 72–73; Ateş, *Rekabet Hukukuna Giriş*, 401; Güven, *Rekabet Hukuku Ders Kitabı*, 36–37.

7 Agâh Kürşat Karauz and Halil Alperen Işık, "Rekabet Kurallarının Yer Bakımından Uygulanması," *Yıldırım Beyazıt Hukuk Dergisi* 1 (2016): 288.

of mergers and acquisitions which shall decrease competition to a significant extent, and transactions related to the measures, establishments, regulations and supervisions aimed at the protection of competition fall under this Act.

The focus of this doctrine lies with extraterritorial jurisdiction in the application's context of the Turkish competition provisions, in case of an anti-competitive activity affecting the domestic market. In such a case, the undertaking in question will be subject to Turkish competition law, regardless of its nationality, because the conduct has an effect within the State, even though it has occurred beyond its borders.[8]

C. The Focus

The focus of the APC lies with the prohibition of all the restrictive anti-competitive behaviors in all the markets in order to protect and maintain the liberal economy from adverse impacts of the prevention or distortion of the competition.

It should be noted that, in Turkish law, the competition law distinguishes from the unfair competition rules which regulate unfair trade practices covered by Turkish Commercial Code and Code of Obligations. The unfair competition rules are part of the tort law rather than competition law because they regulate compensation of the harmed competitor as a result of the violation of the fair trade and good faith, or by means of deceptive behaviors. In brief, the competition law maintains the proper functioning of the liberal economy, whereas the unfair competition rules mainly protect the competitor from tort.[9] In a nutshell, one promotes fair trade while the other protects free trade.[10]

Moreover, the competition law distinguishes from the consumer protection law which involves all the regulations and statutes that seek to create a fairer balance for consumers in the marketplace, prevent sellers from using dishonest tactics, and safeguard consumers against unfair practices and contract terms. In Turkish law, the consumer protection is covered by the Act on Consumer Protection.

---

8 See also, the decisions of TCA: dated 26.02.1998, no. 54/394–46; dated 26.03.1998, no. 59/439–60; dated 07.05.1998, no. 64/485–77.

9 For further information see supra: *Chapter V – Commercial Law.*

10 Şirin Güven, *Haksız Rekabet Hukukunun Amacı ve Koruduğu Menfaatler* (Ankara: Adalet Yayınevi, 2012) 137 ff.; Hamdi Pınar, "Rekabet Hukuku ve Haksız Rekabet Hukuku İlişkisi," *Rekabet Dergisi* 15, no. 2 (2014): 59–87; Ebru Ekşioğlu, *Sorularla Kolaylaştırılmış Rekabet Hukuku* (İstanbul: Aristo, 2017), 5; İ. Yılmaz Aslan, *Rekabet Hukuku*, 5th ed. (Bursa: Ekin Kitabevi, 2017), 15–16.

IV. The Competition Authority (TCA)

The official institution administering the Turkish competition policy is the Turkish Competition Authority ("Authority"). It is responsible for ensuring and protecting the competitive environment on behalf of the State.

According to the article 20 of the APC;

> *The Competition Authority having a public legal personality, and an administrative and financial autonomy is established in order to ensure the formation and development of markets for goods and services in a free and sound competitive environment, to observe the implementation of this Act, and to fulfill the duties assigned to it by the Act.*

The Authority is an autonomous public institution using public power. It is independent in fulfilling its duties. No organ, authority and person may give commands and orders to influence the final decision of the Authority.[11]

The central office of the Authority is based in Ankara. The organization of the Authority comprises the competition board, the chairmanship and service units. The Competition Board ("the Board") is the Authority's main body as well as its decision-making body. According to the article 27 of the APC, the Board has various duties and powers.

The Board mainly carries out, upon application or on its own initiative, examination, inquiry and investigation about the activities prohibited in the APC, takes the necessary measures for terminating infringements, and imposes administrative fines on those responsible for them.

Moreover, it evaluates the requests for exemption and negative clearance, and grants an exemption and negative clearance certificate if it is appropriate. In addition, it authorizes mergers and acquisitions.

The Board may also issue communiqués and make the necessary regulations as to the implementation of the APC and opine directly or upon the request of the Ministry, concerning the amendments to be made to the legislation with regard to the competition law.

§ Part II Undertaking

I. The Legal Definition

The subject of the competition law is an economic player, whatever its legal status, size and sector, which is named as "undertaking" by the APC. In the

---

11 Ebru Öztürk, *Türk İdare Sisteminde Rekabet Kurumunun Yeri Ve Diğer Bağımsız İdari Otoritelerle Karşılaştırılması* (Ankara, 2003).

article 3 of the APC, an undertaking is defined as natural and legal persons who produce, market and sell goods or services in the market, and entities which can take decisions independently and do constitute an economic unit.

Thus, for the purposes of the Turkish competition law, any entity engaged in an economic activity, which is an activity consisting in offering goods or services on a given market, regardless of its legal status and how it is financed, is considered an undertaking.[12] To qualify, no intention to earn profits is required, nor are public bodies by definition excluded.[13]

II. The Elements

A. *Economic Activity*

An undertaking is an economic actor which engages in economic activity.[14] It should be noted that any activity consisting in offering goods and services on a market is considered as an economic activity.[15]

The firms and individuals engage in economic activity to gain profits. A company, through its commercial activity, seeks to attract customers and thereby make profit. Individuals such as lawyers, artists, athletes, sportsmen, patent-holders etc. engage in economic activities since their acts have commercial value. All of these shall be considered as economic activity because they have an economic impact on the market.

In this consideration, the purpose of the actor is irrelevant, the impact, the footstep left on the market is important. Therefore, foundations and associations established for an ideal purpose shall be considered as an undertaking, when they engage in economic operations in order to be financed for their ideal goals. For example, a football club, which strives to succeed in sport, or a university,

---

12 Güven, *Rekabet Hukuku Ders Kitabı*, 53; Cevdet İlhan Günay, *Rekabet Kanunu Şerhi* (Ankara: Yetkin Yayınları, 2010), 92. See similar decisions in EU Competition law: Höfner & Elser v. Macroton, Case 41/90, ECR (1991) I-1979; Aeroport de Paris v. Commission ECR (2000), II-3929; Commission v. Italian Republic Case 35/96, ECR (1998) I-3851; Fédération Française des Sociétés d'Assurances Case 244/94, ECR (1995) I-4013.

13 Nazmi Ocak, *Rekabet Hukukunda Teşebbüsler ve Teşebbüslerin Hakim Durumunun Tespiti* (İstanbul: Beta Yayınevi, 2016), 17 ff.; Ateş, *Rekabet Hukukuna Giriş*, 226–228. See similar decision in EU Competition law: Fédération Française des Sociétés d'Assurances Case 244/94, ECR (1995) I-4013.

14 Oğuzkan Güzel, *Rekabet Hukukunda Teşebbüs Ve Teşebbüs Birlikleri* (Ankara, 2003).

15 See similar decision in EU Competition law: Commission v. Italy Case 118/85, ECR (1987) 2599.

which is founded for education, shall be considered as undertakings in the eye of the competition law.

In a different example, case about ticket sales, Turkish Football Federation has been considered as an undertaking which operates in ticket sale market.[16]

In addition, the public institutions, which do not seek economic profits, may also operate in market as any other companies. In that case, they shall be considered as undertakings and subject to competition law.[17] For instance, a public employment agency engaged in the business of employment procurement may be classified as an undertaking to apply the competition rules since, in the context of competition law, that classification applies to every entity engaged in an economic activity, regardless of its legal status and how it is financed.

B. *Economic Unit*

An undertaking is an economic entity, an economic unit that engages in economic activities and operates in the market. The legal status of this entity is irrelevant in terms of competition law. Competition law takes into account the player in the market, the economic unit rather than the legal person. For this reason, the APC does not use the legal concept of "company" or "person".

This implies that, the legal person is not the subject of an investigation, but the economic entity may be subject to competition law. For example, in an exemplary case, the Board has carried out an investigation on "Google economic entity" rather than Google Inc. or Google International LLC.[18]

C. *Independent Decision-Making*

An undertaking must be able to determine its economic policies and decide which business risks it will take.[19] The legal nature is irrelevant in this matter.[20] To illustrate, a company in a conglomerate may have a legal entity, however it shall not be considered as an undertaking by competition law, if it operates under the economic control of the parent company. In other words, a legal entity is not

16 See the decision of TCA: dated 12.09.2018, no. 18–31/532–262.

17 See the decisions of TCA: dated 13.03.2001, no. 01–12/114–29; dated 08.03.2002, no. 02–13/126–53.

18 See the decision of TCA: dated 19.09.2018, no. 18–33/555–273.

19 *Ocak, Rekabet Hukukunda Teşebbüsler ve Teşebbüslerin Hakim Durumunun Tespiti,* 28; Ateş, *Rekabet Hukukuna Giriş*, 239.

20 Güzel, *Rekabet Hukukunda Teşebbüs Ve Teşebbüs Birlikleri.*

an undertaking if it has no initiative or if it cannot decide on its own economic future.[21]

In some conglomerates, the parent company has power to decide about commercial policies on behalf of others. In these cases, although the conglomerate in question consists of more than one legal entity, the whole corporate group shall be considered as a single undertaking, since the economic body is under the control of the parent company. The source of this control is irrelevant. It might arise from various legal instruments.

Similarly, in a joint venture, all participants have their own separate legal entities. This is a business arrangement in which participants agree to pool their resources to accomplish a specific task. In this task, the venture has its own economical entity, separate from the participants' other business interests. In this case, the joint venture carrying out its business shall be considered as an undertaking, even though it may not have legal status.

Agency might be another example. An agency is a business which conducts the financial or commercial affairs of an organization in return for earnings. In case it is capable of making independent decisions while carrying out these tasks, it shall be considered as an undertaking. An agency taking its own commercial and financial risks by offering independent services to customers like promotions or discounts shall be seen as an independent undertaking.[22]

§ Part III Relevant Market

I. In General

Market definition is an instrument used in establishing the limits of competition between undertakings. This instrument allows the Board to set the framework for the application of the competition law.

The market to be taken into consideration in terms of competition law is referred as "relevant market" which combines the relevant product market and the relevant geographic market. It means that, in any investigation, the Board defines the limits of the market in terms of geography and products.

A relevant product market comprises all those goods or services which are regarded as alternatives to each other. The products are deemed to be in the same market if they are substitutes because of their characteristics, prices and/or intended use.[23] On the other hand, they are in different markets in case they are

---

21 Güven, *Rekabet Hukuku Ders Kitabı*, 54.

22 Ateş, *Rekabet Hukukuna Giriş*, 251.

23 Günay, *Rekabet Kanunu Şerhi*, 986.

not interchangeable. To illustrate, the famous quote "let them eat cake if there is no bread" might be given as an example. It should be noted that cake and bread are not substitute to each other simply because nobody would switch their choice from bread to cake when there is no bread. In this example, there are two products in two separate markets.

A relevant geographic market comprises the area in which the firms concerned are involved in the supply of products or services and in which the conditions of competition are sufficiently homogeneous. If the conditions of competition alter significantly for the undertaking leaving its territory, this means that the market has a geographic limitation. For example, a bakery which produces bread in a city cannot compete with another bakery which operates in a different city. Although the products in question are identical, it is not reasonable for a bakery to send its product to another city because either the product will lose its quality in the way or the bakery will spend enormous money to send it rapidly. This implies that those bakeries cannot be rivals, they shall not be considered in the same market. In this example, the market is geographically limited.

II. Market Definition

A. Information Gathering Process

In order to define the market, first of all, a preliminary opinion is prepared based on the existing information or the information provided by the undertakings parties to the case. Chief customers and undertakings in the market may be contacted, in order to acquire the necessary information for the relevant market definition.

Sometimes it may be necessary to define separate relevant product markets concerning different levels of the production or distribution of the goods and services under examination. In such cases, in order to define the aforementioned markets, professional organizations or undertakings in the downstream and upstream markets may be contacted.

When deemed necessary, letters requesting information may be sent to the abovementioned players of the market.

Additionally, professional staff of the TCA conducts interviews with the officials of the undertaking under examination and get more information about market definition. Professional staff may also visit and conduct examinations in the facilities of the parties, their customers and/or competitors in order to better understand how the products are manufactured and sold.

B. Criteria

The market is where the competition happens. Accordingly, it should be defined regarding to the competitiveness of the products or undertakings of different regions. This means that the products or the undertakings of different regions shall be considered in the same market if they compete with each other.

The definition lies with "substitutability". When substitutability is assessed, it is examined which products customers consider substitutive of the product in question and from which geographical markets customers may purchase the substitutes.

Therefore, in order to understand the limits of a relevant market, it should be examined whether the products are substitutes for each other or the undertakings can compete with others operating in different regions, with no significant change in the conditions of competition.

C. Factors for the Definition of Relevant Product Market

In order to define the relevant product market, it is examined which products compete or may compete with the products under investigation. A relevant product market is a catalog of all the goods or services which are seen as alternatives (substitutes) to each other.[24] The criteria that the Board shall take into consideration when assessing whether the products in question have substitutability may be classified as follows:

1. Features of the Products

The characteristics, price and intended use of the products are the first step in determining whether the products are substitute to each other. However, these are not decisive factors when the definition of the relevant product market is concerned. To illustrate, while the characteristics, price and intended use of the woman's shoes and man's shoes are similar, they are not considered as in the same market because of customer choices.

2. Findings Indicating the Products Substituted Each Other in the Recent Past

In some examinations, it may be possible to analyze information concerning cases in the recent past or changes in the market, which may constitute examples that two products were substitutes for each other.

---

24 See the decision of TCA: dated 26.11.1998, no. 93/750–159.

Where there was a change in relative prices in the recent past (other factors being equal) responses in demand shall be decisive in determining the substitution level. It is also possible to conduct an analysis concerning which products lost sales where new products were introduced into the market in the past.

3. *Quantitative Tests Specifically Developed for Determining the Market*

The substitutability of demand and supply shall be considered when the relevant product market is defined.[25] The substitutability of demand is the most direct and efficient factor which affects the behavior of undertakings on the market because an undertaking cannot significantly influence the prices if the customers may easily switch to substitutive products.[26]

In competition law, a hypothetical test known by the name "Small but significant and non-transitory increase in price test" (SSNIP test) is used to define the relevant market in a consistent way. It is an alternative to ad hoc determination of the relevant market by arguments about product similarity. This test includes an econometric and statistical approach to calculate the demand or supply elasticity and cross-price elasticity for certain products.

The SSNIP test is designed to analyze whether that increase in price would be profitable or if, instead, it would just induce substitution, making it unprofitable. It consists of observing whether a small increase in price (in the range of 10 %) would provoke a significant number of customers to switch to another product. In fact, if the customers switch their choices, this means that products are seen as substitutes or alternative to each other.[27]

In economic terms, the SSNIP test calculates the residual elasticity of demand of the firm, which is how a change in prices by the firm affects its own demand. If the price increase of one product leads to a change in demand in favor of another one, both products in question shall be considered in the same market.

For example, the water is indispensable for life, therefore, there is no elasticity of demand from water to another beverage whatever the increase in price may occur.

---

25 Murat Çetinkaya, *İlgili Pazar Kavramı Ve İlgili Pazar Tanımında Kullanılan Nicel Teknikler* (Ankara, 2003), 5.

26 Ateş, *Rekabet Hukukuna Giriş*, 306.

27 Güven, *Rekabet Hukuku Ders Kitabı*, 165–166; Günay, *Rekabet Kanunu Şerhi*, 988–989.

4. *Opinions of the Customers and Competitors*

The relevant market consists of a "catalog" of goods and/or services which are considered substitutes by the customers. Therefore, customer choices may provide useful information on the market definition. In a famous case, banana is seen in a different market than other fruits because the old people and babies prefer banana rather than other fruits, considering the fact that it is easier to eat it without teeth. In a different example, the diet milk may be considered as different than the usual milk because of customer choices.

5. *Costs and Barriers (Related to Switching the Demand to Potential Substitute Products)*

Some barriers and costs related to the sector may cause the Board to decide that two products which, at first glance, appear to be substitutes, in fact belong to separate markets. For example, the intended use and characteristics of a luxury car and family car may seem to be similar, however, they belong to different segments in the eyes of customers because of the significant price differences.

6. *Supply Substitution Analysis*

In general, demand substitution shows the similarity of the products, which is essential to the assessment of the definition of the relevant product market. Moreover, supply substitution may also be taken into consideration where it has an equivalent effect on the market to demand substitution.[28] For this, suppliers must be able to switch their production to other products when faced with small and non-transitory increases in relative prices and they must be able to market these products without having to tolerate significant additional costs and risks in the short term.[29]

To illustrate, supply substitution in paper production may be given as an example. Paper is generally introduced to the market in a range that includes products of various quality, changing from standard writing papers to high-quality papers used in the printing of art books. From the perspective of demand, it may be seen that papers of distinct quality cannot be used in the printing of the same publications. For instance, low-quality paper cannot be used when printing an art book or a high-quality book. Nonetheless, since paper mills are ready to

28 Ateş, *Rekabet Hukukuna Giriş*, 309; Güven, *Rekabet Hukuku Ders Kitabı*, 170; see also the decision of TCA: dated 2.12.2010, no. 10–75/1537–591.

29 Aslan, *Rekabet Hukuku*, 166; Güven, *Rekabet Hukuku Ders Kitabı*, 170; Günay, *Rekabet Kanunu Şerhi*, 990.

manufacture papers of all qualities, suppliers can switch from manufacturing paper of one quality to another with negligibly low costs and in a short time. In cases where there are no special problems related to distribution and especially where delivery period for orders are long enough to allow the necessary changes in the mill of the paper manufacturer, paper manufacturers can compete with each other to win the orders for different qualities of paper. In such cases, investigating paper manufacturers, the Board shall not define separate markets for each quality of paper and their areas of use. In the contrary, all papers shall be included in the relevant market.[30]

On the other hand, in case the suppliers have to make significant changes to their supply costs and technology, make additional investments, take strategic decisions and spend significant time for all these operations in order to switch their production to different products, there is no supply substitutability. In that case, supply substitution shall not be taken into consideration during market definition stage.

D. Factors for the Definition of Relevant Geographic Market

In order to define the relevant geographic market, it is examined which undertakings taking place in different geographies compete or may compete with the undertaking under investigation.[31]

A relevant geographic market is an area in which the conditions of competition are sufficiently homogenous, and which can easily be distinguished from neighboring areas as the conditions of competition differ significantly from these regions. The criteria the Board shall take into consideration when taking a decision concerning geographical markets may be classified as follows:

1. Market Features

When defining the geographic market, first of all, a preliminary opinion is prepared based on the indications concerning the distribution of the market shares of the parties and competitors, as well as on the price differentiations.

Afterwards, it is examined to see whether undertakings in different regions really serve as an alternative source of supply for the customers. In this examination, demand structure is taken into consideration. The basic question in this matter is whether the customers can switch their orders to undertakings operating in different regions in a short period of time and at negligible costs.

---

30 Günay, *Rekabet Kanunu Şerhi*, 990.

31 Çetinkaya, *İlgili Pazar Kavramı Ve İlgili Pazar Tanımında Kullanılan Nicel Teknikler*, 8.

2. *Findings that Indicate Orders were Switched to Different Regions in the Past*

In some examinations, it may be possible to analyze information concerning cases in the recent past. Supply and demand structure of the market and customer tendencies analyzed in the past cases may give an answer to the question whether or not the undertakings operating in different regions compete with each other at negligible costs.

3. *Quantitative Tests Specifically Developed for Determining the Market*

The substitutability of demand shall also be considered in the definition of relevant geographic market because an undertaking cannot significantly influence the prices if the customers are able to obtain the products from suppliers acting elsewhere.

Therefore, SSNIP test may also be used to understand whether the customers switch to easily accessible substitute products or to suppliers in other regions when faced with a small but evident and non-transitory hypothetical price increase.[32] In cases where the orders modify in favor of an undertaking of different region, there is no geographical limitation for the competition between these undertakings in question.

In addition, the Elzinga-Hogarty test may be applied to assess whether significant product flows are present between two areas relevant for the competition case.[33] If product flows are found to be insignificant (based on a certain threshold), it is concluded that firms in one area do not face competition from firms in the other area. In particular, the test sets criteria for imports to a region and exports from a region: (1) the “little in from outside” (LIFO) criterion states that the percentage of consumption not produced locally should not exceed 10 %; (2) the “little out from inside” (LOFI) criterion states that the percentage of production not consumed locally should not exceed 10 %.

If one of these criteria is not met, it is concluded that the region under consideration is subject to effective competitive constraints from suppliers outside the region. The market should then be defined more broadly until both criteria are met.

32 See the decision of TCA: dated 18.11.2009, no. 09–56/1338–341.

33 See the decision of TCA: dated 03.08.2011, no. 11–44/979–329.

4. Opinions of Customers and Competitors

The existing geographical trends of purchases, trade flow, goods delivery trends and other tendencies of the customers and competitors may be important to define the relevant geographic market.

§ Part IV Prohibition on Cartels

I. Introduction

In the absence of legal remedies provided by the competition law, undertakings could follow a mutual anti-competitive plan, in order to maximize their profits, by creating cartels or cartel-like cooperations which would restrict or prevent competition by market sharing, price-fixing, supply restriction etc.

Coordinated actions are more profitable than competitive actions because the existence of an effective competition leads firms to decrease their prices or increase the quality of their products or services. Moreover, competing firms may lose their profits in order to attract customers. In addition, undertakings operating in a competitive market have a tendency to avoid competition in order to decrease the risks of competition. Therefore, in case competition law fails, undertakings may cooperate in order to maximize their common profits by reducing competition among them.

This cooperation between plural undertakings is often called a "cartel", which may be defined as a group of undertakings which collude with each other in order to improve their profits and dominate the market.[34] In brief, a cartel is an alliance of rivals who cooperate instead of competing.

A perfectly functioning cartel can achieve monopoly power and dominate the market. Thus, cartels or cartel-like cooperative structures created by undertakings constitute one of the main concerns of the competition law, which prohibits anti-competitive agreements, concerted practices and decisions establishing cartels or cartel-like economic structures.

II. Markets Prone to Cartels

Successful collusion arises from considerable coordination, which may result from the facilitating market structure. Indeed, there are some suitable market

---

34 Herbert Hovenkamp, *Federal Antitrust Policy, The Law of Competition and Its Practice* (St. Paul, Minn.: Hornbook Series, West Group, 1999), 144; Daniel G. Goyder, *EC Competition Law*, 4th ed. (New York: Oxford University Press, 2003), 140.

conditions to form and maintain cartels. Because of some features of these markets, creating and preserving cartels are easier than other markets.

First of all, the barriers to market entry may offer a suitable situation for the formation and maintaining of a cartel because it protects the inside undertakings from the potential competition which would come from external forces. Barriers may arise from legal or economic reasons. For example, undertakings cannot operate in some markets without the State's license, or they can be skeptical to enter a market because of the technological requirements or the necessity of enormous costs. Second, markets where economic or technological conditions are predictable, are also prone to cartel. In these markets, demand is not flexible, customers do not shift to other products or services. Third, markets consisting of symmetrical undertakings of products are open to cartels.

It should be added that a cartel may be maintained only if cartel members remain loyal to it. If disloyalty is not punished, it is possible that cartel members cheat on cartel. Therefore, the detection of cheating and the retaliation against it without delay is crucial for the cartel in order to prevail.[35] This is possible in case monitoring, detection and retaliation mechanisms already exist in the market or have implemented by the cartel. Undertakings will be eager to follow the common plan or to continue their coordinated actions if they know that others will retaliate without delay in case of cheating. They would certainly not like to find themselves in the middle of a cut-throat competition, which may be triggered by retaliation against cheating.[36]

Accordingly, transparency in the market is important to the sustainability of any cartel because it creates an environment in which undertakings carry out monitoring and detection mechanisms smoothly. They do not need any communication to agree upon terms of the collusion or to coordinate their actions because they have access to any economic data needed, due to the transparent market conditions.

---

35 İzak Atiyas and Gönenç Gürkaynak, "Uyumlu Eylem Karinesi Üzerine Hukuki ve Ekonomik Çözümlemeler," *Rekabet Hukukunda Güncel Gelişmeler Sempozyumu IV*, 2006, 86; Damien Neven, Pénélope Papandropoulos, and Paul Seabright, *Trawling For Minnows, European Competition Policy and Agreements Between Firms* (London: Centre for Economic Policy Research, 1998), 49; Simon Bishop and Mike Walker, *The Economics of EC Competition Law: Concepts, Application and Measurement*, 2nd ed. (Sweet&Maxwell, 2002), no.5.27.

36 Aydın Çelen, *Oligopolistik Pazarlarda Gözlenen Paralel Davranışların Rekabet Hukuku Açısından Değerlendirilmesi: Uyumlu Eylem Ve Birlikte Hakim Durum* (Ankara, 2003), 8–9.

It should be noted that especially oligopolies are prone to cartels because of the high level of transparency. Oligopoly may be defined as a market structure in which a few firms dominate. It arises when a small number of large firms have all or most of the market share, which means that it is a highly concentrated market structure.

III. Prohibition

A. Legislation

Similar to the article 101 of the Treaty on the Functioning of the European Union (TFEU), the article 4 of the APC states that;

> *Agreements between undertakings, decisions by associations of undertakings and concerted practices which have as their object or effect the prevention, distortion or restriction of competition directly or indirectly in a market are illegal and prohibited.*
> Such cases are, in particular, as follows:
>
> a) *Fixing the purchase or sale price of goods or services, elements such as cost and profit which form the price, and any terms of purchase or sale,*
> b) *Sharing markets for goods or services, and partitioning or controlling all kinds of market resources or elements,*
> c) *Controlling the amount of supply or demand in relation to goods or services, or determining them outside the market,*
> d) *Complicating and restricting the activities of competing undertakings, or excluding firms operating in the market by boycotts or other behavior, or preventing potential new entrants to the market,*
> e) *Except exclusive dealing, applying different terms to persons with equal status for equal rights, obligations and acts,*
> f) *Contrary to the nature of the agreement or commercial usages, obliging to purchase other goods or services together with a good or service, or tying a good or service demanded by purchasers acting as intermediary undertakings to the condition of displaying another good or service by the purchaser, or putting forward terms as to the resupply of a good or service supplied.*
>
> *In cases where the existence of an agreement cannot be proved, that the price changes in the market, or the balance of demand and supply, or the operational areas of undertakings are similar to those markets where competition is prevented, distorted or restricted, constitutes a presumption that the undertakings are engaged in concerted practice.*
> *Each of the parties may relieve itself of the responsibility by proving not to engage in concerted practice, provided that it is based on economic and rational facts.*

Hence, in Turkish competition law, cartel ban lies with anti-competitive agreements, concerted practices, and decisions of associations between undertakings which have as their object or effect the prevention, restriction, or distortion of competition. We will analyze those below.

B. Anti-Competitive Agreements

1. In General

Competition law chooses the word "agreement" rather than contract for a purpose. A contract is a legal agreement which is intended to be binding for the parties and enforceable by law. However, an agreement encompasses anything which encapsulates the "faithful expression of the joint intention of the parties", irrespective of its form or legal status.[37] It has a wide meaning and covers all kinds of consensus, whether or not legally enforceable, written or oral.[38] It also includes so-called gentlemen's agreements, which is not a legally valid and binding contract under the rules of law of obligation, but an agreement in the eyes of competition law.[39]

Anti-competitive agreements are mutual understandings (consensus) which aim to restrict competition. In order for there to be an agreement, it is sufficient that the undertakings in question have expressed their joint intention to conduct themselves on the market in a specific way.[40]

An agreement is prohibited when it intends to create an anti-competitive, cartel-like cooperation, coordination, or collusion between undertakings to restrict competition. If the undertakings under examination have reached to a consensus on a subject related to their economic actions in order to avoid competition, this will be considered as a violation of the competition law, even

37 Güven, *Rekabet Hukuku Ders Kitabı,* 71–72.

38 Emel Badur, *Türk Rekabet Hukukunda Rekabeti Sınırlayıcı Anlaşmalar* (Ankara, 2001), 58 ff. Contra. Metin Topçuoğlu, *Rekabeti Kısıtlayan Teşebbüsler Arası İşbirliği Davranışları ve Hukuki Sonuçları* (Ankara, 2001), 170; Günay, *Rekabet Kanunu Şerhi,* 151; Richard Whish, *Competition Law,* ed. LexisNexis, 5th ed. (London, 2003), 91–92; Alison Jones and Sufrin Brenda, *EC Competition Law, Text, Cases, and Materials,* 2nd ed. (New York: Oxford University Press, 2004), 130–131. See also the decisions of TCA: dated 23.03.2000, no. 00–11/109–54; dated 27.2.2001, no. 01–10/100–24.

39 Aslan, *Rekabet Hukuku,* 206–207; see also the decisions of TCA: dated 26.11.1998, no. 93/750–159; dated 25.10.2005, no. 05–73/986–273; dated 01.02.2002, no. 02–06/51–24; dated 08.02.2002, no. 02–07/57–26; dated 05.01.2006, no. 06–02/45–7; dated 19.10.2006, no. 06–77/991–286; dated 13.9.2005, no. 05–57/850–230; dated 27.2.2001, no. 01–10/100–24.

40 See the decisions of TCA: dated 24.11.1999, no. 99–53/575–365; dated 19.10.2006, no. 06–77/992–287.

though the agreement has never come into force. The prohibition is on the consensus which is intended to restrict competition.[41]

It should be highlighted that the fact that a party may have played only a limited role in the setting up of the agreement, or may not be fully committed to its implementation, or may have participated only under pressure from other parties does not mean that it is not party to the agreement, although these facts may be taken into account in deciding the level of any financial penalty.

The types of anti-competitive agreements discussed in this part are, in particular, agreements which have the object or effect of directly or indirectly fixing purchase or selling prices or any other trading conditions, sharing markets, limiting or controlling production or investment, applying dissimilar conditions to equivalent transactions with other trading parties, thereby placing them at a competitive disadvantage, make the conclusion of contracts subject to acceptance by the other parties of supplementary obligations which, by their nature or according to commercial usage, have no connection with the subject of such contracts,[42] collusive tendering (bid-rigging), joint purchasing or selling, exchanging information, setting technical or design standards etc.

It should be noted that any agreements prohibited pursuant to the article 4 of the APC shall be automatically void according to the article 56 of the APC and the article 27 of the Turkish Code of Obligations which declares as void any contract against law.

2. *Horizontal Agreements*

This is an anti-competitive agreement between competing undertakings operating in the same economic sphere in order to avoid competition.[43] They agree upon coordinated actions which restrict or distort competition at the same stage of competition to create market advantages. Horizontal means that undertakings are at the same level of production, distribution or sale.

---

41 See the decisions of TCA: dated 17.06.1999, no. 99–30/276–166; dated 19.12.2005, no. 05–85/1182–336; dated 24.4.2006, no. 06–29/365–94. See similar cases in EU Competition law: Hüls AG v. Commission, T-9/89, ECR (1992) II-499; Hüls AG v. Commission Case 199/92P, ECR (1999) I-4287; Thyssen Stahl AG v. Commission, T-141/94, ECR (1999) II-347.

42 See Hasan Karakılıç, *Rekabet Hukukunda Bağlama Uygulamaları* (İstanbul: Onikilevha Yayınevi, 2013).

43 Mücteba Altun, *Yatay İşbirliği Anlaşmalarının 4. Madde Kapsamında Değerlendirilmesi* (Ankara, 2012), 61; Badur, *Türk Rekabet Hukukunda Rekabeti Sınırlayıcı Anlaşmalar,* 61; Güven, *Rekabet Hukuku Ders Kitabı*, 74.

For example, horizontal agreements which lead to price fixing, market sharing and limiting competition, which violate competition law, thereby aim to avoid the risks of competition by following the terms of this agreement, are prohibited.

3. *Vertical Agreements*

This is an anti-competitive agreement between undertakings which operate at different levels of the supply chain like production, distribution or sale.[44] For instance, the vertical agreement of a manufacturer with a retailer upon fixing resale prices to customers or sharing the market is prohibited by competition law.

To illustrate, imposing limitations regarding the terms of purchase in case of resale to the buyers and forcing them to sell it to the customers with these particular conditions shall be illegal according to competition law. Another example may be the selective distribution system whereby the provider undertakes to sell, directly or indirectly, the goods or services that are the subject of the agreement, only to distributors selected by it, based on designated criteria, and whereby such distributors undertake not to sell the goods or services to the non-selected buyers.[45]

C. *Concerted Practices*

1. *In General*

The prohibition on cartels applies to concerted practices as well as to agreements. The difference between agreements and concerted practices lies with the form of the collusion. In agreements, undertakings agree upon an anti-competitive course of action, which is prohibited even though it is never legally binding or enforceable, and the performance is irrelevant. However, in concerted practices,

---

44 İ. Yılmaz Aslan, *Rekabet Hukuku Bakımından Dikey Anlaşmalar* (Bursa: Ekin Kitabevi, 2004), 139–140; Badur, *Türk Rekabet Hukukunda Rekabeti Sınırlayıcı Anlaşmalar*, 61; Meltem Küçükayhan-Aşçıoğlu, *Rekabet Hukuku ve Dağıtım Sözleşmeleri* (Ankara: Adalet Yayınevi, 2011), 140 ff.; Gamze Aşçıoğlu-Öz, "Rekabet Hukukunda Dikey Anlaşmalar," in *Rekabet Hukuku ve Dikey Anlaşmalar*, ed. Kerem Cem Sanlı (İstanbul: Onikilevha Yayınevi, 2009), 2; Metin Topçuoğlu, *Rekabet Hukuku Açısından Acentelik ve Dağıtım Sözleşmeleri* (Ankara, 2006), 106; Güven, *Rekabet Hukuku Ders Kitabı*, 75.

45 Özge Ay, *Otomotiv Sözleşmelerindeki Dağıtım Sözleşmelerinden Kaynaklanan Hukuki İlişkilerin Rekabet Hukuku Açısından İncelenmesi* (İstanbul: Onikilevha Yayınevi, 2017), 31 ff.

undertakings knowingly substitute cooperation between them for the risks of competition.

Concerted practices are intentional anti-competitive parallel behaviors which restrict, prevent or distort competition. The parallel behavior is prohibited only if it is a harmonized or coordinated action, which has the object or effect of lessening (restricting, distorting) competition.[46]

While not reaching the stage of the existence of an agreement, concerted practices are intentional actions of the undertakings, which form coordination providing practical cooperation between them against the risks of competition, and which lead to a competition condition that do not reflect the normal conditions of the market considering the structure of the market, characteristics of the product, and the size and importance of the undertakings.[47]

Therefore, the actions must be intentionally harmonized in order to be prohibited. This may come out from an information shared by the undertakings about their intended commercial policy, which reduces market transparency thereby removes the risk of future market uncertainty. The exchange of information may be explicit or implicit. It results in concerted practice when the undertakings take this information into account in devising their future commercial policy. If they are aware of a common plan for coordination, or a common policy to follow, their subsequent parallel behavior in accordance with this, will be considered as a concerted practice because it is intentionally harmonized.

This means that the parallel behavior must result from collective, harmonized actions of the undertakings in order to be prohibited. Parallel behavior is not per se collective or harmonized. It may also come out from unilateral actions of the undertakings which reasonably try to adapt themselves to the changing market conditions. Therefore, a random parallel behavior generated by unilateral actions is not prohibited, but collective behavior is.[48] For example, when paper

---

46 Metin İkizler, *Rekabet Hukukunda Uyumlu Eylemler* (Ankara: Seçkin Yayınevi, 2005), 60; Güven, *Rekabet Hukuku Ders Kitabı*, 84 ff.

47 Dilek Cengiz, *Türk Rekabet Hukukunda Uyumlu Eylem ve Bu Eylemin Hukuki Sonuçları* (İstanbul: Beta Yayınevi, 2006), 39. See the decision of TCA: dated 27.02.2001, no. 01–10/100–24; see also in EU Competition law: Imperial Chemical Industries, Case 48/69, ECR (1972) I-619; Suiker Unie and Others v Commission, Cases 40–48, 50, 54–56, 111, 113 and 114/73, ECR (1975) I-1663; Ahlström Osakeyhtiö and others v Commission, Cases 89/85, ECR (1993) I-1307; Commission v. Anic Partecipazioni SpA, Case 49/92, ECR (1999) I-4125; Züchner v Bayerische Vereinsbank AG., Case 172/80, p.14; John Deere v Commission, Case 7/95 P., ECR (1998) I-3111.

48 İkizler, *Rekabet Hukukunda Uyumlu Eylemler*, 137.

price rises, it is expected to observe the parallel price increase in newspapers, which is a reasonable unilateral action aiming adaptation to increase in costs. No undertaking shall face a competition law penalty because of a unilateral, reasonable economic decision.[49]

In brief, an anti-competitive concerted practice arises where undertakings knowingly substitute practical cooperation or coordination between them for the risks of competition.

2. *Elements of Concerted Practices*

a. *Parallel anti-competitive action of plural undertakings*

Parallel behavior alone cannot be defined as concerted practice. This behavior must be anti-competitive in order to be prohibited.[50] Therefore, any concerted practice investigation starts upon the existence of a parallel anti-competitive behavior, which creates an outcome similar to the market conditions where competition is prevented, distorted or restricted.[51]

In a competitive market, undertakings aim to attract customers and obtain most of the market share, thereby make the highest figures of profits if possible. To this end, they usually make discounts, raise the quality of their goods or services, innovate, advertise, keep their commercial secrets etc. When undertakings take adverse steps in parallel, it does not reflect the normal conditions of a competitive market. In such a case, a concerted practice investigation may be carried out against these undertakings.

It should be noted that the coordination or organization existing in one undertaking cannot be defined as concerted practice. Plurality of undertakings is required for a concerted practice case. To illustrate, a conglomerate which is considered as an economic unit as a whole or a joint venture forming an economic entity, will each be considered as a single undertaking and shall not be

---

49 Promoting unilateral actions is the aim of the article 4 of the APC (See the decisions of TCA: dated 26.11.1998, no. 93/750–159; dated 25.10.2005, no. 05–73/986–273; dated 17.06.1999, no. 99–30/276–166 (a); dated 24.11.1999, no. 99–53/575–365; dated 01.02.2002, no. 02–06/51–24; dated 08.02.2002, no. 02–07/57–26; dated 05.01.2006, no. 06–02/45–7; dated 02.12.2004, no. 04–77/1108–277; dated 02.12.2004, no. 04–77/1109–278; dated 19.10.2006, no. 06–77/991–286; dated 13.01.2005, no. 05–05/42–17; dated 18.09.2000, no. 00–35/393–220).

50 İkizler, *Rekabet Hukukunda Uyumlu Eylemler,* 157.

51 Aslan, *Rekabet Hukuku,* 232; see also the decision of TCA: dated 17.07.2000, no. 00–26/291–161.

subjected to a concerted practice investigation because of their internal organization or coordination.

b. Intentional harmonization of behaviors

The parallel anti-competitive action is forbidden only if it is coming out from the collective behavior of the undertakings which follow a coordinated action instead of competing.[52] Accordingly, each undertaking should independently determine the policies which they will follow in the market. Indeed, this requirement does not prevent companies from keeping up with the behavior of their competitors.[53] An occasional parallel behavior or unilateral actions of the undertakings shall not be subjected to penalties.[54]

It is strictly forbidden to interfere directly or indirectly with the object or effect of an attempt to influence the market behavior of competitors, or to explain their own market behavior to competitors aiming to increase market transparency for the sake of collusion.

It should be highlighted that concerted practice requires a "mental consensus" that provides a practical business cooperation, but even if this consensus is not expressed in words, it can arise through contact, which can be direct or indirect, between undertakings.[55]

Therefore, a relationship between undertakings to create an understanding of each other's activities or a meeting of minds for collusion, is one of the fundamental elements of concerted practices.[56] This relationship must involve an intentional exchange of information directly between the undertakings, or indirectly through a third party. The intention and purpose of this communication should

---

52 See the decisions of TCA: dated 14.12.1999, no. 99–57/614–391; dated 17.07.2000, no. 00–26/291–161; dated 23.03.2000, no. 00–11/109–54; dated 24.12.2002, no. 02–80/937–385 dated 31.10.2002, no. 02–66/814–332. See also in EU Competition law: Hüls AG v. Commission, C-192/92P, ECR (1999) I-4287, p. 163–165; Whish, *Competition Law,* 110.

53 See the decisions of TCA: dated 31.10.2002, no. 02–66/814–332; dated 20.5.1999, no. 99–24/211–124.

54 See the decisions of TCA: dated 23.03.2000, no. 00–11/109–54; dated 14.12.1999, no. 99–57/614–391; dated 31.10.2002, no. 02–66/814–332.

55 Zekeriyya Arı, *Türk Hukukunda Danışıklılık Kavramı* (Ankara: Seçkin Yayınevi, 2004), 83; İkizler, *Rekabet Hukukunda Uyumlu Eylemler*, 100; Aslan, *Rekabet Hukuku*, 229; see also the decision of TCA: dated 17.07.2000, no. 00–26/291–161; Onur Yelda Yüksel, *Rekabet Hukukunda Uyumlu Eylem* (Ankara, 2004), 64.

56 See the decision of TCA: dated 26.5.2006, no. 06–36/465–127.

be to remove the uncertainties regarding the future behavior of competitors and, in some instances, aim to change the future structure of the market.

Hence, the parallel action is investigated when it follows a reciprocal contact, an exchange of information which could be direct or indirect and concludes in a coordination in the market.[57]

It should be added that it is also possible that the market transparency itself may offer, especially in oligopolistic markets, the information needed to collude and coordinate the actions of undertakings. In this case, the collusion between undertakings becomes possible through market structure, which eases cooperation without the need of communication.

3. *Presumption*

The legislator seems concerned that, in the course of the enforcement activities, competition authorities struggle to find direct "smoking gun" evidence of anti-competitive agreements because undertakings do not leave direct evidence of an illegal agreement.

At this point, it would not be wrong to stress that it is relatively easy to prove anti-competitive agreements by obtaining direct evidence of an expression from undertakings. When there is direct evidence, it is an uncomplicated task which can be done by the authorities. However, tacit collusion between undertakings "acting in concert" is difficult to be detected by regulators because no agreement or record exists to prove it. In this case, there is no formal or even informal agreement, but intentionally coordinated actions which result in reduced competition.

Therefore, competition authorities need to reveal intentionally coordinated anti-competitive practices when it is not possible to find out an anti-competitive agreement. However, in some cases, it is quite troublesome to distinguish intentional collective actions from unilateral actions of the undertakings under investigation.

The crux of the matter lies in defining the content of the collective action and the conditions required for the Authority to identify a concerted practice, which may frequently be possible based on circumstantial evidence. This means indirect evidentiary elements.

In Turkish competition law, there exists a statutory presumption that the undertakings are engaged in concerted practice when the market conditions in question show some similarities with the markets where competition is

57 See the decision of TCA: dated 26.05.2006, no. 06–36/465–127.

prevented, distorted or restricted.[58] Indeed, similarities must be supported by objective economic data.[59] To illustrate, undertakings usually decrease the prices of their goods or services or increase their quality in order to attract customers in competitive markets. However, parallel increase in prices or parallel decrease in the quality of goods or services are not usual practices between competitors when they compete, thereby they shall be subjected to the presumption of concerted practice.

Nevertheless, the investigated undertakings may relieve themselves of the responsibility by proving that their acts were not collective but unilateral. It means that they cannot be punished by competition law in case they prove that they did not follow a common plan or they did not intentionally coordinate their actions, but they merely followed the actual market conditions. Thus, the unilateral actions based on rational economic facts will not be considered as coordinated or harmonized.

In short, if undertakings can provide any other plausible explanation than concerted practice, they may be relieved from the responsibility arising from the presumption.

4. *Examination of Oligopolistic Interdependence*

In oligopolies, there are few undertakings with significant market power, which means that most of the total market share is controlled by a few numbers of economic actors.[60] Although only a few undertakings dominate, it is possible that many small firms may also operate in oligopolistic markets.[61]

In an oligopolistic market, undertakings are not in a dominant position on their own, but market force is gathered in the hands of small number of undertakings which could act as monopoly when they act together. That is why oligopolies may be subject to cartel investigations under competition law.

In any oligopoly, because of the concentrated structure of the market, the level of attention has increased between undertakings. Competitors are aware of each

---

58 Günay, *Rekabet Kanunu Şerhi*, 152. See the decisions of TCA: dated 24.02.2004, no. 04–16/123–26; dated 02.02.2006, no. 06–08/121–30; dated 24.04.2006, no. 06–29/355–87.

59 Otherwise it would be an imprecise criterion (Atiyas and Gürkaynak, "Uyumlu Eylem Karinesi Üzerine Hukuki ve Ekonomik Çözümlemeler," 111).

60 Ateş Akıncı, *Rekabetin Yatay Kısıtlanması* (Ankara, 2001), 25; Whish, *Competition Law*, 506; Jones and Brenda, *EC Competition Law, Text, Cases, and Materials*, 12; Jonathan Faull and Ali Nikpay, *The EC Law of Competition* (New York: Oxford University Press, 1999), no.1.71–72.

61 OECD, "Oligopoly Report: DAFFE/CLP (99)25," 1999, 18.

other's actions, even with no communication, due to the high level of market transparency. Hence, their strategic decisions are affected by this knowledge.[62]

Therefore, in an oligopoly, each undertaking is aware of the fact that its strategic decisions and actions will have a significant effect on the market and there will be an immediate reaction from other competitors to it.[63] Knowing that any action will be detected immediately because of market transparency and other undertakings will react with retaliation, an undertaking operating in a market with just a few competitors must take the potential reaction of its closest rivals into account when making its own decisions.[64]

Hence, this awareness creates an "interdependence" between undertakings in the oligopoly, which is unavoidable because any logical undertaking would take into account its knowledge of the market.[65] Since undertakings cannot act independently, they must anticipate the likely response of a rival to any given change in their price, or their non-price activity.[66] In other words, they need to plan and work out a range of possible options based on how they think rivals might react.[67]

This is often the case, by implementing the strategy that maximizes their profits, based on the market situation and the information they have on their competitors.[68]

---

62 Cengiz, *Türk Rekabet Hukukunda Uyumlu Eylem ve Bu Eylemin Hukuki Sonuçları*, 165 ff.

63 Valentine Korah, *An Introductory Guide to EC Competition Law and Practice*, 8th ed. (Hart Publishing, 2004), 53.

64 Cengiz, *Türk Rekabet Hukukunda Uyumlu Eylem ve Bu Eylemin Hukuki Sonuçları*, 166–167; Dennis A. Yao and Susan S. Desanti, "Game Theory and The Legal Analysis of Tacit Collusion," *The Antitrust Bulletin* 38, no. 1 (Spring 1993): 116.

65 Arı, *Türk Hukukunda Danışıklılık Kavramı*, 96; Yao and Desanti, "Game Theory and The Legal Analysis of Tacit Collusion," 126. See also the decisions of TCA: dated 24.04.2006, no. 06–29/357–88; dated 27.06.2000, no. 00–24/255–138.

66 Yaşar Tekdemir, "The Principle of Collective Dominance Under EC Competition Law: A New Approach to The Problem of Oligopoly" (London School of Economics, 1999), 6; Yüksel, *Rekabet Hukukunda Uyumlu Eylem*, 7; Çelen, *Oligopolistik Pazarlarda Gözlenen Paralel Davranışların Rekabet Hukuku Açısından Değerlendirilmesi: Uyumlu Eylem Ve Birlikte Hakim Durum*, 9; Goyder, *EC Competition Law*, 71; Gerwin Van Gerven and Navarro E. Varona, "The Wood Pulp Case and The Future of Concerted Practices," *CMLR*, no. 31 (1994): 576.

67 İkizler, *Rekabet Hukukunda Uyumlu Eylemler*, 138–139; Zafer Kahraman, *Rekabet Hukuku Açısından Oligopolistik Bağımlılık* (İstanbul: Beta Yayınevi, 2008), 7–8.

68 See the decision of TCA: dated 24.12.2002, no. 02–80/937–385.

An understanding of game theory and the "prisoners' dilemma" helps appreciate the concept of interdependence.[69] This is the best-known game of strategy in social science. It helps us understand what governs the balance between coordination and competition in economy. In the traditional version of the game, the police have arrested two suspects and interrogates them in separate rooms. Each can either confess, thereby implicating the other, or keep silent. No matter what the other suspect does, each can improve his own position by confessing.

If the other confesses, then one had better do the same to avoid the especially harsh sentence that awaits. If the other keeps silent, then one can obtain the favorable treatment accorded a state's witness by confessing. Thus, confession is the dominant strategy when nobody sees each other, which means that cheating (competitive action) shall be the dominant strategy when undertakings are unaware of each other's actions.

However, game theory explains that if the suspects saw each other, they would stay silent because they are aware that if one of them cheats, the other will see it and retaliate. Hence, coordinated action shall be the dominant strategy in case the market is transparent. Thus, the market transparency is an important feature, which could increase the likelihood of coordination between competitors.

This means that if undertakings are aware of each other's actions, they may choose coordinated actions over competition in order to avoid any destructive (cut-throat) competition. A key feature of oligopolistic markets is that undertakings operating in an oligopoly may attempt to collude rather than compete in order to enjoy the benefits of a cartel, which can provide higher profits over the long term.

It should be noted that it is difficult to distinguish, in oligopolies, the coordinated collective behavior from the unilateral actions of the competitors, which may be parallel to each other when adapting their behavior to the changing

---

69 Kahraman, *Rekabet Hukuku Açısından Oligopolistik Bağımlılık,* 19 ff.; Oskar Morgenstern, "Oligopoly, Monopolistic Competition, and The Theory of Games," *The American Economic Review* 38, no. 2 (1948): 10–18; Carl Shapiro, "The Theory of Business Strategy," *The RAND Journal of Economics* 20, no. 1 (1989): 131 ff.; Hugo Sonnenschein, "Oligopoly and Game Theory," in *The New Palgrave, A Dictionary of Economics, Vol.3* (New York: Palgrave Publishers, 2002), 705–708; James W. Friedman, *Game Theory With Application to Economics*, 2nd ed. (New York: Oxford University Press, 1990); Yao and Desanti, "Game Theory and The Legal Analysis of Tacit Collusion," 121.

market conditions.[70] Parallel actions may arise from concerted practices or unilateral actions triggered merely by oligopolistic interdependence.[71]

Hence, in oligopoly, even though undertakings carry out completely individual actions and have no contact between them, as a result of this interdependence, they might look like acting in a coordinated manner as if there was a cartel-agreement between them.[72] Accordingly, despite the absence of communication, they look like in a cooperation as if there was a cartel. In this case, the results of the cartel can occur in a completely innocent oligopolistic behavior.[73]

In brief, the parallel behavior in oligopolies is not per se anti-competitive. Competition authorities need to distinguish unilateral actions from collective or collusive actions by analyzing the logic behind the parallel actions.[74]

In this regard, the Board considers that parallel behaviors are inherent to oligopolies, thereby a normal feature of the market.[75] It looks for an exchange of information in order to assess the investigated parallel behavior as an infringement of the cartel ban.[76] In doctrine, it is suggested that oligopolistic interdependence alone cannot be considered as a valid defense against the concerted practice allegations.[77]

---

70 This is called as "oligopoly problem". See Donald F. Turner, "The Definition of Agreement Under the Sherman Act: Conscious Paralellism and Refusals to Deal," *Harvard Law Review* 75, no. 4 (1962): 655–706; Richard A. Posner, "Oligopoly and the Antitrust Laws: A Suggested Approach," *Stanford Law Review* 21 (1969): 1562–1606; Jonathan Baker, "Two Sherman Act Section I Dilemmas: Parallel Pricing, The Oligopoly Problem, and Contemporary Economic Theory," *The Antitrust Bulletin* Spring (1993): 143–219; James W. Brock, "Antitrust Policy And The Oligopoly Problem," *The Antitrust Bulletin* 51, no. 2 (2006): 227–80.

71 Cengiz, *Türk Rekabet Hukukunda Uyumlu Eylem ve Bu Eylemin Hukuki Sonuçları,* 185.

72 See the decisions of TCA: dated 17.6.2003, no. 03–43/490–229; dated 24.4.2006, no. 06–29/357–88; dated 01.08.2002, no. 02–46/557–227.

73 See the decisions of TCA: dated 20.5.1999, no. 99–24/211–124; dated 27.06.2000, no. 00–24/255–138; dated 01.02.2002, no. 02–06/51–24.

74 Kahraman, *Rekabet Hukuku Açısından Oligopolistik Bağımlılık,* 104; Nurkut İnan, *Rekabet Hukuku Yazıları, Rekabetin Korunması Hakkında Kanun'un İçeriği ve Uygulanması Hakkında Görüşler* (Ankara, 2014), 76.

75 See also the decisions of TCA: dated 01.02.2002, no. 02–06/51–24; dated 23.09.2005, no. 05–60/896–241.

76 See also the decisions of TCA: dated 14.12.1999, no. 99–57/614–391; dated 23.03.2000, no. 00–11/109–54; dated 31.10.2002, no. 02–66/814–332; dated 26.05.2006, no. 06–36/465–127; dated 17.06.2003, no. 03–43/490–229; dated 10.10.2014, no. 14–37/713–318.

77 Aslan, *Rekabet Hukuku,* 233; Kahraman, *Rekabet Hukuku Açısından Oligopolistik Bağımlılık,* 103–104.

D. *Decisions by Association of Undertakings*

A decision made by the association of undertakings must be understood as any initiative, irrespective of its form, which is taken by the association and which has the object or effect of influencing the economic behavior of its members. For instance, the tariffs issued by Unions of Bar Associations may be considered as decisions taken by association of undertakings.[78]

In case these decisions have as their object or effect the prevention, distortion or restriction of competition directly or indirectly in a market, they shall be prohibited by competition law as well as agreements or concerted practices.[79]

IV. Exemption

A. *Legislation*

The article 5 of the APC states that;

> *In case all the terms listed below exist, agreements, concerted practices between undertakings, and decisions of associations of undertakings are exempted from the application of the provisions of article 4:*
>
> *a) Ensuring new developments and improvements, or economic or technical development in the production or distribution of goods and in the provision of services,*
> *b) Benefitting the consumer from the above-mentioned,*
> *c) Not eliminating competition in a significant part of the relevant market,*
> *d) Not limiting competition more than what is compulsory for achieving the goals set out in sub-paragraphs (a) and (b).*
>
> *Relevant undertakings or associations of undertakings may make an application to the Competition Authority in order to have the Board confirm that the agreements, concerted practices or decisions of associations of undertakings falling under Article 4 meet the requirements of the exemption.*
>
> *Exemption may be granted for a definite period, just as the granting of exemption may be subjected to the fulfillment of particular terms and/or particular obligations. Exemption decisions are valid as of the date of concluding an agreement or committing a concerted practice or taking a decision of an association of undertakings, or fulfilling a condition if it has been tied to a condition.*
>
> *In case the requirements mentioned in the first paragraph are fulfilled, the Board may issue communiqués which ensure block exemptions for the types of agreements in specific subject-matters and which indicate their terms.*

---

78 Güven, *Rekabet Hukuku Ders Kitabı*, 80.

79 See the decision of TCA: dated 27.10.1999, no. 99–49/536–337(a).

B. Definition

The term exemption refers to being excused or free from some penalty to which others are subject. While best practice advice suggests that competition law policy should equally apply to all sectors and firms in the economy engaged in economic activity, in practice various types of exemptions are granted for social and economic welfare or political reasons. The granting of exemptions does not necessarily imply the weakening of competition law enforcement. Indeed, it may well be that such instances are beneficial for following the objectives of competition law policy.

It should be noted that an "exemption" is not an "exception" in law. An exception refers to being excluded from or not conforming to a general class, principle, rule, etc. However, an exemption does not provide an exclusion from penalties but an excuse for the behavior.

C. Conditions of the Exemption

The penalties resulting from anti-competitive agreements, concerted practices and decisions will not be applied to some cases when the conditions of the article 5 of the APC are met. According to this article, in case an anti-competitive agreement, decision or concerted practice creates or ensures an economic development or a technical improvement to the benefit of customers, with no significant restriction of competition, no more than what is compulsory, it is exempted from penalties stipulated in the APC.

D. Block Exemptions

In case the terms mentioned in the first paragraph are fulfilled, the Board may issue communiqués which ensure block exemptions for the types of agreements in specific subject-matters and which indicate their terms.

Therefore, in the article 5 of the Act, the Competition Board has been empowered to issue communiqués which ensure granting block exemption to types of agreements bearing certain conditions and which determine the conditions in question.

Actually, the issued Communiqués on block exemptions are as following:

- Block Exemption Communiqué no. 2002/2 on Vertical Agreements (Amended by the Competition Board Communiqués no. 2003/3 and 2007/2)
- Block Exemption Communiqué no. 2003/2 on Research and Development Agreements

- Block Exemption Communiqué no. 2005/4 on Vertical Agreements and Concerted Practices in the Motor Vehicle Sector
- Block Exemption Communiqué no. 2008/2 relating to Technology Transfer Agreements
- Block Exemption Communiqué no. 2008/3 in relation to the Insurance Sector

V. Active Cooperation for Detecting Cartels

A. Introduction

Compared to other types of infringements, it is more difficult to detect and investigate cartels that are secret by nature unless parties to the cartel do not cooperate with the Authority. Therefore, it would be beneficial if penalties are reduced or not imposed on for those who make active cooperation with the Authority independently from other undertakings party to the cartel and their managers and employees for detecting and investigating cartels.

For this reason, article 16.6 of the Act regulates that to those making an active cooperation with the Authority for purposes of revealing cartels, penalties mentioned in the Act may not be imposed (immunity), or reductions may be made in penalties to be imposed in consideration of the quality, efficiency, and timing of cooperation and by means of demonstrating its grounds explicitly.

The last paragraph of the article 16 of the Act states that terms for immunity from or reduction of penalties in case of cooperation, and procedures and principles in relation to cooperation shall be determined by regulations to be issued by the Board.

B. Regulation

The article 4 of the Regulation on active cooperation for detecting cartels grants immunity to the first undertaking which submits the information and evidence and meets the requirements stated in the article 6 before the Board decides to carry out a preliminary inquiry or until the notification of the investigation report on condition that the Authority does not have, at the time of the submission, sufficient evidence to find the violation of Article 4 of the APC (the cartel ban).

The article 5 states that the undertakings which submit the information and evidence, and meets the conditions of the article 6, independently from its competitors, as of the decision by the Board to carry out preliminary inquiry until the notification of the investigation report, but which are not covered by the provision related to immunity from fines shall benefit from reduction of penalties.

In order to be covered by Articles 4 and 5 of this Regulation, an undertaking must:

(a) submit information and evidence in respect of the alleged cartel including the products affected, the duration of the cartel, the names of the undertakings party to the cartel, specific dates, locations and participants of cartel meetings,
(b) not conceal or destroy information or evidence related to the alleged cartel,
(c) end its involvement in the alleged cartel except for when otherwise is requested by the assigned unit on the ground that detecting the cartel would be complicated,
(d) keep the application confidential until the end of the investigation, unless otherwise is requested by the assigned unit,
(e) maintain active cooperation until the Board takes the final decision after the investigation is completed.

It should be noted that the same conditions and requirements are regulated for the immunity or reduction of penalties to be granted to the managers or employees of the undertakings in question.

VI. De Minimis Rule

According to the article 41.2 of the APC, based on criteria such as market share and turnover, the Board may decide not to initiate an investigation concerning cartels which do not significantly restrict competition in the market, with the exception of naked and hard-core infringements such as price fixing between competitors, region and customer allocation, and supply restriction.

To explain the details, the Authority issued a Communiqué on agreements, concerted practices and decisions and practices of associations of undertakings that do not significantly restrict competition (no. 2021/3) which gives the limitations of de minimis rule regulated in the Act.

§ Part V Prohibition on Abuse of Dominant Position

I. Introduction

The aim of the competition law is to maintain and promote the competition in the market. In this competitive environment, every undertaking strives to be superior to its competitors. They all want to maximize their profits, earn as much money as possible and gain the maximum market share.

In case these efforts come to a conclusion and one of the undertakings reach out to dominant position, this shall not be considered per se incompatible with competition law because to win the economic competition is one of the possible outcomes of the liberal economy.

Therefore, the undertaking reaching to a certain economic power as a result of both the structure of the market and the correct economic decisions taken, shall not be punished because of its success. This means that being in a dominant position is not prohibited by competition law, but abusing it is.

II. Legislation

The article 6 of the APC states that;

> *The abuse, by one or more undertakings, of their dominant position in a market for goods or services within the whole or a part of the country on their own or through agreements with others or through concerted practices, is illegal and prohibited.*
> *Abusive cases are, in particular, as follows:*
>
> a) *Preventing, directly or indirectly, another undertaking from entering into the area of commercial activity, or actions aimed at complicating the activities of competitors in the market,*
> b) *Making direct or indirect discrimination by offering different terms to purchasers with equal status for the same and equal rights, obligations and acts,*
> c) *Purchasing another good or service together with a good or service, or tying a good or service demanded by purchasers acting as intermediary undertakings to the condition of displaying another good or service by the purchaser, or imposing limitations with regard to the terms of purchase and sale in case of resale, such as not selling a purchased good below a particular price,*
> d) *Actions which aim at distorting competitive conditions in another market for goods or services by means of exploiting financial, technological and commercial advantages created by dominance in a particular market,*
> e) *Restricting production, marketing or technical development to the prejudice of consumers.*

III. Definition and Elements of the Dominant Position

A. *Definition*

According to the legal definition of the dominant position stated in the article 3 of the APC, the dominant position expresses the power of one or more undertakings in a particular market to determine economic parameters such as price, supply, the amount of production and distribution, by acting independently of their competitors and customers.

The leading cases define the dominant position as "one or more undertakings have sufficient power to act independently of customers, competitors and consumers and to prevent effective competition in the relevant market."[80]

B. Elements

First, the dominance describes "economic power" of the undertaking, sufficient to determine the market parameters and to enable the enterprise to act independently from other actors in the market.[81]

If an undertaking has the economic power to disrupt, restrict or prevent competition without the help of any other, this means that it has dominated the market. It should be noted that the market share (comparing to its competitors) and market entry conditions are the most important criteria in determining such economic power.

To illustrate, an undertaking may dominate the market with a market share of 40 % if its rivals are too small or an undertaking may not be a dominant position with a market share of 60 % if there is significant potential competitors, which may enter easily to the market because of low entry barriers. Due to the unique characteristics of each event, market share must be analyzed case by case, with the help of other criteria.[82]

Second, any undertaking, to be considered as in dominant position, must have the power to act independently from other actors (suppliers, customers, competitors and consumers) in the market. The independence mentioned here is to have "economic independence" while making economic decisions, not to be dependent on others' will, random events or circumstances.[83]

---

80 See the decisions of TCA: dated 06.04.2001, no. 01–17/150–39; dated 23.9.2005, no. 05–60/893–242; dated 12.11.2020, no. 20–49/675–295. See similar definitions in EU Competition law: Hoffman-LaRoche, Case 85/76, ECR (1979) 461; United Brands Co. and United Brands Continental BV v. Commission, Case 27/76, ECR 1978, I-207; Continental Can Company Inc. v Commission, Case 6/72, ECR (1973) 215.

81 Gamze Aşçıoğlu-Öz, *Avrupa Topluluğu ve Türk Rekabet Hukukunda Hakim Durumun Kötüye Kullanılması* (Ankara, 2000), 151; Ocak, *Rekabet Hukukunda Teşebbüsler ve Teşebbüslerin Hakim Durumunun Tespiti,* 168.

82 See the decision of TCA: dated 28.04.1999, no. 99–21/167–86.

83 See the decision of TCA: dated 06.09.1999, no. 99–41/435–274(a).

Third, the economic power should not be temporary, because a temporary economic dominance cannot be a sign of the dominant position.[84] Any undertaking can have a moment of power in any market. However, it may never have been able to determine market parameters in that specific moment, by acting independently of market conditions.

C. Collective (Joint) Dominance

The collective (joint) dominant position is, in the simplest terms, the dominant position of few undertakings in the relevant market.[85] These undertakings are not in a dominant position individually, but they become dominant when they act together in coordination.[86] It should be noted that acting in concert may be subjected to a cartel investigation as well.

In collective dominance, undertakings coordinate their actions in such a way that they exhibit the same behavior in the market.[87] It should be highlighted that it is easier to act in concert and maintain a collective dominant position in oligopolies because of the convenient market structure.[88]

---

84 See the decision of TCA: dated 05.09.2000, no. 00–33/356–200.

85 Whish, *Competition Law*, 520–521; Tekdemir, "The Principle of Collective Dominance Under EC Competition Law: A New Approach to The Problem of Oligopoly," 14. See also the decision of TCA: dated 18.09.2000, no. 00–35/393–220.

86 Aşçıoğlu-Öz, *Avrupa Topluluğu ve Türk Rekabet Hukukunda Hakim Durumun Kötüye Kullanılması,* 154; see also the decisions of TCA: dated 08.12.1999, no. 99–56/599–381; dated 01.02.2000, no. 04–4/41–19; dated 12.01.2000, no. 00–1(b)/11–5; dated 09.06.2003, no. 03–40/432–186. See also in EU Competition law: Gencor v. Commission, Case T 102/96, ECR (1999) II-753; French-West African Shipowners Committees, Case IV/32.450, OJ (1992) L-134/1; Compagnie Maritime Belge, Joined Cases 395–396/96 P, ECR (2000), I-1365.

87 See the decisions of TCA: dated 08.12.1999, no. 99–56/599–381; dated 09.06.2003, no. 03–40/432–186; dated 14.12.2000, no. 00–49/529–291. See also in EU Competition law: Almelo, Case C-393/92, ECR (1994) I-1477; Centro Servizi Spediporto Srl v. Spedizioni Marittime del Golfo Srl, Case C-96/94, ECR (1995) I-2883; DIP Spa v Commune di Bassano del Grappa, Case C-140/94, ECR (1995) I-3257; Sodemare, Case C-70/95, ECR (1997) I-3395.

88 Hasan Sabuncu, *Birlikte Hakimiyet Kavramının Birleşme ve Devralmalar Açısından Değerlendirilmesi* (Ankara, 2003), 19–20; Çelen, *Oligopolistik Pazarlarda Gözlenen Paralel Davranışların Rekabet Hukuku Açısından Değerlendirilmesi: Uyumlu Eylem Ve Birlikte Hakim Durum*, 9; Aslan, *Rekabet Hukuku*, 690–692.

IV. Detection of the Dominant Position

A. *In General*

In order to detect a dominant position, first of all, the relevant market shall be defined since the dominance is not absolute but relative. To illustrate, an undertaking may be dominant in a small "water tank" but insignificant in the "ocean".

Therefore, it is possible, only after the definition of the relevant market, to assess the market power of the investigated undertakings on these markets. An investigation usually starts by looking at the market shares of the undertakings in question and their competitors in order to understand how the economic power in the relevant market is allocated.[89]

However, the market share is not the sole or decisive factor in finding a dominant position, and a specific number of market share cannot be considered as a sign of a dominance.[90] The market power that manifests itself on specific relevant markets and the assessment of potential dominance is frequently based on the examination of several factors.

It is possible to draw conclusions on the degree of concentration of the market from differences in the undertakings' market shares. The wider the difference in market shares between the two biggest undertakings and the more dispersed the market shares of other competitors, the more likely the possibility that the one having the higher market share possesses significant market power.

Nonetheless, the importance of high market shares may be undercut by the low entry barriers creating the threat from potential competition, the deflation trend of the market shares, the bargaining power of the customers, fluctuations in market shares resulting from lump purchases infrequently made, rapid technological progress, or the competitive advantages of major competitors.

An undertaking may possess a large amount of market power, even if its market share is small. An undertaking's market power may be further strengthened, and its independent position reinforced by its economic and financial strength, technology level,[91] the available free capacity,[92] vertical integration,[93] the width of the selection[94] and other synergy benefits.

---

89 Ocak, *Rekabet Hukukunda Teşebbüsler ve Teşebbüslerin Hakim Durumunun Tespiti*, 223 ff.; Aslan, *Rekabet Hukuku*, 678; Güven, *Rekabet Hukuku Ders Kitabı*, 179.

90 Aslan, *Rekabet Hukuku*, 680.

91 See the decision of TCA: dated 12.06.2001, no. 01–27/260–74.

92 Aslan, *Rekabet Hukuku*, 685.

93 See the decision of TCA: dated 19.10.2004, no. 04–66/955–231.

94 See the decision of TCA: dated 02.06.2005, no. 05–38/487–116.

For example, economic and financial strength appearing as a low debt-equity ratio may offer the undertaking better possibilities to use different means of competition such as investments or pricing. An undertaking possessing a large amount of free capacity may react to new competitors by increasing production and introducing so many new products that entry to the relevant market is no longer profitable because prices have decreased due to the increase in supply.

When detecting dominant position, factors restricting market power of undertakings shall be considered as well. The use of market power may be curtailed by the existing and potential competitors, or customers and suppliers. Even an undertaking with a high market share cannot price above the competed level, if it is likely that the customers will switch to buying the more inexpensive products of competing undertakings. When customers or suppliers have a strong position in the market, the bargaining power of the allegedly dominant undertaking decrease.

In some cases, the mere threat that a competing undertaking is expanding its business, or a potential competitor will enter to the relevant market may restrict the use of market power by the undertaking in question. In these examples, there is no dominance since the undertaking cannot design its economic policies without the fear of competition.

In this context, the barriers to expansion and entry shall also be assessed because when the market has high entry barriers, the threat from potential competitors is insignificant, which leaves room for the creation of dominant position in favor of the existing undertakings. We will discuss the entry barriers in the following section.

B. Barriers to Entry

The barriers to entry are obstacles to undertakings when entering a market.[95] As a result of barriers to entry, new firms do not enter the market, thereby reducing the level of competition.

Therefore, barriers to entry, forming a roadblock to potential new entrants, allow existing undertakings to make higher profits than in a perfectly competitive market since fewer competitors mean less downwards pressure on prices.[96] As a result, barriers to entry can contribute to the creation of a dominant position manifesting as a monopoly or an oligopoly.[97]

---

95 Ocak, *Rekabet Hukukunda Teşebbüsler ve Teşebbüslerin Hakim Durumunun Tespiti*, 228.

96 Mehmet Yanık, *Rekabet Hukukunun Hakim Durum Ve Hakim Durumun Kötüye Kullanılması Uygulamalarında Piyasa Giriş Engelleri* (Ankara, 2003).

97 See the decision of TCA: dated 18.07.2002, no. 02–44/518–213.

The barriers to entry may be classified under two main sections: Legal barriers and economic barriers.

1. Legal Barriers to Entry

Legal barriers are legal restrictions imposed by immaterial rights such as patents, copyrights etc., or licenses and permits,[98] and statutory prohibitions such as trade barriers, standards and regulations, high import/export duties, exclusive contracts[99] etc.

2. Economic Barriers to Entry

Economic barriers are about the costs and difficulties existing for potential rivals to enter the market. The expansion or entry of a competitor may be considered unlikely if it is not sufficiently profitable. For this reason, typical economic entry barriers include major economies-of-scale or high start-up costs, sunk costs, strongly branded competitors, high brand trust and loyalty, heavily differentiated products and restraints in the access to the distribution channels.[100]

Economic barriers may result from natural, technical reasons, or may be created artificially. Natural reasons include economies of large scale production, ownership or control of a key scarce resource, high set-up costs etc.

Technical reasons may be arising from high start-up costs, high research and development costs, technical knowledge or technological advantages.

Brand loyalty is another economic barrier to entry since customers have become accustomed to trusting the brand. A strong brand creates loyalty, "locks in" existing customers, and deters entry. In order to break even, the new undertaking needs a large advertising and marketing campaign which increases its costs for market entry. Many of these costs are sunk costs, which are costs that cannot be recovered when a firm leaves a market.

Those natural barriers create considerable obstacles which deter potential entrants since they increase the costs necessary for making profits. It is often difficult for a new entrant to match, or exceed this level of costs in order to compete with existing competitors and make profit in the future.

The artificial reasons creating economic barriers are strategic, including predatory pricing, first-mover advantage, loyalty schemes, predatory acquisition

---

98 Aslan, *Rekabet Hukuku,* 687.

99 See the decision of TCA: dated 03.03.1999, no. 99–12/89–31.

100 Güven, *Rekabet Hukuku Ders Kitabı,* 152–155.

involving taking-over potential rivals, vertical integration tying up the supply chain, etc. and make life tough for potential entrants.

V. Abuse of Dominant Position

The dominant position, which is not per se prohibited, may be subjected to a penalty when the dominant undertaking or undertakings exploit their position to eliminate or restrict competition in the relevant market.[101]

The examples of abuse include especially:

- imposing unfair trading conditions or unfair prices such as over-pricing,[102] rebate systems,[103]
- predatory pricing[104] (including price squeeze, limit pricing, over capacity[105]),
- applying dissimilar conditions to equivalent transactions[106] with other trading parties, thereby placing them at a competitive disadvantage like refusal to supply or price discrimination,[107]

---

101 Seda Ulaş-Kısa, *Avrupa Topluluğu Rekabet Hukukunda Hâkim Durumun Rekabet Karşıtı Eylem ve İşlemlerle Kötüye Kullanılması* (Ankara, 2004), 24; Aşçıoğlu-Öz, *Avrupa Topluluğu ve Türk Rekabet Hukukunda Hakim Durumun Kötüye Kullanılması*, 157–58.

102 See the decisions of TCA: dated 13.03.2001, no. 01–12/114–29; dated 06.04.2001, no. 01–17/150–39.

103 Seda Ulaş Kısa, *Avrupa Topluluğu Rekabet Hukukunda Hâkim Durumun Rekabet Karşıtı Eylem ve İşlemlerle Kötüye Kullanılması* (Ankara, 2004), 34 ff.; Halil Çeçen, *Avrupa Birliği ve Türk Rekabet Hukukunda Hakim Durumun Fiyat Uygulamaları İle Kötüye Kullanılması* (İstanbul: Legal Kitabevi, 2018), 73 ff.; Aydın Öztunalı, *Rekabet Hukukunda Hakim Durumun Kötüye Kullanılması* (Ankara: Seçkin Yayınevi, 2014), 96 ff.; see also the decisions of TCA: dated 06.04.2006, no. 06–24/304–71; dated 23.01.2003, no. 03–06/59–21; dated 16.03.2016, no. 16–10/159–70.

104 Alper Fevzi Kara, *Hakim Durumun Kötüye Kullanılması Aracı Olarak Yıkıcı Fiyat Uygulaması* (Ankara, 2003; see also the decisions of TCA: dated 02.10.2002, no. 02–60/755–305; dated 08.12.1999, no. 99–56/599–381; dated 19.10.2004, no. 04–66/955–231.

105 Barış Ekdi, *Gümrük Birliği Çerçevesinde Damping Ve Yıkıcı Fiyat Uygulamaları* (Ankara, 2003).

106 See the decision of TCA: dated 20.09.2004, no. 04–60/866–205.

107 İbrahim Gül, *Teşebbüsün Alıcılarına Ayrımcılık Yaparak Hakim Durumunu Kötüye Kullanması* (Ankara, 2000); Öztunalı, *Rekabet Hukukunda Hakim Durumun Kötüye Kullanılması*, 147–148; Ümit Görgülü, *Hakim Durumun Kötüye Kullanılması Kapsamında Fiyat Ayrımcılığı Uygulamaları* (Ankara, 2003); see also the decision of TCA: dated 06.07.2001, no. 01–31/313–91.

- refusal of contract upon essential facilities,[108]
- stopping business with another undertaking without any plausible explanation,[109]
- preventing, directly or indirectly, another undertaking from entering to the market, or complicating the activities of competitors in the market[110] like most-favored customer clauses which favors one undertaking against others,[111] or predatory litigation aiming the foreclosure of the market to potential competitors,[112]
- making the conclusion of contracts subject to acceptance by the other parties of supplementary obligations which, by their nature or according to commercial usage, have no connection with the subject of such contracts,[113]
- imposing limitations for resale of the goods,
- limiting production, markets or technical development to the prejudice of consumers,
- distorting competitive conditions in another market by means of exploiting financial, technological and commercial advantages outcoming from the dominant position,[114] etc.

---

108 Yaşar Tekdemir, *AT Rekabet Hukukunda Anlaşma Yapmayı Reddetme Sorunu ve Zorunlu Unsur Doktrini: Anlaşma Yapma Yükümlülüğü Ya Da Sözleşme Serbestisinin Sınırları* (Ankara, 2003); Hakan Suat Ölmez, *Rekabet Hukukunda Zorunlu Unsur Doktrini Ve Uygulaması* (Ankara, 2003); see also the decisions of TCA: dated 12.10.2006, no. 06–74/959–278; dated 10.11.2003, no. 03–72/874–373.

109 See the decisions of TCA: dated 16.04.2002, no. 02–24/244–99; dated 19.10.2004, no. 04–66/949–227.

110 See the decisions of TCA: dated 28.08.2002, no. 02–50/636–258; dated 17.07.2000, no. 00–26/292–162; dated 20.07.2001, no. 01–35/347–95.

111 Aşçıoğlu-Öz, *Avrupa Topluluğu ve Türk Rekabet Hukukunda Hakim Durumun Kötüye Kullanılması,* 160.

112 See the decision of TCA: dated 23.11.2000, no. 00–46/488–266.

113 Kısa, *Hâkim Durumun Kötüye Kullanılması,* 78; Kürşat Ünlüsoy, *Rekabet Hukukunda Bağlama Anlaşmaları* (Ankara, 2003); see also the decisions of TCA: dated 23.01.2003, no. 03–06/59–21; dated 28.12.2015, no. 15–46/766–281.

114 Aşçıoğlu-Öz, *Avrupa Topluluğu ve Türk Rekabet Hukukunda Hakim Durumun Kötüye Kullanılması,* 164–165; see the decision of TCA: dated 14.12.2000, no. 00–49/529–291.

§ Part VI Control of Concentrations

I. Introduction

The actors of competition law are undertakings. The legislator specifically preferred this notion to describe economic units which operate in the market and can make independent decisions, regardless of their legal status or how they are financed. The competition law, which aims to protect the liberal economy by ensuring the continuation of competition in the market, is applied on economic actions rather than legal ones in order to reach to its economic goals.

For this reason, competition law covers all types of concentrations through the purchase of shares or assets, by contract or by any other means (de facto or de jure) causing similar economic impact as mergers and acquisitions even though their consequences vary from a legal perspective. For example, establishing a joint venture or consortium without forming a legal person is considered as a concentration in the relevant market, equivalent to a merger in the context of competition law.[115]

Major corporate reorganizations through merger and acquisitions or establishment of big joint ventures or consortiums may have an important economic impact on the market. In these cases, the market will be more concentrated than it was before the concentration. As a result of this, the effective competition may be lessened. The competition law, which aims to maintain and promote competition, prohibits concentrations that would result in a significant lessening of competition.

As a general rule, the party or parties who will acquire control following the concentration must notify the Board prior to its implementation in case it exceeds the thresholds specified in the Communiqué concerning the mergers and acquisitions calling for the authorization of the Competition Board (no. 2010/4).

The Board is entitled to control the concentration after the formation of the contract which will gain validity when it grants authorization following certain procedure. In case the Board decides (based on an economic analysis) that the concentration will lead to the significant impediment of effective competition, the authorization will not be granted.[116]

---

115 Lerzan Kayıhan, *Rekabet Hukuku Uygulamalarında Ortak Girişimler* (Ankara, 2003); Mehmet Akif Kayar, *Rekabet Hukuku Uygulamalarında Yatay İşbirliği Anlaşmaları: Ortak Girişimler Açısından Bir Değerlendirme* (Ankara, 2003).

116 See in EU Competition law: Airtours v. Commission, Case T-342/99, ECR (2002) II-2585.

II. Legislation

The article 7 of the APC states that;

> *It is illegal and prohibited for one or more undertakings to merge, or for an undertaking or a person to acquire – except by inheritance – assets, or all or part of the partnership shares, or instruments conferring executive rights over another undertaking, where these would result in a significant lessening of effective competition within a market for goods or services in the entirety or a portion of the country, particularly in the form of creating or strengthening a dominant position.*
> *The Board shall declare, via communiqués to be issued by it, the types of mergers and acquisitions which have to be notified to the Board and for which permission has to be obtained, in order for them to become legally valid.*

This article empowers the Competition Board to issue a Communiqué to identify which concentrations require to be notified to and authorized by the Board in order to gain legal validity within the framework of Article 7 of the APC. According to this, the Authority issued the Communiqué no. 2010/4 which covers the procedures and principles concerning the identification of the concentrations requiring authorization.

III. Cases Considered as a Concentration

The merger of two or more undertakings, or the acquisition of direct or indirect control over all or part of an undertaking through the purchase of shares or assets, a contract or any other means shall be considered as a concentration, provided there is a permanent change in control.[117]

Control may be acquired through rights, contracts or other instruments which, separately or together, allow de facto or de jure exercise of decisive influence over an undertaking.[118] In particular, these instruments consist of ownership right or operating right over all or part of the assets of an undertaking, and those rights or contracts granting decisive influence over the structure or decisions of the bodies of an undertaking.[119]

Control may be acquired by right holders, or by those persons or undertakings, who have been empowered to exercise such rights in accordance with a contract,

---

117 Guidelines on cases considered as a merger or an acquisition and the concept of control (https://www.rekabet.gov.tr/Dosya/guidelines/10-pdf); Abdulgani Güngördü, *AT ve Türk Rekabet Hukukunda Yoğunlaşmalarda Kontrol Unsuru* (Ankara, 2003).

118 Aslan, *Rekabet Hukuku,* 805–806.

119 Ercüment Erdem, *Türk ve AT Rekabet Hukukunda Birleşme ve Devralmalar* (İstanbul: Beta Yayınevi, 2003), 53 ff.

or who, while lacking such rights and powers, have de facto strength to exercise such rights.

Moreover, the concentration may be vertical (upstream) or horizontal.[120] Both are equally prone to adversely affect the market.

Formation of a joint venture or consortium, which would permanently fulfill all of the functions of an independent economic entity, shall constitute a concentration of two or more undertakings, which agree to pool their resources for the purpose of accomplishing a specific task or achieving a common purpose that the group intends to carry out. In this case, the separate firms do not merge their legal entities, but they establish a joint (combined) control without any legal partnership or corporate designation.[121]

It should be noted that intra-group transactions and other transactions which do not lead to a change in control; temporarily holding the securities for trade rather than controlling the competition policies of the undertaking issuing the securities (like brokers in stock exchange markets); the cases where the control is acquired by a public institution and organization for the purpose of liquidation, dissolution, insolvency, suspension of payments, concordat, privatization or a similar reason, or the change in control is realized by inheritance, are not considered as a merger and acquisition and is not supervised by the Competition Board.[122]

IV. Concentrations Subject to Authorization

As a result of concentration of undertakings, the decrease in the number of undertakings competing with each other in the relevant market may cause oligopoly or monopoly and effective competition in the market may be adversely affected. That is why concentrations exceeding certain thresholds are subject to the authorization of the Competition Board.

The thresholds are specified in the Communiqué no. 2010/4. Accordingly, in case total turnovers of the transaction parties in Turkey exceed one hundred million TL, and turnovers of at least two of the transaction parties in Turkey each exceed 30 million Turkish Liras, or global turnover of one of the transaction parties exceeds five hundred million Turkish Liras, and at least one of the

120 Şebnem Kulaksızoğlu, *Rekabet Hukukunda Yatay Birleşmeler: Antirekabetçi Etkiler İle Öne Sürülen Savunma Ve Yararlar* (Ankara, 2003).

121 Önder Suat Uluçlar, *Yoğunlaşmalarda Tam İşlevsellik* (İstanbul: Onikilevha Yayınevi, 2017).

122 Erdem, *Birleşme ve Devralmalar,* 88 ff.

remaining transaction parties has a turnover in Turkey exceeding five million Turkish Liras, the authorization is required to gain legal validity, except in cases of joint ventures without any affected market. It is also explained in detail how to calculate these turnovers in the articles 8 and 9 of the Communiqué.

V. Procedure

In case the turnovers of the parties to the concentration exceed the thresholds specified in the Communiqué no. 2010/4, the Board shall be notified by the concerned undertakings prior to the implementation of the transaction. The notification should be made by filling the Notification Form attached to the Communiqué with all requested information and documents. It should be noted that administrative fines are imposed on those who do not notify the Board when it was required or who make false or misleading statements in the Notification Form.

According to the article 10 of the APC, the Board is obliged, following the notification, to perform a preliminary examination within 15 days and either authorizes the concentration, or decides to suspense the transaction until the final decision by sending a preliminary objection letter to those concerned, together with any other measures deemed necessary.

In case the Board does not respond to or take any action concerning the application for a concentration within due time, the agreements on this concentration shall take effect and become legally valid after 30 days as of the date of the notification.

According to the article 11 of the APC, in case the Board is aware of the concentration even without notification, it shall carry out an examination on its own initiative. As a result of this examination, the Board may allow the concentration, but impose administrative fines on the undertakings which have failed to notify when it was compulsory, or may refuse to grant authorization to the concentration. In the latter case, the Board decides that the transaction must be terminated together with all unlawful accessories, and that *status quo* existing before transaction must be restored. It is also possible that the Board takes all other measures deemed necessary.

According to the article 13 of the Communiqué, while assessing mergers and acquisitions, the structure of the relevant market, actual and potential competition among domestic- and foreign-based undertakings, the status of the undertakings within the market, their economic and financial power, their alternatives sources for suppliers and customers, their ability to access sources of supply, barriers to entry into market, supply and demand trends, consumer interests, activities benefiting the consumers and other issues shall be taken into account in particular.

VI. Assessment

A concentration may significantly impede competition by eliminating important competitive pressure on an undertaking and thereby creating market power. The first direct effect of this transaction is the loss of actual competition between the parties. The Board shall consider actual market shares in the assessment of the possible effects of the transaction. The concentration levels in a market provide useful information about the competitive structure on the relevant market. In order to calculate concentration levels, concentration rate (CR4, CR5, etc.) or Herfindahl-Hirschman Index (HHI) or other measures can be used. Then, other economic factors which may affect competition on the market shall be analyzed.[123]

VII. Remedies

It is the responsibility of the Board to find out, during an examination conducted under Article 7, whether a concentration transaction may result in a significant lessening of competition in the relevant market.

Both during the preliminary examination and final examination stages, competition problems expected to arise (in the concentration file) shall be notified to the undertakings so as to ensure that the parties may propose suitable and effective remedies. It is indeed within the undertakings' discretion whether to make proposals aimed at eliminating the competition problems.

Although the Board made such decisions in the past, as concerns future concentration transactions, the Board – also in line with its recent practices- is no longer in a position to unilaterally impose a certain remedy as a condition to the parties and shall neither be able to unilaterally change the proposed remedies of the parties or their commitments to fulfill them.

If the Board is in the opinion that the proposed remedy is insufficient, it may allow the parties to make changes to their commitments. In case the commitments still do not attain the sufficiency to eliminate the competition

123 See the Guidelines on the assessment of horizontal mergers and acquisitions (issued by the TCA, dated 04.06.2013, https://www.rekabet.gov.tr/Dosya/guidelines/8-pdf) and the Guidelines on the assessment of non-horizontal mergers and acquisitions (issued by the TCA, dated 04.06.2013, https://www.rekabet.gov.tr/Dosya/guidelines/9-pdf), accessed 14.07.2021.

problems, the Board may prohibit the transaction after following through the necessary procedural stages.

In order for the Board to be able to authorize a concentration transaction conditionally within the framework of the remedy proposed, it must be sure that the competitive concerns related to the transaction will be eliminated following the implementation of the proposed remedies.

It is the parties to the transaction who hold the most comprehensive information needed to carry out a full and correct analysis of the feasibility of the commitments, or of the sufficiency of the remedies in eliminating the competitive concerns. Therefore, during the Board's examination of the proposed remedy, it is the responsibility of the parties to provide all information that is capable of showing the sufficiency of the commitment in eliminating the competitive concerns.

The parties are also required to submit, together with the proposed remedy, detailed information regarding the content of the proposed remedy, how it will be implemented and how it will eliminate the problem of significant lessening of competition.

The main expectation from a proposed remedy is to serve the protection of the level of competition that existed prior to the transaction. Therefore, the remedy is not expected to make the market more competitive. It shall protect competition, not the competitors. Furthermore, its conditions shall be clear, feasible and capable of being implemented effectively as soon as possible.

The Board shall accept only remedies that have been revealed to be sufficient in eliminating the problem of significant lessening of competition. Thus, proposed remedies shall eliminate the competitive concerns related to the transaction without any room for uncertainty and in a sustainable manner and shall be intelligible in every aspect.

In determining the sufficiency of the proposed remedy in eliminating competitive concerns, the Board takes into consideration -within the framework of the market conditions- all factors such as the type of remedy, its scope, market position of the parties and competitors, whether the remedy proposal is capable of being implemented by the parties fully and timely in an effective manner.

The Board shall evaluate whether the proposed remedies are proportionate to the competition problems related to the transaction and whether they fulfill the main necessary conditions for an acceptable remedy and shall thus make a decision.

In case the authorization is granted with conditions, the Board shall supervise the undertakings' actions to see whether the conditions are respected.

VIII. Types of Acceptable Proposed Remedies

Proposed remedies aimed at eliminating competition problems created by a concentration transaction may be structural or behavioral. Proposed structural remedies generally involve the divestiture of a certain business, while proposed behavioral remedies involve the arrangement of the future market behaviors of the parties.

The main purpose of proposed remedies is to protect the competitive structure that existed in the market prior to the transaction. Therefore, due to their characteristics of bringing about a sustainable result in the short term in terms of eliminating competition problems and not requiring supervision after being implemented, structural remedies -particularly those causing structural changes in the market such as the divestiture of a business or removal of links between undertakings- more properly fit within the purpose expected from proposed remedies.

However, the behavioral remedies such as ensuring access to important infrastructure and raw material in a non-discriminatory manner are also likely to solve competition problems caused by a transaction. In this case, behavioral remedies oblige the Authority to monitor the behavior of undertakings in the market continuously.

In the end, the sufficiency of a remedy in eliminating competition problems shall be evaluated on a case-by-case basis in accordance with the requirements of the case.

§ PART VII Sanctions, Fines, Remedies

I. Procedure

According to the article 40 of the APC, the Board may decide on its own initiative or upon the applications filed, to open a direct investigation, or to conduct a preliminary inquiry for determining whether or not it is necessary to open an investigation.[124]

In case a preliminary inquiry is conducted, a report shall be submitted to the Board, as a result of this procedure. Following the submission of the preliminary inquiry report to the Board, the Board convenes in order to evaluate the

124 Mustafa Okan Yağcı, *Rekabet Kurulu'nun İnceleme ve Araştırma Usulü* (İstanbul: Vedat Kitabevi, 2018), 113 ff.

information obtained and make a decision and decides on whether or not to open an investigation (Article 41 of the APC).[125]

While initiating an investigation, the Board designates a rapporteur or rapporteurs who will carry out the investigation within 6 months. Then, the Board notifies the parties concerned requesting that the parties submit their first written pleas within 30 days.

Relevant undertakings may offer commitments in order to eliminate the competition problems under the articles 4 or 6 of the APC which may arise during an ongoing preliminary inquiry or investigation process. If the Board decides that the suggested commitments can resolve the competition problems, it may render these commitments binding for the relevant undertakings, and decide not to initiate an investigation or to terminate an ongoing investigation.

However, the Board which stopped an investigation may re-launch it in case there is a substantial alteration in any of the factors on which the decision was based, or the relevant undertakings act in violation of the commitments given, or the decision was based on missing, false or misleading information presented by the parties.

After initiating an investigation, the Board may also choose to start the settlement procedure, taking into account the procedural benefits that may arise from a rapid resolution of the investigation process and the differences in opinion concerning the existence and scope of the infringement. In this framework, the Board shall grant a definite period of time to the parties under investigation to present a settlement text wherein they accept the existence and scope of the infringement. In case the process is concluded with a settlement, the parties to the settlement may not take administrative fines.

Finally, following the investigation the Board may decide to impose administrative fines on those responsible for the violation of the provisions of the APC. It should be added that suits shall be filed against administrative sanctions before the competent administrative courts. However, judicial review against decisions of the Board shall not cease the implementation of decisions, and the follow up and collection of administrative fines (Article 55 of the APC).[126]

II. Private Law Remedies against Limiting Competition

According to the article 56 of the APC, any type of cartel agreements or decisions which violate the cartel ban regulated in the article 4 of the Act are invalid. This

125 Yağcı, *İnceleme ve Araştırma Usulü*, 124.
126 Yağcı, *İnceleme ve Araştırma Usulü*, 290.

is in line with the article 27 of the Turkish Code of Obligations which states that a contract is void in case its terms are unlawful.[127] In cases where an agreement exceeding an exempted time limitation is concluded, the exempted part remains valid while the exceeding part is void.[128]

Anyone who restrict competition via cartel or abuse of dominant position is obliged to compensate for any damages of the injured. If the harm has resulted from a collective action, there is joint responsibility of the actors, as stated by the article 57 of the APC.

Article 58 of the APC regulates the compensation for the damages. According to this, those who suffer as a result of the violation of competition law may claim, as the damage, for the difference between the cost they paid and the cost they would have paid if competition had not been limited.

Competing undertakings affected by the limitation of competition may request that all of their damages are compensated by the undertaking or undertakings that limited competition. In determining the damage, all profits expected to be gained by the injured undertakings are calculated by taking into account the balance sheets of the previous years as well.[129]

If the resulting damage arises from an agreement or decision of the parties, or from cases involving gross negligence of them, the judge may, upon the request of the injured, award compensation by three fold of the material damage incurred or of the profits gained or likely to be gained by those who caused the damage. This article imposes "punitive damages" to the undertaking responsible from

---

127 Buğra Kesici, *Rekabet Hukukunun İhlalinden Kaynaklanan Haksız Fiil Sorumluluğu* (İstanbul: Onikilevha Yayınevi, 2017), 7; Kerem Cem Sanlı, "Rekabetin Korunması Hakkında Kanun'un Özel Hukuk Alanındaki Sonuçları: Genel Bakış ve Sorunlar," in *Rekabetin Korunması Hakkında Kanun'un Özel Hukuk Alanındaki Sonuçları*, ed. Kerem Cem Sanlı (Onikilevha Yayınevi, 2013), 19; Başak Başar, *Rekabetin Korunması Hakkında Kanuna Aykırılığın Özel Hukuk Alanındaki Sonuçları* (Ankara: Yetkin Yayınları, 2018), 73.

128 Sanlı, "Rekabetin Korunması Hakkında Kanun'un Özel Hukuk Alanındaki Sonuçları: Genel Bakış ve Sorunlar," 27; Osman Berat Gürzumar and Kerem Cem Sanlı, "Akaryakıt Bayileri İle Akaryakıt Dağıtım Şirketleri Arasında Akdedilen Bayilik ve İntifa Hakkı Sözleşmelerinin 4054 Sayılı Kanunun 4. Maddesine Aykırı Kabul Edilmesi İhtimalinde Ortaya Çıkacak Özel Hukuk Sorunları," in *Prof. Dr. Haluk Konuralp Anısına Armağan Vol.III* (Ankara: Yetkin Yayınları, 2009), 549–577; İ. Yılmaz Aslan and Emre Önal, *Türk Akaryakıt Sektöründe Rekabet Yasaklarından Doğan Sorunlar Ve Çözüm Önerileri* (Bursa: Ekin Kitabevi, 2011).

129 Kesici, *Rekabet Hukukunun İhlalinden Kaynaklanan Haksız Fiil Sorumluluğu,* 232 ff.

damage, which is unusual for Turkish tort law.[130] The aim is to deter undertakings from infringement.[131]

According to the article 59 of the APC, should the injured submit to the jurisdictional bodies proofs such as, particularly, the actual partitioning of markets, stability observed in the market price for quite a long time, the price increase within close intervals by the undertakings operating in the market, which give the impression of the existence of an agreement, or the distortion of competition in the market, then the burden of proof is on the defendants that the undertakings are not engaged in concerted practice. This is the reflection of the presumption of concerted practice regulated in the article 4 of the APC. Because of this presumption, concerted practices may be proven with circumstantial evidence.[132]

It should be added that the existence of agreements, decisions and practices limiting competition may be proved by any kind of evidence.

III. Administrative Fines

In case the competition law is violated, the Board imposes sanctions regulated in the article 16 of the APC. According to this article, misleading information or complicating investigation are sanctioned in addition to the prohibited anticompetitive behaviors. Furthermore, the article 17 of the APC regulates the proportional administrative fines.

A. Sanctions against Misleading Information or Complicating Investigation

These sanctions are regulated against procedural violations.[133] In case any false or misleading information or document is provided to the Board, or concentrations

---

130 Murat Topuz and Gökhan Bakar, *On İki Banka Örneği Üzerinden Uyumlu Eylem İle Kartel Oluşturan Bankaların Hukuki Sorumluluğu* (Ankara: Seçkin Yayınevi, 2017), 169.

131 Murat Şahin, *Rekabet Hukukunda Tazminat Talepleri*, 2nd ed. (İstanbul: Onikilevha Yayınevi, 2013), 204; Metin Topçuoğlu, *Rekabeti Kısıtlayan Teşebbüsler Arası İşbirliği Davranışları ve Hukuki Sonuçları* (Ankara, 2001), 306; Şebnem Akipek-Öcal, Nagehan Kırkbeşoğlu, and Hakan Tokbaş, *Sorularla 12 Bankaya Karşı Üç Kat Tazminat* (İstanbul: Aristo, 2017), 96. Contra. Orhan Sekmen, *Rekabet Hukukunda Tazminat Sorumluluğu* (Ankara: Bilge Yayınevi, 2013), 85.

132 Şahin, *Rekabet Hukukunda Tazminat Talepleri,* 256 ff.; Pelin Uyanık, *Rekabet Hukuku Açısından Delil* (Ankara, 2003)

133 Kazım Eren Gönen, *Rekabet Hukukunda İdari Para Cezaları* (Ankara: Seçkin Yayınevi, 2003), 49 ff.

subject to authorization are realized without the authorization of the Board, or any incomplete, false or misleading information or document is provided, or information or document is not provided within the determined duration or at all when the Board has requested information or while the Board carries out on the spot inspection, the Board shall impose an administrative fine by 1/1,000 (one in thousand) of annual gross revenues which generate by the end of the financial year preceding the decision (or closest to the time of the decision).

Moreover, the Board shall impose an administrative fine by 5/1,000 (five in thousand) of annual gross revenues which generate by the end of the financial year preceding the decision (or closest to the time of the decision) in case on-the-spot inspection is hindered or complicated. The realization of on-the-spot inspection with a court decision shall not hinder the application of this administrative fine.

These sanctions cannot be less than 10,000 Turkish Liras.[134]

B. Sanctions against Prohibited Anti-Competitive Behaviors

These are sanctions against prohibited behaviors.[135] To those who commit behavior prohibited in articles 4 (cartel ban), 6 (abuse of dominant position) and 7 (control of the concentrations) of the APC, an administrative fine shall be imposed up to 10 % of annual gross revenues which generate by the end of the financial year preceding the decision (or closest to the time of the decision).

In case administrative fines mentioned above are imposed on undertakings, an administrative fine up to 5 % of this penalty shall be imposed on managers or employees of the undertaking who have a decisive influence in the infringement. This means that the managers or employees playing an important role in the violation of competition law will be subjected to the penalties in addition to the undertaking.

When deciding on an administrative fine, the Board shall take into consideration issues such as the repetition of infringement, its duration, market power of undertakings or associations of undertakings, their decisive influence in the realization of infringement, whether they comply with the commitments given, whether they assist with the examination, and the severity of damage that takes place or is likely to take place.

To those undertakings or associations of undertakings or their managers and employees making an active cooperation with the Authority for purposes

---

134 It should be noted that this amount may be revised by law in the following years.

135 Gönen, *Rekabet Hukukunda İdari Para Cezaları*, 55 ff.

of revealing contrariness to the Act, penalties mentioned above may not be imposed or reductions may be made in penalties to be imposed taking into consideration the quality, efficiency and timing of the cooperation.

C. Proportional Administrative Fines

Provided that penalties mentioned in article 16 are reserved, the Board shall, for each day, impose on undertakings an administrative fine by 5/10,000 (five in ten thousand) of annual gross revenues which generate by the end of the financial year preceding the decision (or closest to the time of the decision) in the event that obligations introduced or commitments made by a final decision or interim measure decision are not complied with, or on-the-spot inspection is hindered or complicated, or information or document requested by the Board is not provided within the duration determined.

IV. Base Fine, Aggravating Factors and Mitigating Factors

The Board has issued the Regulation on fines to apply in cases of agreements, concerted practices and decisions limiting competition and abuse of dominant position in order to ensure transparency, objectivity and consistency in fining process. Under this title, the calculation of the base fine, aggravating factors, mitigating factors and fines to be applied to managers and employees will be given in details.

A. Base Fine

According to the article 5 of the Regulation, while the base fine is being calculated, a percentage for cartels, between 2 % and 4 %, and for other violations, between 5/1,000 (five thousandth) and 3 % of the annual gross revenues of the undertakings and associations of undertakings or the members of such associations, which generated at the end of the fiscal year preceding the final decision, or if that cannot be calculated, at the end of the fiscal year closest to the date of the final decision, and which shall be determined by the Board, shall be taken as the basis.

In the determination of the percentages written above, issues such as the market power of the concerned undertakings or associations of undertakings, and the gravity of the damage which occurred or is likely to occur as a result of the violation shall be considered.

It should be noted that the amount of fine determined shall be increased by half for violations which lasted longer than 1 year, shorter than 5 years, or shall be increased by one fold for violations which lasted longer than 5 years.

B. *Aggravating Factors*

According to the article 6 of the Regulation, the base fine shall be increased by half to one fold for each repetition in case of the repetition of the violation, or in case the cartel is continued after the notification of the investigation decision.

Moreover, the base fine may be increased by half to one fold, where the commitments made for the elimination of the competition problems raised within the scope of Article 4 (cartel ban) or 6 (abuse of dominant position) of the Act are not met, or by up to half, where no assistance with the examination is provided, or by up to one fourth, where other undertakings are coerced into the violation.

C. *Mitigating Factors*

According to the article 7 of the Regulation, provided that the concerned undertaking proves that assistance with the examination has been provided apart from the fulfillment of the legal obligations, there has been incentive by public authorities or coercion by other undertakings concerning the violation, those who were damaged have been indemnified voluntarily, the other violations have been ceased, those activities which are the subject of the violation have a considerably low share in the annual gross revenues, the base fine may be reduced by one fourth to three fifth.

Furthermore, in an ongoing investigation, the fine to be given to an undertaking which cannot benefit from the Active Cooperation Regulation, shall be reduced by one fourth if it presents the information and documents specified under Article 6 of the Active Cooperation Regulation before the Board decides to conduct a preliminary inquiry into another cartel. The provisions of the Active Cooperation Regulation for non-imposition of fines, or reduction in fines to be given, are reserved.

In case the undertakings or associations of undertakings that engaged in the other violations acknowledge their violations and take active cooperation, the fine shall be reduced by one sixth to one fourth.

D. *Fines to be Applied to Managers and Employees*

According to the article 8 of the Regulation, each of the managers and employees of the undertaking who were detected to have had decisive influence on the cartel shall be separately given between 3 % and 5 % of the fine given to the undertaking, or on the other violations, may be given fines up to 5 % of the fine given to the concerned undertaking. The provisions of the Active Cooperation Regulation are reserved.

Further Readings

Akipek-Öcal, Şebnem, Nagehan Kırkbeşoğlu, and Hakan Tokbaş. *Sorularla 12 Bankaya Karşı Üç Kat Tazminat*. İstanbul: Aristo, 2017.

Akıncı, Ateş. *Rekabetin Yatay Kısıtlanması*. Ankara, 2001.

Altun, Mücteba. *Yatay İşbirliği Anlaşmalarının 4. Madde Kapsamında Değerlendirilmesi*. Ankara, 2012.

Arı, Zekeriyya. "Rekabet Hukukunda Amaç Sorunu." *Süleyman Demirel Üniversitesi İktisadi ve İdari Bilimler Fakültesi Dergisi* 8, no. 3 (2003): 27–48.

Arı, Zekeriyya. *Türk Hukukunda Danışıklılık Kavramı*. Ankara: Seçkin Yayınevi, 2004.

Aşçıoğlu-Öz, Gamze. "Rekabet Hukukunda Dikey Anlaşmalar." In *Rekabet Hukuku ve Dikey Anlaşmalar*, edited by Kerem Cem Sanlı. İstanbul: Onikilevha Yayınevi, 2009.

Aslan, İ. Yılmaz. *Rekabet Hukuku Bakımından Dikey Anlaşmalar*. Bursa: Ekin Kitabevi, 2004.

Aslan, İ. Yılmaz, and Emre Önal. *Türk Akaryakıt Sektöründe Rekabet Yasaklarından Doğan Sorunlar Ve Çözüm Önerileri*. Bursa: Ekin Kitabevi, 2011.

Ateş, Mustafa. *Rekabet Hukukuna Giriş*. 2nd ed. Ankara: Adalet Yayınevi, 2019.

Atiyas, İzak, and Gönenç Gürkaynak. "Uyumlu Eylem Karinesi Üzerine Hukuki ve Ekonomik Çözümlemeler." *Rekabet Hukukunda Güncel Gelişmeler Sempozyumu IV*, 2006, 80–115.

Ay, Özge. *Otomotiv Sözleşmelerindeki Dağıtım Sözleşmelerinden Kaynaklanan Hukuki İlişkilerin Rekabet Hukuku Açısından İncelenmesi*. İstanbul: Onikilevha Yayınevi, 2017.

Badur, Emel. *Türk Rekabet Hukukunda Rekabeti Sınırlayıcı Anlaşmalar*. Ankara, 2001.

Baker, Jonathan. "Two Sherman Act Section I Dilemmas: Parallel Pricing, The Oligopoly Problem, and Contemporary Economic Theory." *The Antitrust Bulletin* Spring (1993): 143–219.

Başar, Başak. *Rekabetin Korunması Hakkında Kanuna Aykırılığın Özel Hukuk Alanındaki Sonuçları*. Ankara: Yetkin Yayınları, 2018.

Bishop, Simon, and Mike Walker. *The Economics of EC Competition Law: Concepts, Application and Measurement*. 2nd ed. Sweet&Maxwell, 2002.

Brock, James W. "Antitrust Policy And The Oligopoly Problem." *The Antitrust Bulletin* 51, no. 2 (2006): 227–80.

Çeçen, Halil. *Avrupa Birliği ve Türk Rekabet Hukukunda Hakim Durumun Fiyat Uygulamaları İle Kötüye Kullanılması*. 2nd ed. İstanbul: Legal Kitabevi, 2018.

Çelen, Aydın. *Oligopolistik Pazarlarda Gözlenen Paralel Davranışların Rekabet Hukuku Açısından Değerlendirilmesi: Uyumlu Eylem Ve Birlikte Hakim Durum*. Ankara, 2003.

Çetinkaya, Murat. *İlgili Pazar Kavramı Ve İlgili Pazar Tanımında Kullanılan Nicel Teknikler*. Ankara, 2003.

Ekdi, Barış. *Gümrük Birliği Çerçevesinde Damping Ve Yıkıcı Fiyat Uygulamaları*. Ankara, 2003.

Ekşioğlu, Ebru. *Sorularla Kolaylaştırılmış Rekabet Hukuku*. İstanbul: Aristo, 2017.

Erdem, Ercüment. *Türk ve AT Rekabet Hukukunda Birleşme ve Devralmalar*. İstanbul: Beta Yayınevi, 2003.

Faull, Jonathan, and Ali Nikpay. *The EC Law of Competition*. New York: Oxford University Press, 1999.

Friedman, James W. *Game Theory With Application to Economics*. 2nd ed. New York: Oxford University Press, 1990.

Gerven, Gerwin Van, and Navarro E. Varona. "The Wood Pulp Case and The Future of Concerted Practices." *CMLR*, no. 31 (1994): 575–608.

Gönen, Kazım Eren. *Rekabet Hukukunda İdari Para Cezaları*. Ankara: Seçkin Yayınevi, 2003.

Görgülü, Ümit. *Hakim Durumun Kötüye Kullanılması Kapsamında Fiyat Ayrımcılığı Uygulamaları*. Ankara, 2003.

Goyder, Daniel G. *EC Competition Law*. 4th ed. New York: Oxford University Press, 2003.

Gül, İbrahim. *Teşebbüsün Alıcılarına Ayrımcılık Yaparak Hakim Durumunu Kötüye Kullanması*. Ankara, 2000.

Günay, Cevdet İlhan. *Rekabet Kanunu Şerhi*. Ankara: Yetkin Yayınları, 2010.

Güngördü, Abdulgani. *AT ve Türk Rekabet Hukukunda Yoğunlaşmalarda Kontrol Unsuru*. Ankara, 2003.

Gürzumar, Osman Berat, and Kerem Cem Sanlı. "Akaryakıt Bayileri İle Akaryakıt Dağıtım Şirketleri Arasında Akdedilen Bayilik ve İntifa Hakkı Sözleşmelerinin 4054 Sayılı Kanunun 4. Maddesine Aykırı Kabul Edilmesi İhtimalinde Ortaya Çıkacak Özel Hukuk Sorunları." In *Prof. Dr. Haluk Konuralp Anısına Armağan Vol. III*, 549–77. Ankara: Yetkin Yayınları, 2009.

Güven, Şirin. *Haksız Rekabet Hukukunun Amacı ve Koruduğu Menfaatler*. Ankara: Adalet Yayınevi, 2012.

Güzel, Oğuzkan. *Rekabet Hukukunda Teşebbüs Ve Teşebbüs Birlikleri*. Ankara, 2003.

Hovenkamp, Herbert. *Federal Antitrust Policy, The Law of Competition and Its Practice*. St. Paul, Minn.: Hornbook Series, West Group, 1999.

İnan, Nurkut. *Rekabet Hukuku Yazıları, Rekabetin Korunması Hakkında Kanun'un İçeriği ve Uygulanması Hakkında Görüşler*. Ankara, 2014.

Kara, Alper Fevzi. *Hakim Durumun Kötüye Kullanılması Aracı Olarak Yıkıcı Fiyat Uygulaması*. Ankara, 2003.

Karakılıç, Hasan. *Rekabet Hukukunda Bağlama Uygulamaları*. İstanbul: Onikilevha Yayınevi, 2013.

Karauz, Agâh Kürşat, and Halil Alperen Işık. "Rekabet Kurallarının Yer Bakımından Uygulanması." *Yıldırım Beyazıt Hukuk Dergisi* 1 (2016): 283–98.

Kayar, Mehmet Akif. *Rekabet Hukuku Uygulamalarında Yatay İşbirliği Anlaşmaları: Ortak Girişimler Açısından Bir Değerlendirme*. Ankara, 2003.

Kayıhan, Lerzan. *Rekabet Hukuku Uygulamalarında Ortak Girişimler*. Ankara, 2003.

Kesici, Buğra. *Rekabet Hukukunun İhlalinden Kaynaklanan Haksız Fiil Sorumluluğu*. İstanbul: Onikilevha Yayınevi, 2017.

Korah, Valentine. *An Introductory Guide to EC Competition Law and Practice*. 8th ed. Hart Publishing, 2004.

Küçükayhan-Aşçıoğlu, Meltem. *Rekabet Hukuku ve Dağıtım Sözleşmeleri*. Ankara: Adalet Yayınevi, 2011.

Kulaksızoğlu, Şebnem. *Rekabet Hukukunda Yatay Birleşmeler: Antirekabetçi Etkiler İle Öne Sürülen Savunma Ve Yararlar*. Ankara, 2003.

Morgenstern, Oskar. "Oligopoly, Monopolistic Competition, and The Theory of Games." *The American Economic Review* 38, no. 2 (1948): 10–18.

Neven, Damien, Pénélope Papandropoulos, and Paul Seabright. *Trawling For Minnows, European Competition Policy and Agreements Between Firms*. London: Centre for Economic Policy Research, 1998.

Ocak, Nazmi. *Rekabet Hukukunda Teşebbüsler ve Teşebbüslerin Hakim Durumunun Tespiti*. İstanbul: Beta Yayınevi, 2016.

OECD. "Oligopoly Report: DAFFE/CLP (99)25," 1999.

Ölmez, Hakan Suat. *Rekabet Hukukunda Zorunlu Unsur Doktrini Ve Uygulaması*. Ankara, 2003.

Öztunalı, Aydın. *Rekabet Hukukunda Hakim Durumun Kötüye Kullanılması*. Ankara: Seçkin Yayınevi, 2014.

Öztürk, Ebru. *Türk İdare Sisteminde Rekabet Kurumunun Yeri Ve Diğer Bağımsız İdari Otoritelerle Karşılaştırılması*. Ankara, 2003.

Pınar, Hamdi. "Rekabet Hukuku ve Haksız Rekabet Hukuku İlişkisi." *Rekabet Dergisi* 15, no. 2 (2014): 59–87.

Posner, Richard A. "Oligopoly and the Antitrust Laws: A Suggested Approach." *Stanford Law Review* 21 (1969): 1562–1606.

Sabuncu, Hasan. *Birlikte Hakimiyet Kavramının Birleşme ve Devralmalar Açısından Değerlendirilmesi*. Ankara, 2003.

Şahin, Murat. *Rekabet Hukukunda Tazminat Talepleri*. 2nd ed. İstanbul: Onikilevha Yayınevi, 2013.

Sanlı, Kerem Cem. "Rekabetin Korunması Hakkında Kanun'un Özel Hukuk Alanındaki Sonuçları: Genel Bakış ve Sorunlar." In *Rekabetin Korunması Hakkında Kanun'un Özel Hukuk Alanındaki Sonuçları*, edited by Kerem Cem Sanlı, 15–82. Onikilevha Yayınevi, 2013.

Sekmen, Orhan. *Rekabet Hukukunda Tazminat Sorumluluğu*. Ankara: Bilge Yayınevi, 2013.

Shapiro, Carl. "The Theory of Business Strategy." *The RAND Journal of Economics* 20, no. 1 (1989): 125–137.

Smith, Adam. *An Inquiry into the Nature and Causes of the Wealth of Nations*, 1776.

Smith, Adam. *The Theory of Moral Sentiments*, 1759.

Sonnenschein, Hugo. "Oligopoly and Game Theory." In *The New Palgrave, A Dictionary of Economics, Vol. 3*, 705–708. New York: Palgrave Publishers, 2002.

Tekdemir, Yaşar. *AT Rekabet Hukukunda Anlaşma Yapmayı Reddetme Sorunu ve Zorunlu Unsur Doktrini: Anlaşma Yapma Yükümlülüğü Ya Da Sözleşme Serbestisinin Sınırları*. Ankara, 2003.

Tekdemir, Yaşar. "The Principle of Collective Dominance Under EC Competition Law: A New Approach to The Problem of Oligopoly." London School of Economics, 1999.

Tekinalp, Gülören, and Ünal Tekinalp. "Türk Rekabet Hukukunda Etki İlkesi." In *Prof. Dr. Tuğrul Ansay'a Armağan*, edited by Sabih Arkan and Aynur Yongalık, 325–346. Ankara: Turhan Kitabevi, 2006.

Tiryakioğlu, Bilgin. *Rekabet Hukukundan Doğan Kanunlar İhtilâfı*. Ankara, 1997.

Topçuoğlu, Metin. *Rekabet Hukuku Açısından Acentelik ve Dağıtım Sözleşmeleri*. Ankara, 2006.

Topçuoğlu, Metin. *Rekabeti Kısıtlayan Teşebbüsler Arası İşbirliği Davranışları ve Hukuki Sonuçları*. Ankara, 2001.

Topuz, Murat, and Gökhan Bakar. *On İki Banka Örneği Üzerinden Uyumlu Eylem İle Kartel Oluşturan Bankaların Hukuki Sorumluluğu*. Ankara: Seçkin Yayınevi, 2017.

Turner, Donald F. "The Definition of Agreement Under the Sherman Act: Conscious Paralellism and Refusals to Deal." *Harvard Law Review* 75, no. 4 (1962): 655–706.

Ulaş-Kısa, Seda. *Avrupa Topluluğu Rekabet Hukukunda Hâkim Durumun Rekabet Karşıtı Eylem ve İşlemlerle Kötüye Kullanılması*. Ankara, 2004.

Uluçlar, Önder Suat. *Yoğunlaşmalarda Tam İşlevsellik*. İstanbul: Onikilevha Yayınevi, 2017.

Ünlüsoy, Kürşat. *Rekabet Hukukunda Bağlama Anlaşmaları*. Ankara, 2003.

Uyanık, Pelin. *Rekabet Hukuku Açısından Delil*. Ankara, 2003.

Yağcı, Mustafa Okan. *Rekabet Kurulu'nun İnceleme ve Araştırma Usulü*. İstanbul: Vedat Kitabevi, 2018.

Yanık, Mehmet. *Rekabet Hukukunun Hakim Durum Ve Hakim Durumun Kötüye Kullanılması Uygulamalarında Piyasa Giriş Engelleri*. Ankara, 2003.

Yao, Dennis A., and Susan S. Desanti. "Game Theory and The Legal Analysis of Tacit Collusion." *The Antitrust Bulletin* 38, no. 1 (Spring 1993): 113–141.

Yüksel, Onur Yelda. *Rekabet Hukukunda Uyumlu Eylem*. Ankara, 2004.

Asst. Prof. Dr. Evrim AKGÜN*

Chapter VII Insurance Law

Günay, Barış and Yazıcı, Sena. "Turkish Insurance Law." In *Turkish Private Law*, 337–353. Edited by Korkusuz, Mehmet Refik and İpekel Kayalı, Ferna. Ankara: Seçkin Yayınları, 2020. Güner Özbek, Meltem Deniz, ed. 2019. *Insurance Law in Turkey*. 2nd edition. The Netherlands: Kluwer Law International; Kender Rayegan. *Türkiye'de Hususi Sigorta Hukuku*. 17th ed. İstanbul: Oniki Levha Yayınları, 2021; Ünan, Samim. *Türk Ticaret Kanunu Şerhi – Sigorta Hukuku – Cilt I – Genel Hükümler*. İstanbul: Oniki Levha Yayınları, 2016; Ünan, Samim. *Türk Ticaret Kanunu Şerhi – Sigorta Hukuku – Cilt II – Zarar Sigortaları*. İstanbul: Oniki Levha Yayınları, 2016; Yavaşi, Mahmut. *An Introduction to Turkish Business Law*. Bursa: Dora Yayınevi, 2015; Yazıcıoğlu, Emine and Şeker Öğüz, Zehra. *Sigorta Hukuku*. 2nd ed. İstanbul: Filiz Yayınevi, 2019.

Introductory Remarks

In life, it is always a possibility to run into unfortunate events. Regardless of age, status, or other factors, these events can happen to anyone and have negative consequences. Therefore, we, all humans, have been looking into ways to feel secure. To provide that much needed security, the idea of insurance was born. Still, it is important to bear in mind that the insurance mainly does not prevent the unfortunate events from occurring, but it helps in the aftermath by lessening the impact of their negative effects or outcomes.[1]

In this respect, insurance is and may be a necessity in every aspect of life, and busines is no exception to that. Insurance may be seen as a backup system for the businesses by transferring their risks. By concluding insurance contracts

* Corresponding author.

1 That being said, nowadays the insurance may play an important role in preventing various risks in case of some insurance types. For example, offering free mammography to women over forty in health insurance may come useful in detecting breast cancer at an early stage.

suitable to their field of activity, the businesses may continue their activities, make profit, and thrive without worrying about unfortunate events and their negative consequences.

In this chapter, the overview of the historical background and the sources of the insurance law in Turkey will be given firstly. Afterwards the insurance contract will be defined along with its essential elements. There are different ways to categorize the insurance contracts; hence, the four most common categories will be explained. Then comes the second part where the conclusion of an insurance contract analyzed thoroughly. Since the insurance is a particularly unique sort of contract, there are different types of duties and obligations for the parties, which will be featured broadly. The next part will answer the question on how the insurance contract may extinct. Explanations about various ways that end the contract such as expiry, withdrawal, and termination will be examined. Finally, a brief overview of the scope of coverage for a few common forms of insurances that are often used by businesses will be provided.

§ Part I General Information on Insurance and Insurance Contract

I. Historical Background of Insurance

Insurance has its origins in Code of Hammurabi (around 1700 BC), which shows us that the idea of mitigating the consequences of the risk is dating back to ancient civilizations. However, the concept of insurance as we know today originated from the maritime trade. First insurance policy was issued for the goods that were carried by the ship named "Santa Clara", which set sail from Genoa to Mallorca in 1347.[2] The concept of insurance was extended to the land only after a major fire catastrophe, namely the Great Fire of London, which happened in 1666 and nearly destructed the entire city.[3]

When we come to the reign of Ottoman Empire, even though there have been some other organizations for the same purpose such as ahi-order (*ahilik*) and guilds (*loncalar*), insurance mainly started with minorities acting as insurance agents offering fire insurance contracts secured by some of the foreign insurance

---

2 Huriye Kubilay, *Uygulamalı Özel Sigorta Hukuku* (İzmir: Barış Yayınları, 2003), 12.

3 Malcolm Clarke, "An Introduction to Insurance Contract Law," in *Research Handbook on International Insurance Law and Regulation*, ed. Julian Burling and Kevin Lazarus (Cheltenham: Edward Elgar Publishing, 2012), 10; Rayegan Kender, *Türkiye'de Hususi Sigorta Hukuku* (İstanbul: Oniki Levha Yayınları, 2021), 19-20.

companies. In 1863 the Code of Maritime Law (*Ticaret-i Bahriye Kanunnamesi*) which was translated from the second book of the French Code of Commerce dated 1807, came into effect.[4] After that, a big fire happened in 1870's Beyoğlu, a prestigious neighborhood of İstanbul at that time, led to the foundation of the first local public insurance company of Ottoman (*Osmanlı Umum Sigorta Şirketi*).[5] Later, after the foundation of the Turkish Republic in 1923, Anatolian Limited Turkish Insurance Company (*Anadolu Anonim Türk Sigorta Şirketi*) was established in 1925 as the first insurance company of Republic and National Reinsurance Company (*Milli Reasürans*) in 1929 as the first reinsurance company.[6]

II. Sources of Insurance Law

A. *Legislation*

The sixth book of the Turkish Commercial Code (no. 6102) is dedicated to insurance law where the insurance contracts are regulated. There is also Insurance Activities Act (no. 5684) which regulates the insurance companies and the industry (hereinafter referred to as IAA).[7] These two regulations are the main sources of the Turkish Insurance Law.

Furthermore, according to the gap-filling article of TCC, related provisions of Turkish Code of Obligations (no. 6098) shall be applied to insurance contracts, if there are no provisions available in the TCC (art. 1451).

In addition to TCC, there are other provisions to be applied that regulate insurance contracts, such as Act on Consumer Protection (no. 6502, hereinafter referred to as ACP), Highway Traffic Act (no. 2918), Catastrophe Insurance Act (no. 6305), and Agricultural Insurance Act (no. 5363). And also, some other acts contain various provisions in regard to insurance, *inter alia*.

---

4 İlknur Uluğ Cicim, "Ticaret-i Bahriye Kanunnamesi'ne Göre Navlun Sözleşmeleri," *Cedrus the Journal of MCRI* 4 (2016): 396.

5 Kubilay, *Sigorta*, 13.

6 There is also reinsurance, which can be defined simply as the insurance for the insurance companies themselves. However, since the reinsurance contracts may be concluded only between the insurer and reinsurer and have a lot of different principles than the insurance, this sort of contract will not be covered under this chapter.

7 Although this Act mainly regulates the insurance activities, there are also some provisions regarding the insurance contracts within the Act.

B. *By-Laws*

In order to regulate in detail the issues, which were basically addressed within laws, by-laws are implemented. In insurance law, these by-laws can be exemplified as "By-Law on Insurance Agencies", "By-Law on Private Healthcare Insurance", "By-Law on Insurance and Reinsurance Brokers" and "By-Law on Implementation Principles for Insurances Relating Personal Loans".

The related provisions of acts and by-laws constitute the (official) regulations on insurance.

C. *General Terms and Conditions of Insurance* (Sigorta Genel Şartları)

General terms and conditions (GTC) are accepted as a part of the insurance contracts, according to the article 11/1 of IAA. GTC are drafted and tailored specifically for each type of insurance contract by Insurance and Pension Regulatory and Supervisory Agency. The provisions of the GTC cannot be against the mandatory provisions of the TCC and other relevant laws.[8] Examples include General Terms and Conditions on Fire Insurance, on Life Insurance, and on Indemnity Insurance, among others.

D. *Special Terms*

The contractual parties of the insurance can agree on adding new terms or revising the existing ones unless such terms are regulated as mandatory in the official regulations. The parties can even add special terms to the contract detaching from the provisions of the TCC as long as their additions and/or revisions do not contradict with the protective provisions of the TCC, which can be found under the articles of 1452, 1486 and 1520.[9] Special terms are neither regulations, nor GTC, they belong to a separate group among the contractual terms.

---

8 Mehmet Bahtiyar, "Sigorta Poliçesi Genel Koşulları," *Banka ve Ticaret Hukuku Dergisi* 19, 2 (1997): 100; Ali Bozer, *Sigorta Hukuku* (Ankara: Banka ve Ticaret Hukuku Enstitüsü Yayınları, 1965), 130; Haydar Arseven, *Sigorta Hukuku* (İstanbul: Beta Yayınevi, 1991), 33.

9 In the doctrine, it is controversial whether the parties could change some of the rules of the GTC by special terms. One opinion defends that the amendment of the rules of the GTC is not possible. See, Arseven, *Sigorta*, 33. Also it is defended that adding special terms to the insurance contract is only possible for the subjects that are not regulated by the relevant GTC. See, Şaban Kayıhan, *Sigorta Sözleşmesinde Prim Ödeme Borcu* (Ankara: Seçkin Yayınevi, 2004), 39; Reşat Atabek, "Sigorta Akdinin Yorumu," *Sigorta Hukuku Dergisi,* Vol. 1, Iss. 2 (1982): 137. However, according to the opposing opinion,

E. *Judicial Sources*

The decisions of the judicial bodies on the insurance contracts are of importance in terms of sources of insurance law; especially those of Regional Courts of Appeal, which are the second instance courts, and Court of Cassation as the highest instance court. Furthermore, there are unifying decisions of the Court of Cassation, which unify the conflicting decisions that were rendered by the different chambers of the High Court on the same subject.

III. Definition of the Insurance Contract

The insurance contract is defined as a contract under which the insurer promises, in exchange for a premium, to indemnify a loss caused by the materialization of a danger (risk), or which, the insurer promises, in exchange for a premium, to make payment or to fulfill other performances based on the life span of one or more persons, or the occurrence of certain events during their lives (art. 1401 of TCC).

IV. Essential Elements of the Insurance Contract

A. *Insurable Interest*

Insurable interest is a vital component of an insurance contract, and the interest is defined as a relation between a person and an active (asset).[10] For example, to take out a property insurance, having an insurable interest which is an economic interest in the property, is a necessity.[11]

The article 1408 of TCC requires an insurable interest to exist in all insurance contracts at all times: from the time of conclusion through the extinction of the contract. If there is no insurable interest at the time of concluding the contract, then the contract will be null and void. If the insurable interest ceased

as the GTC are an administrative act and not a part of a legislative act, the parties should be allowed to change the content as long as the amended provisions are not against the protective provisions. Accepting the latter would prevent the legal effect of an administrative act from exceeding that of a legislative act. See, Işıl Ulaş, *Uygulamalı Zarar Sigortaları Hukuku* (Ankara: Turhan Kitabevi, 2012), 66–67; Samim Ünan, *Hayat Sigortası* (İstanbul: Beta Yayınları, 1998), 227; Mehmet Bahtiyar, "Sigorta Poliçesi Özel Koşulları, Genel Koşullardan Ayırdedilmesi ve Bazı Sorunlar," in *Prof. Dr. Ali Bozer'e Armağan* (Ankara: Banka ve Ticaret Hukuku Araştırma Enstitüsü, 1998), 143.

10 Kender, *Sigorta*, 184.

11 Malcolm Clarke, *Law of Insurance Contracts*, 6th ed. (Great Britain: Informa, 2009), 17.

to exist within the contract period, then again, the contract becomes null and void thereupon.

That being said, if someone with a part of a property or a partial right over a property has taken out the insurance for the common interest, the contract will not be null and void for lacking insurable interest of that person on the whole property or right over property. According to the article 1455 of TCC, the exceeding part of the insurance coverage shall be deemed to have been made in favor of the remaining shareholders if they have the same kind of interest as has the policyholder.

B. Risk

The most essential aspect of the insurance contract is the risk, which is an event that may materialize in the future. If and when it materializes, it causes damage and loss or an inconvenience to a person's needs.[12]

By its definition, for the risk to be insured there should be an uncertainty whether it will be materialized or not. In this respect, there is a difference in the concept of the risk between life insurance and the other types of insurances: In the life insurance, it is guaranteed that the risk going to materialize, since every human has a limited time in life but for other insurance types it is not guaranteed that the risk is going to materialize, like for insurance on the theft or accident. That being said, as the life span of people cannot be known, there is still not a guarantee that the risk will be materialized during the contract period.

In addition to that, by the time the insurance contract was concluded the risk should not be already materialized, nor it should become impossible to materialize. Otherwise, such risk cannot be insured. However, it is possible to start the insurer's obligation to carry risk from an earlier date than the date of the conclusion of the contract ("retroactive insurance"). According to the article 1458 of TCC, if the contract was concluded retroactively but the risk was materialized or the possibility of it was ceased already, then there are different scenarios to consider: The first possibility is the one where neither of the parties are aware of the materialization, or that the possibility of it was ceased. In this case, the contract is valid, and the insurer is obliged to pay indemnity. The second possibility is the one where both of the parties are aware of the materialization, or

12 Meltem Deniz Güner Özbek, "Part II – Chapter 1 (Generalities)," in *Insurance Law in Turkey*, ed. Meltem Deniz Güner Özbek. 2nd ed. (The Netherlands: Kluwer Law International, 2019), para. 150; Emine Yazıcıoğlu and Zehra Şeker Öğüz, *Sigorta Hukuku* (İstanbul: Filiz Yayınevi, 2019), 50.

that the possibility of it was ceased, under which it, then, causes the contract to be invalid. The third and last possibility is the one, where only the policyholder or the insured is aware of the situation, but the insurer is not. In this case, the insurer will not be bound by the contract but entitled to collect the premium.

In terms of insurance technic, it is not possible to insure all the risks that can be faced. It is a necessity to determine and limit the scope of insurance coverage in the insurance contracts. There are two main ways of drafting contract from the risk's aspect. The first type is called "all-risks" and it refers to an insurance contract which covers all the risks unless they are explicitly excluded. The second type is called "named perils" and it provides coverage only for the risks which are explicitly named in the contract and nothing else. TCC accepts named perils type of insurance (art. 1409/1), whereas IAA accepts a version of all risks type (art. 11/4). Since TCC is *lex posterior* and the insurance contract shall be regulated only under TCC but not IAA, the article 1409 of TCC shall be applicable in the first place.[13] Also, being a part of the insurance contract, in the GTC there are some risks commonly excluded from the coverage of the relevant insurance type. The risks of war, hostilities, civil war, armed conflict, riot, and insurrection may be given as example.[14]

Insurer has an obligation to carry the risk, which is regulated under the article 1421 of TCC.[15] According to the article 1429 of TCC, unless otherwise agreed, the insurer shall cover the loss if materialization of the risk is a result of a negligent act. Yet, in case of a deliberate act, in other words, if the loss is caused intentionally, the insurer shall not cover those losses.[16] This is a mandatory provision and also in line with the principles of the insurance law. In the article 1429 of TCC, the policyholder, insured, beneficiary, and the persons that they are legally liable for, whose negligence or intent are sought for the insurer's obligation.

---

13 Samim Ünan, *Türk Ticaret Kanunu Şerhi – Sigorta Hukuku – Cilt I – Genel Hükümler* (İstanbul: Oniki Levha Yayınları, 2016), 95–96. Contra. F. Dilek Kabukçuoğlu Özer, *Sigortacılık Kanunu Şerhi* (İstanbul: Oniki Levha Yayınları, 2012), 16.

14 Güner Özbek, "Part II – Chapter 1 (Generalities)," para. 154.

15 Under this chapter, see supra: *Obligation to Carry the Risk.*

16 The only exception to this is the case in the life insurance. Under the article 1503 of TCC, the insurer is obliged to pay the insurance sum if the insured commits suicide and dies at earliest after three years of the life insurance contract being concluded. In addition to that, if the insured's suicide resulted in death due to a mental disorder, then the insurer is obliged to pay without even waiting for the three-year period to be over.

V. Categories of Insurance Contracts

When it is tried to classify the insurance contracts, it can be seen there are different categories. The most frequently used categories are briefly explained below.

A. Insurance of Fixed Sums – Indemnity Insurance

Under the satisfaction of the need criterion, the insurance contracts are divided into two main different types: "Insurance of fixed sums" and "Indemnity insurance".

In indemnity insurance, the insurer is committed to paying the loss the risk has caused. Whereas in the insurance of fixed sums, the insurer is committed to paying the agreed insurance sum regardless of whether the insured has suffered from damage.[17]

The insurer's obligation to pay insurance indemnity or insurance sum commences after the risk occurs. Upon materialization of the risk, if there is an insurance of fixed sums, then the insurer shall pay the agreed amount of the insurance sum. However, in indemnity insurances, the principle of the prohibition of unjust enrichment is valid. Hence, the insurer is only required to pay the amount necessary to compensate for the loss, nothing more. In this case, the insurer shall only pay the amount of the loss and the maximum amount they pay is limited to the amount agreed upon by the parties in the insurance contract.

B. Active Insurance – Passive Insurance

Active insurance and passive insurance appear in indemnity insurance.[18] In active insurance, the insurer is obliged to compensate the value of the property (e.g. a house, an automobile, or a receivable), whereas in passive insurance, the insurer is obliged to compensate the debts of the policyholder or insured, in other words, to prevent the probable decrease of their assets by providing coverage (e.g. liability insurance).[19]

---

17 Helmut Heiss, "Indemnity Insurance," in *The Max Planck Encyclopedia of European Private Law*, Vol. 2, ed. Jürgen Basedow, Klaus J. Hopt, Reinhard Zimmermann and Andreas Stier (Oxford: Oxford University Press, 2012), 860.

18 Kender, *Sigorta*, 236.

19 Kender, *Sigorta*, 236–240; Güner Özbek, "Part II – Chapter 1 (Generalities)," para. 149.

C. *Compulsory Insurance – Voluntary Insurance*

In the field of insurance law, the main principle is the freedom of contract. Thus, the parties are free to choose concluding a contract or not; however, that does not suggest that the parties are completely free without any limitations. Pursuant to the article 13/1 of IAA, the President may impose compulsory insurances where they deem necessary for public interest. In such a scenario, the insurance companies do not have a choice but to provide such compulsory insurances in the particular branch which they have a license (art. 1483 of TCC). This also means a compulsion for the counterparty, so the persons, who fit the definition of the policyholder for that specific insurance according to the relevant regulation, are also required to conclude the insurance contract (e.g. Compulsory earthquake insurance, Compulsory liability insurance for motor vehicles, Compulsory liability insurance for marine environment caused by shore facilities, Compulsory personal accident insurance for highway transportation passengers, Compulsory liability insurance concerning medical malpractice). If there is no such limitation brought by the regulations, then the parties are not obliged to conclude the insurance contract, which means, in principle, the conclusion of the contract is voluntary.

D. *Indemnity Insurance – Insurance of Persons*

Within the framework of TCC, there are two types of insurance contract: "indemnity insurances" and "insurance of persons", which have also sub-branches. According to the systematic of TCC, the classification of the insurance contract is as following:

- Indemnity Insurance
  - o Property Insurance
  - o Liability Insurance
- Insurance of Persons
  - o Life Insurance
  - o Personal Accident Insurance
  - o Sickness and Health Insurance

§ Part II Conclusion of the Insurance Contract

I. Offer and Acceptance

Similar to any other type of contract, there shall be an offer and an acceptance (mutual assent) for an insurance contract to be concluded.

That being said, according to the article 1405 of TCC, if a person who wishes to conclude an insurance contract with the insurer submits a written application and not get rejected by the insurer within 30 days as of the date of the application, the insurance contract shall be deemed to have been concluded. In this case, payments which made at the time of offer are counted as payment for the first premium.

II. Form of the Contract

The principle of no requirement as to form also applies the insurance contracts, as a rule. However, if the contract is both a consumer transaction and an insurance contract at the same time, and the premium is paid by installments, then the contract has to be concluded in written form pursuant to the article 17/3 of ACP.

Furthermore, insurance contracts may be concluded as a distance contract, which means the parties may conclude the contract in any other way than face to face, for example over phone, via e-mail or a website.

III. Parties of the Insurance Contract

A. Insurer

The insurer is a legal person who concludes the insurance contract, and carries, therefore, the risk. Under the article 3 of IAA, the insurer shall be established either as a joint stock company or as a cooperative. Insurers shall not be engaged in other businesses except insurance transactions and businesses, which are directly related to insurance operations. The criteria, which shall be met to operate as an insurer, and the organization of these companies are also regulated in the IAA. According to the article 5 of IAA, to commence their operations, insurers have to obtain a license for each insurance branch, in which they prefer to operate. Licenses obtained are registered to the Turkish Trade Registry. The license may be cancelled in the cases which are mentioned in the article 7 of IAA. These regulations indicate that the insurance sector is extensively controlled by the State.

B. Policyholder

Policyholder is the person who concludes the insurance contract with the insurer. Policyholder can either be a natural person or a legal person. They are subject to obligations and also have the rights arising from that contract. That being said, in some cases, the rights resulting from the insurance contract may be assigned to not to the policyholder but to other people.

According to ACP, a person is regarded as a consumer if they act for non-commercial or non-professional purposes.[20] If someone concludes the insurance contract for non-commercial or non-professional purposes (such as taking out fire insurance for their home), then they are both a policyholder and a consumer at the same time. In this case, appropriate provisions of consumer law will also be applicable to insurance contracts.[21]

C. *Relevant Third Parties*

1. *Insured (in Indemnity Insurance)*

If the interest insured by the contract belongs to someone other than the policyholder, then this person shall be named as 'insured'. In indemnity insurances, the risk materializes in the interest of the insured. The insured ones receive the rights arising from the insurance contract, since they are the ones who suffer from the loss or damage.[22]

2. *Insured (in Life Insurance)*

Insured in life insurance is a natural person whose life is insured. The insurer is obliged to pay a fixed sum in case of death, or in case the insured survives within the period of the contract. Insured may be the policyholder themselves or a different person.

On the other hand, the beneficiary needs to have an insurable interest in the survival of the insured. This insurable interest may be either material (pecuniary) or immaterial (non-pecuniary). The fixed sum may be paid to the insured if they are also appointed as a beneficiary.

---

20 In addition, insurance contracts are explicitly recognized as consumer transactions in the article 3/1 sub-para. l of ACP.

21 For further information on applicable provisions see, Samim Ünan, *Sigorta Tüketici Hukuku* (İstanbul: Oniki Levha, 2016); Evrim Akgün, "6502 Sayılı Tüketicinin Korunması Hakkında Kanun'un Sigorta Sözleşmelerine Etkisi Üzerine Bir İnceleme," in *Prof. Dr. Feridun Yeniseye'e Armağan* (İstanbul: Beta Yayınları, 2014). Also see, Helmut Heiss, "Insurance Contract Law Between Business Law and Consumer Protection," in *General Reports of the XVIIIth Congress of the International Academy of Comparative Law*, ed. Karen B. Brown and David V. Snyder (Dordrecht: Springer, 2012), 335–353.

22 Meltem Deniz Güner Özbek and Gülfer Meriç, "Part II – Chapter 3 (Parties to the Insurance Contract)," in *Insurance Law in Turkey*, ed. Meltem Deniz Güner Özbek. 2nd ed. (The Netherlands: Kluwer Law International, 2019), para. 205.

According to the article 1490/2 of TCC, additionally to the beneficiary's insurable interest in the survival of the insured, the written consent of the insured or its legal representative is required, if the contract covers the death of the insured and the insurance sum exceeds the regular funeral expenses. Furthermore, if the insured is over the age of 15, their consent shall also be obtained. In this case, a life insurance contract taken out without prior authorization shall be invalid if the consent is not subsequently given.

3. *Beneficiary*

The beneficiary is the person who has the right to claim and collect the insurance sum after the risk materializes. They can be a natural or a legal person and will be appointed by the policyholder. There may be more than one beneficiary. For the case that their shares are not specified in the insurance policy, the article 1494 of TCC provides an equal rate for all the beneficiaries. Moreover, a share not collected by any one of the beneficiaries shall be added to the shares of the others.

To enable to pay insurance sum to the rightful owner, the insurer shall be notified of the appointment. According to the article 1494/2 of TCC, if no beneficiary is appointed by the policyholder for the contracts covering the risk of death, the contract shall be deemed as made in favor of the legal successors of the policyholder. However, in the contracts covering the risk of survival, then the contract shall be deemed as made in favor of the insured.

As above mentioned, the beneficiary needs to have an insurable interest in the survival of the insured, according to the article 1490/2 of TCC. In addition to that, if the contract covers the death of the insured and the insurance sum exceeds the regular funeral expenses, the written consent of the insured or its legal representative is also required.

4. *Affected Party (in Liability Insurance)*

The affected party is the person who is not a party to the insurance contract but affected by the risk, which was materialized by the policyholder or by the insured themselves (if the contract is concluded in favor of them). For example, if a surgeon causes bodily harm to their patient due to negligence, the patient is victim here and will be named as affected party.

The TCC provides the affected party with a right of direct action for all types of liability insurances.

5. *New Holder of Insured Interest*

According to the article 1470 of TCC, the insurance contract shall terminate if the holder of the insured interest changes. However, the parties are allowed to change this by agreement. In the case that parties agree, the contract may not automatically become terminated when the holder of the insured interest changes. In such a case, the insurance contract will then be carried on with the new holder for the remaining period of the contract, with the holder obtaining the title of the policyholder hereafter.

6. Holder of the Right in rem

Regarding the property insurance, there can be a holder of the right *in rem*. According to the article 1456 of TCC, if an insurance contract aims to provide coverage to the ownership interest over a property charged with a restricted right *in rem* such as a mortgage or usufruct, the rights of the holder of the right *in rem* (e.g. creditors) continues on the insurance indemnity, unless otherwise provided by the law. If the risk occurs, the insurer shall not pay the insurance indemnity without consent of all of the holders of the right *in rem*.

IV. Legal Restrictions on Insurance Contract

Pursuant to the article 1404 of TCC, the insurance contract cannot be concluded to cover a loss resulting from breach of protective provisions, moral values, public order or personal rights; otherwise, it shall be null and void.

Within the framework of TCC, protective provisions are regulated under three articles: The article 1452 regards the general terms, the article 1486 covers indemnity insurances and lastly the article 1520 regards insurance of persons. In this context, it should be mentioned that there are two types of protective provisions: Absolutely mandatory provisions are rules that the parties can by no means deviate from, even if the contract terms are in favor of the policyholder, the insured or the beneficiary. Absolutely mandatory provisions can be found under the articles 1452/1–2, 1486/1–2 and 1520/1–2 of TCC. And, the relatively mandatory provisions are the rules that cannot be changed by the contract only if the deviation has an adverse effect on the rights of the policyholder, the insured and the beneficiary. Relatively mandatory provisions can be found under the articles 1452/3, 1486/3 and 1520/3 of TCC.

Moreover, according to the last sentence of the article 1429/1 of TCC, the parties may not agree on insurance indemnity or insurance sum to be paid if the risk materializes with the intent of the policyholder, the insured and the persons, whose actions are legally liable to those aforementioned. It is also regulated as mandatory provision under the article 1452/1 of TCC.

V. Burden of Proof

As it is stated above, it is not possible to insure all the risks and because of that some of the risks will and may be left out of the insurance coverage. Under the article 1409/2 of TCC, the burden of proof about the risk which was materialized is outside of scope of the insurance coverage lies with the insurer.

VI. Concluding the Contract with the Assistance of the Insurance Intermediaries

Distribution of the insurance is mostly established by the insurance intermediaries,[23] since it is not always attainable for the parties themselves to take out the insurance contract. In Turkish Insurance Law, there are two types of intermediaries: "Insurance agent" and "Insurance broker".

A. Insurance Agent

Similar to the definition of agent within the scope of TCC, the article 2/1 sub-para. m of IAA defines the insurance agent as a person[24];

> *who has adopted it as a profession to intermediate to insurance contracts in the name and account of the insurance company for a permanent term within a specific place or region based on a contract without holding a title such as commercial representative, commercial attorney, sales official or employee, or to perform such activity on behalf of the insurance company and who carry out the preparatory works before the conclusion of the contract and assist during the implementation of the contract and payment of claims.*

According to the article 21/18 of IAA, the provisions of TCC regarding agents, which are regulated between the articles 102 and 123, shall also apply to insurance agents.

The insurance agent could either be a real or a legal person. To be eligible to operate, it is mandatory for them to be enrolled in a particular registry (*Levha*), which is kept by the Union of Chambers and Commodity Exchanges of Turkey. Detailed regulations on insurance agents can be found in the article 23 of IAA and Insurance Agents By-Law.

---

23 Meltem Deniz Güner Özbek and İlyas Gölcüklü, "Part VII (Insurance Intermediaries)," in *Insurance Law in Turkey*, ed. Meltem Deniz Güner Özbek. 2nd ed. (The Netherlands: Kluwer Law International, 2019), 526.

24 The translation of this provision of IAA is quoted from the website of Turkish Insurance Association (www.tsb.org.tr), accessed 20.03.2021.

Insurance agent operates based on the agency contract they conclude with the insurance companies. There are two subgroups of insurance agencies. The first type is only allowed to carry out preparatory works before the contract and assist the parties through the implementation period of the contract. The second type is explicitly authorized to conclude the insurance contract on behalf of the insurer, in addition to the above-mentioned duties of the first. The latter may also be additionally authorized to collect the premium.

B. Insurance Broker

According to the article 2/1 sub-para. d of IAA, insurance broker is defined as a person[25];

> *representing the parties who want to conclude an insurance or reinsurance contract, acting impartially and independently in the selection of companies with which such contracts are to be made, observing the rights and benefits of the people who want to purchase coverage, having adopted it as a profession to carry out preparatory works before the conclusion of the contract, and to assist if necessary during the implementation of the contract or payment of claims.*

Both real and legal persons can be an insurance broker. To operate as an insurance broker, they have to obtain a brokerage license from Ministry of Treasury and Finance. Detailed regulations on insurance brokers can be found in the article 21 of IAA as well as Insurance and Reinsurance Brokers By-Law.

In parallel with the insurance agent, insurance brokers could conclude the insurance contract on behalf of the policyholder, or pay the premium, if they are explicitly authorized.

§ Part III Duties and Obligations of the Parties

I. Insurer's Duties and Obligations

A. Obligation to Carry the Risk (Art. 1421–1422 of TCC)

The insurer is obliged to carry the risk. According to the article of 1421 of TCC, unless otherwise agreed, the whole premium or the first installment of the premium shall be paid by the policyholder for the commencement of the liability of the insurer. Thus, if there is a non-payment, the liability of the insurer does

---

25 The translation of this provision of IAA is quoted from the website of Turkish Insurance Association (www.tsb.org.tr), accessed 20.03.2021.

not begin and if the risk occurs within this period of non-payment, the insurer will not be liable, even though the insurance contract is already concluded. The exception is the regulation for the transport insurances about the goods carried by land or the sea. For relevant insurances, the insurer will be liable upon conclusion of the insurance contract even before the payment of the first installment.

B. Pre-Contractual Information Duty (Art. 1423 of TCC)

The aim of this duty is to let the policyholder know about all the important aspects of the contract (*i.e.* the scope of the coverage, their duties and rights), since they unlikely have understanding on the concepts of insurance law. It will assist the policyholders to take out an insurance contract fitting to their needs. That is why before taking out the insurance contract, the insurer has a duty to inform the prospective policyholder. However, this duty is not limited to pre-contractual period: The insurer shall inform the policyholder also during the policy period about important changes.

According to the article 1423 of TCC, this duty of the insurer and its agent shall be fulfilled in written form. If the pre-contractual information duty is unfulfilled, then the policyholder has a right to object to the conclusion of the contract within 14 days.[26] The burden of proof regarding the fulfillment of this duty lies with the insurer. There is also a similar regulation in By-Law on the Duty of Information in Insurance Contracts, which is based on the article 11/3 of IAA. According to the article 7 of this By-Law, if the duty is not fulfilled correctly, the policyholder may terminate the insurance contract and also claim compensation if they suffered any damage. According to the article 8 of the same By-Law, the policyholder shall be given a copy of the information form, the content of which is determined by the Undersecretariat of Treasury in detail.

C. Obligation to Deliver the Insurance Policy (Art. 1424–1425 of TCC)

The insurer shall issue an insurance policy and deliver it to the policyholder either in 24 hours or 15 days. The length of period changes based on how the parties have taken out the insurance contract: If it is concluded by the insurer themselves or by

26 However, it is unclear when the fourteen days would begin and what the "right to object" would entail in insurance law. For more detailed discussion on this subject see also, Ünan, *Cilt I*, 239–241; Meltem Deniz Güner Özbek, "Part II – Chapter 3 (Formation of the Contract)," in *Insurance Law in Turkey*, ed. Meltem Deniz Güner Özbek. 2nd ed. (The Netherlands: Kluwer Law International, 2019), para. 192.

their agent, the insurer is then obliged to deliver it within 24 hours from the conclusion of the contract. However, in other cases, they may deliver it within 15 days. In the preamble for the article 1424 of TCC, the circumstances counted as "other cases" are defined as concluding the contract with a broker, or with an agent who is not authorized to conclude the contract on behalf of the insurer. If the insurer fails to deliver the insurance policy on due time, they will be, then, held accountable for the loss arising from the late delivery of the policy. This obligation has a close relation with the policyholder's obligation to pay premium stated in the article 1431 and with the insurer's obligation to carry the risk stated in the article 1421. Unless otherwise agreed, according to the article 1421, the premium or the first installment shall be paid by the policyholder to begin the liability of the insurer. According to the article 1431, the premium shall be paid upon conclusion of the insurance contract and in exchange of the delivery of the insurance policy. When these provisions taken together, it can be seen that without delivering the policy, the policyholder does not need to pay the premium, correspondingly, without paying the premium, the liability of the insurer does not begin. In a situation like this, if the risk materializes actually the insurer has no obligation to pay. However, considering the article 1424, the insurer will be liable for losses.

Pursuant to the article 1425 of TCC, the insurance policy shall set out the respective rights of the parties, provisions relating to default, GTC and special conditions if there are any. It shall be drafted in a comprehensible and easily readable format.

Since there are no requirements concerning the form of the insurance contracts, the policy constitutes evidence for the existence of the insurance contract.[27] If the policy contains terms that are not consistent or contradict the proposal or the mutual agreement of the parties, such terms become invalid, in case they are disadvantageous to the policyholder, the insured, or the beneficiary.

D. Obligation to Pay Expenses (Art. 1426 of TCC)

The insurer should pay the reasonable expenses made either by the policyholder, the insured, or the beneficiary for the determining the extent of the risk occurred, or the amount of the insurance indemnity, or sum. As long as the expenses are reasonable, the insurer is obliged to pay even if the expenses are ultimately turned out to be in vain.

27 Barış Günay and Sena Yazıcı, "Turkish Insurance Law," in *Turkish Private Law*, ed. Mehmet Refik Korkusuz and Ferna İpekel Kayalı (Ankara: Seçkin Yayınları, 2020), 345.

This obligation shall be fulfilled after the risk materializes. The expenses for the laboratory, technic reports, and medical evaluation can be given as example in this scope.

E. Obligation to Pay Indemnity or Fixed Sum (Art. 1427–1429 of TCC)

In indemnity insurance, upon materialization of the risk, the compensation will be paid for the actual loss of the insured, since there is a principle of prohibition of unjust enrichment for this type of insurance. On the other hand, in insurance of fixed sums, insured sum will be paid by the insurer after the risk materializes. In this type of insurance, the amount of actual loss will not usually get evaluated because the risk does not always cause damage or loss. For example, in a life insurance, if the contract is taken out against the risk of the insured's life, and at the end of the policy period the insured is still alive, the risk is, then, materialized without causing any damage. That is why the insurer will pay not the actual loss, but the insured sum.

According to the article 1427/1 of TCC, unless otherwise agreed (i.e. providing for restitution as in case of a repair policy), the insurance indemnity shall be paid in cash.

Under the article 1427/2 of TCC, this obligation shall be due upon materialization of the risk and when the documents related to the risk are given to the insurer and lastly when the insurer has completed the relevant investigation. In any case, the obligation shall be due within 45 days for indemnity insurance and 15 days for insurance of persons, starting from the date of which the insurer is notified of the materialization of the risk. However, if the investigation is delayed because of a fault that cannot be attributed to the insurer, this period shall not begin to run. In case the investigation is not finalized within 3 months as of the date of notification made according to the article 1446 of TCC,[28] the insurer shall pay at least 50 % of the loss or the fixed sum in advance.

When the payment falls due, the insurer will be automatically in default without any notification.

If there is a partial loss, unless otherwise agreed, the insurance indemnity paid for this part shall be deducted from the sum insured. This rule is applicable for all the insurance types except liability insurance.

28 Under this chapter, see infra: *After Materialization of the Risk.*

II. Policyholder's Duties and Obligations

A. Obligation to Pay Premium (Art. 1430–1434 of TCC)

Premium can be defined as an amount of money, which is paid to the insurer in exchange for carrying the risk. In insurance contracts, the policyholder is the one, who is obliged to pay the premium. The insurance premium shall be paid in advance; yet the parties are allowed to pay in installments if they agree so. Also, the insurance premium shall be paid in cash. The payment shall be made to the insurer themselves or to an insurance agent who is explicitly authorized to collect the premium.[29]

The importance of the premium lays in its relation to the insurer's obligation to carry the risk. Unless otherwise agreed, the premium or the first installment shall be paid by the policyholder for the insurer's liability to begin. According to the article 1431/1 of TCC, the premium needs to be paid upon conclusion of the contract and in exchange of the delivery of the insurance policy. There is an exception for the transportation insurances about the goods carried by land or the sea; in this case the premium shall be paid at the time of conclusion, even if the insurance policy is not issued yet.

In case the parties agreed on having the premium in installments, upon materialization of the risk, the corresponding sum of the premium to the insurance indemnity or insurance sum becomes due. The insurer may deduct the insurance premium due from the insurance indemnity or insurance sum to be paid. However, according to the article 1480 of TCC, in the liability insurance the insurer is not allowed to set off the insurance indemnity against any sum due, which means they shall pay the insurance indemnity to the injured party without cutting back.

Pursuant to the article 1432 of TCC, the insurance premium shall be paid at the policyholder's address indicated in the contract, but the parties may agree otherwise, since the place of payment is not regulated under protective provisions.

It is also possible for the risk to change after the contract's conclusion, as a result of changes on the elements of the risk. In this case, the risk can either be reduced or aggravated. The reduction of the risk is regulated under the

29 Clarke, *Law of Insurance Contracts*, 380. Also, under this chapter, see supra: *Insurance Agent*.

article 1433 of TCC.[30] If this is the case, then the premium shall be decreased or reimbursed.

If the policyholder fails to pay the premium, the sanctions will change depending on which premium the policyholder failed to pay. According to the article 1434 of TCC, if the policyholder fails to pay the full amount of the premium or the first installment in due time, then the insurer may withdraw from the contract within 3 months as long as the payment is not made. The insurer may claim the unpaid premium via litigation. However, if they do not claim it within due time (in 3 months), then the insurance contract is deemed as withdrawn. On the other hand, if the unpaid premium is a subsequent installment which became due, the insurer shall notify the policyholder with a registered letter or a notice served by the notary that they should pay the premium within 10 days, otherwise the insurance contract will be deemed as terminated at the end of that period. If two notifications were sent to the policyholder within one premium period, the insurer may terminate the contract, which will be effective at the end of that premium period.

B. Duties

Duties are deeds which are different than the obligations. Contrary to the obligations (e.g. paying the premium), when breached the duties are not suable. That being said, if the duties are breached; the policyholder, the insured, or the beneficiary may face a loss. This loss could be either in a form of a decrease in the insurance indemnity or insurance sum and getting paid partially or in a form of non-payment, which means that the insurer is no longer obliged to pay the insurance indemnity or insurance sum.

Duties can also be regulated as mandatory in parallel with the obligations. Duties between the articles 1435 and 1449 of TCC are mandatory under the article 1452/3 and cannot be amended against the policyholder, the insured, and the beneficiary. Also, the article 1471/2 of TCC, which regulates a duty distinctively formed for property insurance, is mandatory under the article 1486/3, and cannot be amended against the insured.

---

30 Aggravation of risk is regulated in the articles 1444 and 1445 of TCC within the scope of the duty of disclosure in the contract period. Also, under this chapter, see infra: *Duty of Disclosure*.

1. *Duty of Disclosure*

Duty of disclosure could be examined at three different stages of the insurance contract: a) before concluding the contract, b) during the contract and c) at the time of materialization of risk.

a. *Before concluding the contract*

Similar to the insurer's pre-contractual information duty, the policyholder is also needed to disclose important matters to the insurer.[31] Pursuant to the article 1435 of TCC, important matters are such circumstances that can influence the insurer's decision to conclude the contract under different conditions or not conclude the contract at all, if they would have known these matters. The policyholder is obliged to disclose all important matters before the contract is finalized. They need to declare important matters they have already known or should know.[32] The matters asked by the insurer verbally or in writing shall be deemed as important until proven to be on the contrary.

In the case that the insurer gives a list of questions to the policyholder, they shall solely answer those questions; it means that they do not need to declare anything else on their own. On the other hand, if policyholder withholds information about important matters not included in the insurers list in bad faith, they may face exposure of sanctions (art. 1436 of TCC).

According to the article 1438 of TCC, if the insurer is aware of the real situation with regards to non-disclosed or incorrectly disclosed circumstances or facts, they shall not have the right to withdraw from the contract arguing that the duty of disclosure has been violated. In this case, the burden of proof lies with the policyholder.

The sanctions against the breach of duty of disclosure are regulated considering when the insurer learned of the breach. If they learn of it before the risk is materialized, the article 1439/1 of TCC shall be applied. In this case, the insurer can either withdraw from the insurance contract (and notify the policyholder of it within 15 days as of the date they learned of the breach) or adjust the contract

---

31 There are special regulations related to this duty in regard to life insurance as stated in the articles 1497 and 1498 of TCC. Nevertheless, they will not be analyzed under this chapter since life insurance is not a type of insurance contract suitable for the businesses.

32 Hakan Karan and Kemal Şenocak, "Part II – Chapter 4 (Burdens and Obligations of the Insured)," in *Insurance Law in Turkey*, ed. Meltem Deniz Güner Özbek. 2nd ed. (The Netherlands: Kluwer Law International, 2019), para. 239.

by claiming a premium difference. If the requested premium difference is not accepted within 10 days, the insurance contract is automatically deemed as withdrawn. Pursuant to the article 1441 of TCC, if the policyholder has deliberately provided misleading information before concluding the contract, the insurer is, then, entitled to have premiums for the period of time they carried the risk.[33] On the other hand, the insurer's right to withdraw from the contract cannot be exercised in following three circumstances according to the article 1442 of TCC: a) if the right of withdrawal is waived either explicitly or implicitly, b) if the insurer has caused the breach which leads to withdrawal and c) if the insurer concludes the contract despite some of their questions left unanswered by the counterparty.

On the other hand, if the insurer learns of the breach after the risk occurs, the article 1439/2 of TCC shall, then, be applied. The sanctions may vary based on the severity level of the fault and the presence of casual connection. If the policyholder violates the duty of disclosure with negligence, and if this breach has the potential to affect the realization of the risk or an influence on the amount of compensation or insurance sum, a deduction shall be made in proportion to the degree of negligence from the amount of the compensation or fixed sum the insurer shall pay. Alternatively, if the policyholder breaches this duty with intent, then it is needed to investigate whether there was a causal connection between the breach and the materialized risk. If there is, then the insurer is not obliged to pay any compensation or insurance sum. However, if there is no causal connection, the insurer, then, pays the compensation or insurance sum considering the ratio between amount of the premium paid and the premium which should be paid.

The provisions related to the duty of disclosure before concluding the contract shall apply by analogy to the changes that occurred between the time of the proposal and acceptance.

b. During the contract period

After concluding the insurance contract, there may be some changes that affect the risk. These changes can cause the risk to get aggravated or reduced,[34]

33 Karan and Şenocak, "Part II – Chapter 4 (Burdens and Obligations of the Insured)," para. 252.

34 When there is a reduction of risk, the premium would be reduced by the insurer upon policyholder's demand pursuant to the article 1433 of TCC. Even though it is important to inform the insurer about this, there is no duty of disclosure about reduction of risk.

comparing to the time the contract was concluded. When there is an increase about the possibility of materializing the risk or about the amount of compensation, then there is an aggravation of the risk.

Policyholder may cause the risk aggravation with explicit actions, as well as with passive or tacit behaviors (subjective aggravation).[35] In addition, aggravation may also occur with other people's behaviors or as a result of natural events (objective aggravation).[36] According to the article 1444 of TCC, the policyholder is obliged not to aggravate the risk. However, if the risk is already aggravated, they shall, then, notify the insurer instantly or within 10 days at the latest after they became aware of the situation.

The sanctions against the breach of duty of disclosure during the contract period are also regulated according to the time the insurer learned of the breach, namely before or after the risk materialized. Pursuant to the article 1445/1 of TCC, the insurer may either terminate the insurance contract or revise the contract by claiming a premium difference in 1 month from the time they learned of the risk aggravation.[37] This article indicates that time limit for the latter is 1 month, after which the relevant rights shall be forfeited. If the requested premium difference is not accepted by the policyholder within 10 days, the insurance contract shall be deemed as terminated. The insurer cannot exercise those rights if the change on the risk returns to its previous position. On the other hand, if the insurer learned of the risk aggravation after occurrence of the risk, then the article 1445/5 of TCC will be applied. Similar to the article 1439/2, this article laid down different sanctions according to the level of the fault and presence of casual connection, diverging in a range from a deduction in proportion to the degree of negligence to the right to terminate the contract and non-payment of the indemnity or insurance sum.

Pursuant to the article 1445/4 of TCC, the insurer's right to terminate the contract or claim additional premium is ceased to exist if the risk aggravation

---

35 Merih Kemal Omağ, *Türk Sigorta Hukukunda Rizikonun Ağırlaşması Sorunu* (İstanbul: Sigorta Hukuku Türk Derneği, 1985), 65; Kender, *Sigorta*, 310; Evrim Akgün, "Türk Hukuku ve Avrupa Sigorta Sözleşmesi Hukuku İlkeleri (PEICL) Çerçevesinde Rizikonun Ağırlaşması ve Hafiflemesi," *Bahçeşehir Üniversitesi Hukuk Fakültesi Kazancı Hakemli Hukuk Dergisi,* Vol. 8, Iss. 91–92 (2012): 172; Karan and Şenocak, "Part II - Chapter 4 (Burdens and Obligations of the Insured)," para. 258.

36 Omağ, *Ağırlaşma*, 66–67; Kender, *Sigorta*, 310; Akgün, *Ağırlaşma*, 172.

37 There is also a special article about this duty regarding life insurances stated in the article 1498 of TCC. However, that will not be analyzed under this chapter since life insurance is not a type of insurance contract suitable for the businesses.

arisen from the following cases: a matter related to insurer's interest, a case by the insurer which they are responsible, a matter related to the performance of a humanitarian duty, and a case of any changes in insured's health status in life insurances.[38]

c. At the time of materialization of the risk

If the risk occurs, the policyholder shall notify the insurer immediately (without any delay) upon learning of the situation. For this stage of duty of disclosure, there are no requirements of any form, which means the notification may be done written with a mail or an e-mail as well as verbally via phone.[39] According to the article 1446 of TCC, if the policyholder fails to do the notification and the insurance indemnity or the insurance sum increased because of this failure, the insurance indemnity or insurance sum shall, then, be reduced according to the level of fault. However, in the cases the insurer previously learned of the risk materialization, and then this sanction shall not be applied.

Furthermore, according to the article 1475 of TCC, which is a special provision for liability insurance, the insured shall notify the insurer immediately in case the affected party make a claim for indemnity. Also, the insured is obliged to inform the insurer in 10 days of any event, which will cause their liability in the future.

2. Duty to Provide Information and Allow Investigation

Pursuant to the article 1447 of TCC, after the risk materializes the policyholder shall provide all information and relevant documents to the insurer which may be expected of them because of the contract or upon insurer's request. Required information and documents are the ones that are necessary to determine the extent of either the risk or insurance indemnity or insurance sum. Therefore, they need to be provided in a reasonable time. The policyholder shall also allow the insurer to investigate the scene of the risk occurred and any other relevant places, as well as to take appropriate precautions expected of them.

---

38 Karan and Şenocak, "Part II – Chapter 4 (Burdens and Obligations of the Insured)," para. 260.

39 Ünan, *Cilt I*, 502–503; Karan and Şenocak, "Part II – Chapter 4 (Burdens and Obligations of the Insured)," para. 267.

If the insurance indemnity or the insurance sum is increased because of the breach, the amount shall be deducted according to the level of fault. Therefore, any deduction will not be made if there is no fault.[40]

Additionally, in the liability insurance, the affected party shall provide information if requested by the insurer, pursuant to the article 1479 of TCC.

3. *Duty to Prevent, Mitigate the Loss and Protect the Insurer's Right of Subrogation (Art. 1448 of TCC)*

In the event that the risk is materialized, or it became highly probable, the policyholder shall take precautions to mitigate or to prevent the loss or its increase and shall protect the insurer's right of subrogation against third parties. The policyholder shall comply with the instructions of the insurer regarding to the precautions to be taken as much as possible.

If the breach of this duty affects the insurer in a negative way by increasing the insurance indemnity to be paid, a deduction will be made from the insurance indemnity according to the level of the fault.

The insurer shall pay the reasonable expenses to the policyholder, which they made in order to take precautions within the scope of this duty, even if they ultimately turned out to be in vain. Upon the policyholder's request, the insurer shall pay the necessary amount in advance.

4. *Duty to Refrain from Changes to Damaged Goods and The Place of Occurrence (Art. 1471 of TCC)*

After the risk occurs, the policyholder shall not make any changes, which complicates or prevents the identification of the cause or the extent of the damage, on the scene where the risk materialized as well as on the goods before determination of the damage, unless the change is made with the insurer's approval or in order to decrease the effect of the damage.

In accordance with the article 1471/2 of TCC, if the duty is breached due to fault, insurance indemnity will be deducted proportionate to the severity level of fault provided that there is a casual connection between the damage and the breach.

5. *Contractual Duties*

Besides the duties regulated by law, the parties are allowed to include additional contractual duties in insurance contracts. Aiming to protect the weaker party,

---

40 Günay and Yazıcı, "Turkish Insurance Law," 347.

TCC imposes some restrictions on the sanctions for breaches of contractual duties in the article 1449.

If it is agreed on that the sanction for a breach committed by the policyholder gives the insurer the right to terminate the contract either wholly or partially, then the termination may be possible only if the policyholder has the fault, except for the specific rules provided by TCC and other laws. If the breach is committed by a policyholder at fault, then the right to terminate ends after 1 month as of the date on which the situation was learned by the insurer, unless the law regulates a different period of time. Lastly, the insurer cannot terminate the contract in the cases that the breach has no effect on the materialization of risk and the scope of the insurer's deed.

III. The Impact of the Insured, Beneficiary and Representative's Knowledge and Behavior

Besides policyholders, the knowledge and behavior of some other people may also be considered important. According to the article 1412 of TCC, knowledge and behavior of the insured's (who is aware of the insurance), the representative's (if there is one) and beneficiary's (for the cases of insurance of persons) are deemed as the knowledge and behavior of the policyholder.

§ Part IV Extinction of the Insurance Contract and the Outcomes

I. Extinction of the Insurance Contract

As explained below, insurance contracts may end in a variety of conditions and circumstances.[41]

A. Extinction of contract by termination

According to the article 1413 of TCC, in cases such as the insurer declares composition, its license in the relevant insurance branch being revoked or its power to conclude contracts being abrogated, the policyholder is entitled to terminate the contract within 1 month as of the date they became aware of these facts. Moreover, these reasons are not *numerus clausus*, which means that the

41 There is also a special type of extinction of contract in life insurance according to the article 1500 of TCC. However, that will not be analyzed under this chapter since life insurance is not a type of insurance contract suitable for the businesses.

policyholder may rely on similar grounds for termination. On the other hand, in case the policyholder declares composition of debts before paying the entire premium, the insurer is entitled to terminate the contract within 1 month as of the date they became aware of this fact.

If the insurance contract has an adjustment clause and the insurer increases the premium without changing the scope of the coverage based on that clause (i.e. inflation adjustment clause), the policyholder may terminate the contract within 1 month as of the date they were notified about the increase pursuant to the article 1414 of TCC.

In the case the insurer is entitled to terminate the insurance contract partially with a just cause and if it is evident that the insurer would not have concluded the contract for the remaining part alone with the same conditions, they may terminate the contract entirely. Besides, if the insurer terminates the insurance contract partially, the policyholder may, then, terminate the contract entirely, according to the article 1415/2 of TCC.

Pursuant to the article 1417 of TCC, in the cases that the insurer becomes insolvent or enforcement against the insurer proceeded without result, the policyholder is entitled to request security from the insurer that they will fulfill their obligations. If such a security is not given by the insurer within 1 week, the policyholder may terminate the contract. This is also true if the policyholder fails to give such a security before the payment of the premium. In this case, the insurer has right to terminate the contract as well. However, in accordance with the article 1418 of TCC, if the insurer goes bankrupt, the insurance contract becomes automatically terminated.

If the materialized risk causes partial loss, then both of the parties have the right to terminate the insurance contract. However, according to the article 1428/2 of TCC, to be able to exercise that right, the insurer shall need to pay the partial insurance indemnity.

Pursuant to the article 1434/3 of TCC the insurer has the right to terminate the insurance contract if the policyholder did not pay any of the subsequent installments of the premium. To be able to exercise this right the insurer shall notify the policyholder with a registered letter or a notification through notary that the payment shall be made within 10 days, otherwise the contract is to be deemed as terminated.

And lastly, the insurer has the right to terminate the contract if there is an aggravation on the risk and they learned of that before the risk materializes (art. 1445/1 of TCC), as well as after the materialization of risk, if there is a deliberate act to evade disclosure and a causal connection between the risk and the aggravation (art. 1445/5 of TCC).

B. Withdrawal

According to the article 1430/3 of TCC, the policyholder may withdraw from the insurance contract if they pay half of the premium before the insurer's liability begins. In case of partial withdrawal, the policyholder shall pay half of the premium of the withdrawn part.

If the premium as a whole or the first installment is not paid on due time, the insurer may exercise the right to withdraw in 3 months as long as the premiums have not been paid. Moreover, pursuant to the article 1434/2 of TCC, the insurance contract is to be deemed withdrawn if the insurer did not claim the premium within 3 months after it becomes due and payable.

If the policyholder breached their duty of disclosure before concluding the contract and the insurer learned of the breach before the risk occurred, pursuant to the article 1439/1 of TCC, the insurer has the right to withdraw from the contract.

The above-mentioned explanations on the right of termination that depend on the article 1415 of TCC are also applicable for the right of withdrawal.[42]

C. Expiry

It is not a mandatory element for the insurance contracts to have an appointed period of time, yet the parties usually pick a specific date or time-frame for the insurance contract to be effective. In this case, the insurance contract comes to an end on the expiration date, which may be a specific date or end of a period of time such as 1 or 2 years.

In addition, in some of the GTC it states that the coverage may start and end at 12:00 noon in the specific day (expiry date) written on the policy.

D. Agreement

The parties may agree on discontinuation of the insurance contract mutually at any time during the contract period.[43] In this case, in accordance with the article 1419 of TCC, the premiums paid in advance shall be refunded to the policyholder for the idle days, unless otherwise provided by law.

---

42 Under this chapter, see supra: *Extinction of Contract by Termination.*

43 Kender, *Sigorta*, 404; Yazıcıoğlu and Şeker Öğüz, *Sigorta Hukuku*, 191; Meltem Deniz Güner Özbek and İlyas Gölcüklü, "Part II – Chapter 6 (Termination of the Insurance Contract)," in *Insurance Law in Turkey*, ed. Meltem Deniz Güner Özbek. 2nd ed. (The Netherlands: Kluwer Law International, 2019), 316.

E. *Materialization of the Risk*

If the materialized risk causes total loss, the insurance contract automatically become extinct.[44]

F. *Lack of Insurable Interest*

As it was mentioned before, the regulation of the article 1408 of TCC seeks insurable interest at all times.[45] As a result of this mandatory provision, if the interest ceases to exist at any time during the contract period, then the insurance contract will become null and void.

II. Prescription Period

There are three different prescription periods in insurance law. The first one is for all the claims arising from the insurance contracts for all the insurance types. They shall be prescribed after a period of 2 years as of the date when payment falls due. The second one is for all the claims relating to the insurance indemnity or sum and those shall be prescribed after a period of 6 years as of the date of materialization of the risk, according to the article 1420 of TCC. The last one is applicable only in liability insurance (art. 1482 of TCC). In this case, the claim of indemnity directed by the affected party against the insurer shall be prescribed within 10 years as of the event triggering the subject of the insurance.[46]

III. Subrogation of the Insurer

There are three cumulative conditions for the insurer's right of subrogation: Firstly, the insured needs to have a right to claim compensation from the third party who caused the damage. Otherwise, the insurer would not get a litigation right against the responsible third party. Secondly, the insurer shall make a payment. It is important to mention here that the right of subrogation is limited to the amount the insurer paid.[47] Lastly, the loss should be covered under the contract the parties concluded. If the insurer makes a payment even though the loss is outside of the scope of the insurance coverage, then this payment is called

---

44 If there is not a total loss but a partial loss, the insurance contract does not become extinct automatically and does remain effective.

45 Under this chapter, see supra: *Insurable Interest*.

46 Samim Ünan, *Türk Ticaret Kanunu Şerhi – Sigorta Hukuku – Cilt II – Zarar Sigortaları* (İstanbul: Oniki Levha Yayınları, 2016), 385–386.

47 Kender, *Sigorta*, 407.

ex gratia and the insurer does not get a subrogation right for that amount. For example, in March and April of 2020, most of the insurers worldwide made *ex gratia* payment for the COVID-19 treatments.

If these three conditions are fulfilled, the insurer will have the right of subrogation automatically, as a result of the law alone and without the need for a permit, consent or any other legal action.

According to the article 1472/2 of TCC, after the insurer becomes successor, the insured shall not violate the right of subrogation of the insurer, or else they will be responsible.[48]

The right of subrogation is only for the indemnity insurance contracts, which consist of property and liability insurances. However, in liability insurances, since it is the insured who is responsible for the loss, this right could be exercised only when there are other parties that are jointly and severally liable together with the insured (art. 1481 of TCC). In this case, to become a successor, the insurer needs to pay the affected party first.

§ Part V Special Types of Insurance Contract

In this part, some selected insurances for the businesses will be examined. Although these are all different types of insurances, it is possible to gather some of them together and make a combination, which is called "package policy" in practice. If there is a package policy, the rules of each of the relevant GTC will be applied to the relevant risk which was materialized. This means, if a burglary happens and business' insurance contract has coverage for both theft and fire, then the rules which will be applied to this damage will be Theft Insurance GTC.

As mentioned above, in indemnity insurance the insurer is under the obligation to compensate the loss, which means to pay only the amount compensating the loss, not more. And also, the upper limit for the insurer's obligation is the amount stipulated in the insurance contract. This is a result of the principle of prohibition of unjust enrichment.

48 This duty is similar to the one regulated under the article 1448 of TCC. According to the article 1448, the policyholder shall protect the insurer's right of subrogation against third parties by taking protective precautions before the insurer makes any payment. On the other hand, in cases for the article 1472 to be applied, the insured shall protect the rights even after the insurer makes a payment. Ünan, *Cilt I*, 514.

I. Theft Insurance

The theft may be defined as the assets to be taken away without the consent of the owner. In the theft insurance, insurable assets belonging to the policyholder or the insured are covered as well as their permanent residents and employees.

In the system of TCC, not every type of insurance has special provisions of its own, and theft insurance is one of them. Since it is a type of contract under property insurance, the principles of the property insurance and also indemnity insurance, such as the principle of prohibition of unjust enrichment will be valid for the theft insurance along with other principles and the Theft Insurance GTC.

According to the article A.1. of Theft Insurance GTC, this insurance covers theft or attempted theft at the insured place. This may be happened by forcible entry to the insured place (such as breaking, demolishing, climbing or crossing by means of vehicle, equipment or physical agility); or by entering with a made up or original key or by unlocking the password; or by sneaking in and hiding. If the theft happened by killing, injuring, using force or violence or threats, then the material losses and damages that occurred directly in the insured assets will also be covered. The parties are allowed to conclude the contract by having the insurance coverage for just one or more of these groups.

Some assets getting stolen and theft happening in some specific situations stated in the article A.3. and A.4. of Theft Insurance GTC may be included to the insurance coverage additionally, such as having coverage for fur, silk carpets, collectibles, sculptures, or having coverage in the case of a strike or lockout, also in case of absence of anyone for more than 30 days continuously in the places indicated in the insurance contract. However, if the damage is caused because of the following circumstances stated in the article A.5. of Theft Insurance GTC, then the insurance coverage is excluded: Theft resulting from taking advantage of the war, coup, military action, uprising; theft resulting from taking advantage of the ionizing radiation or radio-active contamination arising from any nuclear fuel or nuclear residues; theft resulting from taking advantage of the public authority's intervention on the insured place or things; theft by people who live with the policyholder or insured; the fire, explosion and internal water damages caused by thieves. Besides, deficits in the inventory are excluded from the coverage.

II. Fire Insurance and Fire-Related Profit Loss Insurance

The fire is defined neither in TCC, nor in Fire Insurance GTC. However, in the doctrine, it is accepted that the fire is something that comes into existence without a designated area (like a stove) and can spread on its own by leaving such a place.[49]

When the fire leaves its source and designated area and also has the ability to spread around on its own, then this fire is called "hostile fire".[50] Designated area may be an oven, stove as well as candle, lighter, pipe, oil or gas lamp.[51] The damage arising from hostile fire is covered under fire insurance contract. On the contrary, if the fire stays in its designated area and does not have the ability to spread, then this fire is "friendly fire".[52] If the damages arise from a friendly fire, then they are not covered.

There are no special provisions for fire insurance in TCC, that is why the regulation and principles for property insurance and also indemnity insurance will be applied along with the Fire Insurance GTC.

Fire insurance provides coverage for the material damages on the insured assets which are direct cause of the fire, lightning, explosion, or smoke, steam, and heat as a result of the fire or explosion (art. A.1. of Fire Insurance GTC).

Unless otherwise agreed, fire insurance does not provide coverage for the situations and assets mentioned in the article A.3. of the Fire Insurance GTC.

If the damage or loss happened because of the following circumstances stated in the article A.4. of Fire Insurance GTC, then the insurance coverage is excluded: Damages caused by the war, coup, military action, uprising; damages caused by the ionizing radiation or radio-active contamination arising from any nuclear fuel or nuclear residues; damages caused by the public authority's intervention on the insured place or things; damages caused by the asset's own default, fermentation, combustion or breakdown, without a fire; damages caused by the exposure of the insured goods to the fire or heat for a useful purpose, by dropping or throwing them to the fire, or by burning of the clothes without fire or by the touch of heating, lightening or ironing devices and also lights, candles or cigarettes and such; damages by induction and heating caused by short circuit, grounding or voltage change on the engines, electrical appliances and electronic instruments, devices, utilities when they are using electricity, without a fire; damages caused by collapse, tearing and other ways of deformation, wearing

49 Tekin Memiş, *Yangın Sigortasında Riziko* (Ankara: Seçkin Yayınevi, 2001), 26.
50 Kubilay, *Sigorta*, 95.
51 Memiş, *Yangın*, 34; Evrim Akgün, "Yangın Sigortası, Yangına Bağlı Kar Kaybı Sigortası," in *Sigorta Davaları*, ed. Mutlu Dinç and Mustafa Topaloğlu (Ankara: Seçkin Yayınevi, 2020), 512.
52 Kubilay, *Sigorta*, 96.

because of the low pressure and centrifugal incidents along with mechanical effects in the insured device and engines.

Regarding the risk of fire, there is also "Fire-related profit loss insurance". The damages that fire may cause are not limited to the material damage, but may also bring the business to a standstill. In other words, there may be also a loss of profit of the business, since the workplace or the business operations are forced to stop partially or completely because of the material damage on such as machines, computers, etc.[53] Hereby, fire-related profit loss insurance aims to cover that loss in the profit. The situations covered with this type of insurance will be agreed by the parties in accordance with the coverage which will be given in the fire insurance (art. A.2. of the Fire-Related Profit Loss Insurance GTC).

According to the article A.4. of the Fire-Related Profit Loss Insurance GTC, the following situations are excluded from the coverage: Profit loss caused from the situations which are covered neither in fire insurance contract, nor in Fire Insurance GTC; risks which are not in scope of the coverage according to the parties' agreement; profit losses arising from the bankruptcy of the insured or arising after business operations came to a standstill.

III. Liability Insurance

If some of the activities of a natural or legal person cause a loss, damage, or personal injury to the third person, namely the affected party,[54] then this liability will be covered with liability insurance. In this type of insurance, the insurance indemnity will not be paid to the policyholder or the insured; instead, it will be paid to the affected party.[55] By doing so, the possible decrease of the assets of the policyholder or the insured will be prevented or minimized.[56]

There are two sides of the insurer's obligation to carry the risk in this type of insurance: On one hand, if there is a justified request the insurer needs to pay compensation to the affected party, on the other hand if the request is unjustified

---

53 Akgün, "Yangın," 561.

54 Under this chapter, see supra: *Affected Party*.

55 Mahmut Yavaşi, *An Introduction to Turkish Business Law* (Bursa: Dora Yayınevi, 2015), 119.

56 Meltem Deniz Güner Özbek and Banu Bozkurt Bozabalı, "Part III – Chapter 5 (Liability Insurance)," in *Insurance Law in Turkey*, ed. Meltem Deniz Güner Özbek. 2nd ed. (The Netherlands: Kluwer Law International, 2019), 383. Also, under this chapter, see supra: *Passive Insurance*.

then the insurer needs to help to the policyholder or the insured to extinguish the demand on court.

The articles between 1473 and 1486 of TCC exclusively regulate the liability insurance in general. Furthermore, there are GTC's for almost every type of liability insurance, such as compulsory liability insurance for motor vehicles, employer's liability insurance, compulsory personal accident insurance for highway transportation passengers, product liability insurance. Most of the compulsory insurances are among liability insurances, since this subject is related to the public interest firmly. It is important to state that that this insurance does not provide coverage for illegal activities. Besides, if the damage is caused by an intentional act of the policyholder or insured, then the insurer will not be responsible for that damage.

Under the article 1473 of TCC, unless otherwise agreed, liability insurance is regulated as occurrence based, which means that the obligation of the insurer arises from an event occurred during the contract period, even if the loss happens after that period. Alternatively, the parties may agree to have a claims-made based policy. In claims-made policy, the insurer provides coverage for only the claims made during the contract period, even if the event happened before or during the contract period. It is also possible to have the insurance contract based on both.

If the insurance contract is concluded for the liability related to the enterprise of the insured, then the insurance shall also cover the liability of the representatives, administrators, auditors, and also the employees of the insured. The parties may agree otherwise.

As explained above, there is a duty of notification for the policyholder or the insured.[57] After that notification, the insurer shall inform the policyholder or insured within 5 days whether they will help the policyholder or the insured, or not. If they remain silent, then they shall pay the compensation determined by the court. Settlements need to be approved by the insurer; otherwise, it will be nonbinding for them. Yet, the article 1476/4 of TCC limits the insurer by stating that the insurer shall not refrain from approving the settlement for unjust causes.

According to the article 1480 of TCC, the insurer shall not set off the insurance indemnity that they will pay to the affected party against any sums due under insurance contract. This is the exception to the rule about the insurer being entitled to deduct the premium due stated in the article 1431 of TCC.

57 Also, under this chapter see supra: *After Materialization of the Risk.*

Lastly, according to the article 1478 of TCC, the affected party may claim their loss directly from the insurer, provided that the claim is brought within the prescription period.[58] In other words, even if it is possible, the affected party does not need to sue the policyholder or the insured at all; instead, they can direct their claim to the insurer alone.[59]

Further Readings

Akgün, Evrim. "Yangın Sigortası, Yangına Bağlı Kar Kaybı Sigortası." In *Sigorta Davaları*, 511–573. Edited by Mutlu Dinç and Mustafa Topaloğlu. 2nd ed. Ankara: Seçkin Yayınevi, 2020.

Akgün, Evrim. "Türk Hukuku ve Avrupa Sigorta Sözleşmesi Hukuku İlkeleri (PEICL) Çerçevesinde Rizikonun Ağırlaşması ve Hafiflemesi." *Bahçeşehir Üniversitesi Hukuk Fakültesi Kazancı Hakemli Hukuk Dergisi*, Vol. 8, Iss. 91–92 (2012): 170–197.

Akgün, Evrim. "6502 Sayılı Tüketicinin Korunması Hakkında Kanun'un Sigorta Sözleşmelerine Etkisi Üzerine Bir İnceleme." In *Prof. Dr. Feridun Yenisey'e Armağan*, 2721–2748. İstanbul: Beta Yayınları, 2014.

Arseven, Haydar. *Sigorta Hukuku*. 2nd ed. İstanbul: Beta Yayınevi, 1991.

Atabek, Reşat. "Sigorta Akdinin Yorumu." *Sigorta Hukuku Dergisi*, Vol. 1, Iss. 2 (1982): 125–140.

Bahtiyar, Mehmet. "Sigorta Poliçesi Genel Koşulları." *Banka ve Ticaret Hukuku Dergisi*, Vol. 19, Iss. 2 (1997): 89–108.

Bahtiyar, Mehmet. "Sigorta Poliçesi Özel Koşulları, Genel Koşullardan Ayırdedilmesi ve Bazı Sorunlar." In *Prof. Dr. Ali Bozer'e Armağan*, 133–148. Ankara: Banka ve Ticaret Hukuku Araştırma Enstitüsü, 1998.

Bozer, Ali. *Sigorta Hukuku*. Ankara: Banka ve Ticaret Hukuku Enstitüsü Yayınları, 1965.

Clarke, Malcolm. "An Introduction to Insurance Contract Law." In *Research Handbook on International Insurance Law and Regulation*, 3–17. Edited by Julian Burling and Kevin Lazarus. Cheltenham: Edward Elgar Publishing, 2012.

Clarke, Malcolm. *Law of Insurance Contracts*. 6th ed. Great Britain: Informa, 2009.

---

58 Since the article 1478 is not mentioned in the protective provisions, namely not amongst the provisions stated in the article 1486 of TCC, it is not regarded as mandatory. However, in the doctrine it is accepted that this right cannot be suppressed by agreement of the parties. Ünan, *Cilt II*, 368.

59 Yavaşi, *Business*, 119; Güner Özbek and Bozkurt Bozabalı, "Part III – Chapter 5 (Liability Insurance)," para. 387.

Güner Özbek, Meltem Deniz. "Part II – Chapter 1 (Generalities)." In *Insurance Law in Turkey*, para. 147–156. Edited by Meltem Deniz Güner Özbek. 2nd ed. The Netherlands: Kluwer Law International, 2019a.

Güner Özbek, Meltem Deniz. "Part II – Chapter 3 (Formation of the Contract)." In *Insurance Law in Turkey*, para. 192–195. Edited by Meltem Deniz Güner Özbek. 2nd ed. The Netherlands: Kluwer Law International, 2019b.

Güner Özbek, Meltem Deniz and Bozkurt Bozabalı, Banu. "Part III – Chapter 5 (Liability Insurance)." in *Insurance Law in Turkey*, para. 377–394. Edited by Meltem Deniz Güner Özbek. 2nd ed. The Netherlands: Kluwer Law International, 2019a.

Güner Özbek, Meltem Deniz and Gölcüklü, İlyas. "Part II – Chapter 6 (Termination of the Insurance Contract)." In *Insurance Law in Turkey*, para. 316. Edited by Meltem Deniz Güner Özbek. 2nd ed. The Netherlands: Kluwer Law International, 2019a.

Güner Özbek, Meltem Deniz and Gölcüklü, İlyas. "Part VII (Insurance Intermediaries)." In *Insurance Law in Turkey*, para. 526. Edited by Meltem Deniz Güner Özbek. 2nd ed. The Netherlands: Kluwer Law International, 2019b.

Güner Özbek, Meltem Deniz and Meriç, Gülfer. "Part II – Chapter 3 (Parties to the Insurance Contract)." In *Insurance Law in Turkey*, para. 200–237. Edited by Meltem Deniz Güner Özbek. 2nd ed. The Netherlands: Kluwer Law International, 2019.

Heiss, Helmut. "Insurance Contract Law Between Business Law and Consumer Protection." In *General Reports of the XVIIIth Congress of the International Academy of Comparative Law*, 335–353. Edited by Karen B. Brown and David V. Snyder. Dordrecht: Springer, 2012a.

Heiss, Helmut. "Indemnity Insurance." In *The Max Planck Encyclopedia of European Private Law*, 860–863. Vol. 2. Edited by Jürgen Basedow, Klaus J. Hopt, Reinhard Zimmermann and Andreas Stier. Oxford: Oxford University Press, 2012b.

Kabukçuoğlu Özer, F. Dilek. *Sigortacılık Kanunu Şerhi*. İstanbul: Oniki Levha Yayınları, 2012.

Karan, Hakan and Şenocak, Kemal. "Part II – Chapter 4 (Burdens and Obligations of the Insured)." In *Insurance Law in Turkey*, para. 238–274. Edited by Meltem Deniz Güner Özbek. 2nd ed. The Netherlands: Kluwer Law International, 2019.

Kayıhan, Şaban. *Sigorta Sözleşmesinde Prim Ödeme Borcu*. Ankara: Seçkin Yayınevi, 2004.

Kubilay, Huriye. *Uygulamalı Özel Sigorta Hukuku*. Izmir: Barış Yayınları, 2003.

Memiş, Tekin. *Yangın Sigortasında Riziko*. Ankara: Seçkin Yayınları, 2001.

Omağ, Merih Kemal. *Türk Sigorta Hukukunda Rizikonun Ağırlaşması Sorunu.* İstanbul: Sigorta Hukuku Türk Derneği, 1985.

Ulaş, Işıl. *Uygulamalı Zarar Sigortaları Hukuku.* 2nd ed. Ankara: Turhan Kitabevi, 2012.

Uluğ Cicim, İlknur. "Ticaret-i Bahriye Kanunnamesi'ne Göre Navlun Sözleşmeleri." *Cedrus the Journal of MCRI*, Vol. 4 (2016): 393–410.

Ünan, Samim. *Sigorta Tüketici Hukuku.* İstanbul: Oniki Levha, 2016.

Ünan, Samim. *Hayat Sigortası.* İstanbul: Beta Yayınları, 1998.

Asst. Prof. Dr. Elif KÜZECİ*

Chapter VIII Personal Data Protection Law

Kuner, Christopher, Bygrave, Lee A. and Docksey, Christopher, ed. 2020. *The EU General Data Protection Regulation (GDPR)-A Commentary*. New York: Oxford University Press; Küzeci, Elif. *Kişisel Verilerin Korunması*. 4th edition. İstanbul: Oniki Levha, 2020; Küzeci, Elif and Kılıç, Şebnem. "6698 Sayılı Kişisel Verilerin Korunması Kanunu'nun İş Sözleşmesi Çerçevesinde Değerlendirilmesi: Veri Sorumlusu, Veri İşleyen ve Diğer Aktörler." *Legal İş Hukuku ve Sosyal Güvenlik Hukuku Dergisi* 16, Iss. 63 (2019): 947–992; Voigt, Paul and von dem Bussche, Axel. *The EU General Data Protection Regulation (GDPR)*. Cham: Springer, 2017.

Introductory Remarks

Personal data is acquired from an increasing number of sources in the 21st century, processed more thoroughly, and the outcomes of these activities have a wide range of implications for human life. On the bright side, these advances provide opportunities for individuals to improve their personal and professional lives. However, on the other side of the spectrum, they have serious negative effects that endanger fundamental rights and values, such as the right to privacy, personal integrity, and human dignity. At this point, personal data protection laws are the most significant legal instruments for reducing the negative consequences of data processing technologies.

There are two main dimensions of data protection for business operations. Firstly, governments and companies are the two main actors that process personal data. Therefore, they oblige to comply with data protection legislation. Many businesses process a large amount of personal data in order to improve their profits. While some of these businesses process data for reasons such as improving customer satisfaction, advertising, and marketing, others may be more directly involved in data processing activities. Companies like social media platforms and online advertising firms fall into the last category.

Secondly, people spend most of their time in business life and workplace is one of the areas where new technologies' effects are most clearly observed. From

* Corresponding author.

recruitment process to establishment of workplace organization, from employee performance monitoring to payroll management, Information Communication Technologies (ICTs) are increasingly used in almost all business processes. All these aspects, in addition to the benefits of ICTs, lead to the emergence of new risks in the business life. Practices that violate the privacy of the employee's private life and the right to personal data protection occupy a prominent place among these risks. Regarding the use of ICTs in the workplace, it is necessary to strike a balance between the employee's right to protection of personal data and the legitimate interests of the employer.

This chapter will begin by discussing the necessity of the right to personal data protection, followed by its historical evolution and its legal resources on international level. The second part of this chapter will focus on Turkish data protection legislation. In this context, provisions of the Turkish Constitution, the Penal Code, the Civil Code and the Code of Obligations will be examined. Following that, Turkey's Personal Data Protection Act will be the focal point. In this sense, fundamental concepts, principles, and processing conditions of Turkey's data protection legislation will be discussed, with a specific focus on cases that are particularly important for business law.

§ Part I The Necessity of Personal Data Protection Legislation and Historical Background

I. The Necessity of Personal Data Protection

The right to personal data protection primarily serves to protect the personality of the individual, and to determine the future of the information about themselves while ICT advancements have a direct impact on the evolution of this right. In fact, the growth of databases, followed by the addition of a slew of new technology products, allowed for the processing of personal data to be more thorough than ever before. These technologies are gradually becoming more affordable, widely available, and sophisticated. The rapid development in ICTs even cause a transformation that can be compared with the industrial revolution.[1]

1 Clara Fritsch, "Data Processing in Employment Relations: Impacts of the European General Data Protection Regulation Focusing on the Data Protection Officer at the Worksite," in *Reforming European Data Protection Law, Governance and Technology Series 20*, ed. Serge Gutwirth et al (Dordrecht: Springer, 2015), 149.

ICT advancements provide plenty of advantages that make our personal lives easier and our professional lives more productive. However, they also have certain negative side effects. As the world becomes more digital, individuals' digital footprints, as well as the digital shadow of their identity, become more accessible. Individuals' images, voices, and places can all be recorded. Moreover, since cross-border information flow is now possible in seconds on the Internet, personal data is getting acquired more extensively through different methods and tools. This data is easily connected, allowing for the drawing of relevant conclusions. Furthermore, this procedure can be carried out automatically, with little or no human intervention. This jeopardizes an individual's autonomy and raises a huge risk: A person who is constantly monitored in the digital environment is at risk of transforming from a subject to an object. The most significant legal tool for mitigating these dangers is the right to personal data protection.

The balance between information demands and individual fundamental rights has shifted in favor of the first as a result of the rapid advancement of data processing technologies. Indeed, many fundamental rights and freedoms are inextricably linked to the protection of personal data. Among these, the right to protect and improve one's physical and spiritual being, as well as the right to privacy and freedom of expression stand out. Personal data protection legislation seeks to strike a balance between the need for data processing and human rights in this regard.

II. Historical Background of Personal Data Protection

In the 1970s, some nations began processing personal data in computer databases. The desire to restore the equilibrium that had been disrupted by the initial use of data processing technology was influential in the establishment of first legal regulations on data protection. The German state of Hessen adopted the first data protection law in 1970.[2]

It was followed by the first national data protection law, namely The Data Act (*Datalagen*), which was enacted in Sweden in 1973.[3] In the meantime, personal data protection had also become a highly controversial issue in other parts of

2 For further information on the developments in Germany see: Viktor Mayer-Schönberger, "Generational Development of Data Protection in Europe," in *Technology and Privacy: The New Landscape*, eds. Agre, Philip E. and Rotenberg, Marc (Cambridge, MA: MIT Press, 1998), 222 ff.

3 Gloria González Fuster, *The Emergence of Personal Data Protection as a Fundamental Right of EU* (Switzerland: Springer, 2014), 58.

the Europe. Many European countries rapidly followed the Hessian and Swedish data protection laws in enacting personal data protection legislation.[4] Besides, in the 1970s not only in Europe but also in the USA, there were some measures discussed to protect personal data. These advancements, however, have not resulted in the adoption of comprehensive data protection laws at the federal level in the USA. There is still a legal battle between the two sides of the Atlantic over data protection standards.[5]

With the rise in data processing activities, defining data protection principles began to gain acceptance also on international level. The OECD was the first international body to issue guidelines on data protection in 1980.[6] One year later, the Council of Europe approved the first and only binding international legislation on this field. They have followed by regulations in EU level. In this sense, Directive 95/46/EC in 1995[7] was one of the most important sources for the protection of personal data, not only within the EU but also beyond its borders. The General Data Protection Regulation (GDPR) has replaced this Directive as of May 25, 2018.[8] The impact of the EU data protection regime on other parts of the world has continued to grow in the aftermath of GDPR. In the 21st century, the right to personal data protection is recognized and regulated in many national legal systems around the globe and most of these countries either follow or closely observe the European data protection regime.[9]

---

4 Andrew Charlesworth, "The Governance of the Internet in Europe," in *The Internet, Law and Society*, eds. Akdeniz, Yaman, Walker, Clive and Wall, David (Great Britain: Pearson Education Limited, 2000), 63.

5 For further information on related court decisions see, Elif Küzeci, *Kişisel Verilerin Korunması* (İstanbul: On İki Levha, 2020), 199 ff.

6 OECD Guidelines on the Protection of Privacy and Transborder Flows of Personal Data were first issued in 23rd September of 1980. These Guidelines were updated in 2013. For further information on the revised version of the Guidelines see, https://www.oecd.org/sti/ieconomy/privacy.htm, accessed 18.9.2021.

7 For the Directive 95/46/EC of the European Parliament and of the Council of 24 October 1995 on the protection of individuals with regard to the processing of personal data and on the free movement of such data see, OJ L 281/31, dated 23.11.1995.

8 For Regulation (EU) 2016/679 of the European Parliament and of the Council of 27 April 2016 on the protection of natural persons with regard to the processing of personal data and on the free movement of such data and repealing Directive 95/46/EC (General Data Protection Regulation) see also, OJ L 119/1–88, dated 4.5.2016.

9 On accelerating growth in data protection legislation around the globe see, Graham Greenleaf, "Sheherezade and the 101 Data Privacy Laws: Origins, Significance and Global Trajectories," *Journal of Law, Information and Science* 23, Iss. 1 (2014): 4–49.

When these legal texts are examined, a common feature can be easily noticed: The basic principles in the protection of personal data are largely preventive. In other words, it is aimed to protect personal data before any damage occurs. It can be said that the basic principles of data protection -for instance, a necessity of determining the purpose for which personal data will be processed, the importance of the consent of data subject or the prohibition of processing sensitive data types- stem from this perspective.

§ Part II The Development of Turkish Data Protection Law

I. Turkish Constitution

Since 2010, the protection of personal data has been a constitutional right in Turkey. Within the constitutional amendments of 2010, the following provision was embedded to the third paragraph of the 20th Article of Turkish Constitution, which guarantees the right to privacy[10]:

> Everyone has the right to demand the protection of their personal data. This right comprises the right to be informed about the personal data concerning themselves, access to such data, right to request correction or deletion of them as well as the right to be informed if such data is used in accordance with the purposes for which it was collected. Personal data can be processed only in cases regulated in a law and upon express consent of the subject individual. Principles and procedures regarding the protection of personal data shall be regulated by a law.

Although the inclusion of a data protection right in the Constitution is undoubtedly a significant step forward, it should be noted that there are some flaws in this clause. To begin with, it can be regarded as legislator's hesitation to provide appropriate confidence for this protection. Because it is referred to as the "right of 'demanding' the protection of personal data" rather than the "right of personal data protection" within the scope of this new clause. Second, there is no mention of establishing an independent authority to monitor the application of the data protection principles. However, these cannot be construed that the Article 20/3 creates a barrier to the protection of personal data. Hence, this provision is interpreted as a right to personal data protection rather than a right to "demand" such protection by the judicial bodies.[11] In addition, as will be discussed further below, Turkey established an independent data protection authority in 2017.

---

10 For the English translation of Constitution of the Republic of Turkey see, https://global.tbmm.gov.tr/docs/constitution_en.pdf, accessed 18.9.2021.

11 Küzeci, *Kişisel Verilerin Korunması*, 323–326.

In other words, the opt of legislator and its practices were used to solve some problems in the mentioned provision.

There are also other constitutional provisions relating to the right to personal data protection in Turkey. One of these is the right to protect and improve one's physical and spiritual being, which is regulated under the Article 17 of the Constitution (Art. 17/1). In fact, the Constitutional Court has relied on this Article in several rulings on the subject.[12]

Various Constitutional Court judgments have addressed the issue of personal data protection in the context of the employment relationship. There has been a significant increase in judicial decisions on the subject, especially since the Constitutional Court began to appraise individual applications.[13] Some of the judgments in this context are related to the employee's right to privacy.[14] For instance, the Constitutional Court ruled that monitoring an employee's e-mail correspondence resulting in the termination of the employment contract is unlawful according to the concrete case.[15]

An indirect constitutional source for personal data protection is regulated under the Article 90 of the Constitution. Accordingly, the Article 90/5 states:

> International agreements duly put into effect have the force of law. No appeal to the Constitutional Court shall be made with regard to these agreements, on the grounds that they are unconstitutional. In the case of a conflict between international agreements concerning fundamental rights and freedoms duly put into effect and the national laws due to differences in provisions on the same matter, the provisions of international agreements shall prevail.

This provision requires the consideration of some important international sources on the protection of personal data as being a legal equivalent of laws.

---

12 For a sample case also see, the decision of the Constitutional Court, dated 24.7.2019, no. 2018/73–2019/65 (OJ, 29.11.2019, no. 30963).

13 For further information also see: *Chapter I- Constitutional Law.*

14 Regarding the unconstitutionality of terminating an employment contract based on the applicant's private affair while working for a private company, also see: The decision of the Constitutional Court, dated 30.9.2020, app. no. 2017/14907 (OJ, dated 9.12.2020, no. 31329). Regarding the unconstitutionality of the applicant's dismissal from the public service as a result of the disciplinary investigation initiated after hearing that sexually explicit images were published on the Internet, see: the decision of the Constitutional Court, dated 3.4.2014, app. no. 2013/1514.

15 The decision of the Constitutional Court dated 3.3.2016, app. no. 2013/9704. For an opposing view on a similar subject, also see: The decision of the Constitutional Court, dated 10.12.2015, app. no. 2013/7666.

In this context, two treaties of Council of Europe can be mentioned in particular: European Convention on Human Rights and Convention for the Protection of Individuals with regard to Automatic Processing of Personal Data.

Turkey ratified European Convention on Human Rights (ECHR) in 1954. Data protection is not an independent right involved in ECHR. The European Court of Human Rights (ECtHR) does, however, frequently use the Article 8 of the Convention as a foundation for personal data protection cases.[16] As it may be seen in many decisions of the ECtHR, the objective of the Convention is to guarantee the rights in an effective and practical way rather than through imaginary or theoretical measures. This approach constitutes a basic but significant principle, which must be born in mind, not only for interpreting the Convention, but also implementing provisions concerning data protection in Turkey. Turkey has also been a signatory to the Council of Europe's Convention no. 108. The provisions of this Convention are also part of Turkey's national legal system pursuant to the above-mentioned provision of the Constitution. The Convention was ratified in lineup with Turkey's Personal Data Protection Act, as will be explained below.

II. Turkish Penal Code and Turkish Civil Code

The legal rules that explicitly regulate the protection of personal data in Turkey were adopted mostly in the 2000s. The Turkish Penal Code (TPC), which came into effect on June 1, 2005, is the most noteworthy example of this. According to this code, unlawful recording, delivering, publishing, distributing, or obtaining personal data and not destroying them after required period are regulated as crime and punished by imprisonment.[17]

Furthermore, some provisions of the Turkish Civil Code relating to personal rights are also directly relevant with personal data protection. Pursuant to the general norms of the Turkish Civil Code, exposing or exploiting personal data may be considered a violation of personal rights. Aside from that, the Turkish Code of Obligations (TCO), which was enacted in 2011, includes a special provision regarding the protection of personal data of the employees. Indeed, the Article 419 of TCO states that: "The employer shall use the employee's personal

16 For a detailed assessment also see, Lee A. Bygrave, "Data protection pursuant to the right to privacy in human rights treaties," *International Journal of Law and Information Technology* 6, Iss. 3 (1998): 254–283.

17 Under this chapter, see infra: *Enforcement System*.

data, only if it is about their predisposition towards the occupation or in the level of essentiality for the contract's fulfillment. Lex specialis are reserved".

Personal data protection is also addressed in the legal provisions covering a variety of industries, including electronic communication, health care, and banking. In addition, there are several by-laws are in force. The impact of these regulations, on the other hand, is limited. The Turkish Data Protection Act, which was passed in 2016, established the main legal basis for the protection of personal data in Turkey. In other words, this Act is the cornerstone of Turkey's legal framework for personal data protection.

III. Personal Data Protection Act

The Turkish Personal Data Protection Act (The DP Act) was published in the Official Journal in April 2016 and fully came into force in October.[18] In the same year, Turkey also ratified the Council of Europe's Convention no. 108, as well as the Additional Protocol to the Convention, 35 years after it was first signed. The DP Act was long awaited: It was first drafted in the late 1990s, and two draft acts were presented to the Parliament in 2008 and 2014, but neither was entered into force. Enacting a data protection act has become more critical since 2010, when personal data protection became a constitutional right under the Article 20/3 of the Constitution. As previously indicated, personal data can only be processed in conditions provided by law or with the explicit consent of the subject person under this constitutional provision. In addition, the rules and procedures for the protection of personal data must be established by legislation.

The DP Act's objective is to protect fundamental rights and freedoms of individuals, particularly their right to privacy, when personal data is processed, and to impose obligations and rules that are enforceable on natural and legal persons that process personal data.[19] In this sense, the DP Act's requirements, as well as the procedures and principles that natural and legal persons must follow, shall be understood through the lens of human rights. The Act's scope has also been adopted in order to attain this goal: This Act applies to natural persons whose personal data are processed, as well as natural or legal persons processing such data entirely or substantially by automated or non-automated means that are part of a data filing system.[20]

18 The Personal Data Protection Act, dated 24.3.2016, no. 6698 (OJ, 7.4.2016, no. 29677).
19 DP Act, Art. 1.
20 DP Act, Art. 2.

However, the scope of the application of the DP Act is constrained by the exclusion clauses. The Act has two categories of exceptions: The matters outside of its scope, and the situations in which specific provisions will not apply.[21] The first group includes such as processing personal data for the purpose of generating official statistics, processing personal data in the context of freedom of speech, and some processing operations by law enforcement agencies. It is obvious that these cases occupy a peculiar position in relation to regular data processing tasks. However, the guarantees are weakened by the fact that no provision of the DP Act would be implemented to such processing activities. Rather than totally exempting them from the scope of the Act, we believe that creating an article that takes into consideration the features of the specific difficulties would have offered a stronger legal protection.

Personal data are processed by natural persons in the scope of purely related to themselves or of family members living together with them, is another issue that is fully exempt from the scope of the Act. In the GDPR, a similar exemption provision is also regulated. However, there is a significant difference between them. While "activities related to oneself" are exempt from the DP Act, it is envisaged that the GDPR will not apply to "purely personal or household activity".[22] A phone directory kept only for personal purposes, for example, will be an exception under GDPR but not under the DP Act. While other exclusion provisions limit applicability of the Act, this clause, in our opinion, excessively expands the scope.

The provisions that do not apply to the certain situations have been identified in addition to those that are totally exempted under the DP Act. These are cases where the processing of personal data is necessary for the prevention of crime, criminal investigation, or, in certain circumstances, disciplinary investigation; where the data has been made public by the data subject, and the processing is carried out to protect the state's economic and financial interests.[23] The majority of these exception provisions relate to data processing operations carried out by government agencies. In this regard, we may conclude that, with few exceptions, the companies should comply with the DP Act in their data processing activities, as a rule.

---

21 DP Act, Art. 28. For further information see also, Küzeci, *Kişisel Verilerin Korunması*, 374–384.

22 GDPR, Art. 2/2, sup-para. c.

23 DP Act, Art. 28/2.

The DP Act specifies the general principles to be followed in processing operations as well as the legitimate conditions of data processing. Furthermore, for the first time in Turkey, a data protection authority was established within this new Act. The authority's decision-making body is the Board of Personal Data Protection, which is made up of nine members: Four selected by the President and five by the Grand National Assembly of Turkey.[24] Since its establishment in 2017, the Board has taken numerous decisions and adopted seven by-laws. The Board's decisions have become one of the most important legal sources of personal data protection over time.

As of the date of entry into force, The DP Act was based on the principles of the 95/46/EC Directive rather than the GDPR. However, GDPR is currently followed in the interpretation of the DP Act. It is expected that this approach is to be reflected in upcoming revisions to the Act. Indeed, there are several sections in the recent government policy documents that state that the DP Act would be amended to conform with the GDPR.[25]

§ Part III The Personal Data Protection Act of Turkey

I. Basic Concepts of Personal Data Protection Law

A. Personal Data

The DP Act stipulates that personal data is "any information relating to an identified or identifiable natural person".[26] In this case, it can be said that basically two criteria are used to distinguish personal data from non-personal data. Accordingly, in order to be able to discuss personal data, the data must be (i) related to a natural person and (ii) this person must be identified or identifiable.

We may give an example to try to illustrate the distinction between identified and identifiable persons. The simplest type of information that identifies a person is their first and last name. In this sense, the name is personal data in most cases. However, it may not suffice for all circumstances. For example, a

24 DP Act, Art. 21/2.

25 See the decision on the Approval of the Eleventh Development Plan (2019–2023); the decision of the Grand National Assembly of Turkey, dated 18.7.2019, no. 1225, par. 479.1; Action Plan on Human Rights, Republic of Turkey Ministry of Justice, March 2021, Goals 6.7.

26 DP Act, Art. 3/1, sub-para. d.

person with a common first and last name is not identifiable if only this information is included. On the other hand, even if a person's name is unknown, their identity can be determined using information gathered from different sources. This is highly evident when it comes to users' online activity. In fact, in many circumstances where regular people believe they are anonymous on the Internet, their identities can be identified. This provision allows them to take advantage of the DP Act's protection in such situations as well.

Any circumstance that allows a person to be identified as a result of a content representing the individual's physical, economic, cultural, social, or psychological identity, or associating it with any record such as an identity, tax, or insurance number, is referred to as personal data. It can be a written document, sound, or video recording, or pictures drawn by a child. Even a computer's IP address might be considered personal data. Indeed, the Court of Justice of the European Union (CJEU) has ruled that dynamic IP addresses are personal data under some conditions.[27] In Turkey, IP addresses are also included in the court decisions as examples of personal data.[28]

Personal data covers a wide range of categories. However, it is worth remembering that some types of information related to people are not considered as personal data. Due to the DP Act, anonymous data are in this group and anonymization refers to the process of making personal data not able to be associated with an identified or identifiable natural person, even when having been combined with other data.[29]

Determining which data is personal data is crucial for the data protection compliance processes of businesses. Enterprises may be exposed to various sanctions if a situation in which personal data is processed is perceived as incorrect and excluded from the compliance process. In this sense, another point is that the DP Act considers special categories of personal data and stipulates different conditions for them.

B. Sensitive Data

Some categories of personal data are recognized more sensitive than others in international and supranational texts such as GDPR, Convention no. 108, and many national regulations. It was thought that if these data were unlawfully processed,

27 The decision of CJEU (Patrick Breyer v Bundesrepublic Deutchland), dated 19.10.2016, no. C-582/14

28 The decision of Turkish Constitutional Court, dated 9.4.2014, no. 2013/122–2014/74.

29 DP Act, Art. 3/1, sub-para. b.

some risks, particularly discrimination, would be amplified.[30] Therefore, they need to have higher guarantees than other personal data. The DP Act takes a similar approach, stating that the following types of information will be considered special categories of personal data: "race, ethnic origin, political opinion, philosophical belief, religion, religious sect or other belief, appearance, membership to associations, foundations or trade-unions, data concerning health, sexual life, criminal convictions and security measures, and the biometric and genetic data".[31] As will be explained below, the processing conditions for sensitive personal data differ from those for other types of data due to the DP Act. As a result, in order to ensure compliance with data protection legislation, it is necessary to determine not only how personal data is processed, but also to which category the processed personal data belongs.

C. *Processing Personal Data*

Personal data processing is another important concept. Since the DP Act's obligations, procedures, and principles apply to anyone who processes personal data, it is necessary to figure out which activities fall under its purview. Processing of personal data includes any operation on personal data that is carried out entirely or partially by automated or non-automated means as part of a data filing system, such as collection, recording, storage, protection, alteration, adaptation, disclosure, transfer, retrieval, making available for collection, categorization, and usage of personal data.[32] Considering these examples, certain conclusions may be drawn about the data processing activities that will be subject to the DP Act. First and foremost, practically every operation conducted on data will fall under the scope of the Act. In this regard, it is essential to note that the activities listed in the corresponding article of the DP Act, such as data storage, classification, and usage are not numerus clauses, but just illustrative. Corollary of this, it is apparent that all automatic data processing activities fall under the DP Act's scope. On the other hand, the application of the provisions of the DP Act to data processing activities by non-automatic means will be in question only if there is a data recording system in which personal data is processed and structured according to the certain criteria.[33]

---

30 Christopher Kuner, Lee A. Bygrave and Christopher Docksey, ed. 2020, *The EU General Data Protection Regulation (GDPR)-A Commentary* (USA: Oxford University Press), 369.

31 DP Act, Art. 6/1.

32 DP Act, Art. 3/1, sub-para. e.

33 DP Act, Art. 3/1, sub-para. h.

D. *Data Subject, Data Controller and Data Processor*

Individuals and institutions must identify the actors involved in data processing activities to define their duties. This is a crucial necessity for businesses to properly complete their compliance requirements.

There are three main actors in personal data protection due to the DP Act: Data subject, data controller, and data processor. Data subject is the person whose data are processed.[34] Only natural persons can be data subjects, but data controllers and processors can be either natural or legal persons. According to the DP Act, the data controller is the person who decides on the aims and methods of processing personal data, and is accountable for establishing and maintaining the data filing system. On the other hand, a data processor is someone who, with the permission of the data controller, processes personal data on the behalf of the controller. These definitions are almost equivalent to the GDPR's relevant provisions.[35]

In this sense, determining who the data subject is likely to be the easiest question to answer. Basically, the natural person whose personal data is processed will certainly be in this position. Other actors, on the other hand, are not necessarily as easy to identify. The two conditions in the mentioned definition (determining the goals and means of processing personal data and being accountable for the establishment and management of the data recording system) should be taken into consideration when assessing who is the data controller. Furthermore, while identifying the data controller, it is also of importance to determine who decides on issues such as the legal basis of the processing activity, which personal data will be processed, whose personal data are processed, whether personal data will be transferred to others, and how long personal data will be retained.[36] The data processor is distinguished from the controller by the fact that it performs processing activities on behalf of, and with the authority of the data controller.

34 For the other actors of personal data protection law also see, Elif Küzeci and Şebnem Kılıç, "6698 Sayılı Kişisel Verilerin Korunması Kanunu'nun İş Sözleşmesi Çerçevesinde Değerlendirilmesi: Veri Sorumlusu, Veri İşleyen ve Diğer Aktörler," *Legal İş Hukuku ve Sosyal Güvenlik Hukuku Dergisi* 16, Iss. 63 (2019): 947–992.

35 GDPR, Art. 4/7–8.

36 For the review of the United Kingdom's independent authority see, "Data controllers and data processors: what the difference is and what the governance implications are" (https://ico.org.uk/media/for-organisations/documents, accessed 18.7.2021). For similar review criteria considered by the Turkish data protection authority see also, *Kişisel Verilerin Korunması Kanunu'na İlişkin Uygulama Rehberi* (Ankara: Kişisel Verileri Koruma Kurumu, 2018) 56 ff.

In this regard, the data processor's existence is contingent on the data controller's decision.[37]

II. Basic Principles of Personal Data Protection Law

The Article 4 of the DP Act mandates the existence of a legal basis for the processing of personal data. Personal data, in fact, can only be processed in compliance with the procedures and principles set forth in the DP Act and other legislation. Overall, there are five general principles that must be followed when processing personal data. The interpretation of them is critical in data protection law. This concise article represents the cornerstone of the personal data protection law. The followings are these significant principles:

A. Lawfulness and Fairness Principle

The main principle in the processing of personal data is "compliance with the law and the rules of fairness". As previously mentioned, the primary purpose of data protection regulations is to provide certainty in data processing processes, and this principle is at the heart of that purpose. The notion of legal compliance is self-explanatory at this point: The provisions of the law must be followed when processing personal data. The extent of the rule of fairness is more difficult to define. The rule of fairness, i.e., rule of good faith, expresses the behavior expected of an honest individual in terms of civil law. The content of this expectation may vary over time.[38] In terms of personal data protection law, fair processing indicates that data was neither processed in an unfair, or deceptive manner nor without the consent of the data subject.[39] This rule emphasizes that when trying to obtain data processing objectives, the data controller shall take into account the interests and reasonable expectations of the data subject.[40]

This principle is also closely linked to transparency. As stated in the relevant Recital of the GDPR: "Any processing of personal data should be transparent to natural persons that personal data concerning them are collected, used,

---

37 Paul Voigt and Axel von dem Bussche, *The EU General Data Protection Regulation (GDPR)* (Cham: Springer, 2017), 20.

38 Kemal Oğuzman and Nami Barlas, *Medeni Hukuk – Giriş, Kaynaklar, Temel Kavramlar* (İstanbul: Vedat, 2008), 222.

39 Kuner, Bygrave and Docksey, *The EU General Data Protection Regulation (GDPR)-A Commentary,* 314.

40 Lee A. Bygrave, *Data Protection Law-Approaching Its Rationale, Logic and Limits* (the Netherlands: Kluwer Law International, 2002), 58.

consulted or otherwise processed and to what extent the personal data are or will be processed".[41] The DP Act, on the other hand, has no direct reference to transparency in contrast to the GDPR.

B. Accuracy Principle

Due to the DP Act, any data should be "accurate and kept up to date where necessary". This principle should be viewed in conjunction with the data subject's right to informational self-determination.[42] Accordingly, anyone with knowledge of who processes data and for what purposes can request that inaccurate or outdated data be updated. On the other hand, accuracy principle is crucial not just for the rights of the data subject, but also for the legitimate interests that data processing serves. In fact, assessments based on defective or out-of-date data may damage legitimate interest of the data controller.

C. Purpose Limitation Principle

Processing personal data for specific, explicit, and legitimate purposes is another pillar of principles in processing. The legitimate purpose is defined in the Preamble of the DP Act as the data processed by the data controller being relevant to and essential for the task they have done or the service they have provided. In other words, in accordance with this principle, personal data cannot be processed for unclear, ambiguous, or illegitimate purposes.

Purpose limitation principle should be assessed in the light of other rules such as the data subject's explicit consent, the obligation of data controller to inform, and the data subject's rights. Many requirements of the DP Act are predicated on the data subject's knowledge of data processing operations, as will be discussed below. The data subject, for example, should be informed about the content of their consent. Likewise, when personal data is collected, the data controller is required to inform the data subject about how their data will be processed. These provisions are necessary for the data subject to be assured that the purpose limitation principle was not violated by the data controller.

41 GDPR, Recital 39.

42 Right to informational self-determination has become an intellectual resource that is frequently evaluated within the scope of personal data protection law after the decision ruled by the German Constitutional Court in 1983. See also, BVerfGE, 65, 1 (*Volkszählungsurteil*), dated 15.12.1983.

D. *Data Minimization Principle*

Due to the DP Act, another core principle of data processing activities is "being relevant, limited and proportionate to the purposes for which they are processed". In other words, the amount and type of personal data processed should be minimal and proportional to the initial purposes. This principle ensures that relevant processing actions are always carried out during all the process, not just when the data processing activity is started.

E. *Retain Limitation Principle*

Another basic principle is to prevent data retention for an unlimited period. Personal data should not be kept or stacked with the thought of "it may be necessary one day". As the discussions on the "right to be forgotten" show, keeping data for an unlimited period intrinsically harms individual autonomy.[43] The fact that personal data is retained, on the other hand, poses a data security risk. It is worth noting at this point that the notion of retaining data for just the required period is linked to the data minimization principle discussed above.

III. Legal Conditions to Process Personal Data

The DP Act's Articles 5 and 6 govern data processing conditions. The Article 5 regulates the conditions of personal data processing, while the Article 6 regulates the conditions of sensitive data processing. The explicit consent of the data subject is required for the processing of personal data under both provisions. However, personal data may also be processed in some cases where the explicit consent of the data subject is not available. In this subpart, firstly, the meaning and conditions of explicit consent will be explained, following by other legitimate data processing activities.

A. *Explicit Consent*

Explicit consent defines as "a freely given, specific, and informed consent" under the DP Act. Certain elements must be met for the expressed consent to form

---

43 The DP Act makes no explicit mention of the right to be forgotten. A special provision on "erasure, destruction, or anonymization of personal data" was included in the Article 7 of the Act. For a legal analysis on right to be forgotten in Turkey also see, Oytun Canyaş and Aslı Bayata Canyaş, "Approach towards the right to be forgotten under Turkish law in comparison with EU and US laws: a need for a reform?," *Juridical Tribune* 11, Iss. 2 (2021): 174–202.

the basis of legitimate data processing activity. First and foremost, the consent must be specific to the subject itself and limited to that subject. To put it another way, blanket consent does not meet the DP Act's requirements. It is also forbidden to resort to fault, fraud, or threats to obtain consent. To give their consent freely, the data subjects need to comprehend what they are consenting to and its consequences. In this perspective, the data controller should use explicit and intelligible language, leaving no space for ambiguity.

The right to informational self-determination is clearly reflected on explicit consent. Even if the consent is provided, the conditions should be carefully examined. There may be a hierarchy between the parties. Indeed, in some situations where one of the parties is weaker, there may be uncertainty that permission is freely provided. The employment relationship can be seen as one of the leading examples for this. Therefore, the free will of the employee (data subject) should be carefully analyzed in those cases. Similarly, if data processing is served to the counterparty as a condition for the contract to be concluded even in cases that is not essential to the contract's execution, the consent should be carefully reviewed to ensure that it is freely given. Furthermore, the Personal Data Protection Board determined that obtaining explicit consent for a matter that is required for contract performance and making it a contract requirement was in violation of the DP Act.[44]

B. Data Processing Conditions Without Explicit Consent

1. Envisaged by Law

Personal data may be processed if there is an explicit law on the relevant processing activity. This legal regulation should be adopted by the Grand National Assembly of Turkey. To put it another way, by-laws, directives, and other legislative sources cannot serve as the sole legal basis for the processing of personal data. Furthermore, the provisions on data processing activity should be precise; hence, a legislation that grants an unspecific authorization is undesirable in this regard. One of the instances of this exception envisaged in the Preamble of the DP Act is gathering fingerprints of crime suspects as part of a crime investigation by law enforcement agencies.

44 For the decision of the Personal Data Protection Board, dated 25.3.2019, no. 2019/81.

2. *Vital Interest*

Another legitimate condition for data processing is related to vital interests of human beings. Due to the DP Act, personal data may be processed if "it is necessary for the protection of life or physical integrity of the person themselves or of any other person, who is unable to explain their consent due to the physical disability or whose consent is not deemed legally valid". As it is seen to rely on this provision data processing activity should meet two conditions at the same time. Firstly, there should be a vital interest in danger. Secondly, it should be impossible to gather data subject's consent.

The scope of this provision has been attempted to be clarified with some examples in the DP Act's Preamble. Personal data may be processed during medical intervention in order to protect life and physical integrity if the subject is unconscious, or whose consent is invalid because of a mental illness, according to the Preamble. The applicable health system can handle data such as blood type, diseases and operations, and pharmaceuticals utilized in this context. However, it should be emphasized that the processing of health data in this example is subject to a different method in line with the Article 6 of the DP Act, as will be discussed below. To put it another way, this example is not appropriate for the scope of this provision. However, it is possible to find more accurate examples. For instance, personal data -such as cell phone traffic information, credit card usage, GPS data- may be processed to locate a missing person. On the one hand, for the private sector, the application of this clause will be limited. Special problems that telecom operators and technology businesses may face, on the other hand, should not be overlooked.

3. *Contractual Necessities*

For the establishment and fulfillment of the contract, it may be necessary to process personal data. According to the DP Act, processing personal data without the explicit consent of the data subject within the context of a contractual relationship may only be permissible if specific conditions are met. These conditions are as follows: (i) The processing activity must be directly related to the establishment or fulfillment of the performance of a contract; (ii) personal data being processed must be related to the contracting parties; (iii) this processing activity must be necessary.

For example, an e-commerce website processes the address of a customer to deliver purchased items. At this point, there is no need to get the consent of the customer, because this information is necessary to the performance of the sale contract. By approving the contract, the parties will be deemed to have approved this processing activity. As stated in the DP Act's Preamble, the bank would be able to get the payroll, title deed documents, or a document indicating that the loan requester has no enforcement debt based on this provision in order to fulfill a loan contract. Furthermore, it must be accepted that using employee data to conduct in-house training or maintaining a supplier database may be considered in this sense if it is part of contractual requirements.

4. *Legal Obligations*

Other than the DP Act, the data controller will also be subject to a variety of legal requirements. In this regard, being in need of obtaining the data subject's consent as the legal basis for data processing may result in the failure of the data controller to meet a legal obligation. The enterprises' processing of data such as bank account number, whether the data subject is married, their dependents, whether their spouse is working or not, and social insurance number in order to pay salary to the employee are shown as examples stated in the Preamble of the related sub-paragraph. It should be mentioned that obligations arising from the legislation of another nation are not evaluated within the scope of this paragraph.

5. *Disclosure of Personal Data by the Data Subject*

If the data subject has made their personal data public, the data can be processed without the data subject's explicit consent, according to The DP Act. The term "publicization" refers to the dissemination of personal information to the general public. It is apparent that information distributed by third parties is not within this scope. Information made public by the data subject, on the other hand, will not be processed in all circumstances or for all purposes. As the Personal Data Protection Board (the DP Board) also stated in a decision, the data subject must intend to make the information public. Furthermore, personal data must be processed with the intention of making it public in order to rely on this rule. For example, an individual who placed a sale ad on a website may have included their phone number in the ad. Potential receivers can process this information; however, it cannot be used for other than sale purpose without the data subject's explicit consent, e.g., for marketing purposes.[45]

6. *Establishment, Exercise or Protection of a Right*

Personal data may be processed without the explicit consent of the data subject when processing is required for the establishment, exercise, or protection of a

---

45 The decision of the DP Board, dated 17.11.2019, no. 2019/331.

right. The DP Act's Preamble presents some examples of this exception. One of them is the use of personal data by a company as legal evidence in a lawsuit brought by one of its employees. Another example is the processing of data of a person who is under the legal guardianship in order to preserve their rights.

7. Legitimate Interests of Data Controller

The data controller's legitimate interests are the final exception under the Article 5 of the DP Act. Three conditions must be met in order to rely on this exception: (i) a legitimate interest must exist for the data controller; (ii) data processing must be required to protect that interest; (iii) the data processing activity should not endanger the data subject's fundamental rights and freedoms. These factors emphasize the importance of conducting a balance test that considers the data subject's fundamental rights and freedoms where the data controller has a legitimate interest. The following are some of the issues that have to be evaluated within this context: The potential effects of the processing activity (for example, the risk of harm to the data subject), and the method of data processing (for example, whether the data will be shared with third parties), the state of relationship between the data controller and data subject (for example, the hierarchical position of the data controller), and whether any additional protections are in place (for example, whether protective policies are available).[46]

The foundation of a personal data protection system, in our opinion, is directly related to how to interpret this clause. In fact, personal data protection legislation has always been aiming to strike a balance between the data controller and the data subject. In other words, the purpose of the data protection law is to provide a protection shield to individuals who are vulnerable to evolving data processing technologies.

C. Data Processing Conditions for Sensitive Data

Under the DP Act, "personal data relating to the race, ethnic origin, political opinion, philosophical belief, religion, religious sect or other belief, attire, membership to associations, foundations or trade-unions, data concerning health, sexual life, criminal convictions and security measures, and the biometric and genetic data are deemed to be special categories of personal data".[47]

46 For further information see, Opinion 6/2014 on the legitimate interests of the data controller under the Article 7 of Directive 95/46/EC, Article 29 Working Party, WP 2018, dated 9.4.2014.

47 The DP Act, Art. 6/1.

Processing of these categories of data (may be referred to as "sensitive personal data") without the explicit consent of the data subject is prohibited by the DP Act. There are, however, several circumstances in which such data can be processed without explicit consent. For the conditions of processing sensitive data, there are two separate regimes. Accordingly, data on health and sexual life are subject to different set of rules than other categories of sensitive data.

Without the data subject's explicit consent, sensitive data such as race, ethnic origin, philosophical beliefs, biometric and genetic data can be processed if it is prescribed by law. While the DP Act requires "prescribed by explicit law" for non-sensitive personal data, it is deemed sufficient "prescribed by law" for sensitive personal data other than health and sexual life. In our point of view, this approach is incompatible with the necessity of enhanced data protection for sensitive data.

On the other hand, processing personal data related to health and sexual life is subject to additional restrictions in terms of purpose and actor. These types of data may be processed by individuals bound by confidentiality obligations, or authorized institutions. Furthermore, without the explicit consent of the data subject, these actors may process personal data only for the purposes of protecting public health, preventive medicine, medical diagnosis, treatment and care services, planning and management of health services, and financing. It is worth noting that the condition of being provided by law is not included for these highly sensitive data categories. However, due to the Turkish Constitution, fundamental rights and freedoms may be restricted only by law.[48] Therefore, also in these situations, there should be legal basis for processing.

Lastly, this provision may cause hesitations for some data processing activities that commonly occur. For example, finding a legal basis for health insurance companies to process their clients' medical data is difficult. This industry must rely on the data subject's explicit consent. However, consent should be freely withdrawn just as freely given. This deficiency in this provision may result serious legal issues in relevant cases, particularly if the processing is required for the performance of the insurance contract.

D. *Transfer of Personal Data Abroad*

Transferring personal data is just a type of data processing activity. The provisions concerning transfer, on the other hand, are regulated separately from other processing activities within two articles of the DP Act. The first is concerned with the

---

48 See also, the Turkish Constitution, Art. 13.

transfer of personal data within the country, while the second is concerned with the transfer of personal data outside of the country. The provisions governing the transfer of personal data to third parties within Turkish national borders are quite similar to the general data processing conditions. However, it is envisaged stronger protection for personal data transferred abroad.

As a rule, the transfer of personal data abroad without the explicit consent of the data subject is prohibited. Apart from this, the transfer is possible only in the presence of certain conditions. First, one of the general data processing conditions that explained above must exist. Second, adequate protection provided by the country of transfer is required. Which countries provide adequate protection will be appraised by the DP Board. Data transfer to a country without an adequacy decision can only be carried out if the data controllers in Turkey and the relevant foreign country have written commitments to provide adequate protection, and the DP Board has given its approval.

Moreover, personal data may only be transferred abroad with the approval of the relevant public body and the consent from the DP Board in circumstances where the legitimate interests of Turkey or the data subject may be adversely affected.[49]

E. Data Security

Data protection and data security should not be confused; in other words, the two terms should not be used interchangeably. The goal of the first is to protect individuals, while the goal of the second is to safeguard data. When personal data is involved, however, data security can also help to protect individuals. Therefore, the data security principle is an essential component of personal data protection. This principle requires the data controller to take steps to prevent personal data from being accidentally destroyed, accessed without authorization, modified, deleted, or published.

In terms of data security, the data controller must take all technical and administrative steps necessary to ensure that personal data is processed lawfully, that unauthorized access to personal data is prevented, and that personal data is preserved. If a data processor is processing personal data on behalf of the data controller, they are both responsible for ensuring that the necessary safeguards are in place. If a data leak occurs, the data controller is required by the DP Act to notify data subjects and the DP Board as soon as possible. The DP Board may, if necessary, announce the relevant breach on its official website or in any other

49 The DP Act, Art. 9/5.

appropriate manner. Several announcements have been made in this regard since the Board's presence.

IV. Enforcement System

The DP Act contains several provisions directed towards monitoring and controlling whether personal data is processed in accordance with the law and sanctioning unlawful practices. These provisions can be evaluated in the context of law of obligations, administrative law and criminal law. The DP Act, on the other hand, calls for the establishment of a registry in which data controllers must register before starting data processing. In this regard, the Registry on Data Controllers, abbreviated as VERBIS, has been established as a registration mechanism that is part of the DP Act's preventive approach.

A. Compensation

The data subject may suffer from material (pecuniary) and immaterial (non-pecuniary) harm as a result of unlawful processing of personal data. In fact, the right of the data subject to seek compensation for damages caused as a result of illegal processing of personal data has been referred under the DP Act.[50] If a damage occurred, the person affected may seek compensation under the general provisions of the Turkish Civil Code.

B. Administrative Fines

The DP Act governs the situations in which the DP Board may impose administrative fines. As a result, if the data controller fails to comply with the obligations of notification, data security, compliance of a Board decision, or VERBIS registration, the DP Board may impose an administrative fine. It is a system in which fines are imposed for violations of data protection principles that has been adopted by many countries. In this regard, the approach of the DP Act can be seen similar to the EU approach in particular. The provision concerning administrative fines, on the other hand, is up for debate in several ways.

First and foremost, the violations of general principles and data processing standards previously mentioned are not counted among the situations in which an administrative fine may be imposed, even though the related articles that regulate general principles and standards are the DP Act's backbone. On the other hand, the obligation of the data controller to prevent the unlawful processing

---

50 The DP Act, Art. 11/1, sub-para. ğ.

of personal data is regulated in the DP Act's data security provision. In situations where the general principles and data processing conditions are violated, the DP Board imposes determined administrative fines based on this legal basis. Hereby, the deficiency is attempted to be mitigated through a Board-developed interpretation.

Another point of debate is the DP Act's lower and upper limits on administrative fines. Fines ranging from 5,000 to 1 million Turkish Liras are possible under the DP Act.[51] To put it another way, proportional fines have yet to be determined. As a result, data controllers of varying economic power may be affected to varying degrees by the asserted provisions. Furthermore, the criteria that the DP Board will use to determine the fines are not specified in the Act.

C. Sanctions

In the DP Act, a reference to the TPC in a short article determines the most severe penalties in terms of the sanction system. This is stated as follows: "The Articles 135 to 140 of the Turkish Penal Code (no. 5237, dated 26.9.2004) shall be applied to the crimes concerning personal data". Within the scope of the TPC's provisions, three types of crimes related to personal data protection have been identified: (i) Recording personal data, (ii) illegally giving, disseminating, or seizing data, and (iii) not destroying them. The actions listed here are types of data processing. As a result, if these actions are carried out illegally, the TPC's provisions will be applied.

The DP Act, on the other hand, broadens the scope of data processing activities as already mentioned. Consequently, some data processing activities are subject to the TPC's provisions, while others are not. Modification and classification of data, for example, are not covered by these provisions even though they are data processing activities. It is worth noting that the TPC's provisions were accepted long before the DP Act went into effect. It would be appropriate to make a new amendment to ensure that those processing activities excluded have also been aligned and included.

1. Recording Personal Data

Due to the TPC, recording personal data is considered as a crime and anyone who illegally records personal data confronts a sentence of 1 to 3 years in prison. Aggravating circumstances are regulated in the second paragraph of the

---

51 It should be noted that this amount may be revised by law in the following years. By 2021, this amount is approximately 9,000 to 2 million Turkish Liras.

provision, and it is stipulated that if the crime is related to the recording of certain data categories, the penalty will be increased by half. A sub-division in this context addresses the relevant data categories.

The aggravation will be applied if the personal data is related to the persons' political, philosophical, or religious views, as well as their racial origins. In addition, if personal data revealing the data subject's moral tendencies, sexual life, health status, or trade union membership has been unlawfully recorded, the penalty will be increased. In other words, the illegality of recording information on "individuals' political, philosophical, or religious views, or their racial origins" was not sought. TPC criminalizes illegal data processing in general, but only considers recording information in the specified data categories to be sufficient for a crime to occur. This approach conflicts with the DP Act's regulations. It could also signal a particular risk in terms of human rights. This issue is being attempted to be solved through interpretation. The statement in the Preamble of the provision that "it is certain that recording information about oneself with one's own consent will not constitute a crime" is particularly important in our opinion. This issue, on the other hand, indicates the need to revise the TPC's personal data protection provisions.

Furthermore, the determination made earlier for the TPC's general provisions might apply to this sub-paragraph as well. As can be seen, the unauthorized processing of some sensitive personal data is cited as a reason for the penalty to be increased. These categories, however, are incompatible with the DP Act's special categories of personal data. There is no explanation available to explain this preference.

2. *Giving, Disseminating and Seizing Personal Data*

In the Article 136 of the TPC, the crime of illegally giving, disseminating and seizing personal data is regulated. According to this article, the person who unlawfully gives, disseminates, or captures personal data confronts a sentence of up to 4 years in prison. If the subject of the crime is related to the statements and images of the victims of a sexual assault or that of sexual abuse of a child, the penalty is increased by one-fold. The law does not define the wording of "give, disseminate or seize". This may pose some challenges in practice, particularly in determining which situations are covered by the scope of this article.

3. *Not Destroying Personal Data*

Due to the Article 138 of the TPC, those who are obliged to destroy the data stored in a system are sentenced to imprisonment from 1 year to 2 years if they do not fulfill their duties despite the expiry of the periods determined by the law. If the crime involves data that must be deleted or destroyed in accordance with the Turkish Criminal Procedure Code, the penalty will be two-folded.

The period here is the time limit, which is among the basic principles in the protection of personal data (retain limitation principle). Accordingly, personal data should not be kept longer than necessary for the purpose. In terms of the principle of purpose limitation, the requirement that personal data not be kept indefinitely is also necessary. To avoid arbitrary practices, it is also essential to delete or anonymize data that is no longer needed. It can be seen that the DP Act makes a special reference to the TPC's indicated provision: Those who do not erase or anonymize personal data as contrary to the provision of the Article 7 of the DP Act, shall be punished in accordance with the Article 138 of the TPC.

Further Readings

Bygrave Lee A. "Data protection pursuant to the right to privacy in human rights treaties." *International Journal of Law and Information Technology* 6, Iss. 3 (1998): 247–284.

Bygrave, Lee A. *Data Protection Law-Approaching Its Rationale, Logic and Limits.* The Netherlands: Kluwer Law International, 2002.

Canyaş, Oytun and Canyaş, Aslı Bayata. "Approach towards the right to be forgotten under Turkish law in comparison with EU and US laws: A need for a reform?." *Juridical Tribune* 11, Iss. 2 (2021): 174–202.

Charlesworth, Andrew. "The Governance of the Internet in Europe." In *The Internet, Law and Society*, 47–78. Edited by Akdeniz, Yaman, Walker, Clive and Wall, David. Great Britain: Pearson Education Limited, 2000.

Fritsch, Clara. "Data Processing in Employment Relations: Impacts of the European General Data Protection Regulation Focusing on the Data Protection Officer at the Worksite." In *Reforming European Data Protection Law, Governance and Technology Series 20*, 147–167. Edited by Gutwirth, S., Leenes R. and de Hert, P. Dordrecht: Springer, 2015.

González Fuster, Gloria. *The Emergence of Personal Data Protection as a Fundamental Right of EU*. Switzerland: Springer, 2014.

Greenleaf, Graham. "Sheherezade and the 101 Data Privacy Laws: Origins, Significance and Global Trajectories." *Journal of Law, Information and Science* 23, Iss. 1 (2014): 4–49.

Mayer-Schönberger, Viktor. "Generational Development of Data Protection in Europe." In *Technology and Privacy: The New Landscape*, 219–242. Edited by Agre, Philip E. and Rotenberg, Marc. Cambridge, MA: MIT Press, 1998.

Oğuzman, Kemal and Barlas, Nami. *Medeni Hukuk-Giriş, Kaynaklar, Temel Kavramlar.* İstanbul: Vedat, 2008.

Reports & Decisions

Action Plan on Human Rights. Republic of Turkey Ministry of Justice. March 2021, Goals 6.7.

The Decision on the Approval of the Eleventh Development Plan (2019–2023).

The Decision of the Grand National Assembly of Turkey, Decision no. 1225, dated 18.7.2019.

Index

www.ingramcontent.com/pod-product-compliance
Ingram Content Group UK Ltd.
Pitfield, Milton Keynes, MK11 3LW, UK
UKHW041822031026
15587UKWH00002B/504

9 783631 848890